PUBLIC PILLARS/PRIVATE LIVES:
The Strengths & Limitations of the Modern American Presidents

PUBLIC PILLARS/PRIVATE LIVES:
The Strengths & Limitations of the Modern American Presidents

Timothy D. Holder
John Anthony Moretta
Carl J. Luna
Jaime Ramón Olivares

Design and Production: Abigail Press
Typesetting: Abigail Press
Typeface: AGaramond
Cover Art: Sam Tolia

PUBLIC PILLARS/PRIVATE LIVES:
The Strengths & Limitations of the Modern American Presidents

First Edition, Second Printing, 2005
Printed in the United States of America
Translation rights reserved by the authors
ISBN 1-890919-34-9

*To all of the wonderful people in the
Red States and the Blue States*

ABOUT THE AUTHORS

John A. Moretta earned a B.A. in History from Santa Clara University in CA., an M.A. in History from Portland State University in Oregon, and a Ph.D. in History from Rice University in Houston, Texas. He is currently Professor of History and Chair of the Social Sciences Dept. of Central College, Houston Community College System in Houston, Texas. Dr. Moretta is also an adjunct professor at the University of Houston, where he has taught both undergraduate and graduate classes on a variety of historical topics, ranging from Texas history to United States history through American fiction. He is also an adjunct professor of history in the university's Honor's College. Dr. Moretta's first book, *William Pitt Ballinger, Texas Lawyer, Southern Statesman,* won the 2003 San Antonio Conservation Society's award for one of the best books in Texas history. In addition to his book, Dr. Moretta has also written several articles on Texas history, published in both local and national historical journals, such as *Civil War History.* He is a co-author of *The Western Dream of Civilization* and *American Dreams, American Reality.* He is currently completing a biography of William Penn for Addison Wesley Longman's Library of American Biography Series. Expected publication date is fall, 2005.

ABOUT THE AUTHORS

Carl Luna is a professor of Political Science and chair of the Accelerated College Program at San Diego Mesa College and is a regular lecturer on American politics, comparative politics, and international political economy at the University of San Diego. Dr. Luna received his Ph.D. from American University, Washington, D.C. and his B.A. in political science, history, and philosophy from the University of San Diego. In addition to teaching and research, he is a recurrent guest on San Diego radio and television, commenting on local, state, and national politics, and writes frequently on politics for the *San Diego Union Tribune* and writes the political weblog "Political Lunacy" for the paper's on-line service. He has also been a commentator on presidential and California politics for PBS's *Online NewsHour*, *USA Today*, CBS news and BBC radio. Dr. Luna is a former Fulbright scholar (lecturing on American politics and political economy at Nizhniy Novgorod State University, Russian Federation during the 1999/2000 academic year). He is a contributing author to *The Western Dream of Civilization* and an editor and revision author for *People & Politics: Introduction to American Government*, Gregory Publishing Company.

ABOUT THE AUTHORS

Timothy D. Holder is an assistant professor at Walters State Community College in Tennessee. He has a Ph.D. and an M.A. in History from the University of Kentucky and a B.A. from Asbury College. Dr. Holder was a contributor to the *Encyclopedia of International Military History* and a co-author of *The Western Dream of Civilization.* He has had numerous reviews published of books in the following genres: history, historical fiction, and culture.

Jaime Ramón Olivares is currently a Professor of History at Houston Community College in Houston, Texas. He earned a B.A in International Relations and an M.A and Ph. D. in History from the University of Houston. Dr. Olivares teaches courses in American History and the History of Mexican Americans. He has published numerous Encyclopedia articles on censorship, labor relations, and foreign policy. He is currently working on revising his dissertation for publication. He has submitted an article on the Latin American Working Class to *Latin American Perspectives.*

Contents

Preface

We live in polarized times. Confrontational book titles are piled in stacks a hundred deep at the local discount superstore: *Deliver Us from Evil: Defeating Terrorism Despotism and Liberalism; Lies and the Lying Liars Who Tell Them: A Fair and Balanced Look at the Right; Treason: Liberal Treachery from the Cold War to the War on Terrorism; Big Lies: The Right-Wing Propaganda Machine and How It Distorts the Truth.* Opinions aired on the AM radio are as ideologically polemical as they are bombastic. On television talk shows, pundits and politicos from the left and right talk (or shout, as often as not) past each other, never finding a common middle ground. News organizations tout their fair and balanced reporting while their "targets" on the other "side" accuse them of being biased and "out to get them." Men may be from Mars and Women from Venus, but from the tone of the contemporary American political debate, conservatives and liberals increasingly seem to reside in different universes, let alone on different planets.

This volume attempts to transcend the fiercely partisan tone of current American public debate and present a balanced assessment of the dozen modern presidents from Franklin Delano Roosevelt to George W. Bush. Each essay consists of an introduction, a biographical portrait of the president under discussion, followed by a positive and negative assessment of each man's tenure in office. In every essay due diligence was given by the authors to be as even-handed in their evaluation as possible. Indeed, even the amount of "space"—page length and word count—given to each president in examining their strengths and weaknesses was calculated to keep the approach as equitable as was possible without disruption of the narrative flow.

Two central themes underscore the positive and negative assessments of these particular presidents. First, there is the issue of what Machiavelli referred to as "virtu'"—the ability of good princes to do what works in their quest to obtain and maintain political power. Thus, each president has been rated at least in part on how effective he was in attaining political objectives and implementing policies, despite any particular partisan analysis of the efficacy of that vision. For instance, the ability of any president to achieve a second term, such as FDR, Eisenhower, Reagan, and Clinton, must figure as a significant accomplishment, just as the failed reelection bids of Jimmy Carter and George H.W. Bush's (Richard Nixon being a case unto himself) must be seen as a public rejection for nonperformance. That FDR, LBJ, and Ronald Reagan all succeeded in realizing large portions of their agendas, regardless of biased reckoning, also must be presented in a favorable context, just as the inability of Ford, Carter, George H.W. Bush, and, to a great extent, Bill Clinton to accomplish their policy initiatives must be seen in a negative light. Finally, each president must be appraised in terms of the verdict of history on their respective achievements and blunders, a task complicated by the limited passage of time that separates many of the presidents discussed in this volume from history's collective judgment.

All presidents are complex individuals, and thus in the biographical portion of each essay, the author presents as thorough a personal portrait of that president as space would allow. Without leaving that particular executive "on the couch" too long, the reader at the very least gets a glimpse of what emotional or psychological issues, stretching back to his childhood, affected him as an adult and, therefore, his "behavior" as president.

Adding to their personal dynamics was the immutable fact that all of presidents discussed were in the Oval Office at times when the United States was (and currently still is) the world's undisputed preeminent power. Such status only compounded an already difficult job. Unlike the majority of their predecessors, who dealt primarily with domestic affairs, every president in this volume had to also contend with a multitude of delicate, complex, and in some instances potentially explosive international events, fraught with dire consequences for both the nation and the world if not handled with the utmost diplomatic dexterity and sensitivity.

The political analyses of the modern pundit class too often draw simple, superficial, and thus unfair characterizations of these men, completely omitting the subtleties, nuances, and other "intangibles," which altogether make presidents much deeper and intriguing human beings. Too many current presidential "experts" portray their subjects in two-dimensional, colorless caricatures of goodness or badness, successes or failures, and heroes or scalawags. However, in their defense, they offer such assessments because that is how many Americans might perceive the president at the time, and thus in an effort to be "heard" (and to sell their books or appear on talk shows), they present facile, perfunctory, and usually one-sided appraisals. What these analyses lack—be they the categorizations of Bill Clinton, which either praised him as the heir of the liberal tradition of FDR, Truman, JFK, and LBJ, or reviled him as the most scandalous rogue to hold office in American history—is "depth of balance." The same problem attends Clinton's successor, George W. Bush, who is portrayed as being either a spoiled Uber-fratboy warmongerer or the greatest thing to hit America since sliced bread (white bread, that is). Indeed, since the passing of Ronald Reagan, many (conservatives especially) hail Bush as the scion of the Reagan years' neoconservatism and look to him to fulfill that legacy. In short, too few assessments give a sense of the totality of the man and his presidency.

All twelve presidents reviewed took actions that most reasonable people would find praiseworthy. Naturally, they all did things that reasonable people would find equally egregious. What we sought to accomplish in this book was a presentation of both viewpoints—the good and the bad —that each president may have shown, leaving the reader to decide on which side of the scale the balance falls. Of course, by attempting to play it "down the middle" in an age where the political middle seems to have fallen out of disposition, the authors of this volume are sure to appear partisan in their recounting of a president's successes as well as equally biased in their presentation of a president's shortcomings. Ironically, despite our attempt to be "neutral" or "balanced" in our approach, we too will appear guilty of partisanship—inevitable in a nation apparently divided fifty-fifty down the ideological center. Yet, it is the hope of all involved with this endeavor that readers will, at minimum, walk away from this work with a clearer, deeper understanding and, thus, appreciation for the American presidency and for those twelve men who have held the highest elected office in the nation beginning with Franklin Delano Roosevelt. It is fitting to remember that, in a Republic of the people, those elected by the people must be seen to possess some virtues beyond the vices all mortals bear, lest the concept of the Republic itself be doomed.

Carl J. Luna & John Moretta

Franklin Delano Roosevelt
1933-1945

The man for whom the majority of Americans—especially the poor—voted for president in 1932 was far from being one of them. Born on an estate in the Hudson River country of upstate New York and into a family whose Anglo-Dutch pedigree dated to the seventeenth century, Franklin Delano Roosevelt never wanted for anything that money could buy. This background is the single most important factor in understanding Roosevelt's career, beliefs, his ability to deal with the Depression, and, most important, his extraordinary relationship with the American people.

Roosevelt was born on January 30, 1882. His father, James Roosevelt, was a Harvard Law School graduate whose inherited wealth, coupled with successful high-risk business ventures, provided a comfortable life for his family. Living mainly on his Hudson River estate in Hyde Park, New York, James also maintained a Manhattan apartment since his work required spending some time in New York City. In his "centenary remembrance" of FDR, distant relative Joseph Alsop asserted that the Roosevelts were not American aristocrats. They were "nice people" but were not at the "apex of the pyramid." Strictly speaking, this was true, at least in terms of wealth. James Roosevelt was "comfortable," but his attempts to attain great bounty were thwarted by the depressions of the 1870s and 1890s. James left an estate of $300,000. His second wife, Sara Delano Roosevelt, was one of eleven children, who inherited approximately $1 million from her father. This may strike some as placing the Roosevelts far above the "nice people," especially when one remembers how much one million dollars was worth in the late nineteenth century. Their worth, however, was a long way from the apex of the pyramid, particularly when one considers individuals like Cornelius Vanderbilt, a Roosevelt neighbor in Hyde Park who left an estate between $70 million and $100 million to his heirs.

In another sense, however, Alsop's contention that the Roosevelts were not aristocrats will not wash. The contrast between the Roosevelts and the Delanos on the one hand and the Vanderbilts on the other proves the point. The Roosevelts were "old money"; the Vanderbilts demonstrated in their ostentatious living the newness of their wealth. Aristocracy is not measured exclusively by wealth, even in the United States. The Roosevelt and Delano family ancestry placed them, without question, at the top of the social order. Sara Delano Roosevelt, the family genealogist, claimed that both sides of the family could boast of ties to numerous European aristocrats as well as to numerous *Mayflower* passengers. Among the more interesting ancestors she listed were William the Conqueror and Anne Hutchinson. Sara Roosevelt was not exaggerating when she remarked that her son "had many advantages other boys did not have."

That FDR had such a noble heritage, rather than that of the self-made man or the nouveau riche, was significant. It provided him with a fundamental security and self-assurance. Perhaps most important, from adolescence on Roosevelt was inculcated with the notion that his birthright carried with it the obligation of being a good citizen, that is, to serve and protect the commonweal from the excesses of unfettered individualism and the abuse of power, especially by those who used it for their own self-aggrandizement at the expense of those less fortunate. In short, FDR believed at an early age that he was to become, like his beloved cousin, Theodore Roosevelt, whom he affectionately called "Uncle Teddy," the people's steward. FDR's achievement was to expand the concept of stewardship and combine it with a heavy dose of democracy, thus uniting Jefferson and Jackson.

The man who would accomplish this remarkable political feat was the product of James Roosevelt's second marriage to Sara Delano. If not a June-December match, it was at least a July-October one. James was fifty-four and Sara twenty-eight when FDR was born. The maternal influence on FDR was overwhelming as Sara doted on her only child as well as on her husband. After the fashion of the day, Sara had Franklin in dresses and long curls until he was nearly six years old. Sara also sought to control her son's behavior. As FDR biographer Geoffrey Ward has noted, "No moment of Franklin's day was unscheduled or unsupervised. . . . There was no such thing as privacy." Not until he turned fourteen could Sara bring herself to send him off to school; he had been tutored at home until that time, always under his mother's watchful eye. What Franklin failed to obtain from his parents, he received from adoring servants. The boy rarely got into trouble, as he always wanted to please and seemed to know what was necessary to do—no small advantage for a politician.

In 1896 FDR entered the prestigious and elite preparatory school Groton in Massachusetts. He arrived two years later than most other students, for as Sara wrote it was "hard to leave my darling boy." Though of similar class background with the majority of his peers, FDR nonetheless found it difficult to adjust to his new environment for he was no longer the center of attention. Other students regarded him as charming but snobbish and insecure. In 1900 he entered Harvard, where his academic accomplishments were marginal, but his grades for extracurricular activities were exemplary. He played scrub football (failed to make the regular football team because he was too light) and captained a club crew. He joined the Harvard Republican Club to work in support of "Uncle Teddy's" campaign to become vice president. Although he had completed coursework for a degree in three years, Franklin returned for a fourth to edit the *Crimson*, the school's newspaper. If his editorials at the age of twenty are a gauge of his concern for the world's problems, the needle was pointing near empty. Editor Roosevelt wrote mainly about the need for school spirit and a winning football team. Most significantly, FDR failed to be selected for Harvard's most elite club, Porcellian. No one knows for certain why he was rejected, but most Roosevelt observers contend that it was one of the best things that happened to him. It may not have made him "more democratic" at the time, but it did reduce the additional elitist influences the club might have had upon him.

James Roosevelt died during Franklin's first winter at Harvard. Sara thereafter spent as much time as possible in Boston to be near her son. To guard against her intrusiveness, Franklin developed what biographer Ted Morgan calls "a core of inner armor"—an ability to dissemble, to mask his feelings by resorting to "protective ambiguity." There was nothing equivocal, however, about his feelings for his distant cousin, Eleanor Roosevelt, whom he began "seeing socially" in 1903. Eleanor was Teddy Roosevelt's niece; her father Elliott was TR's younger brother. At Thanksgiving 1903, Franklin shocked his mother when he announced that he and Eleanor were going to marry, which they did in March 1905. During Eleanor and Franklin's engagement period, Sara Roosevelt did all she could to break up the couple but failed. A year earlier, after graduating from Harvard, FDR moved to New York City to attend Columbia Law School. When FDR finished his first year of law school in June 1905, he and Eleanor left for a three-month European honeymoon.

Although FDR never finished the standard three years of law school, he nonetheless took the New York bar, passed it, and went to work for a Wall Street firm that specialized in defending corporations against antitrust suits. He and Eleanor also began raising a family, and over the course of eleven years, they had six children. FDR found being a Wall

Street attorney not at all to his liking and decided to seek a career in politics. His first foray came in 1910 when he sought the Democratic nomination for a seat in the New York state assembly, but when the Democratic incumbent decided not to retire, FDR set his sights on the state senate seat for Dutchess County, which no Democrat had held for a quarter of a century. After conducting a vigorous campaign, he won a narrow victory.

FDR compiled a moderately progressive record as a state senator, opposing Tammany Hall's nominee for the U.S. Senate (at a time when the election was still in the hands of the state legislature) and lending his support to a bill establishing a fifty-four-hour workweek for women and children. His most thoughtful statement in support of reform and one from which can be gleaned some of his subsequent liberal ideology came in a speech in Troy, New York, in March 1912. Advocating the conservation of natural resources, FDR maintained that the time had come to replace competition with cooperation. The "liberty of the community," he asserted, must sometimes take precedence over "the liberty of the individual to do as he pleased with his own property." The role of government was to protect the general welfare, to guard against the disastrous social consequences that would result "if the individuals are allowed to do as they please with the natural resources to line their own pockets during their life."

FDR was reelected in 1912 as state senator but soon accepted the post of Undersecretary of the Navy in Woodrow Wilson's administration. In so doing, he was almost perfectly emulating the career path of his idol, TR, whom he wanted to be just like in every way possible. Moving from Albany to Washington, FDR assumed responsibility for the Navy's procurement, supply, and civilian personnel policies. With the outbreak of World War I, he pressed for preparedness and naval expansion. After the United States entered the conflict in April 1917, he sought an officer's commission, hoping to command men in battle as "Uncle Teddy" had. Fighting in a war was part of TR's prescription for the strenuous life. It was also, if one was clever enough, a way to parlay such activity into becoming a hero, a great boon to one's political career, particularly for someone with presidential ambitions. TR used his escapades with his Rough Riders during the Spanish-American War to win New York's governorship within a few months of his return. His account of the war, one wag said, should be entitled "Alone in Cuba," by Theodore Roosevelt. Although shameless in his use of the war for political gain, such contrivance worked: three years after the war's end, he was president of the United States. Given these factors, it was to be expected that FDR would attempt to resign his post and enlist as soon as the United States entered the Great War. With visions of a San Juan Hill somewhere in northern France dancing in his head, FDR did just that: *attempted* to enlist. Wilson would no more hear of this than allow TR to raise a "Roosevelt Division," which the old warrior wanted to do. Miffed by Wilson's refusal to allow him to enlist, he nonetheless persuaded Secretary of the Navy, Josephus Daniels, to send him on a mission to Europe. It gave the aspiring politician a chance to "see war" and even come briefly under hostile fire. When he returned, FDR planned to insist on a commission so he could get into uniform before the war ended. His knack for contracting diseases, however, nipped that possibility as he suffered from influenza. By the time he recovered, it was too late; the Armistice was only a few weeks away. Roosevelt's next brush with serious disease was not to turn out as sanguine.

In September 1918, a profoundly disturbing event shook the foundation of Roosevelt's personal life and could have easily destroyed his political career forever. While recovering from influenza, his wife discovered a packet of love letters he had received from Lucy Mercer while he was in Europe. Eleanor had hired Lucy as her social secretary four years earlier. In the summer of 1917, perhaps suspecting her husband's infidelity, Eleanor fired Mercer, who had then taken a job with the Navy Department and so remained in close contact with FDR. Meanwhile, to escape Washington's oppressively hot summers, Eleanor was spending those months with the children at Campobello, allowing FDR and Lucy to spend considerable time together. When Eleanor came across the letters, her worst suspicions were confirmed. She was ready to file for divorce. FDR knew the scandal of a divorce would ruin him politically, and his mother also threatened to cut off his inheritance if he went ahead with it. So he promised Eleanor that he would never see Lucy again (a promise he never kept), and the couple remained together, although their marriage would never again be based on intimacy and mutual trust.

In 1920 the Democratic Party nominated Roosevelt for vice president on the ticket headed by James Cox. Although the Republicans, led by Warren G. Harding, easily won the election, FDR gained valuable national exposure. Interestingly, early in the election year, some of FDR's friends promoted a Hoover-Roosevelt ticket. FDR did not object to the idea, and even after Hoover announced he was a Republican, Roosevelt remained keen on the prospect. That the ambitious Roosevelt was interested may seem surprising. As is still true today, the vice presidency was not only a position of obscurity, it was also the road to political oblivion. Unless an act of God or an assassin intervened, no one was likely to hear of the vice president again. Other than those elevated to the Oval Office by the death of a president, no vice president since Martin Van Buren, nearly a century before, had ever gone on to win a major presidential nomination. Moreover, an interesting postwar "anti-war" backlash had emerged, causing many Americans to blame Wilson and the Democratic Party for pushing the United States into a war that they now believed was unwarranted, resulting in the needless death of thousands of Americans. The public had grown weary of progressivism and wanted what Harding called "a return to normalcy," which meant the end of activist government and reform and the embracing of conservatism with its exaltation of rugged individualism. In short, because public opinion was running rapidly in a conservative direction, the Democrats, and thus FDR, had little chance of capturing the White House in 1920. FDR expected to lose but built up a national following in the process. With such visibility, he could then go back and become New York's governor, a position of great political preeminence and, when the time was right, parlay that office into a presidential nomination when it was worth having. Despite the Democrats resounding defeat in 1920, FDR's political future appeared bright.

In August 1921, while vacationing at Campobello, the second tragic event in FDR's life occurred: he was stricken with poliomyelitis, a dreaded disease also known as infantile paralysis because it affected children more often than adults. In searching for the basis of FDR's compassion and rapport with the downtrodden, the importance of this dream-shattering disease requires in-depth interpretation. Despite years of physical therapy and treatment, FDR never regained the use of his legs. He could stand only with the use of heavy steel braces and when he could lean on something; he could walk only by using crutches or with the support of someone's arm. The pain was excruciating, causing FDR "utter despair, feeling that God had abandoned him." Until this point in his life, FDR had always gotten everything he wanted with minimal effort exerted. In this instance his indulged youth had a positive quality, for it provided FDR with his extraordinary self-confidence, tenacity, and optimism—the result of being persistent in trying to get his way as a child. Those who saw FDR as a "Mama's boy" did not understand his nature at all. Had he succumbed to such meekness, he would have vanished from political life. Indeed, after his crippling attack, that is precisely what his overbearing mother often ruthlessly advocated. She wanted to make him a lifelong invalid and, in the process, rekindle the smothering intimacy and control of his life that she had during his childhood. FDR, however, would have none of it. Thus, his battle against polio was as much psychological as physical, as much an effort to defeat depression as to regain the strength in his ravaged limbs. As Geoffrey Ward notes, FDR's struggle changed him for the better, for it required "patience, application, recognition of his own limitations, a willingness to fail in front of others and try again."

Prior to his illness, FDR had been a carefree playboy. After being stricken, he became inwardly more serious. Most important, Roosevelt's suffering expanded his sense of patrician stewardship into a more genuine feeling of compassion. As future Secretary of Labor Frances Perkins noted, "The man emerged completely warmhearted, with humility of spirit, and with a deeper philosophy. Having been to the depths of trouble, he understood the problems of people in trouble." Perkins' assessment not only is accurate but essential in understanding FDR's later relationship with victims of the Great Depression. Because he had suffered, he was able to empathize with those Americans physically and emotionally devastated by the Depression. To the destitute, the smiling, confident, reassuring "only thing we have to fear is fear itself" attitude FDR displayed in the face of the Depression uplifted the people, for they believed he knew something about their plight first-hand, having himself endured a terrible affliction. Without this "blessing in disguise," FDR's jauntiness in the thirties might have turned people against him as the activities of a privileged man who did not understand life's hardships. When asked years later if he ever worried, Roosevelt responded: "If you had spent two years in bed trying to wiggle your toe, after that anything would seem easy." Roosevelt's paralysis changed him in more than the obvious physical ways. It enabled him to present himself to the public as a magnificent success story, one with which Depression folk could identify far more readily than they could with stories of business achievement. Polio was not alone, however, in providing FDR with sufficient compassion to deal with the collapse. He owed much of his success to his wife.

Anna Eleanor Roosevelt was FDR's fifth cousin, once removed, both sharing the same great-great-great-great-great grandfather, Nicholas Roosevelt (1658-1742), the family patriarch. Eleanor was also the first child of TR's younger brother, Elliot, and his wife, the former Anna Hall. From the moment of her birth, Eleanor suffered rejection. Both of her parents wanted a "precious boy," and when Eleanor arrived, "a more wrinkled and less attractive baby than average," both her parents were sorely disappointed. Especially disturbed was Eleanor's mother, a strikingly beautiful woman, whose disappointment at having such an allegedly ugly child was compounded by a difficult pregnancy in which she almost died. Anna Roosevelt never reconciled to her daughter's less than acceptable looks and called her "Granny."

Given this rejection by her mother and both her parent's subsequent early deaths, Eleanor felt abandoned and unloved. Such feelings were intensified when after her father's death (Anna Roosevelt died two years before her husband) she was placed with her grandmother, who not only ignored her but put her under the "care" of a cruel governess. Thus, even as a child, Eleanor felt sympathy for the poor and rejected, for whom she felt obvious kinship.

Although not the raving beauty of some of the other Roosevelt women, Eleanor nonetheless was attractive enough to catch the eye of young Franklin, who from all accounts initially genuinely loved Eleanor enough to want to marry her, despite his mother's protestations and nasty machinations to prevent the union. Interestingly, the two cousins had often played together when they were children. As noted earlier, Franklin and Eleanor married on St. Patrick's Day 1905 in New York, and President Theodore Roosevelt gave the bride away. Although FDR entered into his relationship with Eleanor based on mutual love and companionship, his marriage to the president's niece undoubtedly served him well personally and politically, bringing him greater social prestige and closer to the family of his idol.

In the first eleven years of their marriage, Eleanor gave birth to six children, an occupation that left her little time for further intellectual and social development. Her mother-in-law continued to dominate the family. Sara Roosevelt tried to turn Eleanor into a conventional society matron, which she was successful in accomplishing during this time. Suffice it to say, Eleanor chafed at Sara's controlling behavior and constant meddling, as the two became rivals for the affections of both Franklin and the children. As the two women in his life engaged in competitive rancor, FDR typically ignored the strife, acting as if all was well in the Roosevelt household.

In addition to her close relationship to TR, Eleanor soon proved in other ways to be an important political asset to her husband. Although still suffering from an inferiority complex, and thus painfully shy and at times awkward, Eleanor nonetheless strove to overcome these handicaps and in the process became a wonderfully gracious and kind person who won many friends for Franklin in both Albany and Washington during his early career. Moreover, at this time she was not nearly as physically unattractive, as unflattering photographs years later would convey, and most important, what she lacked in outward beauty was more than compensated by her warmth and inner radiance. Eleanor's eyes "caressed one with sympathy and studied one with intelligence."

Work during World War I led Eleanor to become more independent. It also saw her make a commitment to public service and helping others. The sleeping princess, as the poet Archibald MacLeish put it years later, had been awakened. It was not, however, the World War I experience alone that changed Eleanor into an independent woman dedicated to social service; there was at the same time a private war: the discovery of her husband's affair with Lucy Mercer. As already noted, FDR's adultery forever changed his relationship with Eleanor. In many ways, literally and symbolically, FDR's infidelity was as much a life-altering event for Eleanor as polio was for her husband. The affair made Eleanor even more determined to become as completely independent of her husband as was politically and socially safe for the both of them. Eleanor concluded that henceforth advancing her husband's career was the key to promoting her own. The more visible FDR became the more good she might hope to accomplish through humanitarian endeavors. In a 1932 interview she stated candidly that she "never wanted to be a President's wife, and I don't want to now." Ironically, she was undoubtedly one of the best "Presidents' wives" this nation has ever had.

Despite their marital estrangement, Franklin and Eleanor proved to be a winning team, especially in the political arena. Their strengths complimented each other. Her compassion was a match for his ambition, and over the years, particularly after their great crises, each of these qualities affected the other spouse. How invaluable was Eleanor in FDR becoming president? Without question, her help was indispensable. Even if he had on his own initiative won the presidency, he certainly would not have been the same beloved, benevolent father figure that he became during the Great Depression. Eleanor was as responsible for that image as FDR was, because she was embraced by the people as being as genuinely concerned about their well being as he was. The volumes of letters Depression sufferers sent to the both of them reflected this perception; indeed, many were addressed only to Eleanor, whom many Americans believed was more understanding or sympathetic to their plight because she was a *woman* and, thus, *naturally* would be more inclined to listen to their problems and to do something about them. In short, being First Lady gave Eleanor Roosevelt a wider arena in which to distribute her love. From her tragic childhood onward, Eleanor's life was a constant search for love. In this quest to be loved by others, she was widely and deeply lavish in her solicitude. She was not the sort of person who claimed to "love everybody" but to have real affection for nobody. On the contrary, her compassion was genuine and was reflected in intensely personal friendships with many individuals. As Joseph Lash has noted, she was "a woman of great vitality, whose affectionate nature overflowed and constantly sought opportunities to dispense love upon those she cared about and those who needed her love."

In recent years, it has been strongly suggested that Eleanor "lavished" her love in a homosexual relationship with Lorena Hickok, an Associated Press reporter who was assigned to cover Eleanor in 1932. The two women apparently became fast "friends, and their correspondence suggests that a passionate, physical relationship developed. During the 1933 inauguration ceremonies, Eleanor wore the ring given to her by Hickok as a symbolic token of their intimacy. It is interesting to compare this clandestine act by Eleanor and Hickok with FDR's secret gift of a car to Lucy Mercer on the same day! "Oh! I want to put my arms around you," Eleanor wrote to Hickok a few days later. "I ache to hold you close. Your ring is a great comfort. I look at it and think, she does love me or I wouldn't be wearing it!"

There is little doubt that Lorena Hickok loved Eleanor Roosevelt and that Eleanor reciprocated those same feelings. It would be natural for Eleanor to feel such tenderness toward Lorena Hickok, especially when one considers Eleanor's quest for love and FDR's lack of affection toward her. Yet, despite the passionate exchanges between the two women, there is strong reason to believe that the sort of love Eleanor longed for was neither heterosexual nor homosexual; rather, it was asexual. She wrote letters similar to the one she wrote Hickok to a number of people, both male and female. What's most important historically was that impelling one of the most preeminent figures in the twentieth century to greatness was a need for love and a desire to express it by helping the downtrodden of the United States and the world. Caring for others, improving their lives, made Eleanor feel needed. Beyond that, it is not necessary to probe deeper into her personal life to find conclusive answers.

Part of FDR's aristocratic heritage entailed stoic acceptance of hardship, not complaining. He previously had little opportunity to practice this virtue, but now he performed it superbly. He refused to admit defeat—or even the possibility of defeat. Always convinced of his own destiny, FDR decided soon after his affliction that he "must have been shattered and spared for a purpose beyond his knowledge." It was a short step to concluding that God's purpose was what it had always been: to make him President of the United States.

FDR began his assent toward his "destiny" by making a dramatic appearance at the 1924 Democratic National Convention. Most pundits and watchdogs of both parties had written Roosevelt off politically, but when he appeared like Phoenix rising at the party gathering at Madison Square Garden, radiating confidence and strength with his irrepressible smile, people knew FDR "was back." He came to nominate fellow New Yorker and longtime rival Al Smith for president, praising the Irishman as "The Happy Warrior of the political battlefield." Despite FDR's endorsement, Smith was not nominated in 1924, but in 1928 when Al Smith became the Democratic candidate for president, he convinced FDR to run for governor of New York, a position Smith had held since 1922. While campaigning for Smith, Americans got a glimpse of their future president's position on labor reform, which became an integral feature of the New Deal. FDR criticized Republicans who he said belonged "to the old school of thought, which held to the theory that when an employer hired working men or working women, that employer became the master of the fate of his employees; that when a worker entered the factory doors it was nobody's business as to how he worked, how long he was worked, or how much he was paid."

Riding the Republican tide, which was at its peak in 1928, Herbert Hoover soundly defeated Al Smith, the first ethnic American (Irish American) and Catholic to run for president. FDR, however, won a narrow victory in that year's New York governor's race but was easily reelected two years later. From the start, FDR proved himself a capable, energetic governor. The Great Depression, which began in the fall of 1929 and worsened by the month, brought out Roosevelt's best: his talent for administration and his ability to manage a crisis. In 1931 he created the Temporary Emergency Relief Administration, the first agency of its kind in any state to provide food, clothing, and housing for the unemployed and to find them jobs if possible. As the Depression deepened, FDR began moving away from his usual centrist position, especially on social reform issues, and began articulating a nascent liberalism (he would argue that it was merely reformulated progressivism), which would become the ideological foundation of the New Deal. Moreover, advocacy of such "radicalism" was not only politically safe but opportune as well.

Both FDR and his party believed it imperative to offer an alternative to Hooverism and traditional Republican ideology, which was still mired in rugged individualism and laissez faire. In a 1931 speech, FDR declared that it was time for social interests to supersede individual concerns. People created government "for their mutual protection and well-being," and consequently, "the duty of the State toward citizens is the duty of the servant to its master." One of those duties "is that of caring for those of its citizens who find themselves the victims of such adverse circumstances as makes them unable to obtain even the necessities for mere existence without the aid of others. . . . In broad terms I assert that modern society, acting through its Government, owes the definite obligation to prevent starvation or the dire want of any of its fellow men and women who try to maintain themselves but cannot." It was not a matter of charity, he concluded, but "a matter of social duty."

By 1932 FDR was a leading contender for the Democratic presidential nomination. In an April radio address called "the forgotten man" speech, Roosevelt put a new dynamic on what he had been saying for twenty years. The Republicans favored top-down policies, he asserted, while he wanted lasting economic recovery, which required new initiatives that "put their faith once more in the forgotten man at the bottom of economic pyramid." He compared the economic crisis to a war and demanded that the nation "mobilize" to meet it. He defined what he thought were a "few essentials of a planned program": restoring agricultural purchasing power, protecting homeowners from the threat of mortgage foreclosures, and obtaining foreign markets for American goods by lowering the nation's exorbitant tariffs. Above all, FDR insisted, people and their leaders had to accept the fact "that we are in the midst of an emergency."

On July 2, 1932, appearing at the Democratic convention in Chicago to accept the party's presidential nomination, FDR promised "a new deal for the American people." Though delivered with great passion and sincerity, FDR's acceptance speech, like that of most nominees, was filled with great hope and expectation but contained little of specific substance. It didn't matter, however, for by 1932, all the majority of Americans wanted was someone to reassure them that he would do all he could to address the crisis and, in the process, lead them out of the abyss and back into the light of security, stability, and prosperity. As FDR told his audience, Americans wanted "Two Things: Work; work with all the moral and spiritual values that go with work. And with work, a reasonable measure of security—security for themselves and for their wives and children." He rejected the notion that inviolable, "natural" economic laws make depressions inevitable. The fact was that "men and women are starving," that "economic laws are not made by nature. They are made by human beings." The states had the primary responsibility for relieving distress, but FDR declared, "the Federal Government has always had and still has a continuing responsibility for the broader public welfare." In a real sense, the history of FDR's presidency was the history of the government's efforts—often halting, always controversial—to shoulder that responsibility.

In November 1932, FDR crushed Herbert Hoover by over seven million popular votes and by a margin of 472 to 59 in the electoral college. The result was a clear mandate for FDR and his proposed "new deal." The Democratic Party also swept to victory in both houses of Congress, giving FDR a 59 to 36 advantage in the Senate and in the House a cushion of 313 to 117. Moreover, FDR was taking office at a time of unprecedented crisis and, thus, could count on an extraordinary amount of cooperation, especially from fellow Democrats and particularly from the ranks of those elected for the first time wanting to hitch their political wagons to FDR's "horses" as soon as possible. As a Midwestern congressman told him, "I will do anything you ask. You are my leader." From FDR's perspective, the stakes could not have been higher. He feared, like many other Americans, that if something was not done soon to address the crisis, the nation was headed for revolution.

During the campaign, FDR asserted that everyone had "a right to make a comfortable living," that the government "owes to every one an avenue to possess himself of a portion of that plenty sufficient for his needs, through his own work." Thus, the focus of the early New Deal was not on reform but on recovery—that is, to give as much government assistance to big business and agribusiness, the foundations of American corporate capitalism, on whose fate, it was believed, an upturn depended. Indeed, FDR was more of a conservative reformer than most businessmen understood. From the beginning of the New Deal to its end, FDR's motivation in his reform policies was to preserve capitalism and democracy. As a recent Roosevelt biographer has asserted, FDR's principal concern throughout the New Deal was "to prevent the extremes of American society from crowding the center and stampeding the masses in unacceptable attitudes. . . . Like Bismarck and Disraeli, and his cousin Theodore, he wished to reform the system sufficiently to immunize it against extremes and ensure that everyone shared in the general prosperity, but meritocratically, not through imposed redistributive equality." Thus, weaker, more marginal groups such as small businesses, blue-collar workers, and landless farmers found themselves on the outside looking in and would have to wait until FDR deemed them "worthy" of his attention, which would not occur until late in the first New Deal. Even then, much of what they received was "tokenism" when compared to the largesse received by corporations and agribusiness. Yet, even the earliest New Deal measures clearly indicated that FDR intended to move the country in a dramatically new direction.

One of the most important new directions was the centralization of power in the executive branch, which FDR implemented almost immediately. From the beginning to the end of the New Deal, Roosevelt made all the important decisions himself. Like his cousin Theodore, FDR created myriad specialized task forces, staffed with experts to help him more effectively deal with the Depression. He created a multitude of new "emergency" agencies instead of relying on the various departments to effect strategies and policies.

Although FDR's imprint was on the New Deal, the programs and policies established and implemented were not entirely of the president's making. The New Deal ultimately drew on many sources, but the most innovative and sometimes the most "radical" were largely the handiwork of the "brain trust," a small but influential coterie of advisers and cabinet members, many of whom came from the nation's most acclaimed universities, such as Columbia professors Rexford G. Tugwell, Raymond Moley, and Adolf Berle. Those cabinet members having FDR's ear were Secretary of the Interior Harold Ickes, Secretary of Agriculture Henry A. Wallace, Secretary of Labor Frances Perkins, and New Deal ombudsman Harry Hopkins. Congressional leaders, such as New York Senator Robert F. Wagner, also played key roles in shaping the New Deal agenda. One of FDR's most difficult tasks was to meld such disparate personalities and personal ideologies into a workable coalition that would deliver the programs needed most by the people at the appropriate time. The New Deal, as historian Michael Parrish has noted, "bore the stamp of many authors, arose from no master plan, and did not fit neatly into a single ideological box."

As reflected in the brain trust's influence on the New Deal, FDR was one of the most accessible presidents in United States history. He was always willing to hear new ideas; he constantly sought information outside the normal corridors. FDR's willingness to listen to any ideas, no matter how unconventional they appeared, opened the door for new thoughts and new thinkers. As the bringing to the White House of the

Columbia professors confirmed, intellectuals played key roles in the Oval Office, the likes of which had not been seen since the days before Andrew Jackson, when Jefferson and the Adamses fit into that category. Even Woodrow Wilson, a university professor, did not give scholars the prominence they had in the New Deal. In short, by employing intellectuals as advisers, FDR was trying to reach Jacksonian ends by bringing together the plowman and the professor.

In addition to helping business and agriculture cope with the ravages of the Depression, FDR put into action his long-held belief that government, especially in crisis times, had a moral obligation to provide relief to the destitute. Funds to aid the unemployed were first dispensed through the Federal Emergency Relief Administration (FERA) and then during the winter of 1933-34 through the Civil Works Administration (CWA), the Public Works Administration (PWA), and then lastly through the Works Progress Administration (WPA). By providing either direct unemployment relief via FERA to those unable to find work, or by issuing outright federal grants to the states through the CWA, PWA, and WPA to employ those able to work, FDR broke decisively with past practice and provided millions of Americans with the necessities of life or, as was the case with the various work programs, a job and, with that, hope and respectability. By providing such relief, either directly or indirectly, FDR was challenging the sanctity of what he believed were the outdated notions of laissez faire and rugged individualism. In his mind, from this point on, the federal government was to assume the responsibility to help those who through no fault of their own could not help themselves. This was not socialism; rather, FDR, through his relief programs, was laying the foundation of the modern welfare state and its concomitant ideology—liberalism. As FDR told Congress in 1938, "Government has a final responsibility for the well-being of its citizenship. If private, co-operative endeavor fails to provide work for willing hands and relief for the unfortunate, those suffering hardship from no fault of their own have a right to call upon the Government for aid; and a government worthy of its name must make fitting response."

No cause was nearer FDR's heart than conservation, and like his cousin Teddy, FDR proved to be a determined naturalist and ecologist. In fact, in no other area did his administration devise more innovative, protective, and lasting measures. "The forests are the 'lungs' of our land," he once said, "purifying our air and giving fresh strength to our people." The Civilian Conservation Corps (CCC), which enrolled half a million young men (initially only white males, ages 18 to 25, were recruited to work on the various projects; however, thanks to Eleanor's exhortations or admonishments, young black men also found employment in their "own" CCC), combined the functions of relief and forestry. The volunteers fought forest fires, planted trees, reseeded grazing lands, and constructed roads, bridges, water-storage basins, and even new national parks, such as Big Bend in southwest Texas. They also built wildlife refuges, fish-rearing ponds, and animal shelters.

Without question the most ambitious, grandiose, and acclaimed project of FDR's rural reclamation/conservation agenda was the Tennessee Valley Authority (TVA). This program called for the government, rather than private corporations, to directly foster economic development through the vast watershed area of the south known as the Tennessee Valley. This extensive river basin winds through parts of six southern states, and in the areas where these rivers flowed, poverty was widespread because of the inhabitants' inability to control these rivers, especially during the rainy season. Flooding was endemic as the surging rivers destroyed towns and farms. Thus, the primary objective of the TVA was to control the flooding of the Tennessee River while simultaneously harnessing its water power to generate electricity, develop local industry (such as fertilizer production), improve river transportation, and in the process ease the poverty and isolation of the region's population. In some respects the TVA's mandate resembled that of the PWA, but the TVA had greater authority over economic development, which reflected the influence of New Dealers such as Rexford G. Tugwell, who were committed to statism: the creation of government-planned and government-operated enterprises. Although advisers such as Tugwell never publicly admitted so, they were drawn to certain socialist ideas such as public ownership of key industries and utilities.

Although the TVA was one of the New Deal's most touted successes and boldest experiments in government planning (as well as coming dangerously close to socialism), it generated little enthusiasm for more ambitious programs in national planning. Contrary to what many conservative critics of the era asserted, and even after the Depression was over, neither FDR nor the New Deal embraced the idea of the federal government as a substitute for private enterprise. Nonetheless, when FDR wanted to sum up his proudest domestic achievement as president, he often cited the TVA. Today, delegates at a Democratic National Convention would snicker in baffled disbelief if a speaker saluted FDR for his greatest accomplishment: rural electrification. But the symbolic significance of the TVA and similar projects can hardly be exaggerated.

They were thought of not as mere public utility companies but as the pilot projects of a new and "futuristic" way of life. FDR, as well as many of his allies and supporters, believed the TVA provided a model for a new kind of technological civilization superior to that of the early industrial era. In 1937, Baker Brownell, a professor at Northwestern University, wrote that the TVA was "building more than a dam. It is building a civilization. The visitor here [at Norris Dam] is looking into the next century."

Power-generating dams were to New Deal state capitalists what steel mills were to communists and what stock exchanges were to the neoliberal free-marketers of the late twentieth-century—not just institutions but icons. Here is a song from *Power*, a 1937 pro-New Deal play: "All up and down the valley/They hear the great alarm;/The government means business/It's working like a charm/Oh see them boys a-comin'/Their government they trust/Just hear their hammers ringin;/They'll build that dam or bust."

By 1935, within two years of taking office, Roosevelt had transformed Americans' expectations by demonstrating that they could reasonably look to government for assistance when faced with economic distress. In the process, he effectively disarmed conservative critics who asserted that New Deal programs were subverting personal initiative. In a fireside chat in June 1934, the president rebutted those "plausible self-seekers and theoretical diehards who will tell you of the loss of individual liberty." He told his listeners to answer that contention "out of the facts of your own life. Have you lost any of your rights or liberty or constitutional freedom of action and choice?" All anyone had to do, he added, was read the Bill of Rights "and ask yourself whether you personally have suffered the impairment of a single jot of these great assurances." He was confident of the answer. "The record is written in the experiences of your own personal lives."

By the end of his first term in office, FDR had expanded the role of government in people's lives. In doing so, he permanently changed citizens' assumptions about what government could and should do to protect them against the excesses and vagaries of capitalism. Nothing better illustrates FDR's repudiation of laissez faire and rugged individualism than the 1936 Democratic Party platform. Drafted by one of FDR's advisers, Samuel I. Rosenman, it contained many of the president's ideas and beliefs, including a line based on the Declaration of Independence: "We hold these truths to be self-evident—that government in a modern civilization has certain inescapable obligations to its citizens, among which are: (1) Protection of the family and the home; (2) Establishment of a democracy of opportunity for all the people; (3) Aid to those overtaken by disaster."

During the 1936 presidential campaign, FDR took dead aim at those he called "economic royalists." His direct appeal to class resentments was unprecedented for a major party candidate. Denouncing the "new economic royalty" that had once dominated American capitalism, FDR claimed that the rich and powerful opposed the New Deal because it had destroyed their dictatorial power. The "privileged princes of these new economic dynasties," FDR asserted, "thirsting for power, reached out for control over the government itself. They created a new despotism and wrapped it in the robes of legal sanction." The Great Depression, however, "showed up the despotism for what it was," and people turned to government for salvation. FDR defended his program without apology: "Governments can err—Presidents do make mistakes, but the immortal Dante tell us that divine justice weighs the sins of the cold-blooded and the sins of the warm-hearted in different scales. Better the occasional faults of a government that lives in a spirit of charity than the consistent omissions of a government frozen in the ice of its own indifference."

Roosevelt turned the 1936 presidential election into a struggle for democracy and social sovereignty between the haves and have-nots. In Depression America the latter were obviously the majority and by 1936 overwhelmingly had embraced FDR, liberalism, and the New Deal. Despite Herbert Hoover's rantings that FDR was preaching "the gospel of class hatred," Roosevelt embarrassed the lackluster Republican candidate Alfred M. Landon by the largest electoral vote ever recorded: 523 to 8. The popular vote was equally devastating for the Republicans, as FDR won by over eleven million votes, giving him 60.8 percent of the ballots cast. In Congress the Democrats won enormous majorities. In the House, the Democrats had an advantage of 331 to 89, and in the Senate their margin was 76 to 16. FDR clearly had won a popular mandate both for himself and his party. Even more important was the electorate's class alignment: 42 percent of upper-income voters backed FDR, compared to 60 percent of middle income and 76 percent of lower income voters. A whopping 80 percent of union members voted for FDR, as did 84 percent of relief recipients. A letter FDR received from a Texas furniture worker summed up the feelings most middle to lower class Americans had for FDR in 1936: "You are the one & only President that ever helped a Working Class of people."

In winning reelection, Roosevelt forged a coalition that would dominate the nation's politics for nearly fifty years. Not until the 1980s, with the Republican Ronald Reagan's two electoral victories, would the powerful voting blocs FDR put together to sustain the Democratic Party as the majority party begin to unravel. The combination embraced southern whites as well as northern blacks, rural folks as well as urban immigrants, farmers as well as blue-collar workers, middle-class homeowners and jobless men and women—all attracted by programs and policies that benefited them and sometimes saved their very lives. In short, FDR in four years took a once weak, leaderless, and polarized party and united it into a partisan juggernaut that would guarantee both him and fellow Democrats election victories for decades to come. FDR also made the Democratic Party the progenitor of the welfare state and with that the promise that, even after he was gone, the party could be trusted to expand such assistance and protection to fit the exigencies of future generations of Americans. The coalition also had an ethnic and religious dimension, for the New Deal gave Jews and Catholics, previously *persona non grata*, especially at the national level, a greater voice in policymaking and, consequently, cemented those groups' loyalties to the Democratic Party. FDR's electoral base, however, was built on pocketbook issues. In the following decades, whenever economic concerns were foremost in the public mind, the Roosevelt coalition reasserted itself. As long as the issues remained primarily economic, with all partners benefiting to varying but satisfactory degrees, the alliance remained intact and concomitantly kept the Democratic Party in power. However, as will be seen, during the presidency of Lyndon Baines Johnson, the major issues became social, causing bitter cultural, class, and racial conflicts, all of which were aggravated by equally divisive foreign policy debates. When that occurred, the tensions inherent in the coalition led to its fragmentation and ultimate demise.

The Roosevelt Presidency: A Positive Assessment

One of FDR's greatest challenges as president, especially as events in Europe and Asia brought those areas of the world closer to war, was to move the American people away from isolationism and into accepting a renewed spirit of internationalism. This was no easy task. As noted earlier, feeling betrayed and duped by both their government and business, Americans were determined in the postwar decades to never again be manipulated into fighting another foreign conflict. They not only blamed the high-minded idealism and naïveté of Wilsonian foreign policy but the private sector as well. Indeed, many Americans believed that the war represented a mischievous conspiracy by munitions manufacturers and bankers to get the United States involved for their own profit. Beginning in the 1920s and intensifying in the 1930s, Americans once again embraced isolationism. They were convinced that the best and only way for the United States to avoid getting "sucked" into another debacle was to retrench the nation's overall foreign relations. To the majority of Americans in the 1920s and 1930s, the international order was corrupt, venal, and beyond redemption. FDR set out to reverse these perceptions. He understood the dire consequences of Nazi ambitions for world hegemony. How to get his fellow citizens to understand the ramifications of German aggression and in the process embrace internationalism, especially given their revulsion toward that idea, was the task at hand for FDR.

As the decade of the 1930s progressed and more menacing signs of both German and Japanese aggression appeared, FDR found it more effective to use the rhetoric of moral values and suasion to get Americans to understand what was at stake if the nation remained aloof from international events. Thus, throughout the 1930s he repeatedly discussed Nazi belligerency as a direct threat to the most cherished American beliefs in freedom of speech, freedom of religion, and freedom of occupational choice. When German actions confirmed his exhortations, the opportunity presented itself for carrying the nation toward another great crusade on behalf of democracy, freedom, and peace. FDR wisely avoided Wilson's penchant for righteous overstatement, but he understood the necessity of generating the moral imperative as a means of moving the nation toward the intervention he knew to be necessary if both the United States' self-interest—and its moral principles—were to be preserved.

The Atlantic Charter, promulgated in conjunction with British Prime Minister Winston Churchill, off the coast of Newfoundland in the summer of 1941, best represents FDR's quest for moral justification of United States involvement in World War II. The Charter set forth the common goals both nations would pursue over the next few years, including those in the war's immediate aftermath. There would be no secret commitments, FDR declared. The United States and Great Britain sought no territorial aggrandizement. They would oppose any violation of the right to self-government for all peoples. They stood for free trade, free exchange of ideas, freedom of worship and expression, and the creation of an international organization to preserve and protect future peace. This would be a war fought for freedom—freedom from fear, freedom from want, freedom of religion, freedom from the old politics of balance-of-power diplomacy and *realpolitik.* In many ways, the Charter was FDR's Fourteen Points—his agenda for the postwar world, which hopefully this time around the American people would embrace, understanding that part of the nation's destiny was to participate in world affairs, not retreat from responsibility as they had in the past. Indeed, FDR believed that the United States must become a viable, active member of the world community, not only to prevent future aggression but to fulfill the nation's moral obligation to humanity to help lead it down the righteous and glorious path toward democracy and liberty. In essence, just as FDR believed the government had a covenant to help those Americans who through no fault of their own could not help themselves, so he believed the United States had a similar commitment to the nations of the world.

FDR deeply believed in these ideals and saw no inconsistency between the moral principles they represented and American self-interest. However, Roosevelt's vision threatened conflict with the Soviet Union, an American ally during the war. Indeed, some would argue that is was our most important ally, whose wartime contributions were far greater and more significant than England's. FDR understood that Russia's battle was America's. "The Russian armies are killing more Axis personnel and destroying more Axis materiel," he wrote General Douglas MacArthur in 1942, "than all the other twenty-five United Nations put together." As soon as Germany invaded Russian in the summer of 1941, FDR ordered that lend-lease supplies be made immediately available to the Soviet Union. Roosevelt knew that American aid was essential to keeping Russia in the war; without such assistance the Germans would prevail, leaving the United States in an untenable position. Frustrated by the slow delivery of American hardware to the Soviets, FDR lambasted his cabinet, shouting he was "sick and tired of hearing what was on order"; he wanted to hear only "what was on the water." Roosevelt's commitment to lend-lease reflected his understanding and conviction that aid to the Soviets was both the most effective way of combating German aggression and the strongest means of building a foundation of trust with Stalin to facilitate postwar cooperation.

Unfortunately for FDR, Josef Stalin's vision of the war's purpose, as well as his postwar priorities, was embodied not in the spirit of the Atlantic Charter but in *realpolitik,* especially in obtaining his country's future security. The Soviet Union sought "spheres of influence" over which it would have unrestricted control—something Stalin deemed essential not only for future security reasons but also to help Russia rebuild its war-ravaged economy. Such spheres would provide the Soviet Union with the resources necessary for reconstruction. The Soviets also wanted territorial boundaries that would reflect the concessions won through military conflict. All these objectives ran counter to the Atlantic Charter. As already established, FDR was never afraid of inconsistency and, thus, often "talked" the same language as Stalin. Frequently, he spoke of guaranteeing the Soviet Union "measures of legitimate security" on territorial questions, and he envisioned a postwar world in which the "four policemen"—the superpowers (the United States, the U.S.S.R, Great Britain, and China)—would manage the world.

As the war drew to an end, two disquietingly different perceptions of the Soviet Union emerged. Some Washington officials believed that Stalin's perception of the war and his postwar vision simply reflected national history in which suspicion of outsiders was natural, given repeated invasions from Western Europe and rampant hostility toward Bolshevism on the part of Western powers since 1917. Former Ambassador to Moscow Joseph Davies believed that the way to alleviate that suspicion and hostility was to adopt "the simple approach of assuming that what they say, they mean." In other words, they needed to recognize the historical imperatives driving Soviet policy and try to accommodate them without jeopardizing the other Allies' interests.

The majority of well-informed Americans endorsed a different position. It was folly, one newspaper correspondent wrote, "to prettify Stalin, whose internal homicide record is even longer than Hitler's." Hitler and Stalin were of the same breed, former Ambassador to Russia William Bullitt insisted. Each wanted to spread his power "to the ends of the earth. Stalin, like Hitler, will not stop. He can only *be* stopped." According to Bullitt, any alternative view implied "a conversion of Stalin as striking as the conversion of Saul on the road to Damascus." Senator Robert Taft of Ohio agreed. It made no sense, he insisted, to base U.S. policy toward the Soviet Union "on the delightful theory that Mr. Stalin in the end will turn out to have an angelic nature." Drawing on the historical precedents of Stalin's infamous purges and traditional American hostility to communism, totalitarianism, and Stalin, those who held these convictions saw little hope of compromise. "There is as little difference between communism and fascism," Monsignor J. Fulton Sheen said, "as there is between burglary and larceny." The only appropriate response to stopping Stalin's aggression was force. Instead of "leaning over backward to be nice to the descendants of Genghis Khan," General George Patton suggested, "we should dictate to them and do it now and in no uncertain terms." Within such a frame of reference, the lessons of history and of ideological incompatibility seemed to permit no possibility of compromise.

FDR, ever the optimist and confident of his abilities to rally public support for his concept of foreign policy, believed it was possible to find a path of mutual accommodation that would sustain and nourish the prospects of postwar partnership while allowing for the exigencies of geopolitics. The choice in his mind was clear. "We shall have to take the responsibility for world collaboration," he told Congress, "or we shall bear the responsibility for another world conflict." FDR was neither politically naïve nor stupid. Even though committed to the Atlantic Charter's ideals of self-determination and territorial integrity, he recognized the legitimacy of the Soviets' need for national security. For him, the process of politics—informed by thirty-five years of skilled practice—involved negotiations and compromises that made both sides feel like winners. FDR acknowledged Stalin's brutal, psychotic tyranny; indeed, in 1940, he called Russia as absolute a dictatorship as existed anywhere. Nonetheless, that did not mean a solution was impossible or that one should disengage from the struggle as a basis for world peace. As FDR was fond of saying about negotiations with the Soviets, "it is permitted to walk with the devil until the bridge is crossed."

As with most political figures, it is very difficult to find the real Roosevelt behind his public persona, which almost always wore a smile. To most of those who knew him or met him, what impressed them the most was his irrepressible charm. He was able to beguile even those who opposed his policies or were not satisfied with his program's accomplishments. Consequently, most Americans during the 1930s credited FDR for everything they liked while blaming others for what upset them. This was especially true for Southerners, who initially welcomed the New Deal, especially its rural reclamation projects and work programs, but who later became uneasy with its call for social reform legislation, which they believed was code for black equality. However, these same Southerners were caught in a conundrum because they wanted to remain loyal to their party and president; yet they opposed his social policies. "Now I understand how it was possible for my family to worship FDR despite all the things he had done during his administration that enraged them," Southern journalist Florence King has written. "It was very simple: Credit Franklin, better known as He, for all the things you like, and blame Eleanor, better known as She or 'that woman,' for all the things you don't like. This way, He was cleared, She was castigated, and We were happy." In essence, FDR was so popular because of his personality (or charm) that he had that rare luxury of having a host of "fall guys," including his wife (also serving in that capacity were Harry Hopkins and Secretary of Agriculture Henry A. Wallace), on whom the public blamed everything that went wrong or that they didn't like about the New Deal. Ironically, Eleanor was the far greater humanitarian and altruist than FDR and in many instances was a key player in formulating New Deal policies, especially the more socially controversial ones. Unfortunately (or perhaps fortunately), she did not possess her husband's gift for dissembling with a smile or cajolery and thus was often the recipient of public criticism and scorn.

Much of FDR's popularity was, and is, attributable to his "times"; that is, to the events, both at home and abroad, that affected the nation during his tenure. In the top five "greatest" presidents, only Theodore Roosevelt (usually ranked fourth, with Andrew Jackson fifth and George Washington third) presided at a time of no major crises, whether domestic or foreign. FDR, second behind Lincoln in "greatness," experienced two of the nation's largest crises during his twelve years in office: the Great Depression and World War II. Yet, facing a crisis does not guarantee popularity, especially a war, as the experiences of Harry Truman, Lyndon Johnson, and Richard Nixon attest. Thus, one must search beyond the "good fortune" of being president in a time of crises to explain the public's extraordinary affection for FDR. One obvious answer is that, during hard times, people want a strong, confident, optimistic, and courageous leader to lead them out of the darkness to the promised land of security, stability, and eventually prosperity. Roosevelt certainly fulfilled that expectation. But that is too simplistic and is thus superficial. As one study demonstrated, to underprivileged people "a tremendously powerful man who still is very personally human and who still champions the little man's cause is the truly admirable man." This, the study rightly concluded, was the way most of the dispossessed and disenfranchised looked at FDR. "He was perceived as a warm, understanding man, a man with great power and status, a man with competence, who was, withal, a champion of the little man."

No other American politician in the twentieth century (and none so far in the twenty-first) has been able to project the image of the populist patrician like FDR. Perhaps Robert Kennedy has come the closest, with Theodore Roosevelt doing a good job in originating the role at the start of the century. But no one else has gotten quite the audience reaction or rave reviews that FDR received. "From his fresh mind and resolute utterance," *The New York Times* said editorially of Roosevelt after his inauguration, "the people accept, with great calm and fine spirit, what would have seriously upset them if it had been set forth by a dying Administration." Famed folklorist and humorist Will Rogers noted that, "The whole country [is] with him. Just so he does something. If he burned down the Capitol, we should cheer and say, 'Well, we at least got a fire started.'"

Poor Americans' admiration for FDR was something so powerful that it has survived for decades after his death. In many homes, especially in those of Depression "survivors," it is not uncommon to see a painting of Jesus tending His flock with a photograph of FDR hanging above or beside it. The association of FDR with Jesus or other religious figures was common among Depression victims. A Wisconsin woman reported that a three-year-old girl who was visiting her home identified a picture of FDR as "Saint Roosevelt." She further declared that, "As long as Pres. Roosevelt will be our leader under Jesus Christ we feel no fear." For those who saw FDR's place in the Chain of Being a bit lower than Jesus, Abraham Lincoln sufficed. "My wife and I consider you to be the most humane man to occupy the chair since Lincoln," an elderly Texan wrote to FDR in 1935. An Arkansas Republican agreed, stating that, "Roosevelt has proved himself to be one of the greatest humanitarians and the most Christian of any President since Lincoln's time."

Why were FDR and the majority of the American people so "connected" during the Great Depression? Did he sincerely want to help the nation, or did he use both the crisis and the New Deal for personal political gain? These and myriad other questions can be asked about FDR but can never be definitively answered because, as Roosevelt's Secretary of the Treasury Henry Morgenthau said, FDR was "a man of bewildering complexity of moods and motives." We can assert, however, with confidence that FDR, with his sense of stewardship and his personal experience with suffering, genuinely wanted to help the people; he also wanted to become president, be reelected, and go down in history as a great leader, all of which he accomplished in the first year of his fourth term.

This most enigmatic of men became the most influential American political leader of the twentieth century. Although he did not achieve all his goals, his accomplishments are nevertheless impressive. He initiated the ideology of liberalism and positive government (the welfare state), that is, that the federal government is not only to regulate the economy, preventing excesses and abuses, but to "fix it" as well when it experiences downturns. It also means that the government has a responsibility to ensure employment for every American and to guarantee a minimum standard of living. FDR transformed, if not revolutionized, the executive branch, especially in its growth in power, creating what William E. Leuchtenberg has called "the first modern presidency." In many ways, FDR simply expanded presidential power by augmenting executive authority established by earlier presidents, most notably Lincoln, Theodore Roosevelt, and Woodrow Wilson. FDR's activism, however, went far beyond his predecessors, especially in the key area of initiating social reform legislation. FDR redefined the concept of executive activism. Beginning with FDR and to the present, we not only expect the president to lead and administer the laws but to have a vision for the country, an agenda to implement, a "program" to present to Congress, who will hopefully legislate it into effect with the president providing guidance and moral and ideological "inspiration." Thanks to FDR's presidential style and leadership, executive activism became the *sine qua non* of liberalism. So dominant was FDR in this capacity that Rexford Tugwell declared, "Nothing could be done at all unless we hung together under a leader . . . we had no real right to make judgments." As will be seen, this was also to be true of another Democratic president, Lyndon Baines Johnson, whose executive activism transcended even FDR's.

Although the New Deal was only moderately successful in combating the Depression and required the increased defense expenditures at the end of the 1930s to restore full employment, in the areas of crisis management and preservation of civil society, it was an unmitigated success. Only a leader of immense political dexterity and persuasion could have presented such a smorgasbord as a coherent program while sorting out conflicting policies and never losing popularity in the process.

In conclusion it would be safe to say that without FDR the history of the 1930s would have been vastly different. As will be seen shortly, not only did that crucial decade reflect FDR's overwhelming imprint but so did the war years, both at home and abroad. If one imagines a Hoover victory in 1932, or that of another Democrat, say Al Smith, it is difficult to picture what might have happened to the country in the remainder of the thirties. No other American political figure in the last century had an impact as great as that of FDR.

The Roosevelt Presidency: A Negative Assessment

Much of FDR's greatness was tied to his character or personality, so it is in that realm one finds his many flaws. John Gunther, in his largely hagiographic *Roosevelt in Retrospect,* presents a substantial list of FDR's shortcomings: "dilatoriness, two-sidedness (some would say plain dishonesty), pettiness in many personal relationships, a cardinal lack of frankness . . . inability to say No, love of improvisation, garrulousness, amateurism, and what has been called 'cheerful' vindictiveness." Most of these blemishes revolved around one fundamental defect, one shared by most politicians: an overarching eagerness to please. This was the root of FDR's "two-sidedness," his "cardinal lack of frankness," his "inability to say No." If anyone could get at the heart of this chink in the Roosevelt armor, it was that most famous of Depression-era demagogues, Senator Huey P. Long of Louisiana, who could easily have the same assessment applied to his character. According to Long, when he spoke with FDR prior to Roosevelt's inauguration, the president elect said, "Fine! Fine! Fine!" to everything Long asked or discussed. The senator went away from his meeting with FDR certain "he says 'Fine!' to everybody." As historian Richard Hofstadter noted, FDR "could say 'my old friend' in eleven languages."

FDR's most recent biographer, the Canadian Conrad Black, contends that Roosevelt was "a natural dissembler and was proud of his deviousness, not only because he was good at it and it had served him well, but because he was convinced that it was always in a good cause." One of those "causes" was his quest to achieve and hold the office of the presidency for as long as he could.

FDR's penchant for wanting to please everyone hurt him on several occasions. Perhaps more important was his failure to recognize the problem. During his 1940 campaign against Wendell Wilkie, FDR secretly recorded many of his conversations with his aides, and in those discussions one hears his remarkable ability at self-deception, at displacement. "Of course, the trouble with Wilkie, as you know, his whole campaign—the reason he's losing—," FDR said in October 1940, "is that he will say anything to please the individual or the audience he happens to talk to. It makes no difference what he promised. Someone will come in and say, 'Now Mr. Wilkie, please will you, if elected, do thus and so?' 'Quite so!' Then somebody else comes in, and he says, 'Of course I won't.'"

The most damaging information revealed in the tapes was FDR's suggestion that his campaign workers "way, way down the line" circulate rumors about Wilkie's affair with a New York woman. FDR further urged that word be spread that Wilkie's wife had been paid to act during the campaign as if they were happily married. *"Now, now,"* FDR said, "Mrs. Wilkie may not have been *hired,* but in effect she's been hired to return to Wendell and smile and make this campaign with him. Now whether there was a money price behind it, I don't know, but it's the same idea."

At the very least, such remarks coming from the lips of a man known for his womanizing and philandering to the point that he died in the arms of his mistress was incredible hypocrisy. Moreover, FDR's comments also reflect his inability to realize he was guilty of the same faults he so glibly and callously attributed to others.

Like many political leaders, FDR was not an intellectual and definitely not in the same league academically as his idol, Theodore. After talking with FDR in 1933, ninety-three-year-old former Supreme Court Justice Oliver Wendell Holmes declared Roosevelt, "a second-class intellect but a first-class temperament." However, it was temperament and personality that lifted the nation's spirits in the depths of the Depression. Perhaps more could have been accomplished if FDR had been "smarter," but given the circumstances, a first-class temperament proved to have been more effective.

Holmes was not alone in his assessment that FDR was an intellectual lightweight. Walter Lippmann labeled FDR "a kind of amiable Boy Scout," while George Creel referred to him more accurately as "a gay, volatile Prince Charming." William Allen White believed FDR's mind was "quick" but "superficial" and that Roosevelt smiled "too easily for one who shakes his head so positively. I fear his smile is from the teeth out. . . . He is a fair-weather pilot. He cannot stand the storm." FDR proved White wrong on the journalist's last observation, but White was not far off in believing Roosevelt's mind was "quick and superficial." FDR had always been a voracious and rapid reader, retaining the gist of what he read, but he was anything but a deep thinker, given to deep reflection or speculation about ideas. Although FDR contributed much to the development of the liberal ethos, he was anything but a systematic thinker himself. Ironically, FDR was a devout advocate of planning; yet he had no plan. Not even the New Deal was "planned"; most of the time programs and policies reflected FDR's "philosophy" of "try anything but do something" fly-by-the-seat-of-his-pants approach. Since he was no deep thinker, he too often wanted simple answers and solutions to very complex socioeconomic problems. In short, he wanted what was most politically expedient and popular at that precise moment. FDR was no long-range planner, nor did he possess the acumen and patience to think complex issues through; he wanted action *now,* regardless of the long-term consequences such actions might bring.

One of the negative consequences of FDR's centralization policies, especially his creation of "emergency" agencies, was that too often the new organizations evolved, with FDR's blessing, into powerful, self-serving entities accountable to no one except the president. They also became a way of pretending to address a problem when in reality they simply existed, creating the illusion that FDR and his experts were solving problems. By creating these special agencies, FDR created the perception that he was on top of the nation's myriad problems, when in reality all the agencies did were create insignificant, paper-shuffling jobs for white-collar bureaucrats. Indeed, the new agencies precipitated the unprecedented growth of the federal bureaucracy, which accelerated during World War II. By the late 1960s, the "bureaucratization" of Washington, started by FDR, had resulted in a bloated, detached, and entrenched conglomerate of institutionalized and often incompetent functionaries. Not until the presidency of Jimmy Carter was this problem addressed.

Another consequence of FDR's arrogation of power in the executive branch was the evolution of what Arthur Schlesinger Jr. called "the imperial presidency." Simply defined, the concept was that beginning with FDR and culminating with Richard Nixon, in the decades between the two presidents, increasing power was usurped by the executive branch at the expense of the other two branches of government. At risk was the sanctity of the checks and balances system, which FDR repeatedly violated with impunity because of his popularity. So "charmed" by FDR and distracted by the Depression were the people that Roosevelt, with the "people's blessing," had a free hand to put forth whatever legislation he personally deemed essential for the nation's welfare without fear of either Congress or the Supreme Court challenging him. Congress virtually became a "rubber stamp" for the New Deal, passing with minimal, if any, debate whatever came from the Oval Office. Such pliancy was largely the result of members of Congress wanting to placate FDR, thus ensuring his support come reelection time. They would be able to show constituents that they were on "the New Deal team" and that the beloved president "favored" their return to the Senate or the House. Conversely, those who opposed FDR, especially if they were Democrats, were guaranteed to incur his wrath, for they not only were defying his will but that of the party as well. The public rarely saw the "Mr. Hyde" side of FDR, but politicians certainly did. He was notoriously vicious in his attacks on Democratic "traitors," and his public disavowal of them was the kiss of political death. He usually kept his upbraiding behind close doors, but if that failed to "straighten" someone out, FDR would then publicly do all he could to discredit them in the voters' eyes. In essence, for FDR, "the personal was political and the political was personal," and consequently, you were either for him or against him, and if the latter was true, then your political days were numbered. Rarely, in the history of the Republic has a president had that much personal, political clout.

By the time of his death, FDR had transformed what was for decades the weakest branch of government into the most dominant, and it would remain so until the Nixon debacle. It was not until the presidency of Richard Nixon and the Watergate scandal that the public became aware of how powerful, and thus immune to checks on its power, the executive branch had become. Thanks to FDR, his successors, both Democrat and Republican, inherited an office not only more powerful than it had ever been, but one that they could, if they so desired, make even more impenetrable by invoking FDR's legacy of executive activism in the name of the people. Ironically, up to the Nixon administration, the American public without much questioning accepted the "imperial presidency," for the "messiah," FDR, had done so much for the country with such power. If that was the case, then certainly subsequent presidents should be allowed to have such authority, especially in crisis times. However, until the Nixon administration, what most Americans failed to realize was that allowing the president such primacy would lead ultimately to corruption and the abuse of power. When that occurred, which it did with the Watergate disaster, the people ended up paying the highest price: a loss of faith in the federal government but especially in the office of the president. Such was a "downside" of Rooseveltian patrimony.

FDR's 1937 "court packing" maneuver serves as the best illustration of the growing power of the executive branch during his tenure. One year after receiving the greatest electoral landslide in American political history and an apparent mandate for his New Deal, FDR committed what proved to be one of the greatest political blunders of his career: his attempt to "pack" the Supreme Court. FDR's "plan" called for adding a new justice for each sitting justice who, having served at least ten years, did not resign or retire within six months after reaching the age of seventy (with a proviso that no more than six additional justices would be appointed). In proposing his plan, FDR reasoned correctly that conservative justices who objected to liberalism—the growth of the welfare state in particular—were permitting their personal ideological biases to determine their interpretation of executive (and congressional) powers under the Constitution. Liberal Justice Harlan Fiske Stone later commented that the "reactionary" Justice Willis Van Devanter did indeed "conceive it his duty to declare unconstitutional any law which he particularly disliked."

Interestingly, FDR's "court packing" plan was a comparatively cautious move in light of other proposals emanating from both critics and supporters. Both sides complained that, rather than attempting to enlarge the Court, FDR should have sought to amend the Constitution, mandating a two-thirds vote by the justices to declare an act unconstitutional, to permit Congress to override a Court decision, or to broaden congressional power to regulate the economy. The last suggestion was actually "code" for the expansion of the welfare state, as well as augmenting executive, not congressional, power. Though on the surface FDR liked these proposals, he believed they had a serious common defect: they would never be approved—and would certainly never be sanctioned quickly enough—by the necessary three-fourths of the state legislatures. More important, each of the proposed amendments meant tampering with the Constitution, when in FDR's view the document's language, "properly construed," could easily allow for the kind of increased federal (executive) control over the economy he so desired.

Despite the above proposals and some support for his "packing" scheme, in the end FDR's attempt to expand the Court proved a serious mistake. What prompted one of the most savvy political presidents in history to commit such a misjudgment? Simply put, in FDR's mind, for the New Deal to move forward, that is, to further the advancement of the welfare state, he had to find a way of "removing" what he perceived to be the last obstacle to that end. He believed the most effective way of doing that without arousing too much opposition was to propose the idea of simply adding more justices to the bench. Naturally, they would be liberals, and thus no further New Deal legislation would go the way of the NIRA, the AAA, and Guffy Coal Act—all shot down by the Court. However, much to his amazement, few Americans "bought" his plan. It was perceived by many to be a high-handed attempt to concentrate even greater power in the executive branch, removing the last check on his already immense control of the government. Moreover, few

Americans supported the idea, for they did not see it with immediate, tangible, or direct benefits as they did earlier New Deal measures such as relief programs, agricultural price supports, old-age pensions, and unemployment insurance. Southerners were especially aroused by the plan, for they read into it a "conspiracy" by FDR and his Yankee New Deal liberals led by "That Woman," Eleanor, to secretly appoint liberal justices who would upset their region's racial order.

Opponents cried that the plan reflected just how dangerously power-hungry FDR was and that he aspired to be a dictator. The charges, exaggerated, resonated well with many Americans, who were troubled by the advance of the European dictatorships. The *Dallas Morning News* expressed these fears when it editorialized: "Perhaps it is a little difficult for Mr. Roosevelt, who is entirely self-convinced as to the integrity of his motives, to see that the objection is not giving the particular present executive unlimited power but to giving it to any President. The objection is to a practical dictatorship, which Mr. Roosevelt seeks in his conviction that the purity of his motives will overcome the drawbacks of a nation in political servitude. Unfortunately, the obsession of all dictatorships is the same."

Stunned by the widespread opposition his plan engendered, once he realized the blunder he had made, FDR decided to back down, allowing the Court "reform" bill to go down in defeat in the Senate in July 1937. From this point on, FDR's earlier zeal to push the New Deal further to the left by expanding the welfare state seemed to dissipate with each passing month. To be sure, there were a few more social welfare programs left in the New Deal, but they were not as enthusiastically nor as adamantly pushed as they were earlier. FDR's hesitant behavior contrasted sharply with the impression of energy and purpose he had conveyed in 1933. The administration became less committed to restructuring the economy and more interested in stabilizing it and producing growth. Alan Brinkley maintains that by 1938 New Dealers "were no longer much concerned about controlling or punishing 'plutocrats' and 'economic royalists,' an impulse central to New Deal rhetoric in the mid-1930s. Instead, they spoke of their commitment to providing a healthy environment in which the corporate world could flourish and in which the economy could sustain 'full employment.'"

That FDR's once supposed passionate devotion to social welfare programs should decline so precipitously after 1937 was not surprising when one remembers that he was never as committed to social reform or to championing organized labor as he publicly let on. FDR was not a left-wing social Democrat. Pressured by leftists in his party and by populists like Huey Long and Francis Townsend, FDR reluctantly consented to the 1935 Social Security Act on the condition that it be solvent and designed according to "insurance principles." (The present pay-as-you-go Social Security system, threatened by insolvency, in which the young subsidize the old probably would have horrified FDR.) He was equally unenthusiastic about sponsoring pro-union legislation. He despised the dole for able-bodied citizens, preferring "workfare" projects like the CCC to welfare checks for non-workers. (Aid to Families with Dependent Children [AFDC] was intended to help widows and orphans.) FDR was also a late convert to Keynesian economic management, which became the centerpiece of liberal political economy only after his death. He also resisted leftist pressure to support federal anti-lynching laws and civil rights legislation. FDR's refusal to endorse such measures was both politically and racially motivated: he did not want to alienate Southern white Democrats, whose support he needed in the early New Deal years, and unlike Eleanor, he shared the racial prejudices of most white Americans of his time—a failing illustrated by his support of Japanese American internment during World War II.

As FDR became increasingly preoccupied with national defense and foreign policy, especially after the fall of France to Nazi Germany in 1940, he became more reluctant to press for reform. During the 1930s FDR had established an interesting *quid pro quo* with Congress: they allowed him carte blanche when it came to domestic affairs—full-fledged support for the New Deal—and, in return, he gave that body control of foreign policy issues. Such an arrangement, however, was destined to be short-lived, especially once world war was unleashed in 1939. Beginning in that year and over the course of the next two years, FDR worked assiduously to wrest control of foreign policy from Congress. By the time of the Japanese attack on Pearl Harbor, he had succeeded. Thus, from 1941 until his death, FDR's power both at home in conducting the war effort, as well as in determining the nation's foreign policy, was complete.

Even before Pearl Harbor, FDR had wrested significant control of foreign policy from Congress, at times demonstrating a far more detrimental isolationist mentality than the most rabid of xenophobes in that body. Such was displayed by FDR during the Spanish Civil War, when his refusal to aid the beleaguered republican government ended in a fascist takeover of yet another European country. In July 1936 the Spanish army led by General Francisco Franco revolted in Morocco. The insurgents crossed to the mainland and plunged Spain into three years of bloody civil conflict. When news of the civil war reached the United States, Roosevelt took an even more isolationist stand than some of the more fervid neutralists. He unwisely accepted the British and French view that only strict non-intervention held any hopes for localizing the Spanish conflict and avoiding a dreadful world war. It must be remembered that at this time, both England and France were well on their respective ways toward the policy of "appeasement" and thus feared that, if they aided the Loyalists (those Spaniards loyal to the republican government established in 1931), such action would "antagonize" the fascist dictators, giving them an excuse to start World War II.   Neither Mussolini nor Hitler adhered to such a policy, sending to the "Nationalists" (Franco's army) all manner of arms, including planes and tanks. Mussolini even had the audacity to send into Spain thousands of his infamous "Black Shirts" to help the nationalist forces.   Indeed, both dictators used the Spanish conflict as a "testing ground" for their latest weaponry. With such aid, the days of the Republic were numbered unless England, France, and the United States came to its rescue. Unfortunately, that was not going to happen. Interestingly, had FDR been willing to come to the aid of a fellow republic, that gesture perhaps would have shamed England and France into doing likewise, and that might have been enough to make Hitler and Mussolini think twice about intervention, for neither were ready for war with the Allies, especially if the United States was part of the triumvirate. However, Mussolini and Hitler had nothing to fear, for FDR treated the Spanish conflict as though it were a struggle between two "foreign" states with equal rights, not as an uprising against a legitimate government, and a democratic government at that. FDR imposed a moral embargo on the sale of arms and munitions to Spain and asked Congress to tighten the neutrality statutes by embargoing shipments of military material to countries engaged in civil wars.

Interestingly, as news of the vicious fighting reached the United States, especially the brutality inflicted by the foreign mercenaries on loyalist citizens, even some of the more hardline neutralists began having second thoughts. Led by Senator Russell Nye, long considered the leader of the isolationist cabal in Congress, a resolution was introduced to repeal the arms embargo to the Loyalists. Others supported the Nye resolution, including members of Roosevelt's cabinet such as Harold Ickes and Henry Morgenthau, both of whom pleaded with the president to lift the embargo to "save the world from a fascist gulf." For many Americans (especially among the ranks of the intelligentsia and academics), the

Spanish Civil War was the crucial event of the decade, for it signified the apocalyptic struggle between the forces of democracy and fascism. Some Americans did more than protest FDR's refusal to help. About three thousand American volunteers fought in the conflict on the Loyalist side, most never returning home, dying for the republican cause.

For a brief moment in 1938, it appeared FDR would lift the embargo. That, however, never occurred because Roosevelt typically considered what was political rather than what was the morally correct thing to do. Persuading him in the end to keep the embargo in place was public opinion, especially the attitude toward the conflict of American Catholics, who overwhelmingly supported Franco because of supposed Loyalist anticlericalism and anti-Catholic policies in general. Most Americans were indifferent, and those who were pro-Loyalist in sentiment paled compared to the large bloc of pro-Franco Catholics. Indeed, polls revealed that the proportion of Catholics who backed Franco was more than four times as great as the proportion of Protestants. The American Catholic press and hierarchy were almost unanimous in their support of Franco, who promised to restore the power of the Spanish Catholic Church the moment he was victorious over the Republican "atheists and communists." How significant was the "Catholic lobby"? According to Ickes, FDR told him that to lift the embargo "would mean the loss of every Catholic vote next fall and that the Democratic members of Congress were jittery about it and didn't want it done." So the cat was out of the bag, Ickes complained, the "mangiest, scabbiest cat ever."

Although typically FDR could always use Congress as his "scapegoat" for failed or obstructed policies, as in the case of the Spanish Civil War, it was FDR, not Congress, who failed to do what was right. Ironically, it was Senator Nye, the symbol of congressional isolationism, who led the move to lift the embargo, while FDR, who had originally opposed such legislation, upheld it. FDR's Spanish policy had unfortunate consequences. It helped sustain Neville Chamberlain's disastrous policy of appeasement, which permitted Germany and Italy to supply Franco while the democracies enforced "nonintervention" against themselves. "My own impression," wrote Ambassador Claude Bowers in July 1937, "is that with every surrender beginning long ago with China [the Japanese invasion of Manchuria in 1931], followed by Abyssinia [the Italian invasion of Ethiopia in 1935] and then Spain, the fascist powers, with vanity inflamed, will turn without delay to some other country—such as Czechoslovakia [which Hitler took in 1938]—and that with every surrender the prospects of a European war grow darker." Bowers could not have been more accurate in his assessment, and FDR should have heeded his council on such matters. Had FDR taken a more courageous stand by coming to the aid of the Spanish Republic, demonstrating American resolve to stop fascist aggression and help preserve democracy, perhaps World War II could have been averted. Instead, FDR helped to guarantee that horrible conflict by doing what was politically "safe" rather than what was right. In this instance perhaps, as Conrad Black has contended, FDR's motives were often "a subtle blend of expediency and principle, both lofty and vindictive."

Although making the winning of the war a priority, FDR nonetheless reassured Americans that the New Deal and continued reform—the expansion of the welfare state—was not dead; it just had to be put on the "back-burner." Naturally, it would be resurrected "after this war is won." The operative phrase, of course, was "after this war is won." FDR's rhetoric may have sounded reformist, but as historian John Morton Blum has observed, "He made no convincing effort to give substance to his oratory." As long as the nation was engaged in an unprecedented global conflict, FDR did not consider it desirable—or necessary—to press for additional reforms or even regulation. This became evident in 1942 when he halted all antitrust prosecutions, fearing such action would hamper military production. "The war effort must come first and everything else must wait," he said. In a 1943 press conference, FDR reiterated his position more graphically, telling his audience that "Dr. New Deal" had outlived his usefulness and should step aside for "Dr. Win-the-War." That statement, Alan Brinkley asserts, amounted to "a belated acknowledgment of an already advanced abandonment of the liberal agenda."

Although the war solved many economic problems, it also created new ones, particularly in the area of civil liberties. Here can be seen the "Mr. Hyde" side of FDR, particularly what John Gunther called Roosevelt's "two-sidedness." In time of peace, FDR was committed to protecting individual liberty and freedom of expression. In time of national crisis and in the name of national security, however, he was prepared to impose harsh restrictions. As Attorney General Francis Biddle later remarked, FDR believed that "it was all very well to be liberal . . . but you must not be soft."

FDR exhibited his hard side in the spring of 1940, when he became convinced that immigrants and aliens were involved in espionage for foreign powers. "Of course we have got this fifth column thing, which is altogether too widespread through the country," FDR told the Council on National Defense. "In the bringing in of new people we have got to be pretty darned careful." Consequently, FDR approved Secretary of State Cordell Hull's recommendation that aliens who applied for visas as temporary visitors should be fingerprinted, and he signed the Smith Act, which made all aliens register with the government. Roosevelt also authorized the use of wiretaps against anyone "suspected of subversive activities." He later explained "wire tapping should be used against those persons, not citizens of the United States, and those few citizens who are traitors to their country, who today are engaged in espionage or sabotage."

FDR also enacted an unprecedented policy of censorship. Never before or since (even the censorship invoked during the Iraq War and the 1991 Persian Gulf War paled in comparison) has any administration denied the public so much information and truth in the name of national security. FDR not only suppressed reports useful to the enemy, such as news concerning troop movements, ship landings, and battle casualties, but also criticism of the government that too frequently violated individuals' and groups' constitutional rights of freedom of speech and press. In 1942, FDR wrote to FBI director J. Edgar Hoover, calling his attention to a pro-fascist sheet, commenting, "Now that we are in the war, it looks like a good chance to clean up a number of these vile publications." He also suggested to Biddle that editorials in the *Chicago Tribune* and *New York Daily News*, criticizing the allies, might warrant some censoring of their writers. "The tie-in between the attitude of these papers and the Rome-Berlin broadcasts is something far greater than mere coincidence. I would raise the question as to whether freedom of the press meant freedom to criticize government policy on the basis of 'factual truth.' I think there is a big distinction between this freedom and freedom to print untrue news."

One of the most difficult tasks confronting FDR during the war years was how to make the war real at home. Despite rumors of impending invasion and Japanese submarine attacks, the nearest battlefield was three thousand miles away. How to make the connection, how to convey a vivid sense of involvement, how to tie American families in Iowa City or Oshkosh to soldiers in foxholes—all these posed a dilemma for Roosevelt and for a nation that had never experienced foreign invasion, a sudden bombing attack, or sabotage on its own soil. FDR not only had to find a way to bond Americans on the homefront with the soldiers fighting abroad, but more importantly, he had to simultaneously make the war emotionally, psychologically, and ideologically a "Good War"—"The

Best War Ever"—fought against incalculable German evil and boundless Japanese military aggression. When it came to the war, just as he had dealt with the Depression, FDR wanted things to be simple. American participation in the war was to be righteous and glorious, the duty and challenge of a great power, a war fought to preserve democracy, the fulfillment of the nation's larger responsibility and destiny to protect humanity. To this end, FDR unleashed one of the most remarkably effective, all-encompassing propaganda campaigns ever experienced by the American people. Through advertising, the mass media, music, and songs, whatever he deemed essential to galvanize patriotism, unity, and unequivocal support for the war, he employed. Moreover, FDR dictated to those institutions, like the motion picture industry or to the individuals involved in the respective mediums, what they should say or promote and how they should say it. To implement the propaganda barrage, FDR created one of his special "agencies," the Office of War Information (OWI). Through this office, the indoctrination was disseminated, and none of it was released without FDR's approval. Messages ran the gamut from the insidious to the shamelessly provocative. Regardless of how they were sent, their meaning was clear: just as Americans had rallied to FDR and the New Deal, they were to do the same for the war effort, for the nation was once again in a crisis with the American way of life at stake. In one of its most popular manifestations, this campaign took the form of vivid reminders that what took place in war factories and kitchens directly affected the fate of GI Joe. One hard-line asked, "Are you comfortable, brother? That's good, brother. Just sleep right through this war . . . what's it to you that a kid just got bumped off in the Solomons . . . because *you* couldn't be bothered with scrap collection?" In another version of the same theme, a short film from Battan featured a wounded GI exhorting his family not to waste food. "We haven't had anything but a little horsemeat and rice for days," the soldier says, "and kitchen fats, mom. Don't waste any. Kitchen fats make glycerin and glycerin makes explosives. Two pounds of fat can fire five anti-tank shells." Lest the message be lost, the film ended with the announcement that the soldier had died in the hospital after making the film.

So successful was FDR's propaganda and censorship, especially of the war's brutality and carnage, as well as the enemies' supposed inferiority in all areas, that the American public came to believe that the United States was handily and single-handedly (Even though we had allies, neither Great Britain nor the Soviet Union would have survived without our entry, and thus their contributions to the war effort, once the U.S. was in, were inconsequential) winning the war with minimal loss of American life. By oversimplifying and over-glamorizing the war, by censoring reports from the battlefields before they were printed in the newspapers, by showing only American victories never defeats, by promoting celebratory, illusionary Hollywood epics, FDR desensitized the American people to war's awful reality. The price for allowing FDR to manipulate Americans emotions and perceptions of war would be paid in the 1960s with the "living-room war" in Vietnam. That war was not "filtered" or censored and was brought to Americans live and in "living color" nightly. For the first time, Americans watched their fellow countrymen die gruesome deaths or, at the very least, being placed on helicopters in body bags. They were emotionally and psychologically unprepared for what they saw and ultimately turned against that war. Unfortunately, despite defeat, the needless death of 58,000 Americans and over one million Vietnamese, most Americans want to see Vietnam as a bad dream, a nightmare, and an aberration, to be erased so that they can return to the glory of the "Good War"—World War II. This was partly what the 1991 Gulf War was about. The magic was back. For example, a young American soldier, deeply depressed by her experience as a prisoner of war in Iraq, was given a hug by Allied Supreme Commander General Norman Schwarzkopf "and then everything was fine," said a TV news reporter. No lingering post-traumatic stress disorder here. That's just the way FDR would have wanted such an episode portrayed.

Without question, FDR's most egregious and unpardonable wartime act in the name of national security was his unhesitating approval for "relocating" 110,000 West Coast Japanese Americans, two-thirds of whom were U.S. citizens. Believing the allegations that Japanese Americans were involved in espionage, recognizing that white Californians wholeheartedly (for purely racist reasons) supported their removal, and preoccupied with matters of global strategy, FDR simply accepted Secretary of War Henry L. Stimson's recommendation for evacuation. Stimson reported that when he raised the issue with Roosevelt, the Secretary "fortunately found that he [FDR] was very vigorous about it and told me to go ahead on the line that I had myself thought the best." On February 19, 1942, FDR issued Executive Order 9066, authorizing the relocation of Japanese Americans to areas removed from positions of military authority. The military justification: "The continued pressure of a large, unassimilated, tightly knit racial group, bound to an enemy nation by strong ties of race, culture, custom, and religion along a frontier vulnerable to attack, constituted a menace which had to be dealt with." According to Executive Order 9066, Stimson was given the power to "prescribe military areas in such places and of such extent . . . from which any or all persons may be excluded." As historian Roger Daniels notes, this "strangely reticent" proclamation "mentions no ethnic or racial group by name, nor does it specify place." Yet everyone knew who the victims were, and so it was. "The country had never been in such peril, and Roosevelt shouldered the awesome burden of wartime responsibility," Peter Irons writes in *Justice at War.* "In this atmosphere of anxiety, the rights of an isolated racial minority had little claim on his sympathies."

White Californians had long feared the presence of Asian immigrants. They had pressured Congress into passing the Chinese Exclusion Act of 1882, which ended most Chinese immigration to the United States. Then, in the early twentieth century they turned their racism on Japanese immigrants, whose numbers in California had reached 24,000. In 1906 the San Francisco School Board ordered the segregation of Asian schoolchildren so that they would not "contaminate" white children. In 1907 the California legislature debated a law to prohibit further Japanese immigration to the state. Anti-Asian riots erupted in San Francisco and Los Angeles, encouraged in part by hysterical stories in the press about the "Yellow Peril."

Suffice it to say, the Japanese government was outraged by white Californians hostile treatment of its citizens. Japanese militarists began uttering "war" if the United States government did not put an end to the discrimination and violence. Theodore Roosevelt, putting aside his own racism, assured the Japanese government that he, too, was appalled by white Californians' behavior. In 1907 he reached a "gentlemen's agreement" with the Japanese, by which Tokyo promised to stop Japanese male laborers from going to the United States in return for Roosevelt's pledge to end anti-Japanese discrimination. TR did his part by persuading the San Francisco School Board to rescind its segregation ordinance, which the board did, but throughout all of California the state's white citizens continued to discriminate and harass Japanese workers and their families. Thus, it was not surprising that FDR found it easy to issue his executive order for the detention of Japanese Americans, for the nation, especially white Californians, already were "predisposed" to embrace such a policy.

Within two months of the decree's promulgation, more than 100,000 Japanese Americans were relocated in America's own version of concentration camps. These citizens were forced to leave behind or sell cheaply their possessions, gather together (like the European Jews being persecuted by the Nazis) at removal stations, and board trains and buses for internment camps. The only difference between what was happening to the Jews and the Japanese Americans was that the latter were not being sent to "death camps." In virtually all other aspects of their respective treatment, there was not great disparity. Although some newspapers insisted that Japanese Americans were "coddled" and "pampered," life in the internment camps was bleak. The camps were isolated in some of the most desolate areas of states like Utah and Wyoming. A barbed wire fence surrounded the camp, and watchtowers at each corner kept the prisoners under surveillance. There were no private toilets or dining facilities. People who had spent their lives fishing the waters of the Pacific or working in the rich fields of California's greenbelt now huddled against the wind, dust, and cold of Wyoming winters.

There is no way to ignore the blatant racism involved in the treatment of Japanese Americans, especially when it is contrasted with that of the nation's two other supposed residents of enemy countries—Italian Americans and German Americans. Neither of those two nationalities experienced anything remotely resembling the incarceration and persecution of the Japanese. Indeed, leniency towards them, like the harshness towards Japanese Americans, owed much to political calculation, something consistently in the forefront of FDR's thinking. After Irish-Americans, German and Italian Americans were the largest ethnic groups in the United States and since the 1936 election had proven themselves loyal FDR supporters. Most important, they were European and white. (At least the overwhelming majority of Germans could claim such "purity." Italians were a little more suspect in that capacity, especially those coming from southern Italy or Sicily because of their "swarthiness.") As FDR told Stimson, "American citizens with German and Italian names are also worried [about evacuation]. I am inclined to think this may have a bad effect on morale [code for the potential loss of votes]."

The portrayal of "Japs" in war movies, the popular songs that referred to "those little yellow bellies," and promises to slap "the Jap right off the map"—all this conveyed a racial animosity never applied to America's white adversaries. The racism embodied in Roosevelt's executive order was simply a polite version of that expressed by the governor of Idaho, another state "hosting" Japanese Americans: "the Japs live like rats, breed like rats, and act like rats. We don't want them." "The United States," Justice Frank Murphy declared in his dissent to the Supreme Court's approval of relocation, had engaged in the "legalization of racism." There was no other way to describe it, and it had FDR's blessing.

Just as tragically, anti-Semitism also remained a corrosive presence in America, and it too had FDR's tacit acceptance. The most devastating impact of anti-Semitism appeared in acts of omission rather than commission. By 1942, the Roosevelt administration knew of Hitler's "final solution" of exterminating Jews. However, typically only Eleanor and a handful of others within the administration were concerned. Indeed, Assistant Secretary of State Breckenridge Long consistently obstructed efforts to facilitate a more flexible visa policy, allowing Jewish refugees easier access to the United States and safe haven. Even Congress denounced the Nazi policy of genocide, but FDR refused to intervene to get the State Department to do something to help those searching for a way to escape. There was a way to escape—not for most, but certainly for some. FDR could have easily mandated a relaxation of the nation's visa policy, as well as put pressure on Latin American nations or the British Commonwealth, i.e., Canada, to provide sanctuaries for Jewish refugees, or offer transportation support to relocate Jewish refugees in neutral countries. If FDR had been willing to implement any one of these measures, thousands of lives could have been saved. State Department officials who advocated such action or who protested the inaction found themselves transferred or silenced. FDR simply did not make the saving of Jews a high priority, which many feel was a reflection of his own "closet" anti-Semitism. The government study that documented this record of abomination was appropriately titled: "Report to the Secretary on the Acquiescence of This Government in the Murder of the Jews."

FDR's wartime record with African Americans was somewhat better, but here as well it fell significantly short of what could have been accomplished. Ironically, had the war not come along, FDR's overall civil rights record would have remained as one of the most disappointing in history, especially given the opportunities to improve African-American life the New Deal and the war gave him. What motivation FDR had to promote racial justice was political, as it was with most sensitive issues. Although the majority of blacks still lived in the South (three-fourths of the nation's 13 million African Americans) and suffered the oppression of Jim Crow and, thus, could not vote, such was not true for black Americans living in the North or West. There, black voters were among FDR's staunchest supporters. Eleanor, who enjoyed a well-deserved reputation as a champion of racial equality, greatly augmented FDR's appeal among blacks. Her husband, however, when pressed to take a stand in behalf of racial justice, typically hemmed and hawed, and ended up replying that economic policy took precedence. To support civil rights legislation, he added, would jeopardize recovery by antagonizing powerful Southern congressional Democrats.

Black leaders, however, refused to let FDR slide so blithely on such an issue. Individuals such as A. Philip Randolph, who was head of the most powerful black union in the country, the Brotherhood of Sleeping Car Porters, were determined to at least see blacks benefit economically from the booming wartime economy. Randolph thus challenged the government's employment policies, demanding equal treatment in the work force, particularly in defense industries. He also knew that suggesting a "march on Washington" would most definitely get FDR's attention. The last thing the president needed in the midst of a war would be a demonstration in the capital protesting racial discrimination when the nation was fighting against just that abroad—not the image the United States wanted to project to the world. Accordingly, FDR promulgated Executive Order 8802 in 1941, establishing the President's Committee on Fair Employment Practices (FEPC) "to receive and investigate complaints of discrimination" so that "there shall be no discrimination in the employment of workers in defense industries or government because of race, creed, color, or national origin."

In retrospect, the FEPC was a hollow concession. The agency lacked all enforcement power and served primarily the purposes of exhortation and propaganda. Most important, it received little support from the White House. It appeared that all FDR wanted to do with the FEPC was use it as a way of silencing African-American demands for equality and not embarrass his administration, which a march on Washington surely would have accomplished. It was blatant tokenism, but it seemed to work at least during the war years. For even militant leaders like Randolph were willing to accept temporarily this perfunctory gesture.

Racism was worse in the Armed Forces, where a wretched mixture of exclusion, discrimination, and segregation prevailed. Enlisting at a rate 60 percent higher than their proportion of the population, African Americans met immediate segregation and prejudice. They could not enlist in the Marines or Air Corps; they could join the navy but only to work in the mess halls; they were rigidly segregated in the army. When Tennessee blacks demanded that the governor appoint African Americans to the State Draft Board, he responded: "This is a white man's country . . . the Negro had nothing to do with the settling of America." Southern training camps were especially infamous for their persecution of black soldiers. When a white policeman shot and killed an on-duty black MP, he was found innocent by a local white jury. A black private at Fort Benning, Georgia, was lynched; military officials refused to act when a black army nurse was brutally beaten for defying Jim Crow seating on a Montgomery, Alabama bus; and religious services were segregated, the sign at the base proclaiming separate worship for "Catholics, Jews, and Negroes."

Stories of racism were legion. The Red Cross, for example, segregated "white" and "colored" blood bottles of plasma (ignoring the fact that a black scientist, Dr. Charles Drew, had perfected the method of preserving blood plasma). Congressman John Rankin of Mississippi, a hardcore racist, denounced "the crack-pots, the communists, and the parlor pinks of this country" for attempting to change the labeling system so that "it will not show whether it is Negro blood or white blood. That seems to be the scheme of these fellow travelers to try to mongrelize this nation." A comparable example of stupidity occurred when black soldiers entered a lunchroom in Salinas, Kansas. "You boys know we don't serve colored here," the manager said. Indeed, the soldiers did know. So they just stood there "inside the door, staring at what we had come to see. German prisoners of war who were having lunch at the counter. . . . It was no jive talk. The people of Salinas served these enemy soldiers and turned away black American GI's."

The searing contradiction between the rhetoric of fighting for democracy and the reality of racism at home galvanized black rage. "Our war is not against Hitler and Europe," one black columnist proclaimed, "but against the Hitlers in America." Another African-American citizen wrote to FDR, stating that "If there is such thing as God he must be a white person, according to the conditions we colored people are in . . . Hitler hasn't done anything to the colored people—it's the people right here in the United States who are keeping us out of work and keeping us down." Reflecting the ideological irony at the heart of America's war was a slogan that circulated among black draftees: "Here lies a black man killed fighting a yellow man for the glory of the white man." Such criticism, however, did not stop African Americans from voting overwhelmingly for FDR in the 1944 election.

Typically, FDR skirted the issues and problems confronting black Americans in the early 1940s, stating rhetorically "the long-range problems of racial and minority-majority antagonisms cannot be settled during the war. . . . The war must be won first." FDR failed to endorse abolition of the poll tax, as well as refusing to allow the Justice Department to join the legal challenge to the "white primary," even after the Supreme

Court invalidated such techniques aimed at black disfranchisement. As historian Harvard Sitkoff has observed, "to Roosevelt, the Negro had always remained an unfortunate ward of the nation—to be treated kindly with charity as a reward for good behavior."

It was perhaps in the area of foreign policy and diplomacy that one sees some of FDR's worst character flaws come to the fore, causing serious problems for the United States in the aftermath of World War II. FDR's over-confidence bordered on hubris, especially in believing in the rightness of his every decision. His overarching penchant to avoid conflict allowed Stalin to aggressively push him into capitulating on some of the more crucial wartime issues. Perhaps most damaging to American foreign policy, particularly in the postwar years, was FDR's general naïveté, especially when it came to grasping the vicissitudes of *realpolitik*. Equally detrimental to American policy was FDR's lack of historical knowledge, which was essential for him to possess when dealing with nations like Russia, whose history had determined so much of its behavior, especially toward the West. In this last capacity, FDR's lack of understanding of Russian history, and credulity in believing Stalin would honor his commitments, proved disastrous for the United States. It allowed Stalin to get exactly what he desired most: all of Eastern Europe as a buffer zone. Ever since the days of the expansionist policies of Peter the Great, Russia had long coveted control of Eastern Europe as a means of protecting Holy Mother Russia from Western invasions. Beginning with Napoleon in 1812, it was from that direction that the most devastating, penetrating attacks into Russia occurred. With Eastern Europe as a buffer, Russia could henceforth meet any Western adversary in that area, preventing any further incursions into the country. FDR should have been aware of this necessity and consequently not allowed the Red Army to cross its frontiers and be responsible for the liberation of Eastern Europe. In his quest for a rapprochement with Stalin, FDR ignored warnings from advisers that if the Soviets were allowed into Eastern Europe they would never get out, for to do so would be a blatant and unacceptable abnegation of a fundamental historical imperative. Once the Soviet army "liberated" Eastern Europe from Nazi oppression—agreed to by FDR in 1943—Stalin would then use it to suppress the right of self-determination of Eastern Europeans, establishing in the process the infamous Iron Curtain. All of this Stalin accomplished by 1948, largely as a result of FDR's unwillingness to confront Stalin on those issues that could have prevented this catastrophe. By 1948 Stalin had created a new Russian empire far larger than that of any of the czars. He also redeemed all the territory his predecessor, Lenin, so unabashedly relinquished to Germany "in the name of revolution" in 1917.

FDR should have listened to his generals like Patton who urged him to "dictate to them" rather than the converse. If necessary, Patton and others exhorted, use force to drive the Red Army out of Eastern Europe before it became a *fait accompli* and the Red Army was entrenched. If that occurred, then it could only be removed by force, and that would automatically precipitate a prolonged, bloody conflict. Unfortunately, FDR insisted the United States must show Stalin that he was trusted and, by doing so, he would feel obligated to adhere to his promise of allowing Eastern Europeans the right of self-determination. No sooner was FDR in his grave, than Stalin reneged on this commitment. The wily Soviet dictator knew that FDR's successor, the poorly prepared and uninformed Harry Truman (FDR was largely to blame for Truman's woeful lack of job preparedness), was still bound by FDR's policy restraints, which meant, in effect, he was powerless to stop Stalin's determination to acquire spheres of influence because it had FDR's tacit "seal of approval." As early as 1943, Ambassador to the Soviet Union Averell Harriman warned FDR that Russian actions were based on "ruthless political considerations." At home, Harriman's admonitions were echoed by Congressman John Dingell who stated publicly, "We Americans are not sacrificing, fighting, and dying to make permanent and more powerful the communistic government of Russia and to make Joseph Stalin a dictator over the liberated countries of Europe."

Although FDR was "acutely conscious of the great importance of the Balkan situation" and wished to "take advantage of" any opportunity to exercise influence in the area, the simple fact was that Soviet troops were in control. FDR accepted the consequences. "The occupying forces had the power in the area where their arms were present," Roosevelt noted, "and each knew that the other could not force things to an issue." The contradiction between stated idealistic war aims and such *realpolitik* would come back to haunt the prospect for postwar collaboration, particularly in Poland and other east European countries.

So committed to winning Stalin's trust and friendship, FDR was willing to betray his most loyal friend and ally, Winston Churchill. FDR would often meet privately and secretly with Stalin, aligning himself with the Soviet leader against Churchill on a number of issues. FDR even taunted the prime minister "about his Britishness, about John Bull," in an effort to forge an informal "anti-imperial" alliance between the United States and the Soviet Union. When his secret meetings with Stalin were over, FDR would tell the American people that he "got along fine with Marshall Stalin. . . . I believe he is truly representative of the heart and soul of Russia; and I believe that we are going to get along very well with him and the Russian people—very well indeed." "Very well" indeed, especially if FDR was willing "to give the farm way." When pressed on what kind of person Stalin was, FDR responded: "I would call him something like me, . . . a realist."

FDR's desire to control foreign policy even exceeded his coveting of the New Deal. As he often displayed during various New Deal controversies, FDR possessed an almost mystical confidence in his own capacity to break through policy differences based on economic structures and political systems, to develop a personal relationship of trust that would (so he believed) transcend impersonal forces of division. In short, he believed he could "charm" a man like Stalin into doing what he wanted the Soviet leader to do. If such an approach worked in winning millions of Americans to embrace him and the New Deal, it would certainly work on one man. As FDR arrogantly told Winston Churchill, "I know you will not mind my being brutally frank when I tell you that I think I can personally handle Stalin better than either your Foreign Office or my State Department. Stalin hates the guts of all your top people. He thinks he likes me better, and I hope he will continue to do so." Such a statement reflected not only FDR's naïveté and outright hubris simultaneously but, perhaps more important, his penchant to reduce complex issues to a simplistic solution: "guile with a smile." Interestingly, FDR's arrogance appeared right in at least one regard: The Soviets *did* seem to place their faith in him, believing that American foreign policy was a product of one man's decision as it was in the Soviet Union. FDR thought the same way, telling Bullitt "it's [foreign policy in general and dealing with the Soviets specifically] my responsibility and not yours; and I'm going to play my hunches."

The tragedy, of course, was that one man who perceived that fostering world peace was his own personal responsibility never lived to carry out his vision. Long in declining health, suffering from advanced arteriosclerosis and a serious cardiac problem, he had gone to his favorite place, Warm Springs, Georgia, to revive after his last conference with Stalin and Churchill at Yalta. On April 12, 1945, FDR suffered a massive cerebral hemorrhage and died.

Given the nature of the personalities and the nations involved, it was not surprising that as the war drew to an end, virtually none of the critical issues of postwar relationships had been resolved. Preferring to postpone decisions rather than confront the conflicts that existed, FDR hoped that his own political genius, plus the reality of postwar exigencies, would allow him to prevail over Stalin and establish his vision of a world of free trade and democratic rule. The Soviets also appeared content to wait, working militarily in Eastern Europe to secure maximum leverage for achieving national security and sphere-of-influence objectives. What neither Stalin nor FDR realized was that, in their delay and scheming, they were adding fuel to the fire of suspicion existing between them (despite FDR's claims to the contrary) and possibly missing the only opportunity to forge the basis for mutual accommodation and peaceful coexistence.

As can be readily seen from the above examples, FDR was far from perfect. He did things in his personal and political life that were simply reprehensible. Using his "the war must be won first" excuse with incredible redundancy, FDR was able to sidestep the demands from a variety of individuals and groups for continued social reform. To such advocates, civil rights legislation and expansion of the welfare state would not jeopardize the war effort but actually enhance it by giving more Americans a greater stake in its larger purpose. Critics also point out that many New Deal programs benefited privileged and powerful groups, not the weak and dispossessed. A fair appraisal of the Roosevelt presidency must address his failures: his unwillingness to advance the cause of racial justice and his inability to convert the Democratic Party at the grassroots level into a vehicle of social reform (most notably in the South). FDR frequently used the presidency to educate his fellow citizens about the real issues before them, but he occasionally resorted to shrill demagogic appeals. In some respects, the Roosevelt record is as paradoxical as the man himself.

None of this, however, prevented FDR from being one of the few people who can truly be said to have personally changed the course of history. Had he not won the 1932 Democratic nomination or had the unemployed bricklayer who attempted to assassinate him in early 1933 been successful, the United States, and perhaps the world, would be a different place today. We can only speculate on how it would be different, but it can be said with certainty that FDR personally had an important impact on the course of history during the ensuing years. The theologian Reinhold Niebuhr defined democracy as "a method of finding proximate solutions for insoluble problems." If the problems Americans confronted in the years 1933-1945 were in some measure insoluble, proximate solutions were found. That, in truth, was FDR's ultimate legacy.

(above) FDR, General MacArthur
and Admiral Nimitz in
Pearl Harbor, Hawaii.
July 26, 1944
(right) FDR at the Grand Coulee
Dam in Washington.
October 2, 1937
(below) FDR, Churchill, Geraud
and DeGaulle in Casablanca.
January 24, 1943
Photo credits:
FDR Presidential Library

Churchill,
Franklin D. Roosevelt,
and Stalin at the
Livadia Palace in
Yalta.
February 9, 1945
Photo credit: FDR
Presidential Library

(right) Franklin D. Roosevelt, Fala,
and Ruthie Bie at Hill Top Cottage
in Hyde Park, New York.
Rare picture of FDR
in a wheelchair.
Photo by Margaret Suckley
(bottom) Franklin D. Roosevelt
and Eleanor Roosevelt with their 13
grandchildren in Washington, D. C.
January 20, 1945
Photo credit:
FDR Presidential Library

Harry S Truman
1945-1953

On April 13, 1945, newspaper headlines across the nation mourned, "President Roosevelt Dead." On January 23, 1945, three days after delivering his inaugural address to begin his fourth term, FDR left for Yalta in the Crimea, where he met with Winston Churchill and Joseph Stalin to discuss postwar issues. In all, the ocean voyages and meetings took more than a month. On March 1, two days after returning to the United States, he addressed a joint session of Congress. He entered the chamber in a wheelchair rather than by supporting himself on someone's arm. He delivered his speech while seated rather than by bracing himself against a lectern, and for the first time during his presidency, he mentioned his disability. "I hope you will pardon me for the unusual posture of sitting down during the presentation of what I want to say, but I know that you will realize that it makes it a lot easier for me not having to carry about ten pounds of steel around on the bottom of my legs."

On March 29, after spending a few days at Hyde Park, FDR left for a two-week vacation at his home in Warm Springs, Georgia, hoping the rest would invigorate him. On April 12, at one in the afternoon, while sitting for a portrait, he suddenly said, "I have a terrific pain in the back of my head," and slumped forward. He had suffered a massive cerebral hemorrhage and was pronounced dead at 3:35 p.m. FDR's body was taken to Washington for a funeral service and then to Hyde Park for burial, as millions mourned in sadness and disbelief. Roosevelt's passing was just a month before Germany's formal surrender and five months before Japan's capitulation, which was the result of one of FDR's most well-kept secrets, the Manhattan Project. That clandestine operation in the desert sands of New Mexico ultimately produced the most devastating weapon ever created by the human mind: the atomic bomb, which the United States unleashed twice on Japan to force that nation's submission. Although FDR authorized the building of the bomb, the momentous decision to use it was made by Roosevelt's successor, Harry Truman, upon whose shoulders rested not only the postwar future of the United States but the world as well.

If ever in the history of the modern presidency there was an individual less prepared to assume that position, it was Harry Truman. Not only was Truman almost completely uninformed about what he was to do, but the unfortunate man also suffered from that potentially most debilitating of all successors' handicaps—the "tough-act-to-follow" syndrome. Indeed, public expectation and scrutiny affected Truman more so than any other president. No doubt, John Adams, Martin Van Buren, Andrew Johnson, and William Howard Taft, all of who followed celebrated predecessors, felt varying degrees of disaffection and the pressure to "measure up." None of them, however, followed a president who was as popular or as powerful or who had served as long as FDR. As one of FDR's White House aides, Jonathan Daniels, noted after seeing Truman shortly after Roosevelt's death, "He [Truman] swung around in the President's chair as if he were testing it, more uncertain than even I was about its size." In short, the Roosevelt legacy would haunt Truman throughout his entire presidency, even after he won that office outright on his own initiatives in 1948.

Why was it so difficult for Truman to move out of FDR's shadow? There are many reasons, but perhaps the single most important was the fact that an entire generation of Americans hardly knew any other president, and their perception was that FDR single-handedly took them through the two greatest crises of their time, if not in the history of the Republic. It wasn't so much the policies and programs of the New Deal or those of the war years they would miss but FDR's ebullient, magnetic, infectious personality. They would yearn for that perpetually smiling face that radiated solicitude, optimism, and confidence that all would be taken care of no matter how serious the problem or grave the calamity. Regardless of where one was or what they were doing when they heard the news of Roosevelt's death, feelings of shock, grief, and a sense of foreboding were surely experienced. No doubt such was the response of the men and women serving in the armed forces, who daily were uplifted by FDR's exhortations that the United States would prevail. Also saddened and anxious about their future were factory workers, farmers, and bureaucrats, for whom Roosevelt symbolized conviction and unity through war and depression. For all these Americans, FDR's imprint on American life would endure for decades to come. "He was Commander-in-Chief, not only of the Armed Forces, but of our generation," wrote an editor of *Yank* magazine.

Truman's uncertainty was entirely understandable given the country's mood, for to millions of Americans, especially the poor, FDR had been the messiah. Equally concerned about the new president were liberals, who had regarded FDR as the very model of strong presidential leadership, particularly when it came to social reform issues. Although after 1938 Roosevelt compromised on such programs in the name of national security and military preparedness, progressive Americans nonetheless blamed Congress and "the interests," not the President, for thwarting the reform impulse. As recently as 1944, FDR had rallied reformers—and raised popular expectations—by calling for an "Economic Bill of Rights" to be implemented after the war. This "bill of rights" represented a litany of treasured New Deal priorities: useful employment, adequate earnings for food, clothing, and recreation, decent housing, protection from the fears of old age and sickness, and a good education.

Compounding the public's sense of having lost their best "friend" was the anxiety many Americans felt about their futures and whether that "new man" in the White House could assuage their trepidation and successfully pick up where FDR had left off relative to the New Deal agenda. As the American people saw victory on the horizon in the spring of 1945, they could not help but wonder at the massive changes that had taken place in four short years. Factories bustled with triple shifts, and virtually every American who wanted a job was employed. Millions of people had secured a new start, a new bank account, perhaps a new family. The nation had dealt courageously and victoriously with one of the most severe attacks on its values and survival. So much had changed. Yet so much remained uncertain. What would happen to the economy, the family, morality, race relations, and politics in the new America that was unfolding?

All of these issues ultimately coalesced into a simple series of questions: Which direction would America follow in the postwar years, which values would it embrace, and what would it stand for? With depression and war hopefully behind them forever, Americans were guardedly sanguine that they were perhaps on the threshold of new beginnings. As the historian Allan Nevins wrote, "Americans suddenly seemed to stand, as the war closed, beholding a new heaven and a new earth, to which they somewhat dazedly tried to adjust themselves." Would the new president carry forth with FDR's 1944 economic bill of rights, or would he buckle to the energized conservatives who came to power in the 1938 congressional elections? Would he allow the conservatives, rather than himself, to dictate the federal agenda? If the conservatives controlled it, they undoubtedly would oppose any further attempts to expand the welfare state. If the new president failed to stand up to the reactionary forces, then he would be betraying both the people and his office's moral responsibility to be the champion and protector of the downtrodden and dispossessed. FDR clearly established that precedent, both in actions and words, on numerous occasions. To do otherwise would be a most egregious perfidy of the Rooseveltian legacy. In short, would the new president help move America toward new measures to correct the ancient injustices of discrimination based on race and sex, or would he allow the resumption of the old attitudes of neglect, racism, and complicity in oppression? These were some of the issues Americans pondered as the war's end finally came into view. It was a time of anxiety and fear but also a moment of great possibility, and Americans wondered whether their new president was made of the right stuff to lead them through such uncertainty.

The man to whom the country looked to deal with these prickly issues was a former haberdasher from Missouri. Harry Truman was born on May 8, 1884, in the small western Missouri town of Lamar. His parents, Martha Ellen Young and John Anderson Truman, were salt-of-the-earth Scotch-Irish, hardworking rural folk. Truman's father was a livestock trader and family farmer, whose "estates" in Independence and then Grandview, Missouri, were only a few hundred acres. Suffice it to say, Truman's "pedigree" was rather meager compared to that of his more illustrious, patrician predecessor.

When Harry was six, the family moved from Lamar to Independence, Missouri. When the Trumans arrived, Independence was a small town of around six thousand people located ten miles east of downtown Kansas City. It was the kind of town where everybody knew everybody, as well as everybody's business. Compared to Kansas City, it was a sleepy backwater, churchgoing (overwhelmingly Protestant, with Presbyterianism and Methodism the two most dominant sects), conservative, rooted-in-the-past kind of place, and that's exactly how its residents wanted it to be. Kansas City was a brassy Yankee town, "money-wise" and full of "new people." Independence was Southern in both spirit and pace, indeed, more Southern than Midwestern and very set in its ways. Although during his early adolescent and adult years he worked and lived in other Missouri towns, Truman considered Independence his hometown to where he would retire in 1953.

Harry tried to please his father but despised the livestock business and farming. "Corn-shucking," he said, was "a job invented by Satan." Perhaps one of the reasons why Harry disliked farm life so much was due to his terrible eyesight. Harry was so nearsighted that he had to wear specially made glasses that were so thick that they looked like the bottoms of two Coca-Cola bottles. Such a disability caused Harry to become a rather timid, bookish introvert who shied away from strenuous physical activity—not a temperament conducive to the daily rigors of farm life. Harry was so disaffected by the drudgery and hard work of his rural existence that he went "aesthetic" (or effete in his father's eyes). He dreamed of a career as a classical pianist. A piano in the home of a small-town American family was a symbol of prosperity and affluence, as well as wholesome home entertainment. The Trumans didn't have just an "ordinary" piano but a Kimball, the most popular piano of the day, costing about $200. ("Music for the multitudes" was the company's slogan.) Interestingly, although a sign of increasing plenitude, learning to play the piano was considered in Harry's "gender-specific" environment to be for the young women of the household, not for its male members who were to be pursuing the more "manly" activities of athletics or other appropriate forms of masculine endeavors. Indeed, because he wore glasses, his mother forbid him to play roughhouse games with other boys. As a result of such coddling, Truman became a "mamma's boy," who compensated for being prevented from engaging in rigorous physical activity by becoming a voracious reader—a bookworm. Truman, however, referred to himself as a "sissy." Interestingly, what few close male companions Truman had as a youth were also "sissies," such as Tasker Taylor, "who could draw better than anyone else," and tall, shy Charlie Ross, "who never missed a day of school," and who, like Truman, read everything he could get his hands on. Ross, later a reporter for the St. Louis *Post Dispatch,* won the Pulitzer Prize for journalism and eventually served as President Truman's press secretary.

Despite his loathing of physical work, Truman's preparation for the presidency began with his early life on the farm. It was the kind of experience that many a lad in the decades before and just after the turn of the century never forgot, for they credited the experiences as being among the most pivotal in shaping who they became in later life. Farm life not only helped mold a young man's personality and disposition but in the process created an individual who, it was believed, represented the "essence" of the American character and its attendant values of hard work, simplicity, honesty, integrity, and, naturally, physical strength. In short, "farm boys" like Truman were still revered as the epitome of the Jeffersonian yeoman farmer upon whose broad shoulders rested the great democratic republican experiment called the United States. After 1950 it no longer was important for politicians to boast that they had been born and raised on a farm. In many ways, Truman was the last of such American types to become president. Not until after he attained that office did he fully appreciate what a boon to his political career his farm years had become; they marked the essential beginning of his ascendancy to the White House. As long as Americans embraced the rustic virtues and plain-folk ethos of heartland America, that last bastion of Jeffersonian agrarianism, its native sons, such as Truman, could parlay such sentiments into a promising political career.

At a time when few farm children went beyond elementary school or junior high, Truman was one of the few in his town who attended high school. Truman was one of forty young men and women of the class of '01 of Independence High School. One of the other graduates was Elizabeth Virginia ("Bessie") Wallace, the future Mrs. Truman, whom Harry had known and had a "crush" on since fourth grade. Bessie lived only two blocks from the Trumans, and throughout grade school and high school, Harry remained smitten by the girl "with the golden curls." Years later, when Truman reflected on his affection for Bess, as well as overcoming his shyness, he admitted that if he "succeeded in carrying her books to school and back home for her I had a big day." Truman not only thought Bess "hung the moon," but like most of the other boys in town was also intimidated by her sheer presence and variety of talents, both physical and aesthetic. In short, she was Truman's (as well as everyone else's) "ideal." She was popular. She stood out in class, always dressed in the latest fashion. A natural all around athlete, Bess was the best baseball and tennis player in town and could iceskate and run faster than any of the boys in her age group. She was also an exceptional ballroom and tap dancer and, of course, could play the piano. Bess could simply do so much more than Truman; she could do things he never learned. She could even whistle through her teeth! Finally, Bess was even the right faith, a Presbyterian, which socially put her among the town's elite. When Mary Paxton, Bessie's close friend and neighbor, was asked if Truman hung about the Wallace house, she responded emphatically, "No! No! Harry was a Baptist!" Although "Bessie" would remain the love of Truman's life, the two went their separate ways after high school graduation. Bess went on to Woodland College for Women, and Harry, who had hoped to get an appointment to West Point, went to Kansas City instead with his parents. Apparently, Truman's terrible eyesight prevented his appointment to West Point. Academically he qualified, but at the time physical "handicaps," such as poor vision, automatically disqualified many a young aspirant. Suffice it to say, Truman was sorely disappointed. He desperately wanted to go to college, and "manly" West Point would be the perfect place to help Truman overcome still feeling a "sissy." Compounding his feelings of inadequacy was the fact that his family was moving to the "big city" not because it represented upward mobility but failure. Truman's father had engaged in grain speculations that turned out badly, and the family lost their home in Independence. Thus, at this point in Truman's life, there could be no hope for college. Perhaps more disappointing, he would not see Bess again for another ten years.

Truman was able to find work in Kansas City, spending the next five years as a bank clerk and "moonlighting" in the evenings as an usher at local vaudeville theatres. In 1906 the Trumans moved back to the "country." They inherited a decent-size farm from Truman's mother, "Grandmother Young." For the next eleven years Truman found himself stuck doing work he had loathed so much as a youngster. The farm, however, was not Truman's sole occupation. Truman was so desperate to escape the drudgery and monotony of farm life that, over the course of the next six years (1911-1917), he haphazardly invested in a variety of get-rich-quick schemes, all of which failed. For example, in 1914, he and a partner, Jerry Culberson, invested in an Oklahoma zinc mine. The venture failed with a personal loss to Truman of $7,500. If he and his partner had had enough money to take a rig into the area, they would have become rich. Truman next tried his hand at oil "wildcatting" in Texas, Oklahoma, and Kansas. In 1917, Truman with Culberson and a third partner, David Morgan, drilled a 900-foot deep well on a 320-acre lease in Eureka, Kansas. Truman, however, gave up on the project, joining the army soon after the United States entered the "Great War" in April 1917. Truman's partners let the lease go. The well was right on top of the famous Teter Pool; had Truman stayed home and run his oil company, he probably would have become a millionaire. Interestingly, instead of becoming wealthy, by the time Truman entered the army his total indebtedness hovered around $23,000.

Like many a president before him, Truman became a Mason, which provided him with a great diversion from farm life and failed business ventures. He joined the secret society in 1909, and a year later, he obtained "dispensation" for a lodge in Grandview, Missouri, Truman's present hometown. He soon became the lodge master and maintained his membership and interest in Freemasonry for the rest of his life. During his time on the farm, he found Masonry so fascinating that he later remarked that he learned all the ritual by reciting it to the plow horses.

Without question, the high point of Truman's life back on the farm was his renewed courtship of Bess Wallace, whom he began seeing in

1910 when he returned a borrowed cake plate to the Wallace household. At the time the Wallaces lived across the street from Truman's Aunt Ella Noland in Independence, so Truman had to travel about twelve miles if he wished to see Bess. Apparently, he didn't mind the journey by train, then streetcar. According to family legend, when the cake plate needed returning, Truman seized the plate, "with something approaching the speed of light," walked across to the Wallace house and rang the doorbell. Bess answered the door, and the courtship was on. A year after this "chance encounter," Truman proposed marriage to Bess, but she refused. Truman, undoubtedly crushed, understood Bess' rejection: she came from a prominent family; he did not. Truman, however, was not to be deterred. He and Bess dated for the next six years. Thanks to Truman's persistence in wooing her, in early 1917 Bess finally agreed to marry the future president. Wedding bells, however, were not to ring until after Truman returned from participation in the "Great War."

In April 1917, when Truman was approaching thirty-three, his bucolic life—courting his boyhood sweetheart, farming, enjoying activities and meetings at the Mason Lodge, pursuing get-rich-quick schemes—all suddenly ended with Woodrow Wilson's declaration of war on Germany. Truman had been in the Missouri National Guard since 1905. When Wilson called up all the guards soon after war was declared, Truman was ready to go. He was made a first lieutenant of the 129th Field Artillery Regiment. For nine months, Truman and his regiment (1100 men) trained at Camp Doniphan in Oklahoma before shipping out to France on March 30, 1918. On April 13, 1918, Truman's transport docked at Brest, and a few days later he went to artillery school at Montigny-sur-Aube to learn how to operate the famous French 75, the principal allied artillery piece used during the war. In April 1918, Truman was promoted to captain.

In July 1918, Truman was given command of Battery D, a collection of hard-drinking, rowdy Irish and German Catholics from Kansas City, who took great pride in their ability to drive out company commanders, four of them before Truman took over. Truman was determined not to be the fifth. Truman undoubtedly was filled with trepidation on taking command of Company D; years later he admitted being "outright scared." Truman, however, was not about to run from the challenge. He called together the corporals and sergeants and told them right out that it was their job to get along with him, not the other way around. He told them that if any of them had trouble with that, they should let him know right now, and he would "bust them back right there on the spot." All saluted and said, "No, Sir," and from that moment on, everyone knew who was in charge. Truman and his men not only "got along," the men of Battery D came to idolize their captain, referring to him fondly as "Captain Harry" for the rest of their lives. Such affection and respect for Captain Truman can be confirmed by the hundreds of letters from his comrades found in the Truman Library in Independence. The contents of the letters run the gamut from the mundane to the extraordinary, as the men of Company D kept their captain informed about their respective lives over the span of several decades. From the births of children and grandchildren to the deaths of spouses and fellow soldiers, Truman's men kept their commander up-to-date on the events of their lives. Perhaps more telling was the fact that Truman responded to every letter he received from his fellow combatants, usually typed but always with a longhand personal note at the end to convey a more intimate reconnection. Most important, participation in the Great War gave Truman the opportunity to finally rid himself of his "sissy" demon. He had been waiting since childhood to prove his masculinity to himself and to others, and World War I gave him the chance to erase any lingering doubts family members or friends still harbored about his manliness. Truman believed if he could endure the physical, moral, and psychological challenges of warfare, his masculinity would no longer be in question for he would have proved himself in that one arena of universal acceptance: valor on the battlefield.

Truman's opportunity to prove his mettle came in August 1918 in a fight later called "The Battle of Who Run," a small but potentially deadly engagement for Truman and his men. The encounter took place in the Vosges Mountains in Alsace near the Swiss border, which was at the extreme end of the Western Front. The battle began at 8:00 p.m. on August 29 when Truman's battery fired five hundred rounds of poison gas shells from their 75's at the German emplacements some four miles away. When Company D finished their barrage, they were to move out before the Germans had time to return the fire. As one of Truman's men remembered, "We were firing away and having a hell of a good time doing it until we woke somebody up over there." The Germans retaliated before Company D could leave their position, the result of a sergeant's failure to do his job in a timely manner—bringing up the horses from the rear so the guns could be hauled away.

When the Germans began shelling the American position, Truman was atop his horse trying to see what was going on. Before he knew what happened, a shell burst so close to him that it knocked him and his mount down, and both horse and rider tumbled into a shell hole with the horse landing on top of Truman, pinning him down helplessly. One of the company's lieutenants helped pull Truman out from the hole who, according to the officer, was "gasping like a catfish out of water." No sooner was Truman up than he saw his men frantically running around trying to put their gas masks on, as well as bringing up the horses to hitch them to the cannons and getting the guns out of there before the Germans blew them up. All the while, German shells were exploding all around the frightened Americans. In the midst of the chaos, one of Truman's men yelled, "Run, boys, they've [the Germans] got a bracket on us." No sooner was such a declaration made than several of Truman's men ran. Truman, seeing this ignoble "retreat," was enraged at his men's cowardice and began shouting every obscenity he could think of to shame them back to do their duty. Truman's barrage of profanity stunned the fleeing soldiers, for it was coming from an officer who prior to this moment had seemed so proper and reserved. "I got up and called them everything I knew," was how Truman remembered the moment. He was livid and terrified. In a letter to Bess, Truman confided that the only reason he didn't run was because he "was too scared to run and that [was] pretty scared." His men never knew that. They came back and hitched the horses. Despite the rain of shells, the explosions, and the clods of dirt heaving in all directions, laced with deadly metal from the shrapnel, Company D got their guns out of there.

The "Guns of August 1914" finally fell silent in November 1918, with the signing of the armistice that ended the Great War. Over ten million men on both sides had perished, but Captain Harry S Truman and the boys of Company D all survived and were coming home "in one piece." Truman arrived home on Easter Sunday, April 9, 1919. As his transport steamed into New York harbor, Truman recalled making "a resolution that if old lady Liberty wanted to see me again she'd have to turn around." After a long rail trip to Camp Funston in Kansas, Truman was officially discharged from the United States Army on May 6, 1919. Truman returned from France a changed man. He no longer saw himself as the scared, bookish, shy boy of his prewar years. He believed he had courage and that he was "tough." Perhaps most important, he saw himself as a leader who could inspire others by his "words" as well as by his actions. Truman also became quite gregarious after his wartime experience, enjoying the camaraderie not only of his fellow combatants but with a variety of other people as well. In short, the war helped Truman find his manhood and with it a cockiness and a savoir-faire that few of his friends and relatives could ever imagine him possessing. He knew he had changed but to what depth he had yet to realize. Perhaps most important, his attractive, new personality was perfect for a career in politics.

Truman's heady war experience made it impossible for him to return to farm life. Not long after his coming home, he moved to Independence, where he married his beloved Bess Wallace on June 28, 1919, the very day the Treaty of Versailles was signed. After a short honeymoon the newlyweds moved into Bess' mother's house, while Truman's mother and sister (Truman's father died in 1914) remained in the Grandview farmhouse. Truman's divorce from farm life was typical of millions of Americans in the aftermath of World War I. Like many of his countrymen, Truman left the farm for both economic and personal reasons. As already noted, all his life he had loathed the hard work required, and now as farm prices began falling in the 1920s, the prospect of returning to such a life for little reward made such an existence even more an anathema. Moreover, his new personality was no longer conducive to the loneliness and isolation of rural life. Truman needed and wanted the expansive vistas, the excitement, refinement, and culture of urban America. Thus, soon after returning from his honeymoon, he and a former army buddy, Eddie Jacobson, decided to open a haberdashery in Kansas City.

In the fall of 1919, the men's clothing store of Truman and Jacobson opened for business on Twelfth Street near the venerable Muehlebach Hotel. They had two good years selling their somewhat haute couture shirts, hats, and ties not only to veterans but to the city's tonier male population as well. For Truman the haberdashery not only represented a new life but also a chance to further hone his interpersonal skills as he interacted with a wide variety of the city's population. His store became a gathering place for his friends and a base from which he moved about the city visiting with other men and encouraging them to come to his store. Unfortunately, the recession of 1921-1922 caught Truman and Jacobson unaware. Ignoring the signs and refusing to sell when they could have made a deal that would have returned their investment, they held on, trying to salvage their business to the very end. When they finally closed the store, they owed $25,000 worth of bank notes, not all of which were covered by collateral. For the next three years Truman and Jacobson did their best to pay off the debt. Jacobson could not and declared bankruptcy in 1925; Truman narrowly avoided it and continued paying off his debts, slowly but surely. For the next twenty years Truman was strapped for money. Sadly, when the family farm was threatened by foreclosure in

1940, Truman could not raise the necessary money to keep it, although it had been in the family for a century. In 1922, however, these problems were yet to come about. The "busted merchant," as Truman referred to himself, at least had the consolation of having married the love of his life and of having enormously benefited from his World War I experience. Even though farm life had been far from idyllic, it had given him a sense of resolution and feeling for life's verities.

Typically, when we think of a future president's early years, we tend (or want) to see an individual whose previous life had been filled with a wealth of wonderful, glamorous, and heroic moments. When faced with adversity, naturally he rose to the occasion and triumphed. In the process, his efforts proved historically pivotal, both for himself and the others around him, if not for the nation as a whole. All the while, the future great man kept perspective, humility, and understanding, appreciating the traditions of place and family, as well as the values of others external to his immediate world. Harry Truman had no such "pedigree" when he ran for his first political office in 1922. There had been no pivotal, history-making moments, no upward movement, economically or professionally, just a bundle of experiences that only later appeared to have a pattern. An accurate account of Truman's early years would have stressed their episodic nature—his trying of various schemes and enterprises to escape the drudgery of farm life and to improve himself financially. At age forty in 1922, the best Truman could say for himself was that he was happily married and had nobly and courageously served his country. At this juncture in their lives, neither Truman nor Bess saw much coming their way in the near future. All that changed, however, when Jim Pendergast, a former lieutenant in Truman's regiment, and his father Mike visited Truman in his haberdashery as he was about to go out of business. Apparently, Truman's "popularity" and gregarious personality had caught the attention of the most powerful political figure in Missouri, Democratic "Boss" Tom Pendergast of Kansas City. Jim was Boss Tom's nephew and, together with his father Mike, persuaded Truman to run for commissioner of Jackson County, Missouri. Truman initially hesitated, not wanting to be associated with the Pendergast machine, which was notorious for its involvement in a variety of illicit activities ranging from gunrunning and prostitution to bootlegging and narcotics. However, the soon-to-be "busted merchant" reconsidered and told the Pendergasts he would do it. Boss Tom needed someone "clean" to run for the office, and Captain Harry Truman, "war hero," fit the bill.

Tom Pendergast was a short, red-faced, barrel-chested man with huge hands, which he undoubtedly often used earlier in his career to physically threaten or do actual bodily harm to some uncooperative Irish, German, Italian, or Anglo-American. Pendergast gained control of Kansas City around the turn of the century, and by the time Truman began his association with him, he no longer had a reputation for strong-arming opponents. Pendergast ruled Kansas City from a dingy downtown office that belied both his power and personal wealth. A devout Catholic, Pendergast attended Mass every Sunday and traveled every summer to Europe with his wife aboard the most luxurious transatlantic liners.

Pendergast was an old-time political boss—moral in his own way, very shrewd, at times ruthless, but utterly reliable when he gave his word. By the time Truman began his affiliation with Boss Tom, the Pendergast machine was one of the most efficient, organized, and complete in its control of any such urban camorra in the country. Indeed, when it came to the exercising of pure power, in the eyes of many other urban bosses, Tom Pendergast was the "beau ideal." Pendergast had his roots in the city's poorest wards and, like his eastern counterparts in New York or Boston, provided his constituents with many necessities. In the days before poor relief, he doled out groceries; if someone needed to be buried but the family didn't have enough money for a proper burial, he made the arrangements. Jobs, of course, were always provided or "created" for relatives and friends and even for those not directly connected but loyal to the machine come Election Day. For such munificence and largesse, all Boss Tom asked for in return was votes and patronage from the ambitious office-seekers whom he helped to get elected. Indeed, patronage was the glue that held the machines together. Patronage employees kicked back part of their pay to the boss or to the boss' organization (which were symbiotic). The boss did larger favors for businessmen and companies desiring franchises or favorable legislation or legal transactions that could prove difficult without the boss' approval or support. Payment for such services naturally went directly into the machine's coffers or into the boss' pocket, which in reality were one in the same. Finally, to ensure electoral victory, bosses like Pendergast when necessary resorted to all manner of fraud: bribery, "treating" with booze, outright purchase, repeat voting, and, of course, voting by absentees and dead people. To keep the machine rolling, bosses never hesitated to pull out all the stops on Election Day, calling in all favors and resorting when necessary to all forms of political chicanery. Truman was only vaguely aware of the "depth" of Boss Tom's network when he agreed to run for his first political office.

A political neophyte, Truman compensated for his lack of political experience by hitting the hustings hard, something he would do consistently even as president. By that time, Truman had nothing but contempt for those politicians who did not earn their office by taking the issues and themselves directly to the people. He believed no lucky breaks made up for ringing door bells, shaking hands, "kissing babies," and speaking in all the little town halls and fraternal places and church basements. To Truman, if you wanted political office and the power that went with it, no matter how great or small, you had to go out and get it, earn it, and win it from the people, especially the common people. That was the attitude Truman brought to his 1922 campaign for county commissioner, and over the course of his political career, he approached every campaign with the same exuberance and intensity of purpose. In many ways, Truman's simplistic approach to winning political office reflected not the mentality of his own time but rather that of Jacksonian America, when supposedly politicians who wanted office and power had to go out and get it directly from the people. If they refused to do that, then the people turned against them and denied them office by either voting them out, if they were already in, or not voting for them when they ran for office for the first time.

Despite support in every way possible from Jackson County veterans, as well as from Tom Pendergast pulling every string he could, Truman won the Democratic primary by less than 300 votes. He carried the general election, however, by 3,000 and for the next twelve years earned a reputation for honesty and efficiency, despite his ties to the Pendergast machine. Truman's main responsibilities, as one of three county commissioners or "judges," were to maintain or build new county roads and bridges and to oversee the county home for the indigent aged. Largely as a result of Henry Ford's production innovations, which allowed his company to produce inexpensive automobiles, Americans became the most mobile people in the world. As a result, "older" industries like steel and oil found new and more uses, while a host of new industries emerged, all thanks to the automobile. One of the more important new auto-related "boom" industries of the 1920s was highway construction. As increasing numbers of middle-class Americans purchased cars, an "automobile culture" emerged throughout the nation, stimulating the building of a massive network of paved roads and concomitant service institutions—filling stations, hot dog stands, and "tourist cabins" (the forerunners of motels)—all heralded a wholly new civilization. By the middle of the decade, the country was a network of paved roads. City dwellers now had easy access to the country and made a ritual of day-long excursions. Camping trips and long-distance vacations became commonplace, especially for the burgeoning urban white middle class. Rural folk and their families could now hop into their cars or pickup trucks and head for the nearest town with its stores, motion picture theaters, amusement parks, and sporting events. Suburbs proliferated, promoted as the perfect mix of urban and rural life. Thus, upon becoming a county commissioner, Truman made the "modernization" of Independence and its surrounding environs, via road construction, a priority. He not only sensed the sociocultural benefits the automobile was bringing his constituents but their potential economic enrichment as well, for road construction would greatly improve Jackson County's connection with the booming Kansas City economy. Truman floated several multi-million dollar bond issues to build more roads. Such enterprises not only enhanced the county's ties to Kansas City but, perhaps more important, created hundreds of jobs as well for county residents. Interestingly, although Truman considered himself to be fundamentally a traditional Southern Democrat (especially when it came to the issues of race), his association with the urban–based Pendergast machine, as well as his promotion of infrastructure development and other reforms, was ideologically transforming Truman into an urban progressive. As will be seen, such a metamorphosis made it easy for Truman to break with his conservative roots and embrace New Deal liberalism in the 1930s as Senator Truman. In short, Truman sensed that the America that was emerging in the aftermath of the Great War was disassociating itself as fast as it could from its rustic past and welcoming ever more rapidly the new urban ethos. The successful future politician had to be able to bridge both worlds, especially if one came from a state like Missouri, which was an interesting amalgamation of both the old America and the new.

The work of the commissioner's court was complicated enough, but the politics surrounding it was extraordinary. Those who failed to grasp who was important and where his "support" came from was destined for defeat in the next election. Truman understood the machinations of syndicate politics, for he lasted twelve years. More impressive than his longevity was the fact that Truman never succumbed to corruption and graft, despite his close ties to the Pendergast machine. The fact that Boss Tom rarely, if ever, pressured Truman to toady to his agenda confirms the respect he had for Truman's integrity. However, that is not to say that Truman was a righteous, high-minded crusader and do-gooder. He knew that Boss Tom expected him to allot patronage jobs, but Truman always drew the line between sinecures and graft, willing to promote the former but not the latter. That Truman was "clean" is also not to suggest that he refrained from the use of personal chicanery or cajolery to get what he wanted done. This was especially true when dealing with his fellow commissioners. As Truman reflected, they "used to shoot craps while court was in session down behind the bench while I transacted the business . . . when I wanted something done I'd let Barr and Vrooman [the other two commissioners] start a crap game and then introduce a long and technical order. Neither of them would have time to read it and over it would go. I got a lot of good legislation for Jackson County over while they shot craps."

When reflecting on his years as a county commissioner, Truman believed his greatest satisfaction came from what he had been able to do for common folk. He saw himself, then and as he would throughout his political career, as their champion and protector. Years later in an interview with journalist Eric Sevareid, Truman related that while a county commissioner he discovered that hundreds of old men and women were being committed to mental institutions by relatives who either could not afford to pay for their care or simply refused to do it. Outraged by such callousness and penuriousness, Truman ramroded a massive overhaul of the county's entire welfare system to ultimately provide at the county's expense (the taxpayers') free care for the indigent aged, abandoned for whatever reasons by their families. This, he told Sevareid, gave him more satisfaction than anything else he accomplished in twelve years as a county judge.

"He loved politics," remembered Ted Marks, one of Truman's closest army buddies, "and he strived for something and never let loose until he got there. I think no matter what job he held he put all he had into it. He enjoyed it and did the best he knew how. . . ." His cousin, Ethel Noland, confirmed Marks' assessment, believing Truman did not find his "real work" until he entered politics at the "old age" of forty. However, observed Noland, Truman had been a late bloomer all his life. "He didn't marry until he was thirty-five. . . . He didn't do anything early." Politics came naturally. "There," she said, "he struck his gait."

In 1934, as Truman approached his fiftieth birthday, he believed his political career was about to come to an end. He could not remain a county commissioner forever, for in machine politics rotation of office was a key component of the patronage system. Moreover, the Great Depression had engulfed the nation, and times were tough, so Truman needed a refuge in which he could continue for the rest of his life. He hoped that haven would be Congress, more specifically the House of Representatives, for Missouri had just undergone redistricting, and in the process, the boundaries gerrymandered by Boss Tom saw Jackson County obtain two seats. Truman was confident that his mentor would help him become the representative of the new Fourth District. Much to Truman's dismay and embarrassment, however, Pendergast endorsed another individual, and Truman was left out in the cold. Truman was devastated, feeling betrayed by Pendergast and depressed by the notion that he was out of politics forever and had no choice but to return to the farm. It turned out that Pendergast had not abandoned Truman but had something else in mind for him: election as United States Senator from Missouri. Suffice it to say, Truman was shocked when Pendergast approached him about running but did not hesitate to accept the offer.

That Truman was "Pendergast's boy" was no secret, and Truman himself accepted this fact. Apparently, Truman's candidacy was part of a larger power struggle between the Pendergast machine of Kansas City and the Champ Clark machine of St. Louis. Clark at the time was Speaker of the House, and he and Pendergast had been feuding for years to see whose urban machine would dominate Missouri politics. Truman's selection and victory in the primary and general election for the moment confirmed Pendergast supremacy. On January 30, 1935, Truman proudly took office as junior senator from Missouri.

Unfortunately, Truman's ten years as a senator weren't his happiest in a personal sense. Because of his long-standing affiliation with the Pendergast machine, few of his colleagues had much to do with him. The majority viewed him as a hick, a country bumpkin, and, most insulting, the stooge of Boss Tom. One fellow solon remarked that Truman had calluses on his ears from taking orders on the long-distance phone from Kansas City. Truman did, however, establish a good relationship with "Cactus Jack" Garner of Texas, FDR's vice president for his first two terms. Senator Burt Wheeler of Montana and Senator Carter Glass of Virginia also befriended Truman, as well as Carl Hatch of New Mexico and Lewis Schwellenbach of Washington, both of whom went out of their way to be friendly. The rest of the upper house, however, rarely gave him the time of day or were cordial at best. Bronson Cutting of New Mexico "had a way of looking through me as if I didn't exist"; Pat McCarran of Nevada declared he "never considered him a Senator"; and the powerful George W. Norris of Nebraska, the great voice of reform in the Senate, believed Truman was "poison" and refused to speak to him. But as the venerable and kindly J. Hamilton Lewis of Illinois told Truman, "Harry, don't start out with an inferiority complex. For the first six months you'll wonder how the hell you got here, and after that you'll wonder how the hell the rest of us got here." Truman heeded Lewis' advice, ignored the slights and condescension, although he admitted to Bess "their [the other senators] snubbing" did hurt his feelings. However, he was there to serve his state and its people, and no sooner did he take his seat in that august chamber than he plunged passionately into bringing the New Deal to "The Show-Me State."

Even before becoming a senator, Truman had embraced the New Deal. It was no surprise that as a senator his support for FDR and his programs and policies continued unabated; indeed, Truman's endorsement and enthusiasm for the New Deal transcended that of most of his colleagues. As alluded earlier, as a county commissioner Truman acted more the progressive reformer than conservative Southern Democrat, opposed to any form of government intervention to ameliorate socioeconomic problems. As presiding "judge" for a large metropolitan county and the official in charge of federal relief for the state once the Depression hit Missouri, he witnessed firsthand what the federal government could do to relieve the needy. Truman had never embraced the concept of laissez faire nor the egoistic individualism and acquisitive ethos that informed American capitalism during the 1920s. To him, the exalted notion of "rugged individualism," which many Americans believed was the essence of the American spirit for it defined the "self-made" man, was simply a ruse used by the "winners" to justify how they got there. The upper classes traditionally felt (and perhaps still feel) justified in holding the losers in disdain, blaming them for their own problems, in telling them that they could find work if they really wanted to. In short, losers in the amoral marketplace of unfettered capitalism are "unworthy," not "truly needy." These "winners"—the callous, self-righteous, self-serving rich—Truman held in contempt. In this regard, Truman was more of a Midwestern Populist than progressive. Truman considered bunk the belief that the poor or unemployed were in such condition because they lived improvident, extravagant, or dissipated lives. As he watched the unemployed of his own state desperately look for jobs—any work, no matter how menial—or the number of Missourians in bread lines and soup kitchens, his scorn for rugged individualism and its proponents intensified. He believed that greedy businessmen, especially the 1920s corporate moguls and their Wall Street lackey stockbrokers, in pursuit of their own self-interest (egoism) at the expense of others, had plunged the country into its worst economic crisis in history. The squalor, despair, hopelessness, and disillusionment that Truman saw all around him and the unwillingness of the private sector to help out convinced him that the government (state and national) had a moral obligation to intervene in various capacities and offer relief to the downtrodden and dispossessed. He also believed that laws must be passed to prevent the common folk's further exploitation.

Truman came into national public life at the start of the "Second Hundred Days," the high tide of the New Deal. The crusade was not just recovery (which was fast becoming an illusion) from the Depression but for reform as well. Truman voted with the Democratic majority consistently, helping to pass some of the most far-reaching legislation in congressional history. Truman was a "behind-the-scenes," quiet but determined New Dealer, who rarely spoke for a measure and never took part in debate. He just voted his approval—for the Wagner Labor Relations Act, guaranteeing the right of workers to join unions and bargain collectively with management for wages, benefits, etc.; for the Works Progress Administration; for the Social Security Act; and for rural electrification. This last measure probably changed the way Americans lived more than any other single New Deal piece of legislation. In 1935 in Missouri, 9 out of 10 farmers were without electricity.

As a member of the Interstate Commerce Committee, Truman worked intensely on what became the Public Utility Holding Company Act, designed as a blow against the public power cartels that monopolized utilities. By 1932 thirteen such companies controlled 75 percent of the nation's private power interests. The results of such consolidation and monopolization were huge profits for company owners and speculators and profiteering at consumers' expense, as the companies charged people exorbitant rates for electricity or simply denied them service, as was the case for the majority of rural Americans. Working on the bill also brought Truman face-to-face with big-time lobbying and high-powered witnesses. He resolved to deny no one a hearing. "I'll take all the dinners he has to put out," Truman would later write of a lobbyist for a Midwestern railroad, "and then do what I think is right. I can see no harm in talking to anyone—no matter what his background. In fact I think everyone has the right to be heard if you expect to get all the facts." Despite pressure from Boss Tom and a "propaganda barrage" from utility companies and their stockholders, Truman remained steadfast in his commitment to get the bill passed, which the Senate did by a wide margin. The original measure (the version Truman supported), the Wheeler-Rayburn Bill, called for the "death sentence" for all utility holding companies if they could not prove they served a "valid" economic purpose—the providing of affordable electricity to all Americans. Unfortunately, the House rejected the death sentence. Congress in the thirties was unwilling to outlaw lynching, but when it came to capital punishment for utilities pyramids, the representatives were more compassionate. A compromise bill was eventually passed by the House, cutting the pyramids down to smaller units and kept to only one level above the operating company. Many New Dealers such as Truman opposed the "watered-down" version, but if FDR accepted it, then Truman and the others would go along. Possibly more important to FDR than the final law was that he had been able to make a tough public stand against a major business abuse. The political mileage FDR gained was significant, for the majority of Americans applauded the bill because they had long viewed the utility holding companies as profiteering demons who made millions at their expense.

"I was a New Dealer from the start," Truman would firmly and proudly say later, and as noted above, his voting record confirmed his declaration. Senator Robert Wagner of New York, one of the New Deal's most prolific legislative stalwarts, constantly praised Truman as "extremely useful." However, in manner, background, language, age, and choice of companions, Truman had little in common with the ardent young New Dealers that surrounded FDR and were his "inner circle." Unlike Truman, they were "Easterners" with patrician backgrounds. They were university-educated, graduates of Harvard or Columbia where they obtained degrees in economics, the law, or public administration. Most had backgrounds steeped in the reformist traditions, especially that of early twentieth-century progressivism. To say the least, Truman often felt uncomfortable, even intimidated, by these young lions, for he had virtually nothing in common with them other than being a pro-FDR, pro-New Deal politician. Thus, Truman didn't really care for these new ideologues, preferring always the company of such Western mavericks as Burton Wheeler, Western in style, habits, and manners; indeed, Wheeler was more than a "bit rough around the edges." To Truman, the young liberals were too theoretical, esoteric, even somewhat effete for his tastes, and most disturbing, they seemed to "lack common sense for all their education." Truman was heart and soul vintage Andrew Jackson-William Jennings Bryan kind of Democrat, a plain-speaking, no frills, rough and ready, straight-shooting fusion of urban progressivism and rural populism. Truman loved politics in large part because he loved the camaraderie of men like Cactus Jack Garner of Texas (who would be remembered for observing that the vice presidency was not worth a pitcher of warm spit). Privately, Truman and his Western colleagues poked fun at "the boys with the 'Hah-vud' accents," although never, as far as is known, at the Harvard grad in the White House.

Truman's unwavering support for FDR was born of his genuine desire to do what was best for the common people at a time when so many were in desperate need of help. Truman empathized with the plain folk because he saw himself as one of them, just a bit more fortunate than they were at this moment because he had "a job." Truman knew why the people were suffering, and it was his job to help make their lives better, not only immediately but in the future as well. Loyalty was paramount to Truman, and once he gave his word to his "Boss" that he was a New Dealer, then he believed he had to give the president his undying support as an article of faith. To do otherwise would be for Truman a violation of the sanctity of his word. Truman also knew the personal political value to be gained by voting with the president. He hoped his unequivocal support for the New Deal would be noticed both by the party's power brokers and by those individuals inside the Roosevelt White House who had the president's ear and tallied for FDR who was a "team player." If that became true, then Truman was confident of his rise to greater status within the party. Alben Barkley of Kentucky (Truman's future vice president) noted how he had liked Harry Truman almost at once, instinctively. "As the old political saying goes, he 'voted right.'" To many liberal senators, he was "go-along, get-along Harry," a decent, sincere man whose company they often enjoyed. "I liked Harry Truman," Claude Pepper of Florida remembered, "but he was not someone to take seriously." As will be seen, Pepper and others grossly underestimated Truman's "seriousness" to be more than someone who simply "got along" and "voted right."

In 1940 Truman was up for reelection. Initially, Truman's return to Washington for another six years was all but guaranteed. However, "out of the woodwork" appeared Missouri Governor Lloyd Stark, whose vast nursery chain produced the nationally known Stark apples, to contend for Truman's seat. Unfortunately for Truman, his mentor Tom Pendergast was no longer on the scene for support, having been finally sent to federal prison in 1939 for voting and tax fraud. If Truman hoped to be reelected, he would have to do it completely on his own for he didn't even have FDR's endorsement, despite his unflagging support for the president and the New Deal. By contrast, Stark had White House support, although FDR personally did not publicly endorse the governor. Fortunately for

Truman, as would be true in 1948, his opponent got "cocky," certain he would cruise to victory, underestimating Truman's competitive nature and desire to win. Interestingly, when the campaign started, it was Stark's to lose, and the governor knew it. However, as Tom Dewey would in 1948, Stark became overconfident and complacent about hitting the hustings hard. Moreover, his certitude quickly transformed into brashness, if not outright arrogance, as he strutted about the state, "deigning" to appear only in those Missouri counties that he deemed "worthy" of his presence. He even forced his police bodyguards to salute him. In short, he gave the impression he owned the state. Truman, by contrast, campaigned in 78 of Missouri's 114 counties, telling voters of his support of the New Deal and FDR and how such advocacy had helped Missourians receive much federal assistance. Once again, Truman's willingness to hit the campaign trail hard paid off. He defeated Stark with a plurality of 7,976 votes. While Truman was busying himself for another senate term, the two largest Missouri newspapers, the Kansas City *Star* and the St. Louis *Post-Dispatch,* were eating crow, for both had opposed his reelection and predicted a Stark rout.

No sooner was Truman back in Washington than he became involved in a project that would ultimately secure his 1944 vice-presidential nomination. World War II had been raging for two years when Truman began his second term, and the United States, although still officially "neutral," was aiding the Allies (Great Britain and, by the fall of 1941, the Soviet Union) with massive amounts of materiel. To many Americans it appeared that the Roosevelt administration was doing all it could to get the United States in the war. Whether such an accusation was true is moot; what was certain, however, was the Roosevelt administration was doing all it could on the homefront to get the nation prepared for war without necessarily alarming the American people. What concerned Truman was not military preparedness—he wholeheartedly believed in that—but rather, the horrible waste of public money in the various military-related construction projects and other preparedness measures. Truman was appalled by the accounts from his Missouri constituents of the rampant boondoggling going on in his own state at various forts and other military installations. He was even more outraged when he heard that many of the army officers at the different posts were involved or looked the other way at such shenanigans. Truman asked his fellow senators for authorization for him to create a special committee to investigate defense expenditures. Truman got the support necessary, and the result was the Special Committee to Investigate the National Defense

Program, chaired by the junior senator from Missouri, Harry S Truman. Truman had barely organized his committee when the Japanese attacked Pearl Harbor, Hawaii, on December 7, 1941, "a day of infamy," as FDR would refer to the act the next day as he asked Congress for a declaration of war on the Japanese Empire. The assault shocked Americans, for most did not see it coming or refused to acknowledge the possibility. Indeed, most Americans believed the nation would be able to "sit this one out," but Pearl Harbor ended such naïve thinking. Within days of the United States' declaration of war on Japan, Germany and Italy declared war on the United States in accord with their alliance with Japan. The United States was now fully in World War II.

From the moment the United States entered the conflict, Truman never doubted the rightness of the Allied cause and the Axis' evil machinations, and he especially abhorred the malevolent purposes of Nazi Germany. He was certain the United States would prevail, and he wanted to directly participate in this most righteous of causes. Truman saw the conflict as the quintessential struggle between good and evil for the salvation of humanity. He was so moved by the righteousness of the cause that he tried to convince the Army's chief of staff, General George C. Marshal, to commission him an officer. When Truman asked Marshall for such status, the general told Truman, "We don't need any old stiffs like you," and advised Truman to go back to the Senate where he could do more good for the war effort than he could as an army colonel.

Truman obviously returned to the Senate and quickly turned his investigating committee into one of the government's best wartime operations. The Truman Committee, as it became known, revealed to the government and the people the seamier side of the homefront. In Truman's words, his committee exposed "the bad contractors on camp construction, airplane engine manufacturers who made faulty ones, steel plate factories which cheated, and hundreds of other such sordid and unpatriotic ventures." Truman's committee investigated procurement, labor hoarding, and the armed services' waste of food and other supplies. General Brehon B. Somervell, in charge of army supply, told FDR that the Truman Committee saved the country $15 billion.

In the summer of 1944, as FDR was gearing up for a fourth term, rumors began flying that the president was not only going to "dump" his current vice president, Henry Wallace, but that he was going to choose Truman as his running mate. Naturally, Truman discounted all such talk, but by the time of the July Democratic Convention in Chicago, it was clear that FDR preferred Truman to the other candidates. Truman's selection as vice-presidential nominee in 1944 was the result of being the perfect compromise. Even though Henry Wallace wanted to run again, FDR and the party chieftains dumped him because he was too left for the times. Largely as a result of FDR's "court-packing" scheme and other high-handed maneuvers, from 1938 on, conservatives from both parties dominated Congress. As a result, any advocacy of moving the New Deal further left (more social welfare legislation), which Wallace constantly supported, was opposed, and those who agitated for such programs fell out of party favor. Thus, to placate the conservatives in his own party, FDR unloaded Wallace. His own favorite was South Carolina Senator James Byrnes, whom Roosevelt had made director of the Office of War Mobilization and who had been "assistant president" in charge of running domestic affairs during the war. Byrnes, however, was a Southerner, hostile to labor, and unacceptable to northern liberals, civil rights advocates, and urban bosses. Truman became the perfect "accommodation" for the party's various factions. Although FDR observed, "I hardly know [him]," the man from Missouri had all the right credentials. Truman was from a border state, had alienated no one, and was sufficiently popular with his colleagues that he might prove useful in promoting FDR's postwar legislative agenda.

Truman was sitting on a hotel bed in Chicago when he received a telephone call from FDR who was on the West Coast campaigning. When the president used the phone, he always talked in such a loud voice that the listener had to hold the phone way from his ear to avoid going deaf. Democratic National Committee Chairman Robert Hannegan answered the phone, and Truman, because of FDR's loudness, could hear both ends of the conversation. "Bob," FDR said, "have you got the fellow [Truman] lined up yet?" "No," responded Hannegan, "he is the contrariest Missouri mule I've ever dealt with." FDR, irritated by Truman's balking, declared, "Well, you tell him if he wants to break up the Democratic party in the middle of the war, that's his responsibility." FDR then slammed the phone with a bang. "Oh shit," Truman said, "if that's the situation, I'll have to say yes."

In many ways, Truman knew he was running for the presidency in accepting. He quietly told a few friends that the president would not survive a fourth term. When Truman and FDR lunched at the White House lawn shortly after the Chicago convention, the president's hand shook so badly he could hardly pour cream into his coffee. Truman was aghast at the physical condition of his "boss." Less than four months after taking office, a call came from the White House Press Secretary Stephen

Early, asking Truman to come the White House. When the vice president walked into the room, he knew the worst had happened. Mrs. Roosevelt placed her hand on his shoulder and said, "Harry, the President is dead." Truman asked what he could do for her and the family, and the response, so typical of Eleanor, was, "Is there anything *we* can do for *you?* For you are the one in trouble now."

The Truman Presidency: A Positive Assessment

Woodrow Wilson told a Princeton friend in 1913 that it would be ironic if foreign rather than domestic affairs became his administration's priority. One year after making that remark World War I began, and the Mexican Revolution, which erupted four years earlier, was impacting the United States as well. In 1914, Wilson sent warships and troops to that beleaguered nation to occupy the city and port of Vera Cruz, allegedly to protect United States' interests. Two years later, Wilson sent General "Black Jack" Pershing into northern Mexico to track down and bring to justice the legendary Pancho Villa in retaliation for Villa's invasion of the United States and the killing of American citizens in the fall of 1916. By 1914, foreign crises enveloped the Wilson administration. Like his earlier Democratic colleague, Truman too found himself immersed and overwhelmed by the exigencies of foreign policy. Like Wilson, Truman too hoped he could focus on domestic affairs, but like Wilson, world conflict and its aftermath forced Truman to put such issues on the backburner and deal instead with the problems of war and peace.

As noted earlier, Truman was one of the most poorly prepared vice-presidents-cum-presidents in the history of the executive branch. Truman's lack of readiness for the job, however, was not his fault. A large part of the blame must be placed on FDR who met with Truman only three times during the period between the inauguration following the 1944 election and the president's death. This lapse in communication between Truman and FDR greatly handicapped Truman, especially in the area of foreign affairs. As vice president, Truman had been excluded from all foreign policy discussions. He knew nothing about the Manhattan Project. The new president, Secretary of War Henry Stimson noted, was "coming into an office where the threads of information were so multitudinous that only long previous familiarity would allow him to control them." More succinct were Truman's own comments: "They didn't tell me anything about what was going on. . . . Everybody around here that should know anything about foreign affairs is out." Confronted with multiple, complex, and sensitive issues sufficient enough to intimidate any individual, Truman had to act quickly on a succession of national security questions. Although never "fancying" himself anything close to an expert on foreign affairs, ironically, some of Truman's greatest successes as president were in this realm. Indeed, Truman can be credited with establishing the foundation of America's cold war policy upon which subsequent presidents simply added new approaches and interpretations, but the "essence" remained the same for over forty years. As will be seen, Harry Truman was the progenitor of that sum and substance.

The wartime alliance between the United States and the Soviet Union had never been anything but a marriage of convenience. Defeat of the Axis powers had demanded that the two governments cooperate, but collaboration scarcely lasted beyond Germany's final surrender in May 1945. From that point on, U.S./Soviet relations steadily degenerated into a cold war of suspicion and constant tension, if not outright hostility, that could have escalated into World War III.

Historians vary in their respective analyses of the origins of the cold war. The traditional interpretation, which gained currency after the Soviet Union's collapse in 1989, asserts that Soviet expansionism, which was a continuation of inveterate Russian/czarist appetite for new territory, coupled with an ideological zeal to spread international communism, was the main cause. Proponents of this view insist that the United States, to stop the spread of such totalitarianism, had to take as hard a line as possible to stop this Russian "historical imperative." Other historians, called revisionists, view the Soviet's postwar behavior less passionately and contend that Soviet expansionism was purely defense, to secure "Holy Mother Russia" from future invasions from the West. The revisionists claim as well that such expansion was historically imperative because the most devastating attacks on Russia had come from the West, beginning with Napoleon's invasion in 1812. Revisionists argue that the Soviet Union's obsession with securing its western borders was understandable, especially after the devastating invasion by Nazi Germany in 1941. The United States, in this view, should have tried to reassure the Soviets by seeking accommodation, instead of pursuing policies that intensified Stalin's fears. Still other scholars maintain that assigning blame obscures the deep-seated clash of rival, inherently antithetical historical and ideological dynamics, that made postwar tensions between the two superpowers inevitable. These historians believe that, given the great historical disparity and reality of the two nations, a clash between the United States and the Soviet Union was destined to occur once the common enemy had been defeated.

Regardless of which interpretation to which one subscribes, Truman's role proved pivotal. Compounding Truman's situation was the fact that FDR had acted as his own secretary of state, sharing with almost no one his postwar vision and plans. Roosevelt mistrusted the State Department and disagreed with its suspicious, anti-Soviet hardliners. In short, FDR believed he alone had the "magic" touch when it came to dealing with the Soviets. In retrospect, if there was an area in which FDR could be rightly criticized, it was his naïve and arrogant insistence (and his unwillingness to listen to Churchill's much more sagacious counsel relative to understanding Soviet history) that the Western allies show Stalin that they trusted him to fulfill his postwar commitments established at Tehran (1943) and Yalta (1945). To no avail, Churchill tried to impress upon FDR that bending over backwards to make Stalin feel secure would only serve to fuel the Soviet leader's determination to establish Soviet hegemony over Eastern Europe, as well as control of East Germany. FDR would not listen to Churchill's clear understanding of such *realpolitik,* and, thus, FDR made the mistake of allowing the Red Army to cross the Soviet border. As Churchill warned FDR, once entrenched in Eastern Europe, Stalin would never get out, for history would not allow him to because that was a region long viewed essential to Russian security. Indeed, Stalin would be one of the biggest fools in history if he did not take advantage of such an imperative handed to him on a silver platter by his friend, Franklin Roosevelt. In short, FDR's overweening desire to placate Stalin, as well as his hubris, resulted in a policy of capitulation to Soviet aggression. Had FDR accepted the advice of those whose knowledge of European/Russian history was far superior to his, as well as personally asserting a more forceful position with Stalin, perhaps postwar relations between the two superpowers would have been less tense, for if there was one thing Stalin understood (and feared), it was power and force, both of which the United States possessed in bountiful amounts in 1945. Had FDR been willing to assert such superiority, perhaps Stalin would have been less bellicose and aggressive and thus more willing to negotiate on American terms rather than being allowed to dictate the postwar agenda, which, in effect, FDR permitted to happen. Truman inherited from his beloved predecessor a scenario destined to end in a "cold war" because Truman, unlike FDR, was unwilling to allow an aggressor to have such an upper hand. However, because of his inexperience and lack of information, Truman decided that, until he had a better, clearer understanding of all the machinations, he would adhere to FDR's "accommodationist" initiatives. Truman felt obligated to continue FDR's approach and implement his policies, even though Truman knew in his gut that the Soviets could not be trusted to live up to their end of the bargain(s). Until events proved otherwise, Truman believed he had no choice but to follow in FDR's footsteps in this arena, for any deviation by an upstart would be considered an egregious disavowal of the Rooseveltian legacy, which Truman knew would be most unpopular, causing his immediate castigation in the public eye.

Given the rapidness with which World War II was ending, Truman did not have time to analyze all the complex issues and exigencies that were daily arising and inundating his office. Initially, he hoped he could somehow "cut a deal" with Stalin, much like his old mentor Boss Tom struck bargains with rogue politicians back in Missouri. "I like Stalin," Truman once wrote his wife. "He knows what he wants and will compromise when he can get it." However, Truman quickly disabused himself of such first impressions of the Soviet premier and over the course of the next several months came to have a completely different view of the Soviet leader. As disagreements between the two leaders mounted, Truman came to rely on advisers who had a more "realistic" assessment of Stalin's intentions. One such individual was Averell Harriman, United States Ambassador to Moscow, who told Truman that "irreconcilable differences" separated the Soviet Union and the United States with the Russians seeking "the extension of the Soviet System with secret police and the extinction of freedom of speech." The ambassador was convinced that the United States' previous policy of accommodation had been "misinterpreted in Moscow," leading the Russians to conclude they had carte blanche to proceed as they wished. In Harriman's view, the Soviets were engaged in a "barbarian invasion of Europe."

Harriman's assessment of Soviet policy was bolstered by Secretary of the Navy James Forrestal's similar conclusion. The secretary was convinced that "the ultimate aim of Soviet foreign policy is a Russian domination of a communist world." Truman shared instinctively Harriman's and Forrestal's mistrust and perception of the Soviets, and as he told a friend, he "would be damned" to let Stalin beat him in such a "poker game." It was time, Truman believed, to "stand up to the Russians. We have been too easy with them. Our agreements with the Soviet Union so far [have been] a one way-street." Truman believed it was time to talk to the Russians "in words of one syllable."

Truman's official break with FDR's accommodationist policy occurred during a late April 1945 meeting with Soviet foreign minister Molotov. The moment Molotov entered the room, Truman asserted his authority, almost immediately cutting off the diplomatic chitchat and, in typical Truman fashion, got right to the point. Poland's future (whether the Poles would be allowed the right of self-determination or would a pro-Soviet regime be forced on them), he told Molotov, was the most important problem facing the Allies. Truman then told Molotov that thus far the Russians have reneged on their Yalta agreements to help democratize liberated countries, most notably Eastern Europe. As far as Truman was concerned, Soviet duplicity on this matter made him wary of all future postwar cooperation. Molotov resented Truman's aggressive tone, telling the president that he had "never been talked to like that in my life." Truman retorted: "Carry out your agreements and you won't get talked to like that." At that juncture, a Truman aide recalled Molotov turning "a little ashy." Then the president said, "That will be all, Mr. Molotov. I would appreciate it if you would transmit my views to Marshall Stalin." Later, recounting the conversation, Truman told a friend: "I gave him the one-two, right to the jaw." "Give'em hell Harry" had spoken.

Truman was equally unequivocal when it came to decisions about the atomic bomb. Astonishingly, it was not until after his encounter with Molotov that he was briefed about the bomb. By that time, $2 billion already had been spent on what Stimson called "the most terrible weapon ever known in human history." When told of the Manhattan Project and what had been produced and what it could be used for, if necessary, Truman immediately grasped the significance. "I can't tell you what this is," he told his secretary, "but if it works, and pray God it does, it will save many American lives." In Truman's mind, if dropping the bomb on Japan saved countless American lives and brought the war in Asia to a swift conclusion, then he was ready without much deliberation to make one of the most fateful decisions in the history of humanity. Truman also was aware of what the bomb's impact would be on the Soviets, whom he was confident, after seeing the results, would henceforth "carry out their agreements." As James Byrnes told the president, the bomb would "put us in a position to dictate our own terms at the end of the war."

Truman's decision to drop the atomic bomb, first on Hirsoshima and then three days later on Nagasaki, resulted, as he had hoped, in Japan's surrender, and in the process, according to George Marshall, the president saved anywhere from five hundred thousand to more than a million American troops. Given these projections, any president who refused to use whatever resources at his disposal to save American lives would be rightly accused of needless sacrifice and moral turpitude for caring more about preserving enemy lives than those of his own countrymen. Truman was "old school" when it came to war: there were good guys and there were bad guys, and naturally the United States had always been the former. He saw both Germany and Japan as evil nations whom he believed the United States must vanquish. In Japan's case, the enemy was the same nation that had unleashed a wanton and brutal attack on Pearl Harbor. As Truman later explained to a journalist, "When you deal with a beast, you have to treat him as a beast." Truman believed it was our moral duty to extirpate such menaces from the world. Entrusted with such a responsibility, Truman believed that as commander-in-chief of the nation's armed services he was to use whatever means necessary at his disposal to overcome the country's enemies with minimal loss of American life. If defeating the enemy on American terms (unconditional surrender) meant the use of weapons like the atomic bomb, in Truman's mind, all such action was justified. In short, Truman was not about to let hundreds of thousands of Americans die out of fear of being labeled a murderer of allegedly innocent civilians.

Marshall and other military leaders based their calculations on the Japanese willingness to fight to the very end as witnessed by their ferocious resistance at Okinawa and Iwo Jima, and the likelihood of even fiercer defense of the main islands if an invasion became necessary. Even some Japanese (certainly not those who lived in Hiroshima or Nagasaki) were relieved by the use of the bomb. "If the military had its way," one Japanese official has said, "we would have fought until all 80 million Japanese were dead. Only the atomic bomb saved me. Not me alone, but many Japanese. . . ." Indeed, subsequent studies of official Japanese decision-making suggest that most top leaders in Tokyo adamantly opposed peace in August 1945; only the A-bombs, bringing on the intercession of Emperor Hirohito, finally forced the Japanese to surrender. Moreover, it now appears that no one in the inner circles of military and political power, not even FDR, ever seriously doubted the bomb *would not* be used. As Henry Stimson later recalled, "it was our common objective, throughout the war, to be the first to produce an atomic weapon and use it. . . . At no time, from 1941 to 1945, did I ever hear it suggested by the president [FDR], or by any other responsible member of the government that atomic energy should not be used in the war." Indeed, historians have shown that from the beginning, the momentum behind the Manhattan Project had as its underlying purpose to perfect nuclear weapons and use them accordingly. Thus, as horrible as it may seem in retrospect, no one ever seriously doubted the necessity (or in Truman's case, the wisdom) of dropping the bomb on Japan once the weapon was perfected.

Russian behavior offered little encouragement for the belief that friendship and cooperation ranked high on the Soviet agenda. Stalin seemed more intent on reviving and validating his reputation as architect of the purges than as one who wished to collaborate in spreading democracy. He jailed thousands of Russian POW's returning from German prison camps as if their very presence on Russian soil made them enemies of the state. Even Molotov's wife was sent to Siberia. In the meantime, hundreds of thousands of minority nationalities in the Soviet Union were forcibly removed from their homeland when they protested the attempted obliteration of their ancient identities. Some of Truman's advisers, most notably Harriman and Byrnes, were convinced Stalin was clinically psychotic, so paranoid about the possible loss of control over the Russian people that he would do anything to close Soviet borders and prevent the Russian people from getting a taste of what life in a more open society would be like. For veteran American diplomats serving in Moscow before the war, Soviet actions and attitudes seemed all too reminiscent of the oppression and terror they remembered from the worst days of the 1930s purges.

As the Soviets tightened their grip on Eastern Europe (a process Winston Churchill referred to as an "iron curtain" descending "across the European continent"), all hopes for reconciliation between the two superpowers dissipated. To Truman, as Eastern European nations fell one by one under Soviet control, it was clear that Stalin had no intention of honoring his earlier commitments to promote democracy in that region nor allow its people the right of self-determination. Despite Stalin's claims to the contrary, Truman declared such aggression blatant proof of Stalin's larger purpose of not only spreading communism but of brutally subjugating other peoples in the process. Consequently, by early 1947, the former allies were well on the way to becoming bitter adversaries, a reality Truman had accepted from the beginning, and now he was proven right. More important, if further Soviet expansion and suppression was to be stopped, Truman had to respond now before it was too late and all of Europe came under Soviet domination, making communism a greater threat to peace and freedom than fascism ever was. If Truman continued to "trust" the Soviets, as FDR and others had urged, believing negotiation and diplomacy still possible, then he would be as guilty as the French and

British had been with Nazi Germany, willing to appease Hitler out of fear of provoking another war. To Truman, it was straightforward: had the Western democracies learned nothing out of six years of horrible conflict? To allow the new aggressor, Stalin, to have his way would be tantamount of repeating the same mistakes made with Hitler in the late 1930s. To Truman, both individuals were brutal dictators whose respective ideologies were essentially the same: totalitarianism and world domination. It was time for the United States to "buck up" and fulfill its role as the liberator of oppressed peoples and protector of those trying to withstand the onslaught of such violent encroachment upon their freedom. Thus, from 1947 on, Harry Truman placed his personal stamp on the presidency by focusing on the fight against the Soviet Union and, in the process, put into place some of the most important foreign policy initiatives in United States history. Indeed, thanks to Truman, the United States in 1947, via the promulgation of the Truman Doctrine, once and for all broke with its isolationist past and tradition and committed itself to being the protectors and champions of freedom and democracy throughout the world. From March 12, 1947, when Truman first articulated before Congress this monumental break with the isolationist past down to the present moment, the United States has faithfully adhered to this most seminal of departures. Only briefly in the late 1970s (during the Carter administration and with disastrous consequences) did the United States abandon its commitment to the world first outlined by Harry Truman.

Prompting Truman to announce his "doctrine" were potential Soviet-inspired and aided communist takeovers in Greece and Turkey, two countries vital to U.S. and Western (European) security interests. According to Truman, since the United States had emerged as the preeminent world power, with such status came responsibility, not only to ensure continued safety of the nation but of "free peoples" worldwide. The United States' first gesture in helping others "who are resisting attempted subversion by armed minorities or by outside pressures" was to extend assistance to the "freedom fighters" in Greece and Turkey. If the United States failed to help those two beleaguered countries, then Truman asserted totalitarian communism would spread around the world and ultimately threaten the United States itself. With backing from both Democrats and Republicans, Truman's request for $400 million in assistance to Greece and Turkey, most of it in military aid, was passed by Congress. This vote signaled broad, bipartisan support for a national security policy that came to be called "containment," which Truman established as the foundation of U.S. cold war policy, which, with only some minor alterations, remained the cornerstone of U.S. policy until the end of the cold war.

Another significant accomplishment of the Truman administration relative to the cold war was the Marshall Plan, which also embodied the concept of containment. Concerned that Western Europe's severe economic problems might embolden leftist, pro-Soviet political movements, Secretary of State George Marshall devised a plan to strengthen the economies of that region. In short, the plan called for the governments of Western Europe to coordinate their plans for postwar economic reconstruction with the help of funds provided by the United States. Between 1947, when the plan was implemented, until its end in 1951, the United States contributed nearly $13 billion to seventeen Western European nations to stabilize and eventually revitalize those economies. The Soviets were also invited to participate in the plan, but American policy-makers correctly anticipated that Moscow would avoid any program that had as its intent the rebuilding of capitalism in Europe.

The Marshall Plan proved a stunning success, even though conservatives charged that it was a "giveaway" program. To counter such accusations, Truman pointed out that the plan opened up both markets and investment opportunities in Western Europe to American businesses. Moreover, it helped stabilize the European economy by quadrupling industrial production within its first few years. Improved standards of living enhanced political stability, which helped undermine Western European left-wing political parties from taking power.

Under the auspices of the Marshall Plan, Truman and his advisers rightly concluded that the key to a revitalized Western European economy was the restoration of the German economy, a country still divided into four zones of occupation. In June 1948, Great Britain, France, and the U.S. agreed to initiate procedures for the reunification of Germany into a federal republic. At this juncture, Stalin's true position on Germany became clear: from the beginning, he had no intention of ever allowing a reunited Germany, whom he considered (after the United States) to potentially be the greatest threat to the Soviet Union. Thus impelled by such fears (or paranoia), in June 1948, the Soviets cut off all highway, railroads, and water routes linking West Berlin, which lay wholly within the Soviet sector of East Germany, to West Germany.

Truman passed with flying colors this first of many Soviet "tests" to come of American commitment to containment. He knew the moment the blockades went up what Stalin intended. He also knew that, if he used military force to smash the blockades to liberate West Berlin, such action could instigate World War III. Although sympathetic to the plight of West Berliners, the American public would not sanction the use of force if it meant getting involved in another major conflagration so soon after the last one ended. By this time, too many Americans were enjoying the benefits of one of the greatest economic booms in history. They did not want to be distracted from enjoying the "good life" after so many years of deprivation. Truman was acutely aware of these factors, but he also knew that, if he didn't stand up to the "test" this time, Stalin would certainly try again somewhere else for he would believe Truman "weak." Truman responded brilliantly with the famous Berlin airlift, which over an eleven-month period saw British and American pilots make 250,000 flights, round-the-clock, and deliver a total of 2 million tons of supplies to West Berliners. Recognizing his defeat, Stalin lifted the blockade in May 1949. He then created the German Democratic Republic out of his East German sector, and West Berlin survived as an enclave tied to the United States. The "two Germanys" and the divided city of Berlin stood as symbols of cold war tensions until that conflict came to an end in 1989, when East Berliners literally smashed the infamous Berlin Wall (built in 1961) down.

Truman's successful cold war policies and tough stand against the Soviets in the first Berlin crisis no doubt helped him win the 1948 election, a victory that marked one of the most remarkable and legendary political comebacks in United States history. Indeed, only two years earlier (fall 1946) Truman's presidential ratings hit an all-time historic low when only 32 percent of the electorate approved of his performance. Insult was added to injury when, in the congressional elections of that year, the Republicans gained control of both houses of Congress for the first time since 1928. So stunned were some Democrats that Arkansas Senator J. William Fulbright urged Truman to name a Republican as Secretary of State and then resign so that, in order of constitutional succession in place at the time, a Republican could ascend to the Oval Office. Suffice it to say, Truman did not take Fulbright's advice, and henceforth, Truman referred to the Arkansan as "Senator Halfbright."

Fulbright was not the only disaffected Democrat. Potentially more damaging to Truman's reelection bid was the challenge of former FDR vice president and Truman cabinet official, Henry Wallace, who had been critical of Truman's cold war policies from the beginning. Wallace, together with other anti-containment liberals, formed the Progressive Party, which in turn selected Wallace as their standard-bearer. Wallace claimed he had "taken leave" of the Democratic Party because, "There is no real fight between a Truman and a Republican. Both stand for a policy which opens the door to war in our lifetime and makes war certain for our children." Both while serving the Truman administration and as a renegade, Wallace had criticized Truman's "get tough" stance with the Soviet Union, labeling such a position as bellicose, militaristic, war mongering, and purposely provocative. Truman's chances for reelection were undermined further when Southern Democrats, in response to Truman's public support for civil rights, bolted and formed the States' Rights Party, or "Dixicrats," and nominated the hardcore segregationist Strom Thurmond of South Carolina as their presidential candidate. The Republicans, smelling an easy victory, if not a rout, made the mistake of picking a "loser," Thomas Dewey, who just four years earlier lost to FDR. With such forces arrayed against him, Truman entered 1948 less than sanguine about his chances of victory. Truman, however, had faced tough election campaigns before, and as in the past when everyone wrote him off, he somehow managed to snatch victory from the jaws of defeat. It would be no different this time.

Interestingly, in retrospect, given the strategy he adopted that garnered the support of key New Deal coalition groups, a Truman victory was almost a certainty. Truman also employed the effective rhetoric of anticommunism. The architect of Truman's campaign tactics was presidential aide Clark Clifford, who told Truman he could win if he cultivated urban areas and minorities with his liberalism, and if he identified and isolated Wallace in the public mind by associating him with the communists. Truman accepted Clifford's plan and immediately implemented it by publicly endorsing the findings of the Civil Rights Committee he had authorized (to be discussed later in this essay). This move helped to erode one of Wallace's strongest claims to being the more liberal candidate, a position Wallace made good every time he refused to speak in a Southern segregated facility. Truman then employed the politics of anticommunism by declaring, "I do not want and will not accept the support of Henry Wallace and his communists. . . . These are days of high prices for anything, but any price for Wallace and his communists is too much for me."

Truman's prospects of victory grew brighter with the support of labor and the recently formed liberal organization—the Americans for Democratic Action (ADA). Two events helped persuade labor leaders to side with Truman. First, the president vetoed the anti-labor 1947 Taft-Hartley Act (to be examined later), reestablishing his credentials as the champion of the working class. Although the law was passed over Truman's veto, his election seemed imperative if even a modicum of the harsh act had a chance of being repealed. Second, the ADA was formed by liberals such as Eleanor Roosevelt, intellectuals like Reinhold Neibuhr, and labor leaders like Walter Reuther, all of whom hoped to distance liberalism from the anti-cold war, pro-Soviet rhetoric of the Progressive Party. "We reject any association with communists or sympathizers with communism in the United States," the ADA proclaimed. The organization staunchly supported Truman's cold war initiatives, especially the Marshall Plan, and believed Truman to be the heir of the Rooseveltian legacy of liberalism at home as well. Certain that endorsing Wallace would both guarantee a Republican victory and ensure even more vigorous red-baiting of the labor movement, CIO leaders embraced the ADA and voted to reject the Wallace candidacy. Young, new liberal lions, such as the mayor of Minneapolis, Hubert Humphrey, supported Truman and jumped on the red-baiting bandwagon when he lambasted Wallace supporters in Minnesota as "fellow travelers of Moscow. If I have to choose between being called a red-baiter and traitor," Humphrey declared, "I'll be a red-baiter." In the face of such attacks, Progressive Party support plummeted in the polls from over 15 percent to less than 4 percent. Truman's (or Clifford's) strategy appeared to be working. As a serious challenger, Wallace was all but through by November.

Meanwhile, unfortunately for the Republicans, their candidate was digging his own grave and the party's as well. Compared to the colorful Truman, Dewey was as exciting as a piece of chalk. Behind closed doors, even Republicans complained about his bland speeches and empty platitudes. As one reporter said: "Dewey doesn't seem to walk, he coasts out like a man who has been mounted on casters and given a tremendous shove from behind." A pro-Truman newspaper caricatured Dewey's standard speech as four "historic sentences: Agriculture is important. Our rivers are full of fish. You cannot have freedom without liberty. The future lies ahead." Despite Dewey's lackluster personality and enervated campaign, reporters, columnists, experts, and "everyone" knew Dewey would win in a canter.

Another component of the Clifford strategy was to have Truman call the Republican-dominated Eightieth Congress into a special session and ask them to pass a host of liberal measures such as social security expansion, a higher minimum wage, and national housing legislation, which he had proposed earlier. Truman employed this particular tactic to show the American people that not only was he FDR's liberal heir but that the Republicans and their candidate, despite their rhetoric to the contrary, were bent on the New Deal's destruction. All through the campaign Dewey had said he favored such legislation. Truman argued that if that was true then the Republicans should vote to pass his obvious liberal agenda. Truman knew the Republicans would "do nothing." (Why should they? Dewey was going to win, and so all they had to do was wait it out and, once Dewey was in the White House, they could then dismantle what was left of the New Deal.) Using that as his text's premise, Truman went on the attack, charging that the "do-nothing" Republicans were responsible for the nation's problems. In typical "Trumanesque" style, Truman hit the campaign trail with a fire in his belly rarely seen in American politics. In a whistle-stop campaign, Truman barnstormed his way across the nation, moving from town to town, stopping to denounce Dewey and Wallace from the back of a railroad car. Feisty, biting, and combative, Truman mocked the Republicans, red-baited the Progressives, ignored the Dixiecrats, and began to win the loyalty of the 6 million people who came to hear his stump speeches. Truman accused Dewey of plotting "a real hatchet job on the New Deal," and that the governor's party was controlled by a cabal of "cunning men" who were planning "a return of the Wall Street economic dictatorship." He told farmers and workers they would be "ingrates" if they did not vote Democratic. "If you send another Republican to Washington, you're a bigger bunch of suckers than I think you are." The crowd would yell back, "Pour it on, Harry. Give'm hell."

When the country awoke the day after the election, the "miracle of 1948" had happened. Truman was elected, scoring the biggest upset victory in American history, rolling up 24.1 million votes (49.5 percent) to Dewey's 22 million (45.1 percent) and a more emphatic 303 to 189 in the electoral college. Both Wallace and Thurmond had the same popular tally, but Thurmond, thanks largely to black disfranchisement, received 39 electoral votes from the states of Louisiana, Mississippi, Alabama, and South Carolina and one vote from Tennessee. Wanting their vote to count for something, other Southern segregationists stayed inside the Democratic tent and hoped to influence the president from within. Wallace was embarrassed by his party's communist coterie and by the brutal Soviet coup in Czechoslovakia, which resulted in the murder of its anti-Soviet Foreign Minister, Jan Masayrk. As the ADA had insisted, Wallace was "the dupe of the communists." Riding on the president's coattails were new liberal senators Hubert Humphrey of Minnesota, Estes Kefauver of Tennessee, and "Landslide" Lyndon B.

Johnson of Texas, who won his race by a "whopping" 87 questionable votes. Although it was the loyalty of voters to the memory of FDR and to his New Deal coalition that put Truman in the victory column, the president nonetheless commanded a constituency of his own by virtue of his anticommunist policies and successful cold war initiatives. In this sense, Truman's presidency established a pattern that would persist for several decades: If Democratic candidates could avoid appearing "soft" or "weak" on national security issues, they stood a good chance of being elected president. If the pubic, however, felt insecure or believed America's world preeminence had somehow faltered, then the candidate perceived responsible would more than likely be defeated. Such was the fate that awaited George McGovern in 1972 and Jimmy Carter in 1980, both of whom in the eyes of the majority of Americans had failed miserably on national security issues and, thus, were resoundingly defeated by their respective Republican opponents. By contrast, Truman stood "tough" in 1948 and had a string of cold war successes to bolster his credentials as someone who would not let the Soviets have their way abroad or communists at home undermine the America way of life.

With an apparent mandate for his cold war policies, Truman believed it was time for the United States to break the last vestige of its isolationist past by establishing a system of worldwide military alliances. Truman's initiative was unprecedented in the history of United States foreign policy. Since 1778, the United States had refused to join military alliances in time of peace. Truman not only was having the United States join one, he was the progenitor of such a momentous association. In April 1949, the United States, Canada, and ten European nations formed the North Atlantic Treaty Organization (NATO). In July of that year, the Senate overwhelmingly (82 to 13) ratified United States membership in the alliance. The signatories pledged that an attack against one would automatically be considered an attack against all and agreed to cooperate on economic and political as well as military matters. When cold war tensions increased in 1950, Truman sought to develop the pact's military potential. After a "great debate" in 1951, U.S. troops were assigned in April of that year to NATO forces where they remained for decades; until recently, the United States provided the bulk of NATO's soldiers.

Although the majority of Americans supported Truman's NATO initiative, there were some who opposed it, believing the concept and especially U.S. membership a provocation to the Soviet Union. They also saw the treaty as an "entangling alliance" that defied common sense, violating the foreign policy traditions that had kept the nation safe for over 150 years and threatened constitutional government by eclipsing Congress' power to declare war. Such were the sentiments of Senator Robert Taft of Ohio, the treaty's most vociferous critic and "America first" advocate (isolationist). The nation's use of military force, Taft warned, could be dictated by a response to events in other countries rather than determined by the United States' own policymaking processes. Taft feared that Truman was using cold war exigencies, much as FDR had used the Depression, to augment the power of the executive branch and, if the economy sagged, involve the nation in another war to end the downturn.

Although Truman believed in a powerful executive and wielded presidential power to its fullest capacity when he deemed it essential to protect the people, his presidency never even remotely approximated the power (or abuse of it) of his predecessor. Truman did believe, however, that the president was to play an active, decisive leadership role when it came to foreign policy, something conservatives such as Taft, a Republican, could not accept. During Truman's presidency, a new concept was established to stop aggression: the idea of "collective security," which to be effective as a deterrent had to be sustained in peacetime. Moreover, as Truman contended, the United States would never have to "go at it alone" against an aggressor, which in the long run would save thousands of American soldiers' lives. Truman believed that the best way to ensure American security was to establish the idea of collective security. Thanks to Truman's and others' persuasive arguments, the NATO concept prevailed, allowing for the creation in the 1950s of other such pacts in regions of the world that the United States deemed geopolitically important for itself and for its allies' interests as well.

Unfortunately, in 1949, Truman's string of foreign policy successes, popularity, and bipartisan support for his cold war agenda suffered a severe blow with the fall of China to the communist forces of Mao Zedong. Between 1945 and 1948 the United States extended to Jiang Jieshi's (Chiang Kai-shek) government a billion dollars in military aid and another billion in economic assistance. But Jiang steadily lost ground to Mao's communist forces. Mao was especially popular among the Chinese peasantry (who still comprised the bulk of the country's population) because he promised what they wanted most: land reform. In 1949, when Mao's armies forced Jiang off the mainland to the offshore island of Formosa (Taiwan), many Americans wondered how, with such massive U.S. aid, the communist forces prevailed. Republicans naturally blamed Truman for the debacle, charging his administration with "selling out" to the communists. Financed by conservative business leaders, a powerful "China lobby" excoriated Truman and his new Secretary of State, Dean Acheson, for being "soft" on communism and, despite friction between Mao and Stalin, spoke of a global communist conspiracy directed from Moscow. China's fall also helped to usher in the "domino theory," which asserted that if the United States did not contain communism to China, it would spread like a deadly contagion, turning all of Asia "red." In short, according to this theory, like a row of dominoes, Asia's "democratic regimes" would fall to communist insurgents directed and financed by Moscow and Beijing.

Truman was not responsible for China's "loss," and to label him the culprit is unfair and historically inaccurate. Like so many other issues and problems, he inherited this particular nightmare from FDR. Interestingly, FDR inherited the China "problem" from the Hoover administration, for it was during Hoover's presidency that the Chinese civil war began between Jiang Jieshi and Mao Zedong. From the beginning of that conflict (early 1930s) to its end, the United States supported Chiang and his Nationalist movement against Mao's communist forces. Throughout the 1930s FDR sent millions in aid to Chiang, who used the money on himself and in building up his army rather than for improving his peoples' lives and implementing necessary reforms. Well before 1949, many Americans close to the scene had come to the conclusion that Chiang's regime had degenerated into a corrupt, vicious, and oppressive dictatorship that was alienating the Chinese people, driving them by the thousands into Mao's arms. In short, Chiang was no different than the warlords of old who terrorized and brutally subjugated the people for their own self-aggrandizement. Such assessments, however, did not deter the Roosevelt administration from continuing to send aid to Chiang.

The final straw for most Chinese came with the Japanese invasion, which saw the Japanese forces ravage the Chinese countryside while slaughtering hundreds of thousands of innocent Chinese civilians in the process. In the meantime Chiang, instead of using his army to try to stop the Japanese, continued to fight the communists. Indeed, he reached an agreement with the Japanese that he would let them have the parts of China they had conquered if they in turn would help him defeat Mao's communist forces. For the majority of the Chinese, Chiang's "deal" with the Japanese was the ultimate betrayal, and now they were ready to join with Mao, who not only was proving himself a patriot by fighting the Japanese but a liberator as well from both Japanese aggression and Chiang's corrupt tyranny.

The civil war somewhat abated from 1941-1945 as the United States insisted that Chiang use his forces to defeat Japan, and together they would worry about the communists once Japan had been defeated. No sooner did the Japanese surrender than Chiang and Mao were once again locked in a vicious civil war. Truman, unlike his predecessor who simply threw money at the problem, wanted to know why, with all this U.S. support, Chiang was not winning the civil war. In 1945-46 Truman sent George C. Marshall to China as an emissary to see what the problem was. Marshall returned, disgusted with Chiang, and told the president that, in effect, the United States had been supporting the wrong side. The majority of Chinese despised Chiang and had come to embrace Mao Zedong, and thus the communists would prevail. After hearing Marshall's assessment, Truman lost all faith in Chiang, concluding that the United States could not save the venal Nationalist regime. They were "all thieves, every last one of them," he said privately of the Nationalists in 1948. Truman and Acheson were correct in saying that Chiang was his own worst enemy and that the United States did not have the economic or military capacity to save him. Indeed, they would be "throwing good money after bad." As Acheson observed, "The unfortunate but inescapable fact is that the ominous result of the civil war in China was beyond the control of the government of the United States. Nothing that this country did or could have done within reasonable limits of its capabilities could have changed the result. . . . It was the product of internal Chinese forces, forces which this government tried to influence but could not."

Truman's critics had varied motivations. Naturally, the Republicans were highly partisan, for they were still reeling from Truman's unexpected 1948 victory and were eager at every opportunity, no matter how inaccurate their vitriol, to tar the administration however they could. More important than the Republicans' partisan rantings were the reactions of the American public. Americans were unable to understand why the most powerful and wealthy nation in the world could not prevent bad things from happening. As one observer put it, people had an "illusion of American omnipotence." When setbacks occurred—the "losing" of China, the Soviets possessing the bomb, which they announced they had in September 1949—the United States must have done something wrong. From this simplistic starting point, it was an easy next step to lash out at the scapegoats, and no one served that purpose better than the president, Harry Truman. Although the American public and Republicans lambasted Truman for "losing" China, as the evidence presented confirms, China was "lost" long before Truman became president, and to hold him responsible is unfair and historically unfounded.

Although the Truman administration placed its greatest priority on constructing a global policy of containment, it also reconstructed the domestic legacy of Franklin Roosevelt. Many New Deal liberals still believed it essential to see FDR's "Second Bill of Rights" become reality and naturally looked to Truman for such action. As noted earlier, FDR's "Economic Bill of Rights" established that all Americans had the "right" to a wide range of substantive liberties, including employment, food and shelter, education, and health care. Whenever people were unable to obtain these "rights," the national government was morally obligated to help people have access to them. Such governmental largesse required constant economic and social planning and government spending for the general welfare.

As already noted, Truman was a loyal FDR supporter during his years in the Senate, and as a result, liberals were confident he would carry forward FDR's vision. That Truman shared FDR's expectation was confirmed by the sweeping legislative program of social reforms that he proposed to Congress in 1945—a full employment bill, a higher minimum wage, and national housing legislation. Truman's legislative agenda, a political aide observed, "was a reminder to the Democratic party, to the Congress, to the country, that there was a continuity between the new national leadership and the old." Moreover, Truman had "a very personal stake" in the program—to destroy the complacent assumption of his opponents that "with 'that man' [FDR] gone, the White House would be 'reasonable,' 'sound,' and 'safe.'"

No doubt Truman benefited from the New Deal legacy. It provided an ideology of sorts, a legislative agenda, a corps of experienced administrators, an expansive view of the executive office, and an effective electoral coalition of big-city, low-income voters. FDR's admirers often forgot that their hero after 1938 was forced to acquiesce to a conservative-dominated Congress on many key reform issues. Indeed, from that point on, Congress, not FDR, had the upper hand when it came to the domestic agenda. Truman inherited an already right-leaning Congress when he became president, and that body only moved further in that direction after the 1946 congressional elections. Truman now had to operate in an atmosphere not at all conducive to reform. His "mission" as FDR's heir was perhaps tougher than even Roosevelt's had been when he came to the Oval Office in 1933. In many ways, all FDR had to do was weather the Depression until World War II began. Truman, by contrast, had to adapt the liberalism of the Great Depression (but never fully realized) to the new exigencies of economic growth and prosperity, the advent of the consumer culture, the cold war and the politics of anticommunism at home, and the beginnings of the civil rights revolution. These were all virtually non-existent issues during FDR's four terms. In carrying out this task, he often met with setbacks. However, the most recent polls of both historians and political scientists have placed Truman in the "near great" category of presidents for reasons best stated by the Truman-era pundit, Elmer Davis: "There are two Trumans—the White House Truman and the courthouse Truman. He does the big things right, and the little things wrong."

One of "the big things" Truman confronted almost immediately was the "politics of prosperity" rather than the anticipated "politics of depression." In other words, reconversion from a war to a peace economy, unlike in the past (post-World War I), saw a boom rather than recession. This "phenomenon" was largely the result of the fact that the American consumer came out of the war with a bulging wallet and a frustrated yen for goods that had too long been unavailable. This same consumer demand threatened to undermine potential prosperity by precipitating inflation, and when Truman attempted to limit price increases, he incurred the wrath of both businessmen and consumers concerning the role of government in the postwar world. Corporations, after more than a decade of regulation, wanted to lift wartime controls. Regardless of the prices charged, consumers supported business' demand to lift all restrictions, for they were eager to spend their wartime savings on goods they had gone without for too many years. Truman wisely wanted to lift the wartime restraints slowly, for he knew that the moment prices soared, workers would demand pay increases and management, greedy for profit, would refuse labor's demands precipitating the inevitable: strikes. As Truman predicted, strikes in virtually every major industry occurred. By February 1946, strikes had devoured 23 million work days across so many key industries that the nation's economy was on the verge of shutting down. Unions, smarting under the cut in take-home pay resulting from the ending of war industry overtime, insisted that wage increases were necessary to maintain real income. Business countered that it was labor's demands for pay increases that were driving prices up. Each group looked to the president to resolve the crisis.

Truman now confronted a problem with which FDR never had to contend during the New Deal years. As Barton J. Bernstein has observed,

"Whereas the politics of depression generally allowed the Roosevelt administration, by bestowing benefits, to court interest groups and contribute to an economic upturn, the politics of inflation required a responsible government like Truman's to curb wages, prices, and profits and to deny the growing expectations of rival groups." FDR somewhat faced this problem during the war years, but he could appeal to patriotism and the sacrifices essential for the "great cause" to defuse potential strikes or to keep big business profiteering at a minimum. Truman, however, did not have the war effort to use to disarm these interest group demands. He was put into the lose-lose position of not only having to restrain businessmen, most of whom were in the Republican camp, but the farmer and labor elements in his own Democratic coalition as well. Truman's troubles, especially with labor, reached a climax in May 1946, when he asked Congress for authority to draft rail strikers into the army. Such action by Truman seemed a blatant betrayal of labor by someone who proclaimed himself to be an FDR disciple. Regardless of the political consequences of his actions, Truman believed it was necessary to come down hard on labor because their strikes were threatening the commonweal, something he believed as president he was obligated constitutionally to protect at all times. As noted earlier, Truman held a Jacksonian view of the presidency, which made it his responsibility to at all times govern in the name of *all* the people. This did not mean that he claimed, as Eisenhower did later, to be above politics. On the contrary, Truman was never happier than when in the company of fellow politicians, and he was intensely partisan. Yet, he considered it his duty as president to rise above what he thought were the more local, provincial concerns of members of Congress, who he knew were more concerned about their constituents' needs than those of the nation at large. Most important, Truman believed that at all times the president must resist succumbing to pressure group demands, which acted against what he considered the *national* well-being. Truman knew the moment he threatened the striking workers with harsh reprisals that he would alienate one of the most important coalition blocs of the Democratic Party, and indeed he did. A CIO conference denounced Truman as the country's "No. 1 Strikebreaker." Pro-labor liberals were also greatly disaffected by Truman's actions. Frances Perkins, Secretary of Labor, who left Truman's cabinet shortly after his "strikebreaking," confided to Henry Wallace, "I find myself wondering profoundly about the political future." Despite alienating labor and liberals alike, Truman, true to character, believed he had acted in the best interests of *all* the people by not allowing a special interest group's "selfish actions," such as striking railway workers, to bring the nation's economy to a standstill.

By the time the first postwar elections were held in November 1946, Truman had been victimized by the politics of the pressure group state. As noted earlier, on Election Day the Republicans swept to victory, claiming a substantial majority in the House and a seven-vote margin in the Senate. The Republican Eightieth Congress that much disparaged progeny of the 1946 election was determined to repeal the New Deal.

Faced with this kind of opposition to FDR's 1944 agenda, Truman needed to find a different approach to policymaking. The 1946 debate over the Full Employment Act helped identify one. The act as initially conceived by Truman aspired to be the centerpiece of liberal hopes for a prosperous, just society. As originally drawn, it would have made the federal government responsible for providing employment for everyone "who was able to work and seeking work," with the president recommending programs to sustain employment whenever his economic advisers projected a dip in the economy. Although such work programs might cause short-term budget deficits, supporters believed that in the long run full employment would generate sufficient taxes both to balance the budget and to finance social welfare programs, such as increased minimum wages and national health insurance. Full employment was the cornerstone of FDR's "Economic Bill of Rights." Without it, Truman and others believed none of the other "rights" could be realized. To the conservatives (Republicans and Southern Democrats), these provisions and the phrase "full employment" smacked of European-style welfare, even socialism.

Unfortunately, Truman could not hold the forces of reaction at bay. By the time Congress finally acted on the measure, most of its key provisions had been gutted. Instead of "full" employment, the new version called for "maximum" employment, a phrase that conceivably could justify a jobless rate of 5 or 6 percent. Other revisions stipulated that the private sector still bore the responsibility for employment, as well as general economic decision-making. The conservatives still allowed for some "government management" of the economy, but they made it clear that the heady days of New Deal regulation and government-sponsored or created jobs were over. With a booming economy, the conservatives argued, there was no longer a need for such intervention. Indeed, it was time to resurrect the laissez faire ethos, which, the conservatives asserted, was the way American capitalism functioned best for all. By the time the measure was finally passed, it represented a vague statement of principles rather than a plan for action, its most significant reform being the creation of a Council of Economic Advisors (CEA) to provide recommendations to the president and Congress regarding long-range economic developments. The creation of the CEA signaled that government policy makers would assume some responsibility for the economy's performance. How far that responsibility would extend remained to be determined.

Ironically, out of defeat on the Employment Act came one of Truman's more lasting contributions in the area of federal economic policy. From this point on Truman sought a domestic program that would not revive the political controversies of the 1930s. Instead, he embraced the idea that the government should encourage economic growth, not through centralized planning but by "updating" through measures like the Employment Act, establishing a cooperative relationship with both big business and organized labor that Roosevelt had introduced during World War II. In fact, Truman and his advisers believed that such cooperation would actually make domestic policymaking easier, and as can be seen in the essays in this book on John Kennedy and Lyndon Baines Johnson, Truman was correct. The Truman administration introduced the idea that economic growth would produce increased tax revenues, which, in turn, would give the national government the money to fund domestic programs. "With economic expansion, every problem is capable of solution," insisted George Soule, an advocate of economic growth. Using the relatively new theory of a "gross national product" (GNP), postwar economists could actually calculate the nation's growing economic bounty. Developed in 1939, the concept of GNP—defined as the total value of all goods and services produced (but not sold!) in the nation in a given year—became the standard measure of economic health. Thus, by the end of 1948, Truman had wisely abandoned calling for the realization of FDR's Economic Bill of Rights and, instead, advocated the much more political and acceptable notion of economic growth.

President for the first time in his own right in 1948, Truman told the American people and Congress in his January 5, 1949, State of the Union address, "every segment of our population and every individual has a right to expect from his government a fair deal." Two weeks later Harry S Truman was inaugurated twenty-eighth President of the United States. The first full-scale inaugural since the war, it was also the first to be seen on television. An estimated 10 million people watched Truman put his hand on the Constitution and be sworn in by the Chief Justice of the Supreme Court. Millions more heard the ceremony on the radio. At age sixty-four Truman seemed to brim with vitality and optimism.

Many unfairly called Truman's administration "Roosevelt's Fifth Term." On the surface the "Fair Deal" appeared to be merely an elaboration of existing New Deal initiatives, but at a deeper level, Truman's agenda was different, especially in the way such programs were to be paid for. Unlike the New Deal, the Fair Deal was based on the assumption that expansion of social welfare programs could be financed from continual economic growth. In short, a constantly expanding economic pie would mean a progressively bigger piece for most Americans (namely, those of the ever-growing white middle class) so they would not resent helping those left behind. "Fair Dealers," unlike their more "radical" counterparts of the 1930s, refrained from advocating "tax the rich to aid the poor" programs. Indeed, few, if any, Fair Dealers, including Truman, believed in such policies.

Although putting aside calling for new social welfare initiatives, Truman nonetheless pushed hard for repeal of the Taft-Hartley Act, a more progressive tax system, a seventy-five cent minimum wage (it was then forty cents), agricultural reform, resource development and public power, Social Security expansion, national medical insurance, federal aid to education, civil rights, and expansion of federal housing programs. Truman was confident he could get much of this agenda passed, for the Eighty-first Congress, in which the Democrats regained majorities, initially seemed inclined to cooperate. Truman's initial optimism faded, however, for the coalition of Republicans and conservative (primarily Southern) Democrats proved too powerful in their obstruction to overcome. Also frustrating Truman's efforts was the formidable obstacle course in Congress—malapportioned representation that overweighed rural areas opposed to spending for urban masses, arbitrary committee chairmen, the filibuster, seniority rule, and the balky Rules Committee. Thus, by the end of 1949-50 sessions, Truman had achieved only three of his goals: a minimum wage increase to fifty cents, an expansion of Social Security, and public housing. Under the 1950 Social Security Act, the level of benefits was increased significantly; the retirement portions of the program were expanded; and coverage was extended to more than 10 million people, including agricultural workers.

Because of the continued shortage of affordable housing in urban areas, polls showed greater support for home-building programs. Private construction firms and realtors welcomed extension of federal home loan guarantees, such as those established under the GI Bill and through the Federal Housing Administration, but Congress voted against Truman's call for the construction of publicly financed housing projects. Yet, even conservatives such as Senator Bob Taft recognized the housing shortage and supported the 1949 Housing Act. This law promised "a decent home and suitable living environment for every American family." It authorized construction of 810,000 public housing units (Truman's original goal was 1.05 million low-income homes). Most important, especially for Truman's Democratic successors, the measure provided federal funds for "urban renewal zones," areas to be cleared of run-down dwellings and rebuilt with new construction. As will be seen, thanks to Truman's early initiative in this area, President Lyndon Johnson made urban renewal one of his Great Society's top priorities. It was Truman, however, who first brought to the nation's attention not only the need for more and better housing, especially in deteriorating inner cities, but also the growing problem of urban blight and the poverty associated with it.

The more expansive Fair Deal proposals either failed or were scaled back by the Republican/conservative Democratic bloc that dominated Congress. For instance, Truman's plan for a comprehensive national health insurance program (something still being agonizingly debated today even though the need is greater than ever) ran into opposition, not only from congressional conservatives but from the powerful medical lobbies—the American Medical Association (AMA) and the American Hospital Association (AHA). Both associations helped block any government intervention in the traditional fee-for-service medical system and steered Congress toward a less controversial alternative—federal financing of new hospitals under the Hill-Burton Act. Meanwhile, opinion polls suggested that most voters, many of whom were enrolling in private health insurance plans such as Blue Cross and Blue Shield, were simply apathetic or confused about Truman's national health proposals.

The fate of efforts for agricultural reform best illustrates the constellation of forces, especially well-organized interest groups that stymied much of Truman's Fair Deal. The reform took the name the Brannan Plan, named after Truman's liberal Agricultural Secretary, Charles Brannan. The secretary sought to scrap the costly system of production controls, government price supports, and benefit payments that had been enacted during the 1930s. Instead, Brannan proposed that farmers raising perishable crops should be encouraged to produce as much as the market would bear—an effort that was expected to increase supply and drive down prices for consumers. In return, the government would compensate these farmers with direct income payments, up to maximums per producer. With these maximums, Brannan expected to limit the amount of benefits that would go to agribusiness and to attract the support of smaller "family farmers." Brannan's larger goal was political: to cement the Democratic alliance between small farmers, urban workers, and consumers that had appeared to be developing in the 1948 election.

Truman supported the Brannan Plan, but a determined coalition of interests opposed it. Naturally, the opposition included the majority of Republicans, who resented Brannan's ill-concealed political objectives. Also against the measure was the Farm Federation Bureau, which represented agribusiness—farmers, food processors, and middlemen who feared the imposition of new and possibly complicated controls and who predicted that the plan's costs would bankrupt the government. Some urban Democrats, too, were cool to a program that proposed direct federal money to rural areas. A number of Southern Democrats, worried that the plan would end up reducing government subsidies for cotton, also joined the anti-Brannan coalition. With such forces arrayed against it, the plan was destined for defeat, especially in the House, which rejected the measure by almost two to one. While it appeared to have some chance in the Senate, the outbreak of the Korean War forced that chamber to put it on the back burner where it eventually died, leaving the old system of farm subsidies in place. Thereafter, as in the past, powerful interests remained firmly in control of the American agricultural system. Although the Brannan Plan was defeated, Truman's fervent support of it was confirmation of his unflagging commitment to do, at all times, what was best for the nation as a whole. Unfortunately, in this particular instance, Truman could not overcome the powerful special interests aligned against the Brannan Plan. Thus, instead of having an agricultural system beneficial to both farmers and consumers, which Truman hoped he could create, the public would have to endure the vagaries of a marketplace controlled by self-serving coteries of privileged groups.

Despite these setbacks, Truman persevered, establishing unprecedented breakthroughs in the areas of human and civil rights. Congress approved the Displaced Persons Act, which allowed entry to 205,000 survivors of the Nazi forced-labor and death camps. On the surface, such a measure seems trivial, but it must be remembered that at the time the bill was passed, the revelations of the Holocaust were just beginning to be made known, thanks in large part to the famous Nuremburg Trials. Moreover, the majority of the 205,000 emigrants were from Eastern bloc countries, and consequently, Truman had to endure right-wing hysteria and hyperbole that these "people" were secretly "fifth-columnists" sent by Stalin to spread communism in the United States. Although such paranoia seems ridiculous today, it was very real for Truman and had to be overcome for the bill to be passed. Truman also requested Congress to act on claims made by Japanese-Americans who during the war had been forced from their homes and confined "solely because of their racial origin"—claims that would not be met until forty-five years later.

Without question, Truman's most lauded accomplishment as president was his civil rights initiatives, which began the long, arduous process, finally realized by the late 1960s by Lyndon Johnson, of black equality. Indeed, Truman supported the fight against racial discrimination more strongly than any previous president, including FDR. Only LBJ's commitment to this most vital of domestic issues exceeded that of Truman's.

Perhaps more than any other group, black Americans in 1945 looked forward to a better life, hoping that their manifold wartime contributions both at home and abroad would at last earn them their full citizenship rights. During the war their share of defense jobs increased from 3 to 8 percent (in large part because of Truman's Senate committee). Almost half a million people belonged to the NAACP. Despite persistent racism and continued government indifference, a new sense of ferment and protest was pervasive in the land, especially in the South. Whether in northern cities or southern towns, African Americans, together with some white allies, were committed to building on the energies of the war years. Black Americans sought to secure a permanent FEPC, to abolish the poll tax, to achieve the basic right of citizenship involved in voter registration, and to outlaw forever the terrorism of lynching. Over a million black soldiers had fought in a war to preserve democracy. Now, many refused to accept passively a return to the status quo or to racism.

Tragically, in the immediate postwar years, what few successes blacks had in securing their rights paled in comparison to white intransigence and the use of wanton violence to keep African Americans a repressed people. When Medgar Evers and four other veterans went to vote, white men with pistols drove them away. In Georgia, Eugene Talmadge won the governor's race, proclaiming, "no Negro will vote in Georgia for the next four years." Talmadge, with the help of white terrorists, made good on his pledge when the only black to vote in one district was killed in his front yard. Nearby, in Walton County, whites shot and killed two other blacks. When one of the victims' wives recognized a member of the shooting gang, the two wives were murdered also. As black veteran Isaac Woodward got off the bus in South Carolina, still wearing his uniform, police beat him unconscious with their billy clubs. In Columbia, Tennessee, whites rioted in protest against "uppity" blacks insisting on their rights. Seventy African Americans were arrested, and a mob broke into the jail to murder two of the prisoners. All these events took place in the first eight months of 1946.

Even before becoming president, Truman endorsed civil rights. As senator, Truman supported legislation to abolish the poll tax, appropriations for the FEPC, passage of antilynching legislation, and an end to the filibuster on an anti-poll tax bill. In a remarkable departure from Roosevelt, President Truman intervened openly with Congress to promote legislation creating a permanent FEPC, writing the chairman of the House Rules Committee that to abandon the FEPC was "unthinkable."

After the above-noted violence, Truman met with a delegation of both black and white activists to discuss antilynching legislation, expressing genuine sympathy for African-Americans' plight. "My God," he told the group, "I had no idea it was as terrible as that. We have to do something." In a private meeting with Southern Democrats, Truman confessed his own forebears were Confederates and that he came from a part of Missouri where "Jim Crowism" still prevailed. However, Truman also told his fellow Southerners, "My very stomach turned over when I learned that Negro soldiers just back from overseas, were being dumped out of army trucks in Mississippi and beaten. Whatever my inclinations as a native of Missouri might have been, as President I know this is bad. I shall fight to the end evils like this."

In a bold response, Truman created a Committee on Civil Rights in December 1946. Comprised of such notables as Charles Wilson of General Electric, Frank Graham Porter of the University of North Carolina, and Franklin Roosevelt, Jr., it surveyed the entire spectrum of American race relations. The commission concluded that the situation for black Americans was so desperate that, if something wasn't done soon to rectify the discrimination, repression, and murder of African Americans, the nation was on the verge of a potential race war. In its report, entitled "To Secure These Rights," the committee recommended a series of actions to correct racial inequality: the establishment of a permanent civil rights division of the Justice Department, the creation of a Commission on Civil Rights, enactment of antilynching legislation, abolition of the poll tax, passage of laws to protect the rights of qualified voters, desegregation of the Armed Forces, elimination of grants-in-aid from the federal government to segregated institutions, enactment of a permanent FEPC, home rule for the District of Columbia, and support for the legal attack on segregated housing. In the meantime, Truman became the first president to address a NAACP rally, declaring, "there is a serious gap between our ideals and some of our practices." Truman pledged, "this gap must be closed. Every man should have the right to a decent home, the right to an education . . . the right to a worthwhile job, the right to an equal share in making public decisions through the ballot. . . . We must assure that these rights—on equal terms—are enjoyed by every citizen. "

Suffice it to say, African Americans were elated by Truman's declaration. Truman immediately endorsed the commission's recommendations and the day after their release ordered the Justice Department to intervene in cases before the Supreme Court seeking to invalidate government-backed segregation of public schools and restrictive covenants in housing. These "covenants" were legal agreements that prevented racial or religious minorities (principally Catholics and Jews) from acquiring real estate. Thanks in large part to Truman's constant agitation and exhortations, in 1946 the Supreme Court declared restrictive covenants illegal and began chipping away at the "separate but equal" principle (a farce) that had been used since *Plessy v. Ferguson* (1898) to justify segregated schools. In 1950, and again thanks to pressure from the White House, the Court ruled that under the Fourteenth Amendment racial segregation in state-financed graduate and law schools was unconstitutional. In light of these decisions, all the traditional legal arguments that had been used since *Plessy* to legitimize racial segregation in all public schools seemed open to successful challenge, which would finally come in 1954. Thanks in large part to Truman's courageous determination to obtain justice and equality for black Americans in the immediate postwar years, such an existence for African Americans might not have become a reality in later decades. It was Truman's willingness to take this most sensitive and volatile of issues head-on in the late 1940s that allowed his successors to have the breakthroughs they had in this most important domestic arena. Despite vicious opposition within his own party and from white Southerners, who accused him of "stabbing the South in the back," Truman made it imperative (no matter how white Americans felt about civil rights) that the president must lead the crusade to eradicate this most egregious domestic postwar issue.

Without question, one of Truman's greatest presidential controversies remains the Korean War. Although many historians blame Truman for this alleged debacle, it can be argued that the event also represented, like the first Berlin crisis, one of Truman's more outstanding presidential moments. Once again, he confronted a blatant act of communist aggression and would have triumphed had it not been for the arrogance and defiance of one of his own generals, Douglas MacArthur, who, more than Truman, was to blame for the war's needless protraction. Even the American public must be reproached for their inability to understand the concept of a "limited war," which was the only type of conflict that could have been feasibly fought, given the fact that both the "greater belligerents"—the United States and the Soviet Union—possessed atomic weapons. The risk of a nuclear exchange with the Soviets was an omnipresent factor throughout the war. Truman knew this and wisely kept the war in "perspective" by not directly antagonizing the Soviets or threatening either them or the Chinese with the bomb, even though MacArthur urged such action. If anything, Truman's sagacity and determination to keep the conflict "limited" to the Korean peninsula, as well as keeping the fighting "conventional," are to be lauded, not condemned. By pursuing such an approach, Truman prevented the war from escalating into a possible nuclear confrontation between the United States and the Soviet Union. Had the United States used nuclear weapons, especially on China after they entered the conflict, the Soviets, despite ideological differences with the Maoist regime, certainly would have come to their ally's aid, threatening to use their weapons of mass destruction in retaliation. Indeed, it could be argued that Truman's restraint and "clarity" prevented Armageddon.

On June 24, 1950, North Korean troops swept across the thirty-eight parallel to attack South Korea. Truman had to respond to this blatant act of aggression on one of the United States' allies. He viewed the assault as another Soviet test via its lackey state of North Korea of U.S. will and commitment to containment. "Korea is the Greece of the Far East," he maintained. "If we are tough enough now, if we stand up to them like we did in Greece [and Berlin], they won't take any next steps." To Truman, the invasion smacked of appeasement, believing the communists were doing in Korea exactly what Hitler, Mussolini, and the Japanese had done in the 1930s: "Nobody had stood up to them. And that is what led to the Second World War." Truman further asserted, "if the Russian totalitarian state was intending to follow in the path of the dictatorship of Hitler and Mussolini, they [had to] be met head on in Korea."

Another important factor omitted in the "Truman-bashing" on Korea was the vital precedent established of involving the United Nations in stopping such aggression, which was one of the mandates entrusted to that organization in its charter. Three days after the invasion, Truman asked the United Nations to authorize action to repel the North Korean attack. Fortunately for Truman, the Soviet delegate was boycotting the Security Council to protest the U.N.'s unwillingness to seat a representative from Mao's China, and Truman gained approval for a U.N. "police action" to restore South Korea's border. He appointed General Douglas MacArthur to command the U.N. effort. From beginning to end, the United States supplied the overwhelming majority of troops, who were immediately ordered into the fray. The cold war had turned hot.

North Korean forces initially routed the surprised and disorganized U.S. and South Korean troops, driving them by September 1950 all the way to Pusan on the tip of the peninsula. There they struggled to avoid being pushed literally into the sea. In a daring and what turned out to be tactically a brilliant move, MacArthur landed U.S. troops at Inchon, behind the enemy lines in the south, in effect, catching the North Korean forces in a pincers. Within two weeks, U.S. and South Korean forces drove the North Koreans back across the 38th parallel. Seeking an all-out victory, MacArthur persuaded Truman to let him cross the border to liberate all of Korea from communism.

As U.N. troops moved across the 38th parallel and neared the Yalu River—the boundary between China and Korea—the Chinese warned that they would not "sit back with folded hands and let the Americans come to the border." Dismissing the threat as "hot air," an overconfident MacArthur deployed his forces in a thin line south of the river. On November 25, thirty-three Chinese Divisions (about 300,000 men) counterattacked. Within two weeks they drove the U.N. forces south of the 38th parallel. By winter's end the contending forces were deadlocked at roughly the original dividing line between the two Koreas.

Largely because of MacArthur's arrogance, the war became the worst kind of conflict: a stalemate. Although frustrated, Truman realized that to end the fighting and preserve American lives, he had to seek a negotiated peace based on the original objective of securing South Korea's integrity. MacArthur, however, felt "betrayed" by Truman, whom he believed was "selling out to the communists." MacArthur wanted to blockade and bomb (with atomic weapons if necessary) Mao's China and to "unleash" Chiang Kai-Shek's forces to invade the mainland. "In war," MacArthur insisted, "there is no substitute for victory." Truman, however, rightly feared that, if MacArthur invaded China, such actions would bring the Soviet Union into the conflict. The president told the general, "We are trying to prevent a world war—not start one."

Despite repeated warnings from Truman to refrain from publicly challenging his policies, MacArthur continued to lambaste the president and his conduct of the war. Truman, exasperated, had no choice but to fire the general on April 10, 1951. The Joints Chiefs supported Truman's decision, but public opinion backed one of the most popular generals in United States history, believing Truman, not MacArthur, was responsible for the setback. Indeed, many Americans believed that Truman should have allowed MacArthur to invade China, as naïvely confident as the general was that the United States had the power to easily defeat China and the Soviet Union as well! Moreover, as noted above, the very idea of limited war, of containing rather than defeating the enemy, baffled many Americans, and the mounting toll of American casualties in pursuit of a stalemate or "a negotiated peace" angered them. It seemed senseless. Despite the warnings of General Omar Bradley, Chairman of the Joint Chiefs of Staff, that MacArthur's proposals "would involve us in the wrong war at the wrong place in the wrong time and with the wrong enemy," a growing number of Americans listened sympathetically to Republican charges that communist agents were in control of American foreign policy.

Unfortunately for Harry Truman, the Korean War proved his undoing. The Fair Deal already stymied by the conservative coalition in Congress, was now put so far on the back burner that it would be impossible to resurrect even if the war ended soon. Moreover, because of their inability to grasp the concept of "limited war" or a "police action," Truman lost favor with the American people, for they blamed him, not MacArthur, for the rising number of American casualties. Although general in command, MacArthur nonetheless was to follow the orders and implement the policies as established by the president, who, contrary to MacArthur's "interpretation" of the Constitution, is commander-in-chief of United States forces when the nation is engaged in war. A field general, no matter how victorious or decorated he might be, is not to dictate wartime policy but to follow the orders of his commander-in-chief, the President of the United States. Somewhere along his career, MacArthur forgot that most important Constitutional nicety. All presidents must be able to rely not only on their general's knowledge and ability but loyalty as well. Unfortunately for Truman, MacArthur possessed none of these qualities and, in the end, the general's arrogance and self-serving personality did both his president and his country an unforgivable disservice.

The last thing Truman wanted was a war in Korea or anywhere. Angry as he may have been over the attack, as determined as he was to do what he believed had to be done, his actions should be respected and understood as those of a president who placed the security and interests of the nation above all personal political gain. No matter what the crisis, Truman always did what he believed best for the American people.

The Truman Presidency: A Negative Assessment

In 1946, liberal stalwart Chester Bowles articulated the liberal vision in his seminal work, *Tomorrow Without Fear.* Bowles asserted that FDR's "Economic Bill of Rights" could become a reality if Truman and other liberals "stayed the course" outlined in his book. According to Bowles, government wartime spending and consumer-forced savings (FDR's "brilliant" rationing program) had so boosted the economy that the projected postwar recession never occurred. Indeed, the opposite happened: a postwar boom that improved everyone's standard of living and showed that government investment in such socially beneficial causes as education and health services could keep the economy rolling. If the government guaranteed "full production and full employment," consumerism would increase, tax revenues would finance social improvements for "the disinherited," and all Americans would learn "to live constantly better." No one would suffer, everyone would gain, and poverty, sickness, and malnutrition could be eliminated.

In the immediate aftermath of FDR's death, many liberals believed Truman would carry forward Bowles' (and FDR's) agenda. As time passed, however, they became disappointed. Truman's tactics and political style appeared to contradict the intent of his legislative program. None doubted his grit. He made bold decisions quickly and executed them briskly. Yet, he was generally unreflective, cocky, and brash. Determined to carry on the New Deal tradition, he sent to Congress a twenty-one-point program that included many of the liberal reforms Bowles suggested. Yet he lacked the grand vision necessary to inspire a nation, and he appointed to office lackluster plodders who suffered by comparison with the New Deal luminaries. "It is more important to have a connection with Battery D, 129th Field Artillery than with [Supreme Court Justice] Felix Frankfurter," remarked one commentator. To FDR loyalists, Truman never measured up. Each time he acted, they would ask, "What would Roosevelt had done if he were alive?" Truman was aware of such constant scrutiny, and so insecure was he that he conferred with Eleanor so frequently "as he might have consulted a medium." As late as 1947, Fiorello La Guardia, former New York mayor and now senator, said of FDR: "How we miss him. Hardly a domestic problem or an international situation today, but we say, 'Oh, if FDR were only alive.'"

As noted earlier, Truman had to deal with the same conservative coalition that had come to power in 1938 that had blocked FDR's attempts to expand the New Deal. "With 'that man gone,'" the conservatives were even more emboldened to destroy liberalism and, thus, went after Truman's programs with a vengeance, obliterating most of his initiatives and enacting such reactionary legislation as the anti-labor Taft-Hartley Act, which was the first serious modification of the 1935 Wagner Act. The Wagner Act established federal guarantee and protection of workers to join unions in any industry and to use their organization to bargain collectively with management on issues such as wages and hours. The Taft-Hartley Act prohibited secondary boycotts, jurisdictional walkouts, and the closed shop; it increased the legal responsibility of unions and authorized the president to seek injunctions to delay strikes for eighty days. The cold war made its presence felt in the requirement that union officials file affidavits that they were not Communist Party officials or affiliated with any subversive organization. Hardly the "slave labor law" union leaders branded it, the statute nonetheless greatly handicapped labor's drives for new recruits. In the same year (1947), the Eightieth Congress approved the Twenty-second Amendment (ratified in 1951), which limited the president to two terms, "a belated act of vengeance" against FDR's long presidency.

Although Truman bore only partial responsibility for these setbacks, liberals felt increasingly betrayed by the new president. "The path Franklin Roosevelt charted," Elliott Roosevelt lamented, "has been grievously—and—deliberately forsaken." Truman's rhetoric was fine. Repeatedly he urged Congress to enact a reform agenda. All too often, however, the president's words did not translate into action. Indeed, Truman doubted that major reforms had much of a chance right after the war. "I don't want any experiments," he told his adviser Clark Clifford. "The American people have been through a lot of experiments, and they want a rest from experiments." Truman even believed that many New Deal ideas—"experiments"—were no longer relevant or viable. While Truman wanted to protect the New Deal, he was uneasy around some of the liberals, a "lunatic fringe," he called them, who had risen to high office under FDR. Truman was uncomfortable even with words like "liberal" or "progressive." He preferred "forward-looking."

Truman's fiscal conservatism also put him at loggerheads with liberals. As a Jackson County commissioner, Truman had prided himself on his attempts to balance the budget. He was a man of modest means—perhaps the poorest U.S. senator while he was a member of that chamber—and he always had to be careful with money. Moreover, Truman's fiscal conservatism was good politics; most Americans at that time believed that the government, like a household, should normally spend no more than it took in. Few politicians in Truman's lifetime favored deficit spending in times of prosperity. Truman's conservative feelings on the subject were powerful and genuine, rooted in all of his experience. Much to liberals' irritation, Truman remained cautious about advancing liberal social programs that would cost a good deal of money. Thus, early on in his presidency, Truman abandoned calling for the realization of FDR's Economic Bill of Rights and instead advocated the much more political and acceptable notion of economic growth. Even conservatives were willing to embrace such an agenda because "costs" would be minimal, especially in the area of social welfare legislation to which Truman only paid lip-service throughout his presidency.

Also alienating many liberals were Truman's appointments. Attempting to repair some of the damaged relationships between the executive branch and Congress that had occurred under FDR, Truman appointed to his cabinet conservatives well thought of on Capitol Hill—people like James Byrnes, Fred Vinson, Tom Clark, and Clinton Anderson. By late summer 1945, only Harold Ickes and Henry Wallace remained from Roosevelt's cabinet. In February 1946, Ickes left the cabinet in protest over Truman's selection of a subcabinet officer who had been involved in suspicious oil deals in the southwest. According to journalist Howard K. Smith, 80 percent of Truman's most important appointments in his first two years had gone to businessmen, corporate lawyers, bankers, and military men. "The effective locus of government," Smith declared, "seems to have shifted from Washington to some place equidistant between Wall Street and West Point."

By the fall election of 1946, liberal hopes for the Truman administration and a progressive Congress seemed crushed. By October only 32 percent of the electorate approved of Truman's performance. The end of most price controls in June had prompted a surge of inflation. Labor unrest, in turn, led to massive strikes. Many believed Truman's vacillation and ineptitude had caused the unraveling. As much as anything, Truman's personal style alienated liberal Democrats. FDR had been Harvard-educated, eloquent, and charming. People warmed to the glow of his buoyant personality. By contrast, Truman had risen from machine politics and had reached the White House by accident. Harry Dexter White, Undersecretary of the Treasury, expressed this feeling well in 1946. When FDR was alive, White said, "we'd go over to the White House for a conference on some particular policy, lose the argument, and yet walk out of the door somehow thrilled and inspired to go on and do the job the way the Big Boss had ordered." Now, White lamented, "you go in to see Mr. Truman. He's very nice to you. He lets you do what you want to do, and yet you leave feeling somehow dispirited and flat."

No one was unhappier with Truman than the cantankerous journalist I.F. Stone, who wrote columns for liberal journals such as *PM* and *The Nation*. Under Truman, he wrote, the New Dealers "began to be replaced by the kind of men one was accustomed to meeting in county courthouses. The composite impression was of big-bellied, good-natured guys who knew a lot of dirty jokes, spent as little time in their offices as possible, saw Washington as a chance to make useful "contacts," and were anxious to get what they could for themselves out of the experience. They were not unusually corrupt or especially wicked—that would have made the capital a dramatic instead of a depressing experience for a reporter. They were just trying to get along. The Truman era was the era of the moocher. The place was full of Wimpys who could be had for a hamburger." *Progressive* magazine echoed Stone's assessment, declaring, "A curious uneasiness seems to pervade all levels of Government. There is a feeling that there is no one at the wheel."

Although many liberals initially believed Truman's 1948 election victory portended well for the New Deal's resurrection (such was the overoptimism of the *New Republic,* which proclaimed: "reaction is repudiated. The New Deal is again empowered to carry forward the promise of American life."), they were soon disappointed. What had happened in 1948 was that Truman, with Clark Clifford's strategy to guide him, had occupied America's middle ground, using civil rights and New Deal rhetoric to hold the liberals, while decimating any leftist alternatives through the politics of anticommunism. As Samuel Lubell would declare later, "no one had ever run harder in order to stand still."

Truman's supposed breakthroughs in civil rights legislation represented more of an astute political understanding than personal belief. Truman reportedly told one Southern colleague: "You know I'm against this [antilynching bill], but if it comes to a vote, I have to vote for it. My sympathies are with you but the Negro vote in Kansas City and St. Louis is too important." On another occasion, Truman held hearings on racial discrimination in the defense industry; yet, a Truman aide told friends: "If anybody thinks the committee is going to help black bastards into a $100 a week job, they are sadly mistaken." The *Pittsburg Courier,* one of the nation's leading black newspapers, viewed Truman's nomination as vice president in 1944 over Henry Wallace "an appeasement of the south." At least some Southerners agreed. After Truman ascended to the presidency, one Southern senator remarked: "Everything is going to be all right—the new president knows how to handle the niggers."

Truman further antagonized civil rights activists when he refused to permit the wartime FEPC to order Washington's transit system to hire black operators. The act so outraged black lawyer Charles Houston that he resigned from the FEPC, protesting the government's failure "to enforce democratic practices and protect minorities in its own capital." Such evidence led one historian to question whether Truman's statements on behalf of civil rights were not simply "an attempt to curry favor with liberal groups in Congress while at the same time not antagonizing those who opposed the FEPC."

Even after his public endorsement of the Committee on Civil Rights report, Truman's appearance of commitment to civil rights did not necessarily translate into action. After his bold civil rights message of February 1948, the president retreated quickly. Southern governors and senators had threatened to bolt the Democratic Party in protest, while white Southern newspapers accused the president of "stabbing the south in the back." Hoping to appease the white South while holding onto his liberal image with blacks, Truman refrained from introducing any legislation to implement the recommendations of his Civil Rights Commission; nor did he issue the executive orders to end segregation in federal employment or in the military that the committee had urged. "The strategy," a Truman aide later explained, "was to start with a bold measure and then temporize to pick up the right wing forces. Simply stated, backtrack after the bang." In short, Truman's actions were shaped as much by the changing political climate as by personal convictions. As one historian has noted, Truman's tactics were designed to win some support from all sides. "While avoiding a bruising fight, he could still make certain ritualistic gestures on behalf of a good cause. A speech here and a letter there would assure him of some liberal support and gratitude for his efforts. In this manner he could keep his lines of communication open with all factions while retaining a free hand to do exactly as he pleased in any given situation."

In the end, black protest succeeded more in generating promises of support than substantive action. Some progress did occur. It was important that Truman became the first president to address the NAACP, to identify civil rights as a moral issue, and to create a National Commission to study racial injustice. Symbolic gestures, however, too rarely resulted in meaningful, tangible action. Although Truman vigorously supported FEPC each year in policy messages, his tactics and follow-through were less than effective, causing some to believe Truman's "commitment" was simply a charade to keep African Americans in the Democratic fold. Without question, Truman's overtures were politically motivated, and once he was ensured of black support or votes, then, as noted above, he quickly retracted many of his commitments to persevere on blacks' behalf. Like many politicians before him (and after him), Truman's grand overtures on behalf of civil rights ended up being merely that—lip service to a cause he had little to no intention of genuinely embracing, let alone vigorously pursuing with definite action.

Truman's Justice Department did little to investigate or prosecute violations of civil rights when blacks tried to register to vote in the South. Although Truman finally issued an executive order to end discrimination in the armed forces in July 1948, it was A. Philip Randolph's threat to call for a massive civil disobedience campaign that "motivated" Truman to do the right thing. Even then, it was not until after the Korean War (1955) that the army was integrated. As liberal Minnesota Senator Hubert Humphrey noted at the time, it would have been more helpful to have less rhetoric and more action in the areas of lynching and voting.

Thus, by the end of the Truman years, African Americans faced a daily reality little different from that which had existed for them before World War II, notwithstanding all the fine gestures and political speeches. On September 8, 1948, Issac Nixon was warned not to cast his ballot in Wrightsville, Georgia. The army veteran dismissed the threat and, consequently, was murdered before the sun had set. A few days later, white terrorists kidnapped the local president of the NAACP branch from his home, threatening to kill him if he didn't leave the area, which he did, fleeing to Atlanta for his safety. In November, an all-white jury acquitted the men accused of murdering Nixon. For these black Americans, the politics of gesture was not enough.

Like a seasonal allergy, anticommunism has recurred at regular intervals throughout twentieth-century history. The Red Scare of 1919-

1920 helped to quell labor revolts of that period, as well as to provide an outlet for frustrations left over from the war. Not surprisingly, many saw the New Deal as a new incarnation of the Red Menace. It was all right, Al Smith said in 1936, if the intellectuals around FDR wished "to disguise themselves as Norman Thomas, or Karl Marx, or Lenin," but it became blasphemy when they attempted to "march under the banner of Jefferson, Jackson, or Cleveland."

In the years after World War II, the politics of anticommunism achieved a new pitch of hysteria. The House Committee on Un-American Activities (HUAC), first established in 1938 to investigate anti-American propaganda, was made a permanent standing committee. The 1940 Smith Act provided a vehicle for prosecuting anyone who even advocated communism. In a postwar atmosphere suffused with fear and suspicion, opportunities were rife to use these acts for political persecution and intimidation.

The Truman administration bore at least partial responsibility for the outrages that would occur in the name of anticommunism over the next several years. To placate the rabid anticommunists in Congress who had been ranting about supposed communists in the federal government, Truman, just nine days after the promulgation of the Truman Doctrine, issued Executive Order 9835, creating a Federal Employee Loyalty Program. The order gave government security officials authorization to screen two million federal employees for any hint of political deviance. The order also authorized the attorney general to draw up a list of "totalitarian, fascists, or subversive organizations." Membership, affiliation, or even sympathy with such groups could then be used as a basis for determining disloyalty.

Truman's response reflected a combination of concerns. Clearly there was a connection with the Truman Doctrine. If the country were to wage a crusade against atheistic communism abroad, a strong commitment to clean out communist subversives at home seemed a logical parallel. If, as Michigan Senator Arthur Vandenberg said, the only way to get the Truman Doctrine through Congress was to "scare hell out of the American people" about Soviet expansionism abroad, a vigorous anticommunist program at home would serve as an appropriate complement. If Truman hoped to get any funding for his doctrine's initiatives or for any of his domestic programs, he had to acknowledge the rabid anticommunism of the powerful chairmen of the Senate and House Appropriations Committees. Both individuals were convinced that communists (often defined as New Dealers) riddled the federal bureaucracy. In acquiescing to the political conservatism of such power-brokers, Truman helped legitimize a form of political inquisition, soon to be labeled "McCarthyism," after the most notorious red-baiter of the immediate postwar years, Senator Joseph McCarthy of Wisconsin. All of McCarthyism's later abuses were anticipated by Seth Richardson, the first president of the Loyalty Review Board, when he declared "the government is entitled to discharge any employee . . . without extending to such employee any hearing whatsoever." Any "suspicion of disloyalty . . . however remote" could provide justification for such dismissal. Using these procedures, civil servants who at any time in their lives criticized United States society or government policy (exercising their right of free speech!) could be arbitrarily dismissed from their job without being given the right to confront their accusers. The attorney general's list of subversive organizations allowed for HUAC and Loyalty Board henchmen to call before them and interrogate any individuals whom they "suspected" of at one time belonging to such "traitorous" groups as the Soviet-American Friendship Society—a World War II organization promoted by FDR as being essential in helping to foster good relations with the Soviet Union. Truman further alienated civil libertarians by having as his attorney general a notorious red-baiter, J. Howard McGrath, who declared that communists were "everywhere—in factories, offices, butcher shops, on street corners, and private business. And each carries in himself the death of our society." CIO president Philip Murray reflected the concern of many when he asked: "What sudden threat can warrant our throwing overboard the democratic principles of fair hearing and fair trial?"

Although Truman denounced HUAC's tactics and charged it with having "recklessly cast a cloud of suspicion over the most loyal civil service in the world," he himself helped to initiate the process. Now the question was what would happen to the liberal New Deal tradition in a context where strong advocacy of left-of-center ideas would be labeled as support of communism. Now, everyone had to conform to the anticommunist line; no one dared deviate. The effect on free political debate was chilling.

Truman's doctrine of containment toward the Soviet Union did not necessarily require an anticommunist crusade at home to be successful. Yet, in the politics of the situation, the Truman administration chose not to take that chance. Instead, Truman used the anticommunist mystique (perhaps paranoia or hysteria) as a means of ensuring support for the cold war abroad. While school children were being taught to dive under their desks or rush to air-raid shelters in the event of a Soviet atomic attack (a wooden desk would not be much protection from such a bomb), they were also enjoined to be on the alert for domestic deviants who might give support to communism at home. For American foreign policy the rhetoric of moralism led to rigidity, a loss of flexibility, and the elimination of any possibility for honest debate and criticism about the cold war. Because of the anticommunist crusade, which the Truman administration helped unleash, domestic dissent was stifled, civil liberties were compromised, and social reform advocates risked being pilloried as agents of a foreign state. The prospect for change that had given hope to activists, African Americans, labor leaders, and women after the war had shrunk before the chill wind of anticommunism. Thus, not surprisingly, the politics of anticommunism rather than the politics of liberalism dominated the nation's political life in the years after 1948.

In the area of foreign policy, there is much to be critical of the Truman administration. Beginning with his decision to drop atomic bombs on Japan to the promulgation of the Truman Doctrine in 1947, Harry Truman placed his personal stamp on the presidency by focusing on the fight against the Soviet Union. Dissenting voices were drowned out as the Truman administration pictured the United States and the Soviet Union locked in a life-and-death struggle. The menace of an "international communist conspiracy" was said to justify extraordinary measures to ensure U.S. national security. The claim of protecting "national security"—an emotionally powerful term, whose meanings seemed infinitely expandable—allowed Truman to justify policy initiatives, in both foreign and domestic affairs, that extended the reach and power of the executive branch of government.

Those repulsed by the incineration of human flesh from the atomic bomb doubted the necessity of dropping it, citing later U.S. intelligence surveys that included, "Japan would have surrendered even if the atomic bomb had not been dropped, even if Russia had not entered the war, and even if no invasion had been planned or contemplated." Distinguished military leaders such as Dwight Eisenhower later opposed use of the bomb. "First, the Japanese were ready to surrender, and it wasn't necessary to hit them with that awful thing," Eisenhower noted. "Second, I hated to see our country be the first to use such a weapon." In light of such statements, some have asked why there was no effort to communicate the bomb's horror to America's adversaries, either through a demonstration explosion or an ultimatum. Others have questioned whether the bomb would have been used on non-Asians, although the fire-bombing of Dresden claimed more victims than Hiroshima. Perhaps, most seriously, some have charged that the bomb was used primarily to intimidate the Soviet Union rather than to secure victory over Japan.

The decision to drop a second bomb two days after Hiroshima, of course, raises other questions. Why, once the weapon's horror had been displayed, was it necessary to use it again so quickly before the Japanese even had time to consider the awesome implications of its destructive power? The only answer seems to be Truman's overweening penchant for all-too-quick decision-making, which he believed was a virtue, not a handicap. Truman never gave the Japanese government sufficient time to fully digest what had happened to one of their cities. How much time should he have allotted? At least a few weeks, which many analysts believed would have resulted in a Japanese surrender. Truman typically acted precipitously with dire consequences not only for the United States at the time but for the world's posterity as well.

Others have asked why the United States did not wait to see whether Russia's entry into the war on August 6, 1945, would have caused Japan's surrender, which many believed at the time would have occurred. What was the hurry, these historians ask, unless Truman's main objective in dropping the bomb was to intimidate Stalin. On the Russian issue, there now seems little doubt that Truman thought long and hard about the bomb's impact on U.S./Soviet postwar relations. Truman and his advisors concluded that the weapon's possession would give the United States unprecedented leverage to push the Soviets toward a more accommodating position. Senator Edwin Johnson stated the equation crassly but clearly. "Almighty God in his infinite wisdom," the Senator said, "has dropped the atomic bomb in our lap . . . and now with vision and guts and plenty of atomic bombs, the United States can compel mankind to adopt a policy of lasting peace or be burned to a crisp." Stating the same argument with more sophistication prior to Hiroshima, Stimson told Truman that the bomb might well "force a favorable settlement of Eastern European questions with the Russians." Truman agreed. If the weapon worked, he noted, "I'll certainly have a hammer on those boys." Thus, it is clear from such remarks that, from the moment he made the decision to drop atomic bombs on Japan, Truman's real motive was to use the weapon to terrify Stalin, forcing the Soviet leader into a more "conciliatory mood."

Already noted for his brusque, cocky, assertive manner, possessing the ultimate weapon made Truman even more recalcitrant in dealing with the Soviets. Such was the arrogance displayed by Truman at Potsdam, his first, only, and last face-to-face meeting with Stalin during his entire presidency. As Winston Churchill noted, possessing the ultimate weapon, such a "trump card," made Truman "a changed man. He told the Russians just where they got on and off and generally bossed the whole meeting." It wasn't until the meeting's third day (Truman told Churchill within hours of the meeting's first day that the United States had the bomb and was going to use it on Japan) that Truman casually told Stalin that the United States had "perfected a very powerful explosive which we're going to use against Japan." No mention was made of sharing information about the bomb with supposedly a co-equal wartime partner or of future cooperation to avoid an arms race.

America's possession of the new weapon proved more a source of provocation than of effective diplomatic leverage. If Truman hoped he could use the bomb to intimidate Stalin, he was sorely mistaken. If anything, the United States' possession of such a weapon made Stalin even more resolved to resist Truman's high-handedness relative to the bomb. As Stalin told an American diplomat later, "the nuclear weapon is something with which you frighten people [who have] weak nerves." If the war had proven anything, it was that Russian nerves were remarkably strong. Rather than daunt the Soviets, Dean Acheson pointed out, the bomb confirmed Stalin's suspicions of Anglo-American cooperation in the Manhattan Project and, to the Soviet leader, that was "unanswerable evidence of a combination against them [the Soviets]. . . . It is impossible that a government as powerful and power conscious as the Soviet government could fail to react vigorously to the situation. It must and will exert every energy to restore the loss of power which the situation has produced." Henry Stimson warned Truman that the atom bomb would dominate America's relations with the Soviet Union. "If we fail to approach them now and continue to negotiate with this weapon rather ostentatiously on our hip, their suspicions and their distrust of our purposes and motives will increase."

Churchill further confirmed Stalin's belief about Anglo-American collusion relative to atomic weapons when, in his famous "Iron Curtain" speech, with Truman by his side the Prime Minister claimed, "God has willed" the United States and Great Britain to hold a monopoly over atomic weapons and called for a "fraternal association of English speaking people" against their common foe—the Soviet Union. Thus was the advent of the most dangerous arms race in human history. Indeed, according to Dr. Harold Urey, a leading atomic scientist, by making and storing atomic weapons, the United States was "guilty of beginning the arms race." Urey was correct. Over the course of the next several decades, both the United States and the Soviet Union, to maintain superiority over the other in nuclear capability, would build thousands of such devices of mass destruction. Interestingly, despite both nations' stockpiling of such weapons, and even when the cold war reached tensions potentially dangerous for a nuclear exchange between the two superpowers (such was the possibility during the Cuban missile crisis), both the Soviet Union and the United States wisely refrained from initiating Armageddon. Thus, to date, the United States remains the only nation to have ever used such weapons.

Truman's policy of "containment" became the catchphrase for a global, anticommunist national security policy. In the popular view, containment linked all leftist insurgencies, wherever they occurred, to a totalitarian movement controlled from Moscow that directly threatened, by heinous ideas as much as by military might, the United States. One of the most serious repercussions of containment was the U.S. support of right-wing totalitarian regimes throughout the world but especially in our own "backyard," Latin America, which saw American anticommunist policy degenerate into obsessive paranoia and blatant interventionism. Indeed, beginning in the early 1950s and over the course of the next three decades (until the mid-1980s), the United States pursued the fanatically reckless policy of toppling, using whatever means deemed effective—covert or blatant military intervention—any government suspected of being too far left ("communist" in Washington's eyes, simply nationalistic in reality) that might threaten the hemisphere's "democratic" stability. After supposedly "cleansing" the communist threat in a particular country, the United States would then promote "freedom and democracy" in that country by installing a new government, which in most instances quickly became a right-wing dictatorship, either civilian or military. As long as it was pro-United States and anticommunist, it would be sustained in power indefinitely. Regardless of the region, beginning with the Truman administration and to the present, the United States historically has supported, particularly during the cold war years, notoriously brutal dictatorships in the name of "containing" supposed communist expansion or takeover. In Africa, for example, this mentality shaped U.S. policies, bringing the United States into an alliance with South Africa. In 1948, the all-white Nationalist Party instituted apartheid. State Department officials familiar with African affairs warned that supporting apartheid in South Africa would damage U.S. prestige, but the Truman administration decided to cement an alliance with South Africa nonetheless. That country, Truman reasoned, possessed important raw materials (especially uranium for bombs and manganese for steel) and a cheap labor force. Moreover, South Africa's Nationalist Party was militantly anticommunist.

In aiding such regimes, the United States alienated the citizens of such countries, driving them into the arms of the insurgents, whom the people viewed as liberators from such repression. In many instances, the forces opposing the dictatorships were indeed communist partisans. However, depending on a country's or region's "value" to the United States, containment allowed for an open-ended labeling of "communist" to any nationalist movement trying to overthrow a corrupt, vicious but U.S.-backed right-wing regime. More often than not, U.S. support for such regimes failed, ultimately seeing a leftist government triumphant largely because of the Truman Doctrine's myopic, anticommunist obsession.

In September 1949, word reached the Truman administration that the Soviets had exploded a crude atomic device, marking the end of the U.S. nuclear monopoly. Already besieged by critics who saw a world with Soviet gains and American defeats, Truman issued reassuring public statements but privately took the advice of hard-line advisers and authorized the development of a new bomb based upon the still unproven concept of nuclear fusion. The decision to build this "hydrogen bomb" wedded the doctrine of containment to the creation of ever more deadly nuclear technology, as well as intensifying the arms race with the Soviet Union.

Prompted by the events of 1949, the Truman administration reviewed its foreign policy assumptions. The task of conducting the review fell to Paul Nitze, a hard-liner who produced a top-secret policy paper officially identified as National Security Council document number 68 (NSC-68). It provided a blueprint for both the rhetoric and the strategy of future cold war foreign policy. The paper opened with an emotional account of a global ideological clash between "freedom" spread by U.S. power, and "slavery" promoted by the Soviet Union as the center of "international communism." Warning against any negotiations with the Soviets, the report urged a full-scale offensive to expand U.S. power worldwide. It endorsed covert action, economic pressure, more vigorously hyped anticommunist propaganda, and a massive military buildup. Because Americans might oppose larger military spending and budget deficits, the report warned, U.S. actions should be couched as "defensive" and be presented as economic stimuli rather than as a drain on national resources. In NSC-68, "freedom" became redefined to mean simply "anticommunism."

As reflected in the above paragraph, Truman initiated a problem that will beset every president henceforth: how to formulate and win support for a foreign policy based on national interest rather than moral purity. At some point in the past, an American diplomat wrote in 1967: "There crept into the ideas of Americans about foreign policy . . . a historic note . . . a desire to appear as something greater perhaps than once actually was. . . . It was inconceivable that any war in which we were involved could be less than momentous and decisive for the future of humanity. . . . As each war ended, . . . we took appeal to universalistic, utopian ideals, related not to the specifics of national interest but to legalistic and moralistic concepts that seemed better to accord with the pretentious significance we had attached to our war effort." As a consequence, the diplomat went on, it became difficult to pursue a policy not defined by the language of "angles or devils," "heroes," or "blackguards."

The tragedy, of course, was that such a policy offered no room for intelligence or flexibility. If the battle in the world, according to Truman, was between good and evil, believers and nonbelievers, anyone who questioned the wisdom of established policy risked dismissal as a traitor. An ideological frame of reference emerged during the Truman years through which all other information was filtered. A "cold war mentality" consumed Americans, shaping everything, defining issues according to moralistic assumptions, regardless of objective reality. The intellectual basis for this frame of reference was provided by Truman's "true believers," men such as George Kennan, to whom Truman turned for advice because of their supposed expertise in foreign affairs. It was Kennan who told Truman that the Soviet Union was "a political force committed fanatically" to confrontation with the United States and world domination. Interestingly, twenty years later, Kennan searchingly criticized those who insisted (as he once had) on seeing foreign policy as a battle of angels and devils, heroes and blackguards. Ironically, it was Kennan again in the 1970s who declared, "the image of a Stalinist Russia, poised and yearning to attack the west, . . . was largely a product of western imagination." However, for more than a generation, that image would shape American life and world politics.

Although in the end, the Korean debacle was largely the result of MacArthur's hubris, Truman nonetheless was partly responsible. It could be said that Truman's failure to demand that MacArthur pull back to the 38th parallel instead of allowing the general to establish a front so close to the Chinese border was the real issue. Why Truman, as commander in chief, did not *insist* that MacArthur withdraw is the question that must be asked. Was Truman, like a good many Americans, in *awe* of this supposedly most magnificent of generals who previously had been credited with victory in the Pacific over the Japanese? Or was Truman simply intimidated by this overbearing, pompous egoist? Both factors possibly affected Truman's decision to allow MacArthur to remain along the Yalu River. There is possibly another reason, and if more accurate than already mentioned, then Truman was just as culpable as MacArthur for the quagmire. Perhaps Truman secretly became "politically greedy" and saw great opportunity if the "right circumstances" emerged to allow MacArthur to invade China and return that country to the "democratic fold." It must be remembered that the right and the "Asiafirsters" skewered Truman for having "lost" China to the communists. If there was a chance to atone for that supposed fiasco, then to avoid being labeled "soft" on communism, Truman was willing to take the chance that perhaps MacArthur was right, that China could be "reclaimed." If that was the *real* reason Truman did not demand MacArthur's retreat, then Truman was just as much to blame as the general for prolonging the war. Instead of thinking clearly rather than politically, Truman costs the lives of thousands of more American soldiers and untold numbers of Koreans and Chinese. By allowing MacArthur to remain along the Yalu River, Truman blatantly reneged on the stated purpose of American intervention, which was to repel the aggressor (North Korea) and to ensure South Korean sovereignty—the status quo antebellum. Truman, for all his supposed decisiveness and clear-thinking, should have realized the ramifications of allowing politics to interfere with *realpolitik*.

The Korean conflict also accelerated the process of globalization of the cold war. When the fighting ended, the United States found itself ever more strongly committed to greater military support for NATO. The United States also redoubled its efforts to rebuild Japan as a bastion of capitalist anti-communism in Asia (a move that would come back to haunt the United States economically by the late 1960s). The United States also felt obligated to protect Syngman Rhee, the tyrannical "president" of South Korea for decades ahead. Most important for the future, the U.S. found itself more engaged in the support of another despot, Chiang Kai-shek, in Taiwan and supporting French imperialism in Indochina. By January 1953, Truman's last month in office, the U.S. was providing 40 percent of the French effort in that little-known but highly incendiary outpost of Southeast Asia. It was Truman who first involved the U.S. in "Vietnam" when he allowed the French to return to its colony after World War II. Why did Truman make such a mistake? Again, the answer lies in containment, for Truman saw a French return as a means of stopping the spread of communism in Southeast Asia, for the leader of the insurgents was Ho Chi Minh, a supposed communist who had spent many years in Moscow. Although Ho Chi Minh was a Marxist, he was first and foremost a nationalist who believed the United States (the Truman administration) would help him liberate his country from French colonialism as a "thank you" for his help in driving the Japanese out of Indochina during World War II. Unfortunately, Truman, so immersed and blinded by his own anticommunist rhetoric and hype, saw only "red" when he looked at Ho Chi Minh, and consequently Ho Chi Minh became, as early as 1947, an American "enemy" who had to be destroyed. Contrary to most Americans' knowledge, U.S. involvement in Vietnam began in the late 1940s, when the Truman administration agreed to support the French return and pay for their presence as a deterrent to the spread of communism. As will be seen later in this book, despite U.S. aid, Ho Chi Minh not only defeated the French but ultimately the United States as well in what became this nation's most divisive and protracted war.

History has been kinder to Harry Truman than his contemporaries ever were. Indeed, as Winston Churchill confessed to Truman, "Sir, I held you in very low regard. I loathed your taking the place of Franklin Roosevelt." But in that same conversation, Churchill admitted, "I misjudged you badly, for you, more than any other man, have saved Western civilization." Churchill then went on to list how Truman accomplished that, lauding the president for his most remarkable courage and fortitude in the face of what seemed to be unending international crises. "When the British could no longer hold out in Greece, you, and you alone, sir, made the decision that saved that ancient land from the Communists. You acted in similar fashion . . . when the Soviets tried to take over Iran. . . . Your Marshall Plan which rescued Western Europe wallowing in the shallows and indeed easy prey to Joseph Stalin's malevolent intentions. Then you established the North Atlantic Treaty Alliance and collective security for those nations against the military machinations of the Soviet Union. Then there was your audacious Berlin Airlift. And, of course, there was Korea." In short, Churchill, like many Americans in the post-Truman years, came to appreciate all he had done, much of which in retrospect was not only momentous at the time but proved pivotal as well for future generations of Americans, if not for humanity in general.

To historian Clinton Rossiter, Truman was a "highly successful Andrew Johnson," who kept the reform tradition intact and even strengthened it. Truman saw himself as more than that. He saw himself as the "common folks'" champion whose duty at all times as president was to protect the common people "against the forces of reaction." In the long line of Republicans who had occupied the White House, Truman admired but two—Lincoln, for his concern for the common man, and Theodore Roosevelt, for his progressive policies, which Truman believed went far in protecting the common people from the excesses and exploitation of the industrial capitalist plutocracy. To Truman, Woodrow Wilson and FDR were the giants of the century, and he had no choice, he felt, but to fight for the Democratic heritage that had been passed on to him. "What I wanted to do personally for my own comfort and benefit was not important. What I could do to contribute to the welfare of the country was important."

Contemporaries and many Americans today still underestimate Truman's presidential significance because of their own confusion about government reform, as well as forgetting the profound change in purpose, power (especially that of the executive branch), and structure the Truman era helped to make permanent for several decades. The federal government's evolution from a small officialdom with limited purposes to a bureaucracy of salvation was firmly established by the end of Truman's presidency. Although much of his Fair Deal legislation was defeated, Truman nonetheless did much through his agenda to not only keep the liberal ethos alive but augment as well the power of the executive branch and the federal government in general. Thanks to Truman, for the next several decades (essentially, until the late 1970s), the principal role of government was to protect the citizenry from unfair actions by their fellows and to redistribute the national wealth (largely through sustained economic growth) to give the underprivileged a chance.

Truman encountered many reverses, but he at least raised new public issues that two decades later would form Lyndon Johnson's Great Society. Yet, Truman left office in ill repute, his legislative proposals stalemated, his administration embroiled in rancorous disputes, and his country bogged down in a land war in Asia. The revelation that an applicant for a government loan had helped the wife of a loan examiner acquire a fur coat and that the president's military aid had accepted a deep-freeze unit enabled Republicans to talk about "the mess in Washington" and made household words of "mink coat" and "deep freeze" early artifacts of the effect of the consumer culture on politics. In the spring of 1952, Truman's popularity rating in the polls plunged to the all-time low of 26 percent. No longer did the president have the stature to unify the nation.

Truman would be the first twentieth-century president, unhappily not the last, to learn the cost of fighting a limited war. Indeed, the Red Scare on Capitol Hill—and elsewhere in the United States during the Korean War—exposed a final legacy of the war: it deeply damaged the Truman administration. This damage was cumulative rather than dramatic, for the Korean conflict, unlike the later quagmire that was Vietnam, was not a "living room war." People could not turn on their television sets and witness the savagery of combat. There was little in the way of organized anti-war protest. Americans either wanted to win or get out. Some 5.7 million men served in the military during the war—about one-third the number in World War II—without much being said against the draft. But the frustrations of stalemate—and the continuing casualties—heightened the Red Scare and rendered Truman virtually powerless to control Congress or effectively lead the country. Well before the 1952 elections, it was clear that the Korean War had divided the nation and that the majority of Americans were ready for a change in leadership.

Despite the war's unhappy results, it is fair to conclude that Truman, once faced with the fact of North Korean aggression, acted in the best interest of world stability. To have stood by while the North Korean dictator Kim Il-sung overran South Korea would have demoralized peace-abiding nations and made a mockery of the United Nations. By intervening, the United States and the UN made North Korea pay dearly for its greed. Truman may also have discouraged the Soviets from supporting subsequent military adventurism by their client states elsewhere in the world. In these important ways, Truman's decision to fight in 1950—and his refusal thereafter to provoke a much wider war in China—not only sent strong signals against aggression but also guarded against the conflict's dangerous escalation.

When many Americans were sick of presidential excesses—lying about Vietnam, Watergate—Truman was often lionized. People especially admired his directness and decisiveness. President Jimmy Carter retrieved Truman's **"The Buck Stops Here"** sign from the archives and put it on his desk in the Oval Office. This adulation, however, would have surprised many contemporaries, not only in 1945 but throughout his seven-year presidency as well. Truman then seemed a poor contrast to FDR, with whom he was incessantly and disadvantageously compared. Bespectacled, apparently short, he looked more like a scholar than a dynamic leader of men. Although he could be an effective extemporaneous speaker when his partisan instincts were aroused, he more often spoke much too fast and stumbled, in part because his poor eyesight made it hard for him to read the text. Clark Clifford, a key White House aide, recalled, "he generally read poorly from prepared texts, his head down and his words coming forth in what the press liked to call a 'drone.' He waved his hand up and down as if he were chopping wood."

Critics have even wondered about Truman's most widely praised trait: his decisiveness. Some have speculated that he celebrated his capacity for decision as compensation for a deeper insecurity, rooted perhaps in his childhood. As a youth, he often called himself a sissy, and even at age twenty-nine he told his fiancée, Bess Wallace, that he was a "guy with spectacles and a girl mouth." His parents' marginal economic situation created other insecurities; the socially more prominent Wallace family always seemed to have looked down on him. His own stumbles in finding success in life, and his ever-embarrassing association with the Pendergasts, further placed him on the defensive. Truman was honest, ambitious, and very determined. However, on little things he could fly into rages that scared his associates (similar to the tantrums his hero Andrew Jackson had). He was sometimes short-tempered, combative, resentful, and extraordinarily touchy.

Truman's decisiveness as president has been exaggerated. Having received little help from FDR, he felt his way carefully for nearly two years after 1945. During this difficult time he depended heavily on the advice of others, and even later he frequently took his time before reaching big decisions, such as committing American ground troops to Korea in 1950 or firing General Douglas MacArthur from his Pacific command in 1951. In his foreign policies, Truman is best described not as a heroic man-of-decision-the-likes-of-whom-we-may-never-see-again-in-the-White-House but as a patriotic, conscientious, and largely colorless man whose fate it was to cope with, sometimes imaginatively and sometimes imprudently, some of the most difficult foreign policy problems in American history. Truman's perceived personal shortcomings have been swept away, forgotten by the aging adults of Truman's time in the White House, and certainly unknown to young adults of the early twenty-first century. However, the essential tenets of last century's liberal revolution that Truman helped shape have held, as have the contours of Truman's foreign policy. Indeed, in the latter capacity, it could be argued that Truman's impact as president in determining America's role in the postwar world was far greater than his more revered and illustrious predecessor, in whose shadow Truman unfairly still remains.

Harry and Bess.
June 28, 1919
Photo credit:
Truman Library

(left) Harry S Truman in his World War I army uniform. ca. 1917
(right) President Truman waving from the rear platform of a train.
June 3, 1948
Photo credit: Truman Library

Senator Truman
during the
Truman
Committee
hearings.
ca.1942
Photo credit:
Truman Library

Churchill, Stalin, and
Truman shaking hands at
the Potsdam Conference.
July 23, 1945
Photo credit:
Truman Library

President Truman and
General MacArthur.
October 15, 1959
Photo credit: Truman
Library

Dwight D. Eisenhower
1953-1961

The presidency of Dwight David Eisenhower encompassed the twentieth century zenith of power of both the United States on the global stage and the institution of the presidency itself. For years after his retirement, however, Eisenhower was dismissed by historians as unremarkable in his leadership and accomplishments and by the public as a nice fellow who had the good luck to preside over a basically self-generating and continuing golden age. With the hindsight of five decades of history, the significance of Eisenhower's achievements has taken on a new golden luster. After Ike came the fiasco of the 1960s and 1970s: Johnson, Vietnam, and social upheaval; Nixon, stagflation, and resignation; the twin failures of Ford and Carter; the more successful but still limited presidency of Ronald Reagan; and the triple post-imperial presidencies of Clinton and the Bushes. Thus do the eight years of Eisenhower appear to be an island of peaceful prosperity with the past deprivations of the Great Depression and the horrors of the Second World War lapping on one shore and with the future insecurities and instabilities of the next five decades—from cold war to wars of terror—crashing like oppressive waves on the other.

This is the reason no twentieth century presidency has gone through as great a reassessment by both historians and the public as has the presidency of Dwight Eisenhower. The war hero general turned politician was popular enough with the public during his tenure in office, with approval ratings hovering in the 60 percent to 70 percent range. Yet, after his retirement, for the next two decades historians typically ranked him in the middle of the presidential pack, typically behind even Herbert Hoover. Starting in the 1980s—in part because of the perception of Ronald Reagan as being in the flesh everything Ike had been accused of being in the press—the figure of Eisenhower as a hands-off and somewhat lackluster chief executive was replaced with Eisenhower as a sharp, competent, and engaged administrator. Thus, the Eisenhower presidency staged a comeback in polls, rising steadily in both the opinion of the public and historians. Recent polls have placed Eisenhower 9th (between 8th-placed Kennedy and 10th-placed Johnson, with Lincoln, FDR, Washington, Teddy Roosevelt, Truman, Wilson and Jefferson heading the pack). A recent Zogby poll placed Ike 5th in the public heart, behind only Franklin Roosevelt, Kennedy, Truman, and Reagan. Under Eisenhower's leadership, the United States achieved peace in Korea and avoided further significant military conflicts even as it navigated the shoals of a cold war whose rules of engagement were still evolving. With his credentials as a leader of Allied—and not just American—forces firmly in place, Eisenhower pursued a global policy building on the Bretton Woods and Marshall Plan framework of the 1940s, affirming an American commitment to multilateral engagement that stands in stark contrast to those pursued by his partisan heirs today. Under "Ike," the American economy posted the better part of a decade of strong growth that wouldn't be matched in overall numbers until the Clinton years four decades later—only the Eisenhower expansion would be more egalitarian, reaching into more average households and raising general prosperity to levels never seen before. Under his "unremarkable" leadership, the nation pursued the largest public works project in its history—the interstate highway system—that did as much, if not more, to transform the nature of American society as had the development of the rail network a century before. Eisenhower embraced and expanded the social welfare state created by Franklin Roosevelt and Truman, and he took the first albeit tentative steps along the path of desegregating a society in which racism had been for generations as American as apple pie and the Saturday cross burning.

Moreover, Eisenhower achieved these accomplishments amidst an era of reasonably amiable bipartisanship (at least once the Robespierre of American politics, Senator Joseph McCarthy, had burned himself out) using the same skills he had developed getting the Americans, British, and French to cooperate during the war to get Republicans and Democrats to cooperate during the peace. This Eisenhower legacy could be found in the words of John F. Kennedy, who, running in 1960 to replace Ike on a platform of "youth and vigor," could still observe, "Both Republicans and Democrats want to do what's right for America. The question is, how to do it?" One is hard pressed to imagine such a nod to the good intentions of the other party being shown between the two major political parties in the first decade of the twenty-first century. Meanwhile, Eisenhower's genial, grandfatherly visage (reinforced by his true grandfatherly nature— hence the renaming of Roosevelt's presidential get-a-way, "Shangri-

La," after his own grandson, David), reinforced by generally positive economic and social news, gave him tremendous public approval. To be sure, there was more than a little tarnish on the Eisenhower golden years: entrenched racism and poverty that a decade of rising general prosperity did little to alleviate tops the list. Eisenhower's failure to directly take on the demagogic McCarthy, as well as his tepid embracing of the Civil Rights movement, allowed the damage done by zealotry and bigotry to fester beyond what otherwise might have been contained. Indeed, Eisenhower's tendency towards the more intractable problems was the epitome of the prairie ethic of his youth: in the face of a big storm, hunker down and hope it blows itself out. Eisenhower, never a revolutionary, was content to competently administer and expand upon what was laid out before. But Eisenhower was not a plodding bureaucrat or a disengaged, disinterested chief executive content to delegate the running of government to his chief aids such as Sherman Adam. Eisenhower was a commander in chief by training and by disposition, a man willing to make the call and take responsibility even when the risks were high and the outcome uncertain, be it to deploy an invasion force to liberate Europe or the U.S. Army to liberate an Arkansas high school. Across his career, from West Point to Supreme Allied Headquarters to the White House, Eisenhower carried with him his Midwesterner's genial nature, steady resolve, and confidence in the ultimate triumph of American ideals.

Dwight Eisenhower was the first of three modern presidents to come from Texas. Born 1890 in Denison, Texas, the third of seven sons, Ike (a childhood nickname) spent little of his youth growing up in the land of his birth. His father, a creamery mechanic, relocated to Abilene, Kansas, in the year after his birth. Young Ike spent his formative years in the quiet heartland of what was only a few decades before the wild frontier but now was part of the pacified and gentrifying middle America. That sense of the frontier turned settled lands—the steady and managed bringing of order to what had once been wilderness and chaos—was a theme that permeated Eisenhower's life. Ike's years in the plains also imbued him with the Midwesterner's patience of knowing that, no matter how hard the January blizzards blow, spring will inevitably follow if one has but the pluck to keep one's head down and endure. Thus steady, even to the point of appearing plodding, and determined pursuit of goals and a genial nature in dealing with adversity were ingrained in the future general and president at a young age.

The young Eisenhower sought to test himself on the traditional fields of Midwestern combat, excelling in baseball and football, staying with the latter right up until a knee injury while playing at West Point ended his sports career. Lacking family connections and family money, and not particularly driven towards the uncertain world of business and entrepreneurial enterprise, Eisenhower pursued a military career as offering the best opportunities to a student of above average physical, if average academic, abilities. The Kansas boy thrived in the disciplined world of West Point. While not graduating at the top of his class (He ended up a respectable 61 out of 164 men.), he was a popular cadet, considered a leader by his peers, and he impressed his superiors with an orderly mind that excelled in two areas—logistics and politics. Eisenhower graduated West Point into a commission in an American Army that, with the exception of the brief Spanish American war a decade and a half before and sporadic Indian campaigns that had ended a generation ago, had not been seriously tested in combat since the Civil War and had not faced a real foreign threat since the War of 1812.

The newly commissioned second lieutenant faced a peacetime military career of endless transfers from small remote military bases in the back reaches of America and on the periphery of the still small American empire, a world in which opportunities to display martial abilities were expected to be few and time between promotions long. In this garrison military, organizational skills weighed as heavily as warrior instincts. The ability to get along and get the job done without too much flash, which might attract the attention—and jealousy—of more senior commanders, weighed most heavily of all. Eisenhower made the usual circuit of small bases before World War I, meeting and marrying Mamie Geneva Doud in 1916 while stationed in Texas. He rose to temporary rank of lieutenant colonel once war broke out, but spent the war years—short as they were—stateside helping to train and organize a vastly swelling military as the commanding officer for the new U.S. Army tank corps. The military, however, collapsed to its prewar size just as rapidly following America's post-armistice return to isolationism.

For the next twenty years Eisenhower rose slowly but steadily through the ranks based on his organizational talents, doing tours in the Panama Canal Zone and as assistant executive (1929–33) in the office of the Assistant Secretary of War and even as a member of the American Battle Monuments Commission. By the late 1930s, as storm clouds brewed over Europe and Asia, Eisenhower served as an aide to Douglas MacArthur in the Philippines. No greater contrast in styles might be found in the American military than between those of the self-deprecating Kansas prairie boy and the imperial-minded general with his habit of referring to himself in the third person. Eisenhower's organizational abilities resulted in his being recalled stateside by George Marshall before the war actually began (though at least one version of events holds that MacArthur pushed the transfer, wanting someone who was more of a warrior on hand once the bullets started to fly). With the actual outbreak of war, Eisenhower's abilities to collegially manage the vast logistics of creating and effectively deploying a modern mechanized multi-national military force were immediately appreciated, resulting in his rapid rise from Chief of Military Operations (1941), command of U.S. Forces in the European Theater of Operations including the North African invasion (1942), Chief of all Allied forces in North Africa (1943), Commander of the invasion of Sicily and Italy later that same year and, by early 1944, appointment as Supreme Commander of Allied European Forces. The rest, as they say, is history (a history that he himself documented in his best selling *Crusade in Europe* published in 1948, a volume most distinguished by its relative lack of self promoting and justification, unlike similar volumes by many other wartime commanders).

Following the war's successful completion, Eisenhower was appointed commander of the U.S. Army of Occupation in Germany and then Army Chief of Staff (1945). He argued for the development of an integrated military command structure and the adoption of universal military training for young American men in an effort to avoid the return to isolationism and unpreparedness that had occurred after World War I. Even as he did so, however, he presided over another rapid demobilization of a vast wartime military as America shifted gears to a peacetime economy.

Having reached the highest pinnacles of military rank and having served for 34 years in uniform, Eisenhower left the military in 1948—in part to seek a "quieter" life, in part to avoid presiding over yet another peacetime military—to become president of Columbia University. While one might have imagined a successful chief executive like Eisenhower moving from uniform into a highly compensated business suit, Eisenhower's background in the military actually made him an excellent candidate for university administration. There are a surprising (and largely unexplored) number of similarities between academic and military institutions. Both types of institutions, for example, operate largely outside the free market model as part of a state centrally-planned apparatus—a socialized system. While military officers know far more personal discipline than do their academic counterparts, at the highest reaches of command military officers, like tenured academics, can act the part of professional prima donnas just as their ivory tower counterparts are notorious for. Thus, the skills Ike learned balancing the egos of Montgomeries and Pattons would have served him well in dealing with turf disputes between political science and economics departments. Such, however, was not to be his future. Just as uncertainties left by the "war to end all wars" begat World War II, the uncertainties left at the end of World War II—the division of Europe, the division of the Korean peninsula, and the general division of the world into one part liberal, one part communist, and one part trying to stay out of the crossfire between the other two—begat the cold war. By 1948, the demobilization of the American military had stopped and had begun to reverse itself. Containing communism short of total war, as the new doctrine evolving out of the Truman administration called for, required a reorganization of the postwar American/European army of occupation into an army of deterrence to Soviet preemptive attack. It also required the organization of a new European command structure committing the military forces and resources of the western European states to collective security. Managing an American-English-French military alliance had been hard enough. The new NATO structure added to the mix the recently rehabilitated West German state, as well as Italy and other smaller states. Managing this new mix required special political skills. Hence, a somewhat reluctant Truman (having already been burned by one World War II hero in the person of MacArthur over Korea) felt compelled to recall Eisenhower to uniform in late 1950 to serve as the new Supreme Commander of NATO forces. If Truman had also hoped that getting the publicly popular general out of the country before the 1952 presidential elections would diminish Ike's political future (and thereby help Truman's own party), he was sorely mistaken.

In 1948, operatives of both parties had sounded Eisenhower out over the possibility of his running on their ticket, a hope the war hero did not encourage. In 1952, it was the Republicans who bought the transatlantic airplane tickets to court Eisenhower in Paris, and this time his answer would be yes. Sitting in NATO headquarters, Eisenhower had become increasingly disillusioned with Truman and the Democrat's handling of foreign policy. At the same time, he had grown apprehensive at the prospects that the Taft isolationist wing of the Republican Party was becoming too powerful in its efforts to disengage the U.S. from its postwar international commitments and "bring the boys back home." Eisenhower, therefore, based his decision to run far more on global rather than domestic concerns and an overarching commitment to continued U.S. leadership in international affairs.

Retiring once more, Eisenhower returned stateside to fight a presidential campaign (and his first political campaign at any level) that was pretty much anti-climatic from the moment he threw his helmet into the ring. With the help of Republican liberals, moderates, and internationalists (all of whom became endangered species within the GOP within two generations, which leads one to speculate whether Eisenhower, were he around today, could win a GOP nomination or whether he might even become a Democrat), he easily triumphed over isolationist conservative Senator Robert Taft, thereby establishing the dominance of the internationalists in Republican politics for the next two decades.

Eisenhower ran on three basic issues: the stalemated war in Korea; public displeasure over high taxes and rising inflation; and a general lack of public confidence in the Truman administration. On the issue of Korea, Eisenhower paraphrased his own mentor/nemesis, Douglas MacArthur, in matters oriental (whose own mess in provoking Chinese intervention into the war now had to be cleaned up by his former subordinate) by proclaiming, if elected, "I will go to Korea." While the promise of a visit to Korea mattered little in the realm of diplomatic realities, it resounded with an electorate looking for strong and proven leadership following a string of postwar policy fumbles, from Berlin to the "loss" of China to the stalemate of Korea. A public used to the overwhelming mobilization of force aimed at decisive victory, as had been the case in World War II, was not well-disposed to the "limited" form of conflict that came to dominate the postwar period.

The Eisenhower campaign, meanwhile, advanced no comprehensive domestic platform, preferring to follow a standard Republican line on lowering taxes and bringing down inflation by dealing with "that mess in Washington" being left by the outgoing Truman administration. Vagueness in a domestic platform mattered little in any event, as the real selling point of the Eisenhower candidacy was Eisenhower himself—a trusted and reassuring face from a time when American confidence was strong, promising a return to such national confidence once again. Where Reagan would ride to reelection 32 years later on the platform of "It's morning in America again," Eisenhower would ride in on the basic claim that night had never really fallen. All that was required to set things right in America and the world was a shuffle in command at the top that would restore public confidence and make Americans realize the U.S. was still the global master. Thus, the simple campaign slogan, "I like Ike"—the personal connection between a generation of veterans and the man who led them—was in and of itself sufficient to guarantee the former general a sweeping victory over Illinois Governor (and former academic) Adlai Stevenson. (As a side note, the 1952 election and its 1956 rematch also marked the last time two bald candidates—both with academic credentials to boot—squared off against each other. The fast closing age of television and image-driven politics soon rendered such candidates a polite affectation of a simpler age.)

Eisenhower took office in January 1953, emphasizing in his first inaugural address the common bond the generations of Americans who had fought in one or more world wars now felt and the common obligation they and America now shared. "Americans," he proclaimed, "indeed, all free men, remember that in the final choice a soldier's pack is not so heavy a burden as a prisoner's chains." Thus was America's commitment to maintain a stable international order—a commitment first proffered, unsuccessfully, as it turned out, by Democrat Woodrow Wilson a generation before—reinforced. Like Wilson, Eisenhower would also now have to deploy the skills learned outside of the political arena to preserve and protect his image of America as the world's principle force to keep people free.

The Eisenhower Presidency: A Positive Assessment

Eisenhower entered the presidency with two central goals. On the domestic front, his goal was simply to maintain the economic boom that had come out of the postwar period and to keep the economy aimed at the lowest possible rates of unemployment and inflation and the highest possible rates of economic growth. On the international front, Eisenhower sought to work towards a viable modus operandi with the Soviet Union. The former general realized the U.S. had to reach a sustainable balance between its commitment of multilateral relationships aimed at containing communism and the dangers such policies poised in terms of the potential to trip the U.S. and Soviet Union into a globally devastating war.

By the time he left office in 1961, Eisenhower could fairly claim he had delivered on his central domestic agenda. By comparison to the decades that preceded and immediately followed it, the Eisenhower years were indeed an age when the American middle class turned golden. As his premier biographer, Stephen Ambrose, wrote of the Eisenhower years:

Indeed, by almost every standard—GNP, personal income and savings, home buying, auto purchases, capital investment, highway construction and so forth—it was the best decade of the century. Surely Eisenhower's fiscal policies, his refusal to cut taxes or increase defense spending, his insistence on a balanced budget, played some role in creating this happy situation.

Eight years of essentially uninterrupted economic expansion had an unprecedented impact on general prosperity—low to no inflation, productivity up 25 percent, real wages for factory workers up 20 percent and family wages up 15 percent—that goes far in explaining Eisenhower's strong popularity through most of his time in office.

Eisenhower, like all presidents, deserves less credit for the favorable economic performance of his tenure just as other presidents deserve less of the blame for bad years. But, as Eisenhower's immediate predecessor observed, if you're sitting behind the big desk in the oval room, the buck stops there, for better or for ill. The postwar prosperity that would be the defining feature of American political life from the Truman years until the day the music died (which would be October 6, 1973, the day the Kippur War began, precipitating the OPEC oil embargo that banged the last nail in the coffin of postwar American economic hegemony) was the product of the convergence of three under-appreciated, converging factors.

Contrary to much current conventional wisdom, it was not war itself that produced the tremendous postwar boom. Indeed, as any good economic historian would tell you, war has usually been a loss-leader in the lives of nations, consuming more real wealth in terms of capital stock destroyed and productivity sidelined than it produced. The only way war had ever "turned a profit" *per se* was by the age old tradition of looting and pillaging, which seems to have blessedly fallen out of favor as a means of wealth enhancement by modern economic states. Pillaging, however, only reallocated quantities of existing wealth from one state to another at what economists might blandly call tremendous transactional costs (devastated cities and countrysides, piles of bodies of what had previously been productive workers, etc.).

The Second World War, for America at least, was a wealth enhancer because, upon the completion of war in 1945, Americans had endured essentially seventeen years of economic deprivation driven by the thirteen years of depression (with its resulting diminished purchasing power due to unemployment) and four years of wartime rationing, as everything from rubber to beef was requisitioned to support the war effort. During those four war years, however, America had experienced a period of as close to full employment as it would ever see, producing rising consumable income, yet with nothing on which to spend it. Hence to fight the war effort, American consumers had simply given much of the money paid to them by the government in wages right back to the government as war bonds. As the war ended and demobilization occurred, ten million American men were pushed out of uniform and into civilian clothes in a matter of months, adding dramatically to the defacto pool of the unemployed. At the same time, government expenditures on war materials—manpower and productive resources included—that artificially inflated the economy also plummeted, practically overnight. What should have occurred was a replay of the economic recession of 1919-1921 (which only ended because of the massive—and ultimately disastrous—infusion of capital from repayment of war debt by America's European allies). Indeed, there was a mild recession in 1946, but it was scarcely noticed by an America rejoicing in victory. As the World War II GI's returned home, they had the nest egg of their government-forced war savings to fall back on, allowing them time to marry the girl next door, start the baby boom, and shop to buy all the things they needed for the transition to civilian life. As they did so, consumer demand began an upward spike that continued relatively unabated for a generation. As demand for consumer goods from autos and housing to clothes and baby food went up, employers could seamlessly shift from war production to peacetime domestic production, hiring the newly released GIs to fill the ranks of industry. Thus, the new civilian veterans could buy today and thereby produce the jobs they would occupy tomorrow.

Intensifying this process was the fact that for the better part of fifteen years following the war, America faced no serious trade rivalries, as all of her traditional rivals were either burned to the ground (Germany, Japan, China, and Russia) or bankrupt (Britain and France). As such, if the markets of the world wanted sophisticated industrial products, they would have to buy them from the U.S. at American-driven prices, triggering a massive positive balance of trade that would only be offset by American willingness (driven both by selfless and self-interested motivations) to flood the developed markets of Europe and Japan with aid moneys to secure their economic recoveries.

Finally, the war had unleashed the accelerated development of numerous technologies—not the least of which would be those of electronic computation—that dramatically enhanced the productivity of postwar workers. Complimenting this was one of the most influential social policies of modern American history, a product of the Truman administration's commitment to a "Fair Deal." The GI Bill allowed tens of thousands of returning veterans to forgo immediate reentry into the jobs market by attending what had hitherto been the economically restricted halls of higher academe, thereby artificially depressing unemployment levels and buoying postwar wages while simultaneously producing a highly skilled labor class that gave Americans a competitive advantage for a generation.

(So, a note to all those who think war will make America rich: unless you precede said war with seventeen years of a depressed economy, destroy all American trade rivals, and pay to send an unprecedentedly large number of Americans to graduate school, do not expect wars to pay off. With the exception of the last option, one would hardly consider it all worthwhile.)

As Ambrose correctly observed, however, Eisenhower could take at least some credit for not adopting policies that might have derailed this postwar miracle. Chief amongst these was his willingness to reject his own party's demands for massive tax cuts. Republicans had chaffed for thirty years as the size of the bite government took out of the economy through taxation increased dramatically. They most particularly objected to the 11 percent increase in income taxes levied in the Truman years to offset the costs of the Korean War. Moreover, Republicans rejected the fundamental shift towards progressive rates of taxation that had begun with the adoption of the income tax, accelerated during the Wilson years, and dramatically increased with FDR's (in their view) redistributive fiscal policies. Now with both Congress and the White House in their party's hands, congressional Republicans expected a rapid rollback of taxes as the first step towards a general rollback of the New Deal itself. However, in the face of great partisan anger, Eisenhower refused, falling back on truly conservative principles that the first order of business of any government was to balance its own books. To cut taxes immediately, he argued, would either intensify the Korean War-induced federal deficit or necessitate budget cuts that would seriously undermine either social welfare programs or foreign aid programs—or both. Eisenhower instead promised to bring down federal spending gradually over several budget cycles, thereby not disrupting economic growth in part stimulated by such spending, and to consider addressing taxes only once the budget was in balance.

The debate over fiscal policy in Eisenhower's first year in office underscored the decisive divide that was to occur within the ranks of Republicans over the next several decades. On the one hand were the traditional fiscal conservative Republicans like Eisenhower who had been brought up on the notion of pay as you go (an quaint idea that seems not to have survived the age of credit cards). Some of these Republicans, such as Eisenhower himself, might embrace the Keynesian heresy that in times of extreme economic deprivation the government might briefly float stimulating deficits, but in a generally good economy they believed the costs of such fiscal profligacy (in terms of inflationary pressures) most certainly outweighed the gains. On the other hand was the emerging anti-tax wing of the party, working towards a formulation of "starving the beast of government" that would take until the Reagan years to fully develop. Such Republicans in the 1950s had an intuitive feeling that rising tax revenues simply made government too powerful and, therefore, reducing taxes would eventually force a return to the small government they cherished. And finally, on the Hindu-goddess-esque third hand were liberal Republicans, primarily from the northeast (what became known as the "Rockefeller" wing of the party in the next decade) who more fully embraced the New Deal commitment to social egalitarianism, which social welfare programs helped advance. While the anti-tax wing of the party grew to domination within a generation, Eisenhower was able to build a coalition of deficit-hawks and liberal Republicans (with more than a passing amount of pure patronage politics, guaranteeing continued levels of federal spending in districts of members of Congress who supported him) and push through a budget that maintained existing tax rates.

Of course, the promised budget reductions never actually developed, an eventuality Eisenhower's chief Republican rival, Robert Taft, had huffed and puffed about while arguing against the president's budget plan. Eisenhower simply refused to make the steep cuts in foreign aid spending that Taft pushed for, because to do so would have undercut the multilateral internationalist approach he favored in foreign policy. At the same time, the president resisted yet the fourth hand of his own party (military hawks) calling for greater defense spending. Eisenhower made substantial cuts instead, arguing that the massive World War II style military model wasn't needed post-Korea and such spending would undercut a balanced budget.

Thus, Eisenhower kept in place top marginal income tax rates in excess of 90 percent and substantial excise taxes—a policy that would see him damned by today's members of his own party as being akin to a closet socialist. For Eisenhower, high top-bracket tax rates (which he realized few actually paid) were simply part of the "soldier's pack" burden Americans must pay to preserve their freedom. His 1954 tax reform bill did effect a net tax cut but by increasing deductions, particularly for middle-class households, while maintaining top marginal rates. Meanwhile, Eisenhower did not move to radically rollback domestic spending, as his budget negotiations of 1953 implied he would. All of this was in keeping with Eisenhower's efforts to create a viable détente between traditional Republicanism and what he referred to as "Modern Republicanism" with his mantra of "liberal on human issues, conservative on fiscal issues."

Indeed, Eisenhower pushed for and obtained a vast expansion of the ranks of those eligible to receive social security benefits, resulting in the number of such recipients doubling under his tenure. Meanwhile, base level benefits were also increased in real terms. Eisenhower's Midwestern roots—where neighbor took it on as their undeniable obligation to help neighbor in times of sickness, hardship, or plain old age—had trumped the increasingly ideological fixation of his party on macroeconomic laissez faire theory. Eisenhower did not forget the working man, securing in 1955 a 33 percent increase in the minimum wage (which put the minimum wage about sixty cents an hour higher, adjusted for inflation, than it was by 2004). While unsuccessful in achieving his campaign promise to reverse some of the more union-busting aspects of the Taft-Hartley Act, his administration successfully resisted pressure by his party to roll back even more of New Deal era pro-labor legislation. Indeed, for Eisenhower the postwar prosperity had meant the end of any notion of an American proletariat labor class. All workers had been rolled into the broad middle class whose interests he saw as his to defend. According to no less an authority than George Meany, head of the AFL-CIO, American labor under Ike had "never had it so good." And as workers' pockets bulged with newfound cash, corporate profits also soared from selling progressively more cars, TVs (successfully advertising the former on vastly expanding medium of the latter), and everything else to this new, triumphant consuming class.

In general, Eisenhower did not seek to turn back the legislation and policies of FDR and Truman but built on and consolidated them. Embracing the core principles of FDR's New Deal was, ultimately, the greatest legacy of the Eisenhower years. A political revolution is only complete when it has survived a peaceful transfer of power to a political opposition who still continues the core policies of the revolution. Such was the under-appreciated role of the Clinton administration which, conservative vitriol to the contrary, maintained the fundamental supply-side policies of the Reagan administration, thereby validating them for possibly another generation. Prior to Clinton, Democrats had run against the Reagan revolution in 1980,

1984, and 1988, getting shellacked each time by a public ready and willing to accept the new dominant American political paradigm. Like the Reagan-era Democrats, Republicans had rejected the core values of popular New Deal programs, seeing in the adoption of policies of minimum wage laws, legalized unionization, and the telltale "social" security program the fast spouting seeds of true socialism. It took another decade for Hayek to complete the intellectualization of this opposition in "The Road to Serfdom," published precisely as New Deal politics achieved mastery with the presidential election of 1944 and another generation for these ideals to emerge triumphant with the election of Ronald Reagan.   Republicans, meanwhile, ran doggedly on anti-Roosevelt, anti-New Deal platforms in 1936, 1940, 1944, and 1948, loosing by large margins in all but the last, and then only because FDR was no longer around to personify his revolution.

It was not until Eisenhower's victory in 1952 that a Republican standard bearer fully embraced the basic principles of the New Deal. Indeed, Eisenhower moved to substantially expand on such social policies over his eight years in office.   Ill-suited by temperament and political predisposition to lead a Republican "Thermidor" reaction to the Democrat's revolution, Eisenhower instead successfully reconciled his party with the new American social contract of social welfare through his formulation of New Republicanism. Eisenhower's acceptance of the New Deal validated its principles as the unquestioned cornerstone of American politics accepted by both Democrats and Republicans for the next twenty-eight years, until the "Reagan Revolution" redefined the nature of the American social contract with his restoration of more traditional conservative values.

Eisenhower left an even larger (and longer lasting) mark on American society through an unprecedented initiative in public works, which exceeded the scope and size of even FDR's New Deal projects. Foreshadowing the rise of "New Federalism" that his vice president, Richard Nixon, proclaimed two decades later, Eisenhower sought to share more power—and money—between Washington, D.C. and the states.   Under Roosevelt and Truman, cash-strapped states had willingly given up increasing levels of autonomy in public works projects to obtain federal funding. Eisenhower, with a professional military man's understanding that centralization does not always produce the beneficial economies of scale its proponents advocate, sought to reverse this trend to a degree. Thus, he pushed for a sharing of power between federal and state administrators of large public power projects. In the Hells Canyon project, for example, he successfully championed a model of the building of three dams by a private utility on the Snake River rather than the construction of one huge depression-era style federal dam. He extended this mantra of decentralization into social welfare, pushing for a program of federal matching funds to states for public health insurance programs and education rather than the creation of outright federal programs. Eisenhower also oversaw completion and dedication of the Saint Lawrence Seaway, stimulating the economies of the Great Lakes region.

The crown jewel of national infrastructure projects would be the creation of an integrated interstate highway system—41,000 miles of new, wide, and fast roads—90 percent of the cost of which to be paid with federal revenues from gas and highway users' taxes. As Eisenhower himself described it, the project would be "not only the most gigantic federal undertaking in road-building," but "the biggest peacetime construction project of any description ever undertaken by the United States or any other country." Phenomenally, from the perspective of today, when completion of even a mile of new highway can take years to complete, half of the proposed system would be in place within a decade. Eisenhower had been impressed by the state of highways in Europe—especially the impressive German autobahn system. Meanwhile, he deplored the haphazard patchwork condition of what constituted the American highway system that had been left to the vagaries of state-funded construction. Construction of a truly comprehensive highway system, allowing easy transportation by road from ocean to ocean and border to border, could only be accomplished by determined federal action.

For Eisenhower, the project served two purposes—one related to national security and the other to domestic economic growth. Creation of an efficient domestic road network facilitated the transport of military men and material in times of war. As importantly, from a political perspective, putting the project under the rubric of national defense went a long way to deflecting any criticism members of his own party might have had towards what amounted to another massive Rooseveltian public works project. From an economic perspective, the creation of the new highway system resulted in tremendous spin-off economic growth—the epitome of the "build it and they will come" school of economic development theory—stimulating everything from the already fast growing auto industry to the rise of national food and lodging chains providing services to weary motorists busily motoring from here to there. The massive nature of the construction project also helped to level out fluctuations in employment for a decade or more—if unemployment started to creep up, federal highway dollars could be released, and resulting acceleration of construction could draw down unemployment. For any who claimed that Eisenhower lacked "the vision thing," as would become painfully obvious with many future presidents, a quick spin on a local interstate highway should be sufficient refutation of said claim.

As if to cap off the massive public works of the Eisenhower era, the U.S. also added two more (and final) states: Alaska and Hawaii. While symbolic at the time of the dynamic evolution of American geography, with the retrospect of time, the additions of the 49th and 50th state take on a slightly more ominous portent. It has been forty-five years since the U.S. has added a state—the longest interregnum in national growth in America's history. Indeed, but for possibly Puerto Rico or the District of Columbia, which would simply be a reclassification of existing American territory, no options for expanding the states of the Union appear likely to emerge at any point in the foreseeable future. As such, the Eisenhower years represented the finality of the development of the American polity. No longer a growing youth, by the 1960s the United States could well be seen to have entered its middle age.

Eisenhower also played a significant, though less dynamic, role in dealing with what became the hot button social issue of his presidency and the bedeviling issue of the next decade of American politics: civil rights. The modern civil rights movement might be said to have started with Truman's desegregation of the military, which progressed slowly in practice even through the Eisenhower years, but the real genesis of the postwar civil rights movement could be traced back to World War II itself. A lasting legacy of World War II had been the easing of ethnic tensions between white European Americans—an unexpected by-product of the creation of a poly-ethnic (though not poly-racial) fighting force. For the first time in American history, Americans of different nationalities who had previously had little truck with each other, residing as they did in their urban ethnic enclaves, were now forced to cooperate together to survive and triumph. This resulted in the genre of World War II movies from "The Sands of Iwo Jima" to "Saving Private Ryan," replete with their stock characters—the country hick, the cowboy, the Puerto Rican, the Jewish kid from the Bronx, and the WASP—all learning to transcend their ethnic and social differences and work as a team so they could "whup 'ol Tojo and Adolph." The postwar years witnessed an unprecedented internal national migration as returning veterans now had the option to pursue economic opportunities in new regions of the country—the West and Sunbelt—where they settled in new, multiethnic suburbs, an Irishman living next to an Italian living next to an Englishman living next to a German. Where a generation or so earlier these ethnicities considered themselves separate and often hostile races, now they could cohabitate in suburban affluence while grilling bratwurst, bangers, and sausage side by side at the weekend neighborhood barbecue. Thus, the rise of ethnic toleration, coupled with rising social prosperity (trickling, albeit slowly at best, even into at least some minority households), served to loosen some of the grip racism had as an institution on the American middle-class mind. The rise of nascent black middle and professional classes after the war gave African-American communities the leadership element it needed to force its demands for equality onto the national public policy stage.

Eisenhower had not sought to pursue an active racial civil rights agenda, even dismissing it as an issue during his campaign. But his appointment of a perceived social conservative in the person of California Governor Earl Warren (a decision he later regretted as one of the worst of his presidency) was to change all that. The 1954 landmark ruling by the Warren Court in *Brown v. Board of Education of Topeka* unequivocally removed the constitutional justification for eighty years of post-Civil War American apartheid. Eisenhower's immediate response to Warren's revolution was tepid, at best, pledging that he would uphold the *Brown* decision as the reigning interpretation of the Constitution but not laying out an executive program to do so. Eisenhower would not move decisively on civil rights until the confrontation in Little Rock in 1957. That confrontation, however, from Eisenhower's viewpoint, had as much to do with federalism and chain of command as it did with civil rights. In denying admission for blacks to Little Rock High School, the Governor of Arkansas had deliberately violated federal law, thereby summoning the poltergeist of state nullification of federal law that the Civil War had theoretically exorcised. In calling out the Arkansas National Guard—part of the federal military system—to enforce his defiance, the governor had essentially thrown the gauntlet right at the feet of the commander in chief. Just days before, Eisenhower had reluctantly signed into law a voting rights act that he had himself introduced and championed. The law called for the creation of a new national civil rights commission with the mandate to investigate and penalize states and individuals that sought to violate civil rights of minorities. Eisenhower was reluctant in signing (the first civil rights legislation in eighty-two years), unambitious as it ultimately was, as its enforcement mechanisms had been seriously watered down by a coalition of southern Democrats and western Republicans (the future grand coalition of the Reagan revolution). While the vote foreshadowed the coming realignment of the Republican Party, for Eisenhower it was just another reminder of the intransigence of even members of the party of Lincoln when it came to meaningful advancement of civil rights.

The Arkansas incident brought Eisenhower to the moment he had feared ever since the handing down of the *Brown* decision three years earlier: a southern state again in outright defiance of federal law. Eisenhower first attempted to resolve the crisis through direct discussion with Governor Orval Fabous. When that failed and Fabous continued in his defiance, the president felt compelled to act. Proclaiming that federal law could not be flouted by anyone, Eisenhower nationalized the Arkansas Guard and also dispatched regular army troops to the southern capitol to reassert federal supremacy. The following day, escorted by the U.S. military, black students enrolled at the high school, and an army of protestors simply dispersed. Eisenhower's success in defusing what could have been a twentieth century equivalent of Fort Sumner has been downplayed by most modern historians. One might argue, however, that on the hot August day in Arkansas, it was the fact that many of the men in uniform—both guardsmen and regular army—had served under Eisenhower a decade before that tipped the charged balance to a peaceful conclusion.

While Eisenhower signed a follow-up civil rights bill in 1960, for the remainder of his presidency he adopted a much more passive approach to the issue, leaving it to play out its natural course towards a gradual resolution, in his hope, to slowly fester, as reality would actually have it.

Ironically, given his professional background, Eisenhower was ultimately less successful in achieving his foreign policy goals. While he achieved his primary goal of avoiding a direct and devastating confrontation with the Soviet Union, he was less successful in moving U.S./Russian relations to a fundamentally more stable foundation or in establishing a foundation for U.S. hegemony that could last for the balance of the century. Eisenhower chose to deal with the Soviet Union the way he dealt with most seemingly intractable problems (such as civil rights) by a deliberate denial that a state of crisis occurred, selectively ignoring the problem while simultaneously optimistically expecting the problem to resolve itself favorably at some point in the future. Thus, for Eisenhower, the existence of the Soviet Union had to be taken as a given. An effort to directly challenge the communist regime could only lead to war and likely mutual atomic devastation. The first hydrogen bomb had been tested in November 1, 1952, just three days before his election. The significance of the event was never lost on Eisenhower across his presidency.

For Eisenhower, the big question of the cold war was not how to defeat communism but how to co-exist with it until its own internal limitations brought on its inevitable collapse. To this end, Eisenhower's foreign policy sat directly between the isolationist wing of the Republican Party represented by the soon to be deceased Robert Taft and the war-hawk wing soon to be represented by the rising Arizona star, Barry Goldwater. While embracing the general strategy of containment as developed under Truman, especially in terms of its reliance on multilateral alliances, Eisenhower also backed away from the more aggressive aspects of the Truman Doctrine and sought to avoid the direct application of American military power, something his successors would be far less hesitant to do. Thus, like his domestic policy, Eisenhower's foreign policy tended to lack flash, making it look plodding and even reactive at the time, but that lack of flash kept gun muzzles from flashing as well.

Eisenhower's first significant foreign policy success was to deliver on his campaign promise and visit Korea (a public relations coup). More substantively, the former general brought to the Korean peace table war-making credentials that were fully recognized by the North Koreans. His credibility as a warrior secure, Eisenhower's subsequent threat to the North Koreans to deploy the full might of the United States on the peninsula should peace not be forthcoming, even presumably to the level of nuclear weapons, convinced the reluctant communist regime to sign a armistice by the summer of 1953. Removing Korea from the global chessboard left one less crisis that might disrupt the development of more stable relations with the Soviet state. The death of Stalin in the spring of 1953 removed another, giving the U.S. an opening to establish a new relationship with the new Soviet leadership. U.S. relations with post-Stalin Russia got off to a rough start following the crushing of East German protestors after the tyrant's death. By the summer of 1955, a summit would be held in Geneva between the leaders of the last war's big four powers (the U.S., Britain, France, and the U.S.S.R.). Eisenhower had great hopes that this first meeting with the new Soviet leader, Nikita Khrushchev, would lead to a significant breakthrough in thawing relations with the communist bloc, but early on discussions bogged down over all the minutia in which Soviet diplomats reveled. Disappointed with the lack of progress at the summit, Eisenhower stunned both the Soviets and the world by making a proposal to establish complete bilateral military transparency for both the U.S. and U.S.S.R.: the Open Skies program. Each side would, under his proposal, exchange blueprints of their military bases and open their airspace to routine aerial inspection to guarantee that neither side might be angling for a first strike upon the other. Taken to be a spur of the moment, heart-felt offer by the president, the proposal had actually been the product of skillful stage-managing by Eisenhower. This was also a hallmark of the Eisenhower style—the ability to execute well-planned strategies while making them seem unexpected and off the cuff. While the proposals were ultimately rejected by the Soviets, caught off guard by it as Khrushchev was, the gambit at least made Khrushchev more wary of the old war leader. And while it did not lead to a permanent détente between the two sides, the Geneva summit did move the U.S. and Soviet Union tentatively towards "peaceful coexistence," with the two sides agreeing to work cooperatively on resolving various disputes, particularly the recognition of a neutral Austria that allowed ten years of joint military occupation to end.

Despite both foreign and domestic pressure, Eisenhower avoided a significant U.S. intervention in the long-roiling swamp of Vietnam. Refusing to intervene to save the ill-fated French after the disaster of Dien Bien Phu in 1954 (rebuffing French requests for the loan of an atomic bomb or two for use against Ho Chi Minh and his guerillas), the administration pushed for a partition of Vietnam after Ho Chi Minh triumphed in national elections but did not seek a large scale U.S. role in protecting the newly-created South Vietnam. Unlike Lyndon Johnson, Eisenhower deliberately sought out alternative viewpoints over Vietnam, listening to interventionists argue that a communist victory in South Vietnam would set off a domino effect across the region, and listening to more conservative voices warning against turning Vietnam into Korea redux—the U.S. getting drawn into a land war in Asia that might trigger a larger war, once again, with China. Rather than directly Americanize the defense of the new Diem regime, Eisenhower employed a measured strategy of deploying limited numbers of American military advisors to the region. Having dealt with the problem at hand, Eisenhower gave limited additional attention to the war-torn country, leaving it to simmer on low until it would boil over during the administrations of his immediate successors. Thus, Eisenhower's fears over Vietnam proved to be prophetic within a decade.

Eisenhower also resisted substantial domestic pressure to take a much harder line with communist China—a stance that could easily have led to renewed conflict in east Asia. In late summer 1954, tensions with Red China mounted as communist forces engaged in the shelling of two Taiwanese islands, Quemoy and Matsu, possibly as a preliminary move to an outright invasion of the Nationalist Chinese stronghold. Resisting public and political pressure for a show of force against China, including possibly even a naval blockade of the mainland that might lead to direct war, Eisenhower opted for caution, arguing that during crises, "The hard way is to have the courage to be patient." Rather than rushing in with guns blazing, the man who had seen global war first hand understood that measured use of force is the hallmark of a superpower. Early the following year, Eisenhower issued his "Formosa Doctrine," a vague piece of rhetoric that asked Congress to essentially give the president a blank check to take whatever steps he felt necessary to protect American interests over Taiwan but without spelling out what steps, if any, the U.S. would take to do so. The resulting international uncertainty over U.S. intentions in east Asia was precisely what Eisenhower had sought. The ambiguous American position kept the U.S. from having to make a hard commitment to defend Taiwan, which the U.S. might actually have had to back down on if presented with the reality of a real shooting war in the region. Yet, the policy introduced enough uncertainty into the equation to give the communist Chinese second thoughts about the efficacy of escalating the crisis to the next level. Eisenhower's China policy of deliberate ambiguity allowed the crisis to die out from inertia and put off the need for any further definitive actions on Taiwan for more than a decade, by which time both the U.S. and China were in better position to work out a new status for Taiwan.

Eisenhower's foreign policy was underscored by a continued commitment to the internationalist framework for postwar security that emerged from the Roosevelt and Truman years. The critical understanding reached by Allied war leaders was that the roots of World War II lay in the political instabilities left from World War I and the resulting economic instabilities that led to economic depression, a collapse of global trade, and the resulting rise of fascism in the 1920s and war in the 1930s. In 1944 at Bretton Woods, New Hampshire, the Allied powers agreed to the creation of a more stable postwar global order premised on the development of global institutions capable of maintaining political and economic stability. Thus, Bretton Woods gave rise to the alphabet soup of Keystone Economic International Organizations (KEIOs): the International Monetary Fund to operate as something of a global central bank, providing monetary liquidity to national governments in times of economic duress; the World Bank to provide capital, first to war-ravaged Europe and later to the developing world to foster economic development; and the General

Agreement on Tariffs and Trade (GATT) process, to lower trade barriers and increase global trade and, thereby, global interdependency. While these international organizations—the brainchildren of the United States—would later come under increased suspicion and mistrust by the American public and even American presidential administrations, Eisenhower saw commitment to this multilateral framework as key to global and American security. Without any flash, these institutions operated quietly and rather efficiently in the background of the global stage for the next generation. The fixed exchange system, whereby the dollar was pegged to the price of gold and all other major currencies pegged to the dollar, provided a level of confidence and stability in global markets that had not been seen since before the Great War when the pound sterling was truly king. (Alas, for those who long for such simpler days, the realities of the contemporary complex global market make a fixed exchange regime highly impractical if not outright impossible.) Meanwhile, the World Bank successfully participated in the rebuilding of Europe, and multiple rounds of GATT between 1952 and 1960 substantially reduced tariffs and increased trade between the major powers. Eisenhower's commitment to forgoing large tax cuts and focusing instead on deficit reduction was in part precipitated by his understanding that large deficits and resulting economic inflation would weaken the dollar in its role as the global stabilizing currency.

Eisenhower remained committed to the United Nations as a principle forum for global discussion. In 1958, Eisenhower went to the UN and made his famous "Atoms for Peace" proposal: the idealistic, if ultimately ill-fated, program that sought to move global use of atomic materials from war to economic development. The International Atomic Energy Commission created by Eisenhower's proposal sought to place stockpiles of the world's fissionable materials under international supervision. Eisenhower's speech was received with unprecedented enthusiasm by the UN audience, Soviets included. Ultimately, though, Russian cooperation with the program faltered and collapsed, the victim of its own paranoia as to the hostile intentions of all non-communist states. Admittedly, Eisenhower saw the UN as a tool to be used to advance American interests, but the American interests he sought to advance were ones predicated on international cooperation rather than American unilateralism. Thus, idealistic proposals like Atoms for Peace and Open Skies were not driven by secret strategies to advance American interests but were the product of Eisenhower's middle American optimism that held that, under the right circumstances, all of humanity could learn to cooperate.

This did not mean Eisenhower was above more unilateral actions when global security was involved. When the British and French attempted one last act of imperial grandiosity during the Suez Crisis in 1956, the Eisenhower position was resolute. The 1950 Tripartite Declaration had committed the U.S. and the two foreign colonial powers to maintaining the postwar status quo of the Middle East, including Egyptian control of the Suez Canal. British and French efforts, with Israeli contrivance, to take control of Suez from Egypt threatened to upset this status quo and ran the risk of provoking a direct confrontation between the U.S. and the Soviet Union, which was making hostile anti-western, pro-Arab noises over the incident. Eisenhower's simple response was to directly—in terms surprisingly blunt for a president more comfortable with policies nuanced to the point of uncertainty—tell his British and French counterparts to back off. The Suez crisis reaffirmed that, even in a multilateral framework, the U.S. was the dominant partner whose will could not be ignored.

Eisenhower's foreign policy was constituted on the belief that an "American" world in which political and economic freedoms flourished was the desired and natural destiny for all people. His views of "American exceptionalism," however, unlike those of neo-conservatives forty years later, recognized a profound limit on the ability of America to achieve such a world by unilateral use of American power. Eisenhower understood the use of American force to resolve all international issues to American satisfaction—be it achieving total victory in North Korea, cowing the Chinese with the U.S. Navy over Taiwan, escalating American commitment in Vietnam, or pushing for head-to-head confrontation with the Soviet Union over Hungary or U-2 planes—could create great risks to American stability and even survival. Moreover, he understood that while political power might, as Mao Zedong said, come from the barrel of a gun, democracy and democratic ideas do not. These ideals grow over time by the creation of a sustainable environment—one marked by economic and social development as well as the creation of stable political institutions—amenable to their development. Both Japan and Germany had had an extended experience in the nineteenth century with the development of nascent ideals of democracy before their subversion by radical ideologies in the twentieth century. Thus, the development of stable postwar democracy was more readily obtainable in these countries than in the emerging post-colonial societies and even more so compared to those societies still under the totalitarian yoke. Forcing democracy in these areas could only be accomplished through direct military means, which in the evolving age of nuclear "MADness" (mutually assured destruction) was simply an unacceptable alternative. Eisenhower understood that a stable peace depended upon the credible willingness of the U.S. to exert force from time to time. In 1957, witnessing a rising wave of anti-western and potentially pro-Soviet nationalist movements in the Middle East, the administration announced the extension of the Truman Doctrine explicitly to the region. Under this new "Eisenhower Doctrine," the U.S. committed to sending military and economic aid to any Middle Eastern nation requesting it to bolster that region against communist aggression. Under this doctrine U.S. Marines were dispatched to Lebanon the following year, achieving a much more successful stabilization of the country than would occur with a similar intervention two decades later. Similarly, when mainland China again threatened Taiwan militarily in 1958, Eisenhower was willing to show the flag by sending in the U.S. fleet, calling the Chinese bluff, yet resisting pressures by both his joint chiefs and Chiang Kai-Shek to take China on more directly.

Eisenhower was content to create a stable multilateral international system to keep the Allies allied, while relying on the stick of containment and the carrot of economic opportunity through cooperation to wear the communist bloc down. A combination of international institutions like the UN, multilateral security organizations like NATO, and the measured use of American unilateral power were sufficient to maintain the global peace and resolve international crises on a one-by-one basis. Eisenhower's cautious approach left most of the underlying causes of these crises—like Taiwan, Israel, the Korean peninsula, and the whole fabric of the cold war—unaddressed and liable to flare up as new crises in the future. For Eisenhower, that was a fair enough trade-off: achieving stability now with the optimistic hope that the underlying causes would resolve themselves favorably later. Moreover, as a republic, Eisenhower realized the United States was ill-suited to any global strategy in which it would set itself up as a truly overbearing hegemon on the model of Rome or Britain (or the global empires dreamed of by Nazi Germany, Imperial Japan, or the Soviet Union for that matter). To exert a more powerful and determinant influence on world events required the creation of a new kind of America, one whose resources were mobilized to a permanent war state and whose national will was bent towards global domination.

Eisenhower's televised 1960 farewell address was directed at precisely this point. If the U.S. were to affect a global empire with itself at the helm, would not its domestic Republican political institutions necessarily give way to more authoritarian tendencies, as had been the fate of Rome? And was not the huge and unprecedented size of the American cold war military coupled with the raising clamor of members of his own party for a more assertive use of this power America's first steps along this Roman road? Thus, Eisenhower warned the American people:

> In the councils of government, we must guard against the acquisition of unwarranted influence, whether sought or unsought, by the military industrial complex. The potential for the disastrous rise of misplaced power exists and will persists.

For Eisenhower the danger poised by this military-industrial complex—the dependence of large sectors of the American economy on a cash-rich military—was not that of an imminent military coup à la the novel and film "Seven Days in May." The real danger was an America comfortable with being on a constant war footing and, therefore, an American public more willing to allow military adventurism in foreign policy because the large standing military insulated them, at least to some degree, from truly bearing the "soldier's pack" burden of such policies. Future chief executives, having such military power at their fingertips, would become increasingly willing to use it, proving the dictum if the toy's in the toy box the kid's going to play with it. The danger, as Eisenhower foretold in 1960, was that of a nation and president accustomed to such imperial uses of American force—even if for good reasons—and imperial tendencies abroad could become imperial tendencies at home.

Such would be the prophetic case with the next three administrations and the debacle of Vietnam. Kennedy, Johnson, and Nixon could commit increasing levels of force to Vietnam, with congressional acquiescence, precisely because they had a military on the shelf. America could fight a bloody decade-long war a half planet away at the cost of almost 60,000 American lives without having to move to a true war economy and without significant impact on their quality of life. It would only be in the late 1960s, as college draft deferments expired and substantial numbers of young men from middle and upper class households (at least those who could not afford graduate school or could not finagle an appointment to the National Guard) that the public turned against the war, but even rising public opposition could not end a conflict the president had troops already on hand to fight. So, too, would be the irony that, even as the cold war ended, the U.S. would end up in its first shooting war in almost two decades in Iraq. Once again, both George H.W. Bush and his son would be able, as presidents, to dispatch hundreds of thousands of troops to the other side of the planet with no congressional action necessary precisely because of the large standing army at their beck and call. Whether such tendencies will ultimately "endanger our liberties and democratic processes," as Eisenhower warned, still remains to be seen.

A golden age is defined as a period of peace, prosperity, and happiness, and on the whole, the Eisenhower years qualify for this label more than do those of any modern American president. If this prosperity did not extend equally across all segments of society, it should also be remembered that it was in the 1950s that, for the first time since Lincoln's assassination, all segments of society might at least dream of inclusion in the American dream of middle-class prosperity even if that dream might be years or decades from realization. Martin Luther King Jr.'s dream was born of the quiet, calm public sleep of the Eisenhower 1950s. During the 1950s, the United States strode the world like a colossus, confronted by a Soviet Union still too uncertain of its capacity to resume pressure on the periphery of the American empire, a China tripping and falling flat after Mao's failed "Great Leap." Under the Bretton Woods framework, the dollar was global king, American industry and technology reigned supreme, trade was growing, and global finance was still in the hands of old school bankers for whom foreign exchange was simply a means to balance accounts between nations and junk bonds were precisely junk. Stability, underwritten by the umbrella of American hegemony, reigned. Under this umbrella a Europe (or, at least, its western region) once locked in fratricidal conflict saw economic prosperity, market integration, political stability, and such peace as was once only dreamed possible as being created through the barrel of a gun.

A golden age, however, is only recognized in retrospect, after the age has already turned to brass. While Eisenhower's presidency may be measured precisely by the restraint with which power was used, his successors would show far less restraint, inserting the presidency more aggressively and divisively into domestic politics and inserting American power more aggressively and less successfully into global politics. The multilateral framework that Eisenhower helped create, strengthen, and expand would be strained and, in some cases, shredded by future administrations pursuing narrower international and domestic political agendas. Moreover, as the twentieth century played out, America's relative strategic advantage—both economically and militarily—vis-à-vis the world declined even as its advantage over any one individual nation reached unprecedented heights. Today the ability of the American tail to unilaterally wag the global dog without increasingly overt and costly resort to military force has become increasingly problematic. By most measures, Americans today are far better off materially than they were in the 1950s. But the increasing size of television screens is only one measure of social welfare. America posted an unprecedented and unmatched expansion of standard of living between WWII and 1973. While Eisenhower did not create this prosperity, he effectively managed it. The 1950s represented the economic triumph of the American industrial middle class following its political triumph with the New Deal. Americans by the 1950s expected and witnessed a generation of expanding opportunity. Just as the shift from an agrarian to industrial economy undercut the prosperity and fortunes of the nineteenth century American agrarian middle class, the shift in the latter twentieth century from an industrial to a post-industrial service economy has put severe strains on the old industrial middle class. Since 1973, American households have witnessed increased pressures on economic aspirations, requiring more hours worked, higher consumer debt loads, greater employment and retirement uncertainties, and diminished wage expectations. In short, while the material standard of living of the households of today's maturing baby boomers greatly exceed that of their parents, the future for boomers and, more importantly, their children appear far less certain. A sign of the times, in 1954, social security was expanding. In 2004, there are serious questions as to its long-term viability.

Thus, the presidency of Dwight Eisenhower represents a dividing line in the modern presidency. From Teddy Roosevelt through Franklin Roosevelt, the power of both the United States and the presidency can be seen as growing—in some ways astronomically—as America emerged as the world's dominant power. Two world wars, unprecedented economic upheaval, and the political earthquake of the New Deal had transformed the nation into the quintessential modern industrial society and transformed the presidency into the quintessential modern executive. Eisenhower and, to a lesser extent, Harry Truman presided over the consolidation of the new role the nation now played in the world and the president now played in the nation. Subsequent presidents would fight to preserve the preeminent position of both nation and presidency, often losing in that struggle.

That Eisenhower seemed a kindly if disengaged leader letting things run on automatic was not beside the point: it was precisely the core point of the Eisenhower years. Future presidents would increasingly resort to employing the power of their office in a "shock and awe" campaign to overwhelm (as opposed to cooperate with) political opposition, attempting to elevate the position and power of their office to such an extent that pundits and historians would warn of the rise of a new "imperial presidency" that sought to run over any and all political opposition. To this end, presidents from Johnson onwards would employ the skills of media manipulation to create images of a powerful president from swinging their pets by the ears to landing on carrier decks in a flight suit, turning Teddy Roosevelt's "bully pulpit" into garish neon-lit political advertisement. A man who had spent most of his life in uniform, Eisenhower never needed to resort to wearing one to establish himself as a bona fide national leader. His credentials having been fully established by a lifetime of public service, his leadership abilities were simply taken as a given by both the public and political class, allowing him to achieve maximum political results with seemingly minimal political muscle, thus giving the impression of being politically disengaged while achieving an impressive policy legacy.

The Eisenhower Presidency: A Negative Assessment

The chief weaknesses of the Eisenhower years were sins of omission rather than commission. Across his presidency, Eisenhower was willing to throw himself into efforts that were already well established and enjoyed substantial levels of public support, such as Social Security expansion or creation of a federal highway system. Eisenhower was not, however, a risk taker by nature (his final decision to deploy the D-Day invasion force in the face of uncertain weather notwithstanding). His military training had taught him victory occurred because of overwhelming force and detailed planning and not because of random acts of heroism on the battlefield. This tendency in thought was what made him a natural for rising up through the bureaucratic, as opposed to the warrior, sides of the U.S. military. Caution in risk taking and challenging institutional norms resulted in Eisenhower avoiding becoming fully engaged in several critical issues during his presidency to the diminishment of his presidency.

First amongst these was Eisenhower's refusal to directly engage McCarthyism. McCarthy had earned Eisenhower's wrath when, on the president's second day in office, the senator moved to block what should have been a straightforward confirmation of a noted conservative to a State Department post on the grounds that the nominee had defended another State Department official whom McCarthy had earlier branded as a "communist." While Eisenhower prevailed with the Republican leadership in getting his nominee confirmed, it was his first direct experience with the red-baiting senator from Wisconsin. Eisenhower personally loathed McCarthy and despised his methods and their implication as government policy in a republic; yet, he refrained from directly taking McCarthy on, preferring a policy of waiting for the senator to either fade away or spontaneously self destruct (as would be the actual case). Eisenhower argued he would not lower the dignity of the presidency to engage McCarthy directly and expressed his personal distaste in even having to think about the man. Such rationalizations, however, seem weak at best. Yet Eisenhower continued his public silence on McCarthy, even as the senator challenged more of his nominees. Eisenhower even remained silent during the infamous Army hearings in which the Senator essentially challenged the loyalty of everyone who had served in positions of authority in the Army from George Washington to George Marshall. While Eisenhower stood by, dozens of careers were tarnished and put in jeopardy.

Eisenhower could claim some credit for deliberately withholding information from McCarthy's Army inquisition and thereby derailing the effectiveness of the hearings. His silence could have been taken for high principles, but it also could have been taken for tacit endorsement or, more directly, as a sign of weakness: a president cowered by a publicly popular senator running a campaign based on fear and emotion at the expense of due process of law. That McCarthy was ultimately out of his league in taking on the U.S. Army and, as a consequence, lost the public support upon which his demagoguery was dependent is a matter of great fortune to the Republic. If McCarthy had been more temperate (in both his own emotion and alcohol consumption) in the absence of the opposition of an effective and popular chief executive, he might well have become the American equivalent of the Roman Dictator Sulla, whose reign of fear effectively ended the great age of the Roman Republic forty years before Caesar. In any event, Eisenhower lucked out, and McCarthy did self-destruct but not before great harm had been done to American society and government.

Eisenhower's refusal to become a more active champion of civil rights looms as an even larger failure than his silence on McCarthyism. His refusal to move aggressively on civil rights can be rationalized at least in part by the limitations of his own development. Born in a southern state barely a generation after the civil war, raised in a middle America that was not just racist but of "pure race"—few African Americans resided in the Kansas of Eisenhower's childhood—and coming to professional maturity in the segregated institution of the military, Eisenhower lacked any frame of reference with which to adjust to the concepts of racial desegregation and true equality emerging from the Warren Court's *Brown* decision. That he did not then try to create such a personal framework out of whole cloth was one of his greatest executive and personal failures.

In Eisenhower's defense, it was true that neither the Republican Party nor the Democratic Party were tremendous stalwarts of desegregation in the 1950s. Democrats, in particular, were limited in embracing civil rights by the great power of their southern Democrat American apartheid wing. Indeed, the tension of reconciling this wing with more liberal northern and midwestern Democrats eventually proved untenable, resulting in the great Reagan realignment moving the south into the increasingly socially conservative Republican camp by 1980. Only after being either purged of its southern traditionalist wing by defections (such as Strom Thurmond) to the Republicans or by recantment of past segregationist values (as with Robert Byrd) did the Democrats emerge as a coherent voice in support of civil rights. As comedian Mort Sahl observed during the 1956 presidential race, however, the difference between the two major parties, especially on segregation, were minor indeed. According to Sahl, Eisenhower wanted to pursue desegregation "carefully," while Stevenson wanted to do so "cautiously." This led Sahl to observe that in the Baskin Robbins of American politics there were really only two flavors— Democrat vanilla and slightly creamier Republican French vanilla.

That Eisenhower was unable to come up with a new Neapolitan or rainbow sherbet flavor of American politics that could overcome racism with appeals to America's true liberal values is understandable, but hardly forgivable. To be a truly great leader is to see where the nation must go and then chart out the path to bring it there. Eisenhower's inability to do so on matters of race, more than any other failure, is what keeps him off the list of the top three or four presidents in history.

The civil rights movement was just one (though the most significant) manifestation of the profound social change America was undergoing in the postwar period. Eisenhower, a product of the early twentieth century, was simply not well-disposed to deal with a nation that had come out of World War II a far different society than as it had gone in. Beneath the stable façade of the Eisenhower years, the seeds of the 1960s social alienation and upheaval were already sprouting. In 1947, in Hollister, California, a group of disaffected young veterans riding motorcycles had unleashed what was to become the youth rebellion a decade hence. From beatniks to Elvis to rock and roll to "I Was a Teenage Werewolf," youth alienation was increasingly on display. From "Death of a Salesman" to "On the Waterfront," similar angst amongst the parents of the day could also be found. Just as the Great War had shaken European faith in the inevitability of European hegemony, the trials and tribulation of depression and war had shaken some of America's faith in its own manifest destiny. While the 1950s prosperity did much to paper over this angst, it remained a developing force beneath the calm, Sunday church and dinner-around-the-family-dining-table Norman Rockwell image of Eisenhower's America.

Indeed, one of Eisenhower's only nod to the quiet anxiety Americans were feeling as the social teutonic plates shifted beneath their feet was his proposal that Congress insert the words "under God" into the national pledge of allegiance. Eisenhower was not a particularly church-going man himself. He only regularly attended a congregation after his election as president. He even once dressed down aide Harold Stassen after Stassen asked him to put a little more religion into a speech saying, "I don't want to deliver a sermon." Yet, by 1954 Eisenhower felt compelled to ask Congress to add the two words to the pledge, believing it would help distinguish America as a society of faith from the ultimate secular society, the Soviet Union. (The following year, the phrase "In God We Trust" was introduced on federal currency.) While the phrase seemed innocuous at the time, it would grow to become an increasing focus of debate in the battle between secular and religious values that came to dominate the American social divide by the early twenty-first century. Eisenhower's introduction of the words, "under God," in retrospect, marked the true legitimate emergence of this divide in modern American culture—one only needs brand name a product when competitors have emerged to challenge the product's market share.

Eisenhower can be criticized on other fronts, such as his inability to ultimately rein in domestic spending, particularly on inefficient agricultural subsidies. His administration was also open to the charge of business favoritism, given the heavy representation of corporate managers in the highest reaches of government. Yet, where subsequent administrations with equal, if not greater, levels of business penetration of the councils of government would be subject to criticisms of crony capitalism if not outright corruption, Eisenhower's administration was remarkably scandal free. (The one exception, of course, being the election year scandal involving his running mate, Richard

Nixon, who went on to survive eight years as vice president despite almost being dumped by Ike in 1956.) Yet, these criticisms pale in comparison to the general domestic prosperity of the 1950s and pale even further in light of Eisenhower's real failings on civil rights.

While Eisenhower succeeded in his core foreign policy goal of avoiding direct confrontation with the Soviet bloc, he dealt less successfully with a number of crises around the periphery of American power. Khrushchev's de-Stalinization, for example, offered promise to U.S./Soviet relations, but the resulting instability it produced across the Soviet empire should have been anticipated by both the Soviets and Americans. The toppling of the daunting figure of Stalin the Terrible led directly to protests by workers and students in Hungary, which exploded into quasi-revolution by October 1956. Encouraged by statements of support from the Eisenhower administration, a new regime led by the communist reformer Imre Nagy pursued a policy of Hungarian independence, abolishing the one-party system, demanding Soviet troops leave the country, and announcing its international neutrality and withdrawal from the Soviet Warsaw Pact. Confronted by outright rebellion in Hungary, Khrushchev was again forced to resort to old methods; the Soviet Red Army invaded and deposed Nagy, killing thousands of Hungarian civilians who fought the invaders in the process. As with the case of George H. W. Bush and his ill-advised encouragement of Shi'ite Muslim revolt in southern Iraq in 1991, once the tanks of repression rolled over the demonstrators, the pro-democracy rhetoric of the Eisenhower administration was replaced with stony silence. While advancing democracy was a cornerstone ideological goal of the nation, neither Eisenhower nor the nation had any desire to enter yet another bloody (and possibly civilization ending) war to achieve that goal. The result, however, was to make the United States look hypocritical and to reassure the world of Soviet mastery over its European colonies.

Eisenhower was also ultimately unsuccessful in his quest to establish something akin to peace with the Soviet Union. In part, this was because the Soviets, even after Stalin, had little interest in forming a lasting peace, believing as they did that ultimate victory in the war against capitalism was inevitable. While it only takes one party to make war, it takes all parties to make peace. Khrushchev sought to establish the Soviet Union as a capable military counterpart to American-led NATO, which necessitated a continued military arms build-up, especially in atomic weapons. While the United States actually enjoyed a comfortable superiority in strategic weapons (the precise gap Khrushchev was desperately trying to close), Eisenhower's failure to match the Soviet arms build-up, bullet for bullet, worked against his claims to be advancing peace from a position of strength. While Kennedy ran against a (erroneous, as it turned out) "missile gap" as a legacy of the lack of defense spending by Eisenhower, it can be argued that Khrushchev himself felt emboldened to push Kennedy over Cuba precisely because of a perception that the U.S., under and after Eisenhower, was truly not ready to pay any price to maintain dominance.

The U-2 crisis in the spring of 1960 ended any last hopes Eisenhower had for a breakthrough in U.S./Soviet relations. Eisenhower refused to "come clean" on the existence of top secret U.S. reconnaissance flights over the Soviet Union, believing that a U-2 plane the Soviets had shot down on May 1, 1960 had been destroyed and the pilot killed, leaving no real evidence of its existence. The Soviets parading of the captured pilot and revelation that the administration that had sought "open skies" over both the U.S. and Soviet Union had been secretly violating Soviet airspace for years did much to reinforce Soviet propaganda that the U.S. was not to be trusted and also tarnished Eisenhower's image of competency.

The Eisenhower administration was also unsuccessful in winning the hearts and minds of third world peoples. The U.S.'s clear strategic preference during the cold war was to support its former wartime allies, Britain and France, within limits. Eisenhower had pulled the plug on the last real vestige of old European imperialism by aborting the Anglo-French Suez venture in 1956. But Eisenhower did so not out of support for Egyptian nationalism but out of fear that peripheral conflicts such as this had the potential to lead to a direct confrontation between the superpowers. While the U.S. was in a strategic partnership with Western Europe, Eisenhower was determined to be the dominant partner. Henceforth, the U.S. decided where and when it would be safe for the West to intervene in the periphery. But the clear alignment of the U.S. with the former colonial powers could only alienate America in the eyes of many peoples of the developing world over the decades ahead, especially as the hopes of post-colonial independence faded before the realities of the poverty a century or more of colonization had done little to alleviate and, in many ways, much to aggravate.

Eisenhower's third world agenda was driven far more by cold war concerns, supporting regimes friendly to American interests and, in the cases of Iran in 1953 and Guatemala in 1954, overthrowing regimes—even democratically elected ones—that seemed contrary to those interests. Thus, incrementally through interventions around the periphery, Eisenhower's policies had the unintended consequence of increasingly recasting the United States from being an ally of the weak and oppressed to being an active oppressor—the new neo-colonial heir to the old European masters. Nowhere was this turn-around in developing world attitudes more evident than in the Middle East. While Eisenhower's intervention in Lebanon attempted to demonstrate continued American willingness to intervene against communists, coupled with the U.S.-engineered coup in Iran three years before and U.S. support for the newly-created state of Israel, the Arab street now saw the U.S. as the new British: an imperial presence.

The Soviets took clear advantage of this climate change, launching a major diplomatic offensive to win friends amongst the newly independent states of Africa, the Middle East, and Asia, portraying themselves as the natural friend and ally of nations that had endured the plight of capitalist colonialism. Russia sided with Egypt against Britain and France during the 1956 Suez crisis, and anti-imperialist revolutionaries such as Castro in Cuba and Ho Chi Minh in Vietnam. Eisenhower's focus on securing American strategic position through alliance with Europe and Japan while either ignoring or overwhelming third world nations established a pattern of American cold war imperialism that would ultimately underwrite the single greatest threat to American security interests by the end of the century—third world radicalism.

Eisenhower's waffling over Cuba was also ineffective, failing as it did to either keep a pro-American regime—albeit a loathsome one under the dictator Batista—in power or to win over the new Castro-revolutionaries to America's sphere. Eisenhower was ultimately right to refuse to intervene to save the corrupt and ineffective Batista regime. Uncertain as to the direction Castro would take the island nation, Eisenhower was at first neutral towards Cuba's new regime. When it became clear the pro-Soviet communist elements were gaining the upper hand in the new regime, American policy hardened against Castro, and the perception grew in the administration that the bearded revolutionary must go. After severing ties with the new regime, the administration greenlighted the CIA to train an army of Cuban exiles, using the model of U.S.-covertly-assisted guerillas to overthrow a hostile regime that had been successfully deployed in Guatemala in 1954. But Cuba in 1961 was not Guatemala, and Castro was not a tepidly popular leader like Jacobo Arbenz. While the Bay of Pigs fiasco exploded in the face of John Kennedy, its fallout blackened the reputation of Eisenhower as well. Eisenhower's willingness to embrace selective regime change in Latin America served to undermine much of the good will towards its northern neighbor that Latin American states had begun to develop since Franklin Roosevelt's adoption of the "Good Neighbor Policy" in the 1930s.

The presidency, by Eisenhower, had emerged as a far more important and, subsequently, powerful institution than had ever been envisioned by the framers of the Constitution. By the 1950s, the president was seen as the guardian of national prosperity, the guardian of national stability, and, with the United States' emergence as the preeminent national superpower, the guardian of global stability (and, in the nuclear age, even human survival). Given the fantastic increase of attention on the office and the awesome responsibility its occupant now held, it was unavoidable that postwar presidents increasingly found the traditional system of checks and balances too constraining and cumbersome to respect to the letter of the law, that is, if they were to effectively accomplish the tasks mandated by the American electorate and the global community. Both Congress and the courts are quintessential eighteenth century institutions created to provide deliberate and, above all, slow reflection on all actions of government, thereby guaranteeing the Enlightenment doctrine that the government that governs least governs best. In an age when global markets could increasingly become unhinged in days or nuclear armageddon could be unleashed (be it by nation states or terrorists) in minutes, such ponderous processes directly undercut the ability of a president to respond to fast-changing events. Eisenhower, for example, experienced more foreign policy crises—from U-2s to Cuba to Taiwan—in his eight years than did all American presidents from the Civil War to World War I.

That modern presidents should seek ways to "cut corners" on such traditional restrictions on presidential power was, thus, largely inevitable (unless one considered a wholesale reform of the American checks-and-balance system to something more akin to a French-style presidency that grants a president far more independence in foreign policy than an American president is constitutionally allocated). But while historians usually lay the blame for the emergence of such "imperial presidents" on Richard Nixon or, perhaps, Lyndon Johnson, it is well to remember that it was under "plodding" Eisenhower that tools of manipulating Congress by obfuscation and controlling foreign policy by executive order were first effectively honed.

Moreover, Eisenhower's actions provided a precedent for further adventurism by subsequent presidents and led to the development of precisely the form of imperial mindset he had warned against in his farewell address. The precedent Eisenhower established with the Formosa Doctrine—Congress granting the chief executive essentially a blank check to conduct a foreign policy—would be used by subsequent presidents to legitimize wars from Vietnam to Afghanistan. When octogenarian Robert Byrd failed in 2001 in his attempt to prevent Congress from granting George W. Bush a blank check to fight a global war on terror, he returned to an earlier Congress' granting of a similar blank check to Lyndon Johnson with the Gulf of Tonkin Resolution thereby producing the Vietnam quagmire, Byrd would have done well to remember that it all began with Ike.

During the 1956 campaign for
re-election, Washington, D.C.
November 1, 1956
(courtesy of Dwight D.
Eisenhower Library)

Formal Cadet Portrait,
West Point, 1915
(courtesy of Dwight D.
Eisenhower Library)

Presentation of a special citation to Dr. Jonas Salk by President Eisenhower
on April 22, 1955. Also present are Oveta Culp Hobby, Secretary of Health,
Education and Welfare, and Basil O'Connor, President of the National Foundation for Infantile Paralysis. (courtesy of Dwight D. Eisenhower Library)

Photograph of
General Dwight
D. Eisenhower by
Yoichi Okamoto
(courtesy of LBJ
Library)

During World War II, the
popular image of General
Eisenhower depicts him wearing
a well tailored, short-waisted,
smart-looking jacket, designated
officially as the "Wool Field
Jacket, M-1944." To the troops
it was known as the ETO
(European Theater of
Operations) Jacket, or even
more popularly as the
"Ike Jacket."
(courtesy of Dwight D.
Eisenhower Library)

FDR, General
Eisenhower and
General Patton in
Castelvetrano,
Sicily.
December 8, 1943
Photo credit:
FDR Presidential
Library

John Fitzgerald Kennedy
1961-1963

For most "baby-boomers" (especially those born between 1946-1950) who were teenagers during the 1960s, it is a time remembered as an "Age of Aquarius," an era, one observer noted, that heralded "a new American identity—a collective identity that will be blacker, more feminine, more oriental, more emotional, more intuitive, more exuberant—and just possibly, better than the old one." Another historian wrote that the year 1960 marked "the definitive end of the Dark Ages and the beginning of a more hopeful and democratic period." Conservative observers naturally would have a different take on the decade, arguing that it was a time of "immediate gratification and exhibitionist display," that "produced little culture" because it was an age of "intellectual rubbish" and "unrelieved excess." Yet, according to Morris Dickstein, regardless of where one is on the ideological or political spectrum, one would be hard pressed to deny that the sixties were as pivotal as the thirties "as a point of reference for the way we think and behave." Perhaps no individual was more responsible for generating the excitement, passion, and overall energy that seemed to pervade the decade than John F. Kennedy, who came to embody and personify a time of such hope and confidence in Americans' abilities to change the United States and the world for the better.

Kennedy's idealism and inspiration were so infectious that one year into his administration, a young Peace Corps (a Kennedy initiative) volunteer named Richard Goodwin (who later became one of Lyndon Baines Johnson's speech writers) exulted, "For a moment, it seemed as if the entire country, the whole spinning globe, rested, malleable and receptive, in our [the United States'] beneficent hands." If ever there was a decade in which an American family was center stage and its progeny inextricably linked with the events of their time, it was the Kennedys and the 1960s. Indeed, rarely in the history of the Republic has one family played so vital a role in shaping the politics of an era, perhaps even for a generation. The Kennedy story is even more remarkable given the fact that the family's original forebears were immigrants from one of the most impoverished and oppressed nations in Europe—Ireland.

Despite their humble beginnings, after two generations the Kennedys were well on their way to becoming one of the nation's preeminent families, whose members would come to influence national political life for several decades. Thus, in many ways the Kennedys' rise to fame and fortune was testimony writ large of the American promise that, regardless of one's background or from where one came, the United States could become a land of opportunity for all those who persevered.

In the brief incandescence of the Kennedy presidency, he is still remembered as the first Roman Catholic "ethnic" to be elected to the nation's highest office, breaking the iron tradition that the executive branch was a Protestant preserve. Kennedy's 1960 victory not only had powerful meaning for fellow Catholics, regardless of their ethnicity, but also for other minority groups: Jews, African Americans, Hispanics, and Asians. To all such groups, the election of this young, charismatic, optimistic, and energetic president marked not only the beginning of the end of a WASP-dominated political system and culture but also the resurrection of postwar liberalism, which the Eisenhower administration had less than passionately embraced or promoted. By the 1960 election (thanks in large part to the civil rights movement, which helped energize activism and the reform impulse in general), increasing numbers of Americans felt an inchoate sense of uneasiness and restlessness, of weariness with the cult of conformity and consensus that seemed to prevail, permeating both American society and the political system. Even 1950s liberalism reflected this "tempering," causing many of its more fervid proponents to worry that the blandness and tameness of the Eisenhower mystique were extending through the entire culture. As historian Richard Hofstadter noted in 1956, "Liberals are beginning to find it both natural and expedient to explore the merits and employ the rhetoric of conservatism. They find themselves far more conscious of those things they would like to preserve than they are of those things they would like to change." Long-time liberal pundit Walter Lippmann echoed Hofstadter's observation of liberal complacency, lamenting "for the first time in history the engine of social progress has run out of the fuel of discontent." As the sociocultural historian Henry Steele Commager rightly noted, "the new loyalty" above all meant "conformity . . . the uncritical and unquestioning acceptance of America as it is." Or as historian Arthur Schlesinger, Jr. worried, American society was dangerously close to becoming "one great and genuinely benevolent company town—the bland leading the bland."

In politics, Democrats appeared confused and uncertain, not knowing where to attack, where to differ from Republican moderation, or to whom to turn to for leadership. However, by 1960, the party found its "voice" again in John Kennedy, who, like few politicians of his day, shrewdly, brilliantly translated Americans' restiveness with the status quo into a call for action, a promise to get the country "moving again." To Kennedy, this meant exhorting Americans to engage in pursuits that would give their lives a larger purpose and meaning; there was more to life than the acquisition of the American dream of prosperity, security, and stability. If Americans were "bored" with suburbia and the consumer culture, then Kennedy had plenty for them to do, for the time was right to usher in a new epoch of heroism and sacrifice for the greater good of all humanity. In his now famous (if not immortal) Inaugural Address, Kennedy enjoined Americans to "Ask not what your country can do for you, but what you can do for your country. . . . Ask not what America will do for you, but what together we can do for the freedom of man." Kennedy appealed especially to the young, giving them a sense that anything was possible if only they would do their part. "We can do better," he repeatedly admonished.

Kennedy in many ways was like a Theodore Roosevelt, similar in charisma, charm, wit, optimism, and confidence in Americans to accomplish great things for the nation as well as for the world. Kennedy's personality was every bit as infectious as "Teddy's," energizing those around him to want to excel in their every undertaking: to live the strenuous, purposeful life. Finally, like TR, Kennedy was a tribune at the head of a legion of social activists and reformers (the Progressives for TR) whose responsibility it was to uplift the downtrodden and dispossessed, leading them to the "promised land" of equal opportunity and justice for all. Perhaps more than anything else, it was Kennedy's charisma, his ability to inspire an idealism (and protest) that helped transform the nation. At least that is what many Americans anticipated in 1960. In the end, however, many were disappointed for in too many crucial areas of social reform, John Kennedy failed to deliver the promised goods. Nonetheless, John Kennedy's brief presidency remains one of the most glamorized, romantic, and vibrant times in American postwar history. Because of his heritage, John Kennedy perhaps is more deserving of such adulation than most other presidents, for his ancestors barely escaped one of the worst "starving times" in European history—the Irish potato famine of the 1840s. Not only did his forbearers surmount destitution but the stigma of ethnicity and religion as well. Thanks in large part to his family's refusal to accept "second-class" citizenship because of their religion and original nationality,

John Kennedy became the first ethnic, Catholic American president. Interestingly, down to the present moment, he has been the only one.

As they watched millions of their countrymen die, Patrick Kennedy (JFK's paternal great-grandfather) and his fiancée, Bridget Murphy, joined the human wave of 845,000 other Irish people who fled the Emerald Isle in the 1840s for the United States, arriving in Boston in 1849. No sooner did they arrive than they were greeted by an unanticipated, often virulent, Anglo-American nativism. Although old-stock Americans were suspicious of other European immigrant groups, such as the Germans, they were especially fearful of the Irish, whom many believed were a "fifth-column" sent over by the Pope to Catholicize the United States. In the teeming streets of Eastern seaboard cities like Boston and New York, their customs and their poverty made Irish immigrants conspicuous and thus easy prey and victims of a host of urban predators like con artists who fleeced them of their meager possessions. Unlike the Germans, who were coming at the same time, the majority of the Irish were impoverished, landless peasants fleeing abject poverty and political and religious oppression. They arrived with little to no money, so they could not move west and purchase land and thus were confined to the Atlantic seaport cities where they first entered the country. Desperate, they accepted jobs and conditions that native-born workers scorned. Because they had no other place to go, one boss observed, the Irish could "be relied on at the mill all year round." The employer of a largely Irish work force in Fall River, Massachusetts, declared coolly: "I regard my people just as I regard my machinery. . . . When my machines get old and useless I reject them and get new, and these people [the Irish] are part of my machinery."

Roughly three out of four Irish immigrants worked as laborers or domestic servants. Irish men dug canals, loaded ships, laid railroad track, and took what other work they could find. Irish women hired out to cook, wash and iron, mind children, and clean houses. Worst of all for Anglo-American nativists was the fact that virtually all Irish immigrants were Catholic, making them particularly visible as targets of long-standing American anti-Catholic prejudices. Nativists also degraded the Irish for their supposed immoral, "inherent" character flaws, portraying them as hard-drinking, obstreperous, half-civilized folk. Such views lay behind the discrimination that often excluded the Irish from better jobs. Job announcements commonly stated, "No Irish need apply." Despite such prejudices, the Irish persevered, and over time, like JFK's grandfather, the American-born Patrick—"P.J.," short for Patrick Joseph—became by the 1880s, one of the most powerful behind-the-scenes political operators in Boston. Indeed, by 1900, P.J., along with "Smiling" Jim Donovan and John "Honey Fitz" Fitzgerald, succeeded in establishing Irish bosses as the dominant force in Boston politics—not bad for the first-generation son of a cooper. Although P. J. represented the classical "rags-to-riches" success story, it would be his son, Joseph Patrick Kennedy, who was really responsible for making the Kennedy name one of the most widely known in the United States. In many ways, the "Kennedy story" began with the now rather infamous Joe Kennedy, "the old man," who more than any other member of the Kennedy family was the most important person in John Kennedy's early life. More than his father or grandfather, Joe Kennedy Sr. devoted his life to proving that an Irish-American family was as good as any "blue blood" family who had arrived on the *Mayflower.* Besides the making of money, which Kennedy believed was symbiotic with erasing the "taint" of being an Irish Catholic, nothing consumed him more than his obsession with gaining recognition and acceptance for himself and his family within WASP society. To that end, he devoted his entire life engaging in any activity he deemed essential for that purpose, regardless of the legality or the adverse effect it may have had on others. As he told journalist Arthur Krock, "For the Kennedys it is the shithouse or the castle—nothing in between." Indeed, Kennedy's fixation with acceptance often drove him to the borders of sociopathic behavior. Despite all his transgressions, to Kennedy it was all worth it in the end, with confirmation coming on January 20, 1961, as he watched his second eldest son inaugurated President of the United States.

Joe Kennedy's assent to wealth and power began on the streets of his Irish ghetto in Boston, where he hawked newspapers and became "street smart," as he associated with the other denizens of that world—pimps, prostitutes, and racketeers. When he reached high school age, his parents committed the "unpardonable sin" of enrolling him in the private but Protestant Boston Latin School. Suffice it to say, Boston's Archbishop William O'Connell was not at all pleased by the Kennedys' "defection." However, the archbishop's admonishments had little effect on the Kennedy decision for they were determined to see their son accepted at Harvard, and they knew his chances were greatly enhanced if Joe attended the prestigious Latin School. They were correct, and Joe entered Harvard in the fall of 1905. Joe Kennedy was far from an exemplary student; indeed, he rarely opened a book because he was too involved in extracurriculars, especially athletics. He was an exceptional baseball and football player, and when not playing those sports, he managed the basketball team, commanded a drill regiment, and got elected class president—not bad recognition and acceptance of an Irish Catholic kid by WASP America. Harvard, more than any institution of higher learning at the time, was still the premier WASP bastion and remained such a preserve until the 1950s. Academically, Joe switched his major from economics to the less rigorous study of classical music. After five years at Harvard, Joe finally graduated with a degree in music. Although recognized for his athletic prowess and sociability, Joe was denied membership in Harvard's most vaunted social clubs. At the time, Joe was convinced it was because of his "Irish Catholic pedigree," but one Harvard faculty member believed he was blackballed because he was an inveterate liar. The truth was probably somewhere in between.

Upon graduation, Joe decided to pursue a career in banking, which he believed would get him the quickest to his goal of becoming a millionaire by his mid-thirties. Despite growing up in the whirlwind of Boston politics, at this point in his life, Joe had little interest in such pursuits. As he later said to his wife, he wanted "the freedom which money provides, the freedom to come and go where he pleased, when he pleased and how he pleased." Joe only worked for his father's bank—East Boston Columbia Trust—for a short while. Thanks to the elder Kennedy's political connections, Joe was appointed an assistant state bank examiner, which he enjoyed because, "If you're going to get money you have to find out where it is."

Joe Kennedy's visibility within the ranks of Boston's Irish elite grew brighter with his courtship and eventual marriage to Rose Fitzgerald, daughter of Boston's colorful mayor, John "Honey Fitz" Fitzgerald. Interestingly, Joe and Rose had known each other since childhood, as the Fitzgeralds and Kennedys interacted socially on a frequent basis. Rose was definitely Irish upper class, and initially her father was not too keen on her seeing the parvenu Joe Kennedy. Academically (and perhaps intellectually), Rose was her suitor's superior. Unlike Joe, Rose was a voracious reader: creative, curious, and generally much more expansive and open in her thinking. She was third in her high school class and was admitted to Wellesley College, but her father, heeding the powerful Archbishop O'Connell's "advice" not to send her to a secular (code for Protestant) school, refused to let her enroll. Rose was devastated by her father's decision. She recalled that not going to Wellesley was her "greatest regret. It is something I have felt sad about all my life." Rose was sent off to northern Germany to attend an austere, rigid Catholic finishing school at Bluementhal. Typically, she made the best of an awful situation, excelling academically, majoring in German and French, which she spoke fluently, while simultaneously absorbing a curriculum of *Kinder, Kirche, and Kuche*—children, church, and cooking. Like her soon-to-be husband, Rose, too, loved music, and upon her return to the United States, she studied piano in Boston at the New England Conservatory of Music. She also was a member of a variety of social clubs that did charitable works throughout the city. Although initially cool toward his daughter marrying Joe, "Honey Fitz" ultimately acquiesced, for at least Joe had a Harvard degree and enough of the right "Irish pedigree" to make him "acceptable." Thus, on October 14, 1914, Joe Kennedy and Rose Fitzgerald were married, settling into a house in Protestant, middle-class Brookline, Massachusetts, soon producing the progeny that would make their union an American dynasty.

For three years Joe worked as treasurer for Old Colony Realty, a slumlord outfit that was notorious for evicting poor Irish and Italian families, repossessing their homes, fixing them up, and then reselling them at a significant profit to upwardly mobile Irish where they would be safe from "the encroachment of undesirable elements." When the United States entered World War I in 1917, Joe became assistant general manager of Bethlehem Steel's shipyards in Quincy, earning $20,000 a year—ten times what the average American worker made at the time, placing him in the top 1 percent of the national income bracket. Joe knew nothing of shipbuilding but all about financing. In competition with other shipyards, Joe out-produced all others, breaking all the records by building thirty-six destroyers in two years. It was while working for Bethlehem Steel that Kennedy had his first confrontation with FDR, who was at the time Assistant Secretary of the Navy and in charge of wartime ship production. FDR had to send four U.S. navy tugs with armed servicemen to get two frigates that Kennedy refused to hand over to the navy until they were paid for. Suffice it to say, FDR was not about to let a "greedy capitalist" obstruct the war effort. Despite FDR's ironhandedness, Kennedy came to respect the future president, declaring to his friend, newspaper magnate William Randolph Hearst, that the secretary was even "tougher" than he was. Thus began the interesting "love-hate" relationship between FDR and Joe Kennedy that lasted until the president's death in 1945.

After the war, Joe parlayed his already substantial income into even more money by investing in the great bull market of the mid-1920s. In that decade Joe learned all there was to know about manipulating the stock market, profiting heavily from insider trading. Kennedy believed corporations existed for the benefit of management, not the stockholders. Despite his increasing wealth and high-profile activities, first in Boston and then in New York where he moved his family in 1926, Joe Kennedy remained on the periphery of patrician society. In short, the Kennedys suffered from "status anxiety," for they were a family in transition, caught between two classes, two cultures. Although financially and materially successful (Joe cavorted around New York City in a chauffeur-driven plum Rolls Royce), many Yankee patricians still considered the Kennedys nouveau riche upstarts not worthy of admittance to high society even though they possessed all the appropriate physical trappings. In their quest for acceptance, the Kennedys increasingly disassociated themselves from their Irish roots, pretending that somehow they were no longer Irish but full-fledged Yankee Americans. Many of their Irish friends resented such pretension and fawning and turned against them. Although his name was constantly in the major New York newspapers for his Wall Street exploits, he was still referred to as an "Irish American." Kennedy was perplexed and angered by such slights, declaring, "I was born here. My children were born here. What the hell do I have to do to be an American [gain WASP acceptance]?"

Like other ethnic Americans (most notably the Italians, Germans, and Jews), Joe Kennedy resented the passage of the Volstead Act and eventual Eighteenth Amendment, which prohibited the manufacture and sale of alcohol. To Kennedy and other "ethnics," prohibition represented yet another WASP assault and degradation of their respective cultures. The temperance movement had long been the bastion of WASP propriety and righteousness, and since their coming to the United States in the 1840s, the Irish in particular had been the focus of that crusade. By the 1920s WASP reformers had become even more fearful of the deleterious effects of drink on the urban working class for its ranks now included millions of Italians and Jews as well. Already suspect for their faith (Catholic or Jewish) and other "strange" habits, drinking was considered by many crusaders to be the immigrant's most egregious vice. If such an indulgence was outlawed, then hopefully their redemption could begin. Nativist prohibitionists hoped the law would ultimately result in a massive exodus of those ethnic groups they believed were causing the "mongrelization" of America—the Italians, Jews, and other southern and eastern Europeans.

For many ethnics the drinking of alcoholic beverage was part and parcel of their daily lives. Whether at home with meals or socially at family gatherings or public events, or at their favorite neighborhood bar, drinking was one of their culture's most important leisure-time activities, a custom practiced and enjoyed for centuries. To an already sensitive Joe Kennedy, prohibition was further confirmation that the Irish were still disdained by WASP America. Joe and other angered immigrants got their revenge on the WASP "drys" by becoming bootleggers, illegally importing liquor from outside the United States, usually from Canada, and making fortunes in the process. Joe Kennedy was never one to pass up any potential moneymaking enterprise, nor did he care if such an endeavor was wholly illegal. Indeed, bootlegging proved to be one of Kennedy's more lucrative undertakings for it was virtually impossible for the government, with only 1,500 federal agents, to police the drinking habits of 110 million people. Thus, Joe Kennedy simply got richer during the Roaring Twenties by providing his "Yankee" friends with all the booze they could consume.

Ever the on-the-make entrepreneur, Joe Kennedy decided that the booming motion picture industry in Hollywood, California, was yet another opportunity to increase his already substantial income from banking, shipping, and bootlegging. In 1926, Joe left for Hollywood where he stayed for three years, immersing himself in an industry ripe with free-wheeling, money-making potential, for it was a business that catered to a demand of its own creation. Every week 60 million Americans went to the movies, and Joe Kennedy made some $6 million providing them with cheaply made Tom Mix westerns and low budget "B" melodramas. Interestingly, with his flair for the grandiose and flamboyant, he did not produce or finance any epic à-la-Cecil B. DeMille blockbusters. He came close to such an effort as a result of a tempestuous affair with the reigning diva of the silent picture era, Gloria Swanson. Joe placed her in the infamous *Queen Kelly,* directed by the *avant garde* German émigré Erich von Stroheim. The picture was never released for ostensibly moral reasons: Swanson portrayed a self-giving prostitute nun! Despite the "loosening" of American morality in the 1920s, the majority of citizens were not ready to embrace such a controversial topic. Suffice it to say, neither was the Catholic Church, and Joe Kennedy certainly did not want to incur its displeasure. Although the film was a bust, the wily Kennedy managed to hand Swanson much of the financial loss and recouped his investment through the earnings of Swanson's first "talkie," *The Trespasser.* Soon after getting his money back, Kennedy decided he was through with the actress and Hollywood and returned to Rose and their eight children. Joe's Hollywood dalliance started a penchant among the Kennedy men for such "action" with Hollywood starlets, and as will be seen in this essay, his son, the President of the United States, upheld the family "tradition" quite well.

Raising eight young Kennedys—four boys and four girls—was a muscular undertaking, requiring both vigor and painstaking care.

Most of the responsibility naturally fell to Rose, who, although a kind, nurturing person, nonetheless imposed on her brood a very disciplined, regimented life. The children had their own personal "file," in which was kept a daily account of all they did, good and bad. Strategically planted reminder notes and abbreviated lectures or news items were on walls and bulletin boards throughout the house, and clocks were placed in every room so the children would not be late for meals or Mass. Speaking proper English was an obsession with Rose and Joe Kennedy, for neither ever wanted any of their children to be denied access to WASP society because they were uneducated or uninformed. They simply wanted there to be no excuses for their children to be seen as anything but "one-hundred percent American"—WASP. Rose thus schooled the children in such points as the correct use of "I" and "me," and before dinner they were required to read the news stories she had tacked on the bulletin board so they could discuss what they read with their father. Occasionally, instead of the day's news or issues, they would be required to read a book about a past historical event or person, such as the Civil War or a biography of Thomas Jefferson, and relate their understanding to Joe. Joe would quiz them about what they had read and try to promote a debate among them or, more often than not, a one-on-one with him. The overall effect of such discourse on young Jack Kennedy was the inculcation of an insatiable desire to read and a capacity to memorize vast quantities of information. As far as their formal education was concerned, the boys attended Protestant preparatory schools, such as Choate, while the girls were sent to Catholic schools.

His sons' physical prowess was as important to Joe Kennedy as was their intellectual development. The Kennedy family compound at Hyannis Port was the perfect place for such growth. During the summer months the boys were up at dawn, jogging and doing calisthenics before a breakfast of Wheaties, and of course while they were eating, Joe lectured on the importance of physical fitness and the necessity of being able to live "the strenuous life." Interestingly, of the four boys, only Joe Jr. came close to being the all-around athlete his father was. However, it didn't matter to Joe Kennedy if none of his sons were his athletic equal. He simply wanted them to be able to endure any physical challenges or tests to their manliness, to never be afraid to compete, and of course to excel and win. As he admonished his sons, "Don't play unless you can be captain," and "Second place is failure." A son who performed badly (at least in Joe's eyes) was ostracized from the family dinner table and forced to eat alone or in the kitchen with "the help." In short, athletic bravado was simply an extension of the ethos of competition that pervaded Kennedy family life. As Kennedy friend and future Supreme Court Justice William O. Douglas observed, "The father particularly laid it hard trying to make the boys, and the girls, excellent in something, whether it was touch football, or tennis, or boating, or something else." Indeed, a "rite of passage" to acceptance within the Kennedy clan required passing the "test" of enduring a roughhouse game of touch football (which more often than not quickly degenerated into "tackle" as tempers flared because of the intensity of competition). As one Kennedy visitor recalled, "You had to show raw guts, fall on your face now and then. Smash into the house once in awhile going after a pass. Laugh off twisted ankles or a big hole torn in your best suit." If one feigned injury or bowed out of the game too early, for whatever reason, the likelihood of being accepted into the Kennedy clan was remote. You were simply not tough enough; you were too "effete" and, thus, not worthy of acknowledgement and acceptance by the Kennedy men.

Joe was especially passionate about sailing, and his sons were going to be as well. The "old man" was a master sailor, and he expected no less from his sons. Moreover, the "sport" of sailing was considered to be the quintessence of the *aristoi*, a most patrician endeavor. During the summer, sometimes from sunup to sundown, the boys were at sea perfecting their sailing techniques as their father followed behind them in a boat barking out their mistakes over a bullhorn. Interestingly, of all his four sons and largely because of a chronic bad back, which limited his physical/athletic ability, Jack Kennedy became the best mariner.

However, the intense competitiveness and the insistence on perfection and winning posed a particularly cruel dilemma for Jack. "At least one half of the days that he spent on this earth," his brother Bobby noted, "were days of intense physical pain." Jack almost died from scarlet fever as a child, suffered a chronic weak back, and spent a substantial portion of his childhood years in bed, rarely finishing a normal school year as one ailment after another required prolonged hospitalization or diagnostic tests. Partly as a result of these illnesses, Jack became a voracious reader, devouring biographies and histories and developing in the process, because of his solitude, the detached, intellectual cast of mind that would later mark so strongly his political persona.

Despite his taciturn ways and overbearing personality, Joe's fatherly attention was returned with love and obedience. Moreover, what children would not admire a father who could bring home for dinner movie stars like Tom Mix or sports legends like Babe Ruth or Red

Grange, and who instantly responded to their letters when away from home? Despite being gone for weeks, if not months, at a time, the Kennedy children rightly sensed they were always on their father's mind. Some successful fathers only transmit their wealth to their progeny; Joe Kennedy also passed on his unyielding determination to triumph over any adversity. The one exception was Rosemary, born retarded, and after an operation cared for at a convent. Joe showed his love for her by donating thousands of dollars to research on her disability.

Joe's first serious foray in politics occurred during the early 1930s in support of fellow "patrician" FDR, whom he believed could ameliorate the effects of the Depression, preventing what he and other capitalists feared most: social unrest. Hungry people, Kennedy said, could turn "ugly and menacing," and thus something needed to be done to relieve them of their distress. The New Deal had yet to take shape, but Kennedy saw in FDR the possibility for national economic reform. He plunged himself into getting FDR elected, raising thousands of dollars for his campaign, and contributing $50,000 personally. He also wrote many position papers for Roosevelt, one of which was a blueprint for the future Securities and Exchange Commission to which FDR appointed Kennedy as chairman in 1934 as a "thank you" for all he had contributed to his election. Many of FDR's advisers were outraged by FDR's choice, for Kennedy had been one of the markets most notorious abusers. But FDR was often as unburdened by scruples as Kennedy, and as the president told an aide, "It takes a thief to catch a thief." Joe left the post in 1935 to help get FDR reelected. He returned to government for a year as head of the Maritime Commission, a position from which FDR hoped Kennedy could invigorate the sickly shipbuilding industry. In 1938, Joe Kennedy's career as a public servant reached its apex: he was selected as ambassador to Great Britain, the most important and prestigious diplomatic appointment a president can make, and long considered the preserve of the Anglo-American aristocracy. Joe Kennedy had finally "arrived." Not yet believing that European events warranted his full concentrated attention, FDR evidently thought it "a grand joke" to tweak the lion's mane by appointing an reconstructed Irishman to the Court of St. James. When he first heard the suggestion that the job should go to Kennedy, FDR "laughed so hard he almost fell out of his wheelchair."

FDR should not have been so cavalier about Joe Kennedy, for no sooner was the hot-tempered Irishman ensconced than he created a whirlwind of trouble for the president with his off-the-cuff, impolitic, crude, and insulting comments about virtually anybody and anything

English. He called the queen of England a "cute trick," and Churchill a "heavy drinker." Those references paled beside a remark to the German ambassador in which he declared, "I'm for Hitler." He praised the Munich settlement, saying he could not imagine anyone (the great powers) going to war over the partition of Czechoslovakia. He also declared soon after Munich, "The democracies and dictators should cooperate for the common good." The final straw for FDR occurred in 1940 when in an interview he announced, "Democracy is finished in England." Such comments and others revealed that Kennedy not only was an "unreconstructed" Irishman but, much to FDR's embarrassment, a hard-core isolationist, anticommunist, and probably an anti-Semite, closet racist, and fascist as well. FDR had no choice but to relieve him of his position, which he did in 1940, thus putting an end to Kennedy's public career but not the use of his money and influence on his sons' behalf who were now to take up his never-ending assault on the ramparts of the Anglo-American elite. He would not rest nor be vindicated until one became President of the United States.

That responsibility initially fell to his eldest son, Joe Jr., who in so many ways was the carbon copy of his father's aggressiveness and drive. Indeed, Joe Jr. was the ideal embodiment of his father's vision—robust, talented, gregarious, strong, and athletic. He was a devout Catholic, praying nightly at his bedside. Even ideologically he was his father's son. His senior thesis at Harvard, "Intervention in Spain," favored the fascist dictator Francisco Franco and condemned the Republic for being governed by communists influenced, if not controlled, from Moscow. Like his father, Joe approved of the Munich settlement, writing to a friend that he believed the Germans were a "marvelous people," and it would be "tough to keep [them] from getting what they want." He related to his father his impression of German Jews: "Their methods had been quite unscrupulous. This [Nazi] dislike of the Jews is well-founded."

Joe Jr.'s relationship with his siblings, especially with Jack, was anything but "brotherly love." Joe simply bullied Jack unmercifully. Later in life JFK admitted that Joe was "hot-tempered: and often outright mean," often reveling in how much pain he could inflict on his brothers. An early photograph shows Jack and Joe Jr. holding hands, with little Jack grimacing because Joe was squeezing his hand so hard. Jack needed twenty-eight stitches after he and Joe collided playing a game that involved running at each other. Joe's "pugnacious personality," Jack remembered, "smoothed out but it was a problem in my boyhood." Unfortunately, tragically, all of Joe Sr.'s hopes that his first-born would someday become President of the United States literally went up in flames in early June 1944, when the PB4Y Navy Lt. Joe Kennedy was flying with eleven tons of explosives on board for a bombing run to destroy German V-I rocket sites in France blew up in mid-air over southern England. It seems the "old man's" inculcation of the glorification of achievement and risk-taking "stuck" with Joe Jr. Before taking off, Joe had left a message for his father: "If I don't come back, tell my dad that I love him very much." In 1948, Jack lost his sister, the vivacious Kathleen ("Kick"), in another plane crash, and Kathleen's English officer husband had died in the war in the same year as Joe.

Meanwhile, on the other side of the world in the South Pacific, the once bullied, sickly younger brother was becoming the hero Joe Jr. had desperately wanted to become. Interestingly, in many ways unnoticed by the "old man," Jack was beginning to outshine his brother long before his World War II heroics. By the time of their Harvard years, Jack was outdoing his brother in both scholarship and popularity. By his senior year Jack had made the Dean's list and graduated *magna cum laude* with a B+ average. His senior thesis, "Why England Slept," won accolades from the faculty and was eventually published as a book with the help of professional journalist, Arthur Krock (a close friend at the time of Joe Sr.), head of the Washington Bureau of the *New York Times,* who massively revised the original manuscript. Within a short time, Kennedy's senior paper became a best selling book hailed by the *New York Times Book Review* for its "mature understanding and fair mindedness," and by the *Boston Herald* for its "grasp of complex problems, its courageous frankness, its good manners, and its sound advice." Not everyone was as enthusiastic in their endorsement of the book as the *Times* and *Herald.* Not nearly as effusive was the English intellectual Harold Laski, who told Ambassador Kennedy, "In a good university half a hundred seniors do books like this as part of their normal work in their final year. But they don't publish them for the good reason that their importance lies solely in what they get out of doing them and not out of what they have to say. I don't honestly think any publisher would have looked at that book of Jack's if he had not been your son, and if you had not been ambassador. And those are not the right grounds for publication."

Despite Laski's less than laudatory comments, the work nonetheless reflected Jack's intellectual curiosity and probing. His thesis was that democracies, in the absence of immediate threats, encouraged "private aims," which hurt a nation like England because it failed to heed fascism's call for militarization. As fascism became more bellicose, aggressive, and interventionist, the democracies needed to rearm, Kennedy argued. They did not and, thus, were unprepared for the fascist onslaught that engulfed the continent by 1940. Although critical of the democracies' rearmament policies, Kennedy praised Churchill for evoking British national purpose, much as he would call for a national renewal during his 1960 presidential campaign. Kennedy's thirst for information and knowledge caused one of his many girlfriends to complain, "He listened to *every* radio news broadcast."

After graduation from Harvard, Jack attended Stanford University's Graduate School of Business. However Jack's presence at Stanford was brief; after a few months he left the school and toured South America. Upon his return to the United States, he decided to enlist, but because of his weak back neither the army nor navy would accept him. However, after some politicking by his father, the navy acquiesced, and Jack entered at the rank of ensign and was assigned to the Office of Naval Intelligence in Washington. Sitting at a desk eight hours a day was not exactly what Jack envisioned when he joined the navy. He wanted to be on a ship, for what better way to put his years of sailing experience into practice than as an officer on a battleship. Moreover, serving on a destroyer or cruiser would undoubtedly put him in "harm's way"—combat—and, thus, he would have an opportunity to prove to the "old man" that he was as physically capable as his revered older brother of not only surviving battle but of performing heroically in the process. After intense personally lobbying of his superiors (Jack also got a "little push" from Joe Sr.), the young ensign got his way and was transferred to seamanship school at Northwestern University and then to the South Pacific to command a PT boat—one of the riskiest, most physically demanding positions in the navy—the perfect assignment for demonstrating that he could hold his own, regardless of the disabilities that afflicted him. During all this time, his back pain was unrelenting; while at Northwestern he slept on a table instead of a bed.

After weeks of maneuvers and practice runs, which usually ended up in "drag" races among the PT boats (Kennedy once raced his boat homeward toward the dock, cutting the engines at the last moment, and crashed into the structure, totally dismantling it), on August 1, 1943, Kennedy's days of being in "McHale's navy" came to an abrupt end. While on an important patrol, with engines improperly set and no one on watch, a Japanese destroyer appeared out of nowhere, striking Kennedy's boat with such force that it split the vessel in half, setting it afire and spilling the entire crew into the waters near the Solomon Islands. Two crewmen died instantly, but Jack towed a badly burned mate across a strong current back to one half of his boat and then for four hours across miles of open water to Plum Pudding Island. Jack's heroics to save his crew not only won him the Navy Cross but front-page headlines as well in American newspapers. He had at last proven to his father that he was as courageous and strong as Joe Jr. (who brooded for days upon hearing the news of his younger, "weaker," brother's gallantry and who would "clench and unclench his fists" after toasts to the young hero) and, thus, now "worthy" of his father's love and attention. After a few more mishaps at sea, Jack returned stateside for an operation on his back. The surgeon apparently botched the job, leaving a gaping hole in Jack's back that "never closed up." As a friend further observed, "You could look into it and see the metal plate that had been put into his spine." The pain was constant, with Kennedy spending months in hospitals seeking relief. In the course of his numerous treatments to cure his back condition, doctors discovered that Kennedy had Addison's disease, an adrenaline deficiency that could not be cured, only "contained" by massive injections of cortisone on a daily basis. Worse, the affliction was believed to be terminal. "I'll probably last until I'm forty-five," the young Kennedy told a friend. Fortunately, oral medication was eventually developed that both isolated the disease and offered relative assurance of a full and normal life. Nonetheless, Joe Kennedy worried that his son's ailments would ruin his plans—his obsession—with having a Kennedy in politics, for in his mind only a son of good health and perfection could withstand the rigors of a campaign. As a friend observed at the time, Jack's illnesses were "an irritation for his father and for himself. It threatened to get in the way of everything they were trying to accomplish"—a Kennedy in the White House. While recuperating in Arizona, Jack and his father, over long phone conversations, concluded that Jack was now the heir apparent; he replaced Joe Jr. in his father's political plans. According to JFK, "My father wanted his eldest son in politics. 'Wanted' isn't the right word. He demanded it."

In retrospect there should have been little surprise that Jack would assume his dead brother's mantle, especially given the "old man's" overbearing insistence that with Joe Jr. gone it was incumbent on Jack to fulfill his father's ambitions. Interestingly, Jack later told newsman Walter Cronkite that he did not feel "obligated" despite his father's pressure to fill Joe's shoes. He added that he certainly would not have entered politics had his brother lived. Ironically, Jack had a better overall political "profile" than Joe: He was a young man with an enviable education, well traveled, with enough money from a family trust fund to live in comfort, and perhaps most important, he was blessed with a keen intelligence. In short, Jack was simply more perspicacious than his revered brother. Politics was a natural career choice. John Kennedy did not start at the bottom when he entered public life. In his first gambit in 1946, he ran for and won election to the House of Representatives for the 11th Congressional District of Massachusetts. His constituents were largely working class Irish and Italians, residing in Charlestown, Cambridge, and Boston. He also served the more affluent Yankee enclave of Beacon Hill. His family's prestige, influence, and wealth were unquestionably important to his victory. During the campaign, however, it quickly became apparent that this skinny twenty-nine-year-old possessed an inherent political savvy that few had recognized. He displayed a boundless energy, a willingness to work hard, and a knack for enthusing volunteer campaign workers. Cultivating local politicians like Dave Powers, shaking hands at factory gates, and speaking to groups of veterans' mothers, Jack learned his trade quickly and skillfully. But as he told a friend at the time, he could also "feel pappy's eyes on the back of my neck."

Kennedy impressed most of his House colleagues as a very pleasant, not overly zealous, young man and somewhat of a loner, even aloof at times. He had a habit of leaving the chamber early, even while someone was speaking, to change into old clothes and dash off to play touch football or softball. Such a penchant underlined his youth and vigor. In character with his upbringing—his father's influence—he took a conservative stance on many issues. Although voting with Northern Democrats most of the time, he could not be categorized as a "liberal." Indeed, during his six years in the House, Kennedy remained an ideological enigma, voting "right" on some issues one day and then the next voting "left" on others. In short, it appeared as if Kennedy was keeping all his options open, perhaps shrewdly watching to see which way the ideological winds of his constituents and the nation were blowing, then voting accordingly. For example, he garnered considerable publicity championing veterans' causes (a high percentage of his district's male constituents had served in the military during World War II), such as his criticism of the American Legion's opposition to low-cost housing. At the same time, he created a mild furor by attacking Truman and the State Department for having "lost" China. Such displays of "conviction," however, were rare as he generally maintained a low profile. In short, he focused on taking care of the needs and problems of his constituents.

Kennedy's solicitude paid off handsomely in 1952 when he surprised the experts by defeating the popular Republican incumbent, Henry

Cabot Lodge Jr., for the Senate. His victory was even more remarkable given the fact that Ike Eisenhower landslided his way to the presidency, carrying virtually every Republican who ran for office that year on his coattails. One of the states Ike swept was Massachusetts. Kennedy owed his victory to his father's money and his brother Robert's crafty, if not brilliant (and at times ruthless), campaign strategies, which soon became legendary. Kennedy money flooded Massachusetts that election year, for as Joe Kennedy proclaimed, "We're going to sell Jack like soap flakes." Large gifts in the Kennedy name went to the largest and most influential Italian and Irish American charities and organizations. The "old man" also created a series of "improvement" groups that targeted the fishing, shoemaking, and textile industries whose employees were overwhelmingly of Irish and Italian "extraction." Most notably, Joe lent $500,000 to the McCarthyite publisher of the Boston *Post*, for as his son commented to a Harvard classmate, "You know we had to buy that f. . . paper, or I'd have been licked."

Robert Kennedy's tactics perhaps proved more valuable in securing victory than all the "tea parties" given by the Kennedy women and the thousands of dollars donated by the "old man." It was Robert who advised his brother to attack Lodge, a noted internationalist, for spending too little time on domestic issues. To a Jewish audience, Jack pointed out that *he* was running for office, not his anti-Semite father. Robert had the powerful prelate Archbishop Richard Cushing of Boston baptize his and Ethel's first child just before Election Day, keeping the Kennedy name in the forefront of Italian and Irish voters' minds. Indeed, the fact that the Irish and Italian population of Boston was so significant a political force, it was a given that the Catholic Kennedy would receive virtually all their votes.

During his Senate years, Kennedy found both joy and sorrow. A recurrence of back trouble almost cost him his life in 1954, and he lost a close race with Estes Kefauver to be the 1956 Democratic vice-presidential nominee. Such pain and disappointment was offset by his marriage to the beautiful and cultured Jacqueline Bouvier, daughter of financier John Bouvier, whose pedigree was exactly what the Kennedys were trying to cultivate. Jacqueline was an alumna of Vassar and the Sorbonne, well read and informed, fluent in French, and most important, from the moment she married Jack, she became, without question, one of his most invaluable political assets. Indeed, as will be seen, her contribution to her husband's popularity and "style" proved indispensable. Her gracious, engaging personality, her sheer "presence," whether in public accompanying her husband or on television giving the nation a one-on-one personal tour of the remodeled White House, Jackie endowed the Kennedy mystique with a panache and *savoir faire* rarely displayed by a First Lady.

Without question one of Senator Kennedy's more controversial "accomplishments" was his winning of the 1958 Pulitzer Prize for his biography *Profiles in Courage*. His receipt of this most prestigious award frighteningly paralleled the contention caused by his earlier publication. Although the book's concept—how politicians reconciled taking positions opposed by their constituents—was JFK's (according to Kennedy confidant Theodore Sorensen), everything else, from the outline to the research, to the actual writing and editing, was largely the efforts of Sorensen and Jules Davids, a professor at George Washington University. Indeed, Kennedy contributed little to the work other than some paragraphs in the preface and conclusion. In short, Kennedy simply did not write the book. To say otherwise, according to historian Herbert Parmet, would be "as deceptive as installing a Chevrolet engine in a Cadillac." Thanks to Arthur Krock, who convinced the 1958 Pulitzer Prize Committee to make an "exception" for the biography award, Kennedy received the nation's most distinguished literary honor. As a result, Kennedy's acclaim as a distinguished writer and intellectual skyrocketed. Most distressing was Kennedy's embracing of that public perception as real. Suffice it to say, the political dividends from the award were huge: he won his 1958 reelection bid by almost 900,000 votes, impressing party moguls that perhaps the young senator from Massachusetts was presidential material. Indeed, Kennedy counted on winning the 1960 presidential nomination.

Although legitimate scholars and academicians had strong reservations about Kennedy's true intellectual prowess, interestingly, in the political arena, neither liberals nor conservatives challenged his aptness. A self-taught speed-reader, Kennedy's voracious reading habits drew attention and envy. His fascination with learning, his insatiable curiosity, and his ability to grasp complexities appealed to many intellectuals. Personally, JFK was an intellectual but, as one historian observed, "of a very special kind . . . more analytical than creative, more curious and penetrating than wide-ranging or philosophically speculative, more skeptical than confident, more catalytic than original or imaginative." Shunning doctrinaire rhetoric and dogmatism, Kennedy felt uneasy with slogans and stereotypes. In many ways Kennedy was an interesting amalgam of Enlightenment rationalism "utilitarian" intellectualism, for like the disciples of both those movements, Kennedy believed that ideas were

184 John F. Kennedy

to be used to solve problems, not for impressing others or as a way to pass time. By the late 1950s, Kennedy actively courted academics and "eggheads," not because they represented political power—they were much too resented for that—but because he admired brilliant people. He never patronized them; nor did he tell them that they were essential. He simply enjoyed and respected the company of practical intellectuals.

Although appealing, Kennedy's brilliance was not as important to his political ambitions as was his ability to *convey* compassion and understanding, regardless of how he truly felt. T.S. Eliot once wrote, "Intellectual ability without the more human attributes is admirable only in the same way as the brilliant chess prodigy." Kennedy's humanity was as important to his political success as his celebrated charm, good looks, and glamour. Yet, like FDR, he was not a "bleeding-heart" idealist. Self-possessed and cool, he once remarked, "I'm not the tragic lover type." Although skeptical by nature and inclined toward a personal fatalism, he was nonetheless sensitive to the afflictions and deprivations of others, aware that few Americans enjoyed the amenities he had known.

JFK, the politician, began to articulate his views on public issues, especially his thinking on foreign policy matters, to which he devoted considerable energy, hoping to establish himself as an "expert." At this juncture in his political career, Kennedy was a hard-line, anticommunist cold warrior, jumping on the "blame Truman, blame the State Department for the loss of China" bandwagon of his Republican associates. "What our young men have saved," Kennedy declared, "our diplomats and our president have frittered away." It was time, he said, to prevent "the onrushing tide of communism from engulfing all of Asia." Yet, on other occasions, Kennedy showed a keen awareness and understanding of the increasing importance of the wars of national liberation taking place in Africa and Asia in the 1950s, as the peoples of those two regions were trying to throw off centuries of European exploitation and subjugation. After a trip to Southeast Asia, he talked about "the fires of nationalism now ablaze. . . . Colonialism is not a topic for tea-talk discussion; it is the daily fare of millions of men." The United States, he warned, would have serious problems it if ignored the "civilizations striving to be born." In particular, Kennedy opposed support for the French in Indochina. "No amount of American military assistance," he noted, "can conquer an enemy which is everywhere and at the same time nowhere, 'an enemy of the people' which has the sympathy and the covert support of the people. . . . To pour money, material, and men into the jungles of Indochina without at least a remote prospect of victory would be dangerously futile and self-destructive." Unfortunately, John Kennedy did not listen to his own words or admonishments relative to U.S. involvement in Indochina after becoming president. Among his colleagues Kennedy was well liked but not particularly influential or sought-after. Unlike LBJ, who reveled in behind-the-scenes maneuvering and power brokering, JFK eschewed such wheeling and dealing over a tumbler of bourbon. He preferred instead to pick and choose carefully whom he befriended and what causes and issues he championed. Interestingly, his closest friends were conservative Southerners like George Smathers of Florida and Richard Russell of Georgia. The man he admired most was Robert Taft. Kennedy even boasted of his good personal relationships with such hardcore racists as John Rankin of Mississippi. When Jack told an interviewer that he was "not a liberal at all," he was not understating the obvious, for he refused to embrace the domestic social welfare measures to which the ADA (Americans for Democratic Action) and other liberal groups were committed. Yet, he was a dedicated supporter of the bread-and-butter issues affecting his blue-collar constituency, such as increases in the minimum wage, veterans' benefits, public housing, and support for organized labor. Despite his endorsement for components of the liberal agenda, as far as "real" liberals were concerned, Kennedy was as far from being one of them as were the Senate colleagues with whom he associated. Nonetheless, by 1958 he was receiving hundreds of speaking invitations each year. Eager to obtain as much public exposure as possible, he accepted many and was frequently absent from the Senate.

As election year 1960 moved closer, interestingly, Kennedy began an ideological "metamorphosis," minimizing his relationships with both Democrat and Republican conservatives, and moving closer to his liberal colleagues, firmly supporting them on welfare issues, civil rights, and civil liberties. For example, in 1959, he worked diligently to secure repeal of the Federal Defense Education Act clause, requiring students to sign a disclaimer of disloyalty if they wanted college loans. Despite his "coming out" for reform issues, many liberals believed Kennedy disingenuous. Indeed, many were certain that Kennedy's newfound liberalism was the result of political expediency—he knew he could not win the party's nomination without liberal support. Others were more cynical, convinced that Kennedy was now embracing the liberal ethos because he wanted to remove the taint of his earlier support (at least tacitly) for Joe McCarthy and his anticommunist reign of terror. As one Kennedy biographer noted, it was "the issue that would not die."

Unfortunately, JFK "inherited" from his father his McCarthyism, for the "old man" was one of the Wisconsin senator's most ardent admirers and strongest supporters. Indeed, all too frequently, JFK's views sounded like his father's. "I know Joe [McCarthy] pretty well," he told a college class, "and he may have something." Kennedy strongly supported the anticommunist McCarran Act, declaring "we have to get all foreigners off our backs." In a speech at the University of Notre Dame, he warned about the "ever-expanding power of the federal government," connecting it to "the scarlet thread that runs throughout the world." However, by 1954 and especially after the Army-McCarthy hearings, which marked the beginning of the end of the senator's inquisition, Kennedy's support for McCarthy waned considerably. According to Theodore Sorensen, Kennedy was prepared to censure McCarthy for his personal excesses, but in a speech prepared for the occasion, he refused to condemn McCarthy's anticommunist crusade. The speech was never delivered, because Kennedy was in the hospital recovering from the back surgery that almost killed him. When McCarthy was finally censured, Kennedy issued no statement of support, nor at any time did he reveal the visceral revulsion toward McCarthy's tactics that characterized most liberals. Indeed, his views seemed to be shaped more by personality considerations than by ideology. He liked McCarthy personally but disliked his crass, ruthless tactics. Kennedy had similar sentiments toward other notorious red-baiters, such as Richard Nixon, whom he was happy to see defeat the liberal Helen Gahagan Douglas in the 1950 U.S. Senate race in California. JFK gave Nixon a campaign contribution from his father. "It isn't going to break my heart if you can turn the Senate's loss into Hollywood's gain [by defeating Douglas]," Kennedy said.

"Practical" politicians defended Kennedy's fence straddling on McCarthyism by contending that, because of the high percentage of Catholics in Massachusetts and because of McCarthy's popularity among Catholics, it made good political sense for Kennedy to waffle on such an emotionally charged issue. According to Kennedy biographer James MacGregor Burns, Kennedy's equivocation was "logical" since "He was shaping his liberalism by fits and starts, out of his experience with concrete problems." Kennedy also underestimated the intensity of feeling among his liberal Democratic colleagues on the subject. As he once ruefully explained, "Some people have their liberalism 'made' by the time they reach their late 20s. I didn't. I was caught in cross currents and eddies. It was only late that I got into the stream of things."

Despite his waffling on McCarthyism, Kennedy soared to national prominence at the 1956 Democratic National Convention. His speech nominating Adlai Stevenson evoked wild enthusiasm. Indeed, so impressed were delegates that Stevenson and other party chieftains agreed to "open up" the vice-presidential nomination. Kennedy seized the opportunity with a vengeance as his staff galvanized a coalition of conservative Southern Democrats and Northern urban bosses that almost catapulted him to victory. In the end, however, Kennedy's Catholicism got in the way. Narrowly defeated on the second ballot by the more liberal Estes Kefauver, Kennedy nevertheless emerged the ultimate winner. "He probably rates as the one real victor of the entire convention," one columnist wrote. "His was the one new face. . . . His charisma, his dignity, his intellectuality, and in the end his gracious sportsmanship are undoubtedly what those delegates would remember." JFK agreed. "You know," he told Dave Powers afterward, "if we work like hell the next four years, we will pick up all the marbles."

In early January 1960, JFK formally announced his candidacy. By that time the field had dwindled to three serious hopefuls—Senators Hubert Humphrey, Lyndon Johnson, and Stuart Symington. For a brief moment Adlai Stevenson made a run, but the stigma of being a two-time loser quickly ended his bid. Only Humphrey, whose long association with civil rights, labor, and the ultraliberal ADA caused many Democrats to regard him as something of a radical, tried to win the nomination like Kennedy by running in the primaries. Kennedy rightly believed that the only way to convince his party's power-brokers that he could win the presidency was to win in the primaries, and Kennedy did precisely that, winning every primary he entered, even West Virginia, a state that was 95 percent Protestant. In winning West Virginia (JFK captured an astonishing 61 percent of the vote), Kennedy shattered the myth that a Catholic could not be elected president, something pervasive in the American electorate's mind since 1928 when Herbert Hoover defeated the Catholic Al Smith. Kennedy had hoped to avoid the Catholic issue, for it was political dynamite; to discuss it openly simply focused attention on it. However, in West Virginia, he had no choice. In roadside comments, major speeches, and television appearances, including one with Humphrey, he challenged head-on the idea that he was the Pope's captive or that a person's faith was a valid criterion for being chief executive. He campaigned at his fighting best, more confident and determined than his staff. His anger flared when it became apparent that his opponents (particularly LBJ, who had chosen not to follow the primary route) were

188 John F. Kennedy

urging West Virginians to back Humphrey in order to stop Kennedy. Despite his challengers' shenanigans, Kennedy swamped Humphrey, and soon after his defeat in West Virginia, the Minnesota senator bowed out of the race. Interestingly, Humphrey was a lone voice in the 1950s, boldly taking forthright positions on sensitive issues such as civil rights in a decade when moderation was the national style. Kennedy's victory over him in the primaries was interpreted as further evidence that the nation would not countenance an assertive candidate in the forthcoming election.

With Humphrey out of the way and despite Johnson's desperate efforts to rally an opposition in other states, Kennedy was unbeatable, winning handily every primary he entered. One of Kennedy's more difficult remaining tasks was to convince liberals that, notwithstanding his waffling on McCarthyism, he deserved their support. Eleanor Roosevelt criticized Kennedy for not exhibiting the courage he wrote about, citing his reluctance to speak out against federal aid for parochial schools and his reliance on his father's money. Suffice it to say, there was no love lost between Eleanor and Joe Kennedy; indeed, the former First Lady despised the elder Kennedy. JFK struck back, however, mobilizing his own stable of liberal supporters, ranging from UAW leader Walter Reuther to intellectuals such as Arthur Schlesinger, Jr. Also helping Kennedy win primaries in key industrial states such as Illinois, Pennsylvania, Ohio, and Michigan were powerful urban bosses such as Mayor Richard Daley of Chicago and big state governors like David Lawrence of Pennsylvania and Michael DiSalle of Michigan. Thus, by the time the Democrats gathered for their 1960 nominating convention in Los Angeles, the Kennedy political machine was unstoppable; he was nominated on the first ballot.

After his victory, Kennedy had less than twenty-four hours to pick a running mate, secure his consent, convince key party chieftains, and prepare his acceptance speech. Kennedy's choice of Senate majority leader Lyndon Johnson of Texas as his vice president provided not only the convention's biggest surprise but one of the hottest behind-the-scenes controversies in Democratic Party history as well. JFK knew the moment he decided on Johnson that party liberals would be outraged for they considered the Texan a conservative anathema. As Arthur Schlesinger Jr. later noted, "The choice of Johnson was regarded as a betrayal. It seemed to confirm the campaign stereotypes of the Kennedys as power-hungry and ruthless." Fortunately for the Democrats, open revolt was nipped in the bud as liberals like Schlesinger and economist John Kenneth Galbraith acted as intermediaries and conciliators between those hostile toward the Texas senator and those within the Kennedy inner circle who pressed for

Johnson's nomination. Johnson helped his own cause by giving strong assurances that he would fully support the convention's civil rights plank. Kennedy's reasons for choosing Johnson varied in detail and emphasis. Theodore Sorensen believed JFK not only admired LBJ, but he believed as well that the Texan simply had all the right credentials for the position. Schlesinger contended that Kennedy hoped the selection would both unite the party and assuage its older members, many of whom believed him too young and inexperienced to win and thus needed the expertise of a savvy, veteran operator like Johnson by his side. Kenny O'Donnell, who objected strenuously to Johnson's selection, claimed JFK reassured him by declaring, "the Vice-Presidency doesn't mean anything" because "I'm not going to die in office." He added, however, "If we win, it will be by a small margin and I won't be able to live with Lyndon Johnson as the leader of a small majority of the Senate." The best interpretation of Kennedy's reasoning came from Theodore H. White's seminal, *The Making of the President, 1960.* According to White, since Kennedy's main strength was in the North and Northeast, it was essential to have someone who could bolster the ticket in the South and Southwest. In his memoirs LBJ confirmed White's (and Kennedy's) contention, claiming that when Kennedy proffered the nomination, "the sectional issue" was emphatically discussed. Moreover, JFK knew the ebullient and persuasive Johnson would be a tireless campaigner. In addition, with Congress still in session, LBJ's position as majority leader would go far toward preventing anything embarrassing for Kennedy from occurring before the legislators went home. Indeed, Johnson shrewdly recognized that much of his prestige as majority leader was because a Republican—Eisenhower—occupied the White House. If Kennedy won, he, not Johnson, would speak for the party. Thanks to a convenient act passed by the Texas legislature, it became possible for LBJ to run simultaneously for vice president (or president) and for another term in the Senate. It was the best of both possible worlds. Even if the Republican nominee Richard Nixon won, Johnson was certain to return to the upper chamber. Finally, Johnson's wife, Lady Bird, whose judgment he respected enormously, urged him to accept Kennedy's invitation to join the ticket. She regarded the vice presidency as a way for her husband to remain politically active while at the same time relieving some of the intense and incessant pressure he experienced as majority leader. Also affecting Lady Bird's decision was LBJ's 1955 heart attack. Becoming vice president, she reckoned, could preserve her husband's health and prolong his life. Finally, LBJ's own ambitions to someday become president contributed to his acceptance. Keenly aware of the handicap of being a Southerner, he hoped that being vice president would help him gain greater national exposure and recognition.

From his opening campaign address in Detroit on Labor Day to his tumultuous Boston homecoming on election eve, in virtually every speech he gave, Kennedy echoed the issues developed by 1950s intellectuals. They saw complacency, lethargy, imminent decline, and decay. So did he. They called for national sacrifice, for energetic executive leadership, for the will to repel communism abroad, and for the revitalization of the public sector at home. So did he. Kennedy's speeches, however, were not deep or profound elaborations of the liberal ethos; they were stripped-to-the-essentials, simplified articulations of liberalism's general ideas for a mass audience. Their purpose was not to amplify the liberal case but to tailor it to the national mood. This JFK did brilliantly by reducing the liberal critique to a single theme: it was time, he proclaimed, "to get the country moving again." At home, this meant clearing the slums, wiping out poverty, bringing prosperity to depressed areas, providing every school child with a decent education, restoring dignity to the aged, and insuring jobs for those adversely affected by automation. In short, Kennedy's proposals were merely the piecemeal reforms Democrats had tried advancing (unsuccessfully) in recent Congresses. It did not matter that his ideas were mere extensions of the already existing welfare state; they were sufficient to permit Kennedy to wrap himself in the Wilson, Roosevelt, and Truman mantle. Most liberals asked no more.

Relative to the cold war, Kennedy's main issue was how to stop losing it. He told audiences that his presidential campaign was "founded on a single assumption, the assumption that the American people are tired of the drift in our national course, that they are weary of the continual decline in our national prestige . . . and that they are ready to move again." He was certain "the people of this country are willing to give, are willing to sacrifice, and will spare no effort" in their responsibilities of meeting the Soviet/communist threat wherever it may manifest itself in the world. Kennedy never doubted America's greatness, that the nation would commit itself to great ends, and that the American people insisted on being "First, period." To Kennedy, keeping the United States "first" meant having more missiles and more conventional weapons than the Soviets, winning the space race as well as the hearts and minds of the newly liberated peoples of Africa and Asia, and having a booming economy. The rhetoric was a bit chauvinistic for some intellectuals, but Kennedy accurately conveyed their sentiments that United States hegemony equated with the good of the human race.

Finally, there was the civil rights issue, which was fast becoming the most emotionally charged political topic in America. At the moment, it posed an insoluble dilemma for Kennedy. To win, he needed the black vote, and to get it, he would have to publicly support civil rights. If he did that, he would certainly lose white southern votes, which he also needed. His liberal advisers urged him to come out now and vigorously campaign as a determined advocate of civil rights. The Democratic Party pros felt otherwise, not convinced that Kennedy could capture the black vote. Moreover, Kennedy's standing within the black community was low. As Marjorie Lawson, a black attorney, told Jack, most African Americans regarded him as "an intellectual liberal" who lacked "in real understanding of Negro problems and goals." Despite the reservations of party chieftains, Kennedy decided to heed the liberals and run as the civil rights candidate, leaving the South to LBJ. His rhetoric was uncompromising: "If a Negro baby is born here," he told a Harlem audience, "and a white baby is born next door, that Negro baby's chance of finishing high school is about 60 percent of the white baby's. This baby's chance of getting through college is about a third of that baby's. His chance of being unemployed is four times that baby's." Kennedy promised that with "a stroke of the Presidential pen" he would do what Eisenhower failed to do—end discrimination in federally supported housing. Sounding like Theodore Roosevelt on his "bully pulpit," Kennedy said that it is the president's job to exert moral leadership "to help bring equal access to facilities from churches to lunch counters, and to support the right of every American to stand up for his rights, even if on occasion he must sit down for them." Whether Kennedy was promising black people enough to improve his image among them remained to be seen.

At the beginning of September, the polls rated the race a toss-up. Veteran pundits, however, gave the Republican nominee, Richard Nixon, the edge, which surprised many because Nixon was the minority party candidate. Indeed, the only reason why Republicans won in 1952 and 1956 was because Eisenhower was a national hero with a nonpartisan image. Moreover, Nixon lacked magnetism, was a mediocre public speaker, and was one of the men most despised by liberals, many of whom were convinced that he was truly an evil man. Although his behavior and tactics prior to 1960 may have warranted such aspersion, by campaign time he had assiduously cultivated the image of a "new" Nixon, a moderate Nixon, and an advocate of Keynesian economics and strong supporter of civil rights. Nixon's critics were unimpressed. Adlai Stevenson believed that Nixon had "put away his switchblade and now assumes the aspect of an Eagle Scout. This is a man of many masks. Who say they have seen his real face?" To many observers Nixon typified the hollow man of a synthetic society. He appeared to be manipulating himself to gain a temporary advantage. As one editor noted, it was not whether the real Nixon was the old Nixon or the new Nixon, but "whether there is anything that might be called the 'real' Nixon, new or old."

Kennedy, too, came under such scrutiny. Many believed him to be a "Democratic Nixon," a man wanting in strong convictions. Indeed, to television commentator Eric Sevareid, "The 'managerial revolution' has come to politics, and Nixon and Kennedy are its first packaged products. The Processed Politician has finally arrived." Remembering how he felt in the 1930s when he was deeply disturbed by the Republic Steel Company massacre and the Spanish civil war, which ended in a brutal fascist takeover, Sevareid added: "I can't find in the record that Kennedy or Nixon ever did, thought or felt these things. They must have been across the campus on Fraternity Row, with the law and business schoolboys, wearing proper clothes, thinking in proper thoughts, cultivating the proper people. I always sensed they would end up running the big companies in town but I'm damned if I ever thought one of them would end up running the country." Despite their perceived similarities, Nixon had two advantages over Kennedy: he seemed the more experienced candidate, and he was Protestant.

Against his aides' advice, Kennedy decided to face the religious issue head-on by speaking before the Houston Ministers Association, a gathering of local Protestant clergy, the majority of whom were openly hostile toward the idea of a Catholic in the White House. At his best in tense situations, Kennedy delivered one of the most impassioned and forceful speeches of his campaign, affirming his belief in an America "where the separation of church and states is absolute—where no Catholic prelate would tell the President (should he be Catholic) how to act, and no Protestant minister would tell his parishioners for whom to vote. There is no Catholic vote, no anti-Catholic vote, no bloc voting of any kind . . . and where religious liberty is so indivisible that an act against one church is treated as an act against all." "By God," Sam Rayburn exclaimed as he watched on television elsewhere in the Rice Hotel in Houston, "he's eating 'em blood raw!" Nixon agreed the next day that the religious issue should be eliminated from the campaign. Kennedy's speech did not end bigotry or silence the barrage of jokes (such as "JFK will rename the Statue of Liberty, 'Our Lady of the Harbor'") about his religion. How many votes his speech before the ministers changed is impossible to say, but the warm response Kennedy received from clergymen gave him a valuable psychological boost and helped him gain the support of previously doubtful Southerners like Speaker of the House Sam Rayburn. In one hour on television, Kennedy buried the issue of his alleged inexperience. On September 25, 1960, the two candidates met in a Chicago television studio to answer questions from newsmen in the first of four historic debates. Seventy million Americans watched the candidates reiterate their campaign arguments and dispute whether the national performance had declined since 1952. Interestingly, the public response to the four confrontations between the two men centered less on their ideas than on which man was the more "telegenic." So little difference did some detect that the veteran political writer Gerald Johnson saw the contest as "Burroughs Against IBM."

Judged by the printed text, the first debate was a draw. However, on television, image counts more than substance of thought or ideas. Grim and confident, Kennedy delivered his message of "imminent danger." "I run for the Presidency," he told viewers, "because I do not want it said that in the years when our generation held political power America began to slip." Nixon smiled nervously and dabbed at the perspiration on his forehead. He looked tired, gaunt, even sickly, the camera detecting the fatigue he felt after a month spent first in the hospital for treatment for a knee infection, then in furious campaigning to make up for lost time. During the debate Kennedy shrewdly concentrated on the audience while Nixon spoke primarily to his adversary, as if he was trying to score points in a debating match. Although Nixon was much more impressive in the final three debates, fewer people were watching. Ironically, radio listeners, according to polls, gave the nod to Nixon but far more people watched the debates than heard them. In short, Kennedy's "image" bested Nixon's. In retrospect, Nixon erred in providing his lesser-known adversary such a valuable forum. In fairness to Nixon, if he had not publicly debated Kennedy on television, Nixon would give the impression that he was reluctant to defend his or the Eisenhower administration's record. He also sensed correctly that the American public wanted a joint television appearance. Thereafter, few disputed the Democratic claim that their man was a bona-fide contender, a "heavyweight." Indeed, Kennedy emerged from the first debate a celebrity. His crowds grew in size; his subsequent speeches were clearer, more refined, and delivered with a confidence that bordered on the bravado; and his receptions seemed more like the "idol-fests" held for romantic leads in the movies. Women shrieked when they saw him, and young girls grabbed at his clothing. Momentum was definitely shifting his way, and Nixon knew it.

Both candidates established a basic theme in their speeches. For Nixon, it was his experience as vice president and his contributions to the Eisenhower administration. Since he could claim no such status, Kennedy instead hammered hard on the need "to move America forward." Repeatedly he declared, "Mr. Nixon says 'We never had it so good.' I say we can do better." Kennedy punctuated his point by engendering a sense of crisis both physical and "spiritual" and an urgency to repair the "harm" inflicted on the nation by eight years of lackluster Republican rule. For example, Kennedy warned of the existence of a "missile gap" (which did exist but in America's favor!) between the United States and the Soviet Union, as well as pointing to the dangers of a communist Cuba and lamenting the condition of the nation's educational system. As both candidates rightly contended, foreign policy was a paramount concern among Americans. Several diplomatic fiascoes marred Eisenhower's last months in office, which benefited Kennedy. The shooting down of a United States U-2 reconnaissance (spy) plane over the Soviet Union caused the scheduled summit conference between Ike and Khrushchev to collapse, while closer to home the growing power and popularity of Fidel Castro in Cuba entrenched a communist regime only ninety miles from the American mainland.

Both candidates developed essentially the same international scenario: this period in time was dangerous, and the United States was struggling for its very survival in its confrontation against monolithic communism directed from Moscow. Both men emphasized the need to cultivate the friendship of underdeveloped nations, but neither showed a particular willingness to accept wars of national liberation as being anything other than Moscow-manipulated communist expansion. They agreed it was imperative for the nation to maintain a strong military posture and preparedness. Nixon, however, in support of his boss' "New Look" (actually that initiative was the handiwork of Eisenhower's Secretary of State, John Foster Dulles) insisted that the strength of the armed forces was adequate to meet any exigency. Kennedy argued to the contrary, assailing the Republican administration not only for the alleged missile gap but also for debilitating conventional forces, which, he maintained, might be needed to fight limited "brushfire" or counterinsurgency engagements. Finally, both Nixon and JFK asserted that national security was best guaranteed by weapon superiority rather than by negotiating arms reduction treaties with the Soviets. Both men embraced the "missile supremacy mentality," despite the fact that any increase in such weapons by either country inevitably led to a new round in an already intense arms race between the two nations with neither side willing to lose the slightest ground in the precarious balance of power game. In the last week of October, an unanticipated development helped put Kennedy in the lead. Martin Luther King, Jr. had been arrested for taking part in a sit-in at the Magnolia Room restaurant of Rich's Department Store in Atlanta. A Georgia judge sentenced King on a "technicality" to four months in jail deep in the rural southern "cracker country." Civil rights activists were certain King would not get out alive. Nixon made no public comment, but behind the scenes he urged the White House via the Justice Department to do "something." Typically, Eisenhower ignored him. The Kennedy team did not hesitate to act. JFK called the distraught and pregnant Mrs. King to express sympathy and pledge help. The next day Bobby Kennedy phoned the local judge on King's behalf. What "exhortation" or admonishment or threat Bobby used on the judge was never fully revealed; at the time the only thing that mattered was King's release, which occurred two days after his sentencing. Naturally, the Kennedys got the credit. In truth, legal developments in the case made the reverend's release mandatory. The Reverend Martin Luther King, Sr. announced that he had intended to vote for Nixon on religious grounds but would now vote for Kennedy. "Imagine Martin Luther King having a bigot for a father," Kennedy said privately, adding, "Well, we all have fathers, don't we?" Although apolitical, King Jr. declared, "It took a lot of courage for Senator Kennedy to do this especially in Georgia. For him to be that courageous shows that he is really acting upon principle and not expedience. . . . I am convinced he will seek to exercise the power of his office to fully implement the civil rights plank of his party's platform." Suffice it to say, the Kennedy phone calls went a long way toward swaying many black voters to vote Democratic that November, especially in the crucial big states like Michigan and Illinois, which Kennedy carried by small margins.

Despite Kennedy's courageous act in helping secure King's release, the country in general gave little indication that it was in a heroic mood or that it was ready to give either candidate a decisive mandate. So evenly did the electorate distribute its ballots on Election Day that, after a long night of television viewing, the nation was still not certain of the outcome. Kennedy's victory margin in the popular vote (two-tenths of 1 percent) was the smallest since 1880, although his edge in the electoral college was more significant, 303-219. He actually won fewer states than Nixon but won the "right" ones in the North and South, which gave him the electoral votes needed for victory. He carried the

South and the populous urban North, the same combination that, since the days of FDR, had formed the foundation of Democratic strength. The first triumph of a Roman Catholic nominee was taken as proof of the country's freedom from bigotry, despite the fact the Kennedy lost the vote of over four million Democrats who would not support a Catholic candidate. Although Protestant voters outnumbered Catholic, Kennedy's preponderant support from those of his own faith enabled him to squeak through. Especially in the electoral college, his religion helped because of the large concentration of white ethnic-Catholic citizens in the populous northern industrial centers. It is conceivable that a Protestant Democrat, even a Protestant Kennedy, might not have done as well.

In the same year Kennedy was elected, noted sociologist Daniel Bell wrote in *The End of Ideology:* "Thus one finds, at the end of the fifties, a disconcerting caesura. In the West, among the intellectuals, the old passions are spent. The new generation, with no meaningful memory of these old debates, and no secure tradition to build upon, finds itself seeking new purposes within a framework of political society that has rejected, intellectually speaking, the old apocalyptic and chiliastic visions."

For many American liberals, however, Kennedy's election offered the promise and, thus, the opportunity to prove Bell's rather cynical assessment wrong. Liberals believed Kennedy not only would resurrect New Deal/Fair Deal progressivism but revitalize it as well with his "intellectual energy" and enthusiastic and optimistic personality. They saw a vigorous chief executive committed to the doctrine of a strong presidency and eager to regain a sense of national purpose. They believed he would help them leave behind the inert Eisenhower years and face up to the challenge of critical public issues, such as civil rights. Kennedy's admirers reiterated that, when Martin Luther King had been jailed, Nixon did nothing but Kennedy intervened to secure his release. They noted, too, that Kennedy had campaigned on a platform calling for the elimination of racial discrimination, federal aid to education, medical care for the aged, and government action to stimulate economic growth. Kennedy's "New Frontier" agenda, which he first articulated in his acceptance speech, called for Americans to challenge the "uncharted areas science and space, [the] unsolved problems of peace and war, [the] unconquered pockets of ignorance and prejudice, [the] unanswered questions of poverty and surplus." The words sparkled. Whether they meant anything remained to be seen.

The Kennedy Presidency: A Positive Assessment

In many ways, Kennedy's Inaugural Address (written by Theodore Sorensen, one of JFK's top aides) came to embody and reflect his entire presidential approach. Every sentence seemed punctuated to heighten the crises allegedly facing the nation, to evoke a sense that Armageddon was imminent. The "revolutionary beliefs" for which Americans sacrificed their lives since the war for independence were "at issue around the globe," Kennedy declared. "Let every nation know . . . that we shall pay *any* price, bear *any* burden, meet *any* hardship, support *any* friend, oppose *any* foe, in order to assure the survival and success of liberty." The words were ennobling, exhorting Americans to a fever pitch of moralism and nationalism. In the Kennedy "frame of reference," the nation truly faced unprecedented crises, especially abroad. If so, then it was time for Americans to "buck up" in national purpose and put their confidence and trust in a heroic leader. That leader, of course, was John F. Kennedy, who would lead them down that most righteous and glorious path in the fulfillment of America's destiny as the leader of the free world and liberator of oppressed peoples. Interestingly, Kennedy made no mention in his Inaugural Address of the crises at home in race or poverty. Nonetheless, according to the *New Republic,* the Inaugural Address had "that ring of command that emboldens men to renew their faith."

Yet, there was also something disturbing about the speech. Its grandiloquent phrases evoked a sense of alarm, of impending, dire consequences for Americans if they did not soon "regenerate" morally, physically, and intellectually. To Kennedy, such rejuvenation was essential to meet *external* challenges or threats, not necessarily to address the social issues at home where the rhetoric of moral fervor would have made far more sense. As will be seen, by making foreign rather than domestic concerns a priority, JFK initially misallocated his administration's resources and energies to problems that could not be solved in the short run. Once he realized this, he refocused his efforts to the home front, realizing his priorities would have to be changed before he could begin to achieve his greatest triumphs.

Although many "true" liberals suspected Kennedy's commitment to that ideology, popular reaction to his call to action was nonetheless enthusiastic. The Kennedy transition team created such fanfare that it seemed the new president was ready to deliver on his promises. Interestingly, his choices for some of his top cabinet officials were hardly known as reformers. Indeed, Secretary of Defense Robert McNamara,

National Security Adviser McGeorge Bundy, and Treasury Secretary Douglas Dillon were all Republicans. JFK nevertheless generated the impression that partisanship was unimportant; what counted were talent, creativity, and bold, aggressive thinking capable of producing the desired results, both at home and abroad. To that end, he brought into his cabinet an interesting array of intellectuals and academics, experts— "technocrats"—from the private sector like McNamara, who was president of Ford Motor Company. This pantheon of supposedly the "best and the brightest" was reminiscent of the halcyon days of FDR and his "Brain Trust." Indeed, similar to their New Deal forbears, the majority came from Harvard and other elite universities and "think tanks." Secretary of State Dean Rusk had been a Rhodes Scholar. Compared to his predecessor, Kennedy appointed three times as many academics to the two hundred most important government posts. In celebrating his advisers' brilliance, Kennedy never missed a chance to accentuate the difference between his presidency and that of the allegedly indolent Eisenhower administration.

If neither the president nor the First lady were the intellectuals many believed them to be, they did read widely, patronize the arts, and exhibit solicitude about the quality of American life. As the journalist Richard Rovere observed, "Kennedy's concern with motels was not only whether Negroes should get into them but with the *idea* of motels—with their function, with the way they looked, with the strange names they bore, and with what they revealed about us."

JFK's administrative style indeed differed dramatically from that of his predecessor. Because of his military career, Eisenhower ran the White House with a "chain of command" approach, a hierarchy of individuals whose job it was to distill all information relative to issues and policies for Ike's approval down to one typewritten page. JFK, by contrast, sought out ideas from an informal, freewheeling group of advisers, whom he often summoned at the spur of the moment to address a problem or to formulate official policy. Chief among them was his brother Robert, whom he had the "audacity" to name at age thirty-five as attorney general. When critics deplored the younger Kennedy's lack of qualifications, the president riposted with, "I don't see what's wrong with giving Bobby a little experience before he goes into law practice." Ike detested "any noisy trumpeting" about national emergencies, preferring "careful calculation and balance." Kennedy, by contrast, to create the impression (or illusion more often than not) that his White House was a flurry of action and decisiveness, relied on moral exhortation and a constant sense of urgency. Such contrivance engendered among his staff and advisers a "crisis mentality" that JFK believed essential to keep his people "fresh" and on their toes so they would never slip into the complacency and intellectual lethargy or sterility that seemed to plague the previous administration.

JFK himself would be the hub of the informal decision-making process. "He wanted all the lines to lead to the White House," *Time* correspondent Hugh Sidey wrote; "he wanted to be the single nerve center." Unlike Eisenhower, who would never make a final decision on issues until they had been thoroughly researched by layers of staff members, Kennedy directly participated in the action. As a result, all too frequently he acted impulsively, making decisions "at the moment," instead of carefully reflecting on his advisers' suggestions. Sorensen celebrated his boss's presence, proudly declaring, "Not one staff meeting was ever held, with or without the president." The emphasis was on informality, flexibility, and hard-hitting advice from energetic aides. As the journalist Henry Fairlie observed, "The Kennedy team lived on the move, calling signals to each other in the thick of the action . . . like basketball players developing plays while the game moved on." As Bobby Kennedy candidly recalled, "We thought we were succeeding because of all the stories of how hard everybody was working." Thus, part of the "Kennedy mystique" was that the nation had a leader so energetic, so inspiring, that he was able to infuse those around him with exalted service to a higher cause. People were so eager to serve their president and country that they would compete with each other to see who could put in the longest hours serving the nation in its supposed time of maximum need. "Senior members of [Defense Secretary Robert McNamara's] staff," one reporter noted, "would hurry to the Pentagon on Sunday mornings to feel the hood of the Secretary's car to determine by its temperature how long he had been at work."

It was also an exhilarating time. According to Arthur Schlesinger, Jr., "Washington seemed engaged in a collective effort to make itself brighter, gayer, more intellectual, more resolute. It was a golden interlude." As one journalist noted, the Kennedy team "aspired to greatness, not just occasionally, but all the time. . . . As the sun rose over the farther most shores of Cathay and began its slow process across the heavens, it was always one minute to midnight somewhere, and something would happen; a government would fall, there would be a significant outbreak of violence. . . . All over Washington, men would rise early to answer the bidding to crisis and to greatness, and the still slumbering public would wake in the morning to find that they had been summoned to meet danger once more; and once more to be rescued from it." In short, the "best and the brightest" of the younger generation were now in charge.

They considered themselves "the cream of the crop," individuals who were both hard-nosed and brilliant—capable of solving any problem and certain they had a special mission at a decisive moment in history. The Kennedy administration, observed Joseph Kraft, "dazzled the nation by intellectual brilliance and social swank," for even White House entertainment sparkled with a panache and refinement not seen in some time. With Pablo Casals playing in the East Room, the American Shakespeare Festival performing at a State Dinner, and Andre Malraux honored for his literary achievements, Kennedy seemed to be transforming Washington into a pantheon of artistic and intellectual preeminence as well as unprecedented governmental energy and effectiveness. Extolling the ambiance, Arthur Schlesinger Jr. later wrote: "Never had girls seemed so pretty, tunes so melodious, and evenings so blithe and unconstrained." Reporters, many of them young and liberal, lavished attention on the high culture and taste that the Kennedys appeared to bring to government. An air of royalty was enveloping the land of the common man. No doubt, Joe Kennedy Sr. was elated by the accolades heaped upon his son by the media and by proper WASP society for the president's *haute* activities at the White House. For through his son, "the old man" finally gained acceptance to a world that had long shunned him.

To those privileged to be part of such an atmosphere, nothing could be more fulfilling. As Walt Rostow's (a top Kennedy adviser) wife, Elspeth, said to him: "I've not seen you for years more cheerful or effective. You're an odd lot. You're not politicians or intellectuals. You are the junior officers of the Second World War come to responsibility." With a PT commander in the White House, surrounded by fellow veterans from either World War II or Korea, the sense of shift in command was almost visceral. There was a downside, however, to the "can do" mentality of Kennedy's people. By the late 1960s and early 1970s, a "hubris syndrome" had emerged within the ranks of many of the people who came to power originally with Kennedy. This was especially applicable to Robert McNamara, Walt Rostow, and others who came to believe that their counsel, decisions, and policies were absolute and, thus, best for the nation. How could their initiatives be anything but correct, for weren't they "the best and the brightest"? If John Kennedy placed such confidence in them, why shouldn't the American people? Such wanton arrogance ultimately led to all manner of failed initiatives at home and disasters abroad, most notably the Vietnam War. Nonetheless, the Kennedy attitude reflected the American mood of optimism in the early 1960s.

Extraordinarily self-assured like the great monarchs of old, Kennedy was highly conscious of his place in history. Indeed, likening himself to the English King Henry V, whom Shakespeare immortalized in one of his historical plays (*Henry V*), Kennedy often quoted Henry's salutation to his army before the battle of Agincourt, which the king won despite being greatly outnumbered by his French adversaries. Kennedy believed the passage accurately described both his summons to national service and his generation's "toughness" and "destiny" to cross the new frontiers of the 1960s. "We . . . shall be remembered; We few, We happy, we band of brothers . . . And gentlemen in England now a-bed Shall think themselves accursed they were not here."

Like FDR, Kennedy wisely endeared himself to the media; he was the first president to allow his press conferences to be televised live. By May 1961 some three-fourths of the American public had seen at least one. Of these viewers, a staggering 91 percent said they had a favorable impression of the president while only 4 percent responded negatively. Thanks, in part, to his élan, Kennedy augmented the already substantial growth in the size and power of the executive branch. Americans increasingly were made aware of the "awesome" responsibilities of the Oval Office. Credulous journalists, especially those of Kennedy's age group, touted the high decision-making taking place in the president's office and relayed to the public their own certainty that the fate of the world depended on the deeds of the American president. Indeed, Kennedy was so eager to promote the image of his abilities to prevent daily cataclysm that, for "posterity's sake," he was the first president (so far as is known) to install hidden microphones in the Oval Office. He had this done in 1962, after which he secretly taped all sorts of meetings, wanting future generations of Americans to appreciate the "perilous" times in which he was president.

Kennedy's celebration of the American presidency greatly pleased liberals, for since the days of FDR, strong White House leadership had become an integral component of the reform ethos. Despite foreign policy debacles and failure to deliver on most of his New Frontier promises, Kennedy remained personally popular throughout his presidency. Along with the booming economy, which after 1962 seemed capable of almost anything, the magnified presidential mystique intensified liberal expectations that government possessed the answers to solve the nation's most serious problems. One of the most important dynamics that shaped the 1960s was the revolution of popular expectations, and such a force owed much to John Kennedy's glorification of presidential activism.

High expectations, especially from liberals, instantly greeted the new president. Such individuals were particularly excited about the possibilities for a New Frontier in domestic policies, for they had been waiting since the end of the Truman era for a harbinger, and they believed Kennedy to be that redeemer. Soon after Kennedy's victory, *Newsweek* predicted that the new president could hope for a "long and fruitful 'honeymoon' with the new Democratic 87th Congress." If JFK "jumps right in with a broad new legislative program," the journal added, "he will find Congress so receptive that his record might well approach Franklin D. Roosevelt's famous 'One Hundred Days.'" The magazine then listed the reasons why Kennedy should have such success, chief among them the support of powerful and effective Democratic leaders such as Speaker of the House Sam Rayburn and Vice President Lyndon Johnson, who would preside over a Senate that he had dominated as majority leader since 1955. With such endorsements, liberals were certain Kennedy could easily enact the Democratic domestic agenda of federal aid to education and to housing, a hike in the minimum wage from $1.00 to $1.25 an hour, and even some form of federal health insurance seemed possible.

Unfortunately, over the course of Kennedy's "1,000 days" as president, only the most modest, "token" reforms were enacted. Indeed, in most instances even less was accomplished, with major initiatives either buried in committee or withdrawn altogether because Kennedy refused to lay his presidency on the line to get them passed. Nonetheless, Kennedy succeeded in enlarging the House Rules Committee, a bottleneck that had long stymied liberal efforts, and Rayburn then shepherded through a two-stage hike in the minimum wage; it would increase to a $1.15 in September 1961 and to $1.25 in September 1963. Congress also approved legislation providing modest public funding for manpower training and depressed areas, notably Appalachia, and in 1962, Congress passed important, though little-noticed, changes to prescription drug regulations, requiring new drugs to be tested for efficacy as well as for safety before they could be sold to the public.

Kennedy also took a few steps toward the advancement of women's interests and rights. Largely as a result of the work done by a presidential commission initially headed by Eleanor Roosevelt (the former First Lady died in 1962), Kennedy issued an executive order that ended sex discrimination in the federal civil service. In 1963 he signed an Equal Pay Act, guaranteeing women equal pay for equal work. Although the measure had no provisions for enforcement, over the course of the next ten years, 171,000 female employees received a total of $84 million in back pay under the act. Most important, Kennedy's commission encouraged women activists on both the state and federal levels to develop networks and to talk seriously about ending long-standing divisions within their ranks. Although certainly no supporter of feminism, Kennedy nonetheless unintentionally helped to encourage a much more self-conscious and assertive women's rights movement after 1964.

Kennedy also actively promoted the cause of mental health. No doubt motivating him to take such initiative was his mentally ill sister. Thanks to his exhortations, in 1963 Congress passed a Mental Retardation Facilities and Community Mental Health Centers Act, which funded local mental health centers that were to provide a range of outpatient services, including marital counseling, help for delinquents, and programs for unwed mothers and alcoholics. The act's principal purpose was to get the mentally disabled out of large state institutions, which many reformers rightly believed were "snake pits" of callous care and abuse. Thanks to subsequent funding for this crusade for deinstitutionalization, the population of mental hospitals declined from 475,000 in 1965 to 193,000 in 1975. Outpatient mental health services meanwhile exploded six-fold between 1955 and 1980. Perhaps most revealing was that such an initiative reflected not only Kennedy's personal interest in such care but an opening salvo as well toward implementing some sort of national health insurance program. The act also expanded federal presence and authority, something that surely pleased liberals.

Reflecting his belief in one of the key tenets of what British journalist Godfrey Hodgson called the "liberal consensus"—confidence in capitalism as an economic system—Kennedy was especially keen on promoting economic growth, which he believed essential for minimizing class conflict. Kennedy also maintained that a robust American economy was equally imperative in fighting communism abroad, especially if the United States hoped to pick up new allies among the recently independent nations of Africa and Asia. Even the most progressive of Kennedy's advisers believed that no inherent flaws existed in America's social and economic order. "Capitalism works," John Kenneth Galbraith declared in his 1958 *The Affluent Society*, "and in the years since World War II, quite brilliantly." In the mind of Galbraith and other liberal Keynesians such as Walter Heller, Kennedy's chief economic adviser, the postwar boom eliminated the issue of redistributing wealth, since an ever-expanding economic pie meant that even America's poorest citizens would someday soon attain middle-class status. In short, the nation had no need for a leftist agenda committed to altering the basic economic structure. As Arthur Schlesinger, Jr. noted, New Deal concerns with "meeting stark human needs for food, clothing, shelter, and employment . . . are now effectively solved." Neither JFK nor his aides were indifferent to the plight of those still at the bottom; they believed remaining inequities could be eliminated within the existing economic structure by simply making it more efficient. Thus, economic growth, not civil rights, aid to education, or national health care, became Kennedy's domestic priority.

In the Kennedy economic "frame of reference" (which was derived in large part from the influence of the Keynesian Walter Heller, who had been an economics professor at the University of Minnesota before Kennedy appointed him to head the Council of Economic Advisors), if the GNP increased at a sufficiently rapid rate, even the most destitute would have the opportunity to participate in prosperity. Thus, increased productivity, which to Kennedy meant a correlative increase in jobs, became the panacea for eliminating social tension or potential class conflict between the "haves" and the "have-nots." Thus, for political and humanitarian reasons, Kennedy was anxious to reduce unemployment and to accelerate economic growth. To Kennedy and Heller, employment was the key, and the only way to ensure job availability was to increase material output. As Heller told the president, "ample employment opportunities are basic requirements for making effective . . . the elimination of discrimination against certain groups of workers" and for "creating a higher standard of living." It did not necessarily matter in what areas production increased—consumer goods, capital goods, or military hardware. All that mattered was keeping production sufficiently rolling to avoid any rise in unemployment. As Galbraith noted, "increasing aggregate output is an alternative to redistribution." Thus, with the full-fledged support of his economic advisers, Kennedy focused on what he called "fine-tuning" the economy.

Since American capitalism had already demonstrated its "revolutionary" productive potential, all that Kennedy and the government now needed to do was to maximize that capacity through monetary, fiscal, and tax policies. For example, Kennedy concluded that moderately higher federal deficits could be risked without causing serious inflation. Cutting taxes also sold well with Congress and the public. Thus, in late 1962 Kennedy came out publicly for one of Heller's main goals: a cut in personal income and corporate taxes. Such reductions, the president argued, would free funds for investment and thereby promote economic expansion. Kennedy was confident that, if the appropriate fiduciary initiatives were implemented, the nation's economy could be put on a course of sustained expansion. Interestingly, the same argument has been used by Republican conservatives since the Reagan years and reinforced and implemented most recently by George W. Bush.

In Kennedy's view, such a task would be relatively easy because the country's problems, according to the president, were "*technical* and administrative. They involve sophisticated judgments which do not lend themselves to the great sort of 'passionate' movements which have stirred this country so often in the past." In short, Kennedy believed that only a few minor adjustments in the status quo were needed for continued prosperity and, thus, for the maintenance of the liberal consensus. At the time, Kennedy's statement reflected a president oblivious to the new "passionate" forces already rocking the country, such as civil rights. As Walter Lippmann acutely observed, Kennedy was "a man of the center . . . far removed from the social struggles of the New Deal."

Kennedy's promotion of "Hellerian Keynesianism" alienated many liberals. They were especially upset by the tax cut proposals, which they believed benefited businesses and upper-income Americans. They had wanted tax reform, which would have shifted the burden of paying away from middle and lower income Americans to the upper classes and corporations. They also wanted an increase in social spending and investment in public works projects to provide jobs for the currently unemployed. Even strong Kennedy supporter John Kenneth Galbraith felt "betrayed" by the president's tax cuts, believing the initiative to be "reactionary Keynesianism," while declaring Kennedy's speech announcing the policy to be the "most Republican since McKinley." Despite liberal opposition, Kennedy believed his decision was based on sound advice, and he thus lobbied hard for congressional approval. He conciliated some reformers by accepting the Keynesian idea of short-run budget deficits to stimulate economic growth. No president before him had dared to publicly assume such a position—not only of cutting taxes in a growth economy but also of simultaneously running (modest) budget deficits. In this sense his quest for a tax cut, which ultimately passed in 1964, left an important legacy to policymaking. In the end, Kennedy's policies helped account for a $100 billion increment in GNP without an appreciable price rise. The economist Seymour Harris praised Kennedy as "the most literate of all Presidents in his understanding of modern economics and revealed great courage in his willingness to risk political losses in putting his economics to the test of the market place." Finally, Kennedy could take satisfaction in knowing that he had brought the country out of the Eisenhower recession and helped stimulate the longest sustained recovery in the nation's history. Interestingly, the success of the Kennedy-Heller economic agenda depended on stability in the steel industry, which was still the nation's most dominant manufacturing enterprise. As Heller told Kennedy, "Steel bulks so large in the manufacturing sector of the economy that it can upset the price applecart all by itself." In Heller's assessment, steel price increases in the years 1947 to 1958 almost single-handedly contributed to the rise in the wholesale price index because steel prices rose faster than other prices, causing inflation; conversely, stability in steel prices after 1958 resulted in zero inflation. Heller believed that the steel corporations could continue to make profits equal to those of the previous years without price increases. Thus, in the summer of 1961, Kennedy used his influence to get both labor and management to establish a new contract that would accept price stability. When the steel union agreed in 1962 to a 2.5 percent wage increase, which was less than its 1950 and 1955 contracts, Kennedy was jubilant because the figure was less than the expected 3 percent productivity increase. Unfortunately, steel magnates such as Roger Blough of U.S. Steel reneged on their agreement not to raise steel prices. The action directly threatened Kennedy's entire economic agenda, and the president, therefore, responded with a passionate commitment and decisiveness heretofore not seen in his other pronouncements on domestic issues. Only the space program received such aggressive solicitude. As Kennedy promised Americans, the nation would land a man on the moon "by the end of the decade." But space was as much a foreign policy issue as a domestic one.

Kennedy responded to the steel industry's affront by galvanizing all his administration's resources. He publicly denounced Blough, contacted either directly or indirectly through his aides the chiefs of the other steel companies, asking them to hold the line on prices, and threatened antitrust action against those companies not willing "to play by the rules" as dictated by JFK. Kennedy was so angry with the steel barons that he told an aide, "My father once told me that all steel men were sons-of-bitches but I did not realize until now how right he was." Blough particularly incurred the president's wrath. He personally insulted Kennedy by arrogantly walking into the Oval Office and handing JFK a press release about the price increase with not even the courtesy of a perfunctory "by your leave." Blough's disrespect for Kennedy's authority caused the young president to respond as though the country were at war, creating a crisis atmosphere that ultimately forced the steel companies to rescind their increases. JFK's rage was justified. He felt betrayed by Blough and the other steel executives, for they imperiously challenged not only his office but his economic vision as well. Moreover, if Kennedy had not responded to the steel moguls' challenge as aggressively as he had, he would have lost all credibility with the unions: they had agreed to accept his agenda on *his word* that management would do likewise. In short, by coming down hard on "big steel," Kennedy preserved not only labor's trust but that of the American people as well. He proved that, despite his age and inexperience, he would not let the interests of a powerful, greedy few dictate to him which "policies" were to be pursued. Interestingly, only on this issue—one so crucial to his economic agenda—did Kennedy mobilize all the forces of his presidency on a question of domestic policy. It should also be noted that steel prices were permitted to rise quickly the next year.

The steel crisis testified to Kennedy's overall approach to domestic affairs. Challenged directly and personally in the one area he deemed critical—the economy—he was capable of using his power vigorously and forcefully to maintain the sanctity and prestige of his office. Kennedy's boldness, however, only amplified his lack of similar commitment on other domestic issues, most notably civil rights, as will be seen later in this essay. As a columnist for the *New Republic* commented, "We get awfully sick of this 'moderation.' All during the Eisenhower administration there was moderation . . . and now instead of Kennedy urgency there is more moderation." In fairness to Kennedy, his failure to be the activist he promised during the campaign was the result of several factors, the most important of which was his narrow election victory. He had triumphed over Nixon by fewer than 113,000 votes out of more than 68 million cast. Although his party had majorities in both houses of Congress, Democratic "numbers" obscured the power of the conservative coalition of southern Democrats and Republicans. Thus, Kennedy, ever the realist and pragmatist, avoided confronting such powerful adversaries on "sensitive" domestic issues such as civil rights, choosing instead to bide his time on such matters until popular opinion was on his side, and then he would act. At the time, JFK was unduly criticized for such complacency. Liberals particularly believed he needed to be more venturesome and aggressive, marshalling his allies and going over the heads of Congress, taking his causes directly to the public and fighting steadfastly for a coherent program of change. Kennedy, however, was acutely aware of the reality of his election, which he rightly interpreted as the American people endorsing change or reform but gradual, not abrupt, not wholesale, and certainly not at the expense literally or figuratively of the middle class upon which the liberal consensus rested. As Kennedy himself succinctly put it: "There is no sense in putting the office of the Presidency on the line . . . and then being defeated," especially on issues middle-class America was not yet ready to embrace. As will be seen, the young president mobilized substantial support for his foreign policy initiatives but refused to put his administration on the line when it came to critical domestic issues. As one wag wryly noted, "The only reason for a man [JFK] to have a popularity rating of 75 percent is to bring it down to 72 percent when he does something he believes in." During his first two years in office, Kennedy evidently failed to find an issue on which he chose to spend that percentage of support. As will be seen, however, by 1963, Kennedy discovered a domestic problem on which he was willing to risk his personal power.

From the moment he took office, Kennedy made foreign affairs an unequivocal priority. Indeed, nothing on the domestic front, not even civil rights, got the president's attention as much as foreign affairs. Kennedy not only fancied himself an "expert" in international affairs (after all, his senior thesis was so well informed it was published) but also was convinced that communism represented the nation's greatest potential crisis and challenge. Kennedy was certain that the United States would lose the cold war to the Soviet Union if it was unwilling to boldly, aggressively, and courageously confront its communist adversaries. Secretary of Defense Robert McNamara bolstered Kennedy's contention that the Soviets were bent on world domination by declaring to an Armed Services Committee, "There is no historical parallel to the drive of Soviet communist imperialism to colonize the world." Like the warring tribes of ancient history, the Russians "sought not merely conquest but total obliteration of the enemy." In this capacity, JFK was no different than Harry Truman who likewise made anticommunism initiatives his administration's priority.

However, beginning in the 1950s, the cold war geopolitically shifted to the third world, where wars of national liberation were being fought, especially in Asia and Africa. As independent countries in those regions were born, Kennedy believed it imperative for the United States "to be there," ready to provide those countries with whatever aid was needed to help turn them toward democracy and make them American allies in the process. However, the Eisenhower-Dulles foreign policy agenda was a one-dimensional program based on the notion of either "massive retaliation"—threatening the Soviet Union with a missile attack if they attempted to "expand" communism elsewhere in the world—or of providing *only* military assistance to the emerging nations. As Kennedy rightly concluded, more often than not, it was not tanks but tractors that were desperately needed to grow food and sustain life. Kennedy's predecessor's agenda had not allowed for what Kennedy called a more "flexible response" to the new exigencies of cold war *real politik*. To be sure, military assistance would still be required to help "stabilize" a newly independent nation, but Kennedy believed that it must come in the form of counter-insurgency units, trained and equipped to fight guerrilla wars effectively. It was time, Kennedy believed, for the United States military arsenal to create "special forces" units, such as the Green Berets, expertly trained in the "art" of guerrilla warfare to crush indigenous (but Soviet supported) communist insurgents. In JFK's view, traditional or conventional units (save perhaps in Europe) were fast becoming obsolete. Operating on the assumption that every local civil conflict was a manifestation of the larger global tension between the Soviet Union and the United States, Kennedy believed it was shortsighted to depend solely on nuclear deterrence to the virtual exclusion of modern forces capable of fighting small "brushfire wars." Also affecting Kennedy was Khrushchev's speech in early January 1961 pledging Soviet support for wars of national liberation, like those in Algeria and Vietnam. Similar to the Peace Corps (also a Kennedy creation to be discussed momentarily), the Special Forces was also a clarion call to young America to help promote and secure freedom worldwide. In this capacity, it was designed to attract the most physically adept and tough-minded young men to carry forward the military and political war against Soviet efforts to control movements for national liberation.

Without question, the creation of the Peace Corps remains one of the Kennedy mystique's most enduring legacies. More than any other of Kennedy's "flexible response" initiatives, the Peace Corps symbolized the high idealism and promise of the New Frontier. To Kennedy, America's fate rested on winning the "hearts and minds" of developing countries. If true, then there was no better way to demonstrate such commitment than the sending of inspired volunteers, the "products" of the most affluent society in the world, willing to put on hold their pursuit of the American dream to help third world people realize their own aspirations. The concept of unselfishly helping others was unarguably noble, representing the very best in the Judeo-Christian tradition. What could be more "American" than young people traversing the globe and living at subsistence pay to share their expertise with those attempting to catch up with the modern world. If nothing else, the idea represented a public relations coup for the Kennedy administration. The program highlighted American idealism and selflessness. Almost immediately, hundreds of dedicated young people responded to the call, willing to sacrifice their own secure futures on behalf of a higher, noble cause. Kennedy's intentions towards emerging nations and the poor countries were honorable. He wanted them to improve their socioeconomic conditions and to enjoy freedom. He was not afraid or paranoid about traditional leftist ideology (socialism) and wanted open-minded diplomats in his administration who shared his sentiments. To Kennedy, it was paramount for the United States to understand why such "thinking" appealed to so many aspiring peoples. He also believed that the democratic left, and not just established elites, should be included in the new governments taking shape in the third world. In short, Kennedy was remarkably attuned to the attitudes, problems, and concerns of the less-developed and newly-independent countries. He established an especially warm rapport with African leaders, including those who embraced socialism. On numerous occasions he publicly announced his support for allowing nations to pursue economic systems that best suited their peculiar needs. Unlike John Foster Dulles, the architect of Eisenhower's foreign policy, Kennedy accepted a nation's right—new or old—to be neutral or non-aligned in the larger cold war struggle between the United States and the Soviet Union. That is not to say that Kennedy stopped trying to woo those nations professing such status—quite the opposite. William Atwood, Kennedy's ambassador to Guinea, expressed the president's desire to compete with the Soviets for new "clients" when he wrote that he refused to accept "defeat" when he was told that "Guinea was down the drain" because the Soviets had "gotten their first." To Atwood (and to Kennedy), the New Frontier meant that the United States was not sitting back and giving up in its competition for new allies among the emerging nations.

Kennedy used American wealth in other ways to do good in the world. He appointed George McGovern to head the sluggish Food For Peace program and vastly expanded the amount of surplus food shipped to hungry people around the world. He also attempted to streamline the nation's foreign aid efforts, creating a new Agency for International Development (AID) and, most important, shifting the emphasis from military to economic assistance.

Kennedy also gave foreign affairs his greatest attention because it allowed him to augment executive power. Despite inherent restraints in Congress' right to declare war, the president had (and still has) a virtually unlimited range of options. From Truman's executive order to send troops to Korea to Eisenhower's decision to land Marines on the beaches of Lebanon in 1958, precedents had been established for granting the president greater discretionary power in the struggle against worldwide communism. In short, in Kennedy's "understanding," *he* was in charge of foreign policy—not the State Department, not Defense, not the NSC, and certainly not the CIA. Thus, he intentionally chose Secretary of State Dean Rusk, who served as an obedient instrument for his own wishes rather than as a decisive, independent source of thought and input. Indeed, under Kennedy, the secretary of state never would be allowed the freedom or latitude to shape the nation's foreign policy, much as Eisenhower had permitted John Foster Dulles to do. The way to get "action" was to formulate foreign policy from the White House, if need be from the Situation Room, where a few trusted aides could make quick decisions and implement them without worrying (or caring) about how various desk officers and their staff would respond. Activism was the watchword, and the only way to make it a reality was for the president and a close, tough-nosed group of like-minded advisers to carry it forward. As Arthur Schlesinger Jr. later summed up the Kennedy approach to foreign policy, "The Kennedys had a romantic view of the possibilities for diplomacy. They wanted to replace the protocol-minded, striped-pants officials by reform-minded missionaries of democracy who mixed with the people, spoke the native dialect, ate the food, and involved themselves in local struggles against ignorance and won." As Kennedy and his inner circle saw it, creative departures from existing patterns of response constituted an indispensable prerequisite for more effectively combating Soviet aggression.

Kennedy was especially concerned about Latin America, long a region suspicious and hostile toward the "Yanqui colossus." Plagued by poverty and an exploding population, their history punctuated by revolutions and coups, Latin Americans correctly regarded the United States as indifferent to their needs and exploitive of their people and resources. However, the Castro revolution and Fidel's subsequent embracing of Marxist-Leninist doctrine forced an abrupt change in the relationship between the United States and its Latin neighbors. No longer could the United States be impassive, allowing American corporations to abuse the region's resources and its peoples. Not only did communism now lie ninety miles from the United States mainland, but if Castroism spread south (which Fidel indeed propagated), the United States would find itself for the first time having to apply the Truman Doctrine of containment to

212 Jobn F Kennedy

its own backyard. Such a scenario could possibly cause the United States to "overextend" itself in the process, thus weakening its global presence. If that occurred, Kennedy was convinced the Soviets would certainly take advantage of American debility by challenging the United States in the underdeveloped nations. Kennedy even worried that, if America became so immersed in fighting communism in the New World, the Soviets might be willing to upset the status quo in Europe. Kennedy believed the best way to avoid such a calamity was to create some sort of Marshall-like plan for Latin America, hence the Alliance For Progress, which became the core of an agreement between the United States and the Latin American Republics, signed in August 1961 at Punta del Este. Kennedy pledged $20 billion of American aid during the next ten years. The other nations promised to invest $80 billion and, most critical of all, to initiate land, tax, and socioeconomic reforms. The 1960s were to be a decade of hope and growth for Latin America.

Kennedy's main objective with the Alliance For Progress was naturally "political stability," meaning that in power at all times in Latin America were pro-United States anticommunist governments. Unfortunately, too often, Kennedy looked the other way at coups that brought to power what proved to be oppressive and brutal military dictatorships. Generally, however, Kennedy followed a pragmatic pattern of nonrecognition and suspension of all aid programs if a new regime blatantly violated human rights or appeared opposed to the Alliance. Despite a willingness to deal punitively with dictators, in the end Kennedy's overarching concern was with any instability that provided communists with an opportunity to take advantage.

Like most cold war presidents, Kennedy was intrigued by the prospect of a summit with his Soviet counterpart, Nikita Khrushchev. Such a possibility seemed imminent as the Soviet premier sent Kennedy friendly messages at the time of his election, and after Kennedy's inauguration, the Russian leader's cordiality continued. Kennedy responded with kind words for improving Soviet-American relations and affirmed his intention not to resume the U-2 intelligence flights over the Soviet Union. Khrushchev made clear to American Ambassador Llewelyn Thompson that he wanted to meet soon with the new president. Unfortunately, the exchange of pleasantries and the possibility of a rapprochement ended abruptly after the Bay of Pigs fiasco (to be discussed in depth later in this essay) in April 1961. Despite the "grave reservations" of many of his key advisers *not* to have a face-to-face meeting with Khrushchev, Kennedy proceeded, agreeing to meet with the Soviet leader in Vienna in early June 1961. Kennedy should have listened to his aides. However, in the end Kennedy prevailed in his first "test" by the Soviets, even though many at the time believed he should have taken a harder line. A "second Berlin crisis" was to be one of Kennedy's more important early foreign policy triumphs in which he proved to be both patient and firm. From the moment at Vienna in which Khrushchev threatened to sign a separate peace treaty with East Germany, allowing that country to take over jurisdiction of East Berlin, Kennedy knew he was being "tested." Moreover, such a treaty would have permitted East Germany to stop a highly worrisome outflow of refugees—actually a "brain drain" of skilled, educated young people—to West Germany. It also would have encouraged the East Germans (whom the United States did not recognize) to cut off Western access to Berlin, an action no cold war president could ever allow. From the beginning of the cold war, Berlin had become the symbol of the Western democracy's determination to stand firm against Soviet threats. In many ways, this latest challenge to the status quo in Berlin was reminiscent of 1948-49, only this time the stakes were higher and more dangerous because both sides possessed massive nuclear capability. As Truman knew in 1948-49, Kennedy knew in 1961 that, if Soviet bluster won, the credibility of America's commitment to contain communism would be dangerously weakened, not only in Europe but also throughout the entire world. Thus, like his predecessor, Kennedy refused to budge or even to negotiate. In Kennedy's view, Berlin was to remain, as it was, until "hell froze over." Kennedy was convinced that, if he acquiesced, he would actually increase the danger of nuclear war by encouraging the Soviets to make new demands. "It will be a cold winter," he told Khrushchev. Kennedy also later told a press conference, "We intend to honor our commitments"—in other words, the United States would never relinquish Berlin. Kennedy then went home and asked Congress for another large increase in defense spending, mobilized 120,000 reservists, and called for a massive fallout shelter program.

The Soviets' response was dramatic. On August 13 they erected a wall—first of barbed wire, later of more solid substance—between East Berlin and West Berlin, putting a halt to the "brain drain." Kennedy wisely refused to be stampeded into provocative action, even though many "hawks" on the "other side of the aisle" (Republicans) urged the president to blow the wall down! Kennedy naturally dismissed such rantings, for to do something as mindlessly precipitous as that would have certainly led to an all-out war between the United States and the Soviet Union. There was simply no way Khrushchev would have allowed American tanks to blow up the wall, kill Soviet and East German workers and soldiers, and do nothing. If he did nothing, he would have been removed from power instantly. Moreover, as Kennedy rightly pointed out, the wall was on the *Soviet side* of the city, on their "turf," and, thus, they had the right to build it regardless of its purpose or what it came to symbolize. In short, Kennedy recognized the Soviet Union's right to close off its zones. Despite Kennedy's refusal to destroy the wall, the situation escalated into one of the most inflammatory moments of the cold war as American and Soviet tanks and soldiers confronted each other menacingly at the borders. Kennedy made it clear to Khrushchev that the United States would defend the beleaguered city. Indeed, Kennedy's declaration, *"Ich bin ein Berliner"* ("I am a Berliner"), delivered in front of the wall to a massive crowd, which cheered his pledge to defend West Berlin, became one of the most memorable lines of his presidency. Once Khrushchev realized that Kennedy was committed to defending Berlin, even if it meant war, he decided to back down. In mid-October 1961, Khrushchev dropped his demands for a separate peace treaty with East Germany, and the impasse gradually faded away. The wall, however, remained and became one of the most imposing physical manifestations of the cold war until East Germans literally tore it down in 1989, symbolizing the end of that forty-five year conflict. Most important, thanks to John Kennedy's calm, patient, but firm resolve not to abandon the American presence in Berlin, the Soviets finally "got the message" that the United States was determined to uphold the status quo in Europe, even if it meant having to go to war to preserve it.

Without question, John Kennedy's finest moment as president came during the most frightening military crisis in world history—the Cuban Missile Crisis of October 1962. It was Kennedy's display of a combination of toughness and restraint, of will, nerve, and wisdom that won him worldwide accolades once the calamity passed. In the most intransigent and dangerous quandary of postwar history, Kennedy proved equal to the task.

Understandably fearful of the American threat to Cuban independence after the Bay of Pigs invasion, Fidel Castro sought and secured Soviet military assistance. Aware that the Russians had been supplying large quantities of arms to the Castro regime, the United States believed that it had a pledge from the Soviets that the weapons would be exclusively defensive in nature. In press conferences in the preceding months, Kennedy made it clear he would not for a moment tolerate anything but defensive weapons in Cuba. If he discovered otherwise, he would take immediate action to protect American security, for he would not allow Cuba to become "an *offensive* military base of significant capacity for the Soviet Union." Then on October 14, an American reconnaissance plane routinely photographing Cuba discovered uncamouflaged sites of Soviet missiles capable of attacking the American mainland with nuclear warheads. Greatly alarmed, Ex Comm (the Executive Committee of the National Security Council), taking care to conceal its activities in order to avoid public panic, began a series of meetings to consider what to do about the threat.

The Soviets' motives for deploying the missiles in Cuba remain obscure. Officially, the Russians claimed they were only protecting the island from attack and no doubt believed such weapons would decrease the probability of an American invasion of Cuba. A more viable explanation of the Soviet action was that it had an international political purpose. It provided them with a relatively cheap way of supporting a fellow Marxist in Castro while simultaneously rebutting Chinese criticism that the Soviets were not vigorously supporting "liberation movements" and, thus, were "betraying" the cause of world revolution. As Barton J. Bernstein observed, "Blocked in Berlin and condemned by the Chinese as unduly conservative, the Soviet Union, by placing missiles in Cuba, could gain prestige in the Communist world and perhaps also be in a stronger position for the next round of negotiations on Berlin." Bernstein's assertion was bolstered by Soviet expert Charles Bohlen, then United States ambassador to France, who believed Khrushchev intended to come to the United Nations in November and deliver an ultimatum to the United States on Berlin, demanding it be given to East Germany. Khrushchev also may have hoped to use the missiles as a way of silencing his own hardliners in the Kremlin, many of who opposed his advocacy of peaceful coexistence. Whatever the reasons for the planting of the missiles, the Soviet leader badly miscalculated his adversary's reaction. Indeed, although Kennedy triumphed in Berlin, acting judiciously but firmly, many both at home and abroad believed otherwise: that the president, when confronted by Russian audacity (the wall), capitulated. Kennedy was acutely aware of this perception and wanted to erase any lingering doubts that he was not "tough" enough to deal with this latest Soviet challenge to his presidency. Thus, this time Kennedy was determined to win a confrontation with the Soviet Union over Cuba.

From the beginning of the ordeal, Kennedy was unequivocal about the missiles' removal; the only question was how. As Robert Kennedy explained in his *The Thirteen Days,* his brother "could not accept what the Russians had done." Out of Ex Comm's far-ranging and candid discussions emerged a number of possible responses: private negotiations with Khrushchev without going public with the missiles' presence; a public announcement then a settlement with the Russian premier, possibly in the United Nations; an air strike and invasion; a "surgical" air strike on the missiles "only"; quarantine or blockade of Cuba; or a "back channel" accord with Cuban leader Fidel Castro.

As the debate continued, Kennedy became convinced that a quarantine—a forceful action but less dangerous than a military attack—was the best option. By not allowing Soviet ships to reach Cuba without first being searched by U.S. naval personnel for "offensive" weapons and designated "accoutrements," such a response demonstrated American determination to stop the Soviet threat while retaining the alternative of a subsequent air strike or invasion. On Monday, October 22, Kennedy revealed his plan to deal with the missile threat, first privately to key congressional leaders from both parties and then to the public on nationwide TV. In his broadcast Kennedy emphasized that the Soviet government had in effect "lied" to him, as they had repeatedly assured the United States both publicly and privately that the arms buildup in Cuba was for purely defensive purposes. The presence of surreptitiously placed offensive missiles was "a deliberately provocative and unjustified change in the status quo which cannot be accepted by this country, if our courage and our commitments are ever to be trusted again either by friend or foe." On the diplomatic front, Kennedy instructed United States ambassador to the United Nations, Adlai Stevenson, to present the photographic evidence of the missiles to the world, which he did. Meanwhile, Secretary of State Dean Rusk obtained unanimous support for the administration's policy from the Organization of American States, a hemispheric-type United Nations, which represented Mexico and Central and South American nations. Valerian Zorin, Soviet ambassador to the UN, at first denied the presence of the missiles, but after Stevenson pushed him for a response with his now famous "I will wait until hell freezes over" admonishment, Zorin admitted that the projectiles were indeed "offensive," in more ways than one!

Tension mounted when Khrushchev declared the quarantine to be "outright banditry" and warned Kennedy that his actions were pushing humanity "to the abyss of a world missile-nuclear war." The Soviets, he announced, rejected the quarantine (which they "interpreted" as a "blockade" and, thus, an act of war), and that, if Soviet ships were halted, they would protect their "rights"—either break the quarantine line or fire on American ships trying to stop them. A press office of the Soviet UN delegation told his American counterpart, "This could well be our last conversation. New York will be blown up by tomorrow and by Soviet nuclear weapons." Although such a comment more than likely reflected irrational panic, information that construction on the Cuban missile bases was proceeding at full speed could not be so easily discounted.

As the Soviet ships steamed toward the quarantine line (originally established 500 miles into the Atlantic, then contracted to approximately 250 miles from Cuba) and the nations stood, in Dean Rusk's now famous words, "eyeball to eyeball" at the brink, the world held its breath. Fortunately, a confrontation at sea was avoided because, as Rusk further announced, "the other fellow blinked [first]." Khrushchev ordered the five ships believed to be carrying either missiles or "embargoed" goods to turn back to the Soviet Union. Hopeful as these actions were, the missiles still remained in Cuba. The rush to Armageddon had been slowed, but the real issue of Soviet missiles in Cuba was unresolved.

Realizing that Kennedy was "serious," Khrushchev made the first overture that the missiles were "negotiable." In an unorthodox diplomatic maneuver, a Soviet intelligence officer approached ABC correspondent John Scali with a possible deal: the Soviet Union would remove the weapons, promise never to reintroduce them, and allow United Nations verification that the missiles had been removed and all bases destroyed; in return, the United States would issue a public pledge not to invade Cuba—in short, public "acceptance" of the Castro regime. Scali immediately passed the offer to his White House contacts and received word back from Ex Comm that the administration was interested in the deal but that time was short.

Kennedy later received the first of two conflicting messages from Khrushchev, which in a rambling way suggested, but did not explicitly offer, a similar bargain. While considering a response, Kennedy received disconcerting news. An American reconnaissance plane had been shot down over Cuba and the pilot killed—the same man who first discovered the missiles, Major Robert Anderson. Equally alarming was Khrushchev's second communiqué, which raised the ante for withdrawing his missiles by demanding that American missiles in Turkey also be removed. As the "blackest hour of the crisis" approached, fearing rash action or errors, Kennedy wisely ordered all atomic missiles defused. However, many in Ex Comm demanded retaliation for the downed American plane and pilot killed. An air strike on the missiles was initially decided, but fortunately Bobby Kennedy prevailed with another idea: he shrewdly suggested that the second letter be ignored and that the president simply answer the first one, giving the Soviets time to respond while postponing the air strike. Interestingly, at the time, some of Ex Comm's military members were genuinely upset that the strike had been momentarily called off. One such individual was Air Force General Curtis LeMay of the Joint Chiefs who "assured" the president that the Russians would do nothing if the United States launched an air strike on their missile sites in Cuba. Suffice it to say, many around the table were just a bit incredulous. After the nightmare was over, Kennedy told one of his closest aides, Kenny O'Donnell, "Can you imagine LeMay saying a thing like that? These brass hats have one great advantage in their favor. If we listen to them, and do what they want us to do, none of us will be alive to tell them later they were wrong." One of Kennedy's greatest "triumphs" in the Cuban missile affair was over some of his advisers.

Kennedy embraced his brother's idea, sending the premier a message agreeing to the conditions of the first letter. Ironically, several months before, Kennedy had ordered the obsolete and useless Jupiter missiles in Turkey to be removed. Although irritated they had not been, as Bobby Kennedy explained, to order withdrawal of the missiles "under threat from the Soviet Union" was something his brother would not do. However, the clock was ticking for Khrushchev; if he did not respond within the next twenty-four hours, Kennedy would order a full-scale invasion of Cuba.

The Soviet premier publicly broadcast his reply to Kennedy's message the next morning without a mention of the Turkish missiles. Khrushchev declared he had "given a new order to dismantle the arms which you described as offensive, and to crate and return them to the Soviet Union." After referring to the UN inspection of their removal and the American pledge not to invade Cuba, he added a welcomed thought about the future. "We should like to continue the exchange of views on the prohibition of atomic and thermonuclear weapons, general disarmament, and other problems relating to the relaxation of international tension." Kennedy quickly wired his appreciation, and the crisis was over.

Kennedy wisely refused to rub Khrushchev's nose in the dirt. When someone suggested he go on television to announce his victory, the president tartly replied, "I want no crowing and not a word of gloating from anybody in this government." Kennedy knew that Khrushchev more than likely would have to endure harsh criticism from his own hardliners and hawks (which he did), as well as from the Red Chinese for having capitulated to the "American imperialists and militarists" and for selling out a fellow Marxist state. Kennedy also wanted to do nothing to further the illusion that all the United States had to do was be tough with the Russians—in effect, Dullesian brinkmanship—and they would collapse. As he told Arthur Schlesinger Jr., the Cuban situation had unique aspects favorable to the American position that would not necessarily be present in other crises. Moreover, despite the concession, the Soviet Union remained a formidable and dangerous adversary and one not to be humiliated or senselessly provoked.

As the world breathed a huge sigh of relief, speculation raged why Khrushchev had backed down. It is impossible to know exactly why, but the most likely explanation was the United States' overwhelming nuclear superiority in all capacities—bomber planes to deliver the bomb, submarines armed with Polaris missiles, and ICBMs. Indeed, there was a "missile gap," but it was in the favor of the United States, and Khrushchev knew it. Also, like Kennedy, the Soviet premier was horrified at the thought of a nuclear war that would have killed 100 million Russians, a like number of Americans, and untold numbers in other nations. Thus, both men realized that the timing was right to discuss and hopefully negotiate some sort of treaty that would lay the foundation for eventual nuclear disarmament. Indeed, Kennedy believed it imperative after the world had come so perilously close to nuclear holocaust to try with renewed vigor for a test ban treaty with the Soviets.

The task was not an easy one. In both the United States and the Soviet Union, their respective military-industrial complexes opposed any form of disarmament and distrusted any whisper of détente. Despite such powerful forces arrayed against them, Kennedy and Khrushchev prevailed, succeeding in the summer of 1963 in establishing a significant "thaw" in the cold war by signing a nuclear test ban treaty. According to the terms, underground tests could continue since there would be no on-site inspections. Atmospheric tests, however, were banned. Other nations with nuclear weapons were invited to join in the agreement. The British agreed to do so; France and China, the two newest members of the nuclear club, refused. Although very limited in scope, the treaty nonetheless was a starting point that hopefully someday would lead to more substantive talks and disarmament treaties. Kennedy summed up this beginning by quoting one of his favorite Chinese proverbs: "The journey of a thousand miles begins with a single step."

The 1963 Nuclear Test Ban Treaty reflected Kennedy's belief that it was time to set aside the hysterical slogans of the cold war and seek a basis of peaceful coexistence with the Soviet Union. Gone was the anticommunist rhetoric and histrionics that characterized his first two years in office. A "new" Kennedy had emerged who disavowed "a Pax Americana enforced on the world by American weapons of war." "We must re-examine our attitudes," Kennedy told an audience at American University where he announced the test ban treaty, "as individuals and as a nation—for our attitude is as essential as [that of the Soviet Union]." It was time for Americans (as well as himself) to stop seeing the Soviet Union as a "government or social system so evil that its people must be lacking in virtue." In effect, Kennedy, the quintessential Cold Warrior, was asking Americans to reevaluate the very assumptions that had driven American cold war policy since the conflict's inception. Kennedy, now the "peacemaker," appealed for a new understanding of the bonds that united all humankind, for as he told his university audience, "in the final analysis, our most basic common link is that we all inhabit this small planet. We all breathe the same air. We all cherish our children's future and we are all mortal."

To most Americans, Kennedy's "toughness" during the missile crisis was nothing short of magnificent. Bohlen called it the greatest moment in his administration, and British Prime Minister Harold MacMillan would later say that the president earned his place in history by this one act alone, for he finally demonstrated that he had more "courage" than "profile." Indeed, there is no doubt that the Cuban Missile Crisis proved to be the critical event of Kennedy's presidency. Throughout his career (even his life), Kennedy obsessed about being "tough" and manly. The missile crisis allowed him to both show his mettle and recognize the dangers of being too manly. The crisis also gave Kennedy a tremendous confidence boost that he could handle any eventuality, for it created a foundation for genuine wisdom and restraint, and for charting a course that involved the substance of leadership and vision rather than just image. Perhaps most important, Kennedy's "victory" in the missile crisis gave him the personal fortitude (and public support) needed to address crucial domestic issues.

As a result of the missile crisis, in many ways John Kennedy became a different president. This was especially true in his last months in office, which saw him finally embrace the liberal ethos instead of pay lip service to it. Consequently, not only did Kennedy push hard for civil rights legislation but other reforms as well, for which liberals had been clamoring since the moment he took office. Of all the domestic initiatives, however, civil rights loomed the largest. As the movement continued to intensify, Kennedy found himself forced to endorse the demands for change swelling from below. Simultaneously, the ethical thrust of the civil rights struggle and the increasing sensitivity of his advisors to the economic plight of the poor propelled Kennedy into a far more activist stance on behalf of those Americans shackled by the chains of poverty. In a presidency thus far marked by moderation at home and a cold war mentality abroad, such changes seemed dramatic.

Without question Kennedy's most momentous breakthrough came in the area of civil rights, an issue he had long avoided. By the summer of 1963, he could no longer ignore black Southerners, as growing frustration in the black community engendered increasing civil rights demonstrations. In Georgia, Alabama, Mississippi, North Carolina, and Florida, African Americans took to the streets once again, angry at the federal government's refusal to act. They were intent through the force of their own moral commitment to bring down the barriers to equal treatment. "Freedom Now" rang like a clarion call throughout the region. Nowhere was the crisis greater than in Birmingham, Alabama, the nation's most segregated and repressive city. Led by Martin Luther King, Jr., the city's black people marched in silence to demand that African Americans have equal access to public accommodations and to petition the city's business leaders to change their hiring practices so blacks could have decent jobs. Unfortunately, the marchers were met by some of the most brutal reprisals ever visited upon American citizens in the history of the Republic. The city's notoriously racist sheriff, Bull Connor, not only unleashed his police force who beat mercilessly any demonstrator they came across, including women and children, but used fire hoses and police dogs as well. The entire nation was transfixed as it witnessed on nightly TV the force of naked racism. As CBS commentator Eric Sevareid observed, "A newspaper or television picture of a snarling police dog set upon a human being is recorded in the permanent photoelectric file of every human brain."

The Kennedy administration responded with unprecedented pressure on Birmingham's political leaders and businessmen to help stop the violence and grant concessions. In the end, all such efforts failed, forcing Kennedy to finally take the issue directly to the American people (Northern whites in particular), who at last, like their president, had grown sickened by the violence and brutality they witnessed nightly on their television sets. In a speech delivered largely extemporaneously because the text had not been completed by the time he went on the air, Kennedy told his fellow citizens that civil rights was above all "a moral issue . . . as old as the scriptures . . . as clear as the American

Constitution." America, Kennedy declared, had been founded "on the principle that all men are created equal, and that the rights of every man are diminished when the rights of one man are threatened." It should be possible, he said, "for American students of any color to attend any public institution without having to be backed up by troops. It ought to be possible for American consumers of any color to receive equal service in places of public accommodation, such as hotels and restaurants . . . without being forced to demonstrations in the street, and it ought to be possible for American citizens of any color to register and to vote in a free election without interference or fear of reprisal . . . But this is not the case. . . . We preach freedom around the world, and we mean it, and we cherish it here at home, but are we to say to the world, and much more importantly, to each other that this is the land of the free except for the Negroes; that we have no second class citizens except Negroes, that we have no class or caste system, no ghettoes, no master race except with respect to Negroes?"

With a passion he had rarely shown before, Kennedy asked his audience: "Who among us would be content to have the color of his skin changed and stand in the Negro's place? Who among us would then be content with the counsels of patience and delay?" The time had come, Kennedy declared, for "the nation to fulfill its promise. . . . A great change is at hand, and our task, our obligation, is to make that revolution, that change, peaceful and constructive for all."

Although late in coming, the president had offered a ringing endorsement of almost every basic demand of civil rights activists. For many, however, the commitment was still too late and too little. Nonetheless, Kennedy's bill called for an end to employment discrimination, equal access to public accommodations, and a stronger role for the Justice Department in initiating desegregation. Although most of the bill had to be substantially strengthened over the course of the next year by his successor, Lyndon Johnson, Kennedy, nevertheless, committed himself to the cause as he never had before, placing his own credit on the line in the process. For a man who always avoided conflict on domestic issues, it was a decisive moment. Kennedy had taken sides—first, because it was right, and second, because he no longer had the option of avoiding a choice.

By 1963 a profound change had occurred in John Kennedy's political perspective. He had found his voice. He absolved himself of the shibboleths of strident, anticommunist rhetoric and advocated instead the pursuit of accommodation and peaceful coexistence with the Soviet

Union. On the home front, Kennedy embraced the civil rights cause as his own and identified morally with black protestors, whom he considered the vanguard of a reform impulse that would help him ameliorate other conditions as well, such as poverty. Indeed, he defined the issue of racial equality as the nation's most pressing issue and was willing to commit the resources of his presidency to make it a reality. During the first two years of his presidency, Kennedy lacked the vision, especially when it came to domestic problems, to give direction to the brilliant technicians who surrounded him. Now, for the moment at least, he had a definite agenda he was willing to "spend" political credit fulfilling and to give structure and order to those pragmatic options his advisors so cherished.

The Kennedy Presidency: A Negative Assessment

Although Kennedy seemed to have "turned the corner" on his presidency in 1963, his overall record in the realm of domestic policies was hardly stellar for a variety of reasons. Perhaps the most important factor was his own lack of interest in such affairs, which in turn made Kennedy an uninspiring leader in this area. As noted earlier, Kennedy prided himself on being a detached, cool, and dispassionate politician, especially when it came to domestic issues. Not until late 1963 did he come to finally embrace the liberal ethos. Until that time he identified with moderates and even conservatives, particularly on the more sensitive social questions such as civil rights. In fact, he disdained liberals, referring to them as "honkers." He told Theodore Sorensen, hard at work on the inaugural address, "Let's drop the domestic stuff altogether." Sorensen did, and consequently the speech focused almost exclusively on foreign affairs, which Kennedy believed was his bailiwick. Indeed, Kennedy made no pretense of hiding his priorities, telling Richard Nixon, "Foreign Affairs is the only important issue for a President to handle, isn't it? . . . I mean who gives a shit if the minimum wage is $1.15 or $1.25, compared to something like Cuba?"

Kennedy also had to contend with a powerful coalition of conservative Democrats and Republicans, whom he was certain would defeat easily major liberal initiatives. In fairness to Kennedy, this alliance had been in place since 1938 and had forced even FDR to cool the reform impulse. Liberals nonetheless expected Kennedy (based largely on his campaign rhetoric) to be more aggressive and venturesome, rallying his allies, going over the heads of Congress, and fighting steadfastly for a coherent program of change. Kennedy simply lacked both the self-assurance and the sense of direction to pursue that path. Even having as his vice president one of the most powerful senators in history was not enough to overcome this conservative obstruction, which defeated or refused to act on a number of Kennedy proposals, including health care for the aged and creation of the Department of Urban Affairs. Interestingly, as vice president, Johnson was far weaker on the Hill than he had been while Senate majority leader. In short, instead of fighting for his bills, Kennedy acquiesced in the face of opposition, constantly reminding liberals of his lack of mandate and of the political realities on Capitol Hill. Such easy capitulation angered and alienated liberals, many of whom rightly believed Kennedy simply lacked the "courage" about which he had written to push his agenda forward. Never one to idly accept such reproof, Kennedy told his liberal critics that presidential prestige depended in part on maintaining an aura of effectiveness. One had to conserve one's resources for major battles. "There is no sense in raising hell and then not being successful," he said. "There is no sense in putting the office of the President on the line on an issue and then being defeated." Although Kennedy may have been somewhat correct in his analysis, liberals believed that, if he bypassed Congress and appealed directly to the people for support for his New Frontier, he ultimately would have prevailed and liberalism would have triumphed. Unfortunately, not until the end of his administration did Kennedy embrace the efficacy of such action.

No issue reflected liberal frustration more than Kennedy's failure to provide the leadership essential for the passage of a federal aid to education bill. The measure was the centerpiece of the Democratic Party's 1960 platform (along with civil rights), and such an initiative would have provided desperately needed federal dollars to help equalize educational opportunity throughout the country. Kennedy, however, vacillated, offering at best "inept guidance" to the bill. The measure's death knell was a March 1961 press conference in which Kennedy created confusion about his own position on federal funds for parochial schools. In his rambling Kennedy implied that some support for religiously affiliated schools might be acceptable. In a country still with a Protestant majority and still suspicious of Catholics in secular positions of power and devoted to the principle of separation of church and state, any hint of aid to private parochial institutions would doom such an initiative, making its defeat a certainty. When Kennedy later retracted such "a possibility," he alienated liberal congressional Catholics such as John McCormack of Massachusetts (who later replaced Sam Rayburn as Speaker of the House) from supporting the larger cause. From that point on, Kennedy lost his capacity to provide leadership on the issue. Liberals viewed the president's position as timid and indecisive, hampering any possibility of forging a majority coalition to see the bill through.

Although fanfare abounded relative to the administration's cultivation of the arts and academia, creating an aura of brilliance and excellence around Kennedy, in reality there was little of substance behind the glamour and "style." Activism seemed an end in itself, with the flurry of hard work and urgent meetings becoming a façade behind which little was actually accomplished, especially when it came to domestic issues. Indeed, "process" became more important than performance. The Kennedy men, journalist Henry Fairlie observed, seemed to "have been in a constant hurry, taking last minute decisions at last minute meetings, making last minute corrections to last minute statements." The point was not always clear; it was as though "they were always trying to catch up with events, or with each other, or even each with himself." In *Profiles in Courage*, Kennedy had written that "great crises produce great men." As far as Kennedy was concerned, he certainly was not writing about himself, for most of his presidency he demonstrated little of the fortitude (or virtue as will be seen) he had *others* so eloquently put into words. A more accurate statement would have been that the appearance of great crises creates the *impression* of great men. The quality of greatness depended (and still does) on wisdom, experience, and reflection than on frenetic activity and a list of advanced degrees from Ivy League schools.

Perhaps most disturbing was Kennedy's penchant for placing greater emphasis on urgency and style, or profile, rather than on creating a coherent vision of the direction he wanted to lead the country. As James Reston of the *New York Times* observed, "When I asked the president what he wanted to have achieved by the time he rode down Pennsylvania Avenue with his successor, he looked at me as if I were a dreaming child. I tried again: Did he not feel the need of some goal to help guide his day-to-day decisions and priorities? Again a ghastly pause. It was only when I turned the question to immediate, tangible problems that he seized the point and rolled off a torrent of statistics." In short, like the men who surrounded him (who, noted the *New Republic*, exhibited "a certain coolness and grayness"), Kennedy lacked an ideological viewpoint to give direction to his moral mission and, thus, entered the White House with more an approach than with a charge.

The most obvious negation of the Kennedy mystique and, thus, potential for "greatness" was Kennedy's egregious foundering on civil rights. Without question, Kennedy's record on civil rights borderlined on the abysmal until the end of his administration. Indeed, in this most crucial area of activism, Kennedy's "contribution" (until late 1963) was as negligible as his predecessor's and certainly not even remotely in the league of his successor. To have expected otherwise, liberals had deluded themselves, for through most of his years in the House and Senate, Kennedy appeared oblivious to the issue of racial equality. Only after it became clear that his presidential candidacy was real did Kennedy seek advisors with strong connections to the black community. Even then, most of these were white. "They were okay," a black associate later said, "but they did not know much at the time about civil rights." Nevertheless, once the Democratic nomination had been won, it became imperative for Kennedy to reach out for African-American support, which was key to winning industrial states like California, Illinois, Michigan, New York, Ohio, and Pennsylvania. Marjorie Lawson, a black Kennedy advisor, urged the candidate to take explicit steps to overcome the negative image that his past record had generated in many sectors of the black community. "Somehow," she wrote, "some warmth has to be added to this image of intellectual liberalism." In particular, she urged Kennedy to heed the civil rights movement and its commitment to the protection of basic human rights. "The candidate who wins [blacks] will be the one who is most able to make them feel, not only that he understands, but that he cares about human dignity. . . . Nothing short of a *national gesture* will erase the doubts that now exist in the minds of rank and file Negro voters."

With shrewdness and skill, Kennedy took Lawson's advice and set out to woo those he had previously ignored. As he campaigned in Northern black communities, he promised he would abolish racial discrimination in federally-aided housing by executive order. He embraced proposals for new civil rights legislation and criticized the Eisenhower administration for failing to provide executive leadership to enforce existing mandates. As noted earlier, Lawson's exhortation for a *"national gesture"* was Kennedy's behind-the-scenes maneuvering to secure Martin Luther King's release from a Georgia jail. On election day, Kennedy reaped the harvest, his thin margin of victory almost certainly owed to black voters grateful for his intervention on behalf of their leader.

Once in office, however, it became all too apparent that Kennedy's promises were all campaign "gas." Urged to give moral direction to the nation through a new emancipation proclamation, Kennedy kept silent. There was always an excuse for not having acted; most often it was connected to a desire to avoid divisive issues that might jeopardize what was most important to him: foreign policy. While House and Senate liberals fought for new civil rights legislation, fulfilling the 1960 Democratic platform to do so, Kennedy offered only nominal support, refusing to spend any of his political credit for such measures. When confronted by these failures, Kennedy invariably responded that existing legislation was sufficient and that "the timing" was not right for him to use his office to advocate such reforms. There were simply other, more pressing concerns, such as a tax cut and defeating communist challenges abroad.

Robert Kennedy, as attorney general, was somewhat more responsive than his older brother on civil rights. Although later confessing that he had never "lain awake at night thinking about civil rights" before becoming attorney general, he nonetheless was a fanatic when it came to law enforcement and, thus, was outraged at the failure of the Justice Department to implement existing legislation. Although legally committed to protecting civil rights activists from the violence perpetrated on them by Southern law enforcement officials, Robert Kennedy's "sympathy" ended there. Indeed, Robert had few qualms when Southern police prevented violence by simply arresting en masse Freedom Riders and other demonstrators and sending them off to jail. Kennedy even tried to persuade activists to call off their protests, concerned that such constant agitation would embarrass the president when he went abroad. As he told Harris Wofford, Kennedy's White House civil rights advisor, "This is too much! I wonder whether [the Freedom Riders] have the best interest of their country at heart. Do you know that one of them is against the atom bomb—yes, he even picketed against it in jail! The President is going abroad and this is all embarrassing to him." The attorney general believed that his own gradualist policy of litigation was the only acceptable response to America's civil rights crisis, and that he alone should define "the line" between protest and accommodation. As reflected in his comments to Wofford, Bobby was more concerned about the disorder and chaos civil rights demonstrators were causing and how such "activity" negatively affected the nation and the president. Unfortunately, Robert Kennedy, like his brother, was more preoccupied with image than with human rights.

For those civil rights activists who believed they had been guaranteed federal protection from white reprisals, Kennedy's failure to provide it amounted to outright betrayal. Promises had been made and then broken. Unhappily, increasingly frustrated black leaders ascribed such feelings to liberals in general, whom they believed "had used up all their credit." As one black newspaper editor wrote, it was time to bid them all "a fond farewell with thanks for services rendered, until they are read to re-enlist as foot soldiers and subordinates in a Negro-led, Negro-officered army, under the banner of Freedom Now." Even some of Kennedy's strongest African-American supporters were disillusioned, tired of hearing from the president that "the time is not ripe for a civil rights fight." Although Kennedy repeatedly cited political obstacles (some of which were legitimate) and legislative logjams (which his lack of commitment and ineptitude often caused) as restraining forces, African Americans, such as Louis Martin, concluded, "it has been my experience that the public will accept with more favor a batter who strikes out swinging with all his might than a batter who takes the strikes with his bat on his shoulders." By 1962, in the minds of many African Americans, Kennedy was in a serious "civil rights slump," striking out repeatedly while watching every pitch blow by him without lifting the bat off his shoulders once!

In almost every respect, the black critique of the Kennedy record on civil rights was accurate. When the authority of the federal government was directly challenged, Kennedy responded. Or if northern white public opinion seemed discomfited by the brutality and violence they saw on television that was being perpetrated on civil rights marchers and they wanted something done (largely to ease their own revulsion and consciences), then Kennedy acted. Even such grand *gestures* as having federal troops and marshals safeguard James Meredith's admission to all-white University of Mississippi seemed reactive, coming only after extensive federal efforts to work with local white Southern officials. Martin Luther King, Jr., trenchantly summed up Kennedy's record when he wrote, "if tokenism were the goal, the administration has moved us adroitly toward it."

Most distressing of all was Kennedy's indifference, if not outright detachment, from the nation's most pressing domestic crisis. No doubt Kennedy saw on the nightly news the violence and brutality inflicted on black citizens; yet, he remained unmoved, never displaying any sense of moral outrage at such wanton abuse. During his first two years in office, Kennedy simply put civil rights on a back burner, concentrating all his energy and interest on foreign policy while black citizens at home suffered segregation and discrimination. Harris Wofford was so disturbed by the president's callousness that he resigned in March 1962 to join the Peace Corps staff. Wofford's resignation letter encapsulated the frustration and anger many felt within the Kennedy administration about their boss's insensitivity. "You should understand," Wofford wrote Kennedy, "why the larger problem of our integration in this new world represented by Africa interests me, as it does you, more than dealing with the albeit important remaining *rear-guard actions* on the domestic front." Written thirteen months before the Birmingham demonstrations, eighteen months before Martin Luther King Jr.'s March on Washington, and twenty-four months before Mississippi's Freedom Summer (which saw the murder and disappearance of three young voter-registration workers, two white and one black), the letter spoke volumes about the reigning assumptions in the Kennedy White House relative to the civil rights issue. For all too many Kennedy people, civil rights was still a "rear-guard action" even at the moment when black citizens were, in King's words, moving from "sporadic, limited actions to broad-scale activities different in kind and degree from anything done in the past."

It took a "confrontational conversation" between twelve black leaders and Robert Kennedy to finally get Kennedy to understand the depth and intensity of black alienation largely caused by the president's indifference. The encounter shocked and stunned Bobby, who conveyed to his brother how enraged black people had become because they believed the administration had betrayed them. They simply had run out of patience, no longer willing to accept the Justice Department's legal initiatives as "all that can be done." The entourage, led by the novelist James Baldwin and noted sociologist Kenneth Clark, vented their rage at the administration's insensitivity and inaction, which they found egregious in the face of the brutal beatings and insufferable harassment that were daily occurrences for civil rights workers. How, they asked, could Kennedy be so smug and self-congratulatory when churches were being bombed and civil rights workers shot at while federal agents claimed they had no authority to intervene? No longer, Baldwin declared, would African Americans accept white dictation of the pace and substance of progress on civil rights. Although Robert Kennedy's first response was to resent the attack on his own and his brother's integrity, the meeting ultimately helped to generate a new and clearer sense of the dimensions of the crisis and the urgency of a meaningful response from the president.

Although Kennedy ultimately responded with a proposed civil rights act in 1963, for many black leaders it was too little, too late. In the end, virtually all of Kennedy's domestic initiatives were stalled in committee, defeated outright, or so "watered down" or emasculated that they no longer reflected their original purpose. The deadlock delaying the civil rights bill served as an apt symbol of Kennedy's larger record in domestic policy between 1961 and 1963. Largely because of his own lack of legislative experience and reluctance to put his "office on the line" when it came to controversial social welfare initiatives, Kennedy's prospects in pushing his measures through Congress seemed no better in 1963 than they had been earlier. On November 12, 1963, the *New York Times* noted, "Rarely has there been such a pervasive attitude of discouragement around Capitol Hill and such a feeling of helplessness to deal with it. This has been one of the least productive sessions of Congress within the memory of most of its members." The *Times,* one of the nation's most "liberal" papers, was no doubt intimating the liberal disillusionment and disaffection relative to Kennedy's lack of leadership and concern for domestic issues. Kennedy's rhetoric had aroused liberal expectations, but he refused to commit the power and prestige of his office, as well as his own personal popularity, to bring about domestic change. In short, New Frontiers at home still stood in the distance.

Although priding himself on being an expert in foreign policy, some of Kennedy's worst failures as president occurred in this arena. Indeed, Kennedy was only four months into his presidency when he suffered his first serious setback, the Bay of Pigs fiasco. Kennedy's attempt to covertly overthrow the Castro regime on Cuba not only reflected his obsessive anticommunism but his equally pronounced preoccupation with being "tough." Such a compulsion contained a potentially dangerous machismo, which, more than likely, was the result of growing up in an extraordinarily competitive family. Bobby displayed it as well. Kennedy's machismo may also have been a reflection of insecurity, caused by his overbearing, critical, and repressive father. Thus, he constantly felt the need to prove himself as worthy of his office as the youngest elected president in the Republic's history. Whatever the explanation, Kennedy had an overriding desire to prove his mettle. To face crisis and to prevail was to demonstrate one's strength and manliness. As he prepared in May 1961 for his first meeting with Khrushchev, he said, "I'll have to show him that we can be as tough as he is. . . . I'll have to sit down and let him see who he is dealing with."

Nothing exposed these tendencies more clearly than Kennedy's attempt to overthrow Fidel Castro. The scheme that he and his equally zealous anticommunist advisors concocted was to use anti-Castro, CIA-trained and equipped exile-insurgents, land them at the Bay of Pigs on Cuba's southern coast, and support them covertly in a guerrilla war to bring down the Castro regime. The invasion took place on April 17, fewer than three months after inauguration day and proved to be one of the most disastrous military ventures in modern American history. Indeed, for a president who read history voraciously, Kennedy should have known that his "expedition" to Cuba smacked of good, old-fashioned mid-nineteenth-century American (largely Southern-inspired and financed) filibustering, which invariably ended in disaster and embarrassment for the United States.

Kennedy had complicated motives for approving the attack. Perhaps the most important was his desire for a quick and dramatic victory over communism ninety miles from the United States. Such a triumph would undoubtedly go far in helping Kennedy boost his image not only of being tough but also of being capable of handling any crisis or threat to American security, which many Americans believed the Castro government represented. Politically, Castro's overthrow would help erase any lingering reservations Americans had about their president's age and inexperience. He would have proven himself deserving of their trust and confidence in his abilities to govern the nation. Like Eisenhower, who had cut off diplomatic relations with Cuba in January 1961, Kennedy was angered by Castro's volatility, his virulent anti-American rhetoric, and his growing rapprochement with the Soviet Union. Kennedy was also pressured "to do something about Castro" from his father and other anticommunist right-wingers who were certain that the Soviet Union intended soon to make Cuba another Soviet satellite. Reminiscent of the "yellow journalism" of the late 1890s (which, ironically, helped push the McKinley administration into a war with Spain to help "liberate" Cuba), columnists and editorial writers added to the anti-Castro mania, exploiting Americans' fear of communism and urging the president to act before "bolshevism" was entrenched off the Florida coast. Ironically, the Castro revolution against the corrupt, American-puppet government of Fulgencio Batista represented the kind of democratic insurgency against totalitarian governments with which Kennedy wished to identify. However, when Fidel announced that he was a Marxist, as far as the United States and John Kennedy were concerned, his days were numbered.

Although the operation had been devised and put in motion by the Eisenhower administration, it was Kennedy who gave it the fatal green light, despite knowing very little about the plan's particulars or about how poorly conceived it was from its inception. Even the reservations of a number of advisers, both military (such as Marine Commandant David Shoup, who warned Kennedy that Cuba was too large of an island to conquer) and civilian (Chester Bowles told Dean Rusk that "this [the invasion] would be an act of war"), could not deter Kennedy from making the wrong decision. As Senator J. William Fulbright, chairman of the Senate Foreign Relations Committee, told Kennedy, in the larger picture Cuba was not worth so much attention and energy for, although it was "a thorn in the flesh," it was not "a dagger in the heart." Unfortunately, the saner counsel of men like Shoup and Arthur Schlesinger Jr. went unheeded, while that of the "true believers," Robert McNamara, Robert Kennedy, Allen Dulles and Richard Bissel—all of whom supported the plan—prevailed. Perhaps the most "phenomenal" aspect of the venture was the CIA's plan to assassinate Castro, which Dulles and Bissel were confident could be timed and coordinated with an invasion of exiles from Nicaragua. To ensure success, the United States was to lend "covert" naval and air support as the insurgents hit the beach at the Bay of Pigs. Kennedy was also assured that no sooner would the exiles land than anti-Castro rebels by the thousands would pour out of the jungles of Cuba, supporting the uprising and helping drive the dictator from power.

There is no need here to give a blow-by-blow, hour-by-hour account of the debacle; there are numerous, excellent accounts available for that purpose. Virtually all agree that the invasion was destined to end up a disaster and that, by approving it and subsequently accepting responsibility for its failure, the "profile" of toughness and courage Kennedy had so assiduously cultivated would suffer a serious blow. Indeed, his loss of credibility both at home and abroad seemed irretrievable. Thus, what is most important is the event's impact on the Kennedy presidency. First of all, Kennedy never should have sanctioned something as monumental as an invasion of another country, originally planned by someone else, about which he knew very little. In that context, he was "politically greedy," desperate for a dramatic, immediate success with which he could show the American people (and his communist foes) that he was indeed "tough" and, thus, worthy of their respect and support. Kennedy should have also realized that the likelihood of the CIA training 1,500 anti-Castro Cuban exiles in Nicaragua and Florida and Fidel not finding out about such "exercises" was remote. Indeed, major newspapers often ran front-page stories of the operation, making it apparent to Castro that Kennedy was about to do something. In short, news stories, which Kennedy tried to quash, were full of predictions that an invasion of Cuba was imminent. Pierre Salinger, Kennedy's press secretary, later observed that the assault was the "least covert military operation in history. . . . The only information Castro didn't have was the exact time and place of the invasion." Kennedy, Salinger noted, was upset by the lack of secrecy: "I can't believe what I'm reading," he complained. "All he [Castro] has to do is read our papers. It's all laid out for him."

In a purely military context, Kennedy should have listened to those advisers who warned him that the Bay of Pigs was a poor choice to land the insurgents. It was a swampy region from which soldiers, once trapped, could not melt away or find refuge in the mountains as the CIA predicted. Instead, the brigade was pinned down near the beach and badly exposed to enemy fire. Desperate, they called for air support from fighter planes on the aircraft carrier *Essex,* some ten miles offshore. Kennedy demurred, however, and the invaders soon surrendered to Castro's superior forces—some 15,000 men. In all, 114 "freedom fighters" were killed in the fighting, and the rest—1,189—were taken prisoner and later ransomed back to the United States for food and medical supplies.

Kennedy should have recognized and accepted the fact that Fidel was a popular leader, especially at that moment, for less than two years earlier he had overthrown a hated dictatorship. Even Cubans who disliked Castro resented the assault from the overbearing Yankees to the north and rallied to his support. In shouldering the blame, Kennedy was not alone. The CIA, perhaps even more so than Kennedy, was the real culprit, for they filled the president's ear with all manner of gross misinformation and misjudgment. For one, they disastrously underestimated Fidel's popularity and Cubans' historical general animosity for the United States. Moreover, Dulles and Bissell guessed wrong about Kennedy: if push came to shove following the landings, they thought, rather than suffer a humiliating defeat, Kennedy would snatch victory from the jaws of defeat by committing American forces to save the venture. He refused, perhaps realizing at the last second how he had underestimated the power of nationalism and patriotic fervor. Perhaps George W. Bush should take a page from the history of the Kennedy presidency.

The most disastrous consequence of the Bay of Pigs was Kennedy's failure to learn from it and the vindictiveness displayed toward those who counseled against it or those who expressed concern afterward. Such individuals were castigated as "soft," unmanly, and not tough enough to be counted on during "crunch time." "That yellow-bellied friend of yours, Chester Bowles, is leaking all over town that he was against the invasion," Kennedy's press secretary Pierre Salinger told Harris Wofford. "We're going to get him." Shortly thereafter, Bowles was relieved as under-secretary of state and appointed to the honorific position of ambassador-at-large. Kennedy "froze out" his other critics, who quickly learned that, if they hoped to retain their positions, they best "grab their nuts" and be loyal. Kennedy refused to question the efficacy of counterinsurgency; indeed, he and his aides became even more intent on making the concept work, determined to prove to the country's adversaries that the United States at any time could put into the field forces capable of fighting any type of warfare. Finally, Kennedy continued to entertain ideas to assassinate Castro.

Although most Americans continue to believe that Vietnam was "Lyndon Johnson's war," in actuality, the nightmare began with John Kennedy, who first escalated American troop presence and involvement in the eventual quagmire. Ironically, in the 1950s Kennedy warned that "no amount of American military assistance [in Indochina] can conquer an enemy which is everywhere." However, once in the White House, Kennedy reversed himself completely, believing that anywhere in the world there appeared a communist threat, the United States had to meet that challenge and defeat it. Thus, to Kennedy, the containment Cold Warrior, American presence in Vietnam was axiomatic. If the United States showed weakness, he was convinced that "the whole world would inevitably move toward the communist bloc." To Kennedy, it was imperative that America "move forward to meet communism, rather than waiting for it to come to us." Thus, Kennedy's actions in Vietnam simply reinforced and deepened the unfolding tragedy.

The Kennedy policy toward Vietnam emerged as the product of interrelated cold war perceptions shared by Kennedy and most of his foreign policy advisors. To Kennedy, communism was a monolithic conspiracy spearheaded by China and the Soviet Union and committed to aggressively expand and dominate the world. Still affecting Kennedy and the Democrats was the "loss" of China, the stalemate in Korea, and the McCarthyite accusation that Democrats were "soft" on communism—all factors, as noted in the Truman essay, that brought that administration down. Thus, Kennedy, if he hoped to avoid a similar fate, was determined to prevent further defeats, especially in Asia. Moreover, to Kennedy and many of his advisors, China, more than the Soviet Union, was the culprit in Asia, supporting communist insurgents throughout the Asian subcontinent. Thus, any "compromise" in Vietnam was tantamount to appeasement at Munich, with China simply a modern-day surrogate for Nazi Germany. However, once again, as a president who prided himself on his historical knowledge, Kennedy should have realized that *historically* the Vietnamese hated the Chinese, had fought numerous wars against them to prevent conquest, and thus would never allow their country to become a Chinese lackey state. North Vietnamese leader Ho Chi Minh had made that repeatedly clear as early as the late 1940s to the Truman administration. Unfortunately, too many of Kennedy's aides saw the world through their World War II lens, believing as Walt Rostow did that the world situation in 1961 was comparable to the early 1940s when freedom was under siege everywhere. It was time to "turn the tide," Rostow declared, and Vietnam was a good place to start.

Khrushchev seemed to validate communism's aggressive intentions when he announced that the Soviet Union did indeed endorse "wars of national liberation" as a means of promoting Marxist-Leninism's global strategy. To Kennedy and his advisers, the declaration was interpreted as confirmation of their belief that the Russians were extending their confrontation with the United States into new arenas and, hence, escalating the struggle for world dominance.

Kennedy was convinced that the recent series of embarrassing reversals in other cold war areas, such as the race for space, Berlin, and the Bay of Pigs, had emboldened the Sino-Soviet bloc to become even more aggressive. Thus, it was imperative for the United States to make a strong stand somewhere, lest the communists think America a weak and waning power. In such a context, a forceful policy in Vietnam became essential, not only because the administration believed in the domino theory (first established by the Truman administration) but because it needed to establish a presence somewhere, even if it was 9,000 miles away, to show the Soviets that the United States was far from capitulating to their assaults on freedom.

Finally, United States' involvement in Southeast Asia provided Kennedy with a "laboratory" to test its own new strategy of "flexible response" to Soviet aggression. In this context, the forces to be "tested" were the newly created counter-insurgency, "special forces," such as the Green Berets. As Walt Rostow observed, "It is somehow wrong to be developing these capabilities but not applying them in a crucial theatre. In Knute Rockne's old phrase, we are not saving them for the junior prom." By deploying such forces in areas like Vietnam, General Maxwell Taylor believed the United States could prove to the Soviets that wars of national liberation were not "cheap, safe, and disavowable, but costly, dangerous, and doomed to failure." For all these reasons, Kennedy concluded by the fall of 1961 that America's presence in Vietnam must be deepened. In the final analysis, to Kennedy, America's credibility was on the line as a great power. In Kennedy's view, Vietnam would become the battleground on which the United States would win a decisive victory over the Soviet

236 John F. Kennedy

Union, demonstrating as well Kennedy's pledge that Americans would "pay any price, bear any burden, in the defense of freedom." Thus, the escalation, the toppling of governments by military coups, the self-immolation of Buddhist monks in protest to American presence, and deceit began ultimately causing widespread polarization at home and the downfall of a president. When Kennedy entered the White House, there were roughly 500 American military advisers in South Vietnam; by the time of Kennedy's death in November 1963, there were over 16,000 U.S. troops (allegedly still only serving as advisers and helping South Vietnamese peasants with "flood control") in that beleaguered country. Contrary to Kennedy's claim that American troops were not fighting, in reality they were, accompanying ARVN (Army of the Republic of South Vietnam) on "search and destroy" missions as well as fighting Viet Cong on their own initiative. By December 1963, some 100 American soldiers had been killed in combat. By the time of his own death, Kennedy had revealed virtually none of this reality to the American public, nor had he reassessed the situation, and he had no well-considered, long-range plans. To the very end, Kennedy believed that places like Indochina were the new and vital battleground in the cold war. Interestingly, by the end of 1961, one of the most important components of the "monolithic" Sino-Soviet conspiracy theory had unraveled: the Soviets and the Chinese had become bitter adversaries and, thus, their collusion in wars of national liberation was no longer valid. Kennedy knew this but failed to adjust his approach and thinking accordingly. He also neglected to heed what some advisers (a minority, to be sure) were saying: the battle in Vietnam was a civil war first and foremost, not a struggle to expand communism throughout Southeast Asia.

In summing up Kennedy's foreign policy, troubling failures and misconceptions affected him to the end. Although knowing there was no missile gap (and if there was, it was in favor of the United States), Kennedy eagerly increased defense spending, thereby intensifying the arms race. Despite the Bay of Pigs debacle, he persisted in plans to harass and frighten Castro. Ignoring evidence to the contrary, he held fast to clichés—especially in public—such as the domino theory and the insistence of an international communist conspiracy directed from Moscow and Beijing to take over the world. On many occasions, as reflected in his Vietnam policies, Kennedy proved poor at sorting out good information from bad and at developing long-range plans. Contrary to his acolytes' claims, by the time of his death Kennedy had not grown very much on the job.

Although John Kennedy was hardly the first president to be a womanizer, his philandering remains the most legendary of all chief executives. Interestingly, it was in this capacity that Kennedy appeared to resolve the tension between his own frailty and intellectualism on the one hand and his father's insistence on perfection and physical prowess on the other—by emulating his father. Kennedy had purely sexual relationships with numerous women before and after his marriage to Jackie. Many believed his insatiable sexual appetite was caused by the cortisone treatments he took for Addison's disease. At first, Kennedy "confined" his randy behavior to "ordinary" women, but as his fame grew, he engaged in sexual relationships with Hollywood starlets, luxuriating in their eminence and the gossip they conveyed about other stars. His most famous rendezvous, of course, was with Marilyn Monroe, with whom he had an affair while president. Perhaps his most "careless" philandering while president was with a woman who was also intimate with leaders of organized crime. Kennedy seemed oblivious to the fact that his mistress would be under FBI surveillance. It was almost as if, having received a sentence of early death because of Addison's disease, there were no rules that mattered.

Kennedy's obsession with sex and machismo spilled over into his political world as well. He detested those who were indecisive, equating their trepidation with effeminacy. The way to make a difficult decision, he said, was to calculate the odds, make a choice, and "grab our balls and go." Those who vacillated were, by implication, not men. Kennedy loved to use sexually-loaded imagery. When he urged a friend to attack Arthur Krock, an old benefactor who had turned against him, he wanted his comrade to "Tuck it to Krock. Bust it off in old Arthur. He can't take it, and when you go after him he folds."

John Kennedy glittered while he lived like few of the modern presidents in this book, and the world grieved when he died. In the years since that tragic November day in 1963, his memory has undergone vicissitude. Bereavement nourishes myth. JFK, the slain hero, robbed of fulfillment by tragic fate, is the stuff of legend. However, as Emerson poignantly observed, "Every hero becomes a bore at last." Thus, in retrospect, John Kennedy, the fallen hero, the bonny prince, the king at the Round Table, the incarnation of youth and glamour, has become the object of disillusion and harsh criticism.

With the passage of more than four decades, it is still difficult to place the Kennedy presidency in perspective. Few would contest that he was (and remains) a larger-than-life political figure. Part of this he purposely cultivated himself through his extraordinary style and image. With as much contrivance as conviction, Kennedy helped to generate the Camelot myth—the beautiful and stylish wife, the active and attractive leader, the high culture, the court entourage of brilliant, dedicated public servants—a time that belonged, by design, with the legends of chivalric courts. In short, for a brief moment, Kennedy succeeded, even more than FDR, in creating a "bond" between the ordinary lives of his fellow citizens and the glamour and glitter of the Oval Office. Yet, there was something disturbing about the Kennedy style and method. Kennedy seemed never to have experienced in his gut the travail of the common people's struggle to live and overcome. This was especially true with the civil rights movement and understanding what it was like to be black in America in the early 1960s. Kennedy, like FDR and Theodore Roosevelt, embodied a patrician noblesse oblige, believing that only "the best and the brightest"—those to the manor born—should rule. As a result, he helped to create what Arthur Schlesinger, Jr. has called the "imperial presidency"—a president surrounded by the panoply of power, directing the fate of the universe, unconstrained by the realities and tribulations of the common folk.

There is something else as well. Photographs of Kennedy still hang on the walls in the homes of black Americans, together with those of Martin Luther King, Jr. and Jesus. Although personally detached from concern with the plight of African Americans or the poor, he succeeded politically in conveying to the disenfranchised a sense of caring, and a commitment to uplift them. He had, his aide Richard Goodwin wrote, "that rare quality of strengthening men's belief in themselves, in giving them something grand to look toward. . . . He took a country that was on its back, fat and purposeless, lifted it up, gave it momentum, direction, and purpose and a sense of its strength and possibility." Perhaps most important, Kennedy ignited a fire, a passion in an entire generation of Americans to want to change the way things were and to work for the way things might be. Indeed, in the months prior to his death, Kennedy gave new hope to those who believed that he might yet fulfill his potential. Thus, the Kennedy presidency can be summed up as one of unrealized possibility, for as James Reston wrote, "What was killed in Dallas was not only the president but the promise . . . the death of youth and the hope of youth, of the beauty and grace and the touch of magic. . . . He never reached his meridian: we saw him only as a rising sun."

President and Mrs. Kennedy arrive at the National Guard Armory in Washington for the Inaugural Ball.
Jan. 20, 1961
Photo credit: Abbie Rowe, National Park Service/JFK Library

(right) Lt. John F. Kennedy aboard the PT-109 in the South Pacific, 1943
Photo credit: JFK Library
(bottom) Pres. Kennedy greets Peace Corps volunteers on the South Lawn of the White House.
August 8, 1962
Photo credit: Abbie Rowe, National Park Service/JFK Library

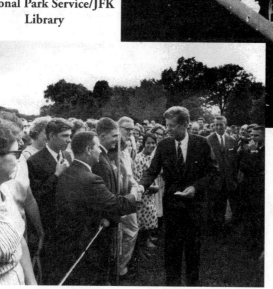

Pres. Kennedy, Director F.B.I. Hoover, and Attorney General Kennedy, White House, Oval Office. Feb 23, 1961 Photo credit: Abbie Rowe, National Park Service/JFK Library

Watching the lift-off of the first American in space. (L-R) Vice President Johnson, Arthur Schlesinger, Adm. Arleigh Burke, Mrs. Kennedy, White House, Office of the President's Secretary. May 5, 1961 Photo credit: Cecil Stoughton, White House/ JFK Library

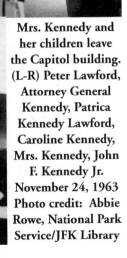

Mrs. Kennedy and her children leave the Capitol building. (L-R) Peter Lawford, Attorney General Kennedy, Patrica Kennedy Lawford, Caroline Kennedy, Mrs. Kennedy, John F. Kennedy Jr. November 24, 1963 Photo credit: Abbie Rowe, National Park Service/JFK Library

Lyndon Baines Johnson
1963-1969

President John F. Kennedy's assassination on November 22, 1963, affected the United States—and the world—unlike any single event up to that point in modern (post-World War II) history. No American born prior to 1960 can forget where he or she was or what they were doing on that somber, surreal day. Most could not believe that an American president had been murdered in broad daylight in a major city until they turned on the TV and saw Walter Cronkite crying as he announced the news. "I have lost my only true friend in the outside world," Sekou Toure, the President of Guinea, declared. Soviet premier Nikita Khrushchev was stunned, later recalling how he and Kennedy together had avoided Armageddon by defusing the 1962 Cuban missile crisis. The Soviets, a reporter wrote, had the feeling that "here was the man who understood the problems between the United States and the Soviet Union," and now he was gone.

For four days, Americans sat before their television sets as the nation collectively mourned a loss that seemed both personal and immediate. They watched the equally popular and adored, now grief-stricken First Lady, Jackie, dressed in black, walk alongside her husband's coffin, borne by a riderless horse to Washington's St. Mathew's Cathedral for funeral services. The Kennedy children, five-year-old Caroline and three-year-old John, were at her side. Following the service, in what has since become a classic, poignant, photograph that captured the moment's essence, John Junior stood at attention, as he had seen the soldiers do, and saluted the coffin. The horse-drawn procession then moved in stately slowness through Washington to Arlington National Cemetery in Virginia. There, Kennedy was laid to rest, his grave marked by an eternal flame overlooking the city. "This was the death of a democratic prince," British journalist Godfrey Hodgson observed, but a prince who somehow, someway had become part of everyone's psychic and emotional life. Even among many anti-Kennedy Southerners, 62 percent experienced the assassination as a loss of someone very close and dear.

Five days later, Jackie called journalist-historian Theodore White to the Kennedy compound in Hyannisport, where she told him a story that White placed in *Life* magazine on December 6, 1963. People should realize, she said, that Jack had been a sickly boy and had spent hours reading about King Arthur and the Knights of the Round Table. Just a week before he was killed, he had seen Lerner and Loewe's Broadway musical *Camelot,* which sentimentalized those chivalric days of heroism. At night in his bedroom he played the recording from Camelot before going to sleep, and he especially loved the lines: "Don't let it be forgot,/ that once there was a spot,/ for one brief shining moment/ that was known as Camelot." Jackie added in White's article, read by millions, that the Kennedy administration had been Camelot, "a magic moment in American history, when gallant men danced with beautiful women, when great deeds were done, when artists, writers, and poets met at the White House and the barbarians beyond the walls were held back." But, she lamented, with her husband gone, "it will never be that way again. . . . There'll never be another Camelot again."

An alive John Kennedy would probably have derided his wife's fanciful tribute and rightly so, for it was myth-making of maudlin proportions. Still, it had lasting appeal to millions of people who had been shaken by the assassination and who were looking for ways to affirm the meaning of Kennedy's life and presidency. Jackie momentarily gave them the context to define her husband's thousand days as president. At the same time, as they had felt after the death of Franklin Roosevelt, many Americans wondered if their new president would be able to carry forth and make real his predecessor's vision, which they believed Kennedy was on the verge of realizing when he was killed. Ironically, Kennedy was quite far from attaining, let alone implementing, his liberal New Frontier agenda. Indeed, many of his initiatives were token gestures to placate various interest groups to sustain their support for the Democratic Party. At best, they were half-heartedly promoted or pushed in Congress, and many were stalled in committee when he died, especially those, such as civil rights, certain to raise whirlwinds of controversy. However, it would be Kennedy's successor, a "politician's politician," an individual who was the complete antithesis of Kennedy in every personal way imaginable, who would make the "Kennedy dream" come true.

Indeed, Lyndon Baines Johnson of Texas, in the span of five years, took the liberal ethos first outlined by FDR in the New Deal farther than even the most diehard of liberals thought possible, and in the process, for a brief moment, it seemed that Americans truly lived in a "great society"—a society in which all citizens had equal access to the American dream of a job, a home, an education, and health care—a nation free of poverty, hopelessness, and discrimination, a beacon of promise and assurance for the rest of the world to emulate. In short, "LBJ" was responsible for both the greatest triumphs and the worst defeats of postwar liberal democracy.

Indeed, issues of social change exploded into the nation's consciousness as African Americans, women, and the economically disadvantaged pressed for reform. Affected both politically and ideologically by such demands, liberals enacted an array of progressive legislation unmatched in the annals of congressional history. The passage of such measures, however, was not enough, for in the process the expectations of so many groups were raised so high that even the most far-reaching and all-encompassing social reform initiatives were not enough to satisfy such heightened hopes for a better life. Thus, by 1968, LBJ's vision and promise of a "great society" had unraveled, for his administration could no longer "deliver the goods" of social reform fast enough to those who believed they were "entitled" to such largesse. Perhaps most injurious to the reform impulse of the Johnson years was the Vietnam War, which, as will be seen, deprived the various programs and initiatives of the revenue essential to sustain them. As the war increasingly sucked the funds (thus the life) out of these programs, tensions borne of broken promises and rising expectations mounted, finally exploding into open, often violent protest by 1967-68. Indeed, by 1968, many Americans believed the nation was on the verge of another civil war, only this time it would be a class conflict between the politicized and "liberalized" have-nots of the lower classes and the "vital-center" haves of the middle class. It was believed that Johnson's liberal agenda and war were responsible for polarizing the two antagonistic, hostile groups—one in opposition to "the Establishment" for its betrayal of the liberal ethos—the other a reaction to liberalism's wanton empowerment of the previously disadvantaged. By 1968, Americans of all classes, creeds, and colors had become disillusioned, alienated, and embittered by the failure of Johnsonian liberalism to provide the unity, stability, and social progress promised by a man who had spent his entire life transcending conflict to find ways to unite people of opposite persuasions in order to achieve the greatest good for the greatest number.

In all of this, one man sought to occupy center stage, harnessing all the power of the executive branch, to direct and shape the decade's history. Ultimately, the events of the 1960s testified to the disappointment of his desire and to the underlying contradictions within the "liberal consensus," which frustrated its fulfillment. To fully understand the external problems that destroyed his dream, it is necessary to examine Johnson's life. Just as the personality of his hero, Franklin Roosevelt, so imbued the New Deal, so it was with LBJ, whose larger-than-life temperament affected both the limits and potential of his Great Society.

In her poignant biography of Johnson, Doris Kearns describes the conversations she held with the former president: "We talked mostly in the early hours of the morning," Kearns wrote: "Terrified of lying alone in the dark, he came into my room. . . . Gradually, a curious ritual developed. I would awaken at five and get dressed. Half an hour later Johnson would knock on my door, dressed in his robe and pajamas. As I sat in a chair by the window, he climbed into the bed, pulling the sheets up to his neck, looking like a cold and frightened child. . . . Later, he said that all along he had been hiding from me the fact that I reminded him of his dead mother. In talking with me, he had come to imagine he was also talking with her, unraveling the story of his life."

(Note to reader: Doris Kearns Goodwin, author of *No Ordinary Time: Franklin and Eleanor Roosevelt: The Home Front in World War II* (1933), received the 1995 Pulitzer Prize for history. She is also the author of *Lyndon Johnson and the American Dream* and *The Fitzgeralds and the Kennedys: An American Saga*. Ms. Goodwin worked as an assistant to President Johnson during his last year in the White House and later assisted him in the preparation of his memoirs.)

Through these early morning meetings, Johnson revealed to Kearns the crucial events of his life, which since childhood helped shape the man he would become and, by extension, the role he would play in leading America. In many ways, the early morning rendezvous became valuable exercises in history and in self-revelation.

Kearns' "cold and frightened child" was born on August 27, 1908, in his parent's comfortable farmhouse on the Pedernales River in the heart of the Texas Hill Country. Although raised in a rural environment, Johnson, contrary to his later retelling of his childhood, did not grow up in poverty. His parents were essentially "middle class" for their time and place. From his birth on, Lyndon was the pride and joy of adoring parents who indulged their son's every whim. From all the evidence, Johnson was a precocious child, healthy, active, and happy. Johnson's mother, Rebekah, perceived him as the brightest, jolliest, best baby ever. Johnson's father, Sam, agreed, writing to a kinsman that, "I do know he is the sweetest, prettiest, smartest baby in the world." Johnson's parents' boasting had some basis in fact. Early photographs reveal a baby exceptionally personable, one who seemed to love people, to want to reach out to them, to woo and win their affection. He basked in the attention and seemed to have been born a charmer, a natural leader. These traits gave some substance to a grandfather's prediction that Johnson would some day be a United States senator. However, such parental and familial doting naturally made Johnson a spoiled child, at times petulant and demanding, traits that would follow him to the White House.

Unfortunately for Johnson, being center-stage lasted until he was five; within a relatively short time, he became merely the oldest child. By the time he was eight, he found himself surrounded by four siblings—three sisters and a brother, all of whom took his parents' attention away from him. As a result, Lyndon became a bit wild, given to running away or hiding or other attention-getting ploys, just what one would expect from a pampered first child after the birth of siblings.

As Johnson matured, he began to realize that his parent's doting masked what he in later life realized was an unhappy marriage; indeed, in retrospect his parents' union could not have been a joyous one, for Rebekah Baines and Sam Johnson could not have come from two more different worlds. Rebekah grew up in a family that was cultured, prudent, dependable, ambitious, and pious, the very opposite of that of her husband's family, which was impulsive, risk-taking, and exuberant—hardscrabblers always on the make for better opportunities without having to work too hard to get them. By contrast, Rebekah was the daughter of one of Texas' leading citizens—Joseph Wilson Baines—college teacher, lawyer, Texas secretary of state, and member of the Texas House, a leading layman in the Baptist church, literate and refined in taste, and by all accounts a person of unimpeachable integrity. Like her husband Sam, Rebekah too was raised in the Hill Country, in Blanco, where her family was recognized as one of the most respected and wealthiest in the area. Unfortunately, in 1904, Rebekah's rarefied world came to an end, the result of economic disaster. After years of disastrous crops and a failed speculative venture, Joseph Baines, on the verge of bankruptcy, had to sell the Blanco house to pay debts. A broken man, he moved his family to the largely German town of Fredericksburg (also in the Hill Country). Two years later, Rebekah's father died.

During her family's painful collapse, Rebekah completed her college work at Baylor Female College (now Mary Hardin Baylor) in Belton, Texas. She eventually had to work to pay her way through school, which no doubt affected her emotionally and psychologically. She always kept up a front, however, concealing her insecurities behind a mask of gentility, camouflaging her painful past in Victorian homilies. After graduation, Rebekah taught elocution in Fredericksburg and wrote articles for local and then Austin newspapers. It was while doing a series of articles on long-time Hill Country families that she met Sam Johnson, whose courtship was so overwhelming and flattering that it proved irresistible to such an incurable romantic as Rebekah. Other than a shared interest in politics and in the outside world, Sam and Rebekah had little else in common. Thus, the resulting marriage proved unfortunate. Despite all her pretense, Rebekah suffered a loss of self-esteem. She had married beneath her self-perceived station in life or, at least, beneath the image of gentility and piety she struggled to maintain even in the worst of times. Her husband's larger-than-life personality, his bursts of temper, his love of a good time with the boys, his occasional excessive drinking, his jokes and folksy but often crude humor, his financial recklessness, and even his lax church attendance all symbolized a major cultural and psychogenic gap. On her part, Rebekah placed unwanted demands or fetters on Sam, never played well the role of a political wife (Sam served as a populistic-inclined state legislator for a number of years), at times retreated into romantic fantasies, and put a damper on the playful, convivial impulses of her husband and his family.

The strains afflicting his parents' marriage left their mark on young Lyndon. Johnson's childhood became a battleground, each of his parents warring for his soul. For Rebekah, Johnson became the vessel through which she sought to rescue, and then achieve, her own now-deferred dream of a graceful and refined existence. Interestingly, like FDR, Johnson's mother, despite having other children to care for, focused most of her attention on Lyndon, hovering over him, curling his hair like that of a girl, and reading to him Romantic poetry, particularly the works of Longfellow and Tennyson. Such maternal smothering angered Sam, who tried to make Johnson a little man, doing all he could to undermine his wife's controlling and emasculating impulses. The young boy was torn. He believed his mother needed him, not because she necessarily wanted what was best for him but rather to displace her own failed ambitions and fulfillment. At the time, Johnson did not recognize that his mother's coddling was an attempt to vindicate her own life, and neither did he realize that her desire was to remake Lyndon in her father's image (certainly not her husband's), her ideal of the educated, sophisticated gentleman. Despite his mother's ulterior motives, Johnson reveled in his mother's attention. "It made me feel big and important. She made me believe I could do anything in the whole world." On the other hand, she froze him out if he did poorly in school or refused to finish his violin lessons; he felt abandoned, bereft, and alone. In those instances, he found solace from his mother's emotional and psychological abuse by immersing himself in his father's more gregarious, forgiving, and exciting world of local politics. During adolescence he would accompany his father on his political sojourns. Johnson loved going out into the countryside, listening to his father talk to constituents, eating homemade snacks offered by voters—Johnson and his father were in their element. "Christ," he later said, "sometimes I wished it could go on forever."

The type of individual Johnson ultimately became was shaped by his parents' ongoing conflict to control his life. Perhaps as a result of his mother's manipulation and withholding of affection from him when he displeased her, Johnson rebelled by following his father's example—wheeling and dealing in politics, using crude language, intentionally violating "proper behavior" by having aides and government officials accompany him to the bathroom when he was president—all the habits his mother detested about his father. Yet, there remained a longing for his mother's approval. Johnson seemed to feel, however, that he could never measure up to her elite standards. As he yearned to win the love of his very different parents, Johnson always seemed desperately eager to make people love him. He also became adept at conciliation, a wonderful skill for anyone with political ambitions. Throughout his life, he labored long and hard to bring people together.

Largely out of a desire to please his mother, Johnson did well in school, a straight-A student in elementary school, but his high school grades reflected that all along he had been at best an indifferent student, not particularly challenged by books or by academic subjects but did well with his mother's prodding or, at times, her completion of his homework assignments. In short, Johnson did best in subjects that allowed him to coast along on the basis of his natural intelligence, worst in courses that required sustained study or memorization. In high school he gained a reputation for his abundant skills in flattery and in persuasion to woo his teachers. Classmates recollected a boy gifted with leadership skills and preternaturally addicted to politics. Johnson graduated in 1924 from Johnson City High School and, much to his mother's grave disappointment, decided that, instead of going immediately to college, he was going to take a trip with friends to California, which he did that summer. Johnson simply wanted to get away for his mother's suffocating "love." As he told Doris Kearns, he had "to get away."

Like many young Americans in the 1920s, Johnson saw California and its booming economy as a chance to make a fortune. However, after a year of working at odd, menial jobs, Johnson concluded that California was not all that it was purported to be and returned to Texas. For two years he worked on a road-building crew for which his father was the foreman. Suffice it to say, Johnson found such hard labor not at all fulfilling, and, thus, this period represented a very unhappy interlude in his life. He fell in with wilder, older boys, joined cronies in minor thievery, in exaggerated pranks, and in the drinking of moonshine whiskey. He became volatile, quick to quarrel, given to overstated posturing and poses to impress girls. It was almost as if Johnson wanted to defy his parents or to embarrass them by his behavior as a way of ventilating his rage toward them for having made him the victim of their tug-of-war for his soul. In February 1927, Johnson enrolled as a freshman at Southwest State Teacher's College (renamed Texas State University in 2002) in San Marcos, Texas.

Johnson prepared himself for teaching in both elementary and high schools. He majored in history and minored in English and social studies. He took no languages and only the bare minimum courses in mathematics and the sciences. Johnson was far from an exemplary student; indeed, throughout his years there, he struggled, even coming close to flunking out several times. However, he persevered, graduating with minimal hours and a grade point average of 2.5, a C+ in 1930. Although only a marginal student, while at Southwest, Johnson believed he learned much more than just history or English. "The enduring lines of my life lead back to this campus," Johnson later said. Intensely ambitious, Johnson understood that success often depended on winning the favor of those with power. Thus, during his second year Johnson attached himself to the college's president, Cecil Evans, making himself indispensable as Evans' private secretary. Once firmly entrenched in that position, Johnson used the implicit power of his closeness to authority to draw other students into his fold. Handing out jobs, making life easier for students and administrators, Johnson became a central figure at the college. Shrewdly, he put together a political coalition designed to win all the major college offices for his followers, working tirelessly to court student votes in elections and to win student respect through his editorials in the campus newspaper. In his editorials, Johnson celebrated the virtues of paternalism and patriotism. In times of trouble, he wrote, it was the father who had to "square his shoulders, resolutely grit his teeth, suppress his emotions and with renewed courage meet the issue." The strong must care for the weak, the older for the young, men for women. If in his own father Johnson had not found an adequate model to transcend conflict within the family, at San Marcos he would create his own paradigm and, by service to authorities, such as the college's president, begin to take part in the image he had created.

"Place" rivals family in most people's sense of identity. In America, where one comes from is as important as what one does for a living or the pedigree of one's forebears. The "where" involves much more than mere geography; it encompasses a regional culture, as well as distinctive and familiar beliefs and values. For Lyndon Johnson, the Texas Hill Country remained peculiarly vivid and compelling. Few presidents have been more conscious of their roots or introduced more images of place in their speeches. Johnson's fondness for the Texas Hill Country reflected both pride and a certain defensiveness about where he grew up.

Almost everyone grows up with duel allegiances. Broader bases of identity—being an American—may supplant local ones—being a Texan—especially if one is away from the home place for extended periods, long enough to forget attachments. What was so clear in LBJ was the depth of local loyalties. Although maintaining throughout his life a strong affection for the Hill Country, such sentiments did not lessen his broader allegiances. In only one area did he reveal some confusion about his provincial loyalties. Born and raised not just in central Texas, but in the heart of the state's most distinct region, the Hill Country, caused Johnson to have an interesting "identity crisis"—that is, whether Texas, particularly Johnson's home town, "Southern" or "Western" in its cultural orientation. Johnson never fully identified with either and, as politics dictated, alternatively claimed one or the other. Because of stereotyping and because of his supposed "southern" twang, most Americans considered Johnson a Southerner. After all, they asserted, weren't the majority of original Anglo-Texans from the South? Wasn't Texas a slave state? Didn't Texans vote to secede from the Union and join the Confederacy? As a result of such historical verities, Johnson could not escape the label and often the burden of being "southern," and he often did the best possible job exploiting the occasional assets that went with that imposed identity. However, like most Texans whose families had been in the state for generations, Johnson considered himself not a Southerner or Westerner but foremost a "Texan." He transferred his regional loyalties to his home state. To him, Texas was his section and region, and, in many ways, even his nation. As much as any Texan, he identified with the state's unique history, taking great pride in having come from such a wonderful mélange of different cultures. Indeed, Texans are as varied, if not more pluralistic, than the people of any other state. In the Lone Star state merge Anglo, African American, and Hispanic cultures, all leavened by a scattering of German, Czech, and other central European traditions, and in the last twenty years an Asian influence is readily visible, especially in Gulf Coast cities such as Houston.

Of course, not all Texans are proud of their state or its heritage. Texans, however, are at least by necessity self-conscious about their identity. Outsiders, especially those from the Northeast, force them to be. "Texan pride," or the braggadocio of a few, has created such perceived chauvinism. Being a Texan is often not just an accident of birth but a state of mind, a cause. A form of Texas nationalism is particularly beguiling for those who grow up in the center of such a large state. It is their middle kingdom, the center of their world. LBJ could not escape this identity. He did not try, although he often tried to change outsiders' images of Texas. In most respects he suffered from the image and from his Texas accent, no matter how hard he tried to subvert it when speaking. People viewed him as a Texan and filled in all the stereotypes associated with that identity. Long before Texas became chic, or so prosperous and populous as to invite envy rather than derision, the images of the state held by outsiders were largely pejorative, and such aspersions stung Johnson, a proud and vain man.

Interestingly, as Johnson became politically powerful and wealthy, he seemed to become less sensitive and defensive about his Texas heritage and, in fact, embraced it and even reveled in it. In short, he became the stereotypical Texan in look, manners, and behavior that for years he tried to minimize. He bought a cattle ranch, in which he took great pride. He relished the chance to put on his boots and cowboy hat, load visitors into his Cadillac (which, of course, all rich Texans owned, complete with longhorns on the hood) and drive them, terrified, at ninety miles per hour about his far-flung property, showing them along the way his prize bulls, pointing out how "well" they were "hung" and how they would soon be in the pastures "ready for action."

Although ultimately enfolding and demonstrating pride in his "Texaness," the source of Johnson's liberalism can be found at a deeper level in Johnson's Hill Country roots. The Hill Country is physically, spiritually, ethnically, racially, and culturally unlike any other place in Texas. The Texas Hill Country is the traditional name of the Edwards Plateau, the southernmost extension of the Great Plains, the elevated shelf that runs along the eastern edge of the Rocky Mountains from Canada to

Central Texas. From the stone ridges of the Edwards Plateau, a handful of shallow rivers descend hundreds of feet down the Balcones escarpment and then drain east in parallel stripes across the Gulf Coastal Plains to the sea: the Pedernales, Blanco, Guadalupe, Lampasas, and San Gabriel. One of these, which winds through the Johnson ranch, is the Pedernales River, where Johnson was born near its banks in 1908 in nearby Stonewall.

Well before Johnson was born, the Hill Country had become a bastion of nascent liberalism thanks largely to its German inhabitants, who came to Texas in the 1840s and 1850s. For years they were virtually the only "white" folk in the area. Most engaged in farming, but businesses of all variety also flourished in their communities. By the eve of the Civil War, their Hill Country towns such as Comfort, Boerne, and Fredericksburg had become completely self-sufficient enterprises, whose citizens took great pride in their respected communities for having carved out of the Texas wilderness such successful endeavors. "Their places can be recognized by their thorough and systematic cultivation," historian Frank Goodwyn wrote. "By picking their own cotton and wielding their own hoes, they have grown wealthy." Goodwyn also noted the distinct "cultural gap" between the Germans and many of their white counterparts elsewhere in Texas, especially those who came from the Lower South: "Having come directly from countries where slavery did not prevail, they [the Germans, Czech, and Scandinavian emigrants of the Hill Country] show no disposition to depend on servile labor, be it either Negro or Mexican." Another Texas historian agreed: "Life on the plantation, cultivated by slave labor, was quite different from that on German farms or in German settlements. The planter and slave owner with his family generally indulged in a life of indolence, while on the German farms every member of the family worked continuously, often even on Sundays, using in Texas the same intensive agriculture as formerly in Germany." In short, there were few helpless poor and few rich people in the Texas Hill Country, which came as close to an egalitarian society as any in the United States. Most people did their own work. Labor was not considered a dishonorable activity to be carried out by helots of a different race or class. In those areas of Texas with plantations, giant ranches, and mines, forced servile labor rather than free labor was used.

Just as they did not despise labor, the German Texans did not loath leisure or learning. Their beer-gardens rang with melodies of their singing clubs, and scholarship, journalism, and the composition of verse in German and English were valued in a society founded by surplus nobles and refugee professors from Central Europe. The obsession of the Southern evangelical Protestants to the east and north regarded the Germans' dancing, drinking, and card playing as sinful activities—a concept completely alien to the Lutherans, Catholics, and free-thinkers alike of the Hill Country. The Germans and other Hill Country residents voted against candidates who supported Prohibition—in an era in which the Baptists and other evangelicals wanted to outlaw liquor.

The symbol of the philosophical and religious pluralism of the Hill Country is the *Vereinskirche*, or "Society Church," a striking octagonal building in the central square in Fredericksburg (the "official capital" of the Hill Country). During the German colony's early years, the *Vereinskirche* was used as a church or meeting place by Catholics, Lutherans, and free-thinkers who respected one another's rights, if not one another's beliefs.

After the Civil War, the area saw an influx of poor Southern whites from the Ozarks and Appalachia. Like their brethren in the Highland South from West Virginia through Tennessee to Texas, these "hillbillies" were often squatters on land they did not legally own. They fluctuated between being a white rural proletariat and a white rural underclass. Like their Ozark-Appalachian counterparts, these white newcomers to the Hill Country tended to be apolitical and suspicious of authority. To the extent that they influenced politics, it was in the direction of populism and radicalism. Like other poor whites of the southern hills, these Hill Country folk were hostile to the rich white planters who monopolized the good farmlands along the Texas river bottoms and coasts—lands often appropriated from squatters who lacked title or were cheated because they had no political connections or legal knowledge. In the mixture of influences that created the relatively progressive culture of the Texas Hill Country, the populist instincts of poor back-country Southern whites must be added to the anti-slavery tradition and liberal nationalism of the more educated and affluent German pioneers. Such "traditions" can be readily seen in LBJ's father, Sam, whose politics as a state legislator, reflected the populism of his non-German white constituents, and in his mother, Rebekah, whose love of literature and sense of refinement and "culture" mirrored as well the unique Hill Country ethos.

Another Hill Country influence was the presence of small groups of former slaves and *tejanos,* both of whom established "colonies," the name given to their communities by the area's local white residents. As will be seen, Johnson, who did as much for black Americans as any president, grew up not far from the African-American enclave called Peyton Colony, founded around 1865 by Peyton Roberts, a former slave from Lockhart, Texas. During Reconstruction, Roberts and other Texas freedmen acquired land in eastern Blanco County. The center of the colony was Mount Horeb Baptist Church; there was also a schoolhouse, a post office, and a boarding house. Surrounded by German families, the freedmen were far safer among the German Texans than they would have been elsewhere.

Most German Texans tended to be conservative in mores and definite in their sense of propriety, and many of them were, and are, devout Lutherans and Catholics. Why, then, over the generations did the Hill Country become a haven to an assortment of freed slaves, *tejanos*, early free-thinkers, anarchic hillbillies, and eventually college-town hippies? (During the 1960s, the University of Texas and the city of Austin for its size boasted of having one of the nation's more active and dynamic counter-culture communities.) The answer is simple: even if they disliked strangers and nonconformists, conservative German Texans respected their rights and freedom of choice and, thus, would not attack them in any way. By contrast, in the regions of Texas infused with traditional Southern culture (i.e., East Texas or, interestingly, in the central-western area around Waco, where the Bush family ranch is located), deviance in political views, religious belief, behavior, or even dress could—and sometimes still can—subject one to ostracism, verbal harassment, physical beatings, or even murder.

Lyndon Johnson, unlike any other Texas politician who gained national stature (including George W. Bush), grew up in a pluralistic society of German Lutherans and German Catholics, Southern evangelical Protestants, *tejanos,* and African Americans, in which the Southern Protestants were a minority in much of the area. Although raised in a Baptist household, LBJ never joined a Baptist church, and as far as doctrinal issues were concerned, he never embraced Baptist beliefs or those of any other Protestant sect. Indeed, Johnson never delved deeply into doctrinal issues, and when he did, he more often than not displayed the "free-thinking" of his Hill Country roots, dismissing such dogma as more harmful than beneficial to humanity. From this indifference, if not disdain for adherence to doctrine, sprang an ecumenical openness, a broad tolerance and respect for so many varieties of Christianity. Except in the most general and attenuated form, Christian doctrines seemed to have little to do with Johnson's career. He was not only tolerant but also undiscriminating. Religion, however defined, seemed good, like motherhood, and thus Johnson endorsed it; at times he even indulged in a little of it.

To amplify the significance of LBJ's diverse environment, by contrast, George W. Bush grew up in a West Texas that was homogeneous in race, ethnicity, and religion—a land of Anglo-Celtic Southern Protestants for whom the three major world religions were the Baptists, the Methodists, and the Church of Christ. Bush's neighbors in West Texas were predominantly Southerners whose ancestors supported the Confederacy and often the KKK. Johnson, although he was predominantly of Southern descent, matured in a community that had been the center of Texas Unionism during the secession crisis and the Civil War, who voted Republican out of loyalty to the party of Lincoln and despised Jefferson Davis and Robert E. Lee. Interestingly, Bush spent his boyhood in a part of Texas in which many right-wing segregationist Democrats in 1964 voted for Goldwater, as opposed to LBJ. Johnson's Texas was one shaped by two local traditions of opposition to the conservative Democrats who dominated Texas politics—the traditions of the liberal and socialist German Unionists and the radical white Southern Populists.

While Texas as a whole was a Southern state, Johnson came from an anomalous section of Texas with the Midwest embedded in its core. To achieve national prominence, he sometimes had to disguise his principles in order not to alienate the state's Southern majority. His native region, in its liberal and nationalist political culture and its German and central European influences, resembled the progressive prairie states like Wisconsin, Nebraska, and Minnesota, which produced his vice president and fellow champion of racial equality, Hubert Humphrey. Cultural geography is a valuable social science and an especially valuable area of study when it can help provide insights into a politician's "politics." Political leaders are shaped by many influences, and as politicians grow in stature (and ambition), they must appeal to more diverse constituencies and in the process may have to alter their policies and views. Even so, successful politicians reflect the values of their neighbors and constituents; if they did not, they would never have risen to high office. Where you are on the political spectrum depends a lot on where you are from.

In the summer of 1930, Johnson graduated from Southwest Texas State University with a Bachelor of Arts degree in history and an English minor. He hoped to find a teaching position, but recent college graduates faced a dearth of jobs, and none suffered more than new teachers. Johnson, however, would be one of the few who were fortunate to find employment in their chosen profession. Thanks largely to family connections (a paternal Uncle George), in October 1930, Johnson found himself teaching not history but speech in Houston, Texas, at Sam

Houston High, one of the city's largest and best high schools. Johnson was paid $1,600 a year, a wondrous beginning salary in the deepening depression. In addition to teaching public speaking, Johnson also taught two courses in commercial geography and one in arithmetic for remedial students. Typically, Johnson threw his enormous energies and talents into his work, leaving little time for any social life. He had older students, and he pushed and prodded them to excel. He especially liked his public speaking classes, for he had absorbed from his mother a fascination with public declamation. He believed speech and drama were perfect vehicles for student growth, for giving students a sense of mastery and self-confidence. In Johnson's perspective, poise, pride, and the ability to communicate were more critical for young people than even academic attainment. He screened the best students for forensic competition and coached both the boys' and girls' debating teams. Always one to exploit opportunities, he gave all his infectious enthusiasm to his young debaters, transfusing them with his energy and pushing them to the limit of their ability. His teams participated in debate events all over the state, and his male team won every match until the state finals and lost there only by a split vote. His ablest male debaters—Gene Latimer and Luther E. Jones—became lifelong friends; both would later work for him in Washington. Johnson took advantage of every opportunity to publicize and promote his team's success, turning debate into one of Sam Houston High's most popular extracurricular activities. In less than one year, his team made him a hero in the school, as well as giving him citywide recognition. He received a rare raise and a contract for another year. However, the twenty-three-year-old high school teacher was destined for a different career.

While home in the Hill Country for the summer, Johnson got direct exposure to Texas politics, assisting his father in an election campaign for Austin lawyer Welly Hopkins, who was running for state senator. LBJ accompanied his father on Hopkins' junkets, and at a rally in Henley, Johnson gave his first political speech, one that catapulted him into the local limelight and one that would soon put him on a completely different career path. At the Henley gathering, one of the scheduled speakers was former governor Pat Neff, a renowned orator, who was currently state railroad commissioner and was up for reelection. Neff never arrived, and only silence followed the call for him from the speaking platform. LBJ knew and admired Neff, for the former governor had appointed his father, Sam Johnson, to his current position as state bus inspector. Lyndon, sensing the crowd's disappointment at Neff's failure to show, stepped forward and gave an impromptu talk in Neff's behalf. Although a speech void of much substance, it wasn't what Johnson said but how he said it that astounded everyone. Hopkins and others were so impressed by Johnson's maturity and gall that no sooner had he finished than Hopkins asked Lyndon to help in his six-county campaign, with primary responsibility for Hays and Blanco counties. As with everything he did, and especially when it came to politics, Johnson immersed himself in the moment, attentive to every detail, all the while displaying an energy and enthusiasm that seemed boundless. He organized support groups in those two counties, printed campaign material, and spent days among local farmers and ranchers, convincing them Hopkins was "their man." An astounded and grateful Hopkins won Hays and Blanco counties and the election that August. As a result, Hopkins spread the word in Austin about the "wonder boy" from the Hill Country.

No sooner had LBJ returned to his Sam Houston High classroom than he received a phone call from Richard Kleberg, the recently-elected congressional member from the Fourteenth District who had heard of Johnson's "unusual gifts for meeting and greeting the public"—the perfect qualifications for a congressional secretary. Kleberg interviewed Johnson in his Corpus Christi office, a meeting that proved to be one of the most important in Johnson's life. Kleberg offered Johnson the job, even telephoning Lyndon's high school principal to explain his need for Johnson and request for him a leave of absence. The flattered principal of course obliged, granting a year's leave and later extending it year after year. Sam Houston High never terminated Lyndon's contract, and LBJ later joked about reclaiming his old job after being president. But as he surely sensed, his teaching career was now over. Politics henceforth consumed all his interests and talents. In fact, it is hard to believe that any American was ever more committed to politics than LBJ.

Johnson's political career was one of the most meteoric in United States history. Within six years of becoming Kleberg's secretary, he was elected to Congress in his own right. Johnson's 1937 victory (to fill a vacancy left by the death of James P. Buchanan of the Tenth Congressional District, which included LBJ's boyhood home in Johnson City) owed much to his relationship with FDR, who became his political "daddy" during the New Deal years. Johnson first got the president's attention while serving as an FDR-appointee to head the National Youth Administration in Texas. From the moment he became the agency's chief (1934), Johnson excelled, gaining a reputation for being a youthful bureaucratic genius, as the ablest (and youngest) NYA director in the country. Even Eleanor

Roosevelt visited his Austin offices, marveling at Johnson's and his staff's efficiency, energy, and enthusiasm. As an administrator, Johnson worked tirelessly. He traveled continuously around the Lone Star state and drove his co-workers with the same relentless intensity. His staff's productivity had no rival, finding jobs during Johnson's tenure for approximately 15,000 Texas youngsters, ranging from building and improving playgrounds to making improvements in state parks or constructing shoulders on state highways. One of the Texas NYA's most imaginative and unique projects, eventually imitated by other states, was the building of 250 small "roadside" parks, with pull-off spaces and picnic tables. Thanks to LBJ's early initiative, Texas still has one of the finest, most extensive roadside park systems in the country.

Under Johnson, the NYA also carried out its work-study program with equally exemplary finesse and success. By the time LBJ left the agency, the Texas NYA had provided over 11,000 high school students and over 7,000 college students with work-study grants. The Texas NYA also established and paid for textbooks and college instructors for freshman college centers, which offered credit courses (usually in high schools) for young people who could not enroll in college, another innovation copied in other states. Other educational programs involved on-the-job training, some at newly-created residence training centers. In the summer the Texas NYA also conducted a few special camps for unemployed or culturally-deprived youth. These camps, prophetic of the later Job Corps, not only taught job skills but hygiene, English, and fine arts as well. Many graduates were able to get jobs after such training.

More impressive was LBJ's brilliant surmounting of the greatest hazard to having a popular Texas NYA program—race. To an extent rivaled by few other New Deal agencies, the national NYA tried to offer fully equal opportunities to African Americans, and in this capacity, LBJ exceeded all other directors, ensuring at least black Texas youth were treated equally even when separate. He appointed a black advisory board; he included all black colleges in the student aid program; and even though blacks did not receive grants in proportion to their numbers in the state population, a much higher percentage of black college students qualified for and gained aid (24 percent compared to 13 percent for whites). In short, more than any other director in the rigidly segregated South, LBJ worked assiduously to provide as many black Texans as was possible access to his agency's largesse. Indeed, thanks to LBJ, black Texas youth fared better when it came to getting jobs in depression America than anywhere else in the country, including those in many Northern states.

During his 1937 run for Congress, LBJ distinguished himself from a crowd of candidates by making the election a referendum on FDR, proclaiming himself to be a true New Dealer and FDR supporter, even to the point of defending Roosevelt's high-handed court-packing scheme. FDR liked what he heard "down in Texas" and, consequently, indirectly aided LBJ at his every turn. Johnson easily won the election, and shortly thereafter, he was invited to join the president on FDR's return from a fishing trip in the Texas Gulf. LBJ wasted little time ingratiating himself with FDR by declaring himself a die-hard New Dealer. Within months of coming to Washington, LBJ had easy access to the president's closest advisers, turning such intimacy into profit for his Texas financial backers, such as the construction firm of Brown and Root. Indeed, when one of the company's projects encountered obstacles from administration officials, Johnson importuned the president so vigorously and persistently that the president, with the nonchalance of a father, finally capitulated, telling an aide to "give the kid the dam." Significantly, LBJ served his conservative Texas supporters while simultaneously maintaining a good rapport with White House liberals. After 1938, as FDR's power over Congress waned, Johnson rarely spoke out on the House floor for New Deal measures. Nonetheless, Johnson retained FDR's confidence and used his access to power as a means of avoiding conflict with those he served. The two men had a special bond. FDR once predicted that LBJ would be president some day! "That's the kind of man I could have been if I hadn't a Harvard education," he remarked. The ironies were everywhere, and never more so than when, on FDR's death, Johnson declared that he felt like he had lost his father.

From the perspective of his Tenth District constituents, Lyndon Johnson was an ideal member of Congress. No one ever served his people more assiduously or with greater success. He quickly became the willing servant, lobbyist, agent, and ombudsman of everyone who asked for his help, whether rich or poor. By the natural order of things, people of wealth and influence most often needed and used his talents. Because of his intense commitment to his district, because of the time he devoted to his people's demands, and because of ambitions to become a senator, Johnson was rarely involved with major national issues, had limited time to work on committee and legislative tasks, and usually tried to avoid highly partisan or controversial issues.

While still serving as Kleberg's secretary, LBJ met and married in a matter of four months a woman who became one of the nation's most gracious First Ladies, Claudia Alta "Lady Bird" Taylor. Interestingly, Lady

Bird, or just Bird as LBJ always called her, was a blind date. Lady Bird proved to be a jewel of great value to LBJ's career but in 1934 one hidden by a plain exterior. Lady Bird was painfully shy, conscientious to a fault, and gracious to the point of stereotype. Because of her reserved manner and plain attire, she did little to compensate for rather sharp features. She was no beauty (certainly not a Jackie Kennedy) but far more attractive physically than Eleanor Roosevelt. She lacked social confidence and on first encounter seemed submissive and deferential. However, appearances were misleading, and as everyone knew her well, a true "steel magnolia" lay just behind the shy surface. She had as much self-discipline as her husband but, unlike him, never displayed a temper or had tantrums when things didn't go her way. She never relaxed her outward calm, was never negative, never publicly complained, and never put people down, a behavior in stark contrast to her husband's penchant for disparaging others. Kind, generous, and supportive, she was continually involved in self-improvement, in reading, learning and growing. In time she gained mastery at almost any task she undertook, and in a pattern reminiscent of Eleanor Roosevelt, she eventually developed the self-confidence needed to build an identity and a career quite distinct from that of her egotistic and demanding husband. In a sense her greatest achievement was to stay with Lyndon, to endure and rebound from his childish petulance, pettiness, and rages, his crudeness and obscenity, his overbearing impositions, and his ego boosting at her expense. She not only stayed with him throughout one of the most intense times in United States history but also gained his gratitude, his respect, and even his dependence. She basked finally in his political success, shared his enormous power and used some of it to further her own goals, and enjoyed his exuberance and his overwhelming acts of kindness and affection.

In 1941, as a result of death once again (in April of that year, Senator Morris Shepherd unexpectedly died), Johnson seized the opportunity he had been waiting for to become a senator. He immediately put his hat in the ring, and the risks were low if he lost. Because it was a "special election," he could retain his seat in the House and still compete for the Senate vacancy. In a regular election he would have had to give up his House seat to run for the Senate, because he could not be a candidate for two offices at once. Johnson's opponent was the popular demagogic governor, W. Lee "Pass the Biscuits" O'Daniel, a former Fort Worth flour manufacturer, who had no talents to recommend him as a senator or for any political office. Nonetheless, in one of the most corrupted elections in modern Texas history, O'Daniel "stole" victory from LBJ. Everyone knew how O'Daniel had "won," even Johnson, but LBJ had little recourse for inquiries would have revealed "irregularities" in Johnson's campaign. Johnson thus withdrew rather than fight back. He still had his House seat, and most important, FDR never loved him as much. Moreover, in 1942, he would be able to run again for O'Daniel's regular Senate seat. Next time he knew he would not lose by trickery. He might win by it. However, 1942 would not be the year. Pearl Harbor forced LBJ to put his political ambitions on hold as he went off to serve his country as a navy lieutenant commander.

Initially, LBJ was stuck in Washington but knew that to advance his political career, he needed to see combat and soon. After several months spent agitating superiors for a chance to see combat, Johnson finally enjoyed a brief moment of glory, a bombing mission over Lae, a Japanese base on the north shore of New Guinea. Johnson's plane, a B-26 medium-range bomber, called the *Heckling Hare,* was part of a twelve-bomber attack on Lae. However, as the planes approached their target, two dozen defending Zero fighters attacked the U.S. planes. Johnson's plane lost power in one engine, had to jettison its bombs, and turned back toward its home base. As the wounded plane departed the squadron, it became an easy target for the Zeros, which damaged the fuselage before they turned away to engage the remaining bombers. Johnson's plane returned to base safely, and his one taste of combat was over. The rest of Johnson's military career proved anticlimactic. On July 1, 1942, FDR issued an order calling back to Washington all congressional members still on active duty. The order, however, did not mean that they had to leave their military units. They had the choice of resigning their seats and remaining on active duty (which four did). Johnson apparently never considered this. He flew back to the states and by August was once again devoting his full energies to serving his Tenth District constituents.

After FDR's death, Johnson somewhat surprisingly moved to the right ideologically. He supported the Taft-Hartley Bill, voted to override Truman's veto of it, opposed anti-lynching legislation, but staunchly defended Truman's national security/cold war initiatives. "I am in favor," he declared, "of letting Stalin know that he cannot run over the world and enslave us . . . and impound our children as captives behind the Iron Curtain." Despite earlier inclinations to accommodate the Soviet Union and criticizing HUAC's red-baiting, by 1947, Johnson now embraced fully the politics of anticommunism, for he saw, like others, great political value in supporting such policies and attitudes. In a time of increasing public hysteria and paranoia about communism,

Johnson determined never to be labeled or accused of being "soft" on communism or labor. If he hoped to run for the Senate, such intimations by opponents could destroy his chances. Thus, in his 1948 race for the Senate, Johnson accused his opponent, Governor Coke Stevenson, of being "soft" on communism, who retaliated in kind. By the end of the election, Johnson had disillusioned former liberal allies, although private assurances persuaded several that his red-bating was just "politics" and that he was still "one of them" in his heart. State conservatives were equally suspicious of Johnson's supposed "conversion" and, thus, never trusted him. By playing to both sides, Johnson was able to avoid alignment with any ideological camp but at the same time did not have the solid support of either, which caused the race to be even closer than in 1941. Indeed, the "final" results changed several times over a two-week period. In the end, Johnson prevailed, beating Stevenson by only 87 votes. Everyone knew, especially Stevenson, that fraud had occurred, and the counties responsible were all in South Texas, an area legendary for its machine politics and corruption. In Duval, Jim Wells, and Zapata counties, election officials carried ballot boxes home, left official tallies at a school or in unlocked rooms, and eventually, before legal deadline, even destroyed ballots. Tampering was a very easy process in 1948 and no doubt occurred this time in Johnson's favor. Johnson had long cultivated the South Texas bosses, both Anglo and *tejano*, and in a typical pattern gained almost all the votes in such controlled counties. Although LBJ carried the three counties, no one ever found evidence that he had any direct involvement in the "vote switching" or tampering that obviously occurred. By eighty-seven votes, "landslide Lyndon" returned to Washington as the junior senator for Texas, thus finally achieving a long-term goal. Although the victory was not sweet, the fruits of victory would prove sweet indeed. This close, contested, corrupt election proved the most important turning point in Johnson's political career.

Johnson came to dominate the U.S. Senate as no one ever had before. Quickly attaching himself to the powerful conservative patriarch of Georgia, Richard Russell, as the key to his own ascendancy, Johnson argued against any change in the filibuster rules in his initial speech on the Senate floor. Such a position won the support of conservative Southerners. Simultaneously, he engaged in the politics of anticommunism, lambasting liberal Leland Olds as a "fellow traveler" and potential "commissar," thereby blocking Olds' reappointment to the Federal Power Commission and delighting his Texas oil and gas friends. As one columnist said in the midfifties, "the tall traveler who came to

Congress as a follower of Franklin Roosevelt is now riding in the first-class coach of Republicanism." Yet, LBJ was more liberal on race than most Southerners, refusing to join the Southern caucus, and by getting to know and do favors for virtually all of his Democratic colleagues, he soon found himself Minority Leader and, two years later, in 1955, Majority Leader of the U.S. Senate.

All of his previous training had prepared him for the position—his skill at avoiding conflict and forging compromise, his keen observation of individual personalities and eccentricities, knowing what made people "tick," and his genius at placating, flattering, and wooing potential allies. As he told his aide, Harry McPherson, there were "two kinds of senators—the minnows and the whales," and Johnson knew how to cultivate both. Among "the whales," no one was larger than he. Johnson got to know every senator intimately, his likes and dislikes, his weaknesses and strengths, his family situation, and the nature of his constituency. His greatest skill lay in his ability to convince those who were ambivalent or neutral of his position, persuade those on the other side, and talk into neutrality those who opposed him. Johnson was far from being a great orator; yet, as one colleague said, "I never saw Lyndon Johnson win a debate conclusively on the Senate floor, and I never heard him lose one in the cloak room." It was off the Senate floor, in his private chambers over drinks, that the famous "Johnson Treatment" was put into effect, encompassing, enveloping, and ultimately exhausting into capitulation the recipient with the intense power of persuasion. According to columnists Rowland Evans, Jr. and Robert D. Novak who coined the term, LBJ would "move in close, his face a scant millimeter from his target, his eyes widening and narrowing, his eyebrows rising and falling. From his pockets poured clippings, memos, and statistics. Mimicry, humor, and the genius of analogy made the 'treatment' an almost hypnotic experience and rendered the target stunned and helpless." In the process, Johnson told whomever he was trying to convince that the entire future of a given piece of legislation depended on that person's response. As one recipient of the "treatment" described it: "Lyndon got me by the lapels and put his face on top of mine and he talked and talked. I figured I was either getting drowned or joining."

The "Johnson Treatment" represented more than the wily tactics of a shrewd, manipulative politician. At a deeper level, Johnson's behind-the-scenes maneuvering reflected a passionate devotion to "consensus building" among disparate groups and individuals who would otherwise never share a common position and move forward an idea or legislation.

Johnson told each person who encountered his "treatment" something different, and then he held the individual to the personal agreement each had made with him. To LBJ, nothing could be worse than allowing divisions to surface publicly or different sides to become emotionally polarized. Thus, virtually all of Johnson's public declarations invoked ideals to which few could take exception. Americans must support the president, regardless of which party they belonged or where they were on the ideological spectrum, uniting behind an unequivocal anticommunist policy. In almost a parody of this consensus approach, in 1958 Johnson announced he was "a free man, a U.S. Senator, and a Democrat in that order. I am also a liberal, a conservative . . . a businessman, a consumer . . . and I am all these things in no fixed order. . . . At the heart of my own beliefs is a rebellion against this very process of classifying, labeling, and filing Americans under headings." To LBJ, to do so was to acknowledge that there might be divisions worth fighting over, and in Johnson's mind, that was something guaranteed to destroy the consensus essential to move the country forward. In short, to LBJ, nothing could be accomplished at home or abroad if Americans were divided on those key issues affecting the nation's well being. It was, thus, his job as an elected official, as a steward of the people, to unite his countrymen behind ideas and programs that would benefit the nation as a whole while protecting it from foreign enemies or challenges to America's leadership of the free world.

Johnson could not understand and, in fact, even belittled those who boasted of their "principles." He dismissed such individuals as self-righteous, impractical ideologues who cared more about the "purity" of their ideas rather than making something happen. In this context, he equally condemned both liberals and conservatives, for both were inflexible, arrogant, and unwilling to bargain or compromise. They always tried to make a point or to fight futile ideological battles and were thus abstract, unable to get anything accomplished. To LBJ, the worst members of Congress were the ideologues because they too often proved to be the greatest obstructionists and perennial impediments to any legislative achievement at all. Where was LBJ ideologically at this point in his career? Somewhere in the middle but always willing to move right or left to accommodate a constituency or to get something passed. More than any other senator, he approached legislation with a body-count mentality—the more bills passed, the better, even if some had to be compromised to the point of emasculation. To Johnson, even a small program, or an opening engagement of some critical issue, was better than no action at all. In many ways, Johnson was like his mentor FDR, whose "try anything but do something" shotgun approach to New Deal legislation was very similar to his protégé's belief that no matter how watered-down a bill might have to be to get passed, even in its debilitated state, the measure marked a start for something better to come.

Although not a standard liberal, neither was LBJ a conventional conservative. Indeed, he was a unique amalgam of antithetical political ideologies tempered by an inherent, indigenously-inspired paternalism. The self-serving, power-hungry wheeler-dealer was Johnson's "Mr. Hyde side," while his loyalty to FDR and New Deal liberalism represented his softer "Dr. Jekyll" side. Johnson never displayed the class resentments and the anti-business biases of the populists and New Dealers. To defend "the people" did require one to alienate opponents to the point that they became inveterate enemies and villains. In private, Johnson often condemned the callousness and shallowness of the rich but rarely rabble-roused, inciting and promoting class warfare. Indeed, he deplored divisiveness and constantly, passionately cultivated "consensus." He never forgot that, as the Texas director of the National Youth Administration, federal programs had enabled young Texans to stay in school and had brought to the Hill Country the blessings of modern appliances through the rural electrification program. He hobnobbed with liberals as well as with powerful Texas business friends and supporters. During his years in the House, he and Lady Bird regularly attended gatherings at the Georgetown home of Arthur "Tex" Goldschmidt and his wife Elizabeth, two liberal Texans. Other guests included Abe Fortas, a brilliant young Yale Law School graduate from Memphis who worked with Goldschmidt in the Interior Department; liberal Southerners Clifford and Elizabeth Durr, relatives of Supreme Court Justice Hugo Black; and future Supreme Court Justice William O. Douglas, who until 1939 was a Securities and Exchange commissioner. Although not always agreeing with his Georgetown liberal friends, Johnson never lost touch with them or his New Deal roots. Indeed, he would later say, "FDR was like a daddy to me."

Regardless of where LBJ was on the ideological spectrum, he was genuinely a tender-hearted man who felt the pain of the downtrodden and oppressed. One of his closest White House aides, Larry O'Brien, recalled, "It was his nature to become almost emotionally involved in this subject [poverty]." LBJ's war on poverty "underscored his often-mentioned concern about the poor, his often-repeated stories about his childhood and his youth." Another confidant, White House counsel and outspoken Texas lawyer, Harry McPherson, admitted soon after LBJ left the Oval Office that Johnson was "as self-centered a man as ever was," but he also had a rare capacity "to empathize." When "an old woman falls down in the street his shins ache a little." LBJ also reveled in the role of the magnanimous benefactor. Since his days as a young teacher in Cotulla, Texas (where he taught for one semester before joining the faculty at Sam Houston High) when he fought to get hot lunches and sports equipment for his poor *tejano* students, he had played "Big Daddy" to others in need, reflecting the acculturation of a Southwestern type of paternalism—he became the South Texas patron writ large—that more aptly described his "ideology" than either conservatism or liberalism. Simply, LBJ wanted to be loved. He had a mean, vindictive streak and an explosive temper that he often could not contain. He was a hard-driving taskmaster who had a callous disregard for his subordinates' personal lives and well being. At the same time, however, he was capable of startling acts of generosity toward people who worked for him. In the political realm, he loathed to make enemies if that could be avoided. Ideally, opponents should be converted, not defeated.

Unlike Harry Truman, Johnson was financially secure by the time he became a senator. Indeed, this was thanks in large part to his wife's Texas Broadcasting Company, which by 1949 included television as well as radio stations. The company had developed into a secure, increasingly valuable, steadily growing enterprise, one augmented by its monopoly of the only VHF channel in Austin. Other investments—in scattered lots, in land, and in bank stock—began a rapid appreciation in value in the postwar years. The Johnsons' income from such investments was about $50,000 annually, and by 1950, Johnson estimated the market value of all his land and Lady Bird's assets at close to $1 million. Despite his wealth, Johnson had no desire to establish a permanent home in a "city" like Austin or Washington. Instead, Johnson longed to return to his beloved Hill Country, and, thus, he and Lady Bird began scouting ranches for sale in the Johnson City and Stonewall areas. Clearly, LBJ yearned to be back on the Pedernales.

In 1951, Johnson finally acquired his dream: a ranch on the Pedernales, which he would quickly dub the LBJ Ranch, and which today (especially during the months of March and April, "bluebonnet season" in Texas) is one of the most visited historic sites in the Lone Star state. Within two years of the purchase, Johnson was treating a parade of famous guests to his own overwhelming style of Texas hospitality. He basked in the limelight. To Johnson, his ranch became an extension of his very self. He simply loved it and could not wait to get back to the ranch no matter how busy he was in Washington either as a senator or as president. When he bought it, he knew virtually nothing about ranching; his father had farmed not "ranched," and there was a world of difference in those two endeavors. Johnson, however, was a quick learner, and with the help of other ranchers and cowboys, LBJ became a true Hill Country rancher in a very short time. The moment he got to his ranch, off came the suits and on went the cowboy boots and hat. The ranch became his only real passion outside of politics, his one avocation. He knew every field, counted every cow, rode or drove across the land in reckless abandon, hunted deer and turkey in the fall, and during periods of depression yearned to be back at the ranch. It symbolized peace, simplicity, honest friendship, and a manageable world. Interestingly, LBJ had little interest in making his place a profitable enterprise, and only toward the end of his life, after he acquired several other ranches, did the LBJ ranch become remunerative. In a pattern stretching back to George Washington, Johnson established his roots in the soil, acquiring his "plantation," his country home. His Western Senate cronies—Everett Dirkson of Montana, Clinton Anderson of New Mexico, Robert Kerr of Oklahoma, and Wayne Morse of Oregon—all had farms or ranches. From time to time the "boys" gathered in Senate cloakrooms, temporarily forgot their political differences, compared notes about ranching, and on occasion swapped real bulls.

Johnson's obsession with consensus had its most clear-cut manifestation on an issue central to the fissures in the American social structure—the question of race. Johnson understood instinctively that no Southerner could achieve the presidency without breaking with traditional Southern attitudes toward civil rights. In 1957, Johnson began assembling the key figures for a consensus behind civil rights legislation in Congress. Brilliantly, he used his private connections to secure agreement to a bill that would never have withstood public debate. To Southerners like Richard Russell, he argued that the only way to keep "uppity" blacks from wreaking havoc with the Constitution was to give them some reform. He promised Russell and other Southerners that he would eliminate from the proposed bill federal intervention in the South to promote voting rights and school desegregation—if Southerners agreed not to filibuster. To Northerners, he conveyed the impression that he was a "secret liberal," as devoted as they supposedly were to racial equality. (When Eleanor Roosevelt was told that Johnson had called himself a "secret liberal," she responded, "You're crazy.") Despite liberal suspicions,

Johnson nonetheless persevered, telling liberals that at this juncture in the nation's history, if they really wanted progress on civil rights, then they would accept his compromise initiative. With the compromises all in place, a jubilant Johnson led the final, anticlimactic floor fight. The bill passed seventy-two to eighteen; a miffed and frustrated Eisenhower reluctantly signed it. Johnson heralded it as a great step forward, good for all Americans, a solution for the problems of 1957. He knew tougher bills would come later, but for the moment he had won all his immediate goals—he kept the Democratic Party together, prevented deeper sectional conflict, gained enormous publicity for this impossible accomplishment (the first civil rights bill since Reconstruction), and, most important, enhanced his presidential nomination possibility. The bill turned out to be largely ineffective, as Johnson had probably anticipated. His main purpose in promoting the bill was to obtain a mild voting rights measure, the one issue that Southerners had the most difficulty opposing. However, thanks to Johnson's maneuverings, a permanent Commission on Civil Rights was established, which over the course of the next few years played an increasingly significant role in a slowly developing civil rights movement and was crucial in the maturation of later, tougher bills. Typically, Johnson stressed the fact that a bill passed, not its content. The bill marked a start; it opened the door; and in that sense, it was more important than any subsequent civil rights legislation.

One of Johnson's more surprising senatorial endeavors was his keen interest in space exploration and related technology, areas in which he surprisingly became somewhat of an expert. As early as 1949, Johnson revealed his penchant for such issues while serving as chairman of the Preparedness Subcommittee. Rocket research and space exploration remained secondary in defense planning and public consciousness until October 4, 1957, when a tiny Soviet satellite, the Sputnik, beeped its way around the earth. Although militarily insignificant, the launching unleashed a wave of hysteria, for it seemed to indicate that the Soviets were ahead of the United States in rocketry and possibly even in science and technology. The symbolic impact was immeasurable. Sputnik provoked the most protracted and intense critical examinations of American achievements in all areas, a phenomenon not witnessed in several decades. Especially scrutinized was education, which apparently was woefully lacking in many areas but especially in science, mathematics, and engineering. Perhaps more important, Sputnik reinforced the cry that the United States was becoming a society of mediocrity, a plastic, conformist, quantity-driven culture. No one did more than LBJ to abet, orchestrate, and politically exploit this developing critique, ultimately parlaying it not only into a great boon for himself but for the nation as well.

Under Johnson's supervision, the special subcommittee formed soon after Sputnik's release launched one of the largest and best conducted congressional investigations in American history. In his reports, Johnson talked of the "most serious challenge" to national security in all American history and lamented how far behind the United States was in the "weapons of tomorrow." Yet, he typically interpreted the problem as a challenge, one that Americans could overcome in the next few years if they put forth now the maximum effort to "catch up." Thus, he no sooner added to the cries of alarm than he tried to convert the concern into forceful action.

Johnson's subcommittee's report led to one of the most massive military buildups in American history by stressing the short time the nation had to narrow the gap. The committee advocated certain immediate responses, which were put into effect with unprecedented dispatch—a rebuilt fleet of bombers, an accelerated timetable for the four types of rockets already in development, and a new early-warning network. At a broader level, it suggested a reorganization of the Department of Defense to end service rivalries, increased research and development programs, increased defense appropriations, higher military salaries, a new civil defense shelter program, an increased exchange of scientific intelligence with allies, new but as yet nonspecific educational programs, and, finally, a new civilian effort in outer space.

This final proposal set the stage for a bill sponsored by Johnson entitled the National Aeronautics and Space Act of 1958, possibly the most important legislation ever to bear his name. The act, as approved, created the National Aeronautics and Space Administration with a board and a civilian director. The new agency reflected LBJ's growing interest and expertise in space exploration. Johnson's constant promotion and support for such endeavors was later repaid by establishing one of the agency's largest facilities near Houston, Texas. Johnson also chaired a new committee on aeronautics and space science, areas in which he read voraciously, and much to the surprise of scientists and other experts in these fields, he not only understood what they were saying but could talk their "language" as well when asking questions or commenting on their proposals. In 1958, he basked in all the publicity and proudly assumed the role as America's foremost spokesman on space-related issues. In a speech before the United Nations, Johnson told the world that Americans were united in favor of a peaceful use of the heavens. Here, all people could escape the legacies of distrust, fear, and ignorance. Johnson had never been in as much demand as a speaker, and he developed sections of speeches on space that he continued to deliver all through his vice-presidential years. On this issue, unlike civil rights, Johnson could easily present himself as a voice of reason and responsibility and, in 1959 and 1960, used his statesmanship on space as a vindication of his on-again, off-again presidential aspirations.

Johnson's obsession with both dominance and consensus provides a partial explanation for his failure to secure the 1960 Democratic presidential nomination and his acceptance instead of the vice-presidency. Apparently, Johnson believed that his behind-the-scenes maneuvering with party moguls, his friendship and patronage of powerful Democratic (Texas) business interests, and his dominance of the Senate was all that was needed to win the nomination. In short, out of recognition and deference, the party would confer on him the legitimacy to lead the Democrats nationwide. While Johnson was "internally" working the party's power brokers, Kennedy was out scouring the states for delegate votes. If Johnson was the master of legislative legerdemain, Kennedy understood far better the politics of presidential nominations. In the end, Kennedy's charisma prevailed over Johnson's cloakroom machinations. When one of the Senate's youngest and politically weakest senators offered that body's most powerful member the vice-presidential nomination, Johnson had only two choices: he could join Kennedy on the ticket for the sake of party unity and victory, or he could turn down the offer and possibly foment personal antipathy and party rancor, finding himself in the potential position of having to take orders as Senate Majority Leader from a man who was his inferior in every aspect of legislative politics. In many ways, Johnson was in a no-win situation. If he rejected the vice-presidency, he would be held responsible for creating party division; if he accepted it, he would be subordinate to an "inferior" politician. However, if he said yes—even if it involved the temporary ignominy of holding a powerless office—at least there was the possibility of moving up to the presidency when Kennedy's tenure was over. In effect, there was no option for Johnson but to accept the vice-presidency.

Suffice it to say, LBJ was miserable in the office. After unsuccessful efforts at securing authority in his own right, he reconciled himself into accepting the classic position of second-in-command. As Johnson later recalled, "The vice-presidency is filled with trips around the world, chauffeurs, men saluting, people clapping, chairmanships of council, but in the end, it is nothing. I detested every minute of it." Only in his trips abroad, when foreign heads of state recognized and accepted him as the nation's spokesman, an acknowledgment of his power, did his natural ebullience and air of authority return. In the meantime, back at home, he performed loyally and effectively those tasks he was asked to carry forward, frustrated that, with all its rhetoric and "style," the Kennedy administration, in one of Johnson's aide's words, was at best "racing in neutral." Then came November 22, 1963.

The Johnson Presidency: A Positive Assessment

Suddenly, the Oval Office was Johnson's, but it had come through such tragic circumstance. How to carry on, how to convey both sadness and leadership, how to sustain and nurture a sense of national continuity and direction, particularly given the aura of romance surrounding the fallen leader and the inevitable foreboding, even bitterness, that would follow? As Harry McPherson noted when the phone call came with the news of the Kennedy killing, "Dallas—insane city; insane, wide-eyed, bigoted Dallas bastards . . . a Texan become President after Kennedy is killed in Texas. There would be perilous suspicions." Yet, no one was better prepared and more able, based on an entire career of conciliation, to provide the healing hand that the country so desperately needed. "I will do my best," he told the mourning crowd at Andrews Air Force Base when Air Force One returned. "That is all I can do. I ask for your help, and God's."

No sooner was he in the Oval Office than Johnson marshaled all his coalition-building skills and tirelessly set about to bring the country together under his leadership. "Everything was in chaos," he later told Doris Kearns. "We were all spinning around and around, trying to come to grips with what had happened, but the more we tried to understand it, the more confused we got. We were like a bunch of cattle caught in the swamp, unable to move in either direction, simply circling 'round and 'round. I understand that; I knew what had to be done. There is but one way to get cattle out of the swamps, and that is for the man on the horse to take the lead, to assume command, to provide direction. In the period of confusion after the assassination, I was that man."

Johnson typically rose above the conflict and confusion, calling labor leaders, civil rights leaders, old political enemies, religious leaders, and friends, exhorting them all to unite in this moment of crisis. "People must put aside their selfish aims," he told each leader, "in the larger cause of the nation's interest. They must start trusting each other; they must start communication with each other; and they must start working with each other."

To further his consensus crusade, Johnson believed it was incumbent on him to carry forward the mission of the slain leader. "Everything I had ever learned in the history books," he said, "taught me that martyrs have to die for causes. John Kennedy had died. . . . I had to take the dead man's program and turn it into a martyr's cause. That way Kennedy would live on forever, and so would I." Many of Kennedy's Harvard clique had never welcomed nor liked Johnson; indeed, they considered him a rough-hewn, self-serving, unsophisticated (or perhaps "uncultured") cunning political operator and consequently wanted to leave Johnson at this most crucial moment. Johnson, however, refused to let them abandon his administration, telling them that they all must put aside past tensions and together work to make Kennedy's New Frontier become reality. Reflecting his obsession with unity and consensus building, while cleverly exploiting their sense of loyalty to Kennedy and the nation, Johnson pleaded with them to stay. "I know how much he needed you. But it *must* make sense to you that if he needed you I need you that much more. And so does our country." Intuitively, Johnson understood the importance (for the moment) of being linked to the Kennedy mystique—to heal the country's anguish, to build consensus behind his own legislative commitments, and to win the support of those who otherwise might become his major critics.

Five days after Kennedy's assassination, Lyndon Johnson addressed Congress, delivering what many pundits have since regarded as one of the most inspiring and reassuring speeches ever given by a president in the aftermath of a national tragedy. As millions of Americans across the country watched anxiously, the new president, speaking slowly and clearly (painstakingly, so trying to temper his Hill Country Texas twang), declared, "All I have I would gladly have given not to be standing here today." Johnson then moved to his main theme, that he would finish what JFK had started: "John F. Kennedy lives. . . . No words are sad enough to express our sense of loss. No words are strong enough to express our determination to continue forward the thrust of America that he began."

Kennedy, Johnson reminded his audience, had proclaimed in his 1961 inaugural address, "Let us begin." Now, LBJ said, "*Let us continue.* In this critical moment," he declared, "it is our duty, yours and mine, to do away with uncertainty and delay and doubt and to show that we are capable of decisive action; that from the brutal loss of our leader we will derive not weakness but strength, that we can and will act and act now." If the message were not clear, Johnson punctuated it by invoking the memory of another martyred president killed by a bullet of hate one hundred years earlier. "Let us here highly resolve that John Fitzgerald Kennedy did not live or die in vain."

In the months following Kennedy's death, Johnson never wavered in his certainty that he, like FDR, could simultaneously deliver to the American people programs to uplift the downtrodden and impoverished at home while securing the progress of the "Free World" by having the United States become a beacon of inspiration for the benefits of government-sponsored welfare capitalism. Johnson was confident that the United States had ample resources to accomplish these objectives. Indeed, in many ways Johnson became the embodiment writ large of the postwar liberal penchant for grand expectations. "I'm sick of all the people who talk about the things we can't do," he told an aide in 1964. "Hell, we're the richest country in the world, the most powerful. We can do it all."

Johnson knew the moment he became president that the successful passage and implementation of his expansive liberal agenda rested with Congress. He devoted unprecedented attention to Capitol Hill, unabashedly using over the course of the next five years all the skills and wiles he had so assiduously honed since first coming to Washington in 1937. "There is," he later explained, "but one way for a President to deal with Congress, and that is continuously, incessantly, and without interruption. If it's really going to work, the relationship between the President and Congress has got to be almost incestuous. . . . He's got to build a system that stretches from the cradle to the grave, from the moment a bill is introduced to the moment it is officially enrolled as the law of the land." He added, "A measure must be sent to the Hill at exactly the right moment. . . . Timing is essential. Momentum is not a mysterious mistress. It is a controllable fact of political life that depends on nothing more exotic than preparation."

Johnson's accommodation (or exploitation) of congressional sensibilities remains unprecedented in the annals of the modern presidency. Not even FDR was as savvy or as effective at wooing, cajoling, browbeating, or outright intimidating or emotionally or psychologically bludgeoning members of Congress to get a bill passed. Leaving nothing to chance, he insisted that his political aides be on the Hill at all times. With characteristic crudeness he told them, "You got to learn to mount Congress like you mount a woman." He told one of his aides, Joseph

Califano, never to take a congressional member's vote for granted. "Don't ever *think* about those things. Know, know, *know!* You've got to *know* you've got him, and there's only one way you know." Johnson raised his right hand, made a fist, and looked at it. "And that's when you know you've got his pecker right here." LBJ then opened his desk drawer, unclasped his fist as though he were dropping something, slammed the drawer, and grinned.

Focusing on domestic issues (which Kennedy did not in his inaugural address, nor did his administration really give them as high a priority which it should have), Johnson enumerated some of the "dreams" Kennedy allegedly was pursuing before his death—"Education for all our children," "jobs for all who seek them," "care for our elderly," and above all, "equal rights for all Americans whatever their race or color." To Johnson, the civil rights issue was paramount. Indeed, as will be seen, no president before or since LBJ pushed as boldly or as vigorously as he did to achieve this most important tenet of postwar liberalism. For the moment, however, until he was secure in his own right as president, LBJ cleverly and wisely knew that to get such a bill passed, he had to exploit the people's (and by extension Congress') sense of guilt and shame for allowing such a travesty as a presidential assassination to taint the nation's image. Thus, for the moment Johnson wrapped himself totally in the Kennedy mantle, portraying himself as "the dutiful executor" of Kennedy's program, telling Congress, "No memorial oration or eulogy could more eloquently honor President Kennedy's memory than the earliest possible passage of the Civil Rights Bill for which *he* (supposedly) fought so long." If Johnson faced any single threat to his leadership, it was northern and liberal suspicion that this southern president would betray Kennedy's alleged leadership on this issue. As was noted in the essay on JFK, for most of his brief tenure, Kennedy's commitment to civil rights was at best tokenism, and only when events forced him politically to embrace the cause did he do so. By the time of his death, Kennedy had finally taken sides on the issue, first, because it was right, and, second, because he no longer had the option of avoiding a choice. Regardless of the Kennedy record on civil rights and liberal doubts that LBJ was committed to such reform, Johnson had no choice but to promote the Kennedy illusion for the moment if he hoped to assuage such reservations. Thus, with a passion rarely previously heard from a national leader, he swept away that suspicion. "We have talked long enough in this country about equal rights," Johnson told Congress. "We have talked for one hundred years or more. It is time now to write the next chapter—and to write it in the books of law." Johnson would not only seek consensus. He would seek it in the name of racial equality, in the name of abandoning once and for all the teaching and preaching of hate and violence.

Without question, Lyndon Johnson embraced the New Frontier out of conviction. However, to LBJ, as it was to his mentor, FDR, there was a political dimension to every personal or philosophical decision made. Nineteen sixty-four was a presidential election year, and Johnson wanted a record of achievement on which to run. To look good, he must get as much of the deadlocked Kennedy agenda through as possible. Even if he failed, he would gain—by blaming Republicans for obstructionism, similar to what Harry Truman did in 1948 on the way to his surprising victory that year. Although passage of a civil rights bill was *the priority*, Johnson rightly believed that the measure's only chance of getting passed was if he got the Kennedy tax cut package through first, thus placating and earning the support for civil rights legislation from the most important sector, "the vital center," as LBJ called white middle-class America. It was upon that class that Johnson believed he could build his "consensus." If they believed they were an integral part (or equal recipient) of liberal largesse, then out of feelings of either genuine commitment to reform or out of guilt for having so much, they would come to support such measures as civil rights and other social welfare legislation. Thus, simultaneously with civil rights, Johnson pushed through Congress the 1964 tax cut, securing its passage only four months (in February) after taking office. The bill called for a $10 billion tax cut spread over 1964 and 1965. The results were spectacular. By 1965 unemployment was down to the 4 percent that the experts considered "frictional," that is, the result of normal job turnover. In short, the United States had reached the great Roosevelt-Truman dream of "full employment." Over the next two years, consumer spending increased an unprecedented $45 billion, the gross national product soared, and the government took in more money under the new tax schedule than it had previously. Fears of automation diminished, as the economy developed 10 million new jobs, a rate of a million a year. From 1961 to 1968, over 14 million Americans moved above the "poverty line," as the proportion of the impoverished in the nation was halved from 22 percent to 11 percent. Median annual family income (under $4,000 in 1958) approached $8,000 a decade later, and by 1970, 30 percent of American families took in over $13,000 annually—all this without serious inflation. During this period, price increases averaged only a little more than 1.5 percent a year. The tax appeared to be proof positive that liberal economists could put their theories into practice with gratifying results. This feat of social engineering, said Secretary of Labor W. Willard Wirtz, marked "the ultimate triumph of the spirit of John Maynard Keynes over the stubborn shade of Adam Smith," and the country's leading conservative economist, Milton Friedman, conceded, "We're all Keynesians now."

All this would mean, at least for a while, that the Great Society would swim in a sea of prosperity as federal revenues leaped from $94 billion in 1961 to $150 billion in 1967. Now innovative social programs would not require sacrifice (especially from the middle class). Helping the poor, renewing the cities, improving education and health care, cleaning up the environment, making America more beautiful, and encouraging the arts and scholarship could all be accomplished painlessly. No one would have to give up anything he or she already enjoyed. For awhile, Johnson's programs would be blessed by a sustained economic boom almost unique in the Republic's history. In 1968, Johnson's principal economic advisor, Walter Heller, summarized in his professorial way why the 1964 tax cut had been so monumental: "An expanding economy enables the nation to declare social dividends out of growing output and income instead of having to wrench resources away from one group to give to another, and thus enables presidents to press ahead with a minimum of social tension and political dissent." Unfortunately, as will be seen, all of the tax cut's economic benefits were undone by the increasing costs, both economic and political, of the Vietnam War, which in the end destroyed not only Johnson's consensus but the advantages as well of one of his administration's most important pieces of legislation.

With the tax cut secured, and as *U.S. News & World Report* grudgingly noted, "[it] appears to have achieved something like magic," Johnson believed the time was right to push for "Kennedy's" civil rights bill. With the middle class now economically sated, as well as being sufficiently repulsed and fed up with watching on the evening news the violence and brutally being visited by black and white civil rights advocates in the South, Johnson was confident that such factors would allow him to push through the mandate. Thus, no sooner did the tax cut pass than Johnson mustered all his energy and political savvy into securing the first of three civil rights measures during his presidency.

Several factors prompted Johnson to throw himself into the civil rights cause. First and foremost, he believed in it. Having grown up in Texas, he witnessed first-hand the viciousness as well as the debilitating psychological and emotional effects of racial discrimination on both blacks and *tejanos*. He empathized with both victims. As a member of

Congress, he had battled to ensure that federal agricultural programs treated blacks and whites equally. Milo Perkins, a top official in the Farm Security Administration during the New Deal years, recalled that Johnson "was the first man in Congress from the South ever to go to bat for the Negro farmer." When Congress approved appropriations for public housing in 1937, Johnson persuaded officials of the United States Housing Authority to select Austin, Texas, as one of the first three cities in the nation to receive funding. He then got the city to "stand up for the Negroes and the Mexicans" and to designate 100 of the 186 housing units for them. Although as a senator he moved cautiously on the issue so as not to alienate white supporters, Johnson remained well to the "left" of most Southern politicians on a variety of issues during the late 1940s and 1950s. When he spoke of "Kennedy's" civil rights bill in his speech to Congress five days after the assassination, he conveyed an unequivocal sense of sincerity, conviction, and determination to see the measure passed. As Johnson recalled, "If I didn't get out in front on this issue [the liberals] would get me. . . . I had to produce a civil rights bill that was even stronger than the one they'd have gotten if Kennedy had lived. Without this, I'd be dead before I could even begin."

Although Kennedy did have a civil rights bill before Congress at the time of his death, as Johnson told Kennedy aide Theodore Sorensen and Justice Department officials, as presently drafted, the bill would "go down the drain . . . he'll be cut to pieces . . . and he'll be a sacrificial lamb." If the president's bill as is was sent to Congress, Johnson predicted that conservatives like Richard Russell were "going to cut his outfit off and put it in their pocket and never mention civil rights." Instead, Johnson contended, Kennedy should have gotten the rest of his program through first, like the tax cut. "I'd move my children on through the line and get them down in the storm cellar and get it, lock and key, and then I'd make my attack." The Kennedy administration had not done its homework on what would be required to enact a civil rights bill, Johnson said, and until it did, it was simply inviting disaster by submitting the bill in its present form.

What should Kennedy have done to secure the bill's passage? According to Johnson, there were several things that needed to be done before the bill made the light of day in either the House or Senate, which on most accounts JFK had failed to do. When it came to legislative strategy and tactics, particularly on controversial measures such as civil rights, few presidents were as instinctively brilliant as LBJ in getting such bills passed. According to Johnson, if the civil rights bill were to pass, it would require twenty-seven Republican votes in support of a motion to end debate. Thus, the first person solicited should be Senate Minority Leader Everett Dirksen, "assuring" him that he would get all the credit if he cooperated and all the blame if he balked. Next, all the ex-presidents needed to be brought together and while standing in front of television cameras, issue a statement of support for the principles of civil rights. The bill also needed to be presented to Richard Russell—his objections listened to and answers found to them before sending the package to the Hill. That way the opposition could be anticipated and prevented from nitpicking the bill to death. Finally, the message should be taken to the Southern heartland, standing in a place like San Antonio, Texas, or Jackson, Mississippi, where the president opens his speech by talking about the astronauts, and pointing out that no one asked the color of a person's skin before they sent him to die in a foxhole. Having put "first things first and gotten all the rest of his legislative package through [the tax cut]," Kennedy could then "go in for the kill . . . and [not] let anybody deter [him]."

Now, Johnson himself was in a position to carry out his own advice. He intuitively knew the timing was perfect, urgent even, to make passing the civil rights bill the primary legacy of the Kennedy presidency. He thus wooed Dirksen (indeed, "The Wizard of Ooze," as Dirksen was nicknamed for his grandiloquent manner, proclaimed, after Victor Hugo, "Stronger than all the armies is an idea [civil rights] whose time has come."); disarmed Russell, who finally helped end a Southern filibuster; turned to long-time fighter for civil rights, Senator Hubert Humphrey of Minnesota, who provided invaluable assistance; and worked hand in hand with Martin Luther King, Jr. and the civil rights coalition. Perhaps most important to Johnson personally, the civil rights issue became the means by which he would finally transcend all the debilitating effect of regional conflict on his own career. He showed both liberals and Northerners alike that not all Southerners were racists and bigots; that there were many Southerners like himself who believed in equality and integration; and that, as fellow Southerner and journalist Tom Wicker observed, Johnson understood "as a Southerner" that the South had to be brought back into the union both for purposes of national unity and progress and for the sake of his own triumph as president.

By July, Johnson prevailed as both Houses passed the Civil Rights Act of 1964 to be administered by a new Equal Employment Opportunity Commission (EEOC), which was to strengthen federal remedies for fighting job discrimination. The measure also outlawed racial discrimination in public accommodations connected with interstate commerce, such as restaurants, motels, soda fountains, and gas stations. It required equal access to public facilities, such as stadiums and swimming pools, and authorized withholding federal subsidies from recipients, such as schools and hospitals, that continued discrimination. The act prohibited discrimination in voter registration and established a sixth-grade education as presumptive of literacy. Title VII, a provision added to the bill during the legislative debates, barred discrimination based on sex, a mandate that became extremely important to the movement for women's equality. The 1964 Civil Rights Act was not only testimony to Johnson's legislative genius but also to his genuine commitment to justice and equality. Quickly upheld by the Supreme Court, it was enforced with vigor by the Johnson administration. Johnson's willingness to insist on the act's fullest compliance greatly extended the federal government's power, especially in the South, long the bastion of resistance to federal encroachment. Naturally, those Southern white leaders who refused to comply rallied supporters around the cry of states' rights and "Lost Cause" histrionics. Johnson, however, was determined to use the full powers of his office, both moral and political, to destroy Jim Crow. Thanks to LBJ, blacks at last could begin to enjoy equal access to thousands of places that had excluded them in the past. Few laws have had such dramatic and heart-warming effects. As Assistant Attorney General Burke Marshall noted, "The thing that the Act reaches is the official caste system in this country."

Although the heroic efforts by civil rights activists in the preceding years were largely responsible for the act's passage, Johnson nonetheless dominated the Washington stage. Some liberals still distrusted Johnson, to be sure, as did black leaders, who suspected that his commitment was purely momentary and political and that, once reelected, he would relegate civil rights to the back burner. As will be seen, both groups were proven wrong and were forced to concede Johnson's role as a star. As black civil rights activist Bayard Rustin declared, Johnson and his aides did "more than any other group, any other administration. . . . I think Johnson was the best we ever had." Clarence Mitchell of the NAACP added that LBJ "made a greater contribution to giving a dignified and hopeful status to Negroes in the United States than any other President, including Lincoln, Roosevelt, and Kennedy." These were appropriate tributes to presidential leadership of an unusually high order.

Simultaneously, Johnson passionately embraced Kennedy's decision to ameliorate the plight of the poor, telling Congress in his first State of the Union address (January 8, 1964) that it was time for America to declare "an unconditional war on poverty." The struggle would not be easy, but "we shall not rest until that war is won." It would be waged "in city slums and small towns, in sharecropper shacks and in migrant labor camps, on Indian reservations, among whites as well as Negroes, among the young as well as the aged, in boom towns and in the depressed areas." Its weapons would be "better schools, better health, and better homes, and better training, and better job opportunities to help more Americans, especially young Americans, escape from squalor and misery and unemployment . . ."

The anti-poverty initiative, like civil rights, was also first explored by the Kennedy administration but, like much of the New Frontier, had gone nowhere. Kennedy and his advisers had been influenced by Michael Harrington's *The Other America*, a small book that had a big impact. "The millions who are poor in the United States tend to become increasingly invisible," Harrington wrote. It required "an effort of the intellect and will even to see them." Accounts like Harrington's and those of other scholars indicated that in an age of affluence one-fifth of the nation existed, as Johnson said, "on the outskirts of hope" in "inherited, gateless poverty." African Americans made up a disproportionate number of the poor, but 70 percent were whites, many of them in enclaves of distress such as Appalachia. Many of the poor were caught up in what became known as the "culture of poverty," transmitted from generation to generation. This was the "voiceless minority," the people who had no way of getting out of poverty because most of them lacked the requisite skills to find gainful employment. In less technologically advanced eras, the poor had been able to pull themselves up by taking unskilled or semiskilled jobs. But the new poor, according to Michael Harrington, were "the automation poor"—those who lacked the appropriate technological knowledge or skills to advance. The result was perpetuation of misery and an ever-widening gap between those who shared in the prosperity of economic growth and those on the margin, barely able to survive. As one economist observed, it was a kind of "colonial situation" with a successful "white economy," leaving far behind a "meager bush economy" in which "gains in the main economy" rarely "trickle down."

Clearly the problem of poverty in America was profound, an issue involving the complicated dynamics of race, class, gender, power, education, and history. Lyndon Johnson presided over an administration that believed "in doing the greatest good for the greatest number." However, how could poverty be eradicated without altering the very structure of American society and challenging the consensus Johnson so prized? The answer lied in the fact that neither Johnson nor those who advised him believed that it was necessary to alter the basic structure of American society to improve the lives of those at the bottom. In short, the war on poverty did not seek to create different winners and losers. Indeed, as Johnson said in June 1964, "This government will not set one group against another. We will build a creative partnership between business and labor, between farm areas and urban centers, between consumers and producers." Despite his personal commitment to alleviating misery, Johnson was unwilling to accept the notion that improvement for one group meant sacrifice for another. In short, Johnson believed there was no compelling reason to view the poor as anything but an unhappy exception to an overall story of success and prosperity.

Johnsonian liberals viewed the war on poverty as simply another extension or manifestation of America's postwar liberal agenda. They embraced the "culture of poverty" concept that those who were poor were in such a condition because of their values and habits, which over time had created a cycle of poverty from which they believed they could never escape. Recognizing that poverty was rooted, in part, in substandard education, inadequate job training, and poor health care, the war on poverty measures would thus provide the money to enable the poor to acquire the skills, motivation, and attitudes needed to better cope with the existing economic exigencies. Johnsonian liberals also perceived poverty as a problem of attitude. Too many of the poor, it was contended, lacked incentive. If they could be helped to see a way out, if they could be motivated to try harder, to begin climbing the ladder of opportunity, to see their own future as inextricably tied to the full participation in the American dream, then they would be motivated to solve the problem themselves. As Johnson's Council of Economic Advisers declared, the war on poverty would emphasize eliminating "the handicaps that [now] deny the poor *fair access* to the expanding incomes of a growing economy." An unfair distribution of wealth and power was not the problem; instead, it was inadequate availability of opportunity.

The war on poverty was a distinct break with the past. It declared for the first time that it was the policy of the United States to end the age-old scourge of want. The New Deal had also attacked poverty, but that was at a time when a significant number of Americans had become victims of economic calamity, and their condition was viewed as temporary. The few New Deal programs, like the Resettlement Administration and the Farm Security Administration, created specifically to address chronic poverty, were ephemeral, grossly underfinanced, and restricted to rural areas. A possible exception was the TVA, which had as one of its goals the amelioration of endemic poverty in a specific region of the upper South. The TVA, however, was as concerned with conservation and resource-development as it was with eradicating poverty. Johnson's war on poverty might have fallen far short of the expectations and demands of social theorists and revolutionaries, but it broke new ground for liberal capitalism in the United States.

Although the tax cut created more jobs, the anti-poverty program would be designed to provide the impoverished with the requisite and relevant skills to become gainfully employed and get out of poverty. At the same time, the plan called for addressing the educational, health, and medical problems that perpetuated poverty. Kennedy had been prepared to "run with the program," but Johnson embraced the idea in *toto*, telling Walter Heller, "Give it the highest priority."

It would only be natural for a birthright populist like Johnson to be so intensely devoted to the idea of ending poverty in the United States. Perhaps more important, the war on poverty revealed Johnson's ideological "two-sidedness." His liberal, compassionate, paternalistic side made the campaign against poverty naturally congenial. "Big Daddy" would make all Americans happy. Such a mentality meshed easily with his yearning to be included in the liberal pantheon alongside his hero FDR. Lyndon Johnson would be a great president in the only way he knew: by using the power of the federal government, especially that of the executive branch, to make life better for all Americans. Of course, such optimism and confidence in national institutions was before the Vietnam War and Watergate eroded such faith. Until such events took their toll on the public's trust, it was believed the government could solve any problem with the appropriate, intelligent central planning. In 1961, JFK promised to land "a man on the moon and return him safely to earth" during the decade. By 1964, the space program, with its ultimate goal of doing precisely what JFK promised, was at full "throttle," thanks to LBJ's enthusiastic support. If the United States had the resources and will to put a man on the moon, Johnson was certain that it could solve more mundane problems by an equal outlay of brains and energy. In short, Johnson's impending Great Society with its emphasis on eradicating poverty and the moon race were symbiotic: both displayed the same unbridled confidence in human ability to shape reality.

According to Walter Heller and the Council of Economic Advisers, the nation needed a "strategy against poverty" that employed tax cuts, area redevelopment, adult education, health insurance for the aged, and civil rights legislation. All of these, however, should be molded into a "coordinated and comprehensive attack" through community action programs in which the poor would be allowed "maximum feasible participation" in the various programs created for their benefit and eventual rise out of poverty. Thus, Johnson took Kennedy's slowly emerging plan, revamped it, and drove it through Congress with great fanfare. Reporters for London's *Sunday Times* commented that it "was not the most daring, but it was perhaps the most bellicose program of social reform in history. It was to be a war on poverty. Federal funds were to be 'fired' into pockets of poverty in what was known in Washington as 'the rifle-shot approach.'. . . He actually spoke of 'throttling want.'" The Economic Opportunity Act of 1964 appropriated nearly a billion dollars for projects such as Head Start, which provided free nursery schools to prepare disadvantaged preschoolers for kindergarten; the Job Corps and the Neighbor Youth Corps provided jobs and vocational training for the young; Volunteers in Service to America (VISTA), modeled on the Peace Corps, promoted community service among youths in impoverished rural and urban areas; and what would prove to be the most controversial departure, a Community Action Program (CAP), which encouraged the poor to demand "maximum feasible participation" in decisions that affected them. Community Action organizers worked closely with 2,000 lawyers employed by the Legal Services Program to provide the poor with free legal aid. The 1965 Public Works and Economic Development Act added over $3 billion more and an Appalachian Regional Development Act another $1 billion to revitalize that section. "We are not helpless before the iron laws of economics," LBJ said. Although from the beginning the war on poverty was under funded, it represented a promising beginning, and as Johnson hoped, he, not Kennedy, would be given the credit for this unprecedented, bold initiative. Indeed, the African-American novelist Ralph Ellison proclaimed Johnson to be "the greatest American President for the poor and for the Negroes." The war on poverty was to be waged through the Office of Economic Opportunity, headed by JFK's brother-in-law and former Peace Corps director, Sargent Shriver.

Clearly, Johnson understood how to shape a consensus. To bring together the necessary groups essential to passing the above legislation, he cleverly and skillfully presented himself as merely carrying forward his fallen predecessor's "ideas." He used his own mastery of legislative politics and the art of conciliation to forge an overwhelming coalition of support, with each victory rolling into another. During his first months in office,

Johnson believed his principal task was to finish what Kennedy had started with the New Frontier. Thus, after the tax cut, civil rights, and the war on poverty initiatives had been passed, then he believed it was time to "unwrap" himself from the Kennedy mantle and become president in his own right with a vision and agenda for the nation far grander than that of any of his predecessors. He wanted to achieve a record in his own name and have an historic place as master of his own administration. To that end, from his first days in the White House, Johnson sought to find a label, a theme, that he could use not only to finally break with Kennedy but also one that would convey to the American people that this president, more than any other in history, was going to make the United States a truly "Great Society."

In most instances, Johnson's Great Society reflected the main objectives of postwar liberalism. However, Johnson not only wanted to make those ideals reality but also wanted to go beyond the achievement of FDR (and, to a limited degree, Truman) to create an America worth of emulation and leadership in the twenty-first century. Although using the phrase in various speeches, it was not until giving the baccalaureate address at the University of Michigan in May 1964, that LBJ did make the concept an ideological statement. Indeed, to Johnson and 1960s liberals, the Great Society was to become the quintessence of postwar liberalism. The United States had come far, the president said to the Michigan graduates. "An order of plenty for all our people." But was material growth enough? Johnson believed it was not. The challenge of the next half-century was "whether we have the wisdom to use that wealth to enrich and elevate our national life, and to advance the quality of American civilization." The time had come for the United States to build a Great Society, "to prove that our material progress is only the foundation on which we will build a richer life in mind and spirit." Clearly, in this "second New Deal" as one pundit called it, there would remain a commitment to social reform. As Johnson said, "the Great Society rests on abundance and liberty for all. It demands an end to poverty and racial injustice, to which we are totally committed in our time." Johnson's vision, however, was even grander than completing the social reform agenda initiated by FDR, for it included not just providing all Americans with the abundant life but with a "quality" of life as well. Thus, the Great Society would be a place where "the city of man serves not only the needs of the body and the demands of commerce but the desire for beauty and hunger for community." In short, Johnson's vision for America, as articulated in his graduation address, not only was to achieve the reality of equality of opportunity for all Americans but simultaneously to create a level of civilization that enhanced the cultural, aesthetic, and physical existence of every citizen. Perhaps most important, the Great Society reflected Johnson's final shedding of the Kennedy mantle, for his conception far transcended that of the New Frontier.

Nothing helped Johnson more in his quest for a popular mandate for his Great Society than the selection of Senator Barry Goldwater of Arizona as the 1964 Republican nominee for president. Until that summer, LBJ used the crisis of the Kennedy assassination and his own role as the conciliator and harbinger of "Kennedy's" ideas to push legislation that under JFK appeared divisive and controversial. All that changed, however, with Goldwater's nomination as the self-appointed champion of right-wing Republican conservatism. Indeed, Goldwater was a reactionary who opposed virtually all efforts of the federal government to intervene in domestic social policy, including civil rights. The graduated federal income tax, he believed, "violated" individual freedom—his highest value. A rabid anti-communist, he advocated sending troops to settle overseas challenges to American preeminence. Goldwater's outspoken, often vitriolic rantings of Johnson's policies attracted a fanatical, well-financed coterie of conservatives and reactionaries, the majority of them upper-middle class, who were bent on making Goldwater the GOP presidential candidate in 1964, which they succeeded in doing. Goldwater's selection was perfect for LBJ, for now he could portray his Great Society as the essence of moderation and his leadership as preeminently centrist. Goldwater defiantly threw down the ideological gauntlet in his acceptance speech, declaring that "extremism in defense of liberty is no vice . . . and moderation in the pursuit of justice is no virtue." LBJ, by contrast, soared to nomination as a fatherly figure and voice of reason who had continued with brilliance the policies of a fallen leader and was now prepared to carry the nation to new heights of glory and progress.

In the ensuing campaign, Goldwater tried to convey his ideological opposition to "Big Government," as it had evolved in the United States under the New Deal, Fair Deal, and the "Dime Store New Deal" of the Eisenhower administration. "Socialism through Welfarism," he maintained, was the greatest threat to freedom. No presidential candidate in modern American history has been more impolitic, if not outright outrageously absurd and out of touch with the electorate. He once told Joseph Alsop, "You know, I haven't really got a first-class brain," and politically (and perhaps literally) speaking, that became evident during the campaign, as Goldwater seemed to go out of his way to offend and alienate potential voters. He went to Appalachia to denounce the war on poverty and to the South to call for the sale to private interests of the TVA, which was highly popular in the area. He told elderly folk that he wanted to do away with Social Security, and he told farmers that he opposed price supports. "My aim," he insisted, "is not to pass laws but to repeal them."

Some of Goldwater's statements were so immoderate that he invited ridicule. "The child has no right to an education," he proclaimed. "In most cases he will get along very well without it." American missiles were so superior, he said, "We could lob one into the men's room at the Kremlin." Angry at what he considered the arrogance of the liberal "East Coast Establishment," he declared, "Sometimes I think this country would be better off if we just sawed off the Eastern Seaboard and let it float out to sea." Democrats had a field day playing with his supporters' motto, "In Your Heart You Know He's Right." "In your guts," they quipped, "you know he's nuts," or retorting with "Yes, far right."

Goldwater's bellicose and preposterous foreign policy statements left him especially open to criticism. "Our strategy," he said, "must be primarily offensive. . . . We must—ourselves—be prepared to undertake military operations against vulnerable Communist regimes." When asked earlier in the year about Vietnam, he replied that he would bomb the supply routes in North Vietnam. What would he do about trails hidden in the jungle? Goldwater answered, "defoliation of the forests by low-yield atomic weapons could well be done. When you remove the foliage, you remove the cover." Although Goldwater tried to clarify and deny these remarks—he meant tactical weapons, not atomic bombs—he was consistent on one point: let the generals have a free hand, and they would deliver victory.

Johnson, meanwhile, campaigned eighteen hours a day as the voice of experience and responsibility, desperately seeking an electoral mandate that would exceed even the victory margin of his hero, Franklin D. Roosevelt. It was simply not in Johnson's character to just win; he had to dominate, to annihilate Goldwater, which would then give the greatest electoral victory in history. Thus, he sanctioned unprecedentedly harsh, negative, and outright crass television spots. One featured a large saw cutting through a wooden map of the United States while the narrator cited Goldwater's comment about the East Coast. Another depicted a pair of hands tearing up a Social Security card. The most controversial spot characterized Goldwater as a maniac whose foreign policies would destroy the world. It showed a little girl picking petals off a daisy and counting, "one, two, . . . five." Then the girl looked up startled and the frame froze on her eyes until she dissolved into a mushroom-shaped cloud and the screen went black. While she disintegrated, a man's voice, loud as if at a test site, intoned, "ten, nine. . . ." An explosion followed, where upon LBJ's voice was heard. "These are the stakes—to make a world in which all of God's children can live, or go on into the dark. We must either love each other, or we must die." The spot closed with the familiar message, "Vote For President Johnson on November 3. The stakes are too high for you to stay home." The daisy spot provoked outrage amongst many Americans, prompting Johnson to remove it, but television news programs continued to show it for several more weeks. It was later estimated that 40 million Americans saw it at one time or another.

When Goldwater urged American military victory in Vietnam, Johnson responded, using almost verbatim the same words FDR used prior to America's entry into World War II: "We're not about to send American boys nine or ten thousand miles from home to do what Asian boys ought to be doing for themselves." While Goldwater might dismantle thirty years of social reform, Johnson not only would augment past achievements but also would take New Deal/Fair Deal liberalism to even greater heights. In short, with LBJ there was stability, continuity, and responsibility. Not surprisingly, on November 3, 1964, Johnson received the mandate for which he had longed. Now president in his own right, the country's thirty-sixth president had won 61 percent of the popular vote, exceeding (appropriately) even FDR's 1936 victory. Voters gave LBJ 43.1 million votes to Goldwater's 27.2 million. Carrying all but six states, LBJ swept the electoral college, 486 to 52. Democratic congressional candidates coasted in on his coattails. They would control the House by a margin of 295 to 140 and the Senate by 68 to 32. Johnson's victory confirmed (for awhile) that he indeed spoke for a consensus, uniting the entire country.

Johnson wasted little time in capitalizing on his victory. Understanding instinctively that he needed to "get while the getting was good"—while the popular mood was conducive to new, liberal initiatives—he instructed his aides to draw up an arsenal of new legislation. "Look," he said, "I've just been re-elected by an overwhelming majority . . . [but] everyday while I'm in office, I'm going to lose votes. I'm going to alienate somebody . . . We've got to get this legislation fast. We've got to get it during my honeymoon." When an aide questioned his haste, Johnson responded: "You've got to give it all you can that first year. . . . It doesn't matter what kind of majority you come in with. You've got just one year when

they treat you right, and before they start worrying about themselves."
Expending his political capital with the genius of someone who knew in
his body's every fiber how fickle a working congressional majority could
be, Johnson established task forces of "the best minds" in the nation and
drove his staff to come up with the programs and legislation that would
make the Great Society a reality.

The results were astounding. A whirling-dervish of energy, Johnson
presided over the most extraordinary display of presidential legislative
action the nation had ever seen—the achievements of the 1965-66
Congress exceeding even the dazzling array of programs enacted during
the first two years of the New Deal. Indeed, from the moment he was
reelected, Johnson had it in his mind to do precisely that—to break all
of FDR's records. In fact, between January 4 and October 23, 1965,
(when the core of the Great Society was created), Congress became a
juggernaut of legislative action, approving eighty-four of the eighty-seven
bills Johnson submitted—a batting average of .960 for LBJ. Two of these
measures—national health insurance for retirees and the poor and the
first-ever general federal-aid-to-education law—were historic landmarks
of the social welfare state. But several others—the higher education bill,
the revision of the immigration laws, highway beautification, the National
Foundation for the Arts and Humanities, the Clean Air and Clean Water
Acts, a new department of housing and urban development—were major
pieces of legislation in their own right, for they reflected reforms that
went beyond New Deal/Fair Deal progressivism. Indeed, the "fabulous
Eighty-ninth" Congress wiped clean the Fair Deal's legislative slate.
When Congress approved a Medicare program of health insurance for
the aged under Social Security, LBJ flew to Independence, Missouri,
so that Harry Truman could witness the signing and to honor him for
having first proposed such legislation. Congress also provided Medicaid
for the indigent to be paid for by general tax revenues.

Truman also saw another one of his initiatives enacted, also in 1965,
with the passing of the Elementary and Secondary Education Act, which
provided more than a billion dollars in grants for low-income pupils and
authorized, for the first time, assistance to Catholic and other private
school children. This departure resulted from Kennedy's easing of fears
about Catholics and the ecumenical spirit fostered by Pope John XXIII,
as well as from Johnson's acumen as a legislator. By the time of Johnson's
presidency, federal aid to elementary and secondary education had
become a key component of the liberal arch, sanctified by a generation of
reformers. LBJ considered it his mandate to complete that arch. Johnson

also felt an intense personal commitment to improving and expanding the nation's public and private education system. No American had greater confidence in the efficacy and power of schools to cure and transform than LBJ. His years as a teacher, first in Cotulla, Texas, and then at Sam Houston High School in Houston, gave him the hands-on experience in education that few presidents in this century have had. LBJ believed his own life confirmed the power of education to uplift. Although often intimidated by the "Harvards" and prep schoolers that surrounded Kennedy, Johnson nonetheless recognized that his Southwest Texas State Teacher's College education had given him an essential leg-up in his climb to the heights of political power. George Reedy, his press secretary, contended that LBJ had "an abnormal, superstitious respect for education. I believe he even thought it would cure chilblain."

Regarded by many of the literati as anti-intellectual, Johnson prided himself on being the "Education President." That same year he shepherded through Congress the Higher Education Act for assistance to college students. In one year, the president claimed that Congress had done "more for the wonderful cause of education in America than all the previous 176 regular sessions of Congress did, put together." Johnson further enhanced his standing among the nation's intellectual and artistic community with the creation of the National Endowment for the Arts and the National Endowment for the Humanities. Indeed, nothing reflected the soul of the Great Society more faithfully than these two endowments. For generations American painters, sculptors, writers, and musicians had tried to solicit public support for their vocations. Unlike Europe where such artists and performers could count on public patronage, their American counterparts had not fared as well. What support the arts and humanities received prior to the New Deal had come from either local government or private patrons and, occasionally, from Washington. No other New Deal activity endeared itself to historians, writers, and artists as the federal arts, federal writers, federal music, and federal theater project of Harry Hopkins' WPA, which kept scholars and creative men and women from starving during the Great Depression and allowed them to continue in their crafts.

The WPA experience, however, was short-lived. In 1943, FDR cancelled all WPA programs, and thereafter, direct federal contribution to high culture and humanistic studies in America virtually disappeared or, at best, was sporadic and begrudgingly given. Once again, it was the New Frontier/Great Society (especially the latter) that breathed new life into an earlier era's liberal impulses. In his January 1964 State of the

Union address, LBJ endorsed a national foundation for the arts. "We must also recognize and encourage those who can be pathfinders for the Nation's imagination and understanding," he told the opening session of the Eighty-ninth Congress. In fact, LBJ's inaugural outdid Kennedy's in its tribute to art and culture. Amid the more traditional hoopla, there was a reception for the nation's prominent artists and writers hosted by Roger Stevens, a prominent New York businessman and Broadway impresario, a ballet performance by Margot Fonteyn and Rudolf Nureyev at the inaugural gala, and a concert by Isaac Stern and Van Cliburn with the National Symphony.

The bill proposing the creation of the endowments emphasized the qualitative dimension of the Great Society. During America's early history, it "was largely engaged in mastering its physical environment. . . . More recently, advancing technology, defense and space needs have put a claim on energies that might have gone into humane and artistic endeavors with the result that our social, moral, and aesthetic development has lagged behind our material advance." It was the "national interest that social, cultural, and educational imbalance be redressed." After several unanticipated months of congressional wrangling, the bill creating the new agencies finally passed the House and Senate in September 1965. The new agency would be called the National Foundation on the Arts and Humanities. Under this umbrella title would be two separate "endowments" administered by national councils or boards of trustees and coordinated by a federal council on the arts and humanities. The National Council of the Arts, established in 1964, became the arts endowment's advisory body. The humanities equivalent would be a new body. The endowments distributed federal grants to deserving individuals and organizations, including sums on a matching basis with private money. Each endowment got $5 million, and half of this diminished sum, in turn, was reserved to meet matching private grants. At most, it was a beginning, but when LBJ signed it into law, he announced that it would have "an unprecedented effect on the arts and humanities of our great nation."

Also at Johnson's behest, the Eighty-ninth Congress established two new Cabinet-level departments, for Transportation and for Housing and Urban Affairs, in recognition of the railroad crisis engendered by the ubiquitous automobile and of the fact that the United States had become a nation of cities. To further carry out the Great Society's emphasis on improving the quality of American life, legislation made provision for the beautification of highways, an abiding interest of Lady Bird Johnson.

As somewhat noted already, Johnson had a long-standing commitment to natural beauty and quality of life, dating back to his childhood in the scenic Hill Country of central Texas. Indeed, he had created a Texas-style arcadia at his ranch on the Pedernales that gave him great joy and serenity. He told visitors: "I'm going to show you the greatest treasure that no money could buy—sunset on the Pedernales." He took a special interest in the roads people traveled as they traversed the countryside. The most potent force in the beautification movement, however, was Lady Bird Johnson. Indeed, the First Lady made it her signature cause, and like her husband, it represented a long-standing interest in natural beauty. While First Lady, she devoted her amazing energies to the outdoor landscaping of Washington and ending blight along the nation's highways. Historian Lewis Gould observed, "Her commitment to the beautification of the environment was of lasting importance." Thanks to the Johnsons, the 1965 Highway Beautification Act marked a significant break with past conservation efforts, which had tended to concentrate on maintaining natural resources and national wealth. Under Secretary of the Interior Stewart Udall, Great Society programs emphasized quality of life, battling the problem "of vanishing beauty, of increasing ugliness, of shrinking open space, and of an overall environment that is diminished daily by pollution and noise and blight."

Taking advantage of the Great Society's reform climate, liberal Democrats also brought about significant changes in immigration policy. The 1965 Immigration Act abolished the 1920s quota system that had discriminated against Asians and southern and eastern Europeans, replacing it with more equitable numerical limits on immigration from Europe, Asia, Africa, and countries in the Western Hemisphere. Since close relatives of individuals who were already legal residents of the United States could be admitted over and above the numerical limits, the legislation led to an immigrant influx far greater than anticipated, with the heaviest volume coming from Asia and Latin America.

In his single most dramatic example of legislative leadership, Johnson even secured congressional approval for the Voting Rights Act of 1965. Confronted by mass demonstrations in Alabama that highlighted the oppressiveness of a social system that refused to give blacks even the basic protection of the franchise, the president went to Congress and, in a voice thick with a heavy Southern accent (something until now he had purposely tried to curtail in his speeches), demanded the enactment of voting rights protection with the promise: "We *shall* overcome," and Johnson did, as he and his aides applied unrelenting pressure for passage of a voting rights bill. The measure received strong bipartisan support, save members of Congress from the South. The House approved it overwhelmingly, 333 to 85. Southerners filibustered in the Senate but lost on a vote for cloture, 70 to 30, after twenty-five days of debate. The measure then passed 77 to 19. For the bill's signing, LBJ assembled a large audience of civil rights leaders and congressional members in the President's Room at the Capitol—the same place where Lincoln had signed the Emancipation Proclamation. "Let us say to every Negro in this country," he said, "You *must* register. You *must* vote. . . . The vote is the most powerful instrument ever devised by man for breaking down injustice and destroying the terrible walls that imprison men because they are different from other men."

The 1965 Voting Rights Act greatly extended federal power in the United States. However, as everyone knew at the time, it was really a regional measure, for it took aim at Deep South states by abolishing the literacy tests and other measures most southern states used to prevent blacks from registering to vote. The act authorized the attorney general to send federal examiners to register voters in any county where less than 50 percent of the voting-age population was registered. The law covered state and local as well as federal elections and protected not only the right to register but also the right to vote. Together with the 1964 adoption of the Twenty-fourth Amendment to the Constitution, which outlawed the poll tax in federal elections, and successful legal challenges to state and local poll taxes, the Voting Rights Act allowed millions of African Americans to register and vote for the first time. Within a year, the strong arm of the federal government had helped to increase the registration of eligible black voters in the six southern states wholly covered by the law from 30 to 46 percent; by 1971, the number of registered black voters in the South had risen to 62 percent.

"The Congress of Fulfillment" completed almost the entire agenda of twentieth-century progressivism. Under Kennedy and more markedly under Johnson, the quarter-century deadlock had been broken. The Eighty-ninth Congress, wrote one Washington reporter, "brought to a harvest a generation's backlog of ideas and social legislation." Arthur Krock observed that it had "moved the country nearer to state collectivism at the federal level than in any previous period." For those who since the Great Depression had waited in vain for another era like that of the New Deal, LBJ and his Great Society caused them to rejoice, for it reminded them of the halcyon days of 1935. "It is the Congress of accomplished hopes," declared Speaker John W. McCormack. "It is the Congress of realized dreams."

By anyone's standards, it was a time of unparalleled accomplishment. "Johnson asketh and the Congress giveth," one wag observed. In a performance unprecedented in the annals of American legislative leadership, Johnson maximized his moment in the sun, expending his political capital almost flawlessly in pursuit of his dream to become one of the Republic's greatest presidents. He had brought the nation together after one of its greatest tragedies, and now that nation was fast approaching its moment of greatness. It was all thanks to Johnson's Herculean efforts to "provide the greatest good for the greatest number." No other president cared so much as Johnson did about domestic policies or about civil rights, and none since FDR in the 1930s had come close to securing so many laws, many of them long awaited by reformers. It was a high tide of American liberalism in the postwar era.

No one could deny Johnson's achievements. He wanted to be "the greatest of them all, the whole bunch of them," and in many ways he was. As Tom Wicker noted in the *New York Times*, "the list of achievements is so long that it reads better than the legislative achievements of most two-term presidents." In the areas of education, Medicare, urban development, social welfare, and, above all, civil rights, LBJ accomplished what few could even envision. As one civil rights leader observed at the time of Johnson's death, "when the forces demanded and the mood permitted, for once an activist, human-hearted man had his hands on the levers of power. . . . Lyndon Johnson was there when we and the nation needed him, and oh my God, do I wish he was there now." Johnson's greatness perhaps lied in his ability to conceptualize and articulate the American dream, to convey to all Americans that it was open to all of them, and if it was not, then he *personally* guaranteed it soon would be, for he would use all the power and persuasion of his office to make it so. "We seek," he told a Howard University audience, "not just equality as a right in theory, but equality as a fact and result." Without overstatement, Senate Majority Leader Mike Mansfield summed up the Johnson legacy: "He has outstripped Roosevelt, no doubt about that. . . . He has done more than FDR ever did, or ever thought of doing."

The larger question, however, was whether Johnson's vision was adequate, whether it realistically addressed the problems of society, and whether the values and methods of the liberal consensus were consistent with the objectives desired. Could Johnson, through his own personal will and obsession with dominance, find the answers to the nation's problems? Or would that obsession itself become a tragic impediment to success?

The Johnson Presidency: A Negative Assessment

The first warning that all was not right with the Great Society and Johnson's "consensus" liberalism occurred only five days after he signed the 1965 Voting Rights Act. On August 11, rioting broke (largely as a result of endemic police brutality and pent-up rage among an adult black male population of which three-fourths were unemployed) out in the Los Angles black ghetto of Watts, and at the end of five days of looting, sniping, and the burning and vandalism of mostly white-owned businesses (property damage was estimated at more than $35 million), thirty-four people were dead, more than 1,000 injured, and some 4,000 arrested. The neighborhood disturbances in New York and other Eastern cities the previous summer had not set off national concern, but Watts touched a sensitive collective nerve. Johnson fretted, and with reason, that such violence would undermine his fragilely collated consensus and public support for continued social welfare legislation. Whatever the causes of the riots, they impacted several of the most visible Great Society programs, especially the war on poverty, which was to white America an initiative that, from its inception, unfairly favored black Americans at the expense (literally) of the white middle class. If such outbursts continued, how long would white America be willing to extend such "goodwill" toward blacks?

Although perceived at the time as an "aberration," in retrospect the Watts riot was an ominous omen of the future. One domestic crisis after another ensued over the course of the next two years, including even bloodier racial confrontations in the cities. Such events shattered the optimism of social engineers and put liberals on the defensive. By late 1965, Johnson himself was beginning to despair. "What do they want?" he asked. "I'm giving them boom times and more good legislation than anybody else did, and what do they do—attack and sneer. Could FDR do better? Could anybody do better? What do they want?" From this perspective, the first twenty months of the Johnson presidency stand as a shining light but relatively brief era in the postwar history of American liberalism.

For all his political dexterity and even sincere, moral commitment to such issues as civil rights and eradicating poverty, in the end in many ways Johnson was responsible for the unraveling of his Great Society. Johnson's immense ego was one of his greatest handicaps, driving him to outdo in monumental proportions FDR and every other president in history. As a result, he measured accomplishment in quantitative rather than qualitative terms—the more all-encompassing programs passed, the better. Thus, too many Great Society programs, like OEO, were pressed into law without much research to sustain them and without much thought about potentially divisive political consequences, which Johnson believed he could mitigate if not obviate completely by the sheer force of his personality and will. Other programs, such as aid to education, were dependent on constant infusions of money to sustain them and, like the war on poverty, needed more careful study than they received if they had any chance of success and acceptance. In short, despite long hours of work, neither LBJ nor his aides did their "homework" as meticulously as they should have to guarantee their programs' viability.

For all of his bravado and possessing an immense ego, from the moment he became president, Johnson was one of the most insecure men to ever sit in the Oval Office. He felt particularly anxious around members of the Eastern Establishment, many of whom Kennedy had placed in positions of power or as confidants during his tenure. They also (in Johnson's mind) dominated the media as columnists and reporters for such Establishment newspapers as the *Washington Post* and the *New York Times*. They were all cut from the same cloth in Johnson's view— highly educated esthetes and snobs from expensive eastern schools and universities. As a result, Johnson believed he was never welcomed or embraced by the Establishment, whom, he was certain, believed him to be nothing more than an uncouth, barely "educated" closet bigot, a stereotypical Texas braggadocio whose main motivation was personal power. The *Times,* Johnson complained in 1967, "plays a leading part in prejudicing people against me. Editors won't use the word, 'President Johnson,' in anything that is good. Bigotry [against Texans] is born in some of the *New York Times* people." Especially agitating Johnson were the Establishment's "Kennedy lovers." Bewildered by the adulation Kennedy received while he was president, Johnson resented the "Kennedy people" when they did not rally to his side after the assassination. "It was the goddamnest thing," he told Doris Kearns. "He [Kennedy] never said a word of importance in the Senate and he never did a thing. But somehow . . . he managed to create the image of himself as a shining intellectual, a youthful leader who would change the face of the country. Now, I will admit that he had a good sense of humor and that he looked awfully good on the god-damn television screen and through it all was a pretty decent fellow, but his growing hold on the American people was a mystery to me."

If Johnson had been a more introspective man, he might have understood why many Americans did not enfold him as he so desperately hoped they would, especially after proving to them by his actions that he deserved their adulation. Americans failed to warm up to Johnson because he was simply not a very likeable person. One reason was his vanity, which knew no limits. As a senator, he offered a calf from his ranch to parents who named their children after him. When he became president, he ordered White House photographers to record his every move for posterity. One estimate contends that he had 500,000 photos taken of himself. Johnson poured over these photos, selecting his "best ones" to give as mementoes to visitors and dignitaries. Johnson also had plastic busts made of himself, which he was known to stroke affectionately while conversing with people in the White House. When he paid a visit to Pope John XXIII, the Holy Father presented him with a fourteenth century painting as a gift. In return, he surprised the Pontiff by giving him a bust of himself.

Johnson's urge to dominate demanded total loyalty among associates and aides. From the moment they joined the Johnson administration, staff members understood that they not only had to work long hours but that they also had to pay homage to Johnson and surrender to his imperious will. Johnson established dress codes for his aides, and if they failed to wear the appropriate, prescribed attire and he noticed it, he would explode and unleash upon that person a most vitriolic and profane tirade. He insisted that aides be reachable at all times of the day or night. To be assured of getting in touch with Joseph Califano, one of his most trusted advisers, Johnson had a telephone installed next to the toilet in Califano's office bathroom. Perhaps the most legendary example of Johnsonian despotism was when he summoned a staff member for a conference while he was sitting on the toilet.

Johnson demanded not only unwavering loyalty but also subservience from the people around him. Those who refused to be a total team player incurred his wrath, which meant having to endure a most vile verbal harangue or upbraiding. Such tirades also served to further inflate Johnson's own sense of self, and if by humiliating or intimidating others he could bend others to his will, then not only was he satisfied but he believed that he had now complete control over them and, henceforth, there would be no questioning of where their "loyalty" lied. Johnson demanded an obsequiousness that ultimately alienated many of his most valuable advisers. As he explained to an aide, "Just remember this: There's only two kinds at the White House. There's elephants and there's pissants. And I'm the only elephant." One of those "pissants" disaffected by Johnson's despotic behavior was press secretary George Reedy, who later observed that Johnson "as a human being was a miserable person—a bully, sadist, lout, and egoist. . . . His lapses from civilized conduct were deliberate and usually intended to subordinate someone else to do his will. He did disgusting things because he realized that other people had to pretend that they did not mind. It was his method of bending them to his desires."

To Johnson, as it was to his "daddy," FDR, "the personal was political and the political was personal." Indeed, Johnson was perhaps the most affected president by such a mentality, ultimately contributing to his undoing. No doubt FDR possessed an immense ego that at times adversely affected his decisions. Egomania is an occupational disease of most politicians and virtually all presidents. Johnson, however, carried the illness to its most extreme form. Johnson simply possessed unbending faith in his own will and power to right all the wrongs and, thus, personally save the nation. Like most egomaniacs, Johnson displaced his own shortcomings onto other individuals. If a Great Society initiative failed, it was his staff's fault, not his, for in Johnson's mind his ideas or "visions" were so right, so just, so noble that if they fell short of what he expected, then that was a failure of implementation and that responsibility rested with his staff. He had done his job, all the hard work of getting the measure through Congress. Now it was up to his charges to make the program come to fruition. If it did not, then his staff failed—they failed not only Johnson but the people as well. "Big Daddy" certainly never would have allowed that to happen. As Johnson told Doris Kearns, "When I looked out at [my cabinet members] I realized that while all of them had been appointed by me, not a single one *was really mine.* . . . Here I was working day and night to build the Great Society, conquering thousands of enemies and hurdling hundreds of obstacles, and I couldn't even count on my own administrative family for complete support. I felt like a football quarterback running against a tough team and having his own center and left guard throwing rocks at him. It was an impossible situation and I was determined to change it. I was determined to make them more dependent on me than I was on them."

Fantasizing about his role as president, he told Kearns, "if only I could take the next step and become dictator of the whole world, then I could really make things happen. Every hungry person would be fed, every ignorant child educated, every jobless man employed." Indeed, helping others often seemed to be the instrument by which he could most directly satisfy his own ego. It was almost as if Providence had singled him out to become the "messiah of the masses." As William Leuchtenburg has shown, Johnson was driven to surpass FDR, and in his mind the only way to accomplish that was to take New Deal liberalism beyond anything FDR or his New Dealers would have even contemplated as a possibility—the eradication of poverty in America—the ultimate uplifting of the downtrodden, something FDR only mused about. As one White House correspondent wrote, Johnson saw himself in the "image of a great popular leader something like Franklin Roosevelt, except more so, striding over the land and cupping the people in his hand and molding a national unity that every President dreams about but none is ever able to achieve." If Johnson could achieve what had eluded FDR, then he would become (in his mind) one of the world's greatest leaders, for he had "created" a society in which all citizens lived in prosperity, security, and stability. Johnson believed the American people entrusted him with that mission when they voted overwhelmingly for him in 1964. As he told Doris Kearns, "for the first time in all my life I truly felt loved by the American people." Hence, his abject despair, when by the end of his tenure, a good number of Americans had turned against him, many of whom had benefited from his reforms. "How was it possible," he asked, "that all these people could be so ungrateful to me after I have given them so much?"

No Great Society program better illustrated Johnson's overweening ego and messianic view of himself than the most ambitious, grandiose, and eventually the most flawed Great Society initiative, the war on poverty, an idea and program doomed to failure from its inception. In almost every respect, Johnson's commitment to an unconditional war on poverty reflected the belief that people were poor because they lacked opportunity and, thus, impoverished individuals must be given access to opportunity so they could be motivated to climb out of the poverty cycle. As sociologist Christopher Jencks observed, the administration's premise was that poverty existed "not because the economy is mismanaged, but because the poor themselves have something wrong with them." Yet, as Sargent Shriver insisted, the government was not going to give "handouts" but, rather, its objective was to change "indifference to interest, ignorance to awareness, resignation to ambition, and an attitude of withdrawal to one of participation." Johnson would never enact a program if he believed it would place in jeopardy his prized consensus. Thus, the approach articulated by Shriver offered a way of attacking poverty with the lowest possible expenditure of dollars and the least disruption of the existing social system.

Ironically, the war on poverty's most important initiative—the Community Action Programs—led ultimately to the entire program's debacle and in the process helped to destroy the politics of consensus upon which Johnson had built his liberal edifice. Interestingly, the CAPs were tied initially to Johnson's civil rights agenda; that is, to guarantee that Southern blacks would have a voice in determining policy for their own areas. The CAP facet of the antipoverty legislation mandated "maximum feasible participation" for residents of poverty areas in developing programs affecting their local communities. The problem, which neither Johnson nor his advisers saw (or admitted), was the idea's inherent potential for radicalization, especially if poor folk took seriously that they would be empowered. So little thought was given to that possibility, let alone believing the poor would actually want or were capable of participation, that only one administration official, Robert Kennedy, mentioned the term before Congress. Kennedy was in favor of allowing the poor "a real voice in their institutions." Much to Johnson's surprise and subsequent dismay, the CAPs became the most important dimension of the overall antipoverty initiative. Johnson should have listened to Sargent Shriver, who perhaps saw the impending problems, and urged Johnson to abandon the CAPS concept and, instead, implement a large-scale employment program that emphasized both creating new jobs (à la New Deal) and training the poor to fill them. However, certain of the rightness of the CAP idea, Johnson ignored Shriver and ordered the CAP program to go into full effect. Johnson typically wanted quick, dramatic, and popular results, and this "mobilization of the poor" on their own behalf seemed a brilliant, cost-effective avenue of success. Shriver, not wanting to incur Johnson's wrath, had little choice but to "get on board." The OEO director, thus, grandiloquently proclaimed that the CAPs would be the "corporations of the new social revolution."

Almost immediately the CAP program backfired, creating the very intergroup conflict Johnson hoped to avoid. Neither Johnson nor the majority of his policy planners believed the poor would take "maximum feasible participation" seriously. It was taken seriously, and soon the Johnson administration found itself in the middle of increasing hostility between CAP leaders and city officials. What had caused the conflict was the unanticipated politicization of the poor and the emergence in certain urban areas of powerful interest groups and individuals determined to empower the poor even if it meant "cutting off the hand that had been feeding them"—the Johnson administration. In cities like Chicago, Philadelphia, and San Francisco, by 1965-66, CAP programs came under the control of radical community leaders and activists who saw city officials as the enemy, preventing them "maximum feasible participation" in remedying their own lives as well as their communities' well-being. Thus, rent strikes, the picketing of City Hall, and attempts to take control of local school boards and antipoverty agencies became commonplace events on an all-too-frequent basis for many city officials to tolerate. Not surprisingly, city mayors and governors responded with outrage. Chicago Mayor Richard Daley declared that putting poor people in control of antipoverty agencies was "like telling the fellow who cleans up [at the newspaper] to be the city editor." The OEO, other politicians insisted, appeared to be "fostering class struggle," with the primary intent to destroy the existing urban structure of political power and representation. The CAPs had created a political dilemma for Johnson, because, as one writer observed, "If the government imposes *any* limits on tactics the poor use, can it really be said that the poor are making the decisions?" On the other hand, if the government retained control and the CAPs became simply manifestations of "tokenism," then wasn't the government being "manipulative and paternalistic?"

By the end of 1965, contention over the CAPs had transformed the war on poverty into precisely the struggle over power that Johnson feared. Johnson was forced to choose between community leaders and poor-rights activists or city officials. He chose the latter, and, thus, the poor felt betrayed by the man they believed wanted to uplift them. As a result, the war on poverty in the minds of poor rights activists became a farce, a form of "political pornography," as Saul Alinsky declared, that sought to "buy off" community leaders. One of the great paradoxes of the CAP initiative was that the federal government found itself in the uncomfortable position of paying the salaries of organizers who, by virtue of their constituency and their own mandate, felt compelled to attack local government institutions. Unfortunately, the war on poverty degenerated into a bitter and disillusioning power struggle between the Johnson administration and the poor and their leaders, and in the end neither side won. The tragedy, of course, was that although some had hoped the OEO would do for the poor what the Wagner Act had done for labor—give them leverage, recognition, and a voice—the Johnson administration seemed to have no such intention. In the end, the antipoverty effort became a *sitzkreig*, or phony war, as the historian Mark Gelfand observed, because it represented "a classic incident of the American habit of substituting good intentions for cold, hard cash." To Johnson, the fiscal conservative, the issue became whether to expend the money needed to create jobs or to simply create cheaper programs that would generate more publicity. Sadly, Johnson chose the latter and, as a result, doomed what could have been one of his more remarkable successes into a bitter and divisive debacle.

In the halcyon days of the Great Society, Johnson proposed to do everything. He would eliminate poverty, heal the sick, educate the illiterate, and restore economic justice to America—all without disturbing what became a most tenuous and fragile consensus. "This program," he told Congress in 1964, "is much more than a beginning. It is a total commitment by this President and this Congress and this nation to pursue victory over the most ancient of mankind's enemies." By 1968, the "total commitment" reflected more the press releases and brochures about antipoverty than the programs developed to do the job. The story of the war on poverty thus became a vignette of the problems—social as well as personal—that ultimately destroyed Johnson's presidency.

And then there was Vietnam. As LBJ was taking the oath of office on that tragic November day aboard Air Force One, Ambassador to Vietnam Henry Cabot Lodge was flying back from Southeast Asia for a meeting that would not take place with John Kennedy but with the new president, Lyndon Baines Johnson. Lodge was coming back to Washington to discuss the consequences of the overthrow of Ngo Diem, in which the Kennedy administration had been an accomplice, but who, like Kennedy, was the victim of an assassination. After conferring with Lodge and the other foreign policy experts in the Kennedy cabinet, Johnson embraced Kennedy's war and, unfortunately, made it his "own." As he told Lodge, "I'm not going to lose Vietnam. I'm not going to be the president who saw Southeast Asia go the way China went." Obviously, Johnson remembered that searing event and its impact on the Truman administration and how his predecessor was publicly skewered for having "lost China" to the communists. Johnson was determined not to let any foreign event tarnish or destroy his presidency. Ironically, however, like Truman, an unpopular and inconclusive war in Asia did indeed ultimately bring Johnson's administration to its knees, undermining all he had accomplished on the homefront for so many Americans. To this day, the Vietnam conflict is still considered to have been "Lyndon's War." The statistics confirm that appellation: when Johnson assumed the presidency, there were 16,000 U.S. troops in Vietnam; when he left five years later, there were over 500,000. The great tragedy of the Johnson presidency was the fact that Johnson had an opportunity to reverse the direction of American foreign policy in that part of the world and thus

avoid, as Godfrey Hodgson observed, "a great mistake. A new president
. . . could have decided right at the start, before his personal prestige was
committed, to cut his losses and get out." Johnson, unfortunately, missed
the opportunity and, consequently, put his presidency on the path of
self-destruction. Why would Johnson allow such a personal calamity
to befall him? The answer is relatively simple: every bone in his body,
every facet of his political personality, compelled him to proceed. On the
same weekend that he gave Walter Heller the green light for the war on
poverty, Johnson directed Lodge and his foreign policy advisers to expand
American involvement in Vietnam. The two wars became the hallmarks
of his presidency, with the tragic paradox that waging one ensured the
defeat of the other.

Like his Democratic forebear, Harry Truman, Johnson also came to
the presidency with minimal exposure to substantive foreign policy issues.
Although privy to many of Kennedy's foreign policy initiatives, Johnson
nonetheless was not involved in some of the more momentous decisions,
such as the Cuban Missile Crisis or the Bay of Pigs fiasco. When it came
to the Vietnam question, Johnson's involvement in high-level discussion
was nonexistent. Moreover, up to this point in his political career,
Johnson had shown little to no interest in foreign policy matters. In fact,
Johnson had relegated such concerns to the bottom of his priority list.
As already noted, Johnson prided himself on his legislative genius and
making the United States a "Great Society." Thus, unlike his predecessor,
who made foreign policy his *raison d'etre*, Johnson focused on improving
life in America. As a perceptive journalist noted in 1966, Johnson "was
the Riverboat man . . . a swashbuckling master of the political mid-
stream, but only in the crowded, well traveled inland waterways of
domestic politics. He had no taste and scant preparation for the deep
waters of foreign policy, for the sudden storms and the unpredictable
winds that can becalm or batter or blow off course the ocean-going man.
He was the king of the river and stranger to the open sea."

Like most of the other issues in Johnson's political life, foreign policy
revolved around two simple, fundamental premises: patriotism and
bipartisanship. Indeed, throughout his political career, Johnson asserted
that foreign policy was merely a reflection of domestic policy—that
they should compliment each other and if they did not, then one or the
other had to be "adjusted" accordingly and appropriately. Also manifest
in his views on foreign policy was his obsession with consensus. "It is an
American, not a political foreign policy we have in the United States," he
said in 1948. "This is a question of patriotism, not politics." Throughout

his political career, Johnson maintained that one must support the president, regardless of the party in power or one's political persuasion. "We've got to be for America first," he said when Eisenhower sanctioned counterrevolution in Guatemala in 1954. "We have got to cut out this distrust and hatred of each other." Johnson was also a thoroughly committed anticommunist, giving his full, unswerving (albeit blind!) support to any and every manifestation of America's containment policy. "When they lead your boy down to that railroad station to send him to boot camp and put a uniform on him to send him somewhere he may never return, they don't ask whether you are a Republican or a Democrat," he told an audience. "They send you to defend that flag and you go."

Johnson's foreign policy perspective also included the dynamics of honor, courage, and credibility. Since the promulgation of the Truman Doctrine, the United States had given its word that it would defend freedom and resist aggression wherever in the world such threats might occur, and in Johnson's mind, the United States at all times must abide by that commitment. Three American presidents had pledged support of South Vietnamese independence, and Johnson was not about to violate that promise. If North Vietnam attacked American troops, it was a matter of honor that the United States "respond in kind" and seek revenge. Johnson once said, "When we are attacked, we must not turn our tail and run, we must stand and fight." In short, Johnson was unequivocal in his belief that at all times the United States must stand behind its commitments. "We love peace," he said, "We hate war. But our course is charted always by the compass of *honor*. . . .We are [in Viet Nam] because we remain fixed on the pursuit of freedom, a deep and moral obligation *that will not let us go.*"

Like many of his other beliefs, Johnson's sense of commitment reflected his Texas upbringing. Johnson grew up in a time and in a Texas environment in which personal bravery, profound fear of humiliation and shame, and a determination to live by one's word were inculcated at a very early age. "If you let a bully come into your front yard one day," Johnson was fond of saying, "the next day he will be up on your porch and the day after that he will rape your wife in your own bed." (Such chauvinism and *machismo* have been somewhat mitigated since Johnson's generation, largely as a result of the influx of "Yankees" and other "foreign," esthete influences.) Texans, of all people, "should go on record against isolationism and appeasement." Retreat, betrayal of a pledge, cowardice—all were (or should) be unthinkable, especially to Texans. Unfortunately, fueling Johnson's bravado was the "Alamo myth" or "syndrome," which down to the present still maudlinly and unwarrantably affects too many Texans. "Hell," Johnson told the National Security Council, "Viet Nam is just like the Alamo." Texas schoolchildren were (and still are) indoctrinated with the legend of how the mission's commander, William Barrett Travis, had supposedly drawn a line in the dust with his sword, instructing all those who would stay and die not to cross the line. Allegedly, only one man chose to leave, and he became the epitome of cowardice and shame for all Texans. Johnson was so affected by the story that he told young soldiers that his own great-great-grandfather had died at the Alamo, when in fact kinsmen on either side of his family had yet come to Texas! To Johnson, the idea of retreating in Vietnam was equivalent to "tucking tail and running" at the Alamo. Such a thought challenged his most profound sense of identity and personal courage. If he accepted such advice, he believed he would be seen in the same light as that lone individual who fled the Alamo: as one who lacked personal courage and skulked away, to live in historical infamy and shame forever.

Johnson also believed that, if he hoped to promote social reform at home, he must never waver in his commitment to defeat communism abroad. "Everything I knew about history," he noted, "told me if I got out of Viet Nam and let Ho Chi Minh run through the streets of Saigon, I'd be doing exactly what Chamberlain did in World War II. I'd be giving a big fat reward to aggression. And I knew that . . . [there] would follow in this country an endless national debate—that would shatter my presidency, kill my administration, damage our democracy. I knew that Harry Truman and Dean Acheson had lost their effectiveness from the day that the communists took over in China. I believed that the loss of China had played a large role in the life of Joe McCarthy. And I knew all these problems, taken together, were chicken shit compared to what might happen if we lost Viet Nam."

As noted earlier, Johnson was convinced that foreign policy must reflect domestic policy and, at all times, be complimentary of one another. Thus, for Johnson, progress on civil rights, poverty, and health and education issues mandated a strong position against communism. Johnson was certain that, if at any time he appeared "soft" on communism, the rightwingers would come out of the woodwork and cut his domestic agenda to pieces just as they had done to Truman's Fair Deal initiatives. As one Johnson aide wrote, "If we wished to pass progressive laws, we had to show that we were firmly committed against the 'ultimate' progressives—the communists."

There is no doubt that Johnson hated the war and understood its devastating potential; yet, because of what he believed, both personally and politically, he saw no alternative but to expand it if such a step meant winning. Defeat was simply unacceptable. Like everything else in his life, the personal became political and the political personal, and Johnson's view and conduct of the war reflected this mentality. These were "his" soldiers, and as he pored over maps in the White House Situation Room at three in the morning and waited to hear from "his" pilots that they had returned safely from a bombing mission, he came to see the entire war as an extension of his own identification with the country—the same connection he had with the Great Society. Johnson even considered the weapons used to be his. When a military aide at Andrews Air Force Base tried to direct Johnson one day toward the correct helicopter, saying "Mr. President, that's not your helicopter," Johnson retorted, "Son, they're all *my* helicopters."

Also impacting Johnson's view of the war, still haunting him, was the Kennedy mystique, which affected him more in foreign policy than domestic. One of Johnson's deepest fears was the possibility that Kennedy's supporters would interpret any change in policy from that of their beloved hero as a betrayal and, thus, a basis for rejecting Johnson's presidency. "There would be Robert Kennedy," Johnson told Doris Kearns, "out in front leading the fight against me, telling everyone that I had betrayed John Kennedy's commitment to Viet Nam . . . that I was a coward. An unmanly man. A man without a spine. Oh, I could see it coming all right. Every night when I fell asleep I would see myself tied to the ground in the middle of a long open space. In the distance, I could hear the voices of thousands of people. They were all shouting at me and running toward me: 'Coward! Traitor! Weakling!' They kept coming closer. They began throwing stones. At exactly that moment I would generally wake up . . . terribly shaken."

Lyndon Johnson did not come to the Vietnam War a free man. He was wrapped in a personal, cultural, political, and ideological straightjacket that over the span of five years would plunge the United States ever deeper into an abyss of war and ultimate defeat. In the process, on the homefront the war unleashed "backlashes" from both the right and the left, which destroyed Johnson's cherished consensus and, in the end, brought down his presidency—all because he could not or would not accept any alternatives to war until it was too late to salvage his presidency. To his credit, Johnson encouraged full discussion of options; he searched for a way out, but ultimately the straightjacket was wrapped too tightly for him to break free of its hold to be able to ask the fundamental questions that needed to be asked about the wisdom of American policy. Instead, he repeated the credo that was perhaps the tightest strap on that straightjacket, the strap that was the essence of his entire understanding of foreign policy—"We are there because we have a promise to keep."

Until 1965, Americans had paid little attention to the unfolding events in that particular corner of Southeast Asia. Both Kennedy and LBJ had kept a very tight lid on what was really happening there. Thus, the issues seemed too remote and confused for serious concern. In August 1964 Congress gave Johnson carte blanche to use force against the communist insurgents (as well as to allow the eventual bombing of North Vietnam) via the Tonkin Gulf Resolution. Only two senators had the courage and perspicacity to vote against the measure (Wayne Morris of Oregon and Ernest Gruening of Alaska), while the rest were willing to let Johnson have a free hand, thus, "absolving" themselves of any complicity in his high-handedness and fault if (and when) intrusion blew up in defeat. The excuse given by the ninety-eight other senators was that they did not consider the resolution a mandate to escalate American intervention. During the fall presidential contest, LBJ deftly skirted the Vietnam problem. Had he truthfully admitted what his policy was, he would lose his trump against Goldwater, which was to label the Arizona senator as a dangerous, war-mongering militarist, and to present himself as a man of rationality, calm, and peace. By early 1965, however, Johnson could no longer hide his Vietnam policies as the war finally registered on the public consciousness (thanks to television and the first "imbedded" newsmen who challenged official accounts).

At the very time the administration was juggernauting legislation through the Eighty-ninth Congress, it was beginning to entangle itself and the nation fatally in Southeast Asia. In February 1965, under the aegis of the Tonkin Gulf Resolution, Johnson authorized Operation Rolling Thunder, a massive bombing campaign of the North to stop the Hanoi government's supplying of the Vietcong communist insurgents in the South. In early March, the first U.S. combat troops stepped ashore on the beach at Nam O. During the summer Johnson took the fatal step of ordering American soldiers to attack—"search and destroy" missions—the communist enemy, the Vietcong, in the South.

Resistance at home to Johnson's Vietnam policy was almost immediate. On March 24, 1964, students and faculty held the first anti-Vietnam War teach-in at the University of Michigan, the very school where Johnson, less than a year earlier, had proclaimed his Great Society.

Teach-ins soon proliferated on university campuses across the nation, driving a wedge between the administration and intellectuals, many of whom had been passionate supporters of many of the Great Society's reform initiatives. It was this growing alienation that Johnson had first experienced at the White House Festival of the Arts. That May 1964, pacifists and the emerging New Left student movement held the first march on Washington to denounce U.S. involvement in Southeast Asia.

Johnson knew very early in the game that the war seriously threatened his Great Society. At a White House task force dinner party, given to honor the various individuals and their committees who had been responsible for the Great Society's early successes, Johnson talked about the potential dangers of escalating American presence in Southeast Asia. He told the gathering that he had consulted with all the foreign policy experts, including ex-President Eisenhower, and they were unanimous in their belief that the United States must not abandon its commitments in Southeast Asia. Nonetheless, Johnson feared for the Great Society. World War I had eclipsed Woodrow Wilson's New Freedom; World War II had aborted the New Deal; and more recently and thus ominously, the Korean War had destroyed Truman and the Fair Deal. "I don't want that to happen to the Great Society. I don't want to get involved in a war. I don't want to get involved in entanglements abroad."

As we know, Johnson's fears were prescient, and that is why he put off major escalations as long as he could and tried to hide the extent of American involvement from Congress and the American people. As he later confessed to Doris Kearns, "I knew from the start that I was bound to be crucified either way I moved. If I left the woman I really loved—the Great Society—in order to get involved with that bitch of a war on the other side of the world, then I would lose everything at home. All my programs. All my hopes to feed the hungry and feed the homeless. All my dreams." Unfortunately, he chose the "bitch" and soon found himself daily immersed, inundated with military matters and forsaking domestic causes that had been closest to his heart. Care and dollars that might have gone to the Great Society were lavished on the most awesome military machine in world history.

Although by 1965 Johnson was already wary of the potential for disaster the war posed for his administration, interestingly, most knowledgeable Americans would surely have considered his fears misplaced. The president and his policies were wildly popular. Polls in the fall of 1965, as the senators and representatives left for home at session's end, showed that no president in three decades enjoyed such consistently strong support from all major segments of the population.

Vietnam, however, would not long remain on the back burner. By the fall of 1965, Vietcong cadres had virtually free reign in the countryside; the majority of southern cities took on the appearance of besieged fortresses; and the military junta in Saigon that had overthrown Diem (and murdered him as well) and now ruled the nation exhibited almost no capacity for developing popular support or waging concerted warfare. Thus, it became time for Johnson to make the fateful decisions that would ultimately lead the United States into its most unpopular war. A phone conversation between Johnson and Arkansas Senator J. William Fulbright perhaps best summarized not only Johnson's thinking at the time but also what he would do over the course of the next three years that dragged the United States ever deeper into the Vietnam quagmire. Significantly, in his dialogue with Fulbright, he defined the options before him in a manner that clearly precluded flexibility and, thus, any hope of getting out. The United States could withdraw from Vietnam, he told Fulbright, but "without our support the government would be unable to counter the aid from the north to the Vietcong. Viet Nam will collapse and the ripple effect will be felt throughout southeast Asia, endangering independent governments in Thailand, Malaysia, and extending as far as India and Indonesia and the Philippines." Clearly, Johnson subscribed completely to the "domino theory." The president also rejected outright the possibility of neutralization suggested by Senator Mike Mansfield and President Charles De Gaulle, arguing, "any such formula will only lead in the end to the same results as withdrawing support." In such a context, Johnson perceived only two possibilities: either continue present policy with increased support of South Vietnam, or embark on a major military escalation. Johnson unfortunately chose the second option, even though he prophetically told Fulbright that committing major U.S. ground forces could result in America becoming "bogged down in a long war against numerically superior forces." Johnson was right at the time, but he nevertheless escalated the number of American troops in Vietnam to over 500,000 by 1968. By the beginning of 1965, U.S. ground forces were fully engaged against the enemy, and American planes were bombing military-industrial targets in the North. At the end of 1965, there were 184,000 American military personnel in Vietnam—by the end of 1966, 450,000. The number of American casualties (killed, wounded, hospitalized, and missing) increased from 2,500 in 1965 to a cumulative total of 33,000 by the end of 1966, to 80,000 by the end of

1967, and to 130,000 by the end of 1968, the peak of U.S. involvement. American planes unleashed more bombs, many of them napalm, on Vietnam between 1965 and the end of 1967 than they had in all theaters of World War II. Toxic chemical defoliants, such as Agent Orange, which were dropped to eradicate enemy cover (something Goldwater "crazily" advocated in the 1964 presidential campaign), hit millions of acres of land in Vietnam and destroyed one-half of the timberlands in the South. A popular bombing crew saying was "Only You Can Prevent Forests." Such statistics revealed that, once Johnson "crossed the Rubicon" of escalation, he would not reverse that decision until it was too late for himself, his Great Society, and, most important, for the American people.

Lyndon Johnson was largely responsible for implementing what became in the end a radical departure from traditional cold war policies by the actions he adopted in Vietnam. As one of his "Wise Men," George Ball, asserted, Johnson could have overruled the hardliners who advised him, listened to those in his inner circle (like Ball) who urged alternative courses of action, and found a way to extricate the United States from Vietnam. Johnson, thanks to the technocrats and number "crunchers" who advised him, such as Robert McNamara, had before him accurate assessments of the repercussions of his decisions, especially if he escalated. Indeed, all during 1965, members of the Joint Chiefs, as well as George Ball, told Johnson that more than likely the infusion of American combat troops into Vietnam would lead to unending escalation, with at least 500,000 troops committed to that country in a war that would last a minimum of five years. Moreover, as national security adviser McGeorge Bundy pointed out to Johnson, "We are fight[ing] a war we can't fight and win as the country we are trying to help is quitting." Bundy also reminded Johnson that U.S. troops were involved in a guerrilla war; yet, "We are sending conventional troops to do unconventional jobs." Finally, Bundy warned Johnson that the war's critics, which were mounting, will ask, "how long—how much? Can we take casualties over five years—are we talking about a military solution when the solution is really political?" George Ball echoed Bundy's assessments, telling Johnson that sending more American troops to Vietnam was "like giving cobalt treatment to a terminal cancer case" and questioned whether "an army of westerners can successfully fight Orientals in an Asian jungle." Johnson countered by telling Ball, "Wouldn't all these countries then say that Uncle Sam was a paper tiger, wouldn't we lose credibility, breaking the word of three presidents?" It was not that Johnson had not heard the other side; he simply had not listened.

Most tragically for the nation, Johnson compounded his military and strategic errors by deceiving the American people and Congress about his decisions. Johnson consistently dissembled, insisting that no major changes had taken place since he became president, and buried his announcements of troop escalations in noontime press conferences full of other news. His obsession with dominance only helped Johnson to further dig his own political grave, for by trying to so tightly control the war by any means possible, he allowed the war to destroy his credibility with the American people, especially once they realized the extent of his deception. Johnson hoped that an American victory in Vietnam would allow him to put his personal stamp on the world, just as he had hoped his Great Society would allow him such stature in the United States. Moreover, as alluded earlier, Johnson's own personal sense of honor, courage, and manliness would never permit him to extricate the United States without a clear-cut victory in Vietnam. In Johnson's mind, the Vietnamese struggle for "freedom" against the communists was no different than that of America's early pioneers who, according to Johnson, "had a rifle in one hand to kill their enemies and an ax in another to build their homes and provide for their families." Such a perspective was hardly in accord with the realities of the conflict in Vietnam. Perhaps more important, the war siphoned funds away from a war of greater significance at home, a war that could have been won if it had sufficient money and the attention and energy of those who had started the war but now could not finish or "win" it because they no longer had the essential "weapons" for victory—the war on poverty. Thus, in the end, by seeking to subjugate the world to his personal vision, Johnson ended up destroying the one thing about which he really cared.

Largely as the result of Johnson's myopia, the Vietnam conflict became the most protracted and unpopular war in United States history. Many of its negative effects have lasted down to the present. While it lasted, the war directed valuable resources to the military-industrial complex, making that entity one of the most powerful, sub rosa institutions in the United States. It intensified the arms race and diverted Johnson's and the American people's attention from foreign problems elsewhere in the world. Because of this all-consuming distraction, the Soviet Union frantically built its nuclear arsenal to the point of parity with the United States. The war also "Americanized" and corrupted South Vietnamese culture and society. It alienated allies, some to the point that they gravitated to the "other side" or decided to join the ranks of the "non-aligned." Spending for the war created huge budgetary deficits that contributed significantly to the problem of stagflation that affected the economy by the late 1970s. Suffice it to say, the economic problems engendered by the war seriously damaged liberalism, which many Americans believed had led us into the Vietnam quagmire in the first place.

Despite the presence of over 500,000 American troops and the incessant bombing of the North, the enemy persevered. American soldiers fought in jungles, forests, rice paddies, and hundreds of villages. It was an unusually bewildering war without clearly defined fronts. Secretary of Defense Robert McNamara and General William Westmoreland, U.S. commander in Vietnam, believed that all the U.S. had to do was kill enough of the "VC" (Vietcong), which, though actually lying, they told Johnson were relatively small in numbers. The war thus became about "body counts" that never seemed to "add up," despite assurances from both McNamara and Westmoreland that the U.S. was indeed killing enough of the enemy for their "soon-to-be" capitulation. Compounding the fact that the VC was far greater in number (over 300,000) than ever admitted, and consequently the U.S. "kill ratio" was having minimal effect in depleting enemy forces, was the South Vietnamese people's maddeningly indifferent attitude toward U.S. presence or, worse, their support of the VC. As a result, American troops came to mistrust the Vietnamese and all too often, out of frustration, unleashed their rage on innocent civilians, committing horrible atrocities in the process. Casualties mounted, gradually intensifying domestic opposition to the war. Even early in the fighting, it seemed that the bloodshed would never end.

Perhaps two of the greatest "casualties" of the war were the American people and government officials, whom the people came to doubt had the capacity to govern honestly and justly. Indeed, by the time the war was finally over (1973), the American people had become so jaded, so distrustful, so cynical toward public officials that it took almost a generation before public confidence was restored. Liberalism also became a casualty, and not until the election of Bill Clinton in 1992 was that ethos somewhat resurrected and then only half-heartedly at best. The war badly damaged the Democratic Party and exacerbated already bitter class and racial divisions and grievances. It called into question the honor and decency for which Americans claimed to stand. Finally, the Vietnam conflict altered the course of post-World War II American society and politics, unleashing emotions that polarized the nation for years to come. Not until the 1980s did Americans begin to put that traumatic episode behind them and move forward.

On January 13, 1969, a week before leaving office, Lyndon Johnson attended a testimonial dinner in his honor at New York's Plaza Hotel. It was a glamorous black-tie affair with dancing in the grand ballroom and entertainment by Cab Calloway. The four hundred guests were an array of high administration officials, prominent New Yorkers, Democratic Party moguls, and liberal businessmen and party benefactors. Johnson gave a brief speech, reviewing his accomplishments in office. He did not give a long-winded litany of the "wonders" of the Great Society, but he did highlight what he considered the most significant features of the most ambitious reform impulse in United States history. Blacks were "finding their voice in the voting booth in every part of the nation," he declared. "The old in their illness . . . know the dignity of independence." Young minds had been "enriched and young horizons expanded." "Families who were poor—and men who were idle—[had] begun to know the dignity of decent incomes and jobs." "A larger share of American earth—of its shores and forests—[had been] set aside for all the American people." Reversing the usual cliché, he noted that what really mattered was "not the ultimate judgment" of historians but "whether there is a change for the better in the way our people live." A week later he handed over the White House keys to his successor and retired to his beloved ranch on the Pedernales.

Did LBJ's Great Society make life better for Americans? Did it augment or diminish the nation's collective happiness and prosperity? Did it make the United States a country to be emulated as a beacon of hope and inspiration, as a model of justice and decency, a land in which all had equal access to the "American Dream"?

Unfortunately, still today, even among many Americans who lived through the sixties and may have even experienced "counterculture" moments, the decade is remembered as a time of turmoil and despair; they conflate the Great Society with ghetto riots, welfare fraud, and campus unrest. That vision has become part of the "street wisdom" of our day. Naturally, such "honest reflections" include dumping much of the supposed "unraveling" on Lyndon Johnson. There were indeed problems with Johnson's presidential leadership, but perhaps more accurate and fair would be to ascribe greater "blame" to the liberal political philosophy he embraced. Johnson *knew* better than any twentieth century politician what was possible in American politics and, thus, knew he had to move quickly if he hoped to advance the liberal agenda. He had a brief window of opportunity thanks to his landslide victory in 1964 to overwhelm the conservatives and interest groups that had blocked reform for a generation. He accomplished that with unprecedented speed and aplomb, delivering in less than a year's time some of the most important and long-lasting progressive legislation in the history of the United States, much of which still benefits Americans. However, critics lambasted Johnson for not trying harder to seek equality of social condition. Such a demand was and is unfair in assessing Johnson's presidency. From the Great Society's inception, Johnson made it clear that he did not even pretend to favor a forced redistribution of wealth and power—of taking from the haves and giving to the have-nots. He had been elected as a liberal—as an advocate of deeply-rooted American ideas about the virtues of equality of opportunity—not as a champion of major structural changes in American life. Johnson understood how little political support there was in the nation for such an idea, which at the least would have called for higher taxation of the middle and upper classes, something Johnson never would have sanctioned because those were the very interest groups (especially the middle class) upon which he had constructed his consensus. In the minds of middle-class Americans, to demand equality of condition would be to burden the nation with taxes, regulation, and bureaucracy, to threaten prosperity, and to destroy the entrepreneurial spirit and individualism that were the essence of the American dream.

The liberal faith of LBJ and others in the 1960s was both attractive and well meaning. Johnson was sincere in his determination that the United States could have it all and do it all—that there were no limits to how comfortable and powerful, how healthy and happy Americans could be. But times have changed, and all aspects of the Great Society are under siege. People now live in an era when "globalization" is creating a deep chasm between "the best and the brightest" and everyone else. A relatively thin strata of highly literate and brainy Americans are leaving the rest behind, distancing themselves emotionally and intellectually to such a degree that they have minimal contact with or much sympathy for those who are not able to keep up. Nor do they care much about public goods. They can buy those they want—better schools, better access to art and culture, better vacation spots, far from those they regard as "less than." Government is not needed to "provide for them."

There was a time, however, a generation ago when a significant portion of the upper middle class and policy professionals felt more closely attached to their fellow Americans and believed they could make a "great society" for all. Out in front of this crusade, totally committed to this vision, was Lyndon Baines Johnson, who in the final analysis—indeed, it could be a most fitting and succinct epitaph for his presidency—"had the best of intentions."

Swearing in of Lyndon B.
Johnson as president,
Air Force One,
Love Field,
Dallas, Texas.
November 22, 1963
Photo credit:
LBJ Library Photo

LBJ on the telephone.
January 10, 1964
by Yoichi R. Okamoto
Photo credit: LBJ Library Photo

President Johnson caused
a storm of protest when
he lifted "Him," one of
Johnson's beagles, by his ears.
May 4, 1964
by Cecil Stoughton
Photo credit:
LBJ Library Photo

(above) Signing of Civil Rights Act
of 1964.
July 2, 1964
by Cecil Stoughton.
(left) LBJ and Harry Truman (day
of Medicare Bill Signing).
July 30, 1965
photographer unknown.
(below) Martin Luther King, Jr.
talks with President Lyndon B.
Johnson in the Oval Office,
White House.
December 3, 1963
by Yoichi R. Okamoto.
Photo credits: LBJ Library Photo

Richard Milhous Nixon
(1969-1974)

If ever an American presidency was worthy of a true, tragic opera in the grand tradition of La Bohème or La Traviata, it would be the presidency of Richard Nixon. Indeed, Nixon has inspired one opera— John Adams' "Nixon In China," which premiered in 1987—but it lacked the full, tragic flair that was Richard Nixon. Perhaps historian Garry Willis captured the true classically Greek tragic nature of Nixon, the man and president, in his aptly titled "Nixon Agonistes." A self-made man rises from mediocre origins to become colleague and friend with a true American prince, only to see their friendship descend into the bitterest of rivalries. The good prince slain, the self-made man then rises to the heights of power, only to be betrayed by his own fears, faults, and all-consuming ambition. Thus, the self-made man falls into disgrace and ruin (and a David Frost interview) while his dead rival enters the pantheon of mythological demigods. Surely a tale such as that is worthy of an operatic score.

Richard Nixon lacked the wealth and connections of many of his predecessors, but that did not prevent him from beating the heavy odds against rising from middle-class roots to become president. Born on January 9, 1913, in Yorba Linda, a town of two hundred, located thirty miles from Los Angeles, California, his father, Frank Nixon, was an intelligent man, despite his sixth grade education, who held a variety of jobs before operating a general store and gas station in Whittier, California. Frank married Hannah Milhous in 1908 over the objections of her parents who were concerned because she had not finished college, and he did not share their Quaker beliefs. Nixon was not born with the advantages of great wealth and power that made the route to the White House an apparent inevitability for the choosing by a Roosevelt, a Kennedy, or a Bush. Neither was he born into a poor dysfunctional family, like a Reagan or a Clinton, who could use the paucity of their childhood to make their own ascent to the towering heights seem all the more magnificent. Nixon was born to a family neither rich nor terribly poor; thus, he would never be part of the American social nobility like his one time friend and later arch nemesis, John Fitzgerald Kennedy. Nor could he lay claim to the Horatio Algers mantle, which can sometimes purchase one a guest pass into the nobility wherein the pauper becomes the prince, as Ronald Reagan did. Nixon always struggled to distinguish himself against the blandness of his own origins in his attempt to reach the heights of American power and society.

Nixon's tragic flaw would lay precisely in the ambition that drove him from his white frame house in Yorba Linda to the White House in Washington, D. C. Across his career, success alone never satiated. No victory was good enough, no success grand enough to earn him the acceptance he sought from the "powers that be"—the East Coast political and economic elite and, in particular, a liberal eastern media that he felt never accorded him the respect he had earned. This personality of driving ambition, coupled with his win-at-all-costs mentality that such ambition necessitated, ultimately led to Nixon's tragic downfall.

Nixon believed that he received his skill as a debater—skills of a sharp tongue and an even sharper mind that would help him offset his other social liabilities—from his father, who had a temper and a love for arguing. So intense was his father's personality that other family members sometimes had to rush to wait on some of the customers in the family store, lest Frank Nixon alienate them. Frank Nixon, though, did more than lead by example. He often drove Richard to the younger Nixon's matches with the debate team, and the two Nixons analyzed the proceedings on the way home. Richard Nixon also credited his father with being his number one supporter in the early days of his political career. Nixon described his father's argumentative nature as simply being the way Frank Nixon related to the world. Though Frank became very heated at times, it usually was not personal. Perhaps this influence did help Richard Nixon develop his debating skills, and perhaps it gave him a more disciplined mind and the mental toughness needed to survive as a politician. But bonding through antagonism was not the best model for relating in an appropriate way on a personal level, and personal relationships were something with which Richard Nixon sometimes struggled as a politician.

Nixon idolized his mother, who was much more reserved than her husband. He referred to her as a saint and admired her religious faith and the privacy she had about it. Her reserve was not limited to religious expression; Hannah Nixon was also very reserved when it came to expressions of emotions, including the expression of love. It makes sense that Nixon prized the strong sense of commitment and the cold, quiet nature of his mother, given that these attributes could be used to describe Richard Nixon as well.

When Nixon was twelve, younger brother Arthur died of tubercular encephalitis. In college, Nixon wrote that when he was down—a more than occasional occurrence—he would remember his brother for inspiration. When Richard Nixon was in college, his oldest brother, Harold, also died after a bout of tuberculosis that had lasted for several years. The struggles of his brothers, the belligerency of his father, and the quiet, steely determination of his mother all worked together on Richard's character, forging him as a tenacious fighter against whatever odds arrayed themselves before him. This inner strength served him well for most of his life, but perhaps it also led to his more self-destructive tendency to see all battles through the lenses of life and death consequences. This tendency, no doubt, contributed to his resolute, yet futile efforts to stonewall the Watergate investigations and to hang onto a diminishing presidency far longer than a person with less inner fortitude might have. But then, persons of limited personal fortitude have seldom become president in the first place.

Nixon went to Whittier College in southern California, a competent but relatively nondescript baccalaureate institution. He had wanted to go to Yale with all the East Coast establishment legitimacy it entailed, but although he had a chance at a scholarship that would have covered tuition, even paying the travel and living expenses would have been too much for his family given the Depression-era economy and the expenses they were already incurring over his brother Harold's tuberculosis. Nixon's paucity of origin was in line with a staple feature of American politics, which would typically pit self-made men either against each other (as in a Goldwater versus a Johnson or a Reagan versus a Carter) or a self-made man against a prince (as in a Clinton versus a Bush). Elections such as that of 2000, pitting two established princes (Bush versus Gore) against each other have been historically uncommon.

Being a member of the college debate team helped to develop Nixon's political views, though his own perception of such views were a bit contradictory. Based on the impact of his father's political outlook and the philosophies of some of his professors, in his memoirs Richard Nixon described his views in college as having "a very liberal, almost populist, tinge," but as a debater, he was required to argue both sides of a topic. From this process, he discovered that he was something of a "free marketer," preferring free trade over protectionism and a laissez faire economy to a state-managed economy. As Nixon himself pointed out, he developed his skepticism for a planned economy when the New Deal was at its zenith of popularity. Nixon was a self-described social liberal with conservative economic views—a combination that would later nicely jive with the ideas of Dwight Eisenhower and "New Republicanism." Aside from debating, another formative aspect of Nixon's college experience that might surprise many people was his involvement in several school plays. Gaining the experience of being in front of a crowd served Nixon well as a politician. Cynics might go on to say that gaining experience at pretending in front of a crowd served Nixon's later purposes.

Nixon went on to the prestigious Duke Law School in North Carolina, where he earned a campus reputation as something of a liberal for speaking out against racism and managed to play a pivotal role in getting an African-American student into a social club, even though the school and its population deeply embraced the racism of the era. During law school at Duke, Nixon lived contentedly in impoverished conditions for three years. Nixon later commented that it was this experience in North Carolina that gave him a profound respect for southern culture, though not the racist outlook that was so prevalent. While at Duke, Nixon applied for a position with the Federal Bureau of Investigations, but he never heard back from them. As vice president, Nixon discovered that his application had actually been approved, but because of a budget cut that year, the FBI could not hire as many new agents as it had planned. The road to the White House had many twists and turns of fate. In Nixon's case, a few more dollars in the FBI's 1930s budget would have steered him away from political ambitions. Had this occurred, the Vietnam War might well have ended differently, and Watergate, of course, never would have happened.

After his schooling was complete, Nixon returned home to California to practice law. He also became highly active in local Californian civic organizations (becoming president of four such groups before he was thirty) as many ambitious men of his generation, such as George H.W. Bush, would do in the years immediately before and after World War II. Nixon's public profile resulted in his being approached by local Republican leaders who wanted him to run for the state assembly. While Nixon never developed the skills of dealing with people on an individual basis that Ronald Reagan or Bill Clinton did, he had a talent for inspiring loyalty and support from groups. Nixon also continued his involvement in local theater, which is where he met his future wife, Pat Ryan.

Nixon took a job in the Office of Price Administration in Washington, D.C. as the United States entered World War II. He could have spent the war overseeing the rationing of rubber and car tires, but despite his mother's Quaker influence, he decided to join the navy. Nixon spent the war stateside for a while before serving in the Pacific Theater. Nixon never had the good fortune to be at the right place at the right time, which allows a man to emerge from war with a hero's medal or wounds that later serve as a badge of honor. He passed through the war like millions of his fellow GIs, nondescript in his small contribution to victory.

After the war, Nixon returned home to California, resumed his social involvement, and was soon elected to Congress as a good, middle-class Republican, conveniently in the year (1946) that Republicans gained back control of Congress for the first time in fifteen years. The bright freshman Congressman from California caught the attention of the new Republican Speaker of the House, facilitating Nixon's appointment to the high profile House Committee of Un-American Activities (HUAC). Nixon had come out of the war with a generally benign attitude toward "Uncle Joe" Stalin, America's erstwhile Soviet ally. After Winston Churchill's Iron Curtain speech in 1946 and repressive Soviet policies toward Hungary in 1947 and Czechoslovakia in 1948, Nixon's attitude towards communism hardened, eventually to hone itself to a razor-sharp anti-red edge, which he soon learned to effectively wield. The Republican-controlled HUAC ran afoul of Democratic President Harry Truman who feared (correctly) that Republicans would try to use their power on the committee for partisan gain; thus, Truman ordered all of his departments not to comply with requests or subpoenas from Congress on security/loyalty issues. Nixon, therefore, joined a committee in a highly public contest of wills with the chief executive (a situation he would later experience from the other side). Nixon saw the error in Truman's tactic: the president's reluctance to be forthright with the committee came across as if he were covering up for subordinates of questionable loyalty (which truly was not the case). Facing negative public reaction, Truman decided to try to ride out the controversy in the hopes that it would die down, which it would, though with notable political damage to his administration, instead of admitting that his tactic of stonewalling Congress was a mistake. Apparently, Nixon did not learn a long lasting lesson from Truman's experience.

Nixon did gain a national reputation with his involvement in the notorious affair of Alger Hiss. During a House Committee of Un-American Activities meeting, Hiss—a first rank member of the eastern political and social establishment—was accused of treason and of being a communist spy, sending shock waves through the political establishment.

Hiss had worked in the State Department, serving as one of Franklin Roosevelt's advisers at the Yalta Conference, and was instrumental in the creation of the United Nations. Though the statute of limitations on the alleged spying had expired, Hiss was convicted of perjury for lies that he told under oath during House hearings in which Nixon figured prominently.

The Hiss case had a much bigger impact on Nixon than simply bringing him into the national spotlight. Historian Anthony Summers argued that Nixon fabricated evidence as he tried to make his case against Hiss. According to Summers, Nixon learned from the FBI that there truly was evidence linking Hiss to the Soviet Union, but the source of the information was too sensitive to be revealed. Rationalizing that his cause was just, according to Summers, Nixon broke the law by creating false evidence, reasoning that in such a case the ends—protecting the nation—truly justified the means. Thus, the Hiss case helped to forge what became Nixon's definitive Machiavellian persona, which emerged repeatedly across his career, culminating in the Watergate scandal when the Nixon administration similarly broke the law for the sake of its own perceived just cause. Like Truman, Nixon similarly refused to cooperate with investigators he saw as politically motivated, failing to recognize that in Truman's case the matter at hand was not allegations of impeachable presidential misconduct. Instead, using Truman as precedent, Nixon clung to an apparently genuine belief that the things done during his time in the presidency were, for the most part, just business as usual.

Even if there is not quite as much linkage between the techniques used in the Hiss case and in Watergate as some might believe, the Hiss case did affect Nixon in another way. According to numerous historians, Nixon's general dislike for rich northeastern liberals, and their dislike for him, was crystallized by Alger Hiss, who deliberately used his Brahman status to try to undercut Nixon during committee proceedings. When Hiss first appeared before the House Committee of Un-American Activities, and Nixon began to question him, Hiss said, "I am a graduate of Harvard Law School." Hiss paused dramatically before adding, "And I believe yours is Whittier?" To Nixon, Hiss was an elitist snob, a product of wealth who went to the finest schools and enjoyed power as a right of privilege rather than an obligation earned by merit. On top of this, Hiss did not even credit Nixon for his law degree from a relatively prestigious school, Duke University. Hiss represented a part of society that Nixon could not join financially or socially despite his own substantial merits.

Nixon was certain that Hiss, a man who had received all the finest things the United States could provide, was a traitor to his country. Yet, "the establishment"—the northeastern, powerful media figures, career government officials, and the like—rallied to the defense of one of their own, labeling Nixon as a red-baiter, a political opportunist with class envy who was attacking his socially superior adversary with charges of treason simply to enhance his career and status. Though Hiss' guilt as a traitor is still debated in some circles, there has been considerable evidence that has come out in the last few years that would seem to incriminate him. At the time, however, a substantial number of people believed that Hiss was the victim of a witch-hunt led by Nixon. These people—both in and out of the eastern establishment—had no love for Richard Nixon, and he had no love for them. For the next several decades, whenever criticism was directed at Nixon, the Hiss case factored into the equation. Nixon often dismissed criticisms of his policies and his conduct, justly or not, as nothing more than personal attacks by long-time enemies who were not interested in the truth. But memories of Nixon's first major appearance on the public stage left a bad taste in the mouths of eastern liberals and left Nixon as a quintessentially polarizing figure for the remainder of his political career.

Nixon served two terms in the House of Representatives before making a run for the Senate in 1950, at which time he received the endorsements of most of the major newspapers in California, which was still a predominantly conservative, Republican state. Nixon campaigned aggressively and successfully against his opponent, Democrat Helen Douglas, portraying her as soft on communism—not "red" but at least "pink." Nixon's people even went so far as to print fliers of Douglas on pink paper. Douglas responded by ideologically grouping Nixon with Hitler and Stalin, saying that all three represented oppressive, totalitarian government. Both sides engaged in "dirty tricks" (i.e., organizing hecklers and protesters to disrupt each other's campaign appearances, which was part and parcel of the politics of the day), but Nixon used them more effectively during the campaign. Hence, Nixon came out of the election with the sobriquet "Tricky Dick" firmly attached. Douglas faced a problem with which Democrats continued to wrestle for the balance of the century. While conservatives continually scored political points with the public by labeling liberals as leftists and, therefore, somewhat communist, liberals were never successful with painting conservatives with a similarly extreme brush. Perhaps that is because the American public had come face to face with the horrors of conservative fascism, thus calling conservatives "Nazis" and "Hitlers" seemed too visceral a charge to stick. Meanwhile, being a more exotic, eastern ideal whose real horrors only slowly penetrated the general consciousness, communism was abstract enough as a label of derision to be accepted by the public. Whatever the reason, Nixon found great success early in his career beating the "red scare" drum.

While in Congress, Nixon had developed a genuine friendship with Joe McCarthy, the very controversial senator whose pursuit of communism in the federal government was the headline dominating political story from 1950 until his downfall in 1954. Nixon and McCarthy were actually very similar in their political ideology, and their friendship furthered the hostility between Nixon and the liberal establishment. Despite their friendship, Nixon believed that McCarthy was too careless in pursuing his agenda, and in McCarthy's final years, Nixon oscillated between maintaining his loyalty and creating some political distance between the two of them.

With his work in Congress and the Senate, Nixon attracted the attention of Republican Party leaders and Dwight Eisenhower, the Republican nominee for the presidency in 1952. The vice presidency had always been considered a minor position in the executive branch. Vice presidents broke tie votes in the Senate, finished out the terms of presidents who died in office, and occasionally filled in at ceremonies the presidents were unable or uninterested in attending. Nixon claimed that if he had presidential ambitions in 1952, he would not have accepted the vice presidential nomination, arguing that it was easier for a person to make a name for himself in the Senate than in the vice presidency. Nixon believed that he was chosen for several reasons. As a man with personal relationships in both the House and the Senate, he would be able to mend fences after the Republican primary battles. As a westerner and a conservative, Nixon would appeal to voters who feared that Eisenhower was too much under the influence of northeastern liberals and moderates. Nixon also realized that Eisenhower wanted to be removed from the political attacks and mudslinging that are so much a part of American political history, but at the same time Eisenhower wanted someone who would fight hard on his behalf. And if there is one thing that both Nixon's supporters and critics agree on, it is that Nixon was a fighter. Thus, Nixon would be used as both the lightning rod and guard dog for the Eisenhower administration.

Nixon hammered away during the campaign on the twin themes that the Democratic Party had mishandled foreign policy regarding communism and that the Democratic-controlled executive branch was plagued with corruption. Nixon saw the executive branch during the Truman administration as an institution guilty of abuse of power. This, too, would impact Nixon's behavior when he was president. As president, he talked frequently about using the offices under his authority to hurt his enemies, believing that he would simply be using these offices the same way that they had been used against himself and other Republicans. He rationalized that the press did not complain about it when his enemies used the government for their own purposes, so it should have been acceptable for him to act the same way.

The run for the vice presidency actually almost ended Nixon's political career. Several newspapers charged that Nixon was the beneficiary of a secret fund supplied by wealthy California businessmen; Nixon allegedly used this money for his own "financial comfort" and was beholden to these businessmen. Nixon tried to explain away his "slush" fund as a perfectly legal way for him to fulfill his obligations as a senator, keeping in touch with his constituents without going broke from travel and postage expenses, but the defense made little headway with either the press or the public. Nixon's misfortune was that, beyond having left himself open to such charges by foolishly allowing the fund to be established, the 1952 race between Eisenhower and Democrat-challenger Adlai Stevenson was truly a bland affair. As a result, the press and the public delightfully seized on the distraction of scandal. Many leaders within the Republican Party urged Nixon to resign, even before he had a chance to mount what he saw as a credible counteroffensive. Eisenhower distanced himself from his wounded running mate (which Nixon would always resent), offering limited public praise but remaining noncommittal regarding Nixon's future on the ticket. Nixon was further frustrated by the fact that stories came out that Adlai Stevenson had a couple of secret funds as well, but the stories were met with no similar outcry for Stevenson's resignation, a situation that Nixon saw as deliberate bias on the part of his old twin nemeses—the press and the establishment.

Nixon was finally compelled to give a speech on national television that became famously known as the Checkers Speech, in which he explained the source of his fund, its purpose, and the generally poor state of his personal finances. Nixon went on to say that the only thing he had received since becoming a vice-presidential nominee was a dog named "Checkers," and that he loved his daughters too much to give Checkers back. The public response to the speech was quite positive, ending the scandal with one well-played scene. While television would be Nixon's undoing in the 1960 presidential race, the nascent medium proved his salvation in 1952.

Even though Eisenhower re-embraced Nixon following the successful public reaction to his speech, this early scandal hindered the development of their relationship over the next eight years. Their relationship received another jolt as they were gearing up for Eisenhower's 1956 re-election campaign. Like his own vice president, Spiro Agnew, would do, Nixon acted exactly as anticipated during his first term as vice president—attacking administration opponents and absorbing political attacks that otherwise would have been directed at the president. Going into 1956, Eisenhower's campaign staff began to weigh whether Nixon could still be an asset for the president or whether his polarizing personality was becoming too much of a liability. Eisenhower tested the waters for change by rather heavy-handedly suggesting that Nixon might want to consider a Cabinet position, such as Secretary of Defense, instead of the vice presidency. Eisenhower overstated the demotion, saying it would actually give Nixon a greater variety of experience and help him in a future run for the presidency. Nixon rightly believed that Eisenhower was trying to dump him from the ticket and that he would be abused in the press because of it. Nixon refused to accept the offer; if Eisenhower wanted him off the ticket, the president would have to push him off. Eisenhower, never one to pursue controversy unnecessarily, did not directly push the issue; however, the story was leaked to the press, which Nixon took to be a means of pressuring him. Nixon refused to take the bait, acting as if he believed he would be the president's choice to continue as vice president.

Ultimately, Nixon held his position for the full eight years, taking a more active role than had Truman or previous vice presidents, marking the beginning of the evolution of the office to more of a "deputy" presidency, as it became for vice presidents like Walter Mondale, Al Gore, and Dick Cheney. Nixon traveled to many foreign countries on behalf of Eisenhower. Nixon's first trip as vice president was a long tour of Asia where he met with several heads of state. He was praised for his diplomacy during this journey by the *New York Times*, which was not a frequent admirer of Republicans in general or Nixon in particular. Nixon also achieved global attention when, during a trip to the Soviet Union, he and Nikita Khrushchev engaged in the famous "Kitchen Debate." The two men argued over the merits of their respective societies in a mock-up of a kitchen at an American Exhibition that had been created so Russians could get an idea of American life. The trip gave Nixon a personal perspective on Soviet communism and reinforced his belief in personal diplomacy (the value of face-to-face contact with leaders of other countries). The interaction prompted him as president to undertake his groundbreaking personal visit to communist China.

Far from being an advocate of "détente" in the 1950s, Nixon actually became increasingly convinced that the best way to deal with the spread of communism was by demonstrating strength and resolve. As the 1950s progressed, Nixon began to believe that Eisenhower's policies of "peaceful coexistence" with communist states, such as his "Open Skies" proposal, opening up the U.S. and U.S.S.R. to complete and voluntary inspection of their military bases, were actually being perceived by the communists as signs of weakness. In 1954, Eisenhower sent 200 military advisers to Vietnam to help French and Vietnamese forces against Chinese-supported communist aggression in Vietnam. As the crisis continued to unfold and it became increasingly clear that the French were losing control of the situation, the Eisenhower administration debated the U.S. response. Beginning with Truman, several presidents adhered to the domino theory, asserting that like a row of dominoes, communism would spread to "democratic regimes" and those countries, like dominoes, would fall one by one to communist insurgents. Nixon advocated a very vigorous stance on the matter, even more so than Eisenhower, believing that stopping the communists in Southeast Asia was even more important than having stopped communists on the Korean peninsula. But Vietnam presented a unique problem to Eisenhower. In Korea the three major democracies of this era, the United States, Britain and France, were united, but they were not united on Vietnam. France was ready to give up in Vietnam, and the British were not interested in helping France keep the colony, since Britain had recently given up so many of its own holdings. Nevertheless, Nixon became a hawk on Vietnam, pushing Eisenhower to take the first tentative steps into what became a twenty-year quagmire.

By 1960, with Eisenhower termed out by the new Twenty-second Amendment (the Republican revenge for Roosevelt inadvertently catching one of their own), Nixon quickly emerged as his clear party standard-bearer. Nixon believed that his name recognition with voters and his years of experience on the national stage, despite his controversial public persona, would prove advantageous. Nixon perceived his main disadvantage to lie in the overall weakness of the Republican Party; in 1960, there were fifty million voting age Americans who considered themselves Democrats but only thirty-three million Republicans. Nixon was also concerned about Kennedy's wealth, charisma, and his Catholicism. Even though many people considered Kennedy's religion a handicap, Nixon reasoned that most people who would vote against Kennedy based on his religion were in states that would vote for Nixon anyway. In other states, Nixon believed that Catholics would overwhelmingly support Kennedy, and some non-Catholics would vote for him just to prove they were not anti-Catholic.

Nixon did not win the presidential election in 1960 for several reasons. He had pledged to campaign in all fifty states, while the election—like all presidential elections—came down to several "swing states." Yet, Nixon's attempt to live up to this promise cost him both in terms of campaign funds and in terms of his own health, as he was constantly on the campaign trail. At one point he was hospitalized for a knee infection; after he was discharged, he overcompensated by campaigning twice as hard because he was behind schedule, only to fall ill again. Nixon's health problems also contributed to his poor physical appearance in the televised debates with Kennedy. Kennedy's people understood that television was a visual medium, far more about image than about abstract concepts. Thus, Kennedy's handlers got him to Los Angeles—the debate setting—days ahead, allowing Kennedy time to relax under the California sun. When the candidates appeared on TV, Kennedy looked tan, healthy, and handsome; Nixon was pale, feverish, and generally sickly looking. While a majority of radio listeners believed that Nixon actually won the debate, the much larger television audience gave their approval to Kennedy. Three more debates followed, but Nixon was unable to regain the critical momentum lost in that first critical debate. Unlike Ronald Reagan, who would successfully rally from a weak first debate against Walter Mondale in 1984, the image of a pale, shaky Nixon contrasted with a young, suave, and confident John Kennedy simply could not be overturned. Beyond the debates, both the media and the public were also taken with Kennedy's energetic message and charisma (a word that, henceforth, Kennedy would serve to define) than they were with Nixon.

Nixon also suffered from the usual problem afflicting vice presidents running for the highest office—the legacy of their predecessor. After eight years of anyone, the public is usually open to the idea of change, and in 1960 JFK was clearly the candidate of change. Eisenhower's general dislike of campaigning and his basic desire to get on with the fine art of retirement meant that Nixon could not depend on the outgoing president even to help mobilize much of the Republican core base of supporters. Given their sometimes tense relationship, Nixon refused to ask Eisenhower for much help, and Eisenhower did not offer much. They had agreed that Eisenhower would campaign shortly before the election, but then Eisenhower's health deteriorated, preventing the limited help that had been promised. Adding insult to injury, Eisenhower actually hindered Nixon's chances when asked at a press conference what Nixon had contributed to his administration. Eisenhower replied, "Give me a week" to think of what Nixon had done. Eisenhower's remark was off the cuff and curt. He was trying to cut the press conference short because of flaring health problems, believing that he could respond to the question the following week at the next scheduled press conference. But the response came out wrong, and although Eisenhower regretted it, Democrats and the media seized on the comment to portray Nixon as ineffective.

Despite all of this, the election of 1960 was razor-close and plagued by allegations of substantial voter fraud in Illinois and Texas. When Kennedy emerged as the victor by a margin of 110,000 votes, Eisenhower and others urged Nixon to contest the election and demand recounts. In a moment of true statesmanship, Nixon refused to do so, believing that a recount would create turmoil and weakness in America when the country needed unity and strength to fight the cold war (although some speculated that Nixon did not want to open up the can of election irregularity worms for fear that some of those worms might have been found to have wiggled over from the Republican side).

Leaving Washington and returning home to the west coast, Nixon went on to lose his bid for the governorship of California in 1962 to popular incumbent Pat Brown. Tired and embittered, he refused at first to read his concession speech to the media, sending a subordinate to do it instead. As the press grilled the subordinate, Nixon changed his mind. He met with the press and scolded them for the years of abuse to which they had subjected him and said that they would not have him to "kick around" anymore. He presented himself so poorly at the press conference that many speculated that this incident, coupled with his election defeats, once again spelled the end of his political career. Like a political cat, however, Nixon had a few more lives to live.

Out of politics for the first time in years, Nixon was disturbed by the treatment that he received from the press and the government. ABC even went so far as to put on a show called "The Political Obituary of Richard Nixon"; one of the guests gloating over Nixon's political obit

328   Richard M. Nixon

was none other than Alger Hiss. Nixon was outraged that a convicted perjurer and personal enemy was picked as a panelist to discuss the state of Nixon's career. Nixon was also upset that the IRS audited him in 1963. In his memoirs, Nixon said he found out ten years later, after he had been cleared of wrongdoing by the audit, that the IRS auditor was pressured three times by supervisors to re-open the case, themselves under pressure from high-level personnel in the Kennedy administration. Nixon was also convinced that a Justice Department investigation of his mother and one of his brothers for a loan they had obtained had been instigated by Attorney General Robert Kennedy as part of what had become a blood vendetta between Nixon and the Kennedys. When Nixon and John Kennedy had been friends in the Congress, having offices across from each other their freshmen year (with Nixon even visiting Kennedy and reading to him to help pass time during a lengthy hospitalization in the late 1940s), the political battles had turned personally ugly. For Nixon, Kennedy came to represent everything he himself could not have—from wealth and social position to the adulation of the people. Even though the Nixons were cleared of any impropriety in the Department of Justice investigation, Nixon believed that these investigations were simply and viciously politically motivated. Such experiences reinforced his resolve as president to use whatever powers were under his control to hurt his enemies as simple payback. Nixon's use of the powers of elected office, powers designed for the public good but that were being used to advance a private and personal agenda, would be justified as being "good for the gander."

The 1964 debacle of Barry Goldwater being crushed by "landslide" Lyndon Johnson (fairly winning the title on this occasion) left the Republican field without a clear dominant contender for 1968. The liberal wing of the Republican Party, led by Nelson Rockefeller, had been badly mauled by Goldwater leading up to the 1964 convention. Meanwhile, Goldwater, a possible heir to the conservative mantle, was forced to fade away after his massive defeat but still loomed on the Republican horizon. Ronald Reagan was only in the second year of his first term as governor of California, and while he positioned himself as a possible contender for the nomination in the event of a brokered convention, he was never a serious candidate. Thus, Nixon, battered and bruised though he was, emerged from the 1968 campaign once again as his party's nominee.

Nixon won the close race for the presidency in 1968 primarily because the nation—and, more importantly, the Democratic Party—was divided over the Vietnam War and race issues. Conservative Democratic Governor George Wallace entered the race as an independent, appealing to southern blue collar workers and social conservatives disenchanted with a Democratic Party dominated by northeastern and upper midwestern liberals, as enshrined in the candidacy of liberal Vice President Hubert Humphrey. Thus, Wallace's candidacy served as a bridge between the conservative route under Barry Goldwater and the conservative triumph under Ronald Reagan. By splitting the Democratic vote (irreparably, as it would turn out), Wallace allowed Nixon, still a polarizing figure for many Americans, to win a plurality of the popular vote and a majority of the electoral college. Yet, despite his triumph, Nixon remained insecure, angry, and paranoid in his conviction that enemies, particularly the "eastern liberal establishment," were conspiring to get him. Richard Nixon finally entered the next and last act of his political drama: the presidency.

The Nixon Presidency: A Positive Assessment

It might seem hard to conceive of a positive interpretation of Richard Nixon's presidency, given the dark shadows that Vietnam, the Watergate scandal, and the legacy of Nixon's proclivity towards political machinations of the most Machiavellian kind cast upon his tenure in office. Yet, such a negative evaluation overlooks Nixon's successes in navigating the U.S. and the world through one of the most dangerous periods of the cold war, of setting into motion the process that ultimately allowed the cold war to reach a peaceful resolution, and of helping the U.S. and global economies adjust to massive destabilizing changes similar in scope and consequence to those experienced during the later 1920s while avoiding a catastrophic system meltdown.

It may be true that Nixon, the man, did not handle the presidency with the grace under fire one hopes to find in a national leader—though Nixon was not the drunken psychotic as many writers have portrayed him. As a man under tremendous pressure (a good deal from his own making), he did not always handle that pressure in an appropriate way (e.g., sometimes he drank substantially too much). An interesting perspective on Nixon is gleaned from John Dean's autobiography, *Blind Ambition*. Dean, who feared that he was the designated administration scapegoat, admitted that there had been a cover-up and that Nixon had ordered it. However, even though Dean explained that the president was a central part of the corruption that engulfed the White House, he also described a man who was brilliant in his capacity for strategic thought (far more so than the man who defeated Nixon in 1960) and capable of inspiring great loyalty from countless talented individuals. Nixon was too flawed to continue as president after the Watergate scandal—indeed, too flawed to avoid the worst scandal in American political history.

Nixon was a highly intelligent man with a great deal of experience and insight into politics (if not human emotion) who served his country during a complex time of shifting global realities—from rising foreign economic competition to escalating cold war tensions—precisely at the times when such qualities were desperately needed. Nixon had built his career on being an anticommunist; yet, his dislike for this political ideology did not prevent him from being remarkably flexible in his dealings with Communist regimes. Indeed, Nixon's credentials as an arch anti-communist was to play a crucial role in his ability to actually sell his policy of "détente" with the Communists to both liberal Democrats and conservative Republicans alike. (Hence, the classic expression that his actions introduced into the American vernacular: "Only Nixon could go to China," —just as only Reagan could reach a peace with Gorbachev a decade and a half later.) Nixon was consistently willing to sacrifice short-term popularity for long-term goals, a characteristic that has traditionally been of short supply in American politics. Nixon had to deal with a lack of congressional support and hostility in the media that had not been seen in Washington perhaps since the nineteenth century (and which would not be replicated until the Clinton years), but he pressed on with his agenda, at times demonstrating exceptional leadership skills. Nixon served the country well as he began the process of pulling America out of Vietnam, provided strong yet restrained leadership during a period of great domestic unrest, and furthered the progress that was being made in race relations, civil rights, and social welfare.

While Watergate unfolded, the United States was in the midst of a cold war with the Soviet Union and a hot war in Vietnam. Indeed, in October 1973, precisely as Watergate moved into a fervent pitch, the Yom Kippur War put the U.S. and Soviet Union on track for their most dangerous head-to-head confrontation since the Cuban Missile Crisis.

Nixon also inherited an increasingly sluggish economy due to increased government expenses because of the war, the rising costs of implementing Lyndon Johnson's Great Society social welfare programs, rising global economic competition, and a country still bleeding from the wounds of its racist pasts that had been reopened (or, better said, had its fetid scabs ripped off) by the civil rights movement. When Nixon took office in 1969, it was the first time in 120 years that a president had to deal with a Congress where the opposition party had a majority in both Houses (a condition that was to become more of the norm, to the bedevilment of the next two Republican presidents and one Democrat—Bill Clinton—as well). This forced Nixon to adopt policies that would have at least some bipartisan appeal, and his capacity to reach compromises surprised and impressed even some of his harshest critics. Nixon was able to enlist bipartisan support on foreign policy issues, such as Vietnam, from several southern Democrats, including but not limited to Sonny Montgomery, William Colmer, and John Stennis of Mississippi and Joe Waggonner and Otto Passman of Louisiana.

But Nixon's difficulty achieving support for his agenda was more complex than simply lacking majority support in the legislative branch. In his memoirs, Nixon identified two major obstacles. First, a majority of the federal government workers were ideologically liberal, which was a problem for the conservative Nixon. The president believed that the liberals had become entrenched after the twenty years of Democratic control of the White House preceding Dwight Eisenhower. Nixon blamed Eisenhower for not encouraging his cabinet officials to replace liberals in their departments with conservatives. As Eisenhower's vice president, Nixon was certainly in a knowledgeable position for such an assessment. These individuals, Nixon believed, who were supposed to be working for him, were too liberal to support his agenda. Supporting Nixon's contentions, a study by Joel Aberbach and Bert Rockman revealed that of the executive branch's upper level career bureaucrats, 47 percent were Democrats, 36 percent were independents who generally leaned to the left, and 17 percent were Republicans. Bernard Mennis did a study on foreign service bureaucrats and discovered that only 5 percent were Republicans. Nixon was frustrated by what he termed the "institutional inertia" that prevented wholesale changes in the make-up of the various departments of the government.

Nixon also believed that there was a strong media bias against him, i.e., a speech given on November 3, 1969. The president's speech described his plans for staying in Vietnam and what he believed the United States had to do to extricate itself from that situation. Television news commentators roundly criticized Nixon's comments, and they questioned his motives. On the other hand, a Gallup poll taken after the speech indicated that 77 percent of Americans approved of Nixon's handling of Vietnam. The president's speech was so popular that

Congress threw itself behind the president, giving him the bipartisan support on Vietnam that he so desperately needed. Of the 300 members of the House of Representatives that signed a resolution supporting Nixon's Vietnam policy, 119 were Democrats. In the Senate, fifty-eight members signed letters similar to the House resolution, and twenty-one of the signers were Democrats. The nation was solidly supporting the president at this point; yet, the media response had been negative. Meanwhile, at an antiwar demonstration in San Francisco twelve days after Nixon's speech, 125,000 demonstrators protested. David Hilliard, a leader of the Black Panthers, said during the protest, "We will kill Richard Nixon. We will kill anyone that stands in the way of our freedom." As 250,000 protesters converged on Washington D. C., an article ran in the *Washington Post* that read in part, "To dig beneath the rhetoric is to discover something extraordinary, and quite beautiful." An evenhanded commentator would be hard-pressed to find "something . . . beautiful" in a movement that sparked death threats against the president. The bias in the media against Richard Nixon can hardly be dismissed solely as a manifestation of Nixon's paranoia. In a society increasingly divided by race, social class, and political and religious ideology, Richard Nixon was a screen onto which his supporters (never overwhelming in number, at least in their intensity) and his opponents (who were legion) could project their hopes and fears. Unfortunately for Nixon, by the late 1960s, as American postwar dominance ebbed, fear greatly exceeded hope.

Despite these obstacles that Nixon faced, he had some noteworthy foreign policy successes. Nixon and his National Security Advisor, Henry Kissinger, ushered in a new era in American/Soviet relations with a diplomatic method known as linkage. Instead of trying to break down and negotiate individually the many divisive issues of the superpowers, Nixon and Kissinger linked them. They took something the Soviets were seriously interested in discussing, like nuclear arms talks or trade, and linked it to an area that was a pressing concern for the Americans, i.e., the Middle East or Vietnam. Through the process of linkage, the United States was able to get the Soviets to compromise on issues that they never would have previously considered.

The idea of linkage was not the only creative wrinkle to Nixon's negotiations with the Soviet Union. For decades the goal of the leaders of the United States was that America must have military superiority over the Soviets. Though this idea had more resonance among conservatives, Nixon came to believe that this type of thinking was flawed for multiple reasons. First, the Soviet Union was primarily a land power, and Nixon saw the United States' strength as a sea power. Second, American nuclear weapons were more effective, but Soviet nuclear weapons were more numerous. Popular support was not present in the United States during Nixon's administration either from a practical point of view to increase the federal budget enough to address the military imbalance or from a strategic point of view. Not enough Americans believed that we needed a massive increase in our numbers of nuclear weapons, and Nixon agreed with popular American sentiment on this point. He saw that there was a threshold beyond which more nuclear weapons would not provide any additional security because both sides already had enough weapons to virtually destroy each other. Instead of focusing on increasing our capabilities against the Soviet threat, Nixon adopted a strategy of striving to keep the United States strong, while at the same time putting an end to the arms race and trying to negotiate some limits. Nixon believed that the United States should focus on *sufficiency* in regard to protection against the Soviet threat, rather than striving in vain for *superiority* over them.

Nixon showed a willingness to have a different type of relationship with communist nations by becoming the first United States president to visit Beijing and Moscow. He was also the first American president to travel to a communist satellite country, going to Romania on August 2, 1969. Nixon knew that the Romanians, somewhat independent minded for erstwhile members of the Soviet bloc, had a strong relationship with communists in Southeast Asia that the U.S. might be able to manipulate to American advantage—another example of the creative negotiations of which he was capable, this time as part of an effort to end the Vietnam War diplomatically. Indeed, Nixon saw most of his major foreign policy concerns as being interrelated. If he could create warmer relations with China, which he accomplished with his groundbreaking visit in February 1972, it could help the United States to compel the Soviet Union to compromise on its differences with the United States. If the Soviets were worried about Nixon's relationship with China, the Soviets might pressure the North Vietnamese to offer some concession towards ending the war. All of these countries' interests were interrelated. Thus, while the Chinese invented the mantra, "the enemy of my enemy is my friend," the dynamic duo of Nixon and Kissinger elevated it to geopolitical perfection.

The most difficult foreign policy issue confronting Nixon was the Vietnam War. Admittedly, Nixon bore some degree of responsibility for Vietnam given his hawkish position in the Eisenhower years and his influence in helping to Americanize the fading French war effort. Yet, the war that Nixon inherited—500,000 combat troops bogged down in military operations that had already stretched on longer than World War II—was arguably like nothing he had envisioned during the heady days of America's 1950s strategic position (though it was precisely what Eisenhower had envisioned—and feared). Nixon ran for the presidency in 1968, promising a "secret plan" to end the war. While some may have taken this to mean that Nixon would simply declare victory and leave (as his opponent in the 1972 presidential election, George McGovern, ultimately advocated), Nixon came into office still committed to, if not, an American victory in Southeast Asia, certainly not a defeat. Nixon would have, all things being possible, preferred a military victory as a clear sign of American resolve not only to Russia and China but to American allies around the world. Nixon believed that there were three avenues to total military success. First, the United States could have used nuclear weapons against North Vietnam, but that would have led to international protests and a possible nuclear response from the Soviet Union. Second, heavy bombing in North Vietnam would have destroyed the extensive irrigation dikes, thus crippling the North Vietnamese, but it would also have resulted in death tolls of North Vietnamese civilians in the hundred thousands. Third, a military victory using conventional forces was feasible, but it would have required a sustained escalation of the number of American troops. In Nixon's opinion, that would have taken at least six months, and the president did not believe that the American people would have supported a policy of sending more troops with an accompanying increase in American fatalities. The president understood that both the public and the troops had grown increasingly weary with the seemingly unending conflict, making a military victory devastatingly controversial and, therefore, politically unobtainable.

In short, the military victory that Nixon would have preferred was not a realistic goal. Many were even calling on the president to simply pull out American forces and let the South Vietnamese fend for themselves. It was even suggested to Nixon that such a move could provide him with political gain. He could then refer to Vietnam as "the Democrats' War," since it was Lyndon Johnson who took an American military presence that numbered about 16,000 under John Kennedy and turned it into a fighting force that totaled 540,000 men. Nixon could make the case that he was making the best of a bad situation, pulling American troops out and saving American lives.

Blaming the Democrats for the Vietnam problem must have been tempting for Nixon. Sentiment in the United States against this war had reached a degree unmatched in any other conflict in American history. During Nixon's inaugural parade in 1969, war protesters threw beer cans, sticks, and stones at the presidential limousine. Someone in the crowd waved a Vietcong flag, and several demonstrators chanted "Ho, Ho, Ho Chi-minh, the NLF is going to win." In December 1969, protesters stormed the State Department building. As they shouted, "Smash the state!" they tore down the building's American flag, burned it, and hoisted the Vietcong flag. During May 1971, 200,000 antiwar protesters went to Washington D. C. and tried violently to shut down the government for a day. They were unsuccessful, but their actions had a powerful impact on government officials. At the University of Pennsylvania, school officials took down all of their American flags so as not to provoke war protesters.

A public opinion poll in 1971 revealed that 71 percent of Americans thought it had been a mistake to send American troops to Vietnam, and 58 percent believed the war was immoral. Nixon could have calmed the passions of the public if he had pulled the United States out of Vietnam, but he did not believe it was right to unilaterally quit on the war—indeed, it could have tremendously destabilizing geopolitical consequences. He refused to consider a policy in 1969 that did not guarantee the return of all our POW's and all possible information concerning our MIA's. And he did not want to leave the President of South Vietnam, Nguyen Van Thieu, or the rest of South Vietnam's population of 17,000,000 people defenseless. Nixon acknowledged in his memoirs that some people considered Thieu less than reputable, but for Nixon the issue was about standing up as a leader against communism. For Nixon, the question was bigger than "How does fighting in a faraway place like Vietnam make America safer?" If the United States abandoned Vietnam, Nixon believed that America's international credibility would be lost and that our allies would feel pressure to accommodate communist aggressors. Also, the Soviets would more likely take a hard line in negotiations with the United States. Plus, Nixon felt concern specifically for the people of South Vietnam. He knew that the North Vietnamese communists had engaged in atrocities against civilians. When the communists took over North Vietnam in 1954, hundreds of thousands of Vietnamese citizens died in labor camps and 50,000 others were executed outright. If the communists had free reign over all of South Vietnam, more horrible acts were sure to come.

336 Richard M. Nixon

It was difficult negotiating with the North Vietnamese because they knew how unpopular the war had become in the United States. During negotiations, the North Vietnamese would sometimes quote antiwar comments made by members of Congress. Nixon's desire to negotiate a settlement in his first year in office was unsuccessful because the North Vietnamese realized that prolonged negotiations played into their hands. They believed that over time Nixon would be pressured by domestic opposition to make more and more compromises. Indeed, Nixon blamed the antiwar protesters when an agreement could not be reached during his first year. Nixon, therefore, believed that the only way to get these concessions from North Vietnam was to make the war unpalatable to them and to show them that the United States had no intention of quitting. Not content to rely on his own instincts, Nixon consulted with Britain's expert on guerrilla warfare, Robert Thompson, who echoed the president's thinking. Thus, by 1970 Nixon actually escalated—dramatically—American military operations in Vietnam, including a massive increase in bombing of northern targets (dropping as many tons of bombs as were dropped on Germany and Japan combined) and invading and attacking North Vietnamese formations that were operating through neighboring (and theoretically neutral) Cambodia and Laos. While Nixon's escalation of the war was greeted with a Vesuvian explosion of anti-war protests (especially on college campuses where an increasing number of students were exhausting their draft deferments), the utter violent intensity of the onslaught succeeded in "bombing" the North back to the negotiating tables. Though Nixon seemed stuck in an almost unworkable situation, he managed to eventually get an acceptable settlement to end hostilities and allow American withdrawal while maintaining the existence of an independent South Vietnam. True, North Vietnam broke the agreement and eventually completed a conquest of the South, but that occurred after Nixon was out of office.

As Nixon escalated the bombing effort, he also increased (with far greater intensity) the policy of Vietnamization of the conflict, which every administration since Eisenhower had pursued as a kind of Southeast Asian holy grail. Vietnamization was the name given to the plan to turn over responsibility for the Vietnam War to the South Vietnamese. The United States continued to supply the war materials that the Army of the Republic of South Vietnam required, but Americans trained South Vietnamese soldiers to defend their own country. South Vietnam was to become more militarily self-sufficient by assuming a larger role in the fighting, and the policy of de-Americanizing the struggle would rob the communists of the advantage of their propaganda about fighting an imperialist enemy. During his first year in office, Nixon reduced the number of American troops in South Vietnam by 60,000. Nixon demonstrated that he was not a bloodthirsty, communist-hating maniac, as some of his critics believed. He was trying to divest us from a complicated situation without compromising one of our allies.

Nixon also decided to put pressure on countries that were aiding North Vietnam. He needed to rely on diplomacy with the communist nations that were helping the North Vietnamese because he wanted their aid in encouraging the North Vietnamese to end hostilities. But he resented the fact that non-communist countries that were receiving aid from the United States were aiding our enemies, so Nixon ordered that aid be cut off to several countries until they stopped undermining our war efforts. As a result, Singapore and Somalia compromised and cut down on their trade with North Vietnam.

Nixon has been intensely criticized for escalating the war in Southeast Asia by the secret bombings and ground incursions that he authorized in Cambodia. Part of Nixon's motive for keeping the bombings secret was to avoid reactions from anti-war protesters, but Nixon was also driven by another concern. Prince Sihanouk, the leader of Cambodia, did not want the North Vietnamese using his country as a route into South Vietnam or as a munitions dump, and the North Vietnamese were doing both of these things. Sihanouk feared, as history would validate horrifically within a few short years, that the presence of communist North Vietnamese in his country encouraged—if not overtly supported—communist guerillas in his own country with destabilizing results. Officially, Cambodia maintained its neutrality, so there were no public requests for the United States to bomb North Vietnamese targets in their country. Such a request, making Cambodia appear to be an American ally in a region of the world where anti-American sentiment was high, would also communicate the message that the Cambodians were too weak to maintain the integrity of their own borders. Nixon later justified the secret bombing, claiming that it had saved the lives of American military personnel, had dealt a harsh blow to the enemy, and had increased the pressure on the North Vietnamese to negotiate in good faith. Nixon's major mistake was forgetting that it is somewhat difficult to engage in such a massive aerial bombardment of a country and have it remain secret for long.

Indeed, Nixon's proclivity for secrecy (while hardly unique amongst modern presidents, especially during times of armed conflict) received substantial criticism from the media and his domestic opponents. Nixon was constantly accused of abusing power by ordering secret wiretaps of political enemies, domestic dissidents, and just about anyone else he saw as a political or personal threat. Yet, Nixon did have a real, potentially security compromising problem with leaks of classified and often highly sensitive information from the government to the media. During Nixon's first year in office, the CIA determined that there were forty-five newspaper articles published that contained information that was supposed to be secret. These articles dealt with topics like arms negotiations with the Soviets, intelligence-gathering options for North Korea, and deliberations over United States policy regarding North Vietnam. When Nixon talked to former President Eisenhower about the leaks, Eisenhower said he believed that anyone who leaked classified foreign policy material should be charged with treason, even if the country had not been in the middle of a war with North Vietnam. Henry Kissinger, Nixon's National Security Advisor, believed that these leaks were a threat to national security. Nixon also consulted with J. Edgar Hoover, the director of the FBI, who recommended wiretaps on the phones of suspects. Hoover said that every president since Franklin Roosevelt had authorized the use of wiretaps. Nixon gave his consent to implementing the wiretaps though he was not involved with each individual decision. The FBI tapped only seventeen people from 1969 to 1971 for the purposes of stopping government leaks, which was less than the number that Roosevelt had tapped. While it is true that warrants were not obtained, previous presidents had not bothered with warrants either. The Supreme Court eventually ruled that warrants had to be obtained (with some rare exceptions), but by that time, Nixon's wiretaps had been removed for over a year. This was not a case of Nixon running a government that was out of control; he was following standard operating procedure as he understood it. Nixon argued, with some justification, that if he had not maintained as much secrecy as he did, several foreign policy breakthroughs, including his highly successful trip to China, the SALT agreement with the Soviets, and the ending of the Vietnam War, would not have happened when and as they did.

In July 1969, the president announced the "Nixon Doctrine," reflecting the president's characteristic pragmatism acknowledged that the United States could no longer maintain its current level of overseas commitments and would only provide war materials and economic assistance in the future. Under the Truman Doctrine, the United States had supplied soldiers, war materials, military training, and economic assistance in helping countries to defend against communist aggression, ranging from Greece to Argentina to Korea and Vietnam, the latter two involving the significant deployment (and loss) of military personnel. The Nixon Doctrine recognized that, after Vietnam, the American public would not tolerate a similar massive long-term deployment of American combat troops into a third-world nation (as, indeed, they would not for over a generation until the occupation of Iraq starting in 2003). Thus, Nixon turned domestic political reality into new geopolitical doctrine. Henceforth, the only time the United States sent troops during future struggles would be if one of the major nuclear powers attacked an ally, which, luckily, was never required across the remainder of the cold war.

American abandonment of the Truman Doctrine and Nixon's phased withdrawal from Vietnam could well have had the regrettable consequence of doing precisely what Nixon had always feared American strategic retreat would do: convince both communist foe and democratic friend alike that the U.S. was a declining strategic power. To offset the real loss of American strategic position in Vietnam and the limitations on projecting U.S. power that the Nixon Doctrine presented, Nixon engaged in his policy of détente, playing the Russians off the Chinese in his own game of geopolitical billiards. Nixon's opening to China helped quell the threat of a direct United States/Sino military conflict and also gave the U.S. some leverage in mitigating rising border tensions between China and Russia (much as Nixon's decision to dispatch U.S. naval forces to the Bay of Bengal during the Pakistani civil war in 1971, which gave birth to the new state of Bangladesh, helped avoid a direct Indian/Pakistani war). In the long term, however, it was Nixon's openings with the Soviet Union that would have the greatest strategic consequence. Russia, apprehensive about rapprochement between China and the U.S., maneuvered closer to American just as Nixon and Kissinger had hoped. Nixon's diplomacy with Russia produced several significant arms accords, including the 1972 Anti-Ballistic Missile Treaty, which helped avoid a costly expansion of the arms race into the realm of missile defenses (which, besides the cost, threatened to introduce new potentially destabilizing uncertainties into the equation of Mutual Assured Destruction [MAD]). The subsequent Strategic Arms Limitation Treaty, while having minimal impact on United States/ Soviet nuclear forces, also helped to bring a greater degree of stability to the nuclear force equation. In addition to diplomatic and cultural exchanges, the détente progressed as Nixon and Brezhnev concluded agreements on trade, including the eventual shipping of $750 million worth of grain from American farmers over three years (to the absolute delight of American wheat farmers), helping Russia to offset their own declining agrarian harvests due to the massive inefficiencies of their already imploding economic system. While the immediate legacy of Vietnam and the Nixon era would be the perception of an America in retreat (which encouraged some degree of Soviet adventurism in Africa and central Asia by the end of the decade, though not to any lasting strategic advantage), Nixon's détente strategy laid the foundation for increasing Russian interdependence with the west that increasingly diminished the prospects of the Soviets initiating major hostilities— literally biting (or nuking) the hand that fed them. The eventual relatively peaceful demise of the Soviet Union, therefore, can be traced in no small part directly back to the seeds of interdependence Nixon planted in the early 1970s.

Nixon was also willing to use force as necessary to demonstrate American resolve even amidst phasing out from Vietnam. When Soviet premier Leonid Brezhnev threatened to introduce Soviet combat troops into the Middle East to stop the Israeli destruction of the Egyptian army during the Yom Kippur War, Nixon countered by warning Russia against any such move, placing American strategic forces on nuclear alert to back up the American demand. At the same time, Nixon successfully pressured the Israelis to allow the Egyptian army to retreat back behind its borders, thereby saving Arab face and ending the crisis. While Secretary of State Henry Kissinger's use of shuttle diplomacy, engaging in revolving rounds of diplomacy between Middle Eastern capitals, failed to broker a sustained peace in the region, Nixon's intervention in the October War directly helped to defuse tensions in the region, setting the stage for the eventually brokering of a sustainable Israeli/Egyptian peace by the end of the decade.

Unfortunately, the successes of Nixon's foreign policy were not matched with his domestic policy. Nixon was not able to enlist bipartisan support for his domestic agenda in the same manner that he had for foreign policy issues. In his first year in office, Nixon proposed more than forty different bills to Congress dealing with domestic issues, twenty of which dealt with crime. Only three of the president's proposed pieces of legislation became law. While Nixon was pleased with what passed—plans to phase out the draft and provide tax reform, and a plan to make the Post Office Department a non-partisan government corporation—he chafed under the almost knee-jerk opposition with which his legislative agenda was greeted. Nixon could, however, pull off surprising victories, such as his early efforts to end the increasingly unpopular draft system, which would be completely abolished by 1973. Nixon, the arch cold warrior who had been a military spending hawk, could pull off the ending of the cold war draft precisely because he was such a strong proponent of having a strong military. Nixon argued that ending the draft would actually make the military stronger because only committed people would enlist into the military. Thus, Americans could trust that Nixon's efforts were not aimed at weakening the military.

Another major Nixon domestic initiative was the Family Assistance Plan, providing the poor with a way out of poverty and cutting through some of the bureaucracy and red tape that hindered welfare assistance. The plan would have helped 13 million more people than were being helped by existing programs, 60 percent of Americans living in poverty would gain the financial resources to be above the poverty line, and it would have given 40 percent more money to African Americans living in the South. While fiscally conservative, Nixon generally accepted the "modern Republicanism" of Eisenhower with its acceptance of the core ideas of the social welfare state. Thus, Nixon was of a different ideological bent when it came to social issues than subsequent Republican presidents, with the possible exception of George H. W. Bush. Nixon's Family Assistance Plan was, in spirit and in kind, an expansion of the Johnson Great Society program. Yet, the Family Assistance Plan never passed. Democrats criticized the proposal, considering the benefits excessively low. Overwhelmingly, conservatives opposed the plan because of its costs and the potential of increasing the number receiving welfare. Conservatives wanted to limit or roll back welfare, not expand it, and, additionally, liberals did not want to hand this president a victory with two of their core constituencies, the poor and minorities.

Race relations were almost as contentious an issue as the Vietnam War during the Nixon years. The intensity of the protests would shock many today. Students, sometimes armed with guns, took over buildings—for example, in 1969 at Cornell University to protest the punishment of three African-American students. Though Lyndon Johnson deservedly gets credit for Civil Rights legislation in the mid-1960s, there were still major inequities at the time Richard Nixon was inaugurated. When Nixon became president, minority businesses only had $8 million in government contracts. By 1972, minority businesses had $242 million. In 1969, 68 percent of African-American school children were going to all-black schools. Six years later, only 8 percent fell into this category.

Nixon did not see similar improvements in the economy. The federal budget deficit had been expanding across the 1960s, driven by the costs of the Vietnam War and the ever-increasing amount of money being spent on social programs (not the least of which being, with rising life spans, social security). Welfare money and benefits for needy families with dependent children was almost three times as great in 1969 as it was in 1960. Concern over rising federal red ink, however, was outweighed for Nixon by the need to maintain military spending and fear that any significant social cuts he might get through the recalcitrant Congress would further alienate the public. The economy was to remain a trouble sport for the United States throughout the 1970s.

By the time Nixon was elected in 1968, the American postwar economic boom was already moving into its terminal phase. Two symptoms of this decline were rising unemployment and rising prices—a combination that became known as "stagflation" in the 1970s. While domestic policies such as increased spending on the war in Vietnam and social welfare and the resulting federal deficit helped contribute to the sluggish American economy that Nixon inherited, the greater problem lay in America's economic relations with the world. For twenty years after World War II the United States was the indisputable global giant, her trade rivals in ruin from the war, the dollar king (pegged to gold in a system of fixed exchange established at the 1944 Bretton Woods conference, all other major currencies were subordinated to the dollar). By the late 1960s, however, the U.S. was sending more money abroad (buying foreign goods and providing aid) than it was taking in through exports. The resulting "dollar glut" (the phenomenon of too many dollars floating around abroad) put downward pressure on the dollar. The correct economic response would have been to devalue the dollar versus other currencies as early as 1965 or 1966. Devaluation, however, comes as a steep cost as the price of imports increase, fueling inflation. (In the long run, that should have been offset by rising exports driven by the cheaper value of the dollar and resulting gains in employment. But the increased pool of cheaper labor in the rapidly developing economies of Asia would blunt much of this theoretical gain when Nixon ultimately devalued the dollar in 1971.) Neither Lyndon Johnson nor Nixon were anxious to take such a step, given the high political cost with which it would come, at least in the short run. By 1971, however, the pressure on the dollar from the rising U.S. trade imbalance became unsustainable, at least under the Bretton Woods gold standard. Nixon attempted to deal with rising inflation and the trade imbalance by announcing a price-control plan unprecedented in peace time (although America was technically at war in Vietnam, it was not truly on a war footing comparable to World War II) freezing prices and wages for 90 days and placing a 10 percent import tariff to dissuade Americans from buying foreign goods. More importantly, Nixon took the U.S. off the gold standard, allowing the dollar to devalue. The measures actually helped stabilize the economy for a short while (long enough to reduce the impact of the plight of the economy on the 1972 election), but by 1973, inflation triggered by the declining value of the dollar began to seriously undermine the economy. The Arab oil embargo in October of that year and the resulting doubling of oil prices greatly exacerbated the problem. (Indeed, rising inflation and unemployment in 1973 and 1974 probably did more to undermine public support for Nixon in the Watergate crisis than the scandal itself did.)

These factors beg the question: If Nixon had been blessed with the booming economy that Bill Clinton enjoyed during his own impeachment, might he actually have ridden out the scandal? While Americans desire "moral" leaders, they do not seem to mind the occasional immorality as much during times of plenty. Nixon moved to devalue the dollar again and implement a second round of price controls, though these actions would be less effective the second time around. Over the next ten years, the U.S. and the world would sink into a global recession the likes of which had not been seen since the 1930s. While Nixon's economic policies failed to avert the general American economic decline that came to characterize the 1970s, he deserves at least some credit for cushioning the fall through his willingness to embrace the politically distasteful task of monetary devaluation. In the 1920s the reigning global economic hegemon, Great Britain, steadfastly refused to devalue its own dominant currency despite its own trade deficits. The American dollar, meanwhile, had not yet established itself as a global currency capable of replacing the weakening pound. The result was ultimately catastrophic: the weakness in the international economy created by the overvalued pound helped turn the financial crisis in the United States into a truly global economic pandemic. Nixon's policy, while far from ideal, at least helped the world adjust over a period of years to the weakening dollar and, therefore, helped keep the recession of the 1970s from turning into the depression of the 1970s, with all of the geopolitical implications therein.

Nixon once remarked that you didn't really need a president for domestic policy—Congress and the Federal Reserve could handle that. Presidents loomed largest, he believed, in foreign policy (which was,

344   Richard M. Nixon

indeed, the predominant reason for the creation of the office in the first place). If Nixon had been able to focus exclusively on the rarefied world of diplomacy and war, stripped of the need to bother himself with mundane electoral domestic politics, he would have undoubtedly left a far less marred legacy. Indeed, Nixon might have done better to have listened to the advice of Eisenhower and hung up the vice presidency back in the 1950s for a cabinet post such as Secretary of Defense. While such a move might have aborted his ultimately ill-fated presidential destiny, it might have left him in a position to take up the mantle of elder statesman of American foreign policy. Nixon as Secretary of State might have accomplished much of the good without all of the damage that Nixon as President created. Indeed, even with a reputation ruined by Watergate, Nixon would still be sought out in retirement for advice on foreign policy by most of the presidents who followed him. Even in areas of domestic policy, such as expanding social welfare and advancing the civil rights agenda, Nixon showed glimpses of visionary leadership. Indeed, his theme of "New Federalism," arguing for the need to devolve at least some of the New Deal federal government back to the states to improve governmental efficiency and rekindle political legitimacy, became the dominant theme of government over the next two decades.

But domestic politics and policy are part and parcel of the presidency, and Nixon's own ambitions would never have been satiated by a corner office in the State Department's headquarters at Foggy Bottom. Nixon was the star of his own operatic drama and, like all great tragic figures, had to ride his destiny to its seemingly inevitable end. This end came with his resignation from office on August 9, 1974, in an attempt to avoid a rapidly encroaching impeachment. For Nixon, his enemies—the eastern establishment, the media, and the snobbish intellectual elite— had finally swayed even the "silent majority" of Americans, whom he had always truly believed were in his corner, against him and were now about to publicly hang him for crimes that he believed were simply "business as usual" of modern American presidential politics, and in which every president from Roosevelt and Truman onwards had engaged. Nixon never fully appreciated that it was the disgrace he brought to the Office of the Presidency and the disreputable behaviors in which both he and those for whom he was responsible engaged that produced the disgrace that had ultimately given voice to the "silent majority"—the voice of outrage.

Yet, in his resignation Nixon demonstrated once again his capacity for graciousness in the face of defeat. In his fascinating book, *Nixon's*

Enemies, Kenneth Franklin Kurz argued that Nixon's fatal flaw was that he was a better loser than a winner. When Nixon had the upper hand, his ugly side manifested itself. Chuck Colson, a special counsel to the president, watched Nixon struggle with the message he was to send George McGovern after McGovern had conceded defeat on election night in 1972. Nixon was hours late with his reply, because the president could not compose any kind words for the man he had beaten. Nixon was still angry about comments made during the campaign. As Colson put it, "Noble in defeat, he (Nixon) was . . . without grace in victory." Nixon had respect for those who beat him, but he was pitiless to those whom he defeated. While this personality characteristic did Nixon great harm across his career, it actually served him well in his final action as a national leader. As with his concession to arch rival John Kennedy in 1960, when Nixon ignored those who urged him to contest the disputable election results, Nixon ultimately brushed aside those around him in 1974 who urged him to fight the impeachment. While it would take a controversial pardon by his successor to finally end the "national nightmare" of Watergate, Nixon's decision to go quietly and not challenge the constitutionality of the impeachment proceedings moving against him—as several advisors and pundits encouraged him to do—ranks with General Douglass MacArthur's decision not to further constitutionally challenge Truman's decision to remove him from command. In both instances, the American constitutional order was placed on the line by the actions of men of driving ambition. In both cases, neither man was willing to put his ambition ultimately above the rule of law by crossing their constitutional Rubicon. Thus, Nixon deserves credit not for the events that led to his demise, but for the manner in which he met his demise.

The Nixon Presidency: A Negative Assessment

Richard Nixon's failures as president can best be divided into two areas: policy and behavior. In the area of policy, Nixon had significant problems on both the domestic and foreign policy fronts. While the economy lagged through Nixon's first term as the postwar boom moved through its terminal phase, both unemployment and inflation, while growing, did not pose such a problem as to seriously threaten Nixon's reelection chances. The economy was sluggish in the late 1960s and early 1970s, and Nixon tried to address the problem, but he was inconsistent with his economic policy. Though he was an economic conservative, he implemented a series of price controls to try to stabilize the economy in the early 1970s. Those price controls provided no lasting benefits, and they actually compounded problems, as some industries raised prices prematurely, so as to have a financial cushion when the next set of price controls was imminent.

Another major issue facing Nixon was race relations. Nixon was troubled by the degree of racial strife in the United States in the late 1960s, but his perception of its roots would strike most people today as politically incorrect at best, absolutely unfathomable at worst. During his acceptance speech for the Republican nomination at the 1968 Republican National Convention, Nixon addressed the issue, complaining about the "unprecedented racial violence" in what he described as "a nation that has been known for a century for equality of opportunity," implicitly pushing the responsibility for racial unrest on civil rights protestors rather than the system they protested. While this appealed to Republican social conservatives, ranging from skepticism to outright hostility in their views of the civil rights movement, it begged the question of the lack of equality of opportunity confronting African Americans denied access to jobs, voting rights, restaurant service, and bathrooms for most, if not all, of the century to which Nixon referred. Since the end of Reconstruction, African Americans had been brutally and murderously oppressed in the United States; Richard Nixon was too smart and well-traveled not to know that. It is hard to interpret this part of Nixon's speech as anything other than an attempt to pander to political interests.

While there is some ambiguity in Nixon's record, overall one gets an unflattering picture of the man in regards to race and gender issues. Nixon placed several Jews in powerful positions, including his National Security Adviser Henry Kissinger, the head of the Council of Economic Advisers Herb Stein, the Federal Reserve Chairman Arthur Burns, and one of his legal counsels Leonard Garment. Yet, according to Nixon's staff, the president also talked about "Jewish traitors" in front of Kissinger. (At times, Nixon seemed to simply forget Kissinger's religion. As Kissinger reported in his own autobiography, on one occasion, while deeply amidst the worst of Watergate, a disoriented Nixon asked Kissinger to get on his knees with the president and pray to their "Lord Jesus Christ" for Nixon's salvation.) Once when talking about the need to ferret out spies, Nixon encouraged his aides to "just find one that is a Jew" because he felt that would fire up Nixon supporters in the country. Haldeman wrote in his diary that Nixon wondered why "all the Jews seem to be the ones that are for liberalizing the regulations on marijuana." The president also told Haldeman that "Jews are all over the government" and "Jews are disloyal."

Nixon's tapes revealed that he thought women in government were not worth the trouble they caused. Nixon believed it was difficult to find any Mexicans or Italians who were honest. Additionally, Nixon believed that Italians did not smell, look, and act like people he considered to be "normal" Americans. Despite the fact that he had spoken out on behalf of African Americans a few times in his past, Nixon believed most African Americans were incompetent, but it was good to hire some for symbolic value. The president had several different racial slurs that he used when referring to African Americans. According to one of his most trusted aides, John Ehrlichman, Nixon believed African Americans "could never achieve parity—in intelligence, economic success, or social qualities." Indeed, Nixon's White House tape recordings of Watergate fame were littered with a constant stream of vulgarities, racial slurs, and epithets to make even the most hardened Klansman blush. Thus, Nixon's public commitment to racial equality and civil rights were at least to a degree undercut by his own private ambivalence.

Domestic policy always took a back seat to foreign policy for Nixon both in terms of attention paid and energy expended. And the biggest issue with which Nixon dealt in office other than Watergate was the Vietnam War. Vietnam was, in fact, the driving force behind virtually every other issue. Nixon realized that the war was too unpopular to commit the kind of manpower resources that would be needed for any chance of a military victory. The best Nixon could hope for was a negotiated peace that would maintain the security of South Vietnam— the kind of settlement that left Korea divided with communists controlling the North, and the South allied to the United States. What Nixon actually obtained was almost the worst of all scenarios. American troops continued fighting until 1973. Nixon wanted the North Vietnamese to agree to a demilitarized zone and keep their forces north of it, but the North Vietnamese were denying that their troops were involved in the fighting in the South, so they refused to sign a treaty admitting otherwise. The years of additional fighting amounted to little for the United States except more dead and wounded soldiers. The United States signed a treaty that left roughly 150,000 North Vietnamese troops in the south, and within two years the communists took over Vietnam. In retrospect, if Nixon had pulled out in 1969, the result would have been the same except fewer lives would have been lost. Nixon talked about securing an honorable peace, which rings as hollow for him as it did for Neville Chamberlain when the British Prime Minister said much the same thing after dishonorable and futile negotiations with Hitler before World War II.

As noted in the essay on Lyndon Johnson, the Vietnam War quickly degenerated into a frustrating, disillusioning, and vicious conflict. American soldiers not only had difficulty defeating a determined foe but also distinguishing who was the enemy and who were innocent civilians caught in the middle. Without question, the most pernicious consequence of this uncertainty was the brutality inflicted by American fighting men on Vietnamese peasants on search and destroy missions. This became especially true as increasing numbers of Vietnamese villagers turned against the United States and supported the Vietcong. As more American GI's lost their lives because of Vietnamese civilians' support for the VC, the more tenacious American soldiers became to wage campaigns of total destruction. As one GI recalled, "we'd go through [a suspected pro-VC hamlet] and that was it. We'd rip out the hedges and burn the hooches and blow all the wells and kill every chicken, pig, and cow in the whole fucking village. I mean, if we can't shoot these people, what the fuck are we doing here?"

Although official policy urged the winning of the "hearts and minds" of the Vietnamese people, battle-hardened veterans believed: "All that is just a *load*, man. We're here to kill gooks, period." Even American medical personnel, whose calling should have made them sympathetic to the plight of Vietnamese civilians, shared such callousness and disregard for their charges' lives. When a reporter heard an American doctor declare that he refused to treat wounded Vietnamese, the reporter asked, "But didn't you take the Hippocratic Oath?" "Yeah," the doctor replied, "I took it in America."

The massacre of the hamlet of My Lai represented the ultimate of such attitudes. On March 16, 1968, Charlie Company, a unit of the U.S. Eleventh Infantry Brigade, was ordered on a "search and destroy" mission into the South Vietnam province of Quang Ngai. Their objective was to destroy the hamlet of My Lai. Already enraged because they had lost several of their unit in an earlier engagement, the 150 GI's descended on My Lai, where they were ordered by their commander, Lt. William Calley, to raze the village as an act of revenge for the loss of their comrades. "When the attack started," one participant recalled, "it couldn't have been stopped by anyone. We were mad and had been told that the enemy was there and we were going to give them a fight for what they had done to our dead buddies." There were no VC in the village, and in fact, its inhabitants opposed the VC. Peasant hamlets "suspected" of being pro-U.S. were often more brutally terrorized by the VC than they were by American troops. On this day, however, such was not the case. Within a matter of minutes, the company opened fire on the villagers. "Off to the right," one observer said, "a woman's form, a head appeared from some brush. All the other GI's started firing at her, aiming at her, firing at her over and over again . . . they just kept shooting at her. You could see the bones flying in the air, chip by chip." The Marines were consumed by rage. "People began coming out of their hooches and the guys shot them and burned the hooches." Another soldier remembered, "Sometimes they would round up a bunch and shoot them together. It went along like that for what seemed like all day. " Some of the dead were mutilated by having "C Company" carved into their chests; some were disemboweled. One GI later confessed that, "You didn't have to look for people to kill, they were just there. I cut their throats, cut off their hands, cut out their tongues, scalped them. I did it. A lot of people were doing it and I just followed. I just lost all sense of direction." That day more than 350 Vietnamese villagers were killed. There was one American casualty, a GI who shot himself in the foot out of disgust for what he was watching. The killing finally stopped after helicopter pilot Hugh Thompson radioed to his section leader, telling him what he was witnessing. In the meantime, Thompson landed his chopper and began rescuing survivors, ordering his machine gunner to open fire on any American soldiers who tried to stop him or who continued to shoot villagers.

Cover-up of the massacre began immediately, with reports declaring the operation "a stunning combat victory against a Vietcong stronghold." *Stars and Stripes* applauded the American soldiers' "courage." In the initial, "official" report sent from Commander-in-chief General William Westmoreland's headquarters, My Lai was a "legitimate" combat operation in which twenty civilians had "accidentally" been killed.

To many Americans, the My Lai massacre was an aberration, an act of momentary insanity—rage—caused by the loss of comrades and frustration of not being able to tell friend from foe. Those were excuses. There was simply no acceptable reason for the wanton slaughter of so many innocent people. The reality and the fact was that My Lai was an extension of the horror that consumed Vietnam and of the policy of massive destruction that had become America's way of winning the war.

Word of the massacre reached the American public in November 1969, ten months into Richard Nixon's administration. The event made the cover story of both *Time* and *Newsweek*. *Life Magazine* published graphic photographs, which horrified and disgusted many Americans, confirming their worst fears that the prolonged, futile conflict had caused American soldiers to lose their humanity, causing them to commit unspeakable atrocities. Suffice it to say, the military establishment was undone by the story and wanted the photographs impounded and the whole affair swept under the carpet as quickly as possible. (The My Lai photographs bear an uncanny comparison to the behavior of the American soldiers in the prison abuse scandal in the Iraqi war and the disagreement on whether to release the photographs for American viewing.)

The My Lai massacre also got the Nixon administration's attention. The last thing Nixon wanted as he was trying to "disengage" slowly from Vietnam (his "Vietnamization" policy, which called for giving the war "back" to ARVN—the now totally demoralized Army of the Republic of Vietnam to fight—was being implemented just as the news of My Lai hit the United States) was for such an unconscionable event to occur, which would only further outrage an increasingly alienated public. Secretary of Defense Melvin Laird briefed Nixon at his San Clemente retreat. The White House proceeded with caution, sensing the incident's potential to embarrass the military and undermine the war effort. Nixon tried to "downplay" the massacre as nothing more than an "isolated incident," an "aberration" born of momentary frustration and the inability of American soldiers to "ferret" out the "right enemy."

Calley's court martial began on November 17, 1970. For over four months, witness after witness came forward to testify before a six-officer jury. Calley's defense was straightforward—he simply followed orders from his superior, Captain Ernest Medina (who, incidentally did not like Calley, calling him "Lieutenant Shithead" in front of the troops). According to Calley, "I was ordered to go in there and destroy the enemy. That was my job that day. That was the mission I was given. I did not sit down and think in terms of men, women, and children. They were all classified the same." Was Calley telling the truth that he had been ordered by a superior officer to kill the My Lai villagers? The court ruled the evidence on that issue inconclusive, and, thus, Medina was not held accountable—only Calley. In his summation, the army's prosecutor quoted an Abraham Lincoln speech given to Union troops during the Civil War about treatment of noncombatants during that horrible conflict. "Men who take up arms against one another in public do not cease on this account to be moral human beings, responsible to one another and to God [for their conduct]."

After thirteen days of deliberations, Calley was convicted of premeditated murder on all specifications. After hearing pleas on the issue of punishment, jury foreman Colonel Clifford Ford pronounced Calley's sentence: "To be confined at hard labor for the length of your natural life; to be dismissed from the service; to forfeit all pay and allowances." Surprisingly, public opinion polls revealed that a majority of Americans overwhelmingly disapproved of the verdict. President Nixon announced that he would "review" the decision. In the meantime, he ordered Calley to be taken to Fort Benning, Georgia, and there held under house arrest. "Confined" to a comfortable apartment, Calley was allowed to have pets, entertain guests, and cook his own meals. Such an order made a mockery of the trial and Calley's punishment, which in most other instances would have been much more severe. Indeed, had Calley been found guilty of committing such barbarity in "saner" times, he more than likely would have been executed. However, the 1960s were anything but sensible times, and the war only exacerbated the excesses. Consequently, Nixon's action (in effect, he "pardoned" Calley) made the whole affair a travesty. He willingly engaged in the worse kind of political maneuvering—that of expediency in order to bury the incident as quickly as possible so he could continue the war's prosecution without having to worry about an "overly sensitized" public. Moreover, Nixon felt no remorse in absolving Calley, for the public, in their disapproval with the original verdict, had already exonerated him. Apparently, many Americans were as "anxious" as Nixon to bury this tragedy as quickly as possible and move on. They were unwilling to accept the fact that the war had degenerated into a senseless, brutal, and emotionally debilitating conflict that brought out the worst in American soldiers.

On November 9, 1974, the Secretary of the Army announced that William Calley would be paroled, after serving only three years under house arrest of what originally was supposed to have been a life sentence served in a military prison with no parole. Thanks largely to Richard Nixon's intercession, William Calley was a free man after having ordered the murder of 350 innocent human beings. The only "good" that came out of the tragedy was that the army high command ordered that its training personnel better "prepare" field officers and enlisted men to "understand" noncombatants.

While Nixon was successful in the grand strategic sense of managing the cold war balance of terror through the policy of détente and in moving the U.S. towards disengagement in Southeast Asia, American policy gains came with significant "collateral damage" in terms of lost human life. The escalating of the bombing of North Vietnam and the expansion of the war into neighboring Cambodia dramatically escalated civilian casualties (in the range of hundreds of thousands). Moreover, the Cambodian incursion ultimately contributed to the very destabilization of that country that the U.S. had desired to avoid, leading to the Khmer Rouge dictatorship and the systematic slaughter of several million Cambodians. Similarly, Nixon's policies in Latin America, particularly the support that the administration gave to the coup by General Augusto Pinochet in which elected Chilean president Salvadore Allende was overthrown and killed, along with the systematic rounding up and execution of thousands of Allende's supporters, directly contributed to massive human rights abuses. Nixon saw the world in the geopolitical abstract, a tendency strongly reinforced by his Secretary of State Henry Kissinger, who likewise thought in terms of nineteenth century balance of power politics in which whole populations could be reduced to pawns on the global chessboard, much as European colonial powers had done in dealing with the millions of peoples living in what they dismissively referred to as "the periphery." Nixon's and Kissinger's failure was to forget that the lesson the U.S. and the industrial democracies supposedly had learned from the horrors of two world wars was that national political objectives could no longer be used to justify imperialism and the callous disregard of human rights. In conducting business as usual on a nineteenth century model, Nixon authorized policies that resulted in genocide and massive human rights abuses—what would be referred to as "crimes against humanity" by the end of the twentieth century. Thus, while Nixon maintained the macro-global peace, he did so at great cost. Some might argue that this was a necessary trade off but certainly not an example of an enlightened approach to foreign policy seeking to correct mistakes of the past.

Richard Nixon will forever be linked with the Watergate scandal, which is seen as the pivotal moment of his presidency. This is unfortunate insofar as it leaves the impression that the only thing wrong with his administration was an involvement with a "third-rate" break-in at the Democratic National Headquarters during the 1972 presidential campaign and foolish (and also incompetent) subsequent efforts at a cover-up. The true significance of the Watergate break in was that it led to investigations that exposed a consistent pattern of scandalous activity. Far from one ill-conceived robbery, the Watergate investigation revealed a presidency rifled by corruption, a profound arrogance of power and contempt for constitutional checks and balances, rampant paranoia, and other manifest symptoms of extreme psychological dysfunction. Watergate, therefore, was not aberrational; it was the natural pathology of an administration that considered the law just another tool to be used and discarded in order to service the higher imperatives of power.

One of the more troubling things about Richard Nixon is that, though his reputation was sullied by the Watergate scandal, he might actually have been guilty of things much worse. Spiro Agnew, Nixon's first vice president, resigned in the face of charges of corruption in a matter unrelated to Watergate. Agnew's legal problems were yet one more headache for the Nixon administration, so no tears were shed in the Oval Office when Agnew offered his resignation. Agnew later, however, alleged that he quit, at least in part, because he feared for his safety, feeling that in the Nixon White House, where the rule of law was continually played fast and loose, even the infliction of physical harm as a means to an end was conceivable. It is one thing for staunch critics from the opposition party to allege that a president is associated with violence against those who can do him political harm. It is quite another for Nixon's vice president to make those allegations.

It might seem extreme (not to mention conspiratorial) to suggest that a president of the United States would be implicated in physical intimidation, but there is more evidence that Nixon might have been capable of such planning in light of his presidential tapes. The tapes feature exchanges between Nixon and Chief of Staff H.R. "Bob" Haldeman in which Haldeman spoke to the president about Vietnam War protesters and how the problems with them were likely to re-occur. Nixon responded by welcoming the thought of more protests, and the two men discussed getting people to attack the protesters. There was talk of "getting" Abbie Hoffman, a well-known protester. As it turns out, two days before that recording was made, Hoffman was "gotten." He had been involved in a demonstration where he was chased into an alley, held, and beaten until his nose was broken multiple times.

There has even been speculation that Nixon was somehow involved in the assassination attempt on May 15, 1972, on presidential candidate George Wallace that left Wallace crippled. According to the Nixon tapes, he expressed concern that the shooting could be linked to him or his people. As Chuck Colson's men got involved, investigating the background of the would-be assassin, Arthur Bremer, and with the official investigation of Bremer, Nixon asked if Bremer was a "left-winger (or a) right-winger." Colson replied that Bremer would be a left-winger by the time the investigation was through. Colson tried to get Howard Hunt to go to Bremer's apartment, break in, and plant left-wing literature, but Colson and Hunt decided that it would be too late by the time Hunt got there. The investigating authorities would have had Bremer's apartment sealed, so Colson scrubbed the mission. It is possible that Nixon and his people were innocent in this matter. Perhaps Nixon was afraid that anyone who would shoot one of his opponents might have made some past connection with the Republican Party machinery. But there is the possibility that Nixon was worried that some connection might be found because there was a connection that existed. Wallace was still open to the possibility a quarter of a century later that Nixon might have been involved. It would seem logical that Nixon and his top aides had not set up Bremer to do what he did. If they had, then they would not have waited until after the fact to create a leftist picture of Bremer. But it is possible that Nixon was worried that someone in his administration might have sanctioned Bremer's deed on their own, thereby taking the initiative to rid Nixon of the meddlesome Wallace because Nixon had cultivated an atmosphere of winning at all costs. Laws and morality did not matter; results did. As the record indicates, Nixon wanted men who were ruthless and loyal. Colson, in his autobiography, said as much in his analysis of Nixon's scandals.

Another piece of evidence linking Nixon to violence and corruption arises from an event in Charlotte, North Carolina, in 1971. The city was hosting a Billy Graham Day in honor of the famous evangelist at which Nixon was scheduled to appear. Haldeman received a memo from one of his assistants who was doing advance work on the appearance. The memo said that Vietnam War protesters would be there, they would probably be violent, and the police would most likely need to use violence to maintain control. Haldeman wrote the word "good" twice on this section of the memo. Where the memo stated that Graham would be the target of some of the protesters' abuse, Haldeman wrote "great." While Nixon or his people may not have been involved in instigating the violence, there was a clear tendency of the administration certainly to use such violence to its political advantage. While it is not fair to blame Richard Nixon for everything said or done by his aides during his presidency, the words and deeds of the president's staff are in fact a reflection on the president.

H. R. Haldeman, who would ultimately serve an eighteen-month jail term for his actions in office, has sometimes been portrayed as something of a Svengali who oversaw dirty deeds while hiding them from his chief executive until their magnitude brooked no concealment. Far from tarnishing Nixon, Haldeman was actually more of an honest reflection of the man. Nixon had a temper that was frequently violent and out of control, especially when he had been drinking. He allegedly struck his wife on at least one occasion. One night April 23, 1970, Nixon called Kissinger ten times because he was mad at CIA operatives for not following his orders in Southeast Asia. Nixon would call, give an order, then hang up, followed by another call shortly thereafter. Kissinger either ignored these presidential orders or determined which orders to obey in these circumstances until the president regained his composure. A similar example was the hijacking in 1969 by Palestinian terrorists of a plane with more than one hundred passengers, forcing it to go to Damascus. The hijackers wanted the Israelis to release a number of Palestinian terrorists being held. Nixon told Kissinger to bomb the Damascus airport. Not wanting to take such a drastic action, yet not wanting to be insubordinate, Kissinger worked with the Secretary of Defense on a third option. They decided to move a couple of aircraft carriers into position to launch a strike, then wait for further orders. The next morning, Nixon asked what had happened. When told that the carriers had been moved but no attack was launched, Nixon replied, "good," and nothing more was said about the bombing. An even more extreme example of Nixon's reckless behavior occurred when the North Koreans shot down an American spy plane in 1969. According to CIA specialist George Carver, Nixon, who had been drinking at the time, wanted to launch a nuclear strike against the North Koreans, and ordered the Joint Chiefs of Staff to pick out targets. After Nixon's conversation, Kissinger convinced the Joint Chiefs of Staff to do nothing until Nixon was sober. When Nixon did become sober, talk of a nuclear strike was never brought up.

Besides the president's temper and his drinking, there were several reporters who claimed that Nixon had spells in which he appeared to be unstable. Helen Thomas recorded that the president "looked like a man in a daze." Nancy Dickerson described him as "mentally erratic." John Osbourne characterized Nixon's temperament as being in "alternating moods of anger and euphoria." During the later stage of Watergate,

Nixon's behavior became so erratic that his own aides sought an outside diagnosis as to the president's competency to stay in office. One of Nixon's speechwriters, Raymond Price, said he had talked to Nixon on more than one occasion when the president's speech sounded slurred, and then Nixon would suddenly drift off, a victim of too much beer and a sleeping pill. Experts listening to Nixon's tapes have also attested to slurred speech. Deputy Assistant Secretary of State William Sullivan described Nixon as a habitual drinker who would telephone Secretary of State Bill Rogers and order someone to be fired. According to Sullivan, Rogers said Nixon would forget about it the next day. Both Rogers and Kissinger were in the unenviable position of disregarding orders from their boss, the president. Though Kissinger has denied the reports of his colleagues that Nixon drank too much, the evidence contradicts him. Roger Morris, who worked on the National Security Council, said that Nixon drank so much, especially when he was at Camp David, that there were occasions late in the evening when matters that should have been taken to the president were saved for the next day.

Beyond his own personal problems, Nixon had surprising difficulty in dealing with and relating to other people. According to Nixon's secret White House tapes released in December 2003, Nixon described Ronald Reagan in August 1972 as "strange" and "just isn't pleasant to be around." Reagan was generally considered an upbeat person with a sunny disposition and a decent sense of humor, which hardly qualifies him as strange. Actually it is Nixon's personality that is usually held up to criticism. Nixon has been faulted for his interactions with others (the press, his critics). Perhaps part of his problem was that he could not see his rivals as they truly were but interpreted them through the somewhat warped lens of his own ambitions. People who criticized his policies were not just people with different opinions; they were traitors to their country. Republican rivals were not just individuals who had a slightly different vision than Nixon; they were "strange." Perhaps this discomfort with people who did not follow his lead is what prompted Nixon to surround himself with so many people who served him blindly. Of course, one can only follow a president blindly if one does not have a well-developed moral code of one's own. The result was an administration peopled by individuals who shared Nixon's win-at-all-costs mentality and were willing to break the law when it suited the agenda of their president.

White House aides prepared "enemies lists," including several hundred Americans who were prominent in various social and political arenas. The list ranged from liberal movie stars like Paul Newman to university presidents. The lists were a manifestation of Nixon's tendency to paranoia, reinforced by an overly loyal staff (and, like all good paranoias, premised on more than a kernel of truth: as a major political figure, Nixon truly did have enemies but not necessarily of the "destroy Nixon at any costs" variety that he imagined). William Buckley, a conservative writer, repeatedly referred to the lists as "fascist" and indicative of a dismissive attitude towards human rights. He also thought the lists indicated a self-righteous mindset on the part of the Nixon administration. Nixon wanted these lists used for the purpose of harassing his political enemies, for example, through IRS audits. Though Nixon aides Haldeman and Colson downplayed the intentions behind the lists, the evidence suggests otherwise. The aides claimed that lists were made to indicate individuals who were not supposed to receive positive treatment, like invitations to the White House, but there were also lists made of people for the Internal Revenue Service to audit. Randolph Thrower, the first IRS commissioner during the Nixon administration, received multiple lists of people to audit. When he refused to authorize the audits without receiving justification for them, Thrower was told that the president wanted it done. When he tried to meet with Nixon regarding this matter, he was rebuffed. After Thrower resigned, Nixon was recorded on the White House tapes as saying that he wanted a commissioner that would go after his enemies, but not his friends. Thrower's successor, Johnnie Walters, also received a list of Nixon's enemies to audit. Walters took no action on the list and only lasted for a short time as IRS commissioner.

Meanwhile, even though the IRS commissioners did not seem cooperative with Nixon's agenda, Nixon's enemies were still vulnerable from retribution from the taxman. Nixon's staff discussed breaking into tax offices after hours to gather incriminating evidence on administration opponents. IRS agents targeted at least one of Nixon's enemies (Robert Greene, an editor of *Newsday*) after the IRS received an anonymous letter regarding wrongdoing. Also, lower level IRS officials were persuaded to conduct individual audits under White House pressure. However, Nixon was not content simply getting audits. A year before the 1972 presidential election, Haldeman recorded in his diary that Nixon wanted information on all of the major Democratic leaders who were potential candidates in 1972. Nixon wanted his people to investigate their finances, their families (one might imagine even their family pets), and anything that might produce dirt on the competition.

Nixon had a legitimate complaint concerning classified information being leaked to the media (a constant struggle in a society desiring security, especially in times of war), but his administration went to extreme and illegal lengths to try to plug such leaks. The worst leak during the Nixon administration from a foreign policy perspective (the single worst leak being the still unknown "Deep Throat," who spilled the beans on Watergate to two reporters) was the publication of the *Pentagon Papers* in the *New York Times* by Daniel Ellsberg, a former assistant to Kissinger and civilian Pentagon employee. This was a top-secret official investigation of U.S. policies in Vietnam prepared in the Johnson administration and of other foreign affairs-related issues, which painted a less than favorable picture of the muddled Pentagon and executive branch decision-making that, for over a decade, had led to the debacle of Vietnam. As damaging as the initial installment the *New York Times* published, Nixon and Kissinger knew that Ellsberg had previously had access to even more damaging material of extensive government duplicity, including covert U. S. activity in southeast Asia. Publication of the papers risked revealing the identity of intelligence assets abroad. Also, the revelation of the flights of American U-2 spy planes over China could become pubic knowledge. The Chinese knew about the flights, but it was not a matter of public record. If it was revealed, the Chinese would be publicly humiliated and forced to respond. This was a particularly sensitive matter for Nixon because he was preparing for his visit to China. The Chinese might call off the visit, which Nixon felt was vital not only to Sino-American relations, but also to the Soviets' attitude towards the United States and the war in Vietnam.

On Sunday, June 13, 1971, the first installment of the *Pentagon Papers* was published. Two days later a federal district judge ordered the *New York Times* not to run the series, but by Thursday the *Washington Post* was running it, followed by the *Boston Globe* and the *Los Angeles Times*. As copies of the papers continued to surface, even the Soviets wound up with the documents, which they returned, they said, in the interests of American/Soviet relations. Though antiwar individuals inside and outside the press believed that Ellsberg was a hero, the attorney general and the FBI considered him a communist spy. The fact that the Soviets returned their copy of the documents was not overly persuasive with the Nixon administration; obviously, the Soviets had read the papers and could have made copies.

The "Plumbers," who became infamous after the Watergate scandal, were men who were picked to stop these leaks that were plaguing the government. While there were real national security concerns in place, the "Plumbers" working out of the White House essentially constituted parallel government working outside of the constraints of law and constitutional protections. Thus, Nixon's quest to protect national security by extra-constitutional means ultimately presented a greater threat to the survival of the constitutional system that he had sworn to uphold than did the leaked information which he sought to plug.

Nixon was not content to merely try to plug leaks. He also sought to sully or destroy the reputations of those who challenged his authority by placing leaks of his own. Such was the case with Ellsberg. The White House wanted to portray Ellsberg as a man with severe mental problems to discredit through association the information that he leaked, but the CIA file on him did not have anything incriminating. In his resultant outrage, Nixon turned to aide Charles Colson, insisting evidence be found to ruin Ellsberg, no matter how it was accomplished. Later, at a meeting with both Colson and Bob Haldeman, Nixon said, "I don't care how it's done. I want these leaks stopped. Don't give me any excuses. Use any means . . . I want results. I want them now." E. Howard Hunt and G. Gordon Liddy went to Los Angeles in search of information, breaking into the office of Ellsberg's psychiatrist to look at Ellsberg's files. Nixon publicly denied any role in the crime when the details surfaced, but he privately accepted responsibility for it.

Paying men to commit crimes and providing them with the equipment and funds to do so was expensive, so Nixon had to be very aggressive at raising money, and it had to be money for which he would not have to account. The White House tapes make clear that one way that Nixon raised money was by putting price tags on ambassadorial positions. It has been customary in American history for political friends and financial supporters to be rewarded with certain ambassadorships, but for a president to demand a specific price ($250,000) in advance was crass—not to mention fundamentally illegal. Thus, a consistent pattern of abuses of power—from illegally raising money to funding dirty tricks, from enemies lists to the illegal use of government resources to harass those on the lists—emerged and grew across Nixon's first term in office, coming to full poisonous fruition with his re-election campaign of 1972.

Watergate is, of course, the best-known scandal associated with Richard Nixon. The scandal grew out of Nixon's basic belief, clearly articulated to his staff and supporters, that a Republican victory in November 1972 was not only necessary for Nixon but for the party (a party that Nixon had surprisingly little interest in when it came to the brass tacks of partisan politics). In Nixon's view, election of a Democrat in 1972 would be inevitably followed by a unilateral U.S. withdrawal from Vietnam, which, like the long-feared dominoes, would irreparably shake the confidence of American allies and embolden the Soviet bloc to the extent that an American defeat in the cold war would become truly conceivable. Thus, the defeat of Richard Nixon was tantamount to the destruction of the Republic. Any means were justified to avoid those ends. Given the temperament of the staff surrounding Nixon—men like G. Gordon Liddy who once tried to impress a date by holding his hand over a lit flame, allowing his skin to char black—the fact that this mandate would be realized as Watergate should have come as no surprise (just as it should have come as no surprise that a man of Nixon's temperament would surround himself with the pathologically loyal like Liddy or Haldeman).

In early 1972, Liddy met with Attorney General John Mitchell, presidential counsel John Dean, and Jeb Stuart Magruder, a White House staff member who helped set up the Committee to Re-elect the President (known as the CRP by Nixon staffers but dubbed CREEP by the press). Their purpose was to hatch a plan for helping Nixon beat the Democrats in the upcoming election by any means necessary. The plan that emerged included such outrageous elements as kidnapping individual delegates so as to disrupt the Democratic National Convention. (The individuals were to be drugged and held in Mexico until the convention was over.) Liddy was going to use mobster hit men to carry out the assignment. Liddy also proposed using prostitutes to seduce high-ranking Democratic officials, presumably for the purpose of extortion, and wanted to place illegal bugging equipment on the Democrats (which actually occurred). When Mitchell rejected the plan, it was not on moral or legal grounds; he cited the proposed cost of one million dollars as being too expensive. The Nixon administration seemed to have a staff divided into two camps: the outright immoral and the fiscally frugal but amoral.

On May 28, 1972, several men in the employ of Nixon aide Howard Hunt broke into the Democratic National Headquarters to plant bugging equipment and to copy papers, as per the Liddy plan. Indeed, one of the things they wanted to find out was what, if anything, the Democrats knew about all the other dirty tricks they were implementing or planning. On June 16, the men returned to the complex because one of the bugs was not working properly. A night security guard discovered their entry and called D.C. police. The rest, as they say, is history. Bob Haldeman claimed for years afterwards that not only did he not know about the break-in, he did not even know why anyone would have ordered it. Nixon echoed this theme, saying repeatedly that he would never have sanctioned such an action because it was such a stupid thing to do (begging the question of whether he would have sanctioned an "intelligent" commission of felony). The White House tapes capture Nixon saying, "The Committee isn't even worth bugging in my opinion. That's my public line." (Of course, the president would have been much better off not uttering that second sentence, or recording such musings in the first place, or surrounding himself with staffers who would take such actions, if even on their own. But then, if Nixon had not done those things, he would not have been Nixon.)

After the men were caught breaking into Democratic headquarters, a two-year investigation ensued regarding who in the White House knew what and when they knew it. It has never been proven conclusively that Nixon ordered the Watergate break-in (though in 2003 one of the key Watergate conspirators, Jeb Stuart Magruder, said for the first time that Nixon had prior knowledge of the plan to break into the Democratic National Headquarters in the Watergate building). There is ample evidence, however, that Nixon and his aides conspired to cover up facts related to the resulting federal investigation and, in Nixon's own words (recorded, as it turned out, on his own secret taping machine), "stonewall" Justice Department efforts to get to the bottom (or the top, if one prefers) of the Watergate scandal. Such actions constitute felony obstruction of justice, a high crime worthy of impeachment. The cover-up activities were orchestrated and far-reaching. White House employees and senior staff began a systematic effort to shred and/or burn documents that might have been related to Watergate or to other illegalities perpetrated by Nixon's people. The Nixon administration also applied pressure through the CIA to discourage the FBI from investigating. Nixon approved of a plan to tell the CIA that, if the FBI dug too deeply into the men involved in the Watergate break-ins, it would lead to embarrassing revelations about previous CIA activities since some of the people involved in Watergate had CIA ties. One theory holds that the "Deep Throat" source for *Washington Post* reporters Woodward and Bernstein was actually one or two of the FBI agents assigned to the investigation who grew frustrated when the information they gathered was not forwarded to the special prosecutor appointed to investigate the scandal.

When it was discovered that Nixon had been secretly taping conversations for his memoirs, something which Franklin Roosevelt, Kennedy, and Johnson also did, Nixon was ordered to turn over the tapes to Special Prosecutor Archibald Cox. But Nixon was reluctant to turn over the tapes, officially on grounds of "executive privilege," but in reality because the tapes later turned out to provide a damning inside portrait of the administration. Nixon offered to make summaries of whatever notes or meetings about which Cox wanted information, and Nixon offered to have a Democratic senator authenticate the validity of the information Nixon provided. When Cox attempted to secure the tapes through a court order in October 1973, the president ordered Attorney General Elliot Richardson to fire him. Richardson refused to comply. The deputy attorney general also rebuffed the president. What followed became known as the "Saturday Night Massacre," as Nixon had to fire both his attorney general and deputy attorney general for refusing to carry out the order to fire Cox. Luckily for Nixon, the number three man at the Justice Department (who would later be unsuccessfully nominated to the Supreme Court by Ronald Reagan—Robert Bork) did comply and fired Cox. Critics considered the "massacre" to be a massive obstruction of justice, but Cox held his position before the independent counsel law was created, so Cox was an employee serving at the pleasure of the president. Firing Cox was not the president's finest hour, but Nixon was operating within the letter of the law. Yet, these actions outraged the public, and the president's popularity rating fell to an unprecedented 27 percent, making potential impeachment all the likelier. Nixon's efforts came to naught, however, as the Supreme Court ultimately ordered him to turn over the tapes to the congressional Watergate inquiry. The subsequent discovery that someone had erased eighteen critical minutes of a key Oval Office conversation that probably would have directly linked Nixon to the cover-up, if not the break-in itself, caused Nixon's already declining public support to largely evaporate. Smelling political blood in the water, Congress (supported by both Democratic and a number of Republican members) moved to remove Nixon from office, precipitating his resignation.

Ultimately, more than a dozen of Nixon's aides went to jail as a result of the various Watergate-related investigations. While a greater number of people went to jail due to the investigation into Bill Clinton's Whitewater activities and even more members of the Reagan administration faced criminal indictment, the crimes committed by Nixon's associates in his name represented a very different and far more dangerous form of public corruption. Clinton's scandals revolved around money and sex; Reagan's scandals revolved around petty influence peddling (with the exception of the Iran/Contra affair—an event more closely associated with Watergate than Whitewater). It is naive to think that Nixon invented political espionage and the dirty tricks that are associated with him or even that such conduct ended with him. The crimes of the Nixon administration, however, were aimed at the procurement and maintenance of political power, even at the expense of the Constitution itself. No president, with the possible exception of John Adams during the "Aliens and Seditions" controversy, has ever taken the Republic so perilously close to violating the Constitution.

America has endured any number of presidents with odd personality traits. George Washington used to delight in scaring the citizens of his new national capitol by driving his ornate carriage at reckless speeds through the streets of New York. Lincoln believed in ghosts; Wilson displayed characteristics of megalomania; Kennedy was addicted to various drugs and sex; Johnson was a certifiable control freak; Reagan fell into a debilitating depression during the Iran-Contra affair; and Clinton had his intern problems. (With a track record like that, little wonder that many Americans, when told their commander in chief—a man with a history of a drinking problem—had bumped his head after passing out from choking on a pretzel while watching a football game, greeted the news with shaking heads and rolling eyes.) What separates Nixon's peccadilloes from those of many of his peers was the systematic way that his own personal failings led to actions that could have—and, indeed, did to a dangerous extent—unravel the very fabric of the American constitutional system of checks and balances. The Nixon presidency underscored the fundamental danger of the modern—or what historian Arthur Schlesinger famously referred to as the "Imperial"—presidency. Over the course of the twentieth century, through war, depressions, and social upheaval, increasing amounts of power devolved to the presidency from the other branches of government. Where Congress existed as the dominant institution of national governance—as the framers of the Constitution intended— across the nineteenth century, by the middle of the twentieth century the president had emerged as the colossus of modern political power. America looks to presidents to wage war (deciding when and how to do so, with little or no meaningful congressional review), write budgets, initiate major policies, and lead the nation in celebration and mourning. Yet, the institution is still dependent upon the character, abilities, and psyche of only one man. If that man is flawed—as all men are in some way—those flaws are magnified to potentially destructive degrees by the prism of power. Richard Nixon was a man flawed to tragic Greek proportions. Through his blind pursuit of power, always justified under the mantle of righteous ends, Nixon came closer than any president to fundamentally subverting American democracy. Such a charge weighs heavily against his many beneficial accomplishments on behalf of the Republic he served. Thus, Nixon truly fit the description of the archetype tragic figure—a man blessed by the gods with abilities, yet cursed by them with ego and ambition. One should look forward to the opera.

Richard M. Nixon in a
campaign motorcade
standing on the back of
car gives the "V" sign.
January 28, 1970
Photo credit: Nixon
Presidential Library

(right) President
Nixon meets with
China's Communist
Party Leader,
Mao Tse-Tung.
February 29, 1972
(bottom) President
and Mrs. Nixon at
the Great Wall of
China.
February 24, 1972
Photo credit: Nixon
Presidential Library

The Shah of Iran, President Nixon, and Mrs. Nixon in formal attire for a state dinner in the White House. October 2, 1969 Photo credit: Nixon Presidential Library

Arrival ceremony welcoming King Faisal of Saudi Arabia. May 27, 1971 Photo credit: Nixon Presidential Library

Nixon with John Ehrlichman. February 12, 1973 Photo credit: Nixon Presidential Library

Gerald Rudolph "Jerry" Ford
1974-1977

Gerald Ford's road to the White House was unique: he was the only United States president to take the job without being elected to either that office or the vice presidency. Appointed vice president when Spiro Agnew resigned and elevated to president after Richard Nixon stepped down, Ford might have been the first president since George Washington to fill that position without having had any real interest in pursuing the office. Indeed, Ford's highest dream had been for high office, but one a few steps removed from the presidency. Across his political career, Ford yearned to become the Speaker of the House, not resident of the White House. It would take a series of unique events to precipitate such an unsought—and unlikely—change of residence for an unassuming member of Congress from Michigan.

Ford was born Leslie L. King, Junior on July 14, 1913, in Omaha, Nebraska—Bastille Day, though it was doubtful that such a fact registered on his solidly middle American family. His father was allegedly abusive to his mother, and two years after Leslie King, Jr. was born, his parents divorced. He and his mother, Dorothy, moved to Grand Rapids, Michigan, to live with her parents. Dorothy later married Gerald Rudolf Ford, a salesman, who formally adopted young Leslie and had his name changed to Gerald Rudolph Ford, Junior (note the Americanized spelling of the younger Ford's middle name). Jerry Ford was not sure exactly when he learned he was adopted, saying he was twelve or thirteen at the time. His biological father showed up unannounced to meet Ford when he was sixteen, but the meeting did not go well; Ford always felt that his biological father did not really care about him.

Ford's mother and stepfather were not prosperous, but Ford saw in them a wealth of character. They prized honesty and hard work and were quite involved in their community. Both were active in their church; his mother was a Daughter of the American Revolution, and his stepfather was committed to the Boy Scouts. Being ambidextrous, writing with his left hand and throwing footballs with his right, was a concern to Ford's parents and some of his early teachers, but Ford, himself, was not troubled by it. However, he did develop a stutter as a young child. But the man who would give hundreds of public speeches outgrew his stutter by the age of ten.

When he entered college at the University of Michigan, Ford was more serious about football than politics and became his team's starting center. He was picked by his teammates as the team's most valuable player, a rare honor for a lineman, and he was selected as a college all-star. Ford credited his football experience with giving him a tough enough skin to withstand the criticisms that all politicians endure. After being on a team that was occasionally booed by the hometown fans and second-guessed in the media, later political criticism was not that daunting.

After graduation, Ford faced a difficult decision. There were pro football teams interested in him, but Ford did not feel that a football career would lead him very far, so he decided to become a lawyer. He wrote in his autobiography that he never saw himself as becoming a great public orator like William Jennings Bryan, but he thought that he could make a difference as a mediator. This mindset was consistent with his moderate political outlook; Ford usually positioned himself in the middle on issues and tried to bring together those with more extreme positions.

Ford wanted to go to law school but could not afford it, so he took a job as an assistant football coach for Yale's football team, hoping to get into Yale's law school. At first, he was too busy with his coaching responsibilities, but eventually, he was provisionally admitted. After making B's his first term, Ford got accepted into the program.

Ford graduated with his law degree from Yale in 1941 and returned to Grand Rapids, Michigan, to start his practice. Conventional wisdom dictated that Ford join an established firm until he made a name for himself, but Ford and a young friend ambitiously opened up their own firm. Through hard work, they were able to turn a profit within their first two years, but the entry of the United States into World War II interrupted Ford's legal career.

Ford joined the navy and was assigned as a fitness instructor in Maryland. However, he wanted a more active role in the war effort. A year later, Ford was finally assigned to an aircraft carrier and stationed in the Pacific. He faced enemy fire several times over the course of the war and was discharged from the navy in 1946 with the rank of lieutenant commander. His wartime experience changed Ford's views on international affairs. Like most Americans, Ford had been an isolationist during the 1930s. By the time World War II ended, Ford believed that the isolationism of the United States had allowed the totalitarian countries to grow into the menaces that they became. Though the Axis powers were defeated, Ford believed that the United States had to stay vigilant on the international scene because of the threat that communism posed to the world.

At the conclusion of his naval experience, Ford returned to Michigan, resumed his career as a lawyer, and got involved in politics. Ford was disturbed by the political situation in his home state. Though he was a Republican, and the Republican Party dominated in Michigan, a millionaire named Frank D. McKay controlled the party political machine. McKay was a committed isolationist and a foe of the Marshall Plan. With the encouragement of his friends, Ford decided to oppose one of McKay's men for a seat in the House of Representatives.

In that same year, 1948, Ford married Elizabeth "Betty" Warren. Because Ford was an upstart politician going against a well-connected veteran, he was encouraged to keep quiet about his desire to run for office as he networked around the district. He did not even tell Betty Warren for a few months. When Ford proposed to his wife in February 1948, he said, "I'd like to marry you, but I can't marry you until next fall and I can't tell you why."

The Fords had a traditional marriage their first several years together, meaning that Jerry Ford pursued his career, and Betty Ford, who had never pressed her suitor on why he had to wait to marry her, took care of their four children. He was the head of the household, so he did what was best for his career. Whatever outside ambitions Betty Ford might have possessed were sacrificed as she looked after the family. But the strain of being a politician's wife was too much for Betty Ford. She had given up a career as a fashion coordinator for a large department store, and she had never really gained access into her husband's world. There were years when Jerry Ford was away from home for up to nine months. Frustration and loneliness drove Betty Ford to a nervous breakdown in 1965. Afterwards, her husband was much more attentive, and they developed into more of a team. The notion of Jerry Ford making a career decision and keeping it from his wife would never occur to the couple again. In fact, when Nixon called Ford to offer him the vice presidency, Ford asked him to hang up and call back so his wife could listen in on the extension. The breakdown did not just change the Fords' marital relationship; it also changed Betty Ford's philosophy on being a politician's wife. Earlier in April 1954, Betty Ford had advised a group of politicians' wives that silence was a virtue. However, after her breakdown, she decided not to keep her feelings bottled up. She frequently spoke out on issues, even when her views differed from her husband.

In 1949, when Ford began a quarter century career as a member of the House of Representatives, one of the first of his fellow representatives that he met was Richard Nixon. The two men became friends, and their careers were intertwined from then on. Ford was one of eighteen members of the House of Representatives who sent a message to Dwight Eisenhower asking him to run for the Republican nomination for the presidency in 1952. And Ford was happy to hear that Eisenhower picked Nixon to be his running mate. When Nixon ran for the presidency in 1960, Ford campaigned for him. When Nixon lost his race for governor of California in 1962, and ABC ran a special called "The Political Obituary of Richard Nixon," speculating on whether it was the end of his career, Ford was one of the panelists on the show.

Demonstrating the moderate tendencies he had possessed all his life, Ford was a frequent supporter of President John Kennedy. The two had previously established a good rapport working as colleagues in the House of Representatives, despite the fact that Ford had campaigned for Nixon. Ford was particularly supportive of Kennedy's foreign policy issues.

In November 1963, in a show of bipartisanship, Ford was picked by Lyndon Johnson to serve on the Warren Commission, which was tasked with investigating the assassination of Kennedy. The commission agreed that Lee Harvey Oswald was guilty of murder, but there was some disagreement over whether Oswald was part of a larger conspiracy. The commission investigated rumors regarding the FBI, the CIA, the Soviets, and the Cubans among others. Ford, along with the rest of the commission, believed that there was not sufficient evidence of a larger conspiracy. They did discover from a bug in the Soviet embassy in Mexico that Oswald had visited the Soviet and Cuban embassies, but the commission decided not to publish it. Some on the commission wanted to conclude in the final report that there was no conspiracy, but others, including Ford, prevailed on the commission to state that there was no *evidence* of a conspiracy. It was a subtle difference, but in Ford's mind, an important one, and the commission concurred.

Ford's involvement on the Warren Commission left him little time to get involved with presidential politics in 1964. He was distressed that Barry Goldwater had won the Republican nomination. Moderate to the core, Ford was uncomfortable with staunch conservatives like Goldwater. Likewise, he regretted that during his tenure in Congress he did not speak out against Joe McCarthy in the 1950s. Ford believed that

Goldwater would be out of touch with the majority of Americans, and Ford was right. Johnson won by a landslide, and the Democrats picked up seats in both Houses of Congress.

Though things were looking bleak for the Republican Party, Ford's personal political fortune was in much better shape. In 1965, he was chosen by his fellow Republicans to serve as the House Minority Leader. Ford's dream was to become Speaker of the House, but the Republicans needed a majority of the seats in the House for that to happen. When Nixon won his party's nomination as president in 1968, Ford was asked if he was interested in being Nixon's running mate. Ford declined the offer because he felt that the Speaker of the House position was still attainable. The Republicans picked up a few seats in the House in the 1968 elections but not enough for Ford to realize his dream.

Ford became disturbed with the mindset that he saw manifested in the White House during the Nixon administration. Nixon's staff seemed disdainful of Congress, including even Republicans in Congress. There seemed to be no sense of equality between the executive and legislative branches. Nixon preferred not to work with Congress, surrounding himself instead in an almost fortress-like way with a small cadre of personal aides accountable only to Richard Nixon. Republican members in Congress were supposed to do the bidding of the White House, but questions were ignored, and those who openly disagreed with the White House were punished. Increasingly, the White House developed an "us vs. them" attitude with the press and Democratic politicians, as well as with any Republicans who crossed them.

Ford's reaction to the Watergate break-in on June 17, 1972, was actually the same as the official White House response. He wondered why anyone would be so dumb and what there could possibly have been to gain by such a foolhardy maneuver. He gave little thought to the incident, until he learned the identities of those involved, men like G. Gordon Liddy. Ford had met Liddy and neither liked nor trusted the man. Ford asked Attorney General John Mitchell directly if Mitchell or anyone at the White House had been involved in Watergate, and Ford was assured that there was no involvement. Naïvely, Ford believed him.

Ford was distracted from Watergate by his opportunity to go to China, which he visited in June of 1972. As a longtime member of Congress, Ford had visited several countries in Asia and Europe over the years, but China had been closed to the United States from the time that the communists had taken over until Nixon's recent visit. Given the circumstances under which Ford became president, he was more ill-prepared than many of his predecessors, but thanks to trips like these, Ford at least had a global perspective.

Despite the Watergate break-in, Ford was optimistic that Nixon would be re-elected in 1972, and Republicans might win a majority of seats in the House of Representatives. Ford, like many Americans, believed Watergate was a minor issue with no connection to the White House. While Richard Nixon won his re-election by a landslide, Republicans still failed to achieve a majority of House seats, depriving Ford once again of his chance to win the speakership. Seeing his dream of becoming speaker dashed yet again, this time in an election that had probably provided his best chance to achieve that goal, Ford concluded that it was time to consider retiring from political life. He decided to run again in 1974, announce his retirement in 1975, and finish out his term in January 1977. He would be sixty-three years old by then, and his wife was already experiencing some health problems, so it seemed a good time to step down.

As 1973 unfolded, the White House was experiencing major problems. Several of Nixon's key men were resigning, and Vice President Spiro Agnew was being investigated for charges of bribery that allegedly occurred while he was both governor of Maryland and vice president. Ford saw Nixon's difficulties as more of a logistical concern, still believing in his innocence. However, Ford was concerned that, with Nixon's administration embroiled in rancorous disputes and accusations, little would get accomplished, and Agnew was yet another unnecessary embarrassment for an administration that already had more than enough problems.

Agnew worked out a plea bargain, resigning October 10, 1973. Ford was contacted that night, inquiring if he had interest in serving as vice president. Ford said he was willing to serve if chosen, but he made it clear that he was not interested in being groomed to run for the presidency in 1976. Ford changed his mind later, but in October 1973 still intended to retire in January 1977. In fact, Ford did not believe that he would actually be selected as vice president. He considered his making the candidates' list a courtesy, a form of political flattery. But Nixon did pick Ford as his vice president, citing at the press conference Ford's suitability to be president in the case of an emergency, the similarity of their views on foreign policy, and Ford's ability to work with Congress. Interestingly, though Nixon had publicly stated that Ford's foreign policy views were of paramount concern, Nixon privately told Ford that, while he should sit in on meetings with the National Security Council, he should predominately involve himself with domestic affairs.

Later, Ford learned that he was actually Nixon's fourth choice for vice president. Nixon had wanted John Connally and made it clear to Ford that Connally was his choice as his successor in 1976, but Nixon's advisors had convinced him that Connally would have a difficult time getting through the confirmation hearings. Nixon had also considered Nelson Rockefeller and Ronald Reagan, but ultimately the former was dismissed as too liberal and the latter as too conservative.

Ford was seen as someone who could help relations between the White House and the media and, even more importantly, the White House and Congress. Nixon's need for such a liaison became even greater after the so-called "Saturday Night Massacre" on October 29, 1973. When Nixon was ordered to turn over the Watergate tapes to Special Prosecutor Archibald Cox, he refused to do so. Cox attempted to secure the tapes through a court order in October 1973. Nixon ordered his Attorney General Elliot Richardson to fire Cox. Richardson refused to comply. The deputy attorney general also rebuffed the president. The "Saturday Night Massacre," followed, as the top two officials of the Justice Department resigned and the special prosecutor was fired at Nixon's behest. The nation was outraged at Nixon's tactics. Ford still believed that the president was innocent of any crimes, though perhaps guilty of extremely poor political sensitivity on the Watergate issue. Many congressional Republicans, however, who generally had never been treated well by the president, had their suspicions.

After a thorough background check by the FBI, Ford breezed thorough his confirmation hearings in the Senate (where he was approved 92 to 3) and the House (387 to 35). At his confirmation ceremony, Ford displayed his sense of humor, saying in reference to his speaking ability, "I am a Ford, not a Lincoln."

Helping Nixon navigate through the Watergate mess dominated most of Ford's attention after assuming the vice presidency. Ford still wanted to believe that Nixon was innocent, but it was impossible to ignore that the corruption went deeper than Ford first realized. Ford grew increasingly frustrated by Watergate and the damage that it was beginning to cause the Republican Party. Politics aside, Ford was also concerned about Nixon on a personal level. Nixon began to corner top officials, such as Ford and Henry Kissinger, and launch into long, rambling monologues about politics, important issues, and personal anecdotes. Such pointless discussions and an unfocused, depressed president were not a reassuring sight.

By the end of July 1974, the House Judiciary Committee had voted in favor of three articles of impeachment against Nixon. On August 1, Nixon's Chief of Staff, Alexander Haig, encouraged Ford to "start thinking about a change" in his life, signally to the new vice president that Nixon's resignation was imminent. A few days later, Ford said in a speech that he could no longer express a "belief that on the basis of the evidence . . . the President is not guilty of an impeachable offense." Ford went on to say that he would no longer intervene publicly on the Watergate matter in support of Nixon.

The next morning, at the regularly scheduled cabinet meeting, Ford was stunned when Nixon began the meeting by saying, "I would like to discuss the most important issue confronting the nation and confronting us internationally too—inflation. Our economic situation could be the major issue in the world today." When Nixon finally did get around to talking about Watergate, he told Ford and his cabinet that he was too involved in foreign affairs when the break-in occurred, and he was not attentive enough to the problem. He told them he intended to fight on for the sake of the Constitution. Nixon tried to focus on other issues, but Ford, Republican National Committee Chairman George Bush, and others kept the focus on Watergate and the trouble it was causing for Republicans and for the country as a whole. Ford saw a man who was in denial and avoiding the inevitable.

On August 9, 1974, Nixon finally bowed to circumstances and resigned, after which Ford was sworn in as president. Ford had not imagined himself as president or spent time campaigning for it. He had not won the presidency after months of staking out positions on the issues, developing an agenda, and trying to think and act "presidential." He did not have months to assemble a group of like-minded men and women to fight for his political interests. He had been thrust into the presidency with one day's warning. Knowing Nixon's demise was going to be a reality, it would have been unseemly for Ford to begin preparations for office before Nixon's departure. Perhaps such a course of action would have been best for the country, but that was not the way Ford was going to treat an old friend, and for all of Nixon's flaws, Ford still considered Nixon a friend. That friendship might well have been Ford's undoing as president.

The Ford Presidency: A Positive Assessment

When Richard Nixon resigned on August 9, 1974, Gerald Ford took over a seriously troubled nation. Public faith and confidence in government had continued to decline amidst deceptions in the Vietnam War, the abuses of power shown by Watergate, and the lingering problem of what to do with Nixon. Many politicians and media figures, not to mention a sizable percentage of the American population in general, wanted to know what was to become of the disgraced former president. Nixon's shadow over the Ford administration was greater than just the Watergate scandal itself. It all had happened so suddenly that Ford did not have months to put together his presidential team the way other presidents had. Ford brought in some of his own people but with many jobs to fill was stuck with Nixon holdovers, resulting with many positions in the White House held, at least temporarily, by people whose loyalty was divided at best—people who wanted to protect Nixon and his legacy. Many of those who stayed had developed an "us vs. them" mentality under Nixon, and they had worked in a climate that valued results over legal technicalities. In many cases these people did not mesh well with Ford's people or with Ford's agenda and political philosophy.

Another task that awaited Ford was re-orienting American foreign policy in the post-Vietnam War world. Vietnam was still a volatile situation even though American troops were out. Also, the chronic conflicts on Cyprus between the Greeks and Turks were flaring up again, and as Ford well knew, fighting anywhere could lead to fighting everywhere during the cold war. On the domestic front, Ford inherited a slumping economy with inflation at 12 percent and a stock market, as Ford put it, "jittery." And the Republican Ford had to deal with all of these problems while sharing power with a Democrat-controlled Congress. Making things even more difficult, Congress had passed laws limiting the president's powers in both foreign policy (specifically the usage of troops) and domestic policy (budget making). As Bob Woodward put it in his book, *Shadow*, "It was as if the presidency were being punished for the excesses and sins of Nixon and Lyndon Johnson."

Ford set about differentiating himself from his predecessor from the outset of his administration. Before being sworn in, he instructed the Marine Band to play the "Michigan Fight Song" instead of "Hail to the Chief." Ford wanted to communicate to the public that Nixon's aloof, secretive "imperial presidency" was being replaced with midwestern

376 Gerald R. Ford

simplicity. Their new president was going to be one of the people. Ford also ordered that all secret recording devices be removed from the White House and asked his key advisors to create a new code of ethics for the White House staff. Nixon had tried to blame his staff for getting him in trouble; Ford was trying to make sure that his staff could not create a similar problem for him.

Some of Ford's people, like speechwriter and senior advisor Robert Hartmann, criticized Ford for keeping so many of Nixon's people for as long as he did. But Ford allowed most of the Nixon people to continue doing their jobs, or if he moved them, it was simply to serve the Ford administration in a different capacity. Ford, as usual, took the principled approach. He believed that it unfair to fire Nixon appointees who were not necessarily corrupt just because they were hired under Nixon. Also, it simply was not practical to replace a large number of high-ranking officials overnight. For Ford to assemble his own cabinet would have been difficult because these people were only guaranteed work for slightly less than two and a half years.

One position in the White House that needed to be filled immediately was the office of the vice president. Ford made a wise move when he chose Nelson A. Rockefeller as his running mate. Ford had to make a fast decision to fill this very important vacancy, and he chose someone that a skeptical public would be convinced was trustworthy. Other leading candidates, like George Bush, Ronald Reagan, and Elliot Richardson, all had previous ties to Nixon. They were not accused of any wrongdoing (except for an unfounded claim that Bush had received an improper contribution for a 1970 Senate bid), but they were linked to the disgraced ex-president. Bush had worked as the chairman for the Republican National Committee, Reagan had campaigned in California for Nixon, and Richardson had been Nixon's Attorney General. Rockefeller was a liberal Republican, and as such, his links with Nixon were few. In fact, there was some evidence that Rockefeller had been a target of Nixon's dirty tricks. What better Republican choice was there than someone who was a victim of Nixon's corruption? Also, besides his intelligence and experience, as a liberal Republican, he was more likely to garner positive comments from leading Democrats and the mainstream media. And praise from those sources was sorely needed for the beleaguered Republican Party.

Ford's pardon of Nixon has been a controversial part of Ford's legacy, frequently described as one of his failures and a major factor in his loss in the 1976 election to Jimmy Carter. By pardoning Nixon, Ford had intended to heal the nation's wounds. So, on September 8, 1974, Ford announced to the press that he had granted Richard Nixon a free and full pardon saying, "My conscience tells me that only I, as president, have the constitutional power to firmly shut and seal this book." Many angry Americans believed that Ford and Nixon had struck some kind of political deal, despite the lack of evidence to support this charge. Some complained that Ford should have at least demanded some kind of confession from Nixon in exchange for the pardon, but such a confession would not have made the pardon "free." Besides, accepting the pardon, which Nixon did, met a legal precedent for a claim of responsibility. Some have complained that it was wrong for Nixon to get "off the hook" when several of his subordinates were already in jail, but it was argued that, given Nixon's higher profile and his loss of the White House, Nixon had already suffered significant punishment.

Ford offered the pardon for several reasons. He felt that the media was too obsessed with the continuing Watergate drama and that it was time for the nation to move forward. Ford believed that there was considerable public and political sentiment that Nixon had been hounded enough. Ford was concerned about reports regarding Nixon's physical and mental health, as the former president tried to cope with what he had lost and what he still faced. When Ford's aides urged him to wait on the pardon, Ford disagreed, believing that those against the pardon would not be mollified with the passage of time. Perhaps Ford best described his feelings to Robert Hartmann, who later wrote about the conversation in his book, *Palace Politics*, saying, "But all you have to do is say you haven't decided." The president replied, "But I *have* decided." Such simple honesty seems like a rare commodity among politicians.

Ford also felt pressed by a sticky legal issue. By tradition when a president left office, all of his personal papers and records were his property. Nixon's tapes and papers made up a massive amount of material, and the Ford administration blocked the removal of that material from the White House because portions of it were subject to being subpoenaed by investigators. If Nixon's people had been allowed to remove the material, which they tried to do one weekend, there would have been a firestorm of protest. And if Nixon and his supporters destroyed the records, critics would accuse Ford and his aides as conspirators to obstruct justice. On the other hand, the material was technically Nixon's property, so the Ford administration was uncomfortable with holding onto it. Besides, Nixon needed his records to help prepare for his legal defense, if it came to that, and he needed them to help him write his memoirs, which would pay his legal bills.

If the pardoning of Nixon had been intended to heal the nation's wounds, so too was the September 16, 1974 proclamation offering clemency to approximately 28,000 Vietnam War era draft evaders and military deserters. A form of limited amnesty would be granted in return for a sworn oath of allegiance and performance of two years of alternative public service. As for those already convicted for draft evasion or desertion, the president created a nine-member clemency board to review their cases. Although Ford's proclamation never used the controversial term "amnesty," it was a step toward what the president called the "reconciliation . . . and restoration of essential unity of Americans within which honest differences of opinion do not descend to angry discord and mutual problems are not polarized by excessive passion." The decision was controversial, with Ford receiving hundreds of medals from veterans as a sign of protest; however, he tried to put the divisiveness of the war in the past.

Ford was derisively called a "caretaker" president by some critics, a guy who was just minding the store until a more presidential figure could be elected in 1976. But after settling into the office, Ford managed to put his own stamp on things. For example, Ford sat down personally with members of the media to go over detailed plans for his 1977 budget proposal. No president had done this since Harry Truman went over the 1953 budget with the press. But Truman's budget was $43 billion and was 80 pages; Ford's budget was $394.2 billion and was 955 pages. Ford knew that such a press briefing was politically dangerous. His aides discouraged him, reasoning that anyone would inevitably make some mistakes trying to explain such a massive volume of material, especially to a critical media audience. If Ford made those mistakes, or if he had to refer some of the more technical or specific questions to others, it could create the image that he did not really know what he was talking about. But Ford decided the risks were worth it. Unlike some of his more immediate predecessors, like Johnson and Nixon who did not want to get bogged down in budget details, Ford thought the budget proposal was one of the most important things he could produce, reflecting the values and priorities of an administration. After an hour and a half and the fielding of fifty-six questions from the press, Ford believed that he had proved that he was competent enough to do the job.

A chronic problem that plagued the Johnson and Nixon administrations and that would plague Carter and the early part of the

Reagan administration was the economy. Social spending had increased dramatically since the 1960s, and military expenditures were high during the Vietnam War. Some in Congress wanted to cut defense spending, but those who were hawkish on defense opposed, as did those whose home districts would be affected by cuts. The growing budgets coupled with the energy crisis led to troubling economic news. The inflation rate was over 12 percent in 1974. The wholesale price index rose 3.7 percent in July 1974, which was the second worst monthly increase since 1946. The stock market looked bleak with the Dow Jones industrial averages at less than 780 when Ford became president. The unemployment rate hit 6 percent in October 1974, with more workers trying to get jobs than at any time in American history.

Although Ford prided himself on his good relations with both Houses of Congress, he had difficulties in working with a Congress controlled by Democrats. And Ford, far less flexible than Nixon, responded to rising inflation in a much more traditional Republican fashion by tightening the money supply, reducing government spending, and raising interest rates. Ford also launched his voluntary "Whip Inflation Now" (WIN). American refusal to buy overly expensive goods and willingness to stop demanding higher wages would supposedly defeat inflation. The president announced the program at a national press conference with WIN buttons for the press corps to wear in their lapels. WIN proved to be totally inadequate in dealing with the economic crisis. The economic problems of the United States continued to escalate.

Ford wanted to remove acreage limitations on farmers of key crops, hoping that greater production would lead to lower food prices. Because of the skyrocketing price of gasoline, Ford encouraged a reduction in the United States' dependence on oil. Ford asked for a one-year tax increase to pay for short-term government programs to stimulate certain industries, to provide more government jobs, and to increase unemployment benefits. However, his advisors informed Ford on November 1974 that the nation was moving from a high inflation rate straight into a recession. They were proved correct as the Gross National Product dropped 8 percent in the fourth quarter of 1974, and unemployment climbed over 7 percent in December. It would be the worst economy downturn since the Great Depression. Ford wanted to act decisively, but doing so actually made him look indecisive. When Ford dropped his WIN agenda in favor of contradictory measures, he appeared to be waffling on the economy, creating the impression that he did not know what he was doing. Ford initially chose to attack unemployment through government programs that cost money, so he had requested the one-year increase in taxes. Because of the looming recession, some Democrats in Congress and newspapers like the *New York Times* called for larger increases in government spending than Ford had advocated. But Ford feared that such an approach would lead to huge budget deficits. Nixon's budget had predicted a $9.4 billion deficit, but Ford feared that new spending proposals would increase the deficit to $25-$30 billion. Interest rates could increase, which would damage the economy, making it harder for businesses and consumers to get manageable loans. Ford believed that the best thing for the long-term economic health of the country was a tight limit on federal growth and tax cuts that would spur the economy by giving businesses and consumers more of their own money to invest. To change from advocating a tax increase to advocating a tax cut in just a couple of months could prove embarrassing for Ford, but he believed that he was acting in the best interests of the country.

Ford also signed the Emergency Jobs and Unemployment Assistance Act and the Emergency Employment Compensation Act, which created 100,000 new public service jobs and extended unemployment benefits by thirteen weeks. The $2.75 billion price tag was higher than Ford would have liked, but it was much less than Congress had originally requested. Budget battles with Congress were seemingly a never-ending problem, but by the election of 1976, he was justifiably pleased with the improved performance of the economy.

By late 1975, New York City was near financial collapse. It was unable to meet its payroll and pay its bonds. New York City Mayor Abraham D. Beame, with the support of most of his state's most prominent politicians, asked the federal government to bail out the city. President Ford let it be known that he would veto any federal bailout bill passed by Congress. A headline in a New York newspaper ruefully summarized his attitude: "Ford to City: Drop Dead." Ford believed that New York City was responsible for its own troubles. From 1965 through 1974, the city's expenses had increased on average 12 percent per year, while its revenue had increased by about 5 percent. The federal government was already paying 25 percent of the city's budget. New York City residents had luxuries that were not offered in other cites, and Ford did not think it was right to ask American taxpayers to pay for these luxuries. Eventually, New York City was provided the opportunity to receive federal loans based on the promise that they pay the federal government back at the end of each fiscal year, and the interest rates on the loans would always be 1 percent higher than the existing rate.

A long-time supporter of the war in Vietnam, Gerald Ford had the misfortune of occupying the White House during the debacle of the final days of that conflict. In April 1975, as the network television cameras recorded the scene, the public watched the pathetic evacuees scramble for helicopters, attempting to flee Saigon.

Two weeks later he achieved a small victory of sorts. The communist regime in Cambodia captured an American cargo ship, the *Mayaguez*. Ford authorized a military rescue. Americans reacted favorably to this macho response, ignoring that forty-one men died to free the ships' thirty-nine crewmembers. One proud senator gloated, "It shows we've still got balls in this country."

Ford deserves credit though for building on the relationship with the communist Chinese that Nixon had fostered. By continuing dialogue with China, a bitter rival to the Soviet Union, Ford was able to negotiate with more strength with the Soviets. Following the withdrawal from Vietnam, Congress was less inclined to support policies that directly confronted the Soviets, especially if it could lead to a renewed commitment of U.S. military personnel to some remote corner of the third world. Hence, when Ford asked Congress in 1975 for permission to dispatch American military advisors to Angola to help shore up that country's military against communist insurgents, Congress quickly denied the request. In the post-Vietnam world the Truman Doctrine, which had led to American military interventions to stop communist movements from Asia to the Americas, was dead. Such a withdrawal of America power could have put Ford at a complete disadvantage when it came to negotiating with the Soviets over things like arms control. But Soviet concerns over a possible alliance between the United States and China was one key factor that kept them from being too demanding in their negotiations with the United States. Ford was not able to reach any truly significant arms control agreements with the Soviets, but he did keep the negotiations alive, leading to further, more productive negotiations under Jimmy Carter. Ford was also able to engage the Soviets in substantive discussions at the international conference held in Helsinki in 1975.

Known as the Conference on Security and Cooperation in Europe, the conference produced the U.S./Soviet Helsinki Accords. In exchange for the western democracies acknowledging the reality of Soviet influence in Eastern and Central Europe, the Soviets promised not to expand their borders in Europe, and they promised to abide by international standards for human rights. The Soviets had wanted such a western acknowledgement of their hegemony over their Eastern European satellites since the 1950s. American presidents had not been interested in such accords previously because it looked like the accords were only designed to benefit the Soviets, so the Soviets had begun to offer concessions in an effort to secure United States participation. By Helsinki, the Soviets were willing to promise to reach an understanding on the status of West Berlin and to engage in negotiations on mutual and balanced force reduction (MBFR) in Europe. The accords were signed by thirty-five nations, including the United States. Ford believed that the decision to participate in the conference and sign the accords was just common sense. If the Soviets failed to observe the human rights standards, their people would be no worse off than before, but if there was a chance the Soviets would abide by the agreement, then their people would be treated better. The United States, Ford reasoned, had no intention of going to war to oust the communists from Eastern Europe. Signing the agreement only recognized the facts on the ground, while defusing any desire the Soviets might have in the wake of U.S. post-Vietnam weakness to reaffirm their position in Europe by some form of foreign policy adventurism. Cold war conservatives such as Ronald Reagan grumbled, but Ford was convinced that he was doing the right thing to help the U.S. peacefully navigate a particularly unstable stretch of the cold war. With this decision, as with so many things during his administration, Ford avoided the extremes and took the more moderate course.

The Ford Presidency: A Negative Assessment

The Ford presidency began under the black cloud left by the scandal-ridden and disgraced Nixon administration. Since Ford was Richard Nixon's choice for the vice presidency, and the public had passed judgment on Nixon as completely corrupt, Ford was tainted at least somewhat in the minds of many by simple association, and his new administration was potentially critically—and perhaps fatally—undermined by the questionable nature of its origins. One of the single greatest successes of the Ford presidency, therefore, was Ford's ability to garner a high degree of public approval, thereby reasserting the legitimacy of the presidency when he first became president. Ford's greatest failure was to squander the popularity he had accrued by bringing honor and integrity back to the Oval Office through his indecision and waffling on numerous issues.

Ford ultimately became unpopular not because he followed Nixon, but because of what he did when he followed Nixon.

Perhaps the roots of Ford's failures as president stemmed from the fundamental ambivalence that he brought to the job. Those close to Ford have often said that he never wanted to be president, supposedly a positive quality, indicating that he was not power hungry or craving adulation. Bob Woodward, the reporter who helped uncover the Watergate scandal and author of many articles about the presidents, believed that Ford's lack of ambition for the presidency was core to the problem. Describing Ford and the presidency, Woodward wrote in his book *Shadow*, "He had not . . . wanted the job. He had not studied for it. He did not have a theory about it. There seemed to be few, if any, dreams. He had not examined what the presidency was." Therefore, Ford conducted his affairs in a less than presidential manner.

Ford had been a career member of Congress. He knew how to sit in a committee and work out compromises. He was familiar with carving out a middle path between contentious individuals with separate agendas, but he was not as adept at getting people behind his own agenda. Having not sought the presidency, Ford had never attempted to retool a leadership and personal style that worked well in the more collegial halls of Congress (at least within the House Republican caucus) into the assertive, commander in chief style necessary to lead a nation rather than the House of Representatives. Used to seeing petty bickering, selfishness, and outright venality displayed as daily-accepted behavior in Congress, Ford was far too tolerant of similar behaviors in his own White House. He did not manage his subordinates appropriately, for example, never either fully resolving the animosity that naturally developed between Nixon holdovers in his administration and the new people he brought in by either knocking heads together or simply purging the recalcitrant members of the ancient regime. Ford did not immediately grasp the importance of finding like-minded individuals to follow him unwaveringly. Other lingering legacies of his congressional days, such as his tendency to drink too much before some of his public speaking engagements—a tolerable congressional foible in the eyes of a press corps jaded in its view of the people's representatives—undercut his effectiveness in the national bully pulpit.

Ford was a moderate, but he became a muddled moderate, spending his presidency searching for an elusive middle ground between Democrats less willing to trust any Republican administration after Richard Nixon and increasingly assertive Republican conservatives typified by Ronald

Reagan who were tired of compromise with the Democratic left. These conservatives would solidify their hopes and support around Ronald Reagan in the Ford years, which almost cost Ford his own party nomination in 1976. All of these things worked against Ford as he tried to guide the country. His first and biggest problem, however, was Richard Nixon.

The Nixon pardon bedeviled Ford not just for his having done it, but also because of the inept manner in which it was done. Ford pardoned Nixon barely a month into his presidency. Thereafter, the press and public learned that Ford had been in a private meeting with Nixon's last Chief of Staff, former General Alexander Haig, scarcely more than a week before Nixon resigned. In the weeks leading up to the resignation, Ford tried to make sure that one of his people was present at such meetings with Nixon staffers, specifically because he wanted to have witnesses around to verify that he was not drawn into the Watergate morass. Ford's wise precautionary stance failed him in the Haig meeting. During their forty-five minute meeting, Haig shared the transcript of one of Nixon's famous secret tapes; it had not been turned over to the authorities yet, though it was about to be, and it would cast Nixon in a very bad light. Haig briefed Ford that Nixon was considering the idea of pardoning himself and then resigning, or resigning and then being pardoned. Ford told Haig he needed time to digest all this information. At the time, Ford was oblivious to how bad this meeting between the two of them would look.

Nixon was considering giving up the fight but was worried about going to jail. Having his aide meet with Ford to discuss a possible pardon, and then Ford's issuing a surprisingly fast pardon for Nixon without even requiring an admission of guilt, tainted both the pardon process and Ford's integrity. Had Ford been more politically adept at the machinations of presidential politics, he would have avoided the private Haig meeting and later demanded far more from Nixon such as a public apology as the price tag for pardon.

Ford also waffled on the issuing of the pardon itself. Just eleven days before the pardon was offered, Ford had declared there was no need to be hasty on the matter. Nixon had not yet been charged with anything, Ford argued, so talk of a pardon was premature. But then Ford issued the pardon within a fortnight. Overnight, Gerald Ford's approval rating dropped from over 70 percent to 49 percent. The public questioned the pardon of Nixon, when his advisers were not accorded the same treatment. Haldeman, Erlichman, and Mitchell were found guilty of participation in the Watergate affair and along with other participants were sentenced to prison. Press coverage, which had been generally positive for the new president overall, became harsher, and pundits became positively vitriolic. The new president began to get booed at public appearances. The day after the pardon was announced, Ford appeared at an urban transportation conference in Pittsburgh, and some of those assembled began to chant, "Jail Ford, jail Ford." The unpopularity of the decision was even present in the president's inner circle: his press secretary, Jerry TerHorst, resigned in protest the day Ford announced the pardon.

That Ford had trouble selling the pardon to his own senior staff merely underscored the trouble he had with the public at large. Ford argued that "compassion for Nixon as an individual hadn't prompted my decision at all." But Phil Buchen, Ford's former law partner and his White House Counsel, and TerHorst separately referred to the pardon as "an act of mercy." Long-time Ford aide Robert Hartmann wrote that Ford had concerns in regards to Nixon's physical and mental health and would never have forgiven himself if Nixon's health deteriorated, or if Nixon committed suicide while Ford delayed his decision for political gain.

But Ford's desire to move on from Watergate misfired. In his second news conference after the pardon announcement, fifteen of the twenty-two questions from the press pertained to the pardon or to Nixon. The Senate, meanwhile, passed a resolution by 55 to 24 opposing any further pardons for Watergate figures until they had been convicted and had exhausted their appeals.

Ford's failure to quickly purge his White House of Nixon holdovers fundamentally undercut the efficacy of his staff and hampered his efforts to achieve the clean break with the past that he sought. The Nixonites continued to be more loyal to Nixon and his policies than they were to the new president. They were not supportive of ideas that differed philosophically with what Nixon had tried to implement during his time as president. Nixon had brought these individuals into the White House because they were kindred spirits, and there was little that they saw in Ford which inspired them to change their views. Hartmann had bitter memories of these Nixon holdovers. In his book on the Ford administration, *Palace Politics*, Hartmann described their methods of operation. "What they could not prevent they could delay. What they could no longer delay they could cause to fail. What they could not make fail they could alter. What they had altered was no longer the President's idea and should be discarded. After awhile initiators of new ideas simply gave up." While Hartmann's description of life in the Ford White House helps to explain the lack of a consistent plan by the president for addressing the country's problems, it does not exonerate Ford. For his part, the president wrote that he knew there was tension within his staff, but he thought Hartmann himself was the cause of a good deal of it. Given the suddenness of Ford's elevation to the presidency, it is not surprising that in the first few months there were staffing problems and loyalty issues. But not confronting these inner staff rivalries hindered his ability for successful initiatives to come out of the White House.

As Ford's subordinates frequently clashed during his presidency with Nixon loyalists, Ford himself tried to stay above the fray (thus contributing to the confusion) though he himself did directly clash with one of the more significant Nixon holdovers, Secretary of Defense James Schlesinger. Schlesinger was amazingly insubordinate, and Ford's slowness in dealing with this problem was equally amazing. As South Vietnam fell in April 1975, Ford was unable to get Congress to empower him to do much of anything besides give the final orders to turn out the lights in the Saigon Embassy. Ford decided that he would at least do what little his situation and resources allowed by ordering Schlesinger to send in an American transport aircraft to rescue as many South Vietnamese loyalists as possible before the inevitable triumph of the North. Schlesinger disagreed with the order, however, believing any reintroduction of American forces into South Vietnam to be foolhardy, so he simply ignored it. Ford, displaying his recurrent pattern of weakness in dealing with subordinates, failed to confront his cabinet officer about it. The rescue planes were never dispatched.

Ford and Schlesinger clashed again the following month in May 1975, when communist Cambodian forces captured an American merchant vessel, the *Mayaguez*, carrying a crew of thirty-nine. Ford ordered a military rescue mission, which succeeded in freeing the crew, though at the cost of the lives of forty-one American military personnel. Ford further ordered four military strikes against Cambodia as punishment for their aggression. Perhaps emboldened by his earlier, unpunished insubordination, Schlesinger decided not to follow these orders either, once again desiring to avoid reengagement in Southeast Asia. He actually lied (or, as Pentagon parlance would have it, he disseminated misinformation) to the president, telling Ford that the first strike had been carried out. When Ford did not follow up and query Schlesinger about the additional attacks, Schlesinger simply committed the sin of omission and did not bring the matter up. When Ford found out that none of the strikes had taken place, he still failed to confront his Defense Secretary. This subject was either so embarrassing or so painful for Ford that he glossed over it in his autobiography. The incidents undercut Ford's authority with other Nixonites, however, and became the subject of the Washington gristmill at the expense of the president's credibility. Ford did not finally decide to fire the man for the better part of another half a year. As described by Woodward, Ford invited Schlesinger into the Oval Office on November 2, 1975, to explain to his wayward Secretary the need for Ford to have his own team in place and how, through his repeated insubordinations, Schlesinger had not made the cut. When Schlesinger realized the purpose of the conversation, he asked the president directly if he was going to be fired. When Ford answered in the affirmative, Schlesinger abruptly walked out on the meeting, demonstrating his disrespect for his president one last time. During the height of the cold war, since America had lost status because of the events in Vietnam, the inability of the President of the United States to hold the respect of his own Secretary of Defense directly undermined the nation's global credibility. Ford should have handled the matter in a more expedient (if ruthless) fashion.

Ford's image problem continued throughout his brief presidency, costing him dearly. The man who never had serious presidential ambitions never tried to develop a presidential image and, thus, came off as less than presidential. Even the man who set him on the path to the presidency, Richard Nixon, had disparaging remarks to Ford's future vice president, Nelson Rockefeller, regarding whether he could imagine Jerry Ford as president. (Ford carried some hard feelings for Nixon over the fact when he became privy to that little piece of Washington gossip.) Beyond the obvious indignities of his frequent physical pratfalls, Lyndon Johnson had once noted, cynically and unkindly, that Ford's problems resulted from having "played football at the University of Michigan too often without a helmet" and Chevy Chase—"Saturday Night Live" style parodies—bolstered the public perception of President Ford as an inept bungler. (The president's propensity to bump his head when disembarking from Air Force One or hitting spectators with golf balls only reinforced this image.) Ford lacked an air of gravitas—he came across as what he was—a man who had stumbled into power. Ford had gotten used to the lifestyle as a member of Congress where media scrutiny was not nearly as intense as it was for a president. Part of that lifestyle for some was, and is, drinking alcohol liberally at lunch. As president, Ford developed a minor image problem due to a "three martini" ethic. While in Congress, it would not have been an issue for the press; it is certainly something more than a few members of Congress and the business world enjoy. As president, Ford no longer got by on his free congressional pass. (Indeed, the road to the White House is littered with the shattered remnants of campaigns by members of Congress and Senators who forgot that behavior acceptable on Capitol Hill did not pass muster on the presidential trail.) Ford's personal habits caught up with him more than once while in the Oval Office. At a speech in Denver, he skipped more than twenty pages of his text; incredulously, the explanation floated by his aides was that the president had been drinking. On at least one other occasion, drinking had led to slurred speech during a public appearance. Several aides, including White House physician William Lukash, concerned with the damage being done to Ford's image confronted the president, urging him to cut back on his libations.

Ford's policy problems and resulting troubles with the public during his brief presidency almost cost him the 1976 Republican nomination, and it did cost him the fall general election. The near miss of the nomination and the fatal hit of the election were closely intertwined. By all measures, an incumbent president (even one who had achieved office through an irregular route) should have had a decisive advantage against a little known one-term governor from a small Southern state. Indeed, Democrat James Earl Carter's limited executive experience at the state level and lack of exposure on the national scene should have given Ford a substantial advantage. The support of Carter by most Democrats could be expected, but he was not the most attractive candidate to independent voters or even socially conservative Southern Democrats who had rallied around the Wallace campaign banner in 1968 and would rally around Reagan in 1980. Despite his incumbency, Ford still lost the election in 1976, and part of the reason was that he lost the support of the increasingly powerful conservative wing of the GOP. Ford lost this support primarily because of three people: Vice President Nelson Rockefeller, First Lady Betty Ford, and Ronald Reagan (who was Ford's challenger for the Republican nomination in 1976).

Rockefeller represented the moderate-liberal wing of the Republican party, which had been on the decline since Goldwater's nomination in 1964. Yet, with his own middle of the road tendencies, Ford was more comfortable with Rockefeller's side of the party than with Goldwater's, which had gravitated towards the leadership of the dynamic new conservative Governor of California (and former actor) Ronald Reagan from the mid 1960s onwards. While Ford chose Rockefeller as his vice president precisely because the moderate Republican stood a good chance of an easy confirmation vote by the Democratic Congress (and, indeed, the nomination was greeted with mostly favorable remarks from Democratic leaders and members of the media), the very fact of such a friendly Democratic reception raised conservative hackles. While conservative Republicans ultimately had to accept Rockefeller as a temporary vice president, they did not have to accept him as having a permanent claim on the position for the 1976 ticket. Indeed, as the election year began, conservatives increasingly questioned whether they would have to have Ford on the ticket, either. With rising pressure from the GOP's right flank, Rockefeller decided, for the sake of party unity and, more importantly, to protect fellow moderate Ford, to voluntarily step aside. Yet Ford derived little benefit from the elimination of Rockefeller from the ticket; the move alienated liberal Republicans and emboldened conservatives, who would now seek to dump Ford from the ticket, too. Ford's pre-election administration shakeup, including the dumping of Rockefeller and the firing of Defense Secretary James Schlesinger, actually produced a negative backlash from both political ends of the media spectrum as well. Conservative George Will called the firing of Schlesinger "a foolish thing done in a foolish way." Liberal Joseph Kraft said Ford's moves "stimulated new doubts as to whether he has the brains to be President." Any points that Ford had wished to gain over Rockefeller's departure were lost.

Conservatives were also upset with public views that First Lady Betty Ford took, and the president's response to the airing of those views. During a controversial interview with Morley Safer on *60 Minutes*, Betty Ford went on the record stating that her children had probably tried marijuana, and had it been popular when she was younger, she probably would have as well. When asked what she thought of the *Roe vs. Wade* ruling, legalizing abortions, Mrs. Ford said the ruling "was the best thing in the world; a great, great decision." To say the least, these were not prim and proper Pat Nixon style responses. Indeed, while one can perhaps debate whether or not the First Lady's comments sounded moderate to the public at large, they enraged social conservatives. President Ford was left in an awkward position; even if he disagreed personally with his wife's statements—which was not a given—it would have been difficult, at best, for Ford to publicly criticize her. While many applauded the First Lady's views and her candor and independence, most of those people were not going to vote Republican.

By 1976, conservative Republicans were increasingly tiring of the accommodations that their more moderate kinsmen had made with the social welfare state. Ford's desires for tax increases to pay for increased social spending was particularly anathema to them. Conservatives were also galled by the policy of détente with the communists begun under Nixon and continued under Ford through the personage of Henry Kissinger. The Secretary of State was one of the few Nixon holdovers who actually worked well with Ford, who had little foreign policy experience coming into office. Conservatives preferred a more red meat anti-communism than Kissinger, with his suspect European-style balance of power diplomacy. Indeed, they found accommodation with the ultimate evil of the twentieth century (and for American conservatives, communism was always seen as the greater evil than even fascism) morally repugnant and longed for a leader willing to pursue not just a peaceful coexistence with this evil but ultimately to triumph over it. Thus, conservatives rallied around the former Governor of California, Ronald Reagan, who used his 1976 presidential run to blast Ford and moderate Republicans on both social and foreign policy grounds. Reagan was steeped in the returning laissez faire ideals of political freedom that came to define postwar neo-conservatism. He rejected the intrusion of government into more and more spheres of economic life (but not into the social sphere to uphold traditionally cultural values—Reagan was no Libertarian) as a fundamental violation of such political freedom. Passionate anti-communism was a natural extension of these views. Reagan, who would thrill the conservative wing of the party by his willingness to forgo the niceties of diplomatic language and call a spade a spade (or a ruthless communist dictator a ruthless communist dictator), was repulsed by Nixon's willingness to compromise with communists and believed that Ford was taking the country further down the line of what ultimately amounted to appeasement of evil.

Reagan believed that Congress had lost the will to fight in Vietnam and had shamelessly let North Vietnam violate its treaty with the United States and overrun South Vietnam. Reagan blasted Ford for not doing more for the South, which was unfair, as Ford was limited by Congress in this matter. (Reagan's administration would later prove itself far more willing to ignore congressionally imposed limits on foreign policy activities.) Reagan also blasted Ford for adopting a policy of timidity, which emboldened the Soviet Union to new acts of adventurism, using proxy troops from their Cuban satellite to support communist movements in Angola and other parts of Africa. Meanwhile, Reagan decried the Soviets taking advantage of American naïveté in deals like the Helsinki Accords, solidifying their own positions at U.S. expense. In Reagan's eyes, everything that was wrong with Ford's foreign policy could be summed up in Ford's treatment of Aleksandr Solzhenitsyn, a Nobel Prize-winning Russian author living in exile. Solzhenitsyn, a hero to Reagan, was openly critical of the oppressive communist system in the Soviet Union. There was talk of a meeting between the writer and Gerald Ford, but Ford did not want to meet the man before an upcoming meeting with the Soviets lest paying such attention to the Russian dissident would embarrass the Soviets and sour the negotiations. Reagan saw Ford's handling of the situation as a sign of weakness, appeasing the Soviets while snubbing a champion of freedom. For Reagan, the United States needed to be far stronger in dealing with the communist menace, far more in the Russians' face—one did not compromise with evil.

Ford, however, proved ineffective in responding to Reagan's challenges on the campaign trail, which increasingly undermined Ford's support even amongst some moderate Republicans. Though Ford benefited during the primary run by the wholesale endorsement of the Republican Party establishment (which he had tremendous influence as incumbent president and party leader), he only squeaked by Reagan in the New Hampshire primary and, a month later, lost the critical North Carolina primary by a substantial margin even though Reagan's own campaign was broke and most major Republican organizations (and even many of Reagan's own advisors) were calling on the former governor to drop out of the race. Reagan continued his challenge to Ford straight through to the Republican convention that summer in Kansas City. While Ford ultimately had the delegates to win the nomination on the first ballot, he had to endure several days of somewhat demeaning and very public negotiations, covered offer by counteroffer in the media, in which he tried to buy Reagan off with an offer of the vice presidency, only to have Reagan humiliating send the same offer back. When Reagan went on to deliver the most electrifying speech of the convention, it was clear to see that, while Ford controlled the party political machine, Reagan owned its heart. Thus, foisted on the party faithful by the final act of a disgraced former leader, Ford was never truly able to win the hearts and minds of fellow Republicans. Even Ford's eventual choice of vice-presidential running mate, Kansas Senator Robert Dole, served to alienate as many members of the party as it appeased. As Richard Nixon's protégé, Dole's selection annoyed liberal Republicans still smarting over the dumping of their champion, Nelson Rockefeller, from the ticket, and it annoyed conservative Republicans who wanted a bone tossed their way for having had their champion defeated. Ford's propensity to always go for the middle ground once again backfired as he lost support on the party's flanks.

Ford was ultimately victorious against Reagan, but the president's image was tarnished by having to go through such a challenge. Next, Ford had to contend with Jimmy Carter, whose moralizing rhetoric enabled the southern governor to steal some conservative votes that might have gone to Ford, had not Reagan so magnificently highlighted Ford's lack of conservatism. Carter also sought to invoke the ghost of Watergate by continuously referring to the Nixon-Ford administration.

During his second debate with Jimmy Carter, Ford committed a significant gaffe, saying, "There is no Soviet domination of Eastern Europe, and there never will be in a Ford Administration." Ford meant to say that the peoples of Eastern Europe were very independent-minded and that, even though Soviet troops occupied their countries, the Eastern European spirit would not be broken. He thought it was obvious that the Soviets physically dominated Eastern Europe and believed that his comments needed no elaboration. Carter, however, reacted to the remark with a studied incredulity, which underscored for the nation a sense of Ford's weakness—if not incompetence—in foreign affairs. The press seized on the gaffe—and Carter's immediate response and the public's growing negative reaction to it. Ford's aides suggested that he offer some kind of clarification of his comments. Ford eventually tried to explain himself on the subject but could not quite bring himself to say that he had misspoken. Even his Chief of Staff, Dick Cheney, asked him if he was trying to sabotage his own campaign. Ford was simply guilty of a problem that had manifested itself throughout his brief presidency—he did not properly consider the political ramifications of the situation. The man who had never sought the presidency simply did not think like a president. By the following January, he would no longer be one.

President Gerald R. Ford listens to a briefing by Secretary of State Henry A. Kissinger on the situation in South Vietnam. April 29, 1975 Photo credit: Gerald R. Ford Library

President Ford announcing his pardon of Richard Nixon from the Oval Office. September 8, 1974 Photo credit: Gerald R. Ford Library

Secretary of State Henry Kissinger, General Secretary Leonid Brezhnev, President Ford, and Foreign Minister Andrei Gromydo during the Helsinki Summit. August 2, 1975 Photo credit: Gerald R. Ford Library

(top) President Ford and Jimmy Carter meet at the Walnut Street Theater in Philadelphia to debate domestic policy during the first of the three Ford-Carter Debates. September 23, 1976.
(bottom left) President Ford and daughter Susan at Camp David. September 4, 1974 (bottom right) President and Mrs. Ford offer each other comfort as they watch the election returns. November 2, 1976.
Photo credits: Gerald R. Ford Library

James Earl "Jimmy" Carter
1977-1981

When Gerald Ford took over the Oval Office in August 1974, Americans were relieved that at least for the moment they had a president whose political career was known for its integrity. Moreover, Ford's ascendancy marked the end of the Watergate crisis, one of the most humiliating and debilitating political travesties in modern American history. Initially embraced by the majority of Americans as the man who would help heal those scars, Ford unfortunately squandered his political capital by a single action. While most of the Watergate henchmen were serving jail sentences for carrying out Nixon's orders to obstruct justice, Ford made the most impolitic move of his brief tenure as president by pardoning Nixon for all his transgressions, freeing him forever from being brought before the bar of justice to answer for his abuse of power. The public was stunned. Ford further alienated Americans by vetoing in one year thirty-nine measures, many of which were Great Society initiatives, such as federal aid to education and health-care bills. Ford's rejection of such measures could not have been more untimely or unwise, for the economy was on the verge of its worst recession since the 1930s. Instead of stimulating the economy, Ford's actions helped bring it to a crushing halt by driving interest rates to an all-time high and by vetoing a tax cut designed to give consumers more money to spend.

Although Ford successfully completed his predecessor's foreign policy initiatives in the Middle East (thanks largely to Henry Kissinger's shuttle diplomacy) and secured a new arms control agreement with the Soviet Union, unfortunately, in April 1975, Ford presided over the humiliating withdrawal of the last American personnel in South Vietnam, as North Vietnamese forces invaded that hapless nation. As the NVA closed in on Saigon, television audiences worldwide witnessed the frenzied flight of the last Americans from the rooftop of the United States embassy. As Americans at home watched with disbelief and disgrace, they realized that the United States had lost its first war to a nation that Lyndon Johnson once described as a "tenth rate piss-ant" country. As the 1976 presidential campaign approached, Democrats were euphoric. As one said, "We could run an aardvark this year and win." Compounding Ford's woes was the reemergence of the Republican "hard" right (the "Goldwaterites" of the previous decade), who rallied behind former California governor Ronald Reagan as their new standard-bearer. Reagan's candidacy divided Republicans, with more moderate party members supporting Ford, while conservatives favored Reagan. In short, a party split occurred, making Democrats even more confident of victory. Luckily for Ford, Reagan's campaign floundered long enough on ill-focused ideas that, even after it caught fire (his advisers urged him to forgo specific proposals and instead highlight his image as a "true conservative" and Washington outsider), it was too late. Ford already had won just enough delegates in the early primaries to eke out a narrow, first-ballot victory at the party's convention. Although winning his party's nomination, Ford nonetheless was perceived by many Republicans, regardless of which way they "leaned," to be a less than inspiring choice. To many voters, the GOP was a divided party, both personally and ideologically, and, thus, would be incapable of solving the nation's mounting problems. The Republican split made Democrats even more sanguine of victory; they just had to nominate the right "aardvark."

Although party stalwarts such as Ted Kennedy and Edmund Muskie hoped to secure the Democratic nomination, as the primary season began, it quickly became apparent that even Democratic voters were tired of insiders and were looking for someone with a different message, a different persona, and perhaps, most important, someone not tainted by "inside the Beltway" corruption and self-aggrandizement. The individual who soon emerged that projected such an image was the one-term governor of Georgia, James Earl "Jimmy" Carter. Carter seemed ideally suited to take advantage of the post-Watergate political atmosphere. A deeply moral, "born-again" Christian who prayed daily and cared deeply about his faith, Carter tirelessly campaigned across the country, telling audiences in small towns that they deserved a government as good, as competent, as moral, and "as filled with love as are the American people." Although beginning his campaign with a name-recognition of only 2 percent, he soon racked up primary victories in Iowa, New Hampshire, and Florida. Resurrecting many of the old Populist rhetoric, Carter told Americans what many wanted to hear: that traditional politicians had become so entrenched, so influenced and corrupted by powerful special interests, that they had forgotten who had elected them and whom they were to serve. It was time for someone completely disassociated from such abuses of power to come in and clean up the mess. Carter trumpeted his credentials as an outsider, attacked the bloated bureaucracy of the federal government, and pledged to restore simplicity, decency, and efficiency to the American political process. To further bolster his image of being an honest, Christian man, Carter confessed in one interview to having sinned against the Fifth Commandment by looking upon women (including his wife Rosalynn) "with lust." Rarely had America seen such a candidate. In his personality, his convictions, and his concern for basic American values, Carter succeeded in creating a new image and a sense of fresh hope. In his acceptance speech at the Democratic convention, Carter further bolstered his Populist impression by railing against corporate corruption and theft, pledging to fight for the "little man," and to cleanse the American system of its tax loopholes and vestiges of racial and economic discrimination. With Martin Luther King Sr. at his side, Carter ended his bid for the nomination in a scene reminiscent of the civil rights movement with blacks and whites holding hands together at Madison Square Garden singing "We Shall Overcome."

Although embraced as a refreshing change and political novelty, by Election Day, Carter had lost much of his initial luster. Indeed he had squandered a 33-point lead in the polls, and he now appeared unsure of the direction he should take, thus losing the direct and simple appeal he had used to garner successive victories in the primaries. "He wavers, he wanders, he wiggles, and he waffles," Ford charged, and there was much truth to the president's assertions. Only Ford's image as a "bumbler," "stumbler, and gaffer" (in a televised debate he said, "There is no Soviet domination of Eastern Europe) prevented the incumbent from squeaking out a victory. More telling was the fact that the overwhelming majority of Americans believed neither candidate possessed presidential qualities—80 percent of voters gave a negative assessment of Carter's leadership ability, 76 percent of Ford's. On Election Day, however, enough Americans pulled the lever by Carter's name (Carter won with 51 percent of the votes) to make him the Thirty-ninth President of the United States. As historian Douglas Brinkley declared, it was as close the country had ever come "to picking a name out of the phone book." Moreover, Carter's victory contained a warning: nearly 70 percent of all voters identified economic issues as their main concern. Carter won 75 percent of the votes of those Americans whose primary worry was increasing economic uncertainty, as inflation and unemployment continued unabated. The key question was whether Carter could remedy the economic downturn and whether his presidency could forge a new consensus on how to function within a world of limits. While Carter had Democratic majorities in both houses of Congress to support such a consensus, it was by no means clear that he possessed the vision or leadership to create it and sustain it. For the moment, however, Americans were willing to give this "simple," honest Southerner from Plains, Georgia, whom they hoped represented a new breed of leader, an "apolitical" politician who possessed the moral rectitude and forthrightness to heal the wounds and unite the country in the aftermath of the Vietnam and Watergate traumas. Who was this man, the soft-spoken, born-again Christian peanut farmer with the brilliant smile?

The man who Americans hoped would restore their confidence in the "system" was born on October 1, 1924 in the small (population 600), southwestern Georgia town of Plains. His parents, James Earl and Lillian Gordy Carter, were rural middle class folk. Carter's father was a fairly successful businessman/shopkeeper (a general store owner) and farmer, who even during the Great Depression remained relatively well off compared to most of his neighbors. He participated in local politics, helping candidates in a variety of ways, and eventually ran for office late in his life, becoming a state senator in the 1950s. Ideologically, he was an "Old South—Lost Cause" sentimentalist and, unfortunately, a hardcore segregationist. Nonetheless, Jimmy Carter idolized his father, declaring that his "greatest ambition was to be valuable around the farm and to please my father. He was the center of my life and the focus of my admiration."

Carter's mother, "Miss Lillian," was the complete antithesis of her husband, who over time exerted a far greater, more indelible influence on Carter than James Earl. A longtime civil rights activists, liberal admirer of the Kennedys and LBJ, a registered nurse and director of a nursing home in Blakely, Georgia, Miss Lillian spent her life aiding the impoverished and championing the needy regardless of race, social status, gender, or religion. As Carter noted, "More than anyone else, my mother made me see the inequities around us." Of all Miss Lillian's deeds, it was perhaps her work with the Peace Corps (at age sixty-seven!) that had the greatest impact on Carter. One night while watching television, Miss Lillian saw a public service announcement for the Peace Corps, entreating people to join with the slogan, "Age is No Barrier." Miss Lillian took the advertisement at face value and signed up. "I wanted to work with people who were the underdogs," she noted at the time. She quit her job at the nursing home, entrusted the family peanut business to her two sons, Jimmy and Billy, and after several weeks of preparation courses, left for Bombay, then Vikhroll, India, in September 1966 where she remained for the next two years. During her stay in India, Lillian performed all manner of health-related tasks, ranging from inoculating children against polio, measles, and tuberculosis to "family planning"—introducing local males to the use of contraceptives to assisting with vasectomies. Miss Lillian immersed herself in Hindu culture and religion, finding the teachings of Ghandi and the Bhagavad-Gita fascinating. Indeed, as she told her son Jimmy, "Hinduism is seeping into my dormant mind." She also learned how to speak Marathi and some of the Gujarati dialects, all while teaching the local population about the need for proper sanitary conditions to help prevent dysentery and other dreaded diseases. "My time in India meant more to me than any other thing in my life," she later observed.

Miss Lillian's Peace Corps experiences left an indelible impression on her son Jimmy. While her peers played canasta in Boca Raton, Florida, in their retirement villas, she was making a real difference in a neglected corner of the world. As Miss Lillian told her children, "If I had one wish for my children, it would be that each of you would dare to do the things and reach for goals in your own lives that have meaning for you as individuals, doing as much as you can for everybody, but not worrying if you don't please everyone." Jimmy Carter took his mother's wishes to heart, becoming one of the most humanitarian presidents in the Republic's history, regardless of the consequences to his political career. In short, Lillian Carter's social activism and general liberal ethos, especially when it came to race, helped mitigate her husband's racism and its effect on Jimmy. Indeed, as Carter matured, he became very much his mother's (not his father's) son, embracing all of humanity on an equal basis and, to this day, exhorting others to do the same.

James Earl's effect on Jimmy was not all bad; he inculcated his son with an incredible sense of discipline and ambition to have a life and career that was meaningful and personally (and monetarily) rewarding. Thus, at a young age, Carter, like so many Southern males of his generation, believed that a military career or service helped to better prepare one for the real world. Moreover, attending one of the academies, either West Point or Annapolis, was still considered *de rigueur* for Southern males, one of the most important rites of passage in the completion of the education of a Southern gentleman. Family honor and service to country was, of course, part of that tradition. Carter chose the Naval Academy instead of West Point largely because of an uncle's influence, as well as a personal fascination and interest in ships and the nation's naval history, which for many young males was far more exciting and romantic than the exploits of the United States Army. Moreover, both James Earl and Miss Lillian were financially relieved by their son's choice of Annapolis because the ravages of the Great Depression made it impossible for them to afford sending him even to a state university.

Carter was an excellent high school student and, thus, had no difficulty meeting the academy's academic requirements. In 1943, Carter enrolled at Annapolis with the United States fully engaged in World War II. Interestingly, although Carter did not graduate from the academy until after World War II, he and his classmates went on training cruises during the summers in the Atlantic, where German U-boats were constantly searching for Allied ships to sink, regardless of the type of vessel they encountered. Indeed, by 1944, because Germany was on the verge of defeat, any Allied ship was fair game. While on one of his training exercises, Carter's ship, the *USS New York,* was fired upon by a German submarine and suffered minor damage. Carter was not hurt. Fortunately, no such attacks occurred on his other missions, and he came out of World War II unscathed.

Carter graduated from the academy in 1946. Carter did well but hardly stood out, graduating in the top third of his class (59th out of 820). In his personal life, however, he had a most fulfilling experience. While at home the summer before his final year, Carter began "courting" Rosalynn Smith, his sister Ruth's best friend. Within months they were engaged and married soon after his graduation in June 1946. Over the next few years, Rosalynn gave birth to three sons: John William (Jack), James Earl III (Chip), and Donnel Jeffrey (Jeff).

Carter majored in engineering, and one of his first assignments was to oversee the electronics operations on experimental radar devices and gunnery. He was also responsible for helping the enlisted men pursue or finish their high school degrees. During Carter's tenure in the navy, there were virtually no educational requirements for enlisted personnel. Indeed, the only stipulation was age—one had to be at least seventeen-years-old to legally enlist, but young boys, especially those from impoverished backgrounds, lied about their age to escape poverty or other disadvantages. The majority of Carter's students came from such backgrounds, and interestingly, a high percentage were fellow Southerners.

Carter's career progressed smoothly as he gained a reputation as an intelligent, disciplined officer. Shipmates remembered him as friendly and helpful but not "one of the boys." Carter was simply more interested in work (and Jesus Christ) than ship or shore leave revelry. On Sundays beginning with his years at the Academy and on through to his ship assignments, Carter held impromptu Bible classes for anyone wishing to attend. Ever since he was a boy, Carter had studied and taught the Bible. Carter had always been a spiritual individual, whose devotion to Christ simply intensified during adulthood. Carter's peers respected his spirituality and Christianity, for as Annapolis classmate Francis Hertzog remembered, "We never swore around Jimmy; it would have been like cussing in front of your grandmother or the Lord." When he returned to Georgia after his twelve-year stint in the navy, Carter immediately pursued his "calling" of teaching the Bible at Plains Baptist Church. He made a commitment then and openly admitted to voters in 1976 that Jesus would always come first in his life.

In 1948, Carter was accepted for submarine duty. During his submarine training class, Carter's political leanings and his willingness to have a political opinion was articulated. (Naval officers are strongly discouraged from voicing any personal political views at any time in their career in the navy. Indeed, such a mandate applies to all military commanders, regardless of the branch of service.) Carter noted that of the sixty-one officers in his class, he was the only one who dared to publicly declare for Harry Truman during the 1948 presidential election. Although frowned upon by his superiors, Carter's *faux pas* did not adversely affect his career.

Although escaping death during World War II, Carter almost lost his life serving in time of peace. The incident occurred on his first submarine assignment aboard the *USS Pomfret*. During a terrible Atlantic storm, the boat surfaced to recharge its batteries, and Carter was on the bridge. According to Carter, while standing on the bridge, a wave rose six feet over his head, pulling him away from the handrail he was holding. The wave literally lifted him off the bridge. Carter desperately tried to keep his head above water and swim through the wave. When the wave finally subsided, Carter found himself on a gun thirty feet behind where he had been standing. If the wave had gone side to side instead of front to back, Carter would have been knocked off the ship completely and sucked into the Atlantic.

After several distinguished years in the submarine service, Carter earned a place in Admiral Hyman Rickover's elite nuclear submarine program.

Carter's assignment to this vaunted and avant garde program proved to be a turning point both personally and professionally, for it brought him under the tutelage of an individual who profoundly influenced his work ethic and eventual leadership style. Indeed, according to Carter, only his parents had a more significant impact on his life than Rickover. Before coming under Rickover's auspices, Carter had already demonstrated a sharp mind, strong work habits, and considerable ambition, but Rickover, whose work regiment was incomparable, inspired Carter to push himself to new limits. When Rickover interviewed Carter for a position with the nuclear submarine program, Rickover asked him if he had done his best at the Naval Academy. Carter, who finished 59 out of 820 cadets, responded honestly, telling the admiral he had "coasted a bit" and that he did not exert himself to his fullest potential. The admiral simply asked, "Why not?" and from that moment on, Carter decided to push himself to new heights. Although Rickover proved to be an inspiration for Carter, not all of the admiral's attributes or behaviors were positive. Nonetheless, Carter worshipped Rickover, emulating his leadership style. Unfortunately, Carter was so enamored of Rickover's approach that he adopted some of the admiral's less than positive qualities. Rickover was notorious for never praising any of his subordinates. He was quick to criticize work that he deemed less than flawless but rarely complimented people when they exceeded his expectations. Silence from Rickover was considered to be praise for a job well done. Although Carter accepted and emulated Rickover's leadership style, many other naval officers came to regard the admiral as a heartless, insensitive martinet. Indeed, if it were not for the admiral's brilliance and political connections, he would have been driven out of the navy for his "eccentricities."

Despite Rickover's controversial behavior, the admiral "favored" Carter, appointing him to help build the reactor for the navy's first nuclear submarine, the *Seawolf*. Carter's dream of someday becoming Chief of Naval Operations seemed within reach. Such was not, however, to become a reality for Carter. Less than a year into this most cherished assignment, Carter received news that his father, James Earl, had cancer and was not expected to live long. During one of his trips home to see his ailing father, Carter was so impressed by the outpouring of affection from friends and neighbors that he decided to leave the navy, return home, and take over Earl's businesses and place in the community. Carter's decision to resign from the navy did not sit well with Rosalynn, who had come to love the independence and excitement of navy life.

"She almost quit me," Carter later remarked. Rosalynn simply did not want to move back to tiny Plains under the watchful eyes of intrusive relatives. Despite some serious "words," Carter prevailed, and in the fall of 1953, the family moved back to Plains, Georgia.

Although acquiescing, Rosalynn Carter was every bit her husband's equal, if not superior in some categories. She was equally intelligent, more pragmatic, kind, supportive but never deferential and certainly not obsequious, devoted to her family, and, above all, much like Lady Bird Johnson, believed in her husband's vision for the nation and humanity and worked assiduously by his side or independently to help make it a reality.

The Carters returned to Plains with little cash and three children to support. They initially had to live in government-sponsored housing until Carter could get his father's various businesses off the ground. Thanks largely to Rosalynn's business acumen, Carter focused on developing and expanding his father's peanut warehouse, modernizing it into a highly successful operation by the early 1960s. By 1961, they had enough money to build a new, comfortable home, enjoyed regular vacations, and had become fully involved in their community. "I had to admit I was enjoying this life," Rosalynn later wrote.

All was not idyllic for the Carters, however, as the issue of race visited their tranquil corner of the world. As a result of the intensification of the civil rights movement, a white backlash invariably emerged in the form of the infamous White Citizens' Councils, which proliferated throughout the South by the early 1960s, penetrating even tiny communities like Plains. The Councils wanted to make sure all whites (as in the days of slavery) were "sound" on segregation and keeping blacks in "their proper place." Unfortunately, the Carters could not escape a "visit" by the local Council, who wanted to make sure that Carter and his family were "fulfilling" their obligation to upholding the racial status quo. Apparently, rumor had it that the Carters were not adhering to the established order, treating their black employees a little "too kindly" and voicing opinions challenging "the way things were." Carter told his two "guests"—the local sheriff and a Baptist preacher, that he indeed opposed segregation and thus had no intention of enforcing it in his business, nor did he have any interest in joining the local Council. Suffice it to say, Carter's attitude shocked and angered his visitors, who returned a few days later with some of Carter's "friends," who told him that his business would suffer if he continued such behavior. Carter was not intimidated, refusing to change his ways and declining to join the local Council. A boycott of Carter's business was called for, but it never materialized, at least to the extent that it negatively impacted Carter's enterprise.

Carter also had to deal with racism in his own Plains' Baptist Church where he was a deacon. Carter refused to support the decision by his fellow deacons and pastor to physically block black worshippers from attending Sunday services. Carter decided to challenge the vote at the next church business meeting, in which two hundred people showed up instead of the usual thirty-five. Only six voted with Carter to oppose the blocking of African Americans from attending church services—his mother, wife, two sons, and one other member of the congregation. Roughly fifty members voted against Carter, so most of those in attendance chose not to vote at all. Afterwards, Carter claimed that dozens of members approached him privately and said they agreed with his position but were afraid to take a public stand. Carter obviously was not, and from this moment on, his reputation grew around Georgia among both blacks and whites that there was an individual, tucked away in tiny Plains, who just might be the harbinger of the "New South" for whom Southerners of both races had been waiting to deliver their section from decades of prejudice, discrimination, and violence. But Carter could not become the "messiah" for the New South if he remained in the private sector. He had to enter politics. Thus, on his thirty-eighth birthday in 1962, he announced to a surprised Rosalynn that he planned to run for a seat in the state senate, a position his father briefly held before his death.

With his family's support, Carter barnstormed his way across the seven-county district that comprised the senate seat. As Carter made the rounds on Election Day, everything appeared to be going his way with victory in sight until he got to Georgetown, Quitman County, where Carter discovered bald-face fraud that in the end denied him victory by a 139 votes. The "victor" was Homer Moore, a hardware store owner from Richland. It appeared that his earlier refusal to support Jim Crow and other segregationist policies were coming back to haunt him, for the local political boss, a diehard segregationist named Joe Hurst, made it known to voters in Quitman County that Carter was a "Negro lover" and, if elected, he would surely help undo "all that was sacred to white Georgians." Hurst was so intent on preserving the status quo, which Carter threatened, that he resorted to all manner of chicanery to ensure Moore's election. Hurst tore up Carter ballots and stuffed the ballot boxes with votes "cast" by people who had moved from the county or who were dead. In short, Carter was the victim of old-style politics that flourished in rural Georgia that kept conservative white Democrats in power at the expense of blacks and white liberals.

An indignant Carter challenged the result, appealing to newspapers and the courts until it was overturned. Thanks largely to Carter's unrelenting efforts to uncover the fraud and the blatant illegalities that occurred, the Georgia state legislature passed a new election code in 1964 that established a much more stringent and better-supervised voting process. Carter began his stint in the Georgia state senate in January 1964 and quickly established a reputation as one of that chamber's most conscientious members, reading every bill and taking on corruption wherever he saw it. As fellow senator LeRoy Johnson observed, "He [Carter] was not a leader of the senate—he was quiet, he was effective, he was deliberate, and he made no waves." Carter had always opposed the various special interests that controlled Georgia politics and, thus, made their curtailment of power and influence one of his crusades. He was especially aroused by those special interests that received preferential treatment by his colleagues, for they were allowing the import of a minority to prevail over the common folk's well-being. Reflecting his Southern populist roots, Carter fought against any bills that showed such favoritism. Although not always successful in his battle with the special interests, Carter nonetheless gained a reputation for being the common people's champion.

One of the more revealing controversies in which Carter became involved during his tenure as a state senator was the writing of a new state constitution, which many of his colleagues insisted invoke "God's sanctification" or "blessing" of the state of Georgia. Carter, a devout Christian, opposed such verbiage, arguing that such wording was a blatant contravention of the United States Constitution, a violation of the sanctity of the separation of church and state. Suffice it to say, Carter's position angered his more fundamentalist colleagues, many of whom labeled Carter an atheist. Despite such vilification, Carter refused to retract, and ultimately his position prevailed. Carter served in the state senate for four years and loved every minute of it. As Rosalynn observed during one session, her husband's political ambitions "were just warming up. I was standing in the back of the senate chamber with him, and the lieutenant governor was going on and on and on, and it was bedlam. And Jimmy said, 'If I were lieutenant governor, this wouldn't be happening.' And I thought, 'Uh-oh. He's really enjoying this.'"

Carter's next gambit for political office initially was for a seat in the national House of Representatives, but when the Democratic front-runner in the governor's race had a heart attack and withdrew his candidacy, Carter was pressured by the party to abandon his congressional race and run for governor instead. Carter was reluctant and tried to get other leading Democrats to pick up the mantle, but they all refused, leaving Carter no choice but to run as his party's nominee for governor. Carter was well-known and respected locally, but around the state he was dubbed "Jimmy Who" by the press. For someone with poor name recognition, Carter did surprisingly well, losing the Democratic primary by 20,000 votes out of about one million that were cast, which boded well for his future. Carter lost to arch-segregationist Lester Maddox, a man he disdained as a hateful bigot. Moreover, for the first time in his life, his defeat by someone like Maddox caused Carter to question his faith. He felt God had betrayed him, for how could He allow someone as "evil" and "un-Christian" as Maddox to defeat a righteous and devout servant of the Lord like Jimmy Carter. After days of agonizing and in spiritual communion with his sister Ruth, Carter concluded that God had not abandoned him but, rather, wanted to momentarily humble him to remind him that one must keep Jesus in his heart at all times in order to perform truly good works. Apparently, Carter had forsaken Christ during the campaign, thinking only of himself as he pursued a life (a political career) rooted in personal selfishness void of Christian humility and good works. This was the "born-again" experience to which Carter referred for the rest of his life. From this moment on, Carter vowed to himself and to God that he would conduct his life, regardless of the endeavor, according to the teachings of Jesus Christ. In short, Carter promised to put his faith in Jesus ahead of all other personal interests, even politics.

The campaign took its toll on Carter, not just spiritually but physically. Carter ended up heavily indebted, physically exhausted, and emotionally drained. He lost twenty pounds during the hustings, but he refused to quit. Despite defeat, financial hardship, and fatigue, Carter resolved to try again in 1970, determined to become Georgia's next Democratic governor. After one month of rest and recuperation, he began campaigning for the 1970 race. He worked hard at the family business to pay off his debts and give himself some of the resources he would need for the next race. To avoid the stigma of being an "unknown," Carter immersed himself in all manner of highly visible, press-catching, statewide activities, all the while "networking" with party moguls. Somehow, among all the politicking, he managed to find time for spiritual enrichment, taking yearly mission trips across Georgia and into other states and countries. He went door-to-door witnessing for Jesus in Pennsylvania and Massachusetts, and he passed out Bibles in Mexico. His sojourns for Jesus initiated what would become lifelong travels to underdeveloped nations, demonstrating Carter's visceral empathy with the world's downtrodden.

Interestingly, as the 1970 governor's race drew nearer, many of Carter's friends and advisers urged him to run for lieutenant governor, because in the governor's race, he would be taking on a heavy favorite in the person of former Governor Carl Sanders. Some even urged him to set his sights lower and run for Commissioner of Agriculture. Carter, however, was not to be deterred and believed he could win the gubernatorial race. Sanders had the support of most of the major newspapers, as well as most of the state's power-brokers (both Democrat and Republican) and special interests. The Sanders' people labeled Carter a bigoted, redneck peanut farmer. Carter naturally dismissed such appellations as typical dirty politics and refused to return in kind. Throughout the campaign, Carter rarely attacked Sanders personally, nor did he criticize the former governor's programs or administration. Instead, Carter focused on what *he* would do for Georgians if elected. He ran a tough, populist campaign against (ironically) the more liberal, urbane Sanders, whom he called "Cufflinks Carl." According to historian E. Stanly Godbold, Carter "wanted to appeal to the large middle class, blue collar type, predominantly white, and most of these people were segregationists. Carter himself was not a segregationist in 1970 but he did say things that segregationists wanted to hear."

Typically, Carter unleashed a whirlwind campaign, a pace Sanders could not keep up with. Family, friends, and a group of political operatives, who would stay with him through his White House years (including Hamilton Jordan, Jody Powell, Bert Lance, Stuart Eizenstat, and Gerald Rafshoon), joined Carter in blanketing the state and getting his name out. Carter estimated that he gave around 1,800 speeches across the state from the moment he decided to run for governor. His tenacity paid off. Carter won the election by a comfortable margin.

As governor, Carter worked tirelessly to help Georgians of all colors improve the quality of their lives. Although shrewdly cultivating the support of white Georgian segregationists during the governor's race, Carter's true feelings on race came out in his inaugural address when he declared, "the time for racial discrimination is over." Carter made good his inaugural declaration by appointing more African Americans and women to state offices than any of his predecessors and by hanging a portrait of Martin Luther King, Jr. in the Georgia State House. He fought with a vengeance against the budgetary and organizational mess that he first became aware of as a state legislator. The state bureaucracy was bloated beyond reason. Many departments had higher payrolls and budgets than their workloads could justify, and too many programs duplicated each other's efforts. Carter believed that the most effective way to deal with such bureaucratic dilation was to adopt zero base budgets—that is, each program and department could not pursue "business as usual" without justifying how they were going to spend the money they were receiving. In short, Carter wanted strict accountability in state government. He also had programs and departments organized according to the services they provided. When duplication of effort was found, cuts were made. Carter did not hesitate to wield the budgetary knife, slicing the bureaucratic waste and fat that had been accumulating on the Georgia body politic for years, sucking the hard-earned money from Georgia taxpayers for little in return.

Career bureaucrats and special interest groups naturally opposed Carter's policies, but he was not going to relent until he had accomplished his goal of a lean and mean, responsible state government that served all Georgians. Of the three hundred state-run agencies that existed when Carter became governor, 278 of them were gone by his second year in the governor's mansion. His "knife" saved Georgia taxpayers millions of dollars in the process.

Carter was also very involved in the preservation of natural resources. He estimated that the only thing he spent more time on was government reorganization. The federal government's efforts in this regard were sporadic at best in the early 1970s, so Carter and other governors stepped into the breech and looked after the environmental affairs of their own states. Carter's most "unusual" endeavor as governor, one that helped him develop a "global vision" even before he became president, was that in his last two years in office he visited ten foreign nations. Carter justified his sojourns (which were taken at Georgia taxpayers' expense) as necessary to promote international trade for Georgia, but it was also a way for Carter to get to know world leaders and to broaden his international vistas just in case he might want to run for president. Indeed, Carter was barely in the governor's mansion before he began thinking seriously about a presidential bid. Shortly after returning from the 1972 Democratic Convention in Miami, Carter and his team began to sketch the outlines of one of the more brilliant political campaigns in American history, encapsulated in a remarkable 72-page memo by Hamilton Jordan. Jordan urged Carter to begin forging national connections and building up his "international" portfolio while still governor. As noted above, he could take such national and international junkets free of personal charge because he could use state funds, which were readily available as a result of his cuts. Of course, his trips were all taken in the name of improving his beloved Georgia's national and global "connections!" So confident was Carter that he could secure the 1976 Democratic nomination that he officially declared his candidacy on December 12, 1974, while still Georgia's governor. After leaving office in January 1975, he and his family traveled about the nation, talking to voters and listening to their concerns. To Carter, it seemed that the deceit, corruption, and humiliation of Vietnam and the Watergate scandal had so disaffected Americans that they yearned for someone to renew their faith in the system. They wanted someone who was honest, sincere, and dedicated to a revitalization of the American spirit. Carter believed he was just the man to "redeem" the nation and deliver its people out of the "bondage" of mistrust and cynicism. Brandishing his "outsider" credentials, "Kennedyesque" smile, and Deep South charm and graciousness, the born-again Christian and successful businessman downplayed the issues and focused on character, vowing never to deceive the public, regardless of personal or political consequences, and to bring honesty and integrity back into government. Despite all his careful preparations, Carter was still a long shot to win the 1976 Democratic nomination. In an effort to gain name recognition and early momentum, Carter committed himself heavily to Iowa, where the first set of delegates would be up for grabs. Some of the major contenders, such as Edmund Muskie, virtually ignored the state, believing its delegate count (forty-seven) was not worth the effort. Carter, however, campaigned heavily, appearing there on 110 different occasions. The strategy paid off, as Carter won 27 percent of the vote. The nearest competitor was Senator Birch Bayh of Indiana with 13 percent of the vote. Overall, the Democrats put forth a confusing array of candidates, who slowly dropped out as the hustings intensified. Frank Church of Illinois and California's maverick governor Jerry Brown threw their hats in the ring even though the primaries had already started. Despite the presence of upstart challengers, Carter persevered, ultimately accumulating enough primary votes to win his party's nomination on the first ballot. Carter triumphed over his challengers largely because of his intelligence, hard work, centrist message, and a tactically brilliant campaign, all of which combined to get him past a field of better-known Democrats.

Taking on the incumbent, Gerald Ford, proved to be a different matter. Although starting out with a 33-point lead over Ford in July, by Election Day the two candidates were dead even. Carter had lost (or squandered) his lead largely because his simplistic message of honesty in government was not substantive enough to endure the rigors of a full-fledged presidential campaign that demanded specificity on issues and a coherent vision and agenda for the country. Carter's campaign did not ring out with the promise to uplift Americans to "New Frontiers," or to create a "Great Society" in which all citizens had a job, health care, and equal access to the American Dream. When pressed about his lack of vision or direction for the country, Carter often answered with convoluted, hollow retorts that seemed to always revert back to his exemplary character. Despite the obvious flaws in Carter's rhetoric, the Georgia governor hung on to win one of the closest presidential elections in American history.

Carter owed his election to a diverse, transitory coalition. Capitalizing on his regional appeal, he carried every Southern state except Virginia. He ran well among Southern whites who belonged to fundamentalist and evangelical churches. Still, his victory in the South rested on a strong turnout among African Americans, the beneficiaries of federal voter protection laws enacted during the 1960s. Meanwhile, across the country, Carter courted the youth vote by promising to pardon most of the young men who resisted the draft during the Vietnam War. Carter's running mate, Senator Walter Mondale of Minnesota, appealed to traditional Democrats, and this helped Carter to narrowly capture three key states that had long been Democratic strongholds—New York, Pennsylvania, and Ohio. Even so, Carter won by less than 2 million popular votes and by only 56 votes in the electoral college. Not only was his margin of victory over Ford slight, but also millions of people had not bothered to vote at all. Only about 54 percent of eligible voters went to the polls in 1976, the lowest turnout since the end of World War II.

The Carter Presidency: A Positive Assessment

As a transitional president, Jimmy Carter's tenure in the White House has been unduly criticized for being void of direction and purpose. It must be remembered that in many ways the Carter presidency—both the man and his time in the Oval Office—represented the end of post-World War II liberalism and the beginning of a revitalized neo-conservatism. Although a moderate centrist, many traditional liberals worried that Carter's position on many issues (especially his fiscal conservatism) and lack of vision and a specific agenda (other than restoring integrity to the executive office), would allow the resurgent right to gain momentum. Particularly disturbing to liberals was Carter's luke-warm attitude toward expansion of the welfare state, which they believed needed to be revitalized not only to keep the reform impulse alive, but to help an ailing economy as well. If Carter was indeed a "closet" conservative, both personally and ideologically, his embracing of that ethos was the result of a reality that many die-hard liberals refused to accept. It must be remembered that the Vietnam War and the "excesses" of the Johnson years caused widespread disaffection among the many traditional blocs that had sustained the Democratic liberal coalition since the days of FDR. This was especially true for ethnic, blue-collar Democrats, who by the 1960s had become the heart and soul of middle America. They took great pride in the fact that they had attained that status on their own initiative. They thus felt betrayed by 1960s liberals for ignoring their needs while focusing instead on "handing out" power and benefits to previously disenfranchised but "undeserving" and "entitled" sectors—African Americans, Hispanics, and other "minorities." As the white middle-class Johnsonian consensus watched the newly empowered burn cities and protest against the "Establishment," they became hostile and alienated, blaming the unravelling on unwarranted redemption.

Carter sensed this estrangement, believing that, in order to bring back to the Democratic fold this most vital sector, he had to articulate a more conservative message. If the party did not at least center itself, then Carter (rightly) believed old-time Democrats like the working class might just vote Republican. Although the 1980 election proved Carter correct about the nation's drift from left to right, during his presidency party liberals saw Carter as an outsider both in terms of the Beltway and within the confines of the Democratic Party. Because Carter was not a traditional liberal, à-la-FDR—Truman—LBJ, he became a sort of political and ideological arch between the final demise of liberalism and the advent (or resurrection) of conservatism.

If Carter is placed in such a context, then the harsh criticisms he has received over the years are unwarranted, especially in light of his many successful foreign policy initiatives, as well as his bringing to the White House an integrity, honesty and morality that had been woefully absent for many years. Refreshingly, Carter valued what was right rather than what was politically expedient or what would enhance his image and power. Carter also disdained the elitism and insular mentality that seemed to have engulfed Washington. Such detachment created the impression among the American people that their elected officials, from the president to Congress, had little interest or concern for their welfare.

Carter was determined to make people believe once again in their government and its officials because in his mind he was simply "the right man." He possessed all the personal prerequisites: he was pleasingly informal, reasonable, industrious, and a church-going, family-oriented man. Carter's roots were rural, but he was also a successful entrepreneurial businessman. Although a Southerner, he was most definitely of the New South, free from race prejudice and Lost Cause sentimentality and defiance. There was also the flair of the Jeffersonian/Populist about him combined with an aura of Rooseveltian New Deal humanitarianism, which helped to reaffirm his New South image. Adding to Carter's mystique that he represented a new breed of politician in the post-Watergate era were his credentials as an Annapolis graduate who had served on nuclear submarines—the ultimate in high technology. In short, Carter presented himself as a candidate who not only cared about the common people, but one who could bring about change efficiently without having to sacrifice his personal integrity or that of the executive branch in the process. Too many of his predecessors had been more than willing to compromise both their principles as well as the probity of their office for the sake of immediate acclaim and power.

Carter's enlightened attitude towards third world countries is to be particularly lauded. He did much to improve United States relations with underdeveloped nations and, in some cases, to help end decades of suspicion and hostility in those countries towards the "Yankee Colossus." Carter realized that it was imperative for the United States to end the overbearing, arrogant, interventionist behavior and policies of past administrations. In many instances, his predecessor's imperiousness caused violent protests against United States presence or interests in such nations and the coming to power of communist or pro-Soviet regimes. By the end of his term, United States relations with many underdeveloped nations no longer were strained because Carter had worked assiduously and sincerely to end the image of the United States as a self-serving exploiter of their people and resources.

It is also unfair to criticize Carter for his failure to cure a sluggish economy, which he inherited from previous administrations. If Carter seemed unable to fix the nation's economic woes, it was because the country was experiencing an unprecedented economic crisis: stagflation, which was high unemployment compounded by high interest rates and high prices. Causing this new type of downturn was the end of the Vietnam War, which had "overheated" the economy, especially in the military-industrial complex. Skyrocketing foreign oil prices and the continued transformation of the nation's economy from the production of capital goods (machinery, steel, etc.) to a more service-oriented and consumer goods production economy also contributed to the problem. Moreover, powerful unions in heavy industry had kept wages and benefits high, but business owners were tired of union power and decided to shop the world for cheaper labor, exporting production of their goods abroad. Thus began the production of American products, consumer as well as capital goods, in underdeveloped nations where labor costs were egregiously low. Increasingly, it became cheaper for the United States to import capital and consumer goods from such countries.

With the Vietnam conflict's end in 1973, over the course of the next few years, unemployment rose steadily because those individuals employed in war-related industries were no longer needed, and there were fewer people serving in the military with the end of the war and the end of the draft. The same became true for workers in capital goods industries. By election year 1976, in the heavy industrial areas of the Northeast and Great Lakes region, unemployment was fast approaching double-digits.

In the early 1970s, the OPEC nations began to raise oil prices. Motivating them to pursue such a policy was not only their desire to increase profits but to send a message as well to the industrial powers that the oil-producing nations were no longer going to be at the mercy of industrialized Europe and the United States. Since the United States had allowed itself to become dependent on foreign oil because it was once so cheap, OPEC's price-hikes naturally adversely affected the nation. The hikes caused price increases at the pump, as well as severe shortages, frustrating and angering Americans not used to lining up and waiting for hours to fill up their gas tanks. In short, few presidents, if any, would have been able to revive an economy mired in such an uncommon state.

Without question, one of the most humiliating events ever to visit a president and the nation was the Iranian hostage crisis. Most Americans remain convinced that Carter was responsible for this most debilitating debacle in American foreign policy. However, upon closer, more dispassionate scrutiny, it becomes apparent that Carter was not at fault. Carter has not only been blamed for failing to negotiate the hostages' release (they were held in captivity for 444 days) but also for the blundered military operation to rescue them. It must be remembered that Jimmy Carter did not cause the Iranian revolution, which led to the taking of American hostages. For years the United States (beginning in 1953 with the Eisenhower administration, which overthrew a supposed left-leaning, pro-Soviet Iranian prime minister, Muhammad Mossadeq) had supported an oppressive regime under Shah Mohammed Reza Pahlevi. U.S. support for the shah was based on oil and on the shah's staunch anti-communism, which the U.S. believed would keep the Soviets at bay in a region they long coveted. The shah was also sustained because he was one of few Middle Eastern Muslim leaders who wanted to Westernize his country, which foreshadowed even stronger ties to the United States. Unfortunately, in his haste and arrogance to modernize Iran, the shah tolerated no opposition to his agenda, silencing with torture and execution Iranians unwilling to embrace his modernization or Westernization policies. During his rule of over twenty years, thousands of Iranians were executed or tortured or left the country to avoid either of those two fates. The shah lived in luxury while too many of his people suffered in poverty. Despite the shah's brutal oppression, Iranians resisted, rallying to Muslim fundamentalist clerics like the Ayatollah Khomeini, who ultimately led the opposition into open, violent revolt against the shah.   As opposition to the shah intensified, the Carter administration urged the shah to leave the country. The inevitable occurred in 1979. The shah was overthrown by revolution, and the ayatollah took over Iran and executed hundreds of people who had either worked for the shah or had supported his policies. The shah was very ill with cancer by the time of his overthrow and came to the United States for medical treatment. Khomeini denounced the United States for allowing the shah to come for medical care, as well as for its years of support for his regime. In response, Muslim radicals stormed the U.S. embassy in Tehran and took those still remaining in the building hostage. A few Americans were released, but for over a year, fifty-two were held captive.

From the moment the hostages were taken, Carter proved a tenacious negotiator. He resisted the temptation to do something immoral and criminal, such as trading weapons for hostages, which his successor was more than willing to do. He also refused to acquiesce to the demands of the Khomeini regime to return the shah, which he was told would secure the hostages release. Carter knew that the moment the shah was back in Iran he would be executed. Since the shah was a known brutal dictator, it would have been easy for Carter to vindicate a return of the shah in exchange for the hostages. Carter refused, accepting the fact that he, as well as his predecessors, had supported the shah and had considered him an invaluable American ally for years. Carter knew that, if his administration betrayed the shah by turning him over to the militants, the United States' credibility with other leaders would have been greatly damaged. Moreover, even though the Iranians' accusations about the shah were correct, Carter knew he could not give into their demand for the shah's return even if it meant the return of the hostages. If he did capitulate, trading the shah for the hostages would establish the precedent that anytime a country hostile to the United States wanted something, all they had to do was take American citizens hostage and the United States would then "roll over" and acquiesce to that country's demands or extortion. Carter was fully aware of these implications and made the hard choice of not succumbing to such terrorism.

Carter deserves credit for the fact that the hostages, all fifty-two of them, returned home safely. At the time of the crisis, Carter could have ordered a major military strike, thus punishing the Iranians, but how many hostages would have survived and how many innocent Iranians would have been killed in the process? If ultimate success on this issue is measured by how many hostages were saved, as well as by how many Iranians were not killed by a U.S. attack, then Carter's determined negotiation and diplomacy is to be lauded, not condemned.

It is unfair to assess Carter's foreign policy solely on the Iranian hostage crisis. Unlike his predecessors, whose foreign policy agendas were largely determined by the exigencies of the cold war (U.S./Soviet relations, Vietnam notwithstanding), even before becoming president, Carter had developed a more global vision, a Wilsonian vision. As already noted, during his last two years as Georgia's governor, he visited ten foreign nations, discussing with heads-of-state a variety of topics, ranging from energy to global warming. Carter believed that such issues would become greater concerns for all countries than simply the staid polemics of cold war geopolitics, which only entailed dialogue and acrimony between the United States and the Soviet Union. Such pre-presidential learning helped Carter to be more aware of different foreign policy questions and, thus, better prepared to deal with them when they arose.

Perhaps most important, Carter realized that in the post-Vietnam era the United States was no longer viewed as the invincible super-power. It had been beaten and embarrassed. For the first time in history, the American people felt the sting and humiliation of defeat. Consequently, by the time of Carter's presidency, there was strong sentiment in the country for the United States to "retrench" from world affairs, that is, to minimize its commitments to other countries, whether they were major powers or underdeveloped nations, whether the aid was economic or military. It was all to be significantly curtailed. The American people no longer wanted to play the role nor have the status as the peacekeepers and defenders of freedom and democracy worldwide. In short, the 1947 Truman Doctrine of containment was to now be reassessed, even though the cold war was still raging. Such commitment got the nation sucked into the Vietnam quagmire. Thus, to avoid any future "Vietnams," the United States must send a message to the rest of the world that they might have to look to someone else to defend them from aggressors or to help them solve their internal problems. The price paid in Vietnam was simply too high to continue such obligations.

Coming into office, Carter was aware of this changed American attitude and tried to construct a foreign policy based on this new reality. Carter believed that it was imperative for his administration to be cognizant of the United States' changed position in the world and adapt to this new reality or America would lose even more prestige. In short, Carter believed that it was time for the United States not only to rethink its world position and image but to create a new one that reflected what Americans wanted but also one that also erased the stigma of Vietnam and the perception of the United States as an overbearing, arrogant power that finally got its "comeuppance" in the jungles of Southeast Asia.

Carter's foreign policy was fundamentally different from his immediate predecessors in three ways. First, Carter emphasized promoting better relations between the United States, Japan, and Western Europe. If these three giants of non-communist, industrial power could more closely cooperate, especially in aiding underdeveloped nations, then, Carter believed, such a commitment would surely demonstrate the superior virtues and rewards to be gained by adopting the economic and political systems of this triumvirate. Communism would thus be seen in a much less positive light and, over time, simply fade into historical oblivion both ideologically and practically. Second, because Nixon and Kissinger had been so clandestine in conducting much of their foreign policy, Congress placed subsequent administrations under increased scrutiny. Such close observation, however, impacted Carter very little. He so disdained the Nixon administration's penchant for duplicity and secrecy that he pledged to conduct a much more open foreign policy, letting both the American public and the world know exactly what the issues were and how he proposed to address them. Finally, and perhaps most importantly, was Carter's commitment to human rights, which became the cornerstone of his foreign policy agenda. Demonstrating an idealism that harkened back to that of Woodrow Wilson, Carter's promulgation of human rights as the essence of his foreign policy was hailed both at home and abroad. Carter wanted the United States to be seen as a "kinder, gentler" nation that promoted American ideals abroad, not by force or economic extortion, but by persuasion and example. He wanted the United States to be seen as a selfless nation of people who were concerned about all humanity's welfare. In Latin America and Africa especially, Carter's dedication to preserving and protecting the freedom of peoples too often oppressed by totalitarian right-wing regimes had made a significant difference in America's reputation. To encourage nations to respect human rights, Carter used American economic aid as an incentive, and where government leaders engaged in a pattern of abuse of their people, Carter often withheld such aid until the oppression was stopped and meaningful reforms instituted.

For Carter, the United States had a mission to help countries improve both the quality and quantity of their citizens' lives. Thus, his foreign policy represented a refreshing, humane departure from the traditional, one-dimensional hard-line anti-communist, anti-Soviet stance of his predecessors. Though Carter believed U.S. foreign policy had to be multifaceted, ready to meet any crisis or exigency that might arise, he was not naïve in thinking that his approach would resolve U.S./Soviet tensions and bring about the end of the cold war. Being a man of peace and wanting to make the world a safer place for all, Carter realized that tough negotiations with the Soviets on limiting nuclear arsenals was required. He negotiated the Strategic Arms Limitation Talks (SALT) II Treaty and the Comprehensive Test Ban Treaty. He also proposed that the United States and the Soviet Union begin to de-militarize Europe by reducing their respective conventional forces. For the Soviets, this meant reducing Warsaw Pact troops and, for the United States, limiting its North Atlantic Treaty Organization (NATO) forces.

The negotiations over a SALT II treaty were actually begun by the Ford administration. When Carter assumed office, he continued the process, wanting to make even deeper cuts than Ford had advocated. At the time, Carter was severely criticized by hawkish Republicans and Democrats who claimed that his reductions were so outrageous that he was jeopardizing American security. Such accusations were groundless. To Carter, if détente was to be real between the United States and the Soviet Union, then significant reductions on both sides were imperative. In the process, Carter, a former naval officer, was not going to leave the United States even remotely vulnerable to a Soviet attack. In short, Carter sought to protect the United States and cut bloated defense budgets while creating a more trusting and open relationship with the United States' most serious adversary.

Though desiring a rapprochement with the Soviets, contrary to criticism, Carter was not going to ignore Soviet aggression for the sake of accomplishing a thaw in the cold war. The crisis in question was the Soviet invasion of Afghanistan in December 1979. Eight months earlier in April 1979, with secret Soviet aid, leftist military forces overthrew Afghani President Mohammed Daoud, replacing him with the pro-Soviet Nur Mohammed Taraki. However, no sooner was Taraki in power than the Afghani people rose in rebellion, eventually toppling the Taraki regime in September 1979. This precipitated the Soviet invasion in December. The Soviets claimed that they invaded Afghanistan to restore order. In reality, the invasion was to try to reinstall another pro-Soviet government. More important, the Soviet invasion reflected the desire of the Brezhnev government to expand into an area of Asia that Russia (dating back to the czars) had long coveted. A Soviet presence in Afghanistan would allow the Russians access to, if not control of, the Straits of Hormuz, near the Persian Gulf through which Middle Eastern oil flowed to the United States and Western Europe. With Iran in political chaos, the Soviets were also poised to invade that beleaguered nation and take control of it.

Carter saw the ramifications of the crisis, making it clear to the Soviets that its actions and intentions would not be tolerated by the United States. He pressured the Soviets to get out of Afghanistan but never threatened them with war if they did not. Finally, on January 3, 1980, before the Senate could vote on it, Carter withdrew the SALT II treaty. Though wanting the treaty ratified, Carter believed that by pulling it such action would force the Soviets to reconsider their southern Asian agenda. Carter also embargoed United States grain and some technology exports. Finally, Carter declared that the United States would boycott the 1980 Olympic summer games to be held in Moscow that summer. Carter did not want the Soviets to benefit economically from such a highly visible event, while Soviet troops killed innocent Afghanis. Carter could not stop the Olympics from taking place, but he had too much integrity to authorize U. S. involvement in something that would reward them.

Another foreign policy victory for Jimmy Carter was the successful Panama Canal Treaties. Many Americans did not believe new treaties were needed with Panama for the right to use the canal, something that the United States built and from which it benefitted. As Republican Senator S. I. Hayakawa of California said, "We stole it fair and square." The 1903 treaty, which the U. S. signed with the new nation of Panama, stated that the U. S. could control the canal and a strip of territory on both sides of the canal in perpetuity. But Carter, wanting to improve the nation's overall relations with Latin America in general, had a different purpose. With the rise of nationalism among third-world countries (and Carter's own sense of fairness and morality), the heavy-handed treaty had been a source of tension between the U.S. and Panama for decades. Moreover, Carter argued that the canal was no longer the economic and strategic necessity that it had once been. On September 7, 1977, Carter convinced the Panamanians to agree to two treaties, which the Senate approved in the spring of 1978. The first treaty limited how long the United States would operate the canal. It was agreed that complete operation of the canal would be turned over to the Panamanian government in 2001. The second treaty allowed the United States to enforce or maintain the canal's neutrality even after turning its operation over to the Panamanian government. In short, the United States feared that, if an overly zealous regime (i.e., anti-U.S.) came to power in Panama, it might try to nationalize the canal, an action no United States president could afford to condone. Even though the treaties, in effect, retained ultimate U.S. hegemony of the canal, many Americans opposed the treaties, believing Carter too conciliatory to "undeserving" underdeveloped countries. Carter believed, however, that his gesture of allowing Panama at least symbolic *de facto* control of the canal would go far as a first step toward realizing his ultimate goal of improving U.S./Latin American relations in general.

Without question, Carter's greatest foreign policy accomplishment was the signing of the Camp David Accords in 1978 between Israel and Egypt, ending decades of tension and hostility between those two nations. The accords represented Carter's firm belief in the efficacy of diplomacy and negotiation to attain peaceful ends, as well as confirmation of his skill as a facilitator. Reviving Henry Kissinger's earlier efforts to mediate Arab-Israeli conflicts, Carter brought Menachem Begin and Answar Sadat, leaders of Israel and Egypt, respectively, to the Camp David presidential retreat. After thirteen days of bargaining, the three leaders announced the framework for a negotiating process and a peace treaty. Although Middle East tensions hardly vanished, the Camp David Accords kept high-level discussions alive, lowered the level of acrimony between Egypt and Israel, and bound both sides to the United States through promised economic aid.

Domestically, the Carter years were not as bleak as critics contend. As noted earlier, Carter inherited an unprecedented economic crisis in the form of stagflation from his immediate predecessors: Ford, Nixon, and Johnson. Americans have an historical penchant for vilifying the president in power when the economy takes a turn for the worse and conversely, for believing the president to be the messiah when the economy is booming. Unfortunately and unfairly, Carter became a victim of the first tendency. Like Herbert Hoover in 1929, who inherited from his two predecessors, Coolidge and Harding, a seriously flawed economy, such was the case for Carter. As Hoover faced the onslaught of an unfamiliar economic downturn, so did Carter. In retrospect, historians and economists know that Herbert Hoover did not cause the Great Depression and that Carter did not cause the stagflation of the late 1970s and early 1980s. Moreover, Carter was not oblivious to the crisis, and in fact, he tried twice to push through Congress tax cuts designed to stimulate the economy. Unfortunately, congressional opposition blocked the bills. This was not a new idea—it had been put into effect before Carter by both JFK and LBJ and most recently by the George W. Bush administration, and in every instance it was embraced by the people.

One of Carter's more successful initiatives, and one he promised during the campaign to immediately implement if elected, was a more stream-lined and efficient federal government, especially the executive branch. Presidents have always promised greater efficiency in the federal government, but Carter, more than most, delivered on his promise. In a repeat of Carter's performance as governor, the White House staff was reduced by 28 percent with several bloated and overlapping agencies abolished in the process. He also prompted Congress to pass the first major civil service reforms since the Chester Arthur administration (1881-1885). The changes called for promoting individuals based on their performance rather than for simply length of service. Carter's new criteria also made it easier for incompetent employees to be fired.

Another of Carter's reform initiatives was to expand government services to the people in areas he deemed essential. For example, the Departments of Energy and Education were created during his presidency. With education now an independent department, the old Department of Health, Education, and Welfare was transformed into the Department of Health and Human Services. Carter demonstrated a statesmanlike spirit of bipartisanship by choosing a Republican, James R. Schlesinger (former Defense Secretary during the Nixon and Ford administrations), to serve as the first energy secretary. Carter correctly expressed concerns about the environment and U.S. dependence on foreign oil. Thanks to Carter's exhortations, Congress passed proposals to double the size of national parks and wildlife preserves, as well as to set up a fund to clean up toxic industrial waste, polluting rivers, lakes, and other areas of the environment.

Most disturbing to Carter was the nation's dependency on foreign oil, which he confronted directly, pointing out that Americans consumed 40 percent more energy than they produced and that, by importing oil, they were also importing inflation and unemployment. Thus, in consultation with Schlesinger, Carter proposed one of the most comprehensive energy bills in United States history. The Carter/Schlesinger plan called for a decrease in U.S. reliance on foreign oil and natural gas and the expansion of domestic energy production through new tax incentives. It also called for the repeal of regulations on the production of natural gas; the levying of new taxes to discourage use of gasoline; the fostering of conservation by encouraging greater reliance on insulation and other energy-saving measures; and the promotion of alternative sources of energy, especially coal and nuclear power.

Though having a vision for the nation and an agenda to implement those ideas, Jimmy Carter's most important contribution to the office of president was his personal sincerity, morality, and dignity. He identified with Americans as a common man, not as a part of the Washington establishment. He endeared himself to the American people when he walked hand-in-hand with his wife, Rosalynn, down Pennsylvania Avenue on inauguration day in a business suit (not a cutaway). He wore a cardigan sweater for a televised "fireside" chat and made a habit of holding "town meetings" in small American communities where he stayed with "average" families. He excelled at the politics of gesture, nominating a record number of African Americans and women to administrative posts. As a presidential candidate, Carter repeatedly promised the public that he would never deceive them. Such rhetoric sounds naïve and righteous, but Carter was determined to restore the people's faith in their elected officials, especially the president.

Carter's moral credibility was enhanced by his declaration that he was a born-again Christian. Such a reference helped to establish him as a man of principles, who would do what was right rather than what was politically or personally expedient, which many Americans believed was what most politicians did to retain the public's favor or that of special interest groups. Carter showed that his commitment to integrity in the White House was not merely campaign pap by endorsing the creation of the office of independent counsel. The Watergate debacle revealed the problem of having the Attorney General responsible for investigating corruption in the executive branch, including the office of the president. To cover up the Watergate scandal, Nixon, exercising his authority, ordered Attorney General Richard Kleindeist to drop the investigation. When he refused, Nixon fired him. After Nixon's resignation, Congress began agitating for the creation of the office of independent counsel—someone who could investigate malfeasance in the executive branch without fear of intimidation from the Oval Office because the independent counsel would not be under executive auspices but would be answerable to the judicial branch. Jimmy Carter could have argued that an independent counsel was not needed because, ultimately, the system had worked. Nixon had violated his oath of office and the laws pertaining to it and had been ousted from power, regardless of an independent counsel investigation. Carter also could have asserted that an independent counsel was not needed because Nixon was an aberration. Finally, Carter could have politicized the debate, blaming the whole episode on Republican corruption, and now that the Democrats were in power, the political climate would naturally change for the better. But Carter believed the creation of the office of independent counsel would help to restore the people's trust in government, something that he deemed essential in the aftermath of the Watergate and Vietnam debacles.

Despite the harsh criticisms that the Carter administration has received, Carter brought healing and unity to a polarized, jaded, and disillusioned America. Carter also helped to unite a divided Democratic Party. At the time of Carter's election, many Americans were skeptical that a Southern candidate could win support even among his own region's black and white populations. Carter surprised both Northern and Southern skeptics, winning the support of both races with his sincerity, longtime commitment to racial reconciliation, and humor, drawling that it was "about time we had a President who doesn't speak with an accent." The fact that he was an avowed born-again Christian also had its appeal, enabling him to reach out to fundamentalist whites and influential African-American religious leaders, key groups to winning in the South. Carter's courting of African Americans was not an election-year stunt; it was something that Carter had successfully done for years, championing and protecting the rights of black Georgians as governor and as a private citizen. Carter also successfully garnered the support of young Americans by promising to pardon most of the young men who had resisted the draft during the Vietnam War, reaffirming his image as a man and candidate of peace and reconciliation. To Carter and for millions of other Americans, it was time to forgive and forget the trauma of Vietnam and move forward. It was time to heal all the emotional and psychological wounds caused by that conflict, and for Carter there was no better way to show such solicitude and compassion than by absolving all those who had resisted and challenged the reasons for what proved to be in the end for many an unjustifiable war.

As can be seen from the above examples and assessment of Jimmy Carter's presidency, much of the criticism he has received over the years was and is unfair. Carter was a pivotal, transitional president who did much to restore the American people's faith in the political process. Carter rekindled Americans' faith in the presidency by personally pledging that he would do all in his power to restore decency, pride, and integrity to the White House. His task was difficult, for he had to overcome the stigma of years of deceit and treachery emanating from the White House. Americans had become so disillusioned and alienated by the entire political process that on Election Day 1976, only about 54 percent of eligible voters went to the polls, the lowest turnout since the end of World War II. Despite the lack of a popular mandate, Jimmy Carter's presidency proved that enough of the American electorate still had sufficient faith in the system to put into office an individual of Carter's sincerity and integrity, and to give that individual a chance to redeem the nation.

The Carter Presidency: A Negative Assessment

Jimmy Carter's lack of a popular mandate after his narrow victory over Ford as well as his image as an outsider proved to be serious handicaps. Powerful constituencies, including both labor unions and multinational corporations, feared that Carter might prove to be an unpredictable leader. Carter also failed to develop the aura of a national leader. Although bringing some people with long experience in government into his cabinet, he relied mainly for advice and affirmation of his vision for the country on a tight, closed circle of fellow Georgians, many of whom had been with him when he first entered Georgia politics in the 1960s. Carter's "kitchen cabinet," dubbed the "Georgia Mafia" by the Washington press corps, overestimated the value of Carter's outsider image and in the end contributed significantly to his demise. Like Carter, they projected a self-righteous hubris that offended and ultimately alienated both the electorate and fellow Democrats. His staff treated key congressional leaders with condescension. Three years after the election, House Speaker Tip O'Neill, a fellow Democrat, noted that he still would not recognize Hamilton Jordan, Carter's chief aide, because Jordan had never bothered to introduce himself to the Speaker. The episode symbolized the standoff that increasingly paralyzed the internal machinery of government during the Carter years. Jettisoning the radicalism of his nomination acceptance speech, upon becoming president, Carter quickly "centered" himself, in James Reston's words, "in the decisive middle ground of American politics." In short, though coming across at times in the campaign as a liberal, heir-apparent to pick up the reform agenda where LBJ had left off, Carter instead moved to the center and eventually to the right by the end of his administration. But he never moved far enough to the right to pick up in conservative support what he was losing in liberal support. It was the same mistake George H. W. Bush would make, only in reverse. Indeed, during the last two years of Carter's presidency, he reduced spending for a variety of social programs, supported a reduction in capital gains taxes paid by wealthier citizens, and began a process of deregulating transportation industries, such as trucking and airlines. Suffice it to say, such abandoning of traditional liberal policies did not endear Carter to many of his party's stalwarts, who believed the Georgian was a turncoat, a conservative wolf in liberal sheep's clothing. Most important, Carter showed a complete inability to function effectively in the political whirligig of Washington. Having run for president as an "outsider," which had initial appeal, Carter, to even have a modicum of success in implementing his agenda, had to transition to becoming an "insider" once elected. His stubborn high-mindedness and self-righteousness prevented him from doing that, and consequently, his administration quickly deteriorated into a morass of indecision, insensitivity, and a permanent deadlock with the major political institutions. The Carter administration had difficulty working with Congress, even though his Democratic Party controlled it, and his administration never developed a strong relationship with the press, which was very influential in helping to shape how the Carter administration was perceived. "If the Carter administration were a television show," political commentator Russell Baker acidly noted, "it would have been canceled months ago." After leaving government, Carter reflected on his difficulties: "I had a different way of governing. . . . I was a southerner, a born-again Christian, a Baptist, a newcomer. . . . As an engineer and governor I was more inclined to move rapidly and without equivocation."

With the exception of the Iran Hostage Crisis, nothing illustrated both the struggles and weaknesses of the Carter presidency better than the energy crisis. Though confronting the energy issue directly and assessing its causes accurately, in the end, and despite sound proposals, Carter's intransigence and self-righteousness caused both his bill's demise and a loss of faith and confidence in his ability to govern the country. When Congress refused to respond to Carter's legislative initiatives, he retreated to the style of his campaign, attempting to reach over the head of Washington officials by delivering a sermon to the American people. Having gone off to a mountaintop retreat to hear the advice of religious leaders, historians, poets, and psychiatrists, he returned with a diagnosis that blamed America's malaise not on energy itself but on the "crisis of confidence [in the American people] . . . a crisis that strikes at the very heart and soul and spirit of our national will." In the past, Carter declared, Americans had "believed in something called progress," characterized by "a faith that the days of our children will be better than our own." Now, he said, the country had lost its bearings: "In a nation that was proud of hard work, strong families, close knit communities and our faith in God, too many of us now tend to worship self-indulgence and consumption. Human identity is no longer defined by what one does but by what one owns." With shrewd insight, Carter delineated the sources of America's troubled spirit: a narrow concern with self over community and a loss of faith in institutions because of political assassination, Vietnam, and the disgrace of Watergate. Carter described the problem but then offered no solutions. Instead, he simply asked fellow citizens to reject the "mistaken idea of freedom" and to restore their "faith and confidence" in traditional American values. The speech was a brilliant jeremiad, the words of a preacher or, more accurately, a therapist, attempting to express and resolve the uncertainty that gripped the population. However, the words failed to break the political stalemate that existed. Indeed, Carter's subsequent dismissal of half his cabinet simply seemed to confirm his ineffectuality as a politician and his utter inability to break "the paralysis and stagnation and drift," which in Carter's own words had come to characterize the American government.

The essence of Carter's problems was his sense of the presidency as a "trusteeship." Reflecting his religious and family background, this concept of being a steward in charge of the nation's well-being led Carter to eschew political negotiation as somehow being equivalent to betraying his mandate. Instead, he saw his role as studying the nation's problems, gathering all the facts, and then rendering an Olympian judgment that, by virtue of the process that had led to it, could not be questioned. In short, words such as compromise, negotiate, concede, and give and take were not part of Carter's political vocabulary, and, thus, he refused to the bitter end of his tenure to accept the reality that to be an effective legislative president one had to make such parlance part of his daily dialogue. Thus, on the energy issue, Carter developed legislation with 113 separate parts but *insisted* that the entire package be accepted *in toto*, since in his view the solution represented Solomonic wisdom, arrived at in a manner that made any change an assault on the integrity of the process, which an overly sensitive Carter regarded as a personal affront. The result, one historian has written, was that Carter tended "to equate his political goals with the just and right, and to view his opponents as representatives of some selfish or immoral interest." To put it in more succinct terms, to Carter, the born-again

Christian, everything political became a struggle between good and evil, righteousness versus wickedness, selflessness versus selfishness—the struggles and problems he had proclaimed were affecting the United States in his now infamous "malaise speech." From civil service reform to foreign policy initiatives, Carter's presidential agenda was suffused with questions of morality and ethics; in this world, political accommodation was somehow sordid.

Such an approach, however, was so antithetical to the realities of Washington politics that Carter had almost no chance of communicating or working effectively with those whom he had to enlist as allies to make his presidency even remotely successful. Dependent on cooperation to implement his goals, he instead guaranteed by his idealistic methods and expectations that such collaboration would never be forthcoming.

Another alienating issue was Carter's penchant for allowing his family, especially his wife, too visible a prominence in his administration. He even allotted his mother ceremonial duties, all of which led to increasing rebukes from around the nation. One national newspaper criticized Carter for treating his family as an "extension of his official self . . ., which is just all wrong in our democratic system. It makes a kind of quasi-royal family out of the president's kin." It was not just Miss Lillian's (Carter's mother's first name) activities that created public outcry but the seeming patronage and privileges granted to his wife, Rosalynn. Although subsequent first ladies (most notably Nancy Reagan and Hillary Clinton) played far more visible, activist roles in their husbands' administrations, the public simply was not ready to embrace a high-powered first lady during Carter's tenure. If Senator Hillary Clinton, whose professional credentials were far more legitimate (she was a very successful attorney) than Rosalynn Carter's, was often criticized for meddling in her husband's domain, then the public wrath that Mrs. Carter incurred is understandable. Moreover, unlike Bill Clinton, who never publicly announced or admitted how much of an advisor his wife may have been, Carter's openness on this subject proved debilitating and impolitic. From Rosalynn's sitting in on cabinet meetings and taking notes to her visiting with foreign heads-of-state, she appeared omnipresent in her husband's administration, causing many Americans to wonder who was actually running the country. They had elected Jimmy Carter president, not his wife, and expected Mrs. Carter to follow precedent and protocol when it came to the "appropriate behavior" for first ladies. Apparently neither "Ros" nor Jimmy were willing to stay within the confines of their respected roles, with the president publicly admitting that he considered his wife an integral component of the decision-making process of his administration. No matter how Carter tried to justify his wife's participation, he simply could not sell this particular folksy candor and spousal intimacy to late 1970s Americans. Indeed, the more Carter revealed about his relationship with Rosalynn and how it impacted policy, the more disdainful and alienated many Americans became from such an "emasculated" president.

Carter further diminished his image with his "honesty" by publicly discussing his interview with *Playboy* magazine, in which he admitted having, even after finding God, "lust in his heart." Carter was so obsessed with having a forthcoming and open administration that he believed that he must reveal even the most personal of "true confessions." What better way to reaffirm his humanity—that is, he was just like any other red-blood American male—than to profess that even the president of the United States has such feelings. Once again, however, Carter's candor backfired, alienating not only conservative Christians, who were appalled by the fact that he had consented to an interview with such a "dirty" magazine, but other Americans as well, who either did not care about his lust or who wondered why Carter felt compelled to discuss such a non-issue. In short, Carter's over-compensating attempt to present himself and his presidency as one of candor and honesty, regardless of the topic, ended up making him appear even less presidential. Americans simply did not care that he may have thought about other women but, rather, how he was going to fix a troubled land.

As noted earlier, during his tenure with the navy, Carter became heavily influenced by the management style of Admiral Hyman G. Rickover, whom Carter admired. The admiral's interpersonal and supervisory skills were not the most supportive or complimentary. Rickover was legendary for expressing supposed approval by simply not saying anything, which translated into "you were doing a fine job." Apparently, only when one was not measuring up would Rickover then speak, unleashing a vicious tirade of verbal abuse. Unfortunately, Carter adopted the admiral's style, bringing to the White House "Rickoverian" management techniques. Such an approach may have been somewhat effective in the navy, but in the White House, Carter's employment of his former boss's methods proved disastrous. After four years, the Oval Office staff was so demoralized and in such disarray that it could not project to the public even a modicum of confidence that the Carter administration had assembled the best and the brightest to cure the nation's ills. Carter became notorious for his tongue-lashings for minor mishaps among his staff, while saying virtually nothing to them for jobs well done. Because of such a management approach, it was no surprise that White House staff and cabinet members changed more often than usual. This image of a revolving door of advisers did not reassure an already skeptical public that their government was in the most secure, competent hands.

The *coup de grâce* to Jimmy Carter's presidency came five months after his energy or "malaise speech": the Iranian hostage crisis. Wanting to make a statement about U.S. intervention in Iranian affairs, militants seized the U.S. embassy in Teheran, taking fifty-two of its personnel hostage on November 4, 1979. Allegedly, the hostages were to be held until the United States agreed to return the deposed shah to stand trial for his years of crimes against the Iranian people. Carter was reluctant to use the military to try a rescue attempt of the hostages, waiting until the spring of 1980. When the military mission was unsuccessful due to mechanical problems with some of the helicopters, Carter gave up on a military option to secure the hostages' release. By not allowing the military to have the time and resources needed to overcome their setbacks and complete the mission, he made the military look incompetent, thus alienating one more national institution. The hostages languished in captivity for 444 days while Carter projected an image of dithering, unsure what to do next to try to get the hostages home.

The hostage crisis and Carter's apparent inability to secure their release only further confirmed the public's perception that Carter was a completely ineffectual neophyte, especially when it came to dealing with the *real politique* of a hostile world. Insult was added to injury relative to Carter and his mishandling of the crisis when the Iranians finally released the hostages on Inauguration Day, January 20, 1981, as the new president, Ronald Reagan, was taking his oath of office.

Carter perhaps could have weathered the hostage crisis better had it not come at the end of a decade that had witnessed American defeat in Vietnam, the constitutional crisis of Watergate, and the OPEC oil embargo. The hostage crisis reinforced and deepened American's sense of having lost control. Humiliated, embarrassed, and powerless to do anything about it, in the eyes of many of its citizens, the United States seemed to have become an emasculated, indecisive, second-rate power, a helpless pawn of external forces that treated the former leader of the free world with scornful contempt. Even before the hostage crisis, Carter's other foreign policy initiatives were in disarray. Even those who supported his goals conceded that Carter's leadership projected a lack of confidence in himself and the nation. Increasingly, his methods and ideas were perceived as detrimental to national security. Conservative critics believed Carter was selective in his human rights initiatives, punishing right-wing dictators, but giving their leftist counterparts the benefit of the doubt. As will be seen, Ronald Reagan's "get-tough-again" 1980 presidential campaign made Carter a symbol of foreign policy ineptitude. Carter's image of being weak and indecisive in foreign policy issues stemmed in part from fundamental flaws inherent in Carter's general foreign policymaking process. Carter himself, although skillful in handling small-group negotiations, had little experience working with long-term foreign policy initiatives. Furthermore, his top policy advisers, Secretary of State Cyrus Vance and National Security Adviser Zbigniew Brzezinski, often had contradictory approaches to policymaking. Brzezinski favored a hard-line anti-Soviet policy with an emphasis on military deterrence—a buildup of the United States nuclear arsenals and other advanced weaponry—while Vance preferred avoiding public confrontations and harsh Dulles-type rhetoric, emphasizing instead the virtues of quiet diplomacy. Pulled in divergent directions, Carter's policy often seemed to waffle.

Just as with Gerald Ford, Carter was sometimes the victim of circumstances that had nothing to do with his ability to be president but which led to a public perception of someone who was less than presidential. A case in point was the "killer rabbit" story. President Carter was out on a boat while vacationing when a crazed rabbit tried to hop aboard. Carter pushed the sick creature away with an oar and later shared the story with some of his aides. The incident made its way into the press where for some reason it was printed in the major newspapers and mentioned on network news. The story was about as relevant to Carter's ability to lead as the story of Ford tripping while getting off an airplane related to Ford's abilities, but the killer rabbit attack somehow became a metaphor for Carter's weakness. The killer rabbit was in the news for a week, and it was referenced whenever anyone wanted to make a point about how weak the United States had become and how much of an inviting target it was.

As a result of such misfortunes, the Carter presidency became permanently disabled. A pervasive sense of impotence spread through the nation, obscuring many of Carter's positive achievements and contributions. His successes, however, seemed ephemeral and could not overcome the cumulative frustration, distress, and anger of the American people. The economy was in a shambles, with inflation rates once again hitting double digits, unemployment threatening to reach 8 percent, and the whole nation watching, day and night for twelve months, as television commentators dissected the latest stories of America's national humiliation in Tehran. Carter had come into office pledging to restore decency, pride, and integrity to the American political process. Instead, he seemed utterly incapable of moving even Congress to enact a handful of his proposals, let alone a fanatical religious leader in Iran. As much a victim of circumstance as anything else, Carter felt—and acted—like a man under siege. Many of his own party, long alienated from the Georgia mafia at the White House, turned against him. Senator Edward Kennedy mounted a primary campaign to challenge the president's renomination (perhaps in hopes of vindicating his brother Robert's attempt to unseat an incumbent president in 1968, LBJ). Kennedy accused him of being a Republican clone with his tight money policies, his failure to do anything about the economy, and his betrayal of campaign promises made four years earlier. "We've exchanged radicals and wits for Jesus and grits," one liberal wag commented. To Democrats, as well as Republicans, it seemed time for a change, time to make one more effort at finally reversing the long nightmare of the seventies with its litany of defeat, humiliation, and decline, which Carter's presidency seemed to personify and exacerbate.

The Republican who rode in from the sunset to redeem America from its supposed "malaise" was Ronald Reagan. Known throughout the country for his movie performances and his television role as the host of both "Death Valley Days" and "GE Theatre," he had also been an effective and popular (especially with southern California conservatives) California governor in the late 1960s and early 1970s. Throughout most of the 1970s, Reagan devoted his energies to mobilizing Republicans with lecture appearances on the "rubber chicken" circuit. Despite his reputation as a staunch conservative, Reagan's appeal in 1980 was remarkably akin to that of Jimmy Carter in 1976. With great shrewdness, Reagan offered America yet another chance to recover what had been lost—this time by going back to rhetoric and a program that reminded the United States of its former power. Mustering as much of his Hollywood persona as he could, Reagan proved brilliant at delivering his message as simple verities: the United States was strong, great, and free. The American people believed in self-reliance, individualism, and patriotism. Communism was a false God; democracy the wave of the future. If America would only respond to Reagan's leadership, it could stand tall against foreign foes, recover the faith that Carter had found missing, and achieve once again the buoyancy of spirit and confidence of character that had distinguished the postwar era until 1973. Reagan offered a message of revival, as Carter had done in 1976, and the American people, once again desperate for a leader to carry them out of the wilderness, responded.

In retrospect, Carter never had a chance of being reelected. According to a 1980 Gallup poll, 46 percent of all Americans rated his presidency as either poor or below average. While Carter symbolized pessimism and doom, Reagan exuded optimism and hope. It was almost a replay of 1932, only this time the Democrat played the role of Herbert Hoover, while the Republican played the role of FDR. (Ironically, Ronald Reagan, as a young man growing up in the 1930s, was a staunch New Deal Democrat, whose first job out of college was with the CWA!) Carter, whom one political scientist called "the most conservative Democrat since Grover Cleveland," had lost credibility on the primary rallying point of the New Deal coalition—the notion that the Democrats were the party of the common folk and cared most about economic problems.

International events also worked decisively in Reagan's favor. Two-thirds of voters believed Reagan would be much more likely to maintain a strong posture against the Soviet Union. Only 27 percent felt the same way about Carter. Three out of four Americans believed Reagan would ensure that the United States was respected by other nations. The major obstacle that Reagan faced—a popular belief that he would be more likely to get the nation into war—evaporated in the aftermath of the Carter-Reagan debate two weeks before the election. Prior to the debate, 43 percent of potential voters expressed concern that Reagan would lead the nation into war, while only 19 percent expressed the same concern about Carter. After the debate, only 35 percent still believed Reagan was a dangerous militarist. Above all, the election was decided by public frustration and anger at the ineffectuality that Carter seemed to represent. Nearly 40 percent of those who voted for Reagan gave as their primary reason "it's time for a change." As one political scientist noted, the 1980 election represented more than anything else a "landslide vote of no confidence in an incompetent administration."

Carter's single term as president was definitely not one of the more illustrious in United States history. However, from the broader perspective that time affords, his foreign policy record in particular looks better and better. First among his many diplomatic accomplishments were the Camp David Accords, a personal triumph that established an unprecedented peace between two of the Middle East's most intractable adversaries, Egypt and Israel. In addition, his negotiating skills rendered the Panama Canal Treaties, which defused a potentially volatile Central American controversy, as well as going far toward helping to eradicate the "Yankee colossus" image of the United States in the eyes of many Latin American nations. Carter also fulfilled Nixon's initiatives with China by formalizing relations with China in 1979. Similarly, his support for Nixon's SALT II agreement with the Soviet Union, although never ratified, confirmed Carter's commitment to détente and arms control. Carter also denounced South African apartheid and helped to oversee the peaceful transition of white-ruled Rhodesia into black-controlled Zimbabwe. Carter also achieved a host of less showy but still significant diplomatic-military goals, including restoring stable relations with Greece and Turkey, NATO's vital southeast flank; reducing U.S. ground troops in South Korea; pardoning Vietnam War draft resisters, including those who had fled the country instead of being inducted; providing assistance to the Afghani rebels trying to drive the Red Army out of their country; making diplomatic overtures to Cuba and Vietnam; welcoming refugees from Indochina; scrapping the costly B-1 bomber; and canceling plans to develop a needless neutron bomb. As foreign policy historian Gaddis Smith observed, the Carter administration's "sheer level and range of activity, if not the results, suggested a foreign policy equivalent of the domestic activity of the first year of Franklin D. Roosevelt's New Deal."

During the 1980s, most pundits and wags criticized instead of praised Carter for his many significant successes. They "acknowledged" Carter only for what he did not do, such as abandon civil rights or send American soldiers to war. As veteran newspaperman Haynes Johnson noted, no matter what Carter did, "he received credit for almost nothing." Even Henry Kissinger recently admitted, "Carter never really got a fair shake." Undaunted by his critics, Carter forged ahead. Equipped with an unusual combination of spiritual strength and remarkable organizational skills, Carter took on some of the world's most volatile trouble spots: promoting democracy, mediating if not preventing potentially murderous conflicts, listening to those whose cries would otherwise go unheard, bringing aid to the afflicted, peace to the beleaguered, and hope to the despairing.

In 1998, an NBC/*Wall Street Journal* poll ranked Carter as having the highest moral character of any president, with 67 percent of those surveyed giving him "very high" marks; Bill Clinton (largely as the result of the Monica Lewinsky or "Zippergate" scandal) hovered near the bottom with Richard Nixon. Jimmy Carter, the penultimate antipolitician, was finally recognized by the American people seventeen years after leaving the White House for the moralistic disposition and unyielding rectitude that were the hallmarks of his presidency.

President Jimmy
Carter and
Rosalynn Carter
at the Inaugural
Ball.
January 20,
1977
Photo credit:
Jimmy Carter
Library

(right) Jimmy Carter at the podium
during a press conference.
October 10, 1978
(bottom) Menachem Begin, Jimmy
Carter, and Anwar Sadat during
one of the Camp David Summit
meetings.
September 7, 1978
Photo credit: Jimmy Carter Library

Jimmy Carter with King Hussein of Jordan. April 25, 1977 Photo credit: Jimmy Carter Library

Jimmy Carter and Giscard d'Estaing at a memorial ceremony for World War II GI's. January 5, 1978 Photo credit: Jimmy Carter Library

Jimmy Carter and Omar Torrijos signing the Panama Canal Treaty. June 16, 1978   Photo credit: Jimmy Carter Library

Ronald Reagan
1981- 1988

In 1999, a congressional member from Arizona proposed that the face of Ronald Reagan, 40th president of the United States, be added to the monumental visages on Mount Rushmore. The member was informed that, regrettably, the rock surface of the monument simply could not fit another face. The member suggested that they chisel off Thomas Jefferson to make room for Reagan, stating that Jefferson had been too much of a radical anyway. To date, the idea has been nixed.

The irony of this little anecdote is that in his own cheery, jovial way Ronald Reagan was as much a radical as was old Tom two centuries before. Both sought to reverse decades of established public thought, both rebelled against the reigning political orthodoxy of their own age, and both succeeded in replacing that orthodoxy with a new one derived, as each argued, from the thinking of an earlier, better time. For Jefferson, the new orthodoxy would be rooted in the classical liberal thought of John Locke and the English Enlightenment of the seventeenth century. For Ronald Reagan, the new orthodoxy would be rooted in American enlightenment ideals which dominated nineteenth century American thought: ideas of self-reliance, free markets, and the guiding mantra that the government that governed least governed best. Reagan argued that these ideals had been subverted by a New Deal agenda that after World War II had progressively moved towards an almost European Socialist, state-centered approach to American politics and society—an approach as alien to the American tradition of individualism as the fascism that America defeated in World War II and the communism that America combated in the cold war. Thus, Reagan entered politics—at first tentatively as a corporate pitchman, then more forcefully speaking on behalf of conservative politicians, and finally dominantly as a conservative candidate—seeking nothing less than to roll back the entire political legacy of the New Deal revolution. That he tried to role back the legacy of Roosevelt has been the basis for criticizing him on the left; that he was not entirely successful in doing so has resulted in criticism from the right. In either case, such criticism has conspired to deny Reagan a generally accepted place amongst the greatest presidents in the popular mind. These views, however, tend to seriously underestimate the true impact of Reagan on modern American politics.

Only one other modern president—Franklin Roosevelt—exerted the magnitude of influence on American politics and society as Reagan. Teddy Roosevelt had tried to fundamentally redefine his times, but his progressive politics of moderate Republicanism became bogged down in internecine party warfare and were then subsumed to the demands of global war. So, too, did Wilsonian idealism and internationalism disappear amidst the flappers and speakeasies of the roaring twenties. Franklin Roosevelt strode the middle of the twentieth century like a political and social colossus. Entering the presidency on a classical platform of balanced budgets and limited government, the cataclysmic disaster of the depression forced him to embrace the economic heresies of John Maynard Keynes, heresies because of their direct rejection of nineteenth century orthodoxy that said governments should never run deficits and the poor should be largely left to their own devices as an incentive to not remain poor. Roosevelt's New Deal was as radical a departure from previous precedent as was Jefferson's revolution. Between the New Deal social welfare and state aide programs and the civil rights movement of the 1950s, the federal government inserted itself ever more unprecedentedly into American society, undermining conservative ideals of state sovereignty to a greater degree than at any time since Reconstruction. Republicans who ran against the Democratic New Deal—from Herbert Hoover to Barry Goldwater—lost. Republicans who at least embraced the basic orthodoxy of government social welfare and social security—such as Dwight Eisenhower and Richard Nixon— might win, but at the expense of conservative Republican ideals and interests, becoming what conservative Republicans of the first decade of the twenty-first century referred to as "Rinos": Republican in name only. When Ronald Reagan won the presidency in 1980, Republicans seemed perpetually sentenced to second place status behind the Democratic Party whose hegemonic New Deal coalition—blue-collar workers, small business owners, social liberals, intellectuals, minorities, Catholics, and Jews—dominated electoral politics.

Yet, Reagan saw and took political advantage of the growing cracks in this Democratic monolith—the increasing divide, for example, between blue-collar workers seeing inflation-adjusted wages decline through the 1970s and minorities just beginning to reap some benefit from affirmative action and other social civil rights policies—which caused the coalition to soon disintegrate (just as he was confident—and correctly so, as history quickly revealed—that the soon to be labeled "Evil Empire" had already entered its Gibbonesque stages of decline and fall). That he may not have correctly analyzed in political terms just why these changes were occurring by 1980 is forgivable enough. In politics it is enough to be a winner, even if one wins for the wrong reasons. Reagan would not erase the New Deal legacy, but he would slow it down and, in some cases, such as in New Deal labor law and Great Society affirmative action, roll it back. Moreover, he reintroduced a tone of limited government that had been largely excluded from meaningful inclusion in public debate for two generations, a tone that dominated American political discussion for the balance of the century. So dominant did Reagan's rhetoric of small government become that the only post-Reagan Democratic president would be forced to admit that "the era of big government" was over.

The Reagan legacy would stride the balance of the twentieth century, as completely as Roosevelt did its middle. Reagan was the catalyst for the great realignment of the Republican Party, the tip point in the transition of Republicanism from the postwar moderate "new Republicanism" of Eisenhower to the so-called kinder, gentler, yet far more ideologically aggressive conservatism of George W. Bush. Reagan tempered the extremism of the pioneers of this conservative backlash to New Deal liberalism—Barry Goldwater and George Wallace—and made their anti-government message more palatable for middle American tastes. In the process, Reagan created a new, great, and unprecedented political alignment, pulling blue-collar workers, southern social conservatives, and corporate America into one alliance against social and economic liberals. Reagan not only reinvigorated conservatives; he set the stage for their domination of the Republican Party and capture of Congress in the 1990s and the election of the most conservative American president, both in rhetoric and action, since the 1920s, if not before.

That neither Ronald Reagan nor Franklin Roosevelt have their faces carved on a South Dakota mountainside is of little consequence. FDR and Ronald Reagan stand as the two antithetical ideological pillars of twentieth century American politics to which all other presidents of their time have served as preludes or reactions—or the consequences thereof. Thus, Reagan, for good or ill (and as American society becomes more politically polarized in the first decade of the twenty-first century, such judgments will no doubt become more, rather than less, contentious), stands out as the most significant Republican president of the twentieth century.

Ronald Reagan was not born into the idyllic middle America of the early twentieth century that he spent his political career trying to recreate. He was born in 1911 in Tampico, Illinois, the second of two sons of an alcoholic and unsuccessful shoe salesman and a protective, religious mother. Ronald's father, Jack, moved the family frequently over the next nine years in a fruitless quest for a larger slice of the American pie. The Reagans eventually settled in Dixon, Illinois, providing a greater degree of stability, though not of the financial kind, in the future president's life. Reagan later joked in his autobiography, *Where's the Rest of Me?* "Those were the days when I learned the riches of rags."

They were also the days that left an indelible mark on him: the desire to learn to live happy no matter what the truth of the day, least one get swamped by the harsher realities of life. Children of alcoholics often have two different paths to follow: they can fall into a life of wallowing in the despair of their upbringing, thus dooming themselves to perpetuate the pathology of their parents; or they can create their own alternative, kinder, and gentler universe and immerse themselves in it. The latter was to be young Ronald's choice. He recreated his childhood, both as he lived it and later, as he relived it, acting as if the motto he wrote in his high school yearbook had been the reality of his life all along: "Life is just one grand sweet song, so start the music." Reagan's first lessons in such acting came from watching his own persevering Scottish mother, Nelle, who escaped the reality of their household's poverty and alcoholism by giving dramatic readings before clubs, in prisons, and in hospitals, young Ronald in tow. From grade school through high school, he learned the joy of performing—of living through the adulation of others—both on school stages and school playing fields. Like a surprisingly large number of modern American presidents (at least, surprising from a platonic guardian or mandarin bureaucracy model of good governance), Reagan was fairly weak when it came to the school books. He excelled, however, when it came to winning the hearts and minds of his classmates.

Across his adult life, Reagan would wax poetic about his middle America upbringing, saying that his early hardscrabble years actually "turned into one of those rare Huck Finn/Tom Sawyer idylls." Indeed, his vision of what America should be like was formed almost in its entirety by his early Dixon, Illinois, days, "a place where life was wholesome . . . people trusted each other, and nobody locked his door at night." Like Walt Disney, another small town boy who endured a rough upbringing and later dedicated his adult life to celebrating an idyllic small town life that never really existed, Reagan spent his professional lives—both in acting and politics—recreating idyllic worlds that had never really been. Disney would be content to recreate a fictional, wholesome "Main Street" in a theme park. Reagan sought to recreate his Dixon on a national scale through the power of the presidency.

Nicknamed "Dutch" by his older brother, Neal, Reagan was a popular high school student, doing well on both the basketball and football teams. He spent seven summers as a lifeguard at a nearby beach, for which he gained local stature—including a front-page headline in the town paper—for saving seventy-seven lives. This image as hero became "the central symbol of his youth," according to one of his later biographers, and contributed to his view of the power of individuals in looking out for each other. Reagan would be one of the minority of his generation to go on from high school to higher education, enrolling in 1928 at a small Christian college near Peoria, Illinois. Unlike some other presidents who spent their college years living a pampered life with the fraternity boys, Reagan put himself through Eureka College by washing dishes in the fraternity house and saving money from his summer lifeguard job. Over the next four years, Reagan studied economics but focused his real energies on sports and acting. While most of his biographers are content to dismiss his academic performance as passing at best, the simple fact that a child of an alcoholic household, consisting of two parents with grade school educations, was able to attend and graduate from any college was a phenomenal personal accomplishment at that time. That Reagan never seems to have realized the magnitude of this accomplishment was just one more example of his basic nature as a self-effacing, self-made man.

Hence, Ronald Reagan was one of those really obnoxious people (from the viewpoint of most mere mortals): the truly self-made man. Through his own effort—and a large dose of the requisite luck with which all self-made men are blessed (the "fortuna" Machiavelli's good prince learns how to master)—Reagan rose from the poverty of his Dixon upbringing to the greatest heights of fame and power. The danger of the self-made man, however, especially the self-effacing one who sees little special enough about himself to have caused Dame Fortune to dally with him, is his later tendency to remember the personal efforts that got him where he was and downplay the luck factor. In his later years Reagan saw nothing unusual in his own success: with hard work and the simple luck to live in America, anyone should be able to achieve what he achieved, he reasoned. The fact that sheer luck—the luck to have gotten that first Warner Brother's contract, the luck to have his movie career peter out by the late 1950s pushing him into other venues, the luck to have Barry Goldwater and Richard Nixon flame out fabulously, leaving the field for conservative leadership wide open—had had much to do with his success became a progressively diminishing plot line in his own personal narrative. Thus, Reagan's own humility actually blinded him to his own uniqueness—and the plight of others far less lucky or self-driven—more than ego would have. Indeed, in looking at modern presidents, it has been precisely the most ego-driven—Wilson, Roosevelt, Johnson, and Clinton—who have reached out to help those "less fortunate" than their self-perceived godlike selves.

It was at Eureka College that Reagan literally had his "eureka" political moment. When the college president proposed cutting back the curriculum and the teaching staff because of a shortage of funds, freshman Reagan gave the main speech at a student rally that won support from the rest of the students for a college-wide strike. The strike resulted in the president's resignation. Reagan later said that he learned then what his skill with an audience could accomplish—a pivotal life lesson. That Reagan should have his first taste of politics supporting a student strike in favor of increased social spending is, of course, one of those little ironies that make life delicious.

Reagan graduated from college in 1932, the year Roosevelt would be elected, during the worst economic depression of modern times. While Reagan had been born into a poor household and had grown up under conditions of material deprivation, he was largely personally unaffected by the economic cataclysm of the 1930s. Passing the first years of the depression in college, within months of graduation he had landed a job as a radio announcer doing play-by-play football broadcasts for an Iowa radio station. Within four years he became one of the top midwestern sports broadcasters, working out of Chicago. For Reagan, who later developed a consuming nostalgia for the golden days of American society prior to the rise of the "crushing" big government unleashed by FDR's New Deal, the depression years themselves were actually the first years of his life in which he experienced a taste of material abundance. Thus, when he accompanied the Chicago Cubs in 1937 to their spring training in Los Angeles, only to be "discovered" in the great Hollywood style and offered a movie contract by Warner Brothers, it was just one more natural step in what was for Reagan a wonderful decade.

Reagan went on to appear in dozens of films over the next few years, most of them of the entertaining but forgettable variety that Hollywood churned out to offer the masses momentary distraction from the hardships of the depression—hardships that the young actor would need never experience again. He was primarily part of the movie studio "B" list of actors—cast most often in supporting roles rather than the leads (leading one network anchor to quip of Reagan's quest for the nomination during the 1976 Republican convention that it should actually be George Raft for president, Ronald Reagan for best friend). In 1940, Reagan married his first wife, Jane Wyman, (with whom he had two children, and would later divorce by the end of the decade). That same year he starred in his most noted film, playing the football legend George Gipp in "Knute Rockne, All American." In that role he uttered his most famous movie line as the dying hero, "Win one for the Gipper," thereby providing himself with both a national nickname and, two decades later, a ready-made campaign slogan that graced uncountable bumper stickers and campaign placards. Having enlisted in the army reserve in 1935, Reagan had risen to the rank of second lieutenant by the time war broke out in 1942. Called to active duty, he spent the war years churning out training and propaganda films, as part of the 1st Motion Picture Unit of the U. S. Army Air Forces in Culver City, California, nearsightedness keeping him from front-line duty. Discharged from the army in 1945 with the rank of captain, he promptly signed a million-dollar contract with Warner Brothers, but his best movie days were already behind him. By 1951, he would be making truly "B" fair, playing second banana to a chimp in "Bed Time for Bonzo."

Even as Reagan's star days wound down, he discovered another avocation—politics. Ronald Reagan was born into a family of good midwestern Democrats. Like his father, he supported Roosevelt in 1932 and cheered on the New Deal, voting for FDR in the next three presidential elections. He came out of his military service in Hollywood adopting progressively more conservative views, however, increasingly mistrusting the increasingly large role government was taking in American society. While brought up with a working class distrust of "big business," Reagan's postwar experience convinced him that "the real enemy" of American freedom and vitality was "big government."

His election in 1947 to the presidency of the Screen Actors Guild (SAG) would be the pivotal year in Reagan's political evolution. That his first real foray into a political role would be as head of a labor union is another Reagan irony. Reagan had been appointed to the board of the Screen Actors Guild in 1941. In 1946, Reagan was asked by the SAG board to mediate a dispute between rival unions, including the Conference of Studio Unions, led by a man suspected of communist connections.

Reagan was not a complete stranger to the issue of communism in Hollywood that came to dominate the community in the late 1940s and early 1950s, having served as an informant for the FBI since 1941. The union mediation experience reinforced Reagan's distrust of communism and communist sympathizers; the following year he testified as a friendly witness—though refusing to "name names" before the House Committee on Un-American Activities (whose hearings resulted in imprisonment of "the Hollywood Ten" and the blacklisting of numerous others). The apparently rising specter of communism as a global menace following the war Reagan found disturbing enough; that it could be found corrupting the "American Dream" factory of Hollywood was intolerable. Reagan also found the tendency of his more liberal colleagues in the film industry to be tolerant of their fellow film professionals' various peccadilloes, including flirtations or outright affairs with communism, increasingly alienating. While Reagan campaigned for Harry Truman in 1948 and Democratic senatorial candidate Helen Douglas in the spring of 1950, he switched his allegiance to the Republican Party that fall, campaigning for anti-communist Richard Nixon. By 1952, Reagan would "Like Ike," leading a "Democrats for Eisenhower" campaign (a role he reprised in 1956). As the fifties progressed, so did Reagan's conversion to conservative principles and politics.

Reagan was re-elected to five more one-year terms as the Screen Actors Guild president. By 1952, though, he had a new wife (the former actress Nancy Davis) and a new career to supplement his declining screen presence. Having taken a job as host and occasional star of General Electric's GE Theatre television show, he also become a spokesman for GE, touring the company's U.S. facilities to give pro-GE, pro-business morale-boosting speeches to company employees and public groups. The experience provided him with, in his words, "a post-graduate in political science," albeit one whose curriculum was written far more by the Harvard Business School and the *Wall Street Journal* than by the University of California Berkeley political science department.

While as president of SAG Reagan had fought successfully to achieve better benefits and working conditions for actors, his experience working for the other side of the corporate table with GE changed his views about management-labor relations. Following a SAG strike in 1960, Reagan resigned from the SAG board. From 1960 onwards, he increasingly saw organized labor as a hindrance to American free enterprise, especially the efficient postwar corporate sort of free enterprise epitomized by General Electric on its endless quest to bring good things—increasing profits included—to life. Thus, the image of "big government" and "big labor," as had grown out of the Roosevelt New Deal, constraining and even strangling the American entrepreneurial spirit, became the stock theme of his GE speeches. The speeches also provided him with the political equivalent of an "off-Broadway" run to hone and improve his own political one-man show prior to taking the act onto the big stage. Reagan was dumped by GE in 1962 from both his television show and his pitchman role, following a change in management at the corporation (and, according to a version of events different from that told by Reagan, at least in part because of attacks he had made in his speeches on the Tennessee Valley Authority, with whom GE had millions of dollars worth of contracts, as an example of "big government" that needed to be cut). But, by then, he was already established as a rising political voice of the new Republican conservatism that bloomed in the deserts of the American west in the post-Eisenhower years.

While Reagan embraced Eisenhower in 1952 and 1956, the brand of conservatism he was gravitating towards by the early 1960s was not Ike's "Modern Republicanism" with its acceptance of core New Deal values tempered by an old-fashioned commitment to a balanced budget. Rising in the western Republican Party was a new brand of conservatism that saw no value in compromise with New Deal Democrats or with what these conservatives saw as creeping (or running rampant, depending how far to the right in the movement one was) socialism. Steeped in a western frontier tradition turned new political mythology, they rejected the Republican Party's eastern establishment divided between Robert Taft isolationists and Nelson Rockefeller social liberals, but they also rejected Eisenhower's internationalism. Instead, they stressed a new formulation: rejection of the social welfare state and a return to doctrines of self-reliance coupled with a commitment to a strong national defense unencumbered by any over-reliance on multilateral commitments.

What good did it do Republicans, asked these rising voices in western state Republican politics like Barry Goldwater from Arizona, to compromise with Democrats on social spending when Democrats, having tasted the wine of deficit spending, would always demand more—more spending, more regulation—until the country drowned in the vintage of state socialism? These new voices in the Republican Party sounded more like southern conservative Democrats on issues of defense and domestic policy—especially the civil rights movement and, to them, the Pandora's box of endless government social meddling it posed—than the traditional northeastern Republicans who had dominated the party since

Reconstruction. That it would fall to a former midwestern sportscaster turned Hollywood actor turned corporate pitchman to eventually fuse these two strains of American politics—western and southern conservatism—was not readily apparent in 1960. But Nixon's defeat at the hands of east coast liberal John F. Kennedy, followed by his 1962 defeat in the race for California governor by west coast liberal Edmund "Pat" Brown, convinced Reagan that the Eisenhower "Modern Republican" model was a political dead end. The only hope to stem the rising tide of Democratic socialism, Reagan began to believe, was nothing less than a new Republican revolution—or, better said, counter-revolution—stressing a return to classic American values of self-reliance and limited government.

Reagan left the party of Roosevelt in the fall 1962, though as he saw it, he had not left the party of FDR; it had, instead, been co-opted by a new strain of big government liberalism that Reagan had never opted for, even as a liberal youth. When Reagan cast his first ballot as a Democrat in 1932, as he wrote in his autobiography, it had been for a Roosevelt who had advocated cutting federal spending, returning power to the states and getting government out of the business of providing relief. Reagan believed that Roosevelt had never intended the New Deal policies to continue beyond the immediate crisis of the depression (a somewhat dubious claim, especially given the Keynesian worldview Roosevelt sought to imprint upon the postwar world through the Bretton Woods Accords). The war had resulted in the creation of a huge government bureaucracy and the mindset of unlimited big government had captured and become entrenched in the post-Roosevelt Democratic Party. By 1960, Reagan became convinced that

> some of our fundamental freedoms were in jeopardy because of the emergence of a permanent government never envisioned by the framers of the Constitution: a federal bureaucracy that was becoming so powerful it was able to set policy and thwart the desires not only of ordinary citizens, but of their elected representatives in Congress.

With Nixon defeated and Eisenhower retired, the Republican Party drifted through the first years of the 1960s without a strong, national voice. The Kennedy assassination and the unexpected elevation of Lyndon Baines Johnson to the presidency completely upset Republican calculations for the 1964 election. Rather than facing an incumbent Democratic president with a relatively weak record of domestic accomplishment and a brewing crisis in Southeast Asia, Republicans now confronted the standard-bearer of a slain national hero whose death instantly thrust him into the American pantheon of political demigods. Barry Goldwater's successful, if contentious, triumph at the Republican national convention signaled the triumph of western Republican conservatism at the national party level. The strident tone of his campaign, however, particularly its early, unrefined message of blatant American exceptionalism and call for a unilateral foreign policy—a message that took the Reagan years to polish and the George W. Bush years to effect—coupled with the pro-Kennedy sentiment of an electorate still enamored with Democratic New Dealism, resulted in Johnson's crushing victory.

The magnitude of the Goldwater defeat forever removed the Arizona senator from future contention as the new conservative leader, leaving the stage door wide open for Reagan to stride through and onto the national political stage—entering stage right, of course. Reagan's entry into national politics was announced by a highly acclaimed televised speech he gave for Goldwater in October 1964. Entitled "A Time for Choosing," the speech was a blistering attack on "big government" and the Great Society programs Johnson had begun pushing through Congress as part of the Kennedy legacy. Having had the better part of ten years to hone his message to a cutting edge, first on the General Electric stump and later in campaign speeches for Republican candidates, and with almost thirty years of professional acting experience to polish off his delivery, Reagan instantly became the first Republican political star of the television era and, following the electoral debacle, the clearleader of the Republican conservative movement. By the end of November, a political support group, the "Friends of Ronald Reagan," had formed, and within a year supporters were steering him towards a run for California governor.

When asked during the 1966 gubernatorial campaign what kind of a governor he would be, Reagan joked, "I don't know; I've never played a governor." A political novice aspiring to his state's highest office his first time out and running against a two-term popular incumbent with a substantial record of achievement, one might have expected the 1966 vote to have been a replay of the 1964 conservative fiasco on a state-size stage. Instead, Reagan's promise to cut property taxes, reduce government waste, especially in social welfare, and curb student unrest on California's campuses, which was rising with the escalating American commitment of troops to Vietnam, resonated with California voters. Reagan beat Pat Brown by over a million votes.

Once in office, however, Reagan quickly discovered the limits to campaign rhetoric that checks and balance government provides, especially when the legislature is dominated by the opposition party. Inheriting a $200 million deficit, his call for 10 percent across the board cuts in services and programs, including education and healthcare, was met with a firestorm of Democratic and popular opposition. Reagan learned that, while in theory the public likes limited and lean government, in practice politicians receive few kudos for limiting those pieces of government that some interest groups care about (which is just about all pieces of government). Thus, Reagan dealt with the state budget crisis by compromise rather than a rigid adherence to conservative principle, a strategy he again embraced in dealing with a Democratic Congress. In California, however, he worked to achieve a balanced budget by agreeing to a substantial tax increase (a move over which he later expressed regret) in return for legislative approval of some of his budget cut package. While president, he compromised in the exact opposite direction, agreeing to budget increases in exchange for a tax cut, with the obvious fiscal results. (The apparent critical difference in the two cases is the fact that the government of California was required to maintain a balanced budget, while such humdrum limitations did not exist at the national level.) Meanwhile, pushed in the spring of 1967 by the more liberal legislature and public opinion, Governor Reagan signed a permissive abortion bill, another act over which he later expressed regret but which he never sought to rescind.

Reagan went into 1968 bitten by that most virulent of maladies that seem to affect all California governors—some sooner rather than later—"Presidentialitis." Indeed, while the governorship of California was a good stepping stone, Reagan's real political ambitions and previous political experience (in terms of campaign activities) were both largely presidential in nature. The California governorship was (and is) to the presidency as television is to motion pictures: a much smaller screen with a much smaller audience and much smaller rewards. By 1968, Reagan was ready to consider regaining stardom on the "Big Screen." While Richard Nixon set about his own campaign for political rehabilitation, during the spring of 1968, a "draft Reagan" movement was begun by Reagan loyalists, including his chief aides and a cadre of millionaires who had backed his run for governor and served as his "kitchen cabinet" (a role they reprised during his presidency). Avoiding any primary challenges (a tactic now all but unthinkable), Reagan only announced his candidacy at the Miami national convention in large part to test the waters for his later viability and, in small part, on the off chance that the convention might deadlock between rivals Nixon and moderate Nelson Rockefeller. When it looked like Nixon's victory was inevitable, Reagan threw him his support and gracefully bowed out. But Reagan had demonstrated that one could mention his name and the word "president" in the same sentence and not get laughed at, which was not bad for a former actor with slightly over a year's experience in elected office. Meanwhile, the most important political development of 1968 for Reagan would be the success of renegade Democrat Alabama Governor George Wallace, whose anti-Liberal, anti-Washington, and anti-civil rights rhetoric resonated with white blue-collar workers and southern social conservatives alike, fracturing irreparably the New Deal Democratic coalition and allowing Nixon to triumph over liberal Democrat and incumbent Vice President Hubert Humphrey. Reagan spent the 1970s pasteurizing the Wallace anti-Washington message and would ride it—and the grand coalition at which Wallace's success in 1968 hinted but that Reagan actually forged— to victory twelve years later.

Re-elected by a comfortable margin in 1970, the centerpiece of Reagan's second term was building consensus around a welfare reform bill that sought to codify some of the key themes of Reagan conservatism: limiting time on welfare rolls and adopting procedures to move people from welfare to work. By 1972, the California budget would be balanced and a tax surplus returned to the voters, but all American politics would soon be overshadowed—for the better part of two years as it turned out— by the developing Watergate scandal. Reagan supported Nixon loyally, only indicating that he thought the president had deceived the country three days before Nixon's resignation. By that time in the summer of 1974, his own aides and supporters were already laying the groundwork for a 1976 presidential run, booking him to deliver speeches, newspaper columns, and radio addresses on a national scale. Gerald Ford's ascension to the presidency threw a slight monkey wrench into the equation, as Reagan's people had not initially counted on running against a Republican incumbent for the party's nomination. Ford's own weakness, however, in dealing with the economic crisis of stagflation—simultaneously rising unemployment and prices that were the byproducts of the 1973 OPEC oil embargo, rising global trade competition, and budget deficits left over from the Vietnam era—reinforced the Reagan camp's view that change was needed and needed quickly.

Moreover, Gerald Ford had made his political career as the "get along" Republican minority leader in the House of Representatives, willing to compromise on core conservative principles in fiscal and social policy with majority Democrats in exchange for marginal influence on policy-making (a condition that House Republicans endured until the Gingrich revolution twenty years later). Thus, by Goldwater-Reagan standards, Ford was something of an ideological throwback to the Eisenhower era, the very "conservative-lite" moderation that Reagan had spent the 1960s working to undermine. Ford's selection of none other than Republican liberal Nelson Rockefeller to serve out the vacant term of vice president only confirmed this verdict in the eyes of conservatives. Indeed, by these same evolving conservative standards, stressing the need to not just check but dramatically roll back government economic intervention, much of Nixon's own domestic agenda, from expanding welfare programs for families to anti-inflationary wage and price controls, smacked of left of centerness, and his policy of détente smacked directly of Eisenhower's push for peaceful coexistence. In retrospect, even Nixon would be too "pink," too pro-government for these Republican conservatives. Ultimately, therefore, the politician in the 1968 and 1972 presidential races closest to the core values of what became the Reagan revolution was southern conservative George Wallace, whose core constituency Reagan accessed with great success in 1980. Beating Gerald Ford for the Republican's 1976 nomination became a first critical, though losing, battle in the final triumph of Republican new conservatives.

Aware of the potential threat that Reagan posed to Ford, the new Republican president tried three times to preempt any California insurgency by offering Reagan a series of positions in his administration: Ambassador to the Court of St. James (the pomp and circumstance of which Ford's people must have hoped would be simply irresistible to a minor member of Hollywood nobility), Secretary of Transportation, and even Secretary of Commerce. Ford pursued a similar tact more successfully with another potential rival, George H. W. Bush, packing the Texan off to China as envoy. Reagan, however, refused to take the bait, even though he was technically unemployed by the end of 1974 after eight years as California governor. (Once again demonstrating the endless fickleness of the California electorate, Reagan would be replaced by the ultra-liberal son of the man he himself had defeated in 1966, Jerry Brown, who, as "Governor Moonbeam," as the press labeled him, spent much of his own two terms in office reversing the Reagan years.)

Reagan's real battle for his party's nomination was in 1976, and even his ultimate loss to Gerald Ford worked dramatically to his own advantage. Had Reagan triumphed over Ford at the convention that summer, it is likely that moderate Republicans would have defected to Jimmy Carter, turning Reagan into a new version of Barry Goldwater and possibly aborting the Reagan revolution before it ever occurred. Had Reagan actually won in 1976, he would have inherited a presidency plagued by an economy even structurally weaker than it would be in 1980 (at least six years from meaningful recovery then versus only two years in 1980) and an America still reeling from Vietnam and, thus, far less likely to embrace his more activist foreign and defense policy. Unlike 1968, Reagan fought a hard uphill battle against Ford across the 1976 primary season, coming close to upsetting the incumbent in New Hampshire and scoring an upset win in North Carolina after blasting Ford for continuing the Nixon policy of détente with the U.S.S.R. and communist China. Strapped for money and under constant pressure by the Republican Party hierarchy to abort his run (ultimately most former national party chairmen, as well as the conferences of Republican mayors and governors, called on the "Gipper" to give it up), Reagan took his struggle right to the convention itself. In a moment of drama, one network anchor compared the situation to something right out of an Allen Drury novel (Drury was the noted writer of the "Advise and Consent" series of political thrillers from the 1950s to the 1970s). Both Ford and Reagan duked it out in the hours leading up to the first convention vote with Ford offering Reagan the vice presidency if he would withdraw from contesting the nomination, and Reagan offering Ford the exact same deal. Ultimately, Ford's incumbency trumped Reagan's chutzpah, winning the nomination on the first ballot. Ford's close November loss to the little-known governor of Georgia, Jimmy Carter, left Reagan the heir apparent for the 1980 nomination, even if moderate Republicans seemed oblivious to that new reality.

Reagan spent the next four years working on his ranch in the mountains above Santa Barbara and laying the ground work for the inevitable 1980 presidential run, making speeches and publishing columns with one unifying theme: under the tax-and-spend domestic policy and détente-appeasement foreign policies of the Carter administration, the United States and the entire free world were fast going to hell in the proverbial handbasket. Meanwhile, both domestic and global events worked to confirm Reagan's charges of mismanagement under Carter. The pattern of stagflation that developed under Nixon continued under Carter, with both unemployment and inflation pushing double digits simultaneously for the first time in American history. Moreover, in the face of American post-Vietnam retrenchment, the Soviet Union seemed on an expansionist roll, with pro-communist regimes coming to power in both the Horn of Africa and southern Africa, and culminating in the 1979 Sandinista communist takeover of Nicaragua and the Soviet invasion of Afghanistan. To compound American problems, the shah of Iran, leader of America's most important Middle Eastern ally after Israel, was toppled by a revolution led by a radical Islamic religious leader, the Ayatollah Khomeini, intractably hostile to all things Western.

On November 13, 1979, nine days after Iranian student radicals stormed the American Embassy in Tehran, taking fifty-two Americans hostage, Reagan declared his renewed candidacy for the presidency, becoming the tenth (and final) Republican to do so in the crowded 1980 field. The other nine, as it turned out, need not have applied. In principle, the 1980 Republican race settled down to a contest between Reagan, heir to the Goldwater conservative movement, and George H.W. Bush, heir to the Eisenhower-Rockefeller moderate wing of the party. Unfortunately for Bush, the Republican Party—especially the activists most likely to participate in the primary contest—had moved farther to the right over the previous twenty years, doing so in response to the continued subordination of the Republican Party as the apparent perpetual junior partner of national politics in the post-Roosevelt era, and also in response to the apparent continued drift of America from "traditional" values under the liberal social policies of the Democrats.

Bush was the favorite of both pundits and the Republican establishment if for no other reason than the "powers that were" did not believe that Reagan's Goldwater/Wallace-esque rhetoric of American unilateralism abroad and rolling back the welfare state at home resonated with the post-modern 1980 voter. At what became known as the "Ambush at Nashua"—a New Hampshire debate between Reagan, Bush and, inadvertently, four of the other candidates—Reagan basically wrapped up the nomination with one well-delivered, crushing line. The debate was originally to be between just Bush and Reagan until other candidates (especially Bob Dole, who would have to wait until 1996 for his day, short as it proved to be, in the presidential sun) protested. Reagan's people ultimately agreed to pay the extra costs of including the lesser candidates, but come the night of the debate, the Bush people pulled a snit (on national television—never a good idea) and refused to allow the other candidates to participate. When Reagan attempted to argue for their inclusion, the editor of the Nashua paper hosting the event ordered his microphone cut off. Reagan's response was a classic line of political riposte, "I am paying for this microphone." With that one line, amidst the backdrop of George Bush looking befuddled and the other candidates looking dependent, Reagan established himself as the only true leader of the Republican Party. That Reagan had spent a professional lifetime learning precisely how to deliver the crucial line on cue—be it "Where's the rest of me?" or "Win one for the Gipper!" or "I'm paying for this microphone"—in no way diminished the impact of his performance on Republican voters (and neither did the fact of knowing how to deliver a line and knowing how to actually write—originally and creatively—the line in the first place, both of which are very different skills). Reagan's 51 percent victory in the seven-way New Hampshire primary essentially clinched the nomination battle at its inception.

Reagan ran for the nomination on a simple three-part plan: cut taxes and cut spending even more, except for defense spending, which must be significantly (that is, massively) expanded to counter the increasing threat of the communist bloc (and to intimidate upstart threats such as Iran). Bush attacked Reagan on his economic plan, which counted on increased long-term tax revenues from short-term tax cuts to eventually eliminate the rising federal budget as "voodoo economics." Except for being anti-Reagan and anti-Carter, however, Bush failed to advance an agenda that resonated with Republican primary voters (foreshadowing how, as president, he would be unable to articulate a vision beyond that of being "pro-Reagan").

Reagan swept his way to the July Republican convention, which, for the first time since the Eisenhower years, had an air of unity and hopefulness about it. In his acceptance speech, Reagan laid out the core message of his fall campaign:

They say that the United States has had its day in the sun, that our nation has passed its zenith. They expect you to tell your children that the American people no longer have the will to cope with their problems, that the future will be one of sacrifice and few opportunities. My fellow citizens, I utterly reject that view.

After Gerald Ford rejected Reagan's overtures to join him as vice president on a dream ticket (once again, the realities of human ego overcoming political expediency), Reagan offered the second place on the ticket to his chief nomination rival, George H. W. Bush, thereby securing the moderate wing of the party (though at the cost of leaving himself no true ideological heir until, ironically, Bush's own son, George W., avenged his father's 1992 defeat and instituted a presidency that attempted to pursue an even purer Reagan vision—at least in foreign policy—than even the Gipper himself had been capable of).

Reagan's single biggest liability in the fall campaign would be his age. At 70, he was the oldest man to ever pursue the presidency. But by 1980, battered by the weakest economy in two generations—an economy that ultimately marked the end of the postwar economic boom—and confidence shaken by defeat in Vietnam, emasculation in Iran and a general perception of looming Soviet triumph, the American electorate was no longer the "New Frontier" society that had embraced a John F. Kennedy. The American electorate had become cautious, worried, and, above all, nostalgic for a day when America's place in the sun seemed as secure as the next sunrise. Jimmy Carter's analysis that America was afflicted by a malaise more psychological than real—correct as it might have been (remembering in hindsight that the Soviet empire was a scant decade away from total collapse and America a equal distance of time from becoming the strongest hegemon in global history)—simply had limited truck with a population looking for someone other than themselves to blame for their malaise. (One does well to remember that the most popular sitcom of the 1970s was the 1950's ode de grandeur, "Happy Days"—who better than a 1950s actor to replace "The Fonz" on the 1980's national stage?)

The Carter campaign completely misjudged how Reagan's message—one they tried across the campaign to paint as far to the right of the American mainstream—resonated with an increasingly conservative public, especially amongst blue-collar workers who had been the mainstay of the Democratic New Deal coalition for almost half a century. Reagan's great success lay in his ability to take such conservative ideas—like his wholesale attack on taxes, government spending, and all manner of social programs—and deliver them with such an air of geniality and humor as to make them far more palatable than when they had been advanced by George Wallace or Barry Goldwater. Carter had won election in 1976 in large part based on his folksy image of honest integrity. In 1980, with the practiced skill of the thespian he was, Reagan was able to out-folksy and out-honest Carter; nothing has as great an image of genuine integrity as a role practiced to perfection. Moreover, Carter's real failures in securing economic recovery, in countering Soviet expansion, and in dealing with the national humiliation of the Iranian hostage crisis (actually made worse by his administration's failed hostage rescue effort the previous spring) undercut Carter's claims that Reagan was dangerous and divisive.

Indeed, by the election, Reagan had succeeded in unifying America in opposition to Jimmy Carter more than it had been at any point since LBJ's electoral landslide against Reagan's mentor in 1964.

(Some mention might be made of the independent run of Republican congressman John Anderson, which foreshadowed similar runs by Ross Perot, Ralph Nader, and Patrick Buchanan but, given Anderson's utter lack of impact on the 1980 election, none will be.) Reagan received 51 percent of the popular vote and 489 electoral votes to Carter's anemic 41 percent and 49 votes, respectively. The Reagan Revolution had begun.

The Reagan Presidency: A Positive Assessment

The Reagan presidency can be summed up by the title of Reagan's definitive biography (to date): "The Role of a Lifetime." For Reagan's supporters, with his strapping shoulders and broad chest (honed through a regular workout schedule), salt and pepper hair (honed, perhaps, by a little help from the makeup squad), and square jaw (honed by his Irish/Scottish midwestern roots), he was a president right out of Republican central casting: a straight-shooting, self-effacing, solid conservative, harking back to the cherished and mythologized days of the Founding Fathers themselves. To his detractors, he was a character out of central casting, too: a character actor good at speaking words written by others and taking direction from the money boys who ran the national studio, a man who kept the public distracted by the smoke and mirrors of a congenial smile while powerful interests worked their wiles. For the public, Reagan was simply reprising the role he had played to great "B" movie success: the straight-shooting, nice, honest fellow whom, even if you did not agree with him or listen to him, you could always like. While each of these views oversimplify a complex man, each grapples with the essential essence of the Reagan presidency (though through the lenses of very different ideological cinematographers). The Reagan presidency, at both its strongest and its weakest, was as much about image and feeling as it was about substance and policy.

That Reagan was able to successfully play on his image, with his supporters, detractors, and the public at large, to his political advantage proved to be one of the greatest assets and achievements of his presidency. By 1980, the Republican Party was desperate for a genuine winner who could once again capture the hearts and minds of the American public as much as Eisenhower had in the 1950s or, dream of dreams, as much as the other party had with Roosevelt in the 1930s. Republicans had had Nixon, but that had not turned out well at all. With Reagan, Republicans—especially conservative Republicans—finally had a leader who looked like a leader and (at least while on script and often, though not always, even on the fly) sounded like a leader. Reagan could dispatch Democratic rivals with a seemingly off the cuff, "There he goes again" (thereby reducing Jimmy Carter in their last presidential debate to a political irrelevancy) or, "I will not make the youth and inexperience of my rival a campaign issue" (thereby neutralizing both his own age issue and Walter Mondale with one line). Reagan could hit his political marks and deliver a line better than any Republican since perhaps Teddy Roosevelt. To that end, as they would with George W. Bush two decades later, Republican supporters forgave him any transgression almost as a knee-jerk reaction and vigorously rejected any criticism, increasingly putting Reagan's critics—rather than the president himself—on the defensive in the op-ed pages and talk shows of America, whether justified or not. As such, unlike his Republican predecessors, Ford, Nixon, and even Eisenhower, Reagan had to exert far less effort in keeping his base support lined up than did Jimmy Carter or Lyndon Johnson (or as would George W. H. Bush and Bill Clinton). Thus, Reagan's image as a forceful Republican leader made him a forceful Republican leader, as nice a bit of stagecraft as any modern president has ever managed.

The tendency of his detractors to dismiss him as a puppet of vested interests—a genial fool without an original thought in his head—was both factually inaccurate and politically ineffectual. It was true that Reagan had a tremendous propensity for making misstatements and outright gaffes when speaking "off-script." His detractors seized on this as a sign of weak intellectual abilities (as they would with George W. Bush) and, therefore, as grounds to dismiss Reagan as a flunky of smarter handlers. What his detractors forgot was that "book-smarts" is no guarantee of popular presidential support, and a successful presidency, as arguably intellectually more gifted presidents such as Richard Nixon, Jimmy Carter, and Bill Clinton could attest. The tendency of Reagan's detractors—both Democrat and Republican—to dismiss him as a light weight actually helped Reagan substantially in two ways. First, underrating Reagan lowered the bar of public expectation such that, even going into his re-election campaign of 1984, simply being able to deliver a few well-turned lines and not actually appear the aging dotard Democrats tried to portray him as was sufficient to deliver to him a crushing victory, even though he had presided over an extremely weak economy for most of his first term and had no major foreign policy triumphs beyond the invasion of a flyspeck Caribbean island to point to.

Second, it actually endeared him to the 90 percent of the American public who were not in the top 10 percent of their high school classes (a ratio always important to keep in mind when calculating the reaction of the electorate to just about anything political). Thus, while Reagan's staff spent the first two years of his presidency always trying to correct for the record Reagan's various public misstatements, by 1983 his communications director was content to simply wave off press criticisms calling the president to account for his statements by saying, "That's just the way the President is." The public seemed to accept it as a simple validation of the image of Reagan as an earnest man trying his best while surrounded by opponents and the press at large trying to trip him up. Indeed, the press corps quickly learned that trying to hold Reagan accountable for his statements was the equivalent of the smart kids snickering when the average kid got a question wrong in class—a guaranteed way not to win endearment in the hearts of the general public. In fact, it was the press corps itself that gave Reagan the title, "The Teflon President," as much because they themselves had given up trying to stick facts on Reagan as had the public. (Indeed, for all the grumbling by conservatives of the liberal bias of the press, Reagan received far easier treatment in being held accountable by the Washington press corps than did either Carter or Clinton.)

Reagan would be dubbed the "Great Communicator," but it would not particularly be for his practiced speeches and most certainly not for his ad libs. Reagan was the "Great Communicator" of feelings and image rather than detailed ideas and substance. One of the most important feelings he was able to communicate to the public during his first term was a feeling of renewed trust and confidence in government or at least in the office of the presidency. That Reagan, the man who ran on an anti-government platform, should be the man to restore trust and confidence in government is yet another in a long line of Reagan ironies. But restore trust he did. Reagan followed an uninterrupted string of five presidents who had each failed to complete two full terms in office. (While it was an assassin's bullet that cut JFK's time in office short rather than electoral ballots, Kennedy's reelection in 1964 was itself by no means a certainty.) By the end of the Carter years, pundits and political scientists who had scarcely a decade before been writing forebodingly of the rise of an all-powerful "imperial presidency" would be writing instead about a declining post-imperial presidency of failed expectations. Coming on the heals of the machinations of the likes of "Tricky Dicky" and "Landslide Lyndon," whose tendency towards prevarication and subversion of the system of checks and balances and given rise to the notion of an "imperial presidency," Jimmy Carter had won election by telling the American people he would never lie to them. He kept that promise, but the public for the most part did not like him for telling what he thought was the truth. Meanwhile, Carter's attempts to de-imperialize the presidency, selling the presidential yacht, and even carrying his own luggage on and off of Air Force One, had served instead to further diminish the office in the eyes of the public.

Reagan managed to fuse both desires of the American public: the desire for seemingly honest leadership with a strong, confidence-inspiring style of leadership that stopped short of the hard to explicitly identify line of imperialism. Thus, Reagan supporters bought back the presidential yacht, and no one except his hardest opponents considered calling him by the diminutive "Ronny": he was Ronald Reagan, President of the United States. And, indeed, as biographer Lou Cannon wrote, it would be his greatest, most natural role. True, there was some element of hypocrisy in the Reagan image. That darling of the newly emerging Moral Majority (a group, which like Bolsheviks in the early twentieth century, learned the advantage of claiming the name "Majority" even when the real membership of the movement constituted a small minority of the population as a whole) was a divorcee who apparently conceived a child out of wedlock with his second wife and, both before and as president, never belonged to any specific religious congregation—just one of those little inconsistencies. But if Reagan did not personally live to themes he portrayed (for example, Reagan never formed a business nor met a payroll, working instead either for large corporate entities or government itself while always advancing the virtues of small business and the American entrepreneurial culture), he was able to consistently project them in manner and speech, winning the American public to his views in the process.

Where Teddy Roosevelt talked of the presidency being a Bully Pulpit, for Reagan it was simply the Silver Screen writ large, a venue in which to sell a role like no other. One of the few advantages that a president of the United States has over a European-style prime minister (who is always guaranteed a voting majority in the parliament and, hence, can always be assured victory in passing legislation—or they cease to be prime minister) is the fact that, in the U.S., the twin roles of political head of state and ceremonial head of state are fused into one person: the president. In a parliamentary system, the prime minister is simply the leader of the majority faction in the parliament. As such, prime ministers have a much harder time commanding the loyalty and support of the segments of the population unrepresented by the prime minister's party. An American president, however, is more than just the partisan leader of one political faction. As the only nationally elected officer (except for the office of the vice presidency, which since the adoption of the Twelfth Amendment has been reduced to the status of a two-for-one add-on to the presidency), the president alone can claim to speak on behalf of the nation as a whole and has over time become the chief representative of the nation, leading the American people through both times of celebration and sorrow. A president whose personality is particularly suited to playing the role of national master of ceremony (as Teddy Roosevelt, FDR, and JFK were while Wilson, Hoover, and Nixon were not) will reap substantial public support. Given that a maxim of American politics is that congressional willingness to give in to a president's demands is a direct function of presidential popular support, this means that the public support a president may derive from the more ceremonial aspects of the job can translate directly into political power. Be it in leading the American celebration to rededicate the Statue of Liberty on its one-hundredth birthday in 1986 or delivering the national eulogy for the crew of the space shuttle Challenger in 1985, Reagan excelled at the role with the resulting increase in political clout.

(After Reagan delivered the eulogy for the dead crew at the NASA Spaceflight Center in Houston, he stood in a receiving line for the crews' families' members. At one point, the young teenage daughter of a crew member broke down in heaving sobs, only to have the president pull her to him and embrace her in a soothing hug. The author, then a graduate student, watched this scene replay on television in the company of a number of other graduate students who predominantly disliked Reagan, some to a matter of sweet intensity. Every eye in the room—and pretty much the entire nation—was tear-filled. If Ronald Reagan had the next day gone to the Congress and asked to be proclaimed emperor, the Congress would have refused—but they might have offered him Rhode Island or California as a future retirement present. Such was the power of the Reagan presidential presence.)

Reagan came to office in an America gripped by a Cartersian malaise and left an America that was militarily stronger, wealthier, and, above all, far more confident that the country had not seen its best days. Reagan's high personal popularity insulated him from the negative things that occurred during his administration (as opposed to a Bill Clinton who got low personal approval marks despite high job approval ratings and a soaring economy). By effectively separating the image of "Reagan the Man" versus "Reagan the Politician" in the eyes of the public, Reagan could keep high personal approval ratings even amidst severe economic recession in his first term and the Iran Contra scandal, amongst others, in his second, allowing him the luxury of never having to fall back significantly into defensive posture (a position that has usually consumed most presidents by their second term, should they have been among the minority fortunate enough to reach a second term).

Reagan's popularity and personality translated into bipartisan appeal as well. Coming into office in 1981 with a sense of national urgency over the deteriorating economy, Reagan enjoyed the most successful first one hundred days of any president since FDR, pushing through the centerpiece of his economic agenda—a major tax cut, more than $43 billion in budget cuts to domestic programs, and significant cutbacks in environmental and business regulation despite having to contend with a Democratic House offset by only a small Republican voting majority in the Senate (the product in itself of Reagan's 1980 coattail effect—the last major example of such coattails until George W. Bush's belated, war-induced coattails in the 2002 midterm elections). Reagan was helped in winning his early victories by his electoral mandate and continued strong public support into 1981, which swelled with his survival of an assassination attempt at the hands of a mentally disturbed young man trying to win the affections of a movie star (that Reagan should almost be assassinated as a consequence of an assassin directly inspired by a movie—"Taxi Driver"—is a further irony of biting depth). These events overwhelmed liberal Democratic opposition to Reagan's budget and tax cut proposals.

While part of Reagan's bipartisan appeal can be attributed to a Democratic Congress responding to the 1980 electoral sea change, it was also a direct consequence of the difference in personal style between Reagan and his predecessor, Jimmy Carter. Carter had come across as something of a self-righteous prig to even majority members of his own congressional part; the dislike Democratic Speaker Tip O'Neil felt for the Carter administration was legendary. Reagan, with his jovial manner and endless supply of Irish jokes and tales, hit it off famously with O'Neil, allowing the two to reach compromises and push through volumes of legislation that Carter could never dream of. Thus, Reagan stands out as the most successful bipartisan president of the twentieth century. The modern history of presidential/congressional relations indicates that personality more than politics plays the definitive role in defining their interactions. Witness the weakness of Carter, Clinton, and George W. Bush (at least pre-9/11) to push their own agendas through Congresses controlled by their own parties, or Ford's, George H. W. Bush's and Clinton's problems with Congresses controlled by the opposition. This reality underscores the fact that Washington, D. C. is actually a very small town (or a very large high school) in which the personality of the players involved often matters as much or more than the politics or ideology they bring to the table.

Reagan also had the good fortune of dealing with a Democratic Party that was entering its long wilderness period in search of a national leader. The death of Kennedy and fall from grace by LBJ, Hubert Humphrey, and Carter had left the party by 1980 with a vacuum of senior and even junior level leadership. Liberal Senator Ted Kennedy's fiery speech at the 1980 Democratic convention, while intended as a call to arms in defense of traditional New Deal values, was ultimately a eulogy for New Deal Democratic activism. The Camelot of Kennedy Democrats was as dead as that of Arthur, and the party spent the Reagan years fighting an unsuccessful rearguard action. As such, Reagan faced no serious national rival figure—either Democratic or Republican—for the national heart and soul. The necessity of the Democrats relying on the failed number two of the Carter ticket—former vice president and liberal Senator Walter Mondale—in 1984 only underscored the paucity of the Democratic political gene pool. Democrats would have to wait until Bill Clinton to regain a coherent national voice, but even Clinton proved incapable of keeping it a sustained national voice, leaving the Democrats going into the 2004 election—twenty-four years after Reagan's first victory—still plagued by weak national leadership. Democrats had after fifty years of near-hegemony exhausted their capacity of innovation and outreach to the American public, becoming instead the party of "status quo," even as the postwar status quo, both domestically and internationally, was unwinding. Incapable of developing new ideas to counter Reagan's new conservative message, Democrats would be reduced to portraying themselves either as "anti-Reagan," thus setting themselves squarely against public sentiment, or as reaching out to create some sort of legislative "détente" (much as the Soviet Union would be forced to do during his presidency) with Reagan, allowing him his victories, but with enough compromises as to allow them to blunt the Reagan agenda to a degree, thereby holding onto the core of New Deal programs, such as public social security and an extant, if reduced, social welfare state. What Democrats have been searching for since Reagan has been precisely new, bold liberal ideas necessary to serve as a counter to Reagan conservatism. Failure to do so has reduced the party to seemingly perpetual second-place status. This had led more than a few conservative commentators to observe that the Democrats have not been able to advance such a new agenda because they are a tired, old party forever devoid of new ideas. If it is any consolation for Democrats, the same was said of Republicans during their own wilderness years between FDR and Reagan.

Reagan can claim at least some of the credit for the overall strong performance of the American economy across the entirety of his eight years in office. His Economic Tax Recovery Act sought to cut tax rates across all tax brackets (and simply the number of tax brackets, bringing top brackets down to levels at which they had not been since before World War II). The theory of what would be labeled Reaganomics, or supply-side economics, was simply a return to nineteenth century classical liberal thought, or neo-liberalism, as it was now called. The neo-liberal economists that infused the Reagan administration built on theories like those of University of Chicago economist Arthur Laffer, who laid much of the blame for the stagflation that had undermined the U.S. economy in the 1970s on excessive government taxes and spending. In this view, the high marginal progressive tax rates (with top brackets above 60 percent) actually served to diminish government revenues as they provided a disincentive for people to earn monies that would only be progressively taxed away. (In reality, the larger effect was to move people and monies into inefficient systems of tax avoidance, such as the underground economy or, more significantly, all manners of tax shelters that made little economic sense other than to take advantage of loopholes in the tax code.) Diminishing revenues coupled with overly generous social welfare spending conspired to create the large budget deficits of the Carter years (averaging $50 billion a year which, in retrospect of the Reagan, "Bush I," and "Bush II" years, seem almost quaint). The large budget deficits, in turn, were funded by sucking capital out of the private sector, leaving a reduced pool of consequently more expensive (in terms of interest rates) capital for private investment, which resulted in fewer jobs being created (and higher unemployment). As classical economic theory dictated, deficits also created inflation as the government pumped money into the hands of consumers. Thus, the combination of the two effects produced "stagflation." (What this analysis left out was the impact of global inflation triggered by the Arab oil shocks and the rising erosion of the U.S. manufacturing sector in the face of rising foreign competition from Europe and Asia adding to unemployment.) The simple solution: cut taxes and cut government spending. Yet, while cutting taxes across the board would be politically expedient, an excessive tax cut for the consuming classes (that is, working and middle classes) actually intensified short-term inflation. Thus, the Reagan tax cuts were deliberately designed to funnel to upper income households the maximum amount of tax relief as would be politically feasible to get out of Congress. These households would then invest their new monies in job-creating enterprises and, therefore, the wealth given by government to them would subsequently "trickle down" into working class households. (This is, in fact, what happened, although the new jobs created were not necessarily on American shores, because American multinational corporations [MNCs] began to scour the world for the cheapest, highest skilled labor. Some of the tax savings would also be diverted to luxury consumption: the Sothesby's indices of precious art appreciated 200 percent across the Reagan years.)

The 1981 tax cut (as well as the follow-up tax reductions in 1986) helped move billions of dollars of federal tax receipts back into upper income households (a much larger amount of federal money than sent through welfare programs down to poor households during the same period). What followed was both an increase in consumer spending and, after 1982, jobs creation, which continued without interruption for eight years—the longest sustained economic expansion in U.S. history—until 1991 when Federal Reserve Chairman Alan Greenspan pulled the plug on the economy by raising interest rates to abort a spike in inflation from an expected spike in global oil prices following the first Gulf War. The oil price spike never materialized, but the rise in interest rates pushed a weakening economy into a recession that cost George H.W. Bush his job.

It was fitting that the Federal Reserve ended the Reagan boom, as the real roots of the 1980s economic recovery lay in the severe anti-inflationary austerity measures implemented by then-Federal Reserve Chairman Paul Volcker between 1979 and 1981. In part, the stagflation of the late 1970s was intensified by the fact that two parts of the U.S. government—the social welfare state and the Federal Reserve—had begun working at cross purposes with each other. With the rising unemployment of the latter 1970s pushing double digits, federal social welfare outlays climbed dramatically with their inevitable inflationary pressure. The Federal Reserve, in turn, had been progressively raising interest rates to combat inflation as economic orthodoxy dictated. Across the 1970s though, the Federal Reserve had been reluctant to increase interest rates too dramatically, as interest rate hikes inevitably increased unemployment (which is, in part, how inflation is brought down: as companies and consumers stop borrowing more expensive money, thereby depressing demand and prices, workers get laid off by companies seeing sales go down). The Federal Reserve was tasked with balancing concerns over inflation with trying to target sustainable levels of low unemployment. In 1979, the Volcker Federal Reserve concluded that both were no longer obtainable goals and, of the two, inflation poised the greater risk to the national economy. "To end inflation," Volcker stated, "the average American must learn to live less well," meaning with less money to spend, thus dampening inflation. Volcker's Federal Reserve moved to significantly tighten the national money supply to a degree not seen since the nineteenth century, which resulted in a prime rate of over 12 percent and a federal funds rate of over 21 percent by 1982. The impact was as dramatic and successful as it was painful, as the Federal Reserve gave Americans a taste of the austerity measures that the global equivalent of the Federal Reserve, the International Monetary Fund, had enforced increasingly in recent years on developing nations plagued by inflation. By November 1982, unemployment levels pushed 10 percent, the highest rate since the Depression, while business failures reached their second highest number since 1933, as tens of thousands of farmers were driven from their lands and hundreds of thousands of blue collar workers lost factory jobs that never returned. Meanwhile, the number of homeless in America soared, as did urban crime rates.

Reagan paid a substantial political price for the deep recession of 1982, with his job approval rating reaching its lowest level of his presidency, but it was not as steep a price as he might have paid. Occurring as the recession did early in his first term, Reagan deflected some of the criticism of his economic policies by pointing out that he had inherited the weak economy from Carter—but that the economy had been even weaker than anyone had guessed (a tact that would be used to some success by George W. Bush's defenders, blaming an economy that remained sluggish into Bush's fourth year in office on the former Clinton administration). More importantly, Reagan benefited from the fact that the Federal Reserve chose to perform its alchemy (in many ways the Federal Reserve has become the modern "medieval barbers" of the American economy, always willing to try to save the patient by bleeding it to death through higher interest rates) during the first two years of his administration, rather than in the run up to reelection. Had Reagan faced reelection in the depths of the Federal Reserve-induced recession (or even on the beginning upswing, as with George H. W. Bush) rather than during an established recovery, a second term would have been far more problematic.

Reagan did ultimately agree to a small tax increase on businesses as a token to anti-deficit critics, but he refused to raise income taxes or to cut defense spending, insisting on "staying the course." By the middle of 1983, even as his public approval ratings bottomed out, the harsh tonic of the Federal Reserve plus the stimulus impact of the Reagan tax cuts (and also the help of collapsing global oil prices) finally began to turn the economy around. By the 1984 election year, economic worries were forgotten with returning prosperity, even though the prosperity of the Reagan years would not be evenly distributed across classes and peoples. (Fortunately again for Reagan, the prosperity was most heavily concentrated precisely amongst those groups that tended to vote.) By sticking to his guns on taxes and spending, Reagan went into the 1984 election looking strong, resolute, and vindicated by economic recovery (unlike his successor, whose cave-in on taxes caused a number of conservative Republicans to "stop lip reading" and vote for Ross Perot). After 1983, except for a sharp correction to the stock market in 1987, economic worries never again posed a significant problem for the Reagan administration.

Ronald Reagan faced three major foreign policy challenges during his presidency: the old challenges posed by the cold war, the new challenges posed by rising third-world radicalism and instability, and the vague yet growing pressures on American economic dominance posed by nascent economic globalization. Of the three, he would be most successful in dealing with the former, though he scored his first foreign policy triumph in the second area in the first minutes of his presidency.

The seemingly endless Iranian hostage crisis had proved to be a humiliation to both the United States and Jimmy Carter and was arguably more responsible for his electoral defeat than even the weak economy. After 444 days of fruitless negotiations and a failed rescue attempt, within minutes of Reagan taking the oath of office, American hostages were loaded onto a plane in Tehran for their final return home. That Carter's people had actually negotiated the hostage's release prior to Reagan's inaugural was a moot point (as would be allegations that Reagan operatives had actually conspired with the Iranians to keep the hostages until after Reagan's election to make Carter look bad). Reagan's triumphant greeting of the hostages on their arrival in America served as a graphic declaration that America was under new foreign policy leadership.

Yet, Reagan would have few other foreign policy triumphs in dealing with developing states. The resolution of the Iranian hostage crisis and the Falkland Islands demonstrated early in the Reagan presidency that foreign policy crises completely unrelated to the cold war, which had dominated American global attention for almost four decades, increasingly confounded Washington. Reagan achieved some moderate success in dealing with regional instabilities, such as with Argentina (by helping the British to put the upstart tin-plated Argentinean military junta in its place) or by dispatching American naval forces to patrol the Persian Gulf to keep its shipping lanes open to the flow of global oil during the Iran-Iraq war. Reagan made some headway in trying to slow the slide of the United States in global economics vis-à-vis the rising sun of Japanese business by negotiating a reduction in the value of the dollar against the yen (the 1986 Plaza Accords) that aimed at stemming the flow of Japanese goods into the United States with the resulting loss of American jobs. In 1988, Reagan also achieved Senate approval of a comprehensive free trade agreement with Canada—the forerunner of NAFTA—to work towards an integrated North American market as a counterweight to Asian and European competition. But American preoccupation with the high stakes cold war left little time during the Reagan years for the development of a comprehensive strategy for dealing effectively with other areas. While Reagan's policies would be instrumental in bringing about a peaceful conclusion to the last round of the cold war, he was far less successful in dealing with the first round of the post-cold war economic globalization and the emerging wars of terror.

Both Reagan's supporters and critics attributed the release of the hostages, at least in part, to the fear that America's new cowboy president inspired in the Iranian leadership. (In actuality, it had more to do with the pathological dislike of Carter, which the Ayatollah Khomeini had developed for reasons never rationality explained.) Indeed, Reagan's campaign rhetoric, calling on America to reassert itself politically and militarily onto the global stage and reverse the better part of a decade of retreat since the unwinding of the Vietnam debacle, was couched in the language of an aggressive application of American Exceptionalism— America's right to act as a global force for good as it saw fit, where it saw fit—that harkened directly back to Barry Goldwater. Johnson portrayed Goldwater (infamously so in the notorious "Nuclear Countdown" television ad) in the 1964 election as a radical militarist who would destabilize the planet and plunge America into cataclysmic war. Carter attempted to paint Reagan with the same warmongering brush.

But where the image of saber rattling Barry Goldwater inspired fear, the image of warrior Reagan inspired jokes—like Jay Leno saying on the *Tonight Show* that Ronald Reagan would give the Iranians back the shah of Iran alright (a key Iranian demand for release of the hostages being the return of the shah from exile to Iran to face justice)—strapped to the nose of an MX missile, that is. Yet, the jokes had an edge of respect to them: if Reagan could restore some degree of global respect for the United States, whose global image had been tarnished by the loss in Vietnam and the fact that an upstart group of Iranian revolutionaries could poke the United States eagle in the eye and seemingly get away with it, even if doing so by rattling a saber or two, godspeed to him. Contrasted with the apparent emasculation of American power under Carter, by 1981 a little warmongering sat well with the American public.

Thus, when Reagan inadvertently (although jokingly) said into a live microphone, "We begin bombing [the Soviet Union] in five minutes" during a mike test for one of his first Saturday weekly radio broadcasts, the American public's response for the most part was a smile and a "there he goes again." (One can only imagine the U.S.S.R.'s ambassador to Washington, Anatoly Dobrinin, sitting in his dining room at the Soviet embassy, sipping tea and listening to Reagan's address, only to spray his tea across the room in momentary shock. It's enough to make one nostalgic for the good old days of the cold war.)

Reagan inherited a cold war that was, in retrospect, heading into its final decade. At the time, however, the conflict seemed to be in the middle of a particularly dangerous stage for American interests. The U.S. withdrawal from Southeast Asia had not resulted in communist dominoes falling across the rest of the region, as American policymakers had feared, a fear that had in large part triggered U.S. intervention in the first place. Indeed, while the dominoes had seemed to initially be falling with the communist take-over of South Vietnam followed by a communist coup in neighboring Cambodia, the resulting war between communist North Vietnam, backed by the Soviets, and communist Cambodia, backed by Red China, exposed the myth of both monolithic communism and the domino theory with one neat, ironic event. America's post-Vietnam retrenchment, however, had encouraged increased Soviet adventurism in Africa, where Cuban troops had been deployed as Soviet proxies to support communist movements in southern Africa and around the Horn. Moreover, communist movements in El Salvador and the successful

Sandinista-dominated revolution in Nicaragua had left communist forces a few days drive from Brownsville, Texas, as Reagan had argued during the campaign.

Since direct confrontation between the U.S. and the U.S.S.R. had been rendered too dangerous by both sides' massive inventories of nuclear weapons, by the 1960s the cold war had evolved into something of a global game of Risk, in which the object was to get as many pro-American or pro-Soviet colored states on the geo-political map, under the theory that the side with the most allies (or satellites) was winning (which harkened in its own way to the "Great Game" European imperialism of the later nineteenth century). Throw in the Afghan invasion, and by 1981, the Soviets seemed to be acquiring a substantial new number of red-colored countries on the global map (that these countries were the bargain basement discount states of the third world notwithstanding) and, hence, were now winning the cold war. A rising number of academic and journalistic texts were trumpeting the eventual demise of the west and the inevitable triumph of communism, and even popular American culture eventually picked up the theme with movies like "Red Dawn" and television miniseries like "Amerika," foretelling of eventual Soviet conquest of the U.S.A. Meanwhile, Western European states, especially West Germany, seemed to be hedging their bets by the late 1970s through policies of "Ostpolitik," which sought to establish new bilateral political and economic relations with the Soviet Union to the exclusion of Washington, D. C.

It was against this background of American retreat and a growing palatable fear of near-term American defeat that Reagan took over the presidency. His first goal, vis-à-vis the Soviets, was to reverse the momentum of the past decade and put America on the offensive, politically at least, rather than militarily. Reagan succeeded in achieving this turnaround by pushing two policies: the implementation of what became known as the "Reagan Doctrine" to counter Soviet expansionism and committing the U.S. to a massive military arms build-up to close and eliminate the military lead that the Soviets had seemingly achieved in both conventional and strategic forces.

Of the two, the Reagan arms build-up had the most significant impact on the conduct of the cold war, though for reasons different than most Reagan supporters tout. (Given the highly problematic long-term impacts of the Reagan Doctrine, it will be discussed below in the "Negative Assessment" section of the chapter.) The conventional view of the success of the Reagan's arms build-up was that the new round of the arms race that it triggered as the Soviets strode to keep up with a 35 percent real increase in U.S. military spending ultimately bankrupted the U.S.S.R., precipitating its abrupt collapse by the end of the decade. Moreover, Reagan boosters argue, Reagan's controversial, if daring Strategic Defense Initiative (famously branded "Star Wars" by the media) scared the Russians into trying to cut deals with the U.S. before America's superior technology rendered their nuclear sword obsolete. Detractors of the Reagan arms build-up, on the other hand, argue that the Reagan arms build-up was a costly and unnecessary provocation that almost drove the world into nuclear war. Neither view truly stands up to historical analysis.

Those who opposed the arms build-up correctly point out that, as the hindsight afforded by post-cold war scholars pouring over Soviet-era records confirm, like the early Eisenhower missile gap that never actually existed, even in 1980 the U.S. was outspending the Soviet Union in meaningful military expenditures (e.g., in what really mattered in a face-to-face contest). However, an America at parity with the Russians, especially coming on the heels of the foreign policy debacles of the 1970s, was not an America able to negotiate with the Soviets from a position of strength. Thus, according to Reagan biographer Lou Cannon, Reagan was committed to build up the U.S. military as a clear sign of resolve to the Soviets and to allow the U.S. to regain a position of strength from which to negotiate a more stable relationship. Moreover, as early as the 1980 primaries, Reagan believed that the Soviets would simply be unable to match the U.S., ruble for dollar, in a new round of arms increases and, therefore, would be compelled to the negotiating table.

Reagan detractors feared that Reagan's arms race, especially the potential threat posed to the Soviets by the Strategic Defense Initiative (SDI) program, might have the unintended consequence of provoking the Soviets to take preemptive action should they feel they were becoming losers in the strategic equation. These fears were only intensified by Soviet rhetoric condemning the Reagan arms build-up, such as Soviet leader Leonid Brezhnev, stating that the U.S. was now pursuing policies of "adventurism, rudeness, and undisguised egoism" that threatened "to push the world into the flames of nuclear war." Indeed, Reagan recognized the risk that SDI posed to the balance of terror and, hence, proposed in a very Eisenhowerian manner that SDI technology, once operational, should be shared amongst all nations. That senior policymakers in the U.S. or the U.S.S.R. actually believed the U.S. would follow through on such a magnanimous act is highly questionable however. Reagan's ultimately successful battle to get NATO allies to agree to the American deployment of a new generation of missiles in Western Europe similarly threatened, for a time, to destabilize U.S./Soviet relations. In theory, a theater weapon intended for use only after a ground war had already started in Europe, the Pershing II cruise missiles, like the newly-deployed generation of American strategic MX and Trident submarine-launched missiles, had sufficient targeting precision to be used theoretically by the U.S. to launch a first strike aimed at destroying the Soviet nuclear arsenal. Their deployment in West Germany in the fall of 1983 was decried by many on both sides of the Iron Curtain as a dangerous provocation and escalation of tension. The previous spring Reagan had referred to the U.S.S.R. as the "focus of evil in the modern world," a theme he returned to that September when he branded the downing of a Korean Air Lines jet (KAL flight 007) by a Soviet fighter, which killed all 269 people aboard including 61 Americans, a "crime against humanity." The day after the "Evil Empire" speech, meanwhile, the Soviet news agency, TASS, proclaimed that Reagan was full of "bellicose lunatic anti-communism," and after the KAL incident, Soviet leader Uri Andropov accused Reagan of risking war that would be "too costly for the whole of mankind." Thus, 1983 stands out as perhaps the most dangerous year of the cold war since 1973 and the Yom Kippur War or even 1962 and the Cuban Missile Crisis. With the deployment of Pershing IIs, the founder of Physicians for Social Responsibility, Dr. Helen Caldicott, stated that she now feared that "Reagan could push the [nuclear] button." Indeed, only three days before their deployment, Americans by the hundred millions watched the nuclear holocaust movie, "The Day After," which sent public anxiety soaring.

Yet, the world survived 1983, and not just out of luck. Reagan had gambled that his more aggressive posture would eventually drive the Soviets to the bargaining table, and he was ultimately proven right. Two things worked to Reagan's advantage mitigating the risks he appeared to be taking. First, the Soviet Union of 1983 was not the Soviet Union of the 1960s and 1970s, when such a provocative American tone might indeed have triggered an unfortunate escalation (as had almost happened over Cuba and the Yom Kippur War). Second, Reagan was simply not the warmongering imperialist that his detractors on both sides of the Iron Curtain made him out to be.

By the early 1980s, significant economic cracks had already developed in the Soviet monolith, which, if not readily apparent from the outside, were increasingly apparent at least to part of the Soviet leadership. Indeed, while Yuri Andropov had risen to the leadership of the Soviet Union from the top of the KGB (the infamous Soviet secret police) he was not the extreme hard-line ideologue who might reasonably have been expected to come from the communist security apparatus. As head of Soviet intelligence, Andropov was uniquely positioned to know the exact details of how bad the Soviet economy had become, with an agrarian sector in a state of near collapse for over a decade and declining industrial output on top of which had been placed the huge financial strain of the unsuccessful war in Afghanistan (which Reagan had successfully conspired to make worse, as discussed below). Thus, Reagan was correct in his assumption that the Soviets were in no position to match a new U.S. arms build-up. While the Americans tended to overestimate Soviet capacities, Andropov was under no delusions as to his country's eroding military posture. The Russians were far less impressed by the threat of "Star Wars" than the Reagan administration supposed; In Soviet eyes, its huge technological barriers and the relatively cheap costs of counter-measures the Soviets could deploy to render it obsolete made it more of a propaganda issue than a real strategic policy threat. Yet, simply matching U.S. increases in conventional and strategic weapons proved economically ruinous for the already tottering Soviet economy.

Thus, Reagan was ultimately correct in his belief that applying pressure on the Soviets precipitated negotiation rather than confrontation. In July 1983, amidst all the flying hostile rhetoric, Andropov sent a letter to Reagan suggesting that they begin discussion over means to eliminate the nuclear threat; Reagan cordially suggested that the two countries formally meet in Geneva. The following January Reagan called for a return nuclear arms talks in Geneva, and a parallel negotiation in Vienna aimed at reducing conventional forces in Europe. Any hopes for a quick pace to negotiations were upset by Andropov's untimely death that February and his replacement by an old, ailing hardliner. Konstantin Chernenko ultimately turned out to be a place-holder fobbed to the top of the Soviet government while Brezhnevian conservatives and Andropovian reformers circled each other in the Politburo. But the rise to power of Andropov's protégé, Mikhail Gorbachev, upon Chernenko's death a year later reopened the process of developing a second U.S./Soviet détente. In Geneva at the end of 1985 and at Reykjavik, Iceland, in 1986, the two leaders, in fits and starts, established both a workable personal rapport and the conditions for a truly meaningful dialogue. At Reykjavik, the process seemed to become hung up on the issue of Star Wars, which Gorbachev wanted shelved as a first, rather than last, step and which Reagan refused to do, ultimately walking away from the conference empty-handed. Here, too, Reagan had gauged his audience well, demonstrating a willingness to stop negotiations rather than making concessions that could be deemed a sign of weakness. Gorbachev later stated that Reykjavik, even with Reagan's apparent intransigence, had gotten the two sides "to the top of the hill, and from the top of the hill you can see a long way." The long way would be a summit the following year in Washington, D. C. where the two leaders signed the Intermediate-Range Nuclear Forces (INF) Treaty, reducing their respective arsenals by 4 percent—a small but significant step. The U.S./Soviet arms race that had consumed trillions of dollars over four decades could be said to have ended with the signing of the INF. Reagan reciprocated the Gorbachev visit with a final 1988 summit in Moscow where he became the first and only American president to be cheered on the streets of the U.S.S.R. by Soviet citizens.

It is to Reagan's credit that he did not live up to the cowboy label that had been so easily applied to him by his detractors. That Reagan deliberately set out from the beginning of his administration to bring down the Soviet Union, which some of his supporters have suggested, in no small part to further polish his historical image, is not substantiated by the historical record. Reagan certainly hoped to reverse the perception of America's strategic decline and ultimately had faith that the Soviet Union would inevitably end up on the ash heap of history. Even amidst his summits and negotiations with Gorbachev, he took time out to deliver his famous speech in Berlin before the Brandenberg Gate with his perfectly delivered line, "Mr. Gorbachev, tear down this wall!" or say in a speech to students at Moscow State University beneath a gigantic bust of Lenin during his final summit with Gorbachev, "we may be allowed that hope: that freedom, like the fresh green sapling planted over Tolstoy's grave, will blossom forth at last in the rich fertile soil of your people and culture." Yet, while Reagan was willing to push for change, he was not willing to commit American forces to achieve such change; rather, Reagan saw his prime role as negotiating a space in which the historic inevitability of Soviet collapse could occur without it taking the world down with it. Usually the collapse of an empire is an extremely messy affair, resolved through war or violent social revolution or both. It is to both Reagan's and Gorbachev's lasting credit that they collaborated to work out conditions under which the Soviet Union might go quietly into the night (though that end was not, of course, Gorbachev's first preference). That Gorbachev negotiated from a position of having a loaded gun at his head—the gun being the escalating unraveling of the inefficient Soviet economy, coupled with rising social discontent, and made massively worse by the Chernobyl disaster in early 1986—and Reagan from one of rising American strategic superiority did, of course, make things easier for Reagan. Reagan, however, wisely resisted overplaying his hand, which he came close to doing by walking out of Reykjavik and pressing the Soviets for more one-sided concessions, as urged by anti-Soviet hardliners such as Defense Secretary Caspar Weinberger. Rhetoric of Evil Empires and American Exceptionalism aside, Reagan understood ultimately that there were limits to American power and that at times negotiation with the devil himself may be preferable to costly war.

Reagan's other major foreign policy success, which related to the conduct of the cold war (and with profound implications for the later twenty-first century war against terrorism), was his re-cementing of the U.S./Britain Atlantic alliance in terms as strong as those that had existed in World War II. While the U.S. and Britain had shared a "special relationship" since the Churchill/Roosevelt days, the relationship had been under varying degrees of strain ever since Eisenhower had pulled the plug on the ill-fated Suez venture in 1956. Reagan and British conservative leader Margaret Thatcher were kindred ideological spirits who had each launched neo-liberal revolutions on their respective sides of the ocean. Moreover, the two quickly established a strong personal bond, which Reagan infinitely strengthened by the strong American commitment to support Britain in the almost operatically comedic (but for the loss of life, which always turns comedy to tragedy) Argentine attack in 1982 on the British Falkland Islands. From then on, Reagan and Thatcher became something of an Anglo-American dynamic duo, mutually supporting each other on the global stage. Indeed, so strong was this bond that Mikhail Gorbachev understood that he had to first win over Margaret Thatcher to his claim that he was not just another communist leader but was a man dedicated to true reform—an audition, if you will—before playing for Reagan. Thatcher's famous report that Gorbachev was indeed a Soviet with whom the West could "do business" served as the letter of introduction he needed to engage in serious discussion with the American president. During the Reagan years, American relations with what would later be referred to as "old Europe" were being somewhat undercut by mass European public opposition to the Pershing II deployment and by general U. S. unease over the policies of Ostopolitik. Although those relations were buoyed by Reagan's personal appeal on visits to Normandy and Berlin, they were somewhat flattened yet again by the flap over Reagan's visit to a German military cemetery containing Nazi-era dead. Nevertheless, the Anglo-American relationship flourished and continued to do so in the post-cold war period, even as American relations with "old Europe" faded from their World War II and postwar congeniality.

The Reagan Presidency: A Negative Assessment

Nostalgia runs deep in all conservative movements—a desire to return to some great past age where things were done at least a tad better than today. Sometimes this takes on a reactionary mode, a desire for wholesale reversal of the "modern" to the "traditional." More often, American conservatism takes the form laid out by the Scottish philosopher and parliamentarian, Edmund Burke, which accommodates change but at a rate that can allow assimilation within a framework of traditional values. Republican conservatives since Barry Goldwater, such as Reagan, have floated somewhere in between. If Reagan could have simply waved a presidential wand and rolled back American domestic policy to the 1920s, he surely would have done so. As it was, with a Congress controlled by the remnants of the New Deal Democratic coalition, he would have to content himself with recreating as presidential policy as much of his childhood memories as Congress allowed.

It should have come as no surprise, therefore, that the presidential portrait that Reagan hung in his cabinet room as a statement of which direction in his presidency he would go was none other than "Silent Cal" Coolidge, the last quasi popular pre-Roosevelt Republican. Reagan, for his personal reasons, had developed his own personal mythology of the glories of early twentieth century American small town life. In his view, pre-New Deal America was an idyllic oasis of limited government, individual responsibility tempered by community support when needed and the triumph of the entrepreneurialism in which rags-to-riches stories were not merely inspirational tales but were the natural order of things. That Reagan himself became such a rags-to-riches story only reaffirmed his life-long view that anyone with a little gumption could make it in this world. To extend a helping hand before people had tried to help themselves—as government "relief" (as it was called in those days) was alleged to do—only created a demoralizing dependency. Reagan never really had the experience of working hard and trying to do everything right, only to have a bank failure in a far-off city or a corporate decision in a far-off headquarters to outsource his job to a far-off country take all his hard work and flush it down the porcelain repository of misplaced faith. Rather, having the prerequisite right mix of talent and luck, Reagan went straight from his midwestern idyllic life to the even more insular world of Hollywood. There he lived a life where hard times henceforth would be defined as not being able to buy a new luxury automobile or forgoing daily fresh flowers in the foyer. Had Reagan endured a few years of random hardship, had the full brunt of the depression weighed as heavily upon him as it did millions of others less fortunate, then perhaps his worldview later in life might have been more like an LBJ than a Barry Goldwater. Then again, had he had a less fortunate life, he probably would have never made it to Hollywood and the White House in the first place. It is good to remember that, for every man who makes it to the presidency, dozens of others tried and failed and tens of millions never had the chance to try at all. Reagan spent his adult professional life in various cities of fantasy—Hollywood, Sacramento, and eventually Washington, D. C.—surrounded by people like himself: successful. Reagan's affinity for Coolidge was fitting as both men shared a common trait of substituting anecdotal personal experience for more accurate, albeit abstract, empirical data. Cowboy comedian Will Rogers' parody of Coolidge could easily have applied to Ronald Reagan: "The economy must be doing well because everyone I meet is doing well. If they're not doing well, I won't meet 'em!"

Reagan saw two aspects of post-1920s American government as being most deleterious to his vision of the limited government paradise that existed before FDR. The first was the rise of the permanent welfare state, which he saw (with some justification) as creating conditions of perpetual dependency. The second was the strangling grasp of federal economic regulation, which he saw as fundamentally choking the American private sector entrepreneurial spirit to death. Reagan desired to see a roll back of government social and economic intervention to conditions prevalent in the great days of nineteenth century laissez faire economics, when the iron fist of the invisible hand ruled free markets and individuals ruled their own economic destinies. To this end, Reagan pursued a triad of policies to roll back the New Deal state: economic deregulation, tax reduction, and, as he had sought as governor of California, social welfare reform.

The deregulatory movement had actually begun in the 1970s, driven by a Democratically-controlled Congress and with the consent of a Democrat president, Jimmy Carter. Spearheaded by no less a liberal figure than Ted Kennedy himself, the Carter years saw a move towards deregulation in trucking, finance, telecommunications, and, most famously, the airline industry. The processes adopted by a coalition of congressional liberals and conservatives was aimed at reducing what was increasingly and broadly perceived as regulatory excess—the burden of forty years of accumulated New Deal bureaucratic economic intervention and inertia, which undermined American economic efficiency and, most importantly, American global competitiveness in the face of rising challenges from East Asia.

The belief that the newly emerging Asian economies' competitive advantage came from their more laissez faire governments was actually more myth than reality. Indeed, the Japanese business model was premised on a level of cooperation between government and business (through economic planning by monolithic bureaucracies like the Ministry of Finance and the Ministry of International Trade and Industry, which sought to identify and directly support export competitive industries) that was completely alien to American economic experience. Asian competitiveness was instead based on a truly simple nineteenth century notion: making workers work harder and longer. And indeed, across the 1960s and 1970s, hours worked by Asian workers increased dramatically while output per worker per hour increased only gradually as new technologies were introduced into industrial processes.

Thus, the single most important deregulatory policy Reagan pursued was in the area of labor law, which Reagan tackled more by example than by actual changes to the laws on the books. When the Paternal Air Traffic Controllers Order (PATCO), a federal employees union, went on strike in August 1981, Reagan wasted no time in applying nineteenth century labor principles: he gave the workers forty-eight hours to return to work and then fired those who did not, effectively crushing the union. When the president of the United States crushed a union, it was an announcement to all that it was now open season on labor unions in general. Union membership, already down from its 1950s peak of nearly 25 percent of the labor force to 20 percent by the late 1970s, declined by a further 25 percent across the 1980s. The combination of the declining power of union-based collective bargaining on a national scale and the rise of "outsourcing" (the shipping of previously American jobs overseas by multi-national corporations (MNCs) seeking cheaper labor costs, beginning with lower skilled blue collar jobs in the 1970s and reaching up to moderately skilled white collar jobs by the 2000s) would have two detrimental effects on the 95 percent of American households dependent upon labor for their income (as opposed to the 5 percent more dependent on returns from invested capital).

First, there would be a constant downward pressure on hourly wages across the 1980s and extending into the 2000s. Thus, maintaining household standards of living from the 1970s onwards increasingly depended on two things: increased use of credit, resulting in average American households amassing increasing and historically high (and probably unsustainable) levels of debt; and increased hours worked, both by individual workers and by more members of the household (that is, women) entering the labor force. While this increase in hours worked amidst stagnant hourly wages boosted American aggregate productivity to levels once again competitive with East Asian economies, it came at the price of creating a new American generation of workers who, unlike either their parents or grandparents, looked forward to working harder and longer without a corresponding increase in take-home pay. In the 1960s, American sociologists began to ponder how America would handle a leisure economy by the end of the century in which average Americans worked less than thirty hours a week. By the 1980s, sociologists were documenting the collapse of America's social recreational culture, as bowling leagues and bridge clubs folded across the country because workers were too busy to "waste time" relaxing.

The dirty little secret of the "new economy" that began under Reagan with the return to supply-side economics was that it would be a "Ben Hur" economy. Like the galley slaves in "Ben Hur" who made the boats go faster by simply rowing harder and faster, American workers in the 1980s made the economy go faster, but it was achieved by working longer and harder and with less security than their parents. Reagan's neo-liberal economists applauded the resulting rise in productivity (and corporate profits that could then be reinvested in further economic growth, though not always within the United States, providing it was not siphoned off to build a new weekend house on Long Island or in La Jolla) and point out how favorably American productivity figures compared to Europeans with their continuing inefficient state socialist economies and social welfare states. Yet, the continuing second dirty little secret of the Reagan revolution is that French workers are actually more productive per hour worked than their American counterparts even to this day—twenty-four years after the revolution began. They simply do not work as many hours over a year, taking long union and state-mandated vacations. In America, vacation time had increased between the 1940s and 1970s but dwindled thereafter. In American corporations today, to take a vacation is tantamount to permanently vacating your desk—if you can be gone for two consecutive weeks, your job is probably not needed after all. Thus, while trumpeting the virtues of the past, Reagan taught Americans to be more content with the diminishing expectations of the present.

Neo-liberal advocates of laissez faire economics often misapply the maxims of their founding guru, Adam Smith, on the role of government and free markets (or, better said, they simply edit out whole portions of Smith's thoughts). To that end, Adam Smith (a moral philosopher looking at the just benefits a free market brought to a free society) did not seek to eliminate all government economic regulation. Rather, for Smith, government regulation was necessary to maintain the rule of law that insured a truly free and fair market in which no interests, particularly wealthy and powerful interests, would be able to cheat and "game" markets to their own advantage (such as through the formation of monopolies). Thus, Smith, the father of classical liberal economics, differentiated between efficient social regulation that protected the public interest and maintained free markets and inefficient micro-regulation of the markets themselves that strangled innovation and added additional economic costs without corresponding social benefits. Like many postwar neo-liberal economists and politicians, Reagan did not differentiate between the two. For Reagan, the impetus for economic deregulation was driven as much by an economic principle turned dogma as by empirical economic rationality.

Conservative critics argued that Reagan did not cut nearly as many regulations as he should have (the most severe of such critics only being content the day that the Federal Register, which publishes new regulations, permanently ceased operation). Yet, liberal critics argued that Reagan was successful—far too much so—in reversing the post-New Deal tide and limiting the number of new regulations being created. Indeed, the general public perception from the outset of the Reagan administration was that Reagan would be extremely pro-business (which was why business interests formed a key part of his 1980 and 1984 campaign constituencies) even at the expense of other interests, such as environmentalists and labor. Reagan's appointments to the regulatory and cabinet bureaucracies only underscored the power of business in Reagan Washington, such as a brokerage firm executive named to head the Securities and Exchange Commission, a construction company owner to head OSHA, and a mining and timber industry lobbyist (James Watt), who was also a born-again Christian with the self-professed belief that the "Second Coming" was imminent so conservation was not necessary, as Secretary of the Interior. Shortly after taking office, Reagan tasked his Office of Management and Budget director, David Stockman, to become the administration hit man on government economic regulation, turning the OMB into the office of the "regulatory czar" empowered to weed out unnecessary rules. Meanwhile, a parallel task force under Vice President George H. W. Bush targeted hundreds of federal regulations for elimination, including many concerning hazardous waste disposal, air and water pollution, worker safety, and nuclear power plant operations. The Reagan administration even sought at one point to remove Reyes Syndrome warnings from aspirin bottles at the behest of a pharmaceutical industry worried about diminished sales. The goal of the Reagan regulatory policy was not just to slow down or roll back the pace of regulation but also to ultimately gut the government's regulatory ability. Under Reagan, regulatory staff at all levels were allowed to decline by attrition while political appointees worked to constrain the activities of their bureaucratic staff. Whole areas of government regulatory enforcement, such as in the area of anti-trust, fell fallow. As a consequence, twenty years of progress towards cleaner air and water was brought to a halt, workplace injuries rose, and corporate malfeasance (a foretaste of the corporate scandals of the late 1990s and early 2000s), as exemplified by the savings and loan scandal, multiplied.

Reagan's commitment to downsizing government did not come at the expense of political expediency however. In 1988, at Reagan's request, Congress created a fourteenth cabinet department, the Department of Veterans Affairs. DVA was previously known as the Veterans Administration, an agency of the Department of Defense. Its elevation to cabinet status, while making little bureaucratic sense and resulting in no real additional monies being spent on veterans, allowed Reagan to deliver on a campaign promise to look after America's veterans. In general, despite Reagan's commitment to cutting the size of the federal government, there was no appreciable decline in the federal workforce across his presidency. It was perhaps in recognition of this fact that two monuments to bureaucratic privilege and girth—Washington's National Airport, which essentially serves as a private airport for members of Congress and executive branch officials, and the nation's second largest government building, the Ronald Reagan Center for International Commerce—were renamed in honor of the faux government-cutting president after he left office.

The deregulatory attitude of the Reagan years—the idea that the governmental rooster was no longer guarding the national hen house—helped to foster an "anything goes" mentality in corporate America. The

Reagan years saw the rise of the "Pretty Woman economy": the mania of mergers and acquisitions fueled by windfall corporate and high income tax cuts, which proved the maxim that too much of anything, even money, can have bad consequences. The central tenet of supply-side economics is the "Field of Dreams" theory of "build it and they will come." In this theory, massive tax cuts targeted at the investment class will result in renewed capital investment in new productive assets (e.g., rich people will take their tax cuts and open factories and businesses). Amidst the depressed consumer demand caused by the recession of the early 1980s, however, American capital investors were not particularly keen to put money into factories that might produce goods no one wanted to buy. As such, much of the capital "liberated" by tax cuts either went off shore in search of more lucrative labor and consumer markets or were plowed into financial speculation, as witnessed by the massive increase in the stock market and the rising cult of "The DOW" as the ultimate benchmark of American economic health. Merging companies to realize corporate savings and enhanced profits by downsizing the merged labor force and the buying and wholesale liquidating of the capital assets through hostile takeovers (as the character played by Richard Gere did for a living in "Pretty Woman") became a primary means to create corporate profits (as opposed to the old-fashioned way of developing new products and markets). Massive insider trading scandals that revolved around the largely unregulated "junk bonds" market that developed to service such takeovers made Ivan Boesky (whose celebration of greed was itself celebrated in yet another Hollywood movie on the excesses of Reagan-era capitalism, "Wall Street") and Michael Milken household names and national "whipping boys" for the sins of capitalist greed. All of this was dwarfed by the massive savings and loan scandal, which essentially amounted to hundreds of less than scrupulous S&L executives implementing schemes to defraud their own institutions of billions of dollars. (Lest there be any doubt, realize that the best and the brightest of the Harvard and Wharton business schools do not drive entire industries into the dumpster unintentionally.) Taxpayers were ultimately left to bail out the resulting industry-wide collapse by the end of the decade to the tune of several hundred billion dollars. Amidst the Reagan-era Wild West mindset, corporate abuses of both the laws of government and markets reached heights unseen since before the stock market crash of 1929. The stock market crash of 1987 took some of the wind out of the sails of corporate "pirates," but the winds of "irrational exuberance," as Alan Greenspan labeled the stock market riot of the late 1990s, would once again propel new fleets of corporate raiders and Enron pirates—until the bursting of the bubble in 2000.

Reagan's commitment to across-the-board business deregulation and the resulting excesses by corporate and capital interests produced a significant broad-based public backlash as early as 1983, contributing to his decreasing approval rating. (Both Republicans and Democrats alike might do well to note, though for very different reasons, even today the only major social institutions that voters distrust more than labor unions—which come in even lower in trust than lawyers, Congress, and reporters—are business corporations. The public outcry pushed the Reagan administration away from deregulation as a major objective by Reagan's second term.

Reagan would actually be more successful in reducing the size of government—or at least the social welfare component of it aimed at poverty reduction—through the massive tax cuts he pushed through Congress in 1981 and the follow-up reductions in 1984 and 1986. The second leg of the supply-side Reagan revolution, the reduction in federal revenues, were supposed to be matched by even greater reductions in federal spending to avoid the inflationary effects of deficit spending and the "crowding out" effects of the resulting massive government borrowing from capital markets, resulting in growth-reducing higher interest rates. Substantial across-the-board federal spending cuts, however, did not occur. Defense spending actually increased across the decade as a necessary component of Reagan's cold war strategy. Meanwhile, Reagan would be unwilling to grasp the so-called "third rail" of American politics, Social Security, even when presented in 1981 with a bipartisan congressional plan to slow down the system's dramatically escalating growth rate (caused by retirees simply living longer) by reducing or freezing the cost of living adjustments. Reagan rejected the proposal for the contradictory reasons that his budget director wanted to hold out for even deeper cuts and his political aides wanted to avoid any cuts at all for fear of losing public and congressional support for tax cuts and deregulation. Instead, President Reagan sought the bulk of his social welfare spending cuts by targeting programs to the young and the poor (who are often one and the same, or at least reside in the same households). Thus, for all his anti-social welfare rhetoric, Reagan was ultimately unwilling to address the inequities of the largest single component of that system, Social Security, which targets the greatest amount of federal social spending at the wealthiest cohort of American society (and also, not coincidentally, the cohort with the highest voting participation): the elderly. Social Security has been one of the greatest success stories of the New Deal social welfare experiment. Between the 1950s and the 1980s, poverty rates amongst the elderly plummeted by almost two-thirds. From the introduction of the Great Society programs of the 1960s to the early 1980s, the poverty rate of American children also declined significantly. Following the Reagan welfare cuts, which intensified the downward pressure on incomes for poorer households, however, child poverty rates actually increased, thereby laying to rest another great myth: that in America children come first.

Reagan's real efforts to reduce social welfare never quite matched his campaign and press conference rhetoric about "welfare queens" driving Cadillacs to the local government office to pick up yet another fat relief check. Yet, Reagan's views on social welfare policy, no doubt influenced by his mother's Scottish Protestantism, were right in line with the strongly neo-Calvinist views of welfare endemic in modern American evangelical conservative politics. These views hold, in good Calvinist fashion, that God smiles on the industrious and pious and grants them the material wealth for which they have worked hard. They seldom remarked on the corollary to the belief that God answers the prayers of the hardworking faithful. Those whose prayers are not answered must, therefore, be lazy or impious or both and, as such, deserve the poverty— both spiritual and material—of their lives. The alternative would be to acknowledge a capricious, Greek-style God of yore who spites some while rewarding others, regardless of their personal worthiness. Underlying neo-conservative social policies is a tendency towards suspicion, if not outright disdain and hostility, for the poor and, with that, a desire to reduce public subsidy of the undeserving. Such thinking led a prominent African-American economist at the time to remark that such conservatives believe that giving money to the rich gives them an incentive to work harder but taking money from the poor achieves the same result.

Reagan's rhetoric on social welfare underscored a fundamental Jekyl and Hyde quality to his presidency. At the personal level, Reagan was a tremendously compassionate man, spending hours each week answering letters from Americans complaining of problems ranging from job loss to medical problems (and often pestering his staff to seek personal solutions to particular cases). At the abstract level of policy, however, he could just as easily cut a program in the name of conservative theory that directly hurt the individual he personally desired to help. According to numerous critics, for example, the Reagan administration was slow to react to the growing AIDS crisis until longtime Reagan friend Rock Hudson died of the disease. Only then did Reagan push for a major policy initiative to deal with AIDS. Yet, in his next budget he actually reduced the level of funding for AIDS-related research. Ultimately, while Reagan considered tolerance and compassion essential personal virtues, he did not believe them to be virtues subject to government enforcement and institutionalization. His efforts to reduce government's role in pursuing such virtues—cutting social welfare, reducing affirmative action—opened his administration to charges of callousness and even outright racism. It would take two Bushes to refine the rhetoric of "compassionate conservatism" enough to wash away some of the stale aftertaste that Reagan's own brand of raw conservatism left on many people's palates.

Reagan saw himself as a unifying leader; yet, his rhetoric and policies often intensified social division on issues ranging from civil rights to abortion. To win his party's nomination, Reagan had to create a new coalition in which a southern vote, dominated by white social conservatives and "state-righters," stood paramount. Reagan's anti-Washington, pro-states' rights rhetoric directly played to the sentiment of many southern whites who felt victimized by the Washington-directed civil rights programs of the 1960s. His triumph at the 1980 Kansas City Republican convention, driven by the conservative wing of the party, finally destroyed the Rockefeller moderate wing of the party that Barry Goldwater had targeted in 1964. Reagan began the conversion of the party of Lincoln with its domination by eastern and midwestern Republicans into the party of Jefferson Davis with the increasing domination of southern (and western) conservatives. This does not mean that Reagan embraced the overt racism of either the old South or anti-civil rights warriors like Strom Thurmond or George Wallace (though more than a little of that rhetoric found its way into his speeches, especially during the 1980 southern primaries). But the states' rights, anti-Washington sentiment that resonated most strongly in the South became the core values of the Republican Party (witness Bob Dole running in the 1996 presidential election at every speech patting his breast pocket in which he kept a copy of the Tenth Amendment), and southern states became the party's core constituency.

Reagan's rhetoric was often more inflammatory than his policies, which would be tempered by congressional opposition. Whipping up opposition on the left and hope on the right, he often then left both sides of an issue hanging and unsatisfied as he compromised on a key point or simply lost interest in pushing the issue. On the abortion issue, Reagan raised the hopes of the pro-life movement with his campaign promises and recurrent speeches, promising to put strict constructionist justices on the Supreme Court who would overturn *Roe v. Wade*. Yet, of his three high court appointments, only one, Antonin Scalia, would clearly fit into that mold. The other two, Sandra Day O'Connor and Anthony Kennedy, would actually be crucial votes in upholding *Roe* after Reagan left office. In fairness to Reagan, he was somewhat surprised by the moderation O'Connor brought to the bench and had tried first to put arch-conservative jurist Robert Bork on the bench before Kennedy. But Bork had been "Borked" by the Democrat-controlled Senate, the new term created by his treatment that meant denial of appointment on ideological grounds. Rather than risking a second controversial appointee, Reagan folded and picked a moderate who was more likely to be confirmed. Reagan's failure to match his rhetoric with action, however, enraged the anti-abortion camp and intensified the already-heated social debate.

Both fiscal conservatives and liberals alike, meanwhile, decried (though for different reasons) the natural outcome of the tax cuts and spending increases of Reagan's first term: unprecedented budget deficits pushing the $100 billion mark in 1982 and the $200 billion mark the following year (levels two to three times higher than those for which Reagan had mercilessly blasted Jimmy Carter). Conservatives complained that the deficits were the result of Reagan being unwilling to really push to dismember the entirety of New Deal and Great Society programs, which would have been required to offset the massive defense build-up. High deficits, they feared, would undercut the economic growth that supply-side tax cuts and economic deregulation were supposed to generate. Meanwhile, liberals saw a more insidious side to the Reagan deficits. As the aggregate federal deficit doubled over the Reagan years (and would double again into the 1990s), federal spending escalated dramatically simply to pay the interest on the multi-trillion dollar debt, pushing debt repayment up to the third largest item in the budget (behind only Social Security and defense spending).

Interestingly enough, massive federal borrowing during the Reagan years did not cause either inflation or interest rates to rise; both actually declined substantially across the 1980s, though stabilizing at rates slightly above their postwar averages. This was due in no small part to the massive infusion of foreign capital into the U.S., primarily from Japanese investors looking to roll over into federal treasury bonds the huge quantities of dollars they were earning from exports to the U.S. The huge influx of foreign capital allowed the U.S. government the luxury of borrowing huge amounts of money without having to raise interest rates to attract lenders and without substantially drawing down domestic capital supplies. (This situation would repeat itself with the huge deficits of the George W. Bush administration, allowing significant deficits without rising interest rates.) Thus, the fears of fiscal conservatives (fears that a simple review of the ultimately positive economic impacts of New Deal and World War II debt should have dissipated) that massive government debt would always be economically ruinous proved to be unfounded. (Additionally, the claims by the George W. Bush administration that Reagan proved "budget deficits don't hurt," were true—to the extent that high deficits do not necessarily significantly hurt aggregate economic growth rates.) Indeed, in retrospect, it should be clear that despite their brand-naming as supply-side economics, the Reagan years owe most of their economic success to the economic stimulus produced by a massive application of old-fashioned Keynesian deficit spending. Had Reagan, in 1981, actually been successful in slashing government social spending as he wanted to do and avoided the major defense spending increases he felt compelled to do, the recession of the early 1980s might well have snowballed into a much deeper and longer-lasting event, the resolution of which Reagan, in turn, would probably have watched from his ranch in Santa Barbara after his 1984 electoral defeat.

But the fear over deficits dramatically changed the policy debate in Washington. From 1982 onwards, reducing the "unsustainable" rate of federal borrowing (so unsustainable that it only lasted for another sixteen years during which time the economy witnessed two long periods of sustained economic growth and endured only one mild recession) became the driving concern of Congress and political pundits. With Social Security sacrosanct and expenditures on defense and debt actually increasing, the only areas of federal spending open to the paring talons of congressional deficit hawks would be social spending on the poor and federal aid to states and cities, which usually underwrote state and municipal social spending on the poor. Decreasing rates of federal aid to states (adjusted for population and inflation) forced states to raise their own taxes (particularly through regressive sales taxes and fees that disproportionately hit lower income households) and reduce social spending. Thus, yet another myth of the Reagan years is exploded: that Reagan's policies lowered taxes across the board for all Americans. While federal income tax rates went down for almost all income brackets, increases in regressive state taxes and in Social Security withholding taxes (which are regressive in and of themselves, as the amount of income subject to withholding is capped, providing upper income households with substantial tax savings) resulted in a net gain in taxes paid by the majority of American households, particularly lower income households.

The double whammy of declining federal and state spending on poverty reduction and increasing taxes and fees on lower income households in conjunction with tax reductions targeting higher income households dramatically reversed the postwar trend towards greater levels of income equality during the 1980s. The myopic political focus on reducing deficits coupled with Reagan's successful rhetorical demonization of even the concept of tax increases, however, meant that the New Deal antidote to rising income inequality—increased social spending and progressive taxation—were no longer politically viable. The Reagan supply-side revolution, while missing its overall target of shrinking government in its entirety, did succeed in a core goal of crushing the New Deal social welfare state. Indeed, according to Reagan budget director David Stockman, the tax cuts were basically a Trojan horse with which to emasculate the poverty portion of the welfare state by "starving the beast" of government with the need for deficit reduction. The Reagan social revolution culminated in 1996 with the welfare reform act agreed to by Democrat Bill Clinton and a Republican-dominated Congress, which amounted to an ending of the New Deal/Great Society-era commitment to provide open-ended support to combat poverty and economic hardship. The Reagan formula of reducing the scope of social welfare by essentially bankrupting government (but first moving massive quantities of national wealth to upper income brackets through tax cuts) proved so successful that it would be dusted off and recycled almost *in toto* by the George W. Bush administration. The only downside of all this was, of course, that, as a consequence, American income inequality is amongst the highest of any industrial democracy and its concentrations of wealth the greatest since the nineteenth century.

Ultimately, Ronald Reagan was largely unsuccessful in his efforts to roll back the clock on American economic and social policy. What Reagan forgot in his desire to return to the glorious days of nineteenth century laissez faire—as do most neo-liberals today—was that the nineteenth and early twentieth century was no golden age for the millions of agrarian and industrial workers who were the bulk of the population. Under the pressure of tight monetary policy that dominated from the Civil War to World War I (towards which the Federal Reserve moved once again in the 1980s), tens of thousands of farmers would be forced off their lands by the combination of declining prices and rising interest rates and forced into taking lower-paying jobs in the sprouting industrial cities, exchanging their lives of blue skies and fresh air for overcrowded, fetid tenements (as also happened in the 1980s, with the exceptions that the low-paying industrial jobs were replaced by low-paying Wal-Mart jobs and the tenements by deteriorating suburbs). In the nineteenth century, what had been a nation of small farmers became a nation of a few very rich owners of capital and many very poor laborers. When these laborers tempted to organize to secure better pay and working conditions, they were often shot by government police and troops acting as agents for capital interests. (Ronald Reagan, in his first political incarnation as a labor leader, would have been incarcerated—or worse—in the age that he idolized.)

In the nineteenth century, life expectancy was almost half of what it is today; yet, no government invested billions of dollars to improve basic sanitation and research wonder cures for disease. The paucity of public health was made all the worse by the wholesale destruction of entire ecosystems—wilderness, rural, and urban—in the name of economic development, resulting in denuded forests, poisonously polluted waterways and air, and agricultural soil erosion on a continental scale. This occurred because, in the nineteenth century amidst the American notion of a manifest destiny to "tame the frontier," no countervailing notion of environmental responsibility and sustainability yet existed (well, actually it did, but those who held such ideals—Native Americans—were being marginalized anyway), and no government intervened to limit the environmental destruction wrought by the personal short-term self interests of the market. In the nineteenth century, racism was an institutionalized fact of life, and ethnic cleansing (as the clearing of Native Americans from desired lands would now be called) was a frontier tradition, in part because no "activist" judges existed to actually give teeth to the Constitution in the face of legislatures caving in to the worst aspects of the tyranny of the voting majority.

Seeing only the benign side of nineteenth century laissez faire thought, Reagan attempted to roll back the clock in each of these areas: fiscal and monetary policy, economic regulatory and labor policy, social policy, environmental policy, and civil rights policy. The one area of nineteenth century policy Reagan tried not to emulate was foreign policy, where he disregarded nineteenth century precepts of avoiding foreign entanglements in favor of a new application of manifest destiny at a global level: the idea of American Exceptionalism.

Due to the beauty of the American system of checks and balances, even as deficits soared, social spending declined, and poverty expanded, Reagan could avoid responsibility for the disorder of the national economic house by pointing fingers at the Democratic Congress. Reagan paid almost no political price (beyond the ego-deflating impact of temporarily low approval ratings) for presiding over the deep recession of 1981-1983 (while George H. W. Bush lost his job for presiding over a much shallower recession), nor would he bear much blame for the unprecedented multi-trillion dollar peacetime debt he left as a parting gift to the American public. Indeed, on issues of economic accountability, Reagan fully deserved his reputation of the "Teflon President." While that label was applied with grudging admiration by the national press and political class, it underscored a significant shortcoming of Reagan as a chief executive—if the president cannot be held accountable for anything, then he is responsible for nothing. Reagan dismissed complaints about his hands-off style of delegating the heavy lifting of government to others by joking, "Hard work never killed anyone but why take the chance." And, indeed, workaholics like Jimmy Carter and, to a lesser extent, Bill Clinton have no greater claim on being successful leaders because of it. Yet, the problem for Reagan was that often being out of the loop as to the day-to-day conduct of the government over which he presided meant that others picked up the slack with deleterious consequences.

While Reagan was by all accounts an honest man with a high degree of personal integrity, one of his great failings, as biographer Lou Cannon pointed out, was his tendency to think that everyone around him operated at the same level of integrity as well. Unfortunately for Reagan and the country, this was often not the case, resulting in an administration rifled by scandals instigated by less ethical and undersupervised underlings, including one such scandal that almost cost Reagan the presidency.

The Clinton administration would be constantly harangued (and Clinton himself impeached) by opponents claiming that his was the most ethically challenged administration in U.S. history. Yet, Clinton actually saw only one of his cabinet appointees indicted and none actually convicted of improprieties. The Reagan administration saw over one hundred officials, including senior policymakers and advisors, investigated, indicted, or convicted on charges of official misconduct. This list included a troika of Reagan's most trusted senior aides who had been with the president since his California gubernatorial days. Two of these aides—Lyn Nofziger and Michael Deaver—would be convicted of influence peddling from the West Wing itself. The third, Attorney General Ed Meese, avoided indictment but was forced to resign his office. Meanwhile, scandals rocked both the Reagan EPA and the Department of Housing and Urban Development with charges of favoritism and corruption, resulting in resignations and felony convictions. As one of Reagan's confidants and biographers pointed out, Reagan had a weakness in thinking that all of those around him shared his own standards of honesty and integrity.

The Iran-Contra affair, in which numerous Reagan aides, including two national security advisors (history may never know exactly how high up in the Reagan administration the chain of responsibility reached due to pardons issued by George H.W. Bush in the last hours of his presidency to the remaining senior members of the Reagan administration implicated in the scandal), conspired to violate congressional law by using profits from illegal arms sales to Iran to fund anti-communist guerillas in Nicaragua almost cost Reagan his presidency. The congressional investigation of the scandal dominated headlines and consumed the attention of the national government for most of 1987, depriving Reagan of the energy and focus to pursue any major domestic or foreign policy initiatives for almost a year. The core of the congressional inquiry came down to one essential Watergate-style question: "What did the President know and when did he know it?" While Reagan denied that he had been involved in the violation of law, for awhile during the spring of 1987, the "I-word" could be heard being whispered around the Capitol, as Congress and the public watched intently to see if a smoking gun directly linking Reagan to a violation of law would be found. (While lying about an affair before a grand jury may or may not be considered by reasonable people grounds for removal from office, deliberately ordering subordinates to violate the law and then to lie about it most certainly crosses that threshold.) Ultimately, two things saved Reagan. First, the televised testimony by one of the accused, Lt. Colonel Oliver North, appearing before Congress in full bemedalled uniform, tipped public opinion towards the president. Second, and most importantly, the public accepted both Reagan's explanation in testimony to Congress that he simply did not remember, "period," what his role in the scandal had been, and a subsequent television apology where he admitted that the facts showed mistakes were made by others over Iran-Contra, but in his own heart he did not believe he had been involved in wrongdoing. Congress, sensing the president had the public on his side, backed down in pursuing impeachment, content to see three of his aides convicted of conspiracy and perjury. Reagan, therefore, survived the scandal but not without cost. The scandal took a severe personal toll, leaving him almost incapacitated by depression for much of the winter of 1987 and leaving his administration running adrift until his wife, Nancy, engineered the replacement of Chief of Staff Donald Regan with Reagan friend and confident, Howard Baker, which snapped Reagan out of his doldrums.

More importantly, the scandal ultimately shook public confidence in Reagan. His defense over Iran-Contra essentially boiled down to an admission that he had been out of the loop in what became a critical scandal at the top of his administration. Reagan's statement to Congress, "I don't know, period!" got him off the hook with the American public. Such words coming from the lips of a British prime minister, however, could only have been followed by "I therefore resign." Reagan got to keep his job, but after Iran-Contra the public would have less awe and the Congress less fear for a president revealed to be a forgetful old man. While Reagan enjoyed several foreign policy successes in 1988 (the culmination of processes begun pre-Iran-Contra), the scandal effectively ended his productive presidency.

In foreign policy, while Ronald Reagan was predominantly successful in accomplishing his twin cold war goals—avoiding nuclear war while working towards a peaceful demise of the Soviet Union—he was less effective in dealing with developing nations, both within and outside of a cold war framework. American cold war strategy had been based on nuclear mutual assured destruction (MAD) to avoid direct atomic war with the Soviets, the policy of containment to keep the Soviet Union militarily within its principle borders, and the Truman Doctrine of providing U.S. support to regimes threatened by communist aggression or subversion. After Vietnam, however, such interventions were no longer as politically or tactically palatable, hence the appearance of weakening American resolve when the U.S. refused to take active steps to stem the tide of Soviet adventurism in Africa in the late 1970s. Reagan's innovation in cold war strategy would be a piece of strategic tit for tat—the Reagan Doctrine. The U.S. began supporting anti-communist insurgencies aimed at rolling back recent Soviet "gains" in Nicaragua (which initially was a more indigenous response to a heinous dictatorship than a calculated move by the Russians on the geopolitical chessboard) and Afghanistan.

Of the two, the Afghani venture—with the United States playing the role which the U.S.S.R. had gleefully played in Vietnam, arming local insurgents with low-cost weaponry like shoulder-launcher anti-aircraft rockets with which to take down multimillion dollar helicopters, thereby inflicting maximum damage on the opponent for minimum risk and cost—was the more successful. Reagan's strategy of arming the Muhajaddin against the Russians unquestionably upped the cost of the Soviet war in Afghanistan in terms of men, money, and materials, helping to compel the Russians to begin withdrawing from the country in early 1988 (the opening stages of what became the complete retreat and collapse of the Soviet empire over the next three years). Yet, with the perspective of time, especially post-9/11, the arming of the radical Islamic fundamentalist Muhajaddin (out of which the Taliban and Al Qaeda would emerge—movements opposed to all things Western and secular, be they Russian communism or American capitalism) stands out as the height of short-term thinking. The biggest American mistakes over Afghanistan were ultimately made during the George H. W. Bush and Bill Clinton years, when the U.S. simply forgot about the country that it had helped fan a fine war in a decade before. But the blithe manner in which the U.S. intervened in Afghanistan under Reagan, without thought to the ultimate consequences of that intervention, underscored a repeated failure of U.S. foreign policy to see the developing world through lenses other than those of immediate U.S. interests.

Such would also be the case with the U.S. intervention in Nicaragua, where the anti-communist "Contras," which Reagan referred to as "the moral equivalent of our founding fathers," turned out to be the cast off dregs of the recently deposed dictatorship. (This leads one to speculate if Saddam Hussein had been overthrown in a communist coup in the 1980s, would the United States have supported the cast-off remnants of his regime—the same people the U.S. would have to crush after the 2003 Iraqi war—as insurgents against the communists? The answer would most likely be yes. Hence, both timing and politics makes the strangest of bedfellows.) While Reagan's arming of the Contras helped to wear down the Sandinista government, ultimately resulting in it allowing popular elections, the Sandinistas continue to be a major political force in the country to the present, and the resulting war devastated the Nicaraguan economy to the detriment of the region as a whole. The venture also had the unintended consequence of almost ending the Reagan presidency in scandal.

The Reagan administration's 1983 invasion of the island of Grenada, while particularly popular with the American public (after defeat in

Vietnam, humiliation by Iran, and tragedy in Beirut, a victory—any victory—played well on the bruised American psyche), smacked too much of American gunboat diplomacy for the comfort of many of the United States' Caribbean and Latin American neighbors. The invasion was ordered ostensibly to protect American medical students on the island from harm at the hands of a pro-communist government that had come to power in a bloody coup and had gotten cozy enough to neighboring communist dictator Fidel Castro to invite Cuban engineers to help build an airport in the country, which might have had a military use. Yet, the regime had been in power for more than a year before Reagan ordered an invasion to be conducted by a Marine amphibious force that had originally been scheduled for deployment as peacekeepers to Lebanon. The attack by a suicide truck bomber in Beirut, killing 241 U.S. Marines just two days before the Grenada invasion, had essentially ended the U.S. Lebanon deployment. Critics of the Reagan administration argue that, with a Marine invasion force all dressed up but with no place to go, Reagan had simply used the pretext of trouble in Grenada to justify an invasion to distract a public angry over the Beirut fiasco. Whether this view is correct or not is still a historical debate, but the Grenada invasion would be a historical precedent for the unilateral—even preemptive— foreign policy that the U.S. later executed against Panama in 1989 and Iraq in 2003 in the face of significant regional and global displeasure.

As the Beirut venture demonstrated, the United States under Reagan saw its position in the Middle East, already shaken by the fall of the shah in 1979, continue to erode. American intervention in Beirut had been precipitated by the Israeli invasion of southern Lebanon in the summer of 1982, which had further destabilized a country wracked by civil war. That fall, Reagan laid out a detailed proposal for Palestinian self-rule in association with Jordan, which was flatly rejected by Israel. The withdrawal of U.S. forces following the Beirut bombing and U.S. preoccupation with escalating tensions with the Soviet Union thereafter moved the Israeli problem to the foreign policy back burner. Reagan's failure to launch any meaningful initiative to follow up on the positive momentum developed by the 1979 Camp David Accords contributed to the 1980s becoming a lost decade for resolving the Israeli-Palestinian conflict.

Reagan also proved ineffective in dealing with what became the biggest threat to American security and global stability after the cold war—radical Islamic fundamentalism and its adherents' chief tactic of confrontation—terrorism. The Iranian hostage crisis had resolved itself even before Reagan officially took office. But this crisis was soon replaced with seven Americans taken hostage by pro-Iranian militias in Beirut. Unlike Carter, Reagan avoided the trap of myopically focusing on a problem that he was basically helpless to redress. Stating that the U.S. would not negotiate with terrorists, he turned a weak position into one of moral strength. At the same time, ever the one to respond to personal situations, Reagan developed his own fixation on freeing the American hostages out of a sense of personal responsibility. From this desire sprang the "arms for hostages" deal, in which the U.S. arranged to shift weapons (with help from Israel) and military spare parts to Iran (who needed the weapons and parts to maintain their war effort against Iraq, with whom the United States was also supplying aid to fight the Iranians) in exchange for Iran to use its influence to free the American hostages held by its allies in Beirut. (Thus, the words "convoluted" and "Middle East" flow smoothly together.) The arms deal blew up fabulously in Reagan's face as part of the Iran-Contra scandal. Moreover, while the deal resulted in several hostages being released, they were quickly replaced by new hostages, thereby rendering the whole episode both damaging and pointless.

Reagan had limited luck in dealing with other terrorist threats as well. In 1986, following a terrorist attack linked to Libyan agents on a West Berlin nightclub that killed a U.S. serviceman, Reagan ordered the bombing of Libyan leader Muammar al-Qaddafi's residence in Tripoli. Qaddafi survived the attack, but the absence of evidence of Libyan-related terrorism afterwards seemed to indicate Reagan had delivered a successful message. In December 1988, less than a month before Reagan left office, a Pan Am plane exploded over Lockerbie, Scotland, killing all 259 people on board and 11 people on the ground. An investigation later revealed that the explosion was the result of a Libyan terrorist attack. Hence, the Reagan years showed that terrorism was a malignancy much like a cancer, which might go into remission for awhile but always threatened to flare up again unless the U.S. would be willing to endure painful military surgery with no guaranteed prognosis of success.

The Iranian-Iraqi war also presented the U.S. with a major foreign policy challenge. Iran had been the second most important American ally in the region and, with Israel, formed the twin pillars of U.S. Middle Eastern strategy. From the fall of the shah in 1979 to the invasion of Kuwait in 1991, however, revolutionary Iran was seen as the greatest threat to American interests in the region, and stopping the spread of Iranian fundamentalism to neighboring oil states the number one policy priority. Meanwhile, when Saddam Hussein sensed weakness in regional arch-rival and neighbor Iran, in a move worthy of any nineteenth century European imperialist state, he attacked, hoping to establish Iraqi regional dominance and grab a little territory along the way. The Reagan administration was caught in a quandary: pleased that Iran would be weakened by war but not desiring to see Iraq (a major enemy of Israel and Soviet client state) emerge in a significantly stronger strategic position. War in the region also put global oil supplies passing through the Straits of Hormuz at risk from Iranian or Iraqi interdiction. The idea of essentially playing both sides off each other, thereby keeping the war running as long as possible and draining both regimes, had a certain Machiavellian appeal that the Reagan administration could not resist.

Like the Afghani strategy, however, the short-term advantage that the U.S. gained in the Persian Gulf from the Reagan strategy led directly to significant, long-term strategic problems in the 1990s and beyond. American support of Iraq under Reagan and later George H.W. Bush served to give Saddam Hussein a false sense of U.S. acquiescence towards his aggressions, while the cost of the Iranian war gave him the incentive to look for new conquests. The consequence of this was Iraq's 1991 invasion of Kuwait, which necessitated two subsequent U.S. interventions to set right. The American intervention in the first Gulf War was itself partly mandated by the executive agreement Reagan reached with the Saudis in the 1980s to establish secret American facilities in that country as bases for the forward deployment of military equipment for use against Iran, should that country become aggressive towards oil-producing neighbors like Saudi Arabia. The trade-off for basing privileges was providing the Saudis with a security guarantee, a guarantee on which they collected when Iraqi tanks rolled into Kuwait. (The U.S. presence in Saudi Arabia would also be used by Osama bin Laden to rally support to his Al Qaeda movement with his call to drive the "infidels" out of the Islamic holy lands.)

Thus, like the British a century before whose every intervention into the periphery of the developing world triggered responses that necessitated further interventions, ultimately resulting in the creation of a costly empire, Reagan's machinations over Iran and Iraq lay the causal groundwork for two wars over the next fifteen years and the introduction of an American military presence into the region that may last for decades into the twenty-first century. Whether the actions precipitated by Reagan will result in completing the cycle ending in empire is already a topic already under fierce debate by political scientists, policy makers, and pundits.

Nancy Reagan looks at her husband, Ronald Reagan, as he takes the oath of office as 40th President of the U. S. January 20, 1981
Photo credit: Reagan Presidential Library

(Right center) President Reagan and Prime Minister Margaret Thatcher on the south lawn during her Arrival Ceremony.
February 26, 1981.
(Bottom)The Reagans honor the victims of the bombing of the U.S. Embassy in Beirut, Lebanon, at Andrews Air Force Base, Maryland.
April 23, 1983
Photo credit: Reagan Presidential Library

(top) President Reagan holds a National Security Council meeting on the Persian Gulf with National Security Advisor Colin Powell in the Oval Office. April 18, 1988 (Right center) President Reagan, Vice President Bush meet with Soviet General Secretary Gorbachev on Governor's Island, New York. December 7, 1988 Photo credit: Reagan Presidential Library

Dedication of the Reagan Library, Simi Valley, California. (L. to R.) Presidents Ford, Nixon, Bush, Reagan, Carter. November 4, 1991 Photo Credit: George Bush Presidential Library

George Herbert Walker Bush
1989-1993

In 1962, a 38-year-old George Herbert Walker Bush, future 41st president of the United States, decided to run for the office of the chairman of the Harris County Republican Party. His mantra during the campaign was "Conservatives Unite!" as the party was on the brink of being hijacked by the ultra-conservative John Birch Society. While campaigning in Houston, he was asked to comment on the "Liberty Amendments," the central plank of the conservative John Birch Society, calling for a radical retrenchment of government and international commitments. Acting as the consummate politician, Bush exclaimed that further study of the amendments was necessary before he could make any sound conclusions in an attempt to mollify the intolerant "Birchers" while distancing himself from their extremist, anti-government rhetoric. Bush won the ensuing election to the important local position.

The election proved to be a precursor of the political life of George H.W. Bush: moderate politician who became the chameleon of the Republican Party, dodging left and right as the politics of the moment demanded. Bush's ability to ideologically shape-shift to match the tenure of his times, his audience, or his opportunities served him well in a political career that led from the conservative hardscrabble plains of west Texas to the urbane internationalist halls of the United Nations to the Oval Office itself. After the 1963 election Bush said, "I took some of the far-right positions to get elected. I hope I never do it again. I regret it." Bush would indeed be required on numerous occasions during his political career to adopt the rhetoric of rising Republican conservatism despite his own commitment to a much more moderate Republicanism in the tradition of Dwight Eisenhower or Gerald Ford. Yet, despite his political flexibility—the ability to famously dismiss the domestic agenda of Ronald Reagan as so much "voodoo economics" and still go on to serve eight years as Reagan's loyal vice president—Bush ultimately remained much more moderate a Republican than either Reagan or his own son, George W. Bush, would be. Both before the 1962 election and afterward, from west Texas party committees to the vice-presidency and presidency itself, Bush tried to reconcile the growing ideological divide within both his party and the nation as a whole. As that divide grew wider, his ability to successfully straddle the diminishing middle ground would be challenged. By 1992, thirty years after his first election victory in Texas, Bush would no longer be able to ride to victory as a moderate in an increasingly polarized age.

George H.W. Bush also straddled the divide between the forty-five year cold war period and the post-cold war world—a New World Order, which fifteen years after the fall of the Berlin Wall is still not readily definable. Indeed, facing dramatic pressure from international events while president, Bush proved consistently incapable of developing a sustained and coherent domestic agenda. Under Bush, America experienced one of its weakest economies since the Great Depression while simultaneously witnessing the collapse of its greatest principle rival and the end of the cold war. Domestic blunderer and international conqueror, winner of two wars and loser of the hearts and minds of the American public, Bush shaped his times but, unlike an FDR, a Reagan, or even a George W. Bush, did not define them. As a result, many scholars and political observers consider Bush a transitional figure between the Reagan years and the onset of the late twentieth century American conservative revolution and the institutionalization of that revolution under the presidencies of Bill Clinton and Bush's own son. Yet, in retrospect, it must be agreed that Bush's presidency was instrumental—in both a negative and a positive manner—in helping to lay the foundations for twenty-first century American and global politics.

George Herbert Walker Bush was born in 1924 into a family that, like the Kennedys, was imbued with a passion for politics and "friendly" competition. Also like the Kennedys, he was born into a family of wealth, power, and ambition. The Bush and the Walker clans' (representing the merger of the Bush line with the firebrand line of Bush's paternal grandmother) earliest known ancestors surface in the early colonial period. Some descendants emigrated to Rhode Island and Connecticut in the seventeenth century. Throughout the period, there were businessmen, ministers, and common workers, which filled the Bush clan. The evidence indicates that the Bush/Walker clans were laborious and hard-working individuals. The modern wing of the Bush/Walker line begins to take shape in the late nineteenth century. Samuel Prescott Bush, who was born in 1863, was a steel company president who achieved fame and financial security during World War I as a U.S. government official charged with supervising major weapons contractors.

On May 15, 1895, Prescott Sheldon Bush was born to Samuel Prescott and Flora Bush in Columbus, Ohio. Prescott's early life was one of relative affluence. He lived a good and prosperous life. At age thirteen, he attended the affluent Douglas School in Columbus, and then he transferred to St. George's in Newport, Rhode Island, when his father moved to the region. In 1913, armed with a private school education, Presscott graduated from the prestigious school and was accepted into the elite Yale University (attendance at which became a multigenerational Bush family tradition). When Prescott enrolled at Yale, he immediately became involved in a number of extracurricular activities, participating in numerous varsity sports, such as golf and baseball, performing with acclaim in these endeavors throughout his enrollment. Prescott also became active in other extracurricular activities, pursuing his love of music and singing, actively creating and dominating the Yale Glee Club in these years. His tenure at Yale was also marked by his induction in 1917 into Skull and Bones, the ultra-elite order marked by its elaborate secret rituals that was founded at Yale in 1833. Many famous Yale alumni belonged to this secret organization, which would later include Prescott's son and grandson. In 1917, the society was a prominent social club, including the likes of H.S. Fenimore Cooper (grandson of James Fenimore Cooper) and E. Roland Harriman. A rumor passed through generations of "bonesmen" that Prescott and his cohorts dug up the bones of the Native American Geronimo as part of one of the society's many unusual rituals. Bush's participation and connections within this society and at the university created countless social and economic opportunities, which is, of course, the central *raison d'etre* of such societies in the first place. With his graduation, Prescott maintained these connections as the nation entered one of the bloodiest wars in its history.

With the commencement of World War I and the subsequent American entry into the conflict looming in the horizon, Bush's life, like many other young Americans, changed dramatically. After graduating from Yale, he enlisted in the U.S. Army, where he quickly rose through the ranks to become an artillery captain in the Allied Expeditionary Forces, serving from 1917 to 1919. During his enlistment, he taught intelligence-gathering techniques to a staff of French officers. He also witnessed intense and concentrated combat experience at the Meuse-Argonne offensive in September 1918. This battle would be the concluding battle in the "war to end all wars." Bush was luckily not one of the thousands of casualties of the battle or the war. With the signing of the Armistice in November 1918, Bush returned to civilian life in the United States. Life after the war for Prescott was not as eventful as the war itself; nevertheless, he was determined to return to a stable and gainful life over the next few years. Securing employment in St. Louis as a salesman at the Simmons Hardware Company, he worked diligently over the next few years building a career in sales. Most significantly during this period, he married a twenty-one-year-old beauty in Dorothy Walker, tying the knot both with his new bride and with a new, dynamic branch of the emerging Bush dynasty on August 6, 1921 in Keenebunkport, Maine. Dorothy was the daughter of a midwest patrician named George Herbert Walker, whose family hailed from St. Louis and was the founder of the Walker Cup, an international golfing competition. Thus, much like Samuel Bush, George Walker was a scion of business with an aristocratic stamp. The marriage also coincided with his failed employment at the hardware company; the union of George and Dorothy was a marriage of convenience and opportunity, as well as one based on a true sense of love. With his new wife and new job prospects, the Bushes moved back to Columbus, Ohio, where he found employment in another ultimately failing business enterprise. Yet, based on his accumulated experience, Bush was hired as president of sales for Stedman Products in Massachusetts. Bush had finally gained a prominent position in a significant corporation. More importantly, Bush had achieved financial stability to support his wife and his impending family.

On June 12, 1924, the Bushes had their second child, George Herbert Walker Bush (their first, Prescott Jr.). Named after his influential maternal grandfather, the young George Herbert Walker would live a life of affluence as had his parents. Six months after his birth, the family moved to Greenwich, Connecticut. As the young George moved through his formative years, his father exchanged his job at Stedman and gained employment at the prominent multinational corporation at U.S. Rubber Company in New York City, as manager of the foreign division. By 1926, both the American economy in general and the Bush family in particular would be in a state of rising prosperity. Shifting jobs yet again, Prescott secured a quintessentially lucrative executive position as a senior investment manager in the prestigious firm of Brown Brothers. By the end of the decade, yet another generation of the Bush family had achieved the social position and economic affluence that could be considered their birthright. Thus, as the Bush family entered the 1930s, the ravages of the Great Depression, inflicting hardship and destitution on millions of Americans, simply passed over the family Bush, as fitting their class. Having met the marketplace head-on and won, Prescott now turned to the arena of social power that is politics, as many victors in the wars of commerce often do.

The elder Bush became politically active in local politics and the Connecticut Republican Party, becoming a moderator of the Town Committee of Greenwich and chairman of the state's Republican Party finance committee. By the 1940s, he had emerged as a respected Republican leader in state politics. In 1950, he retired from Brown Brothers to run for the United States Senate seat against William Benton. Bush lost by a scant margin, but it whetted his appetite for national politics. With the usual helping hand that luck plays in most careers, Bush would gain his political fame. In 1952, the other Connecticut U.S. Senator, Brian McMahon, unexpectedly died, giving Prescott a second opportunity in two years to run for office. Building on the statewide organization he had established in the 1950 race and running as a solid Taft Republican, Bush won the short-term position to act as a substitute for McMahon. In 1956, he campaigned against Democrat Abraham Ribicoff and won a full term outright. Over the next decade, "Pres" (as he was called) served in the U.S. Senate as an honorable and loyal politician. Bush soon distanced himself from the Taft isolationist wing of the Republican Party, however, emerging as an internationalist on foreign policy in the rising Eisenhower tradition and an ardent proponent of a strong foreign defense against an expansionist Soviet Union. Indeed, Bush himself had been instrumental in helping convince General Dwight Eisenhower to seek the presidency as a Republican in 1952. To a certain degree, Prescott became an important figure behind the political scenes in the Republican Party. While never a party kingmaker, he was a trusted political activist who campaigned for the party, demonstrating a strong loyalty to his partisan colleagues. Bush would stress the importance of loyalty, in matters personal and political, above all virtues to his children. George H.W. Bush took careful note.

"Poppy," as the future president would be known, was influenced in a number of different ways by his active parents. While the young Bush lived a sheltered life, or what one historian calls a "protected habitat," it was not a life insulated from all challenge and competition. The Bush home was filled with games, such as golf, tennis, and sailing. An old family friend noted, "there was always a game of catch going on outside the house, and health and energy seemed to burst from each individual pore." The Bush household was definitely an energy-imbued environment. But the activities were not just fun and games. Bush's parents, especially his mother, emphasized to their children that playing for fun was all well and good, but playing to win, fairly and within the rules, was as important, if not more important as the fun itself. And in every contest, Bush's parents noted that one always competed against themselves as much as the other person.

Along with fun and games and a love for competition came strictness and discipline when necessary. As one historian of George H.W. Bush would later comment, "he [Prescott] was a strict father but a just one." Prescott impressed upon his son the value of citizenship and, especially, the responsibility of people of their "station" to give back to society. As George H.W. Bush would later relate, "Dad always impressed on his children the importance of being responsible citizens and instilled in us the concept that we had certain obligations because of the privilege we enjoyed." Along with discipline, religion also played a major role in Bush's upbringing. George's sister noted that the family would read from the Bible at breakfast every day, with "lessons from the parables as applicable to daily life pointed out and emphasized."

George's life of affluence included the requisite eastern establishment educational regime: Greenwich Country School followed by the academically renowned Phillips Academy in Andover, Massachusetts. George attended Phillips for five years, instead of the usual four, partly as a result of a respiratory infection, which caused difficulty in attending class. As he developed and excelled at the school, particularly on the baseball diamond, World War II loomed on the horizon. George graduated from Phillips feeling a fundamental need to leave the nest of his family, having developed a strong trait of individualism that many affluent children fail to exhibit, perhaps a product of an upbringing that stressed personal achievement and responsibility. While most of his classmates decided to attend college, George found in the emerging world war a way to "get out from under" his father's influence.

Like many school age kids at the dawn of World War II, George Bush was enraged by the Japanese attack on Pearl Harbor. After graduating from Phillips, he enlisted in the navy, having reached the tender age of eighteen. Bush entered an intense ten-month preflight naval training program upon completion of which he was commissioned as an ensign in the U.S. Naval Reserve. He was subsequently promoted to a lieutenant (junior grade) on board the aircraft carrier *USS San Jacinto,* serving in the Pacific Theater. While flying on a combat mission to Chi Chi Jima, Bush's aircraft encountered anti-aircraft fire; his plane was shot down, and two of his comrades were killed. After awaiting rescue for four hours in the middle of the Pacific, he was eventually rescued by a submarine, the *USS Finback*. For his bravery, the young Bush received a Distinguished Flying Cross. In November 1944, Bush returned to the *San Jacinto* where he flew an additional fifty-eight combat missions, receiving a Distinguished Flying Cross, three air medals, and the Presidential Unit Citation. In 1945, victory achieved, he was honorably discharged from the U.S. Navy having amassed a truly impressive wartime record. Armed with these experiences, Bush returned home and entered Yale University.

Over the next few years, Bush concentrated on his studies at Yale, focusing on a degree in economics. While studying, he also engaged in a number of extracurricular activities, excelling at baseball. Like his father, he also joined a number of societies, including Skull and Bones (or, more correctly said, he was "recruited into the society"). In 1951, the war hero graduated from Yale with his degree, though not with what he really desired: independence. It was not that Bush sought to divorce himself from his family. Rather, the experiences of war and university had equipped him with the confidence of self to play the greatest game of all—making it in life on his own—or, at least, on his own with a small stake from his family, a national network of family and Yale (and Skull and Bones) alumni connections and the door-opening ability of the name "Bush," son of a soon-to-be senator and friend of the President of the United States.

In 1947, Bush, his wife Barbara (herself the child of New York money whom George had met and married in the heady prewar days of 1941), and their first son, George W., moved away from his father and his family in Connecticut and off to the hardscrabble final frontier of the postwar oil fields of Midland, Texas. Rapidly becoming the heart of the booming Texas oil industry, Midland, located near the oil town of Odessa in west Texas, presented a perfect opportunity for a man of George Bush's ambition to make his money and earn his independence, even as his father had done by moving to New York after the last Great War. Bush took a job as an equipment clerk for a Dresser Industries subsidiary, International Derrick and Equipment Company (IDECO). By 1951, the independence-minded Bush decided to strike out on his own, starting up a small, independent oil company specializing in oil exploration. Over the next few years, Bush's Zapata Oil rode the oil boom of west Texas to success and prosperity, establishing him as a businessman of note in his own right, independent of his broader family. In 1959, Bush split Zapata Oil into two subsidiaries: Zapata Offshore and South Penn Oil Company (later Pennzoil). The evolution of Zapata

504   George H. W. Bush

into an increasingly offshore drilling company, however, necessitated a

504   George H. W. Bush

into an increasingly offshore drilling company, however, necessitated a relocation of the administration of the company and the residence of the Bush family from inland Midland to more coastal Houston. Arriving in Houston, however, Bush was bitten fully by a political bug that had already started to sting him back in Midland. Having already honed his skills of working groups and winning friends both in the business and in the social life—church organizations, school committees, and social clubs—of Midland, Bush set about becoming a player in the bigger world of Houston money and power.

By 1963, Bush was elected as the chairman of the Harris County Republican Party. The turmoil over the Kennedy assassination and the resulting rise of a nascent Great Society liberalism under Kennedy's successor, fellow Texan Lyndon Johnson, provided Bush an opportune time to enter politics. Bush saw the county chair position as a natural stepping-stone to higher office. While he minimized the significance of the position, saying, "my job is primarily an organizational job," Bush understood that he could use that organization to help build a political base and develop his own loyal political organization. Armed with this minimal but potent level of political experience, Bush decided to run for a higher profile public office, if for no other reason than to add to his experiential resume. In 1964, he challenged a local House incumbent, the flamboyant longtime Democratic Texan member of Congress, Ralph Yarborough, for his seat. Being the political rookie in Texas politics, Bush rightfully assumed that he would lose the election. Indeed, in late 1964, he wrote a letter to Richard Nixon (who, after the trouncing of Goldwater, was once again looking like something of a national party leader) saying, "it is too early to analyze the election here in the state but I think objectivity dictates we were caught in a landslide." Bush understood that the 1964 election meant Republicans in general were in for a few lean years at least. For the next two years, Bush focused more on business than on politics while he and Republicans across the state and country nursed the wounds of two successive national defeats. The quiet would not last long. In 1966, Bush once again ran for Congress, and this time the independent-minded Republican, walking a still acceptable line between the ultra-conservatism of Goldwater and the increasingly statist liberalism of Johnson, won his position in Congress. (The pro-Republican bias of the newly-created, heavily gerrymandered 7th congressional district of Texas which he ran also contributing to his triumph). Yet, another branch of the Bush family was going to Washington.

Bush played only a marginal role in the Democrat-controlled Congress, his House record reflecting a conflict between his loyalty to the House Republican caucus and his own moderate conservative views. His record while a member of Congress reflected his devotion to the Republican ideology, with a voting record in 80 percent agreement with the Republicans and Democrats who forged the conservative coalition. While he firmly believed that most social activism should be the product of voluntary action at the local level, in what was perhaps his most controversial action as a member of Congress, he voted against the conservative coalition and for the Civil Rights Bill of 1968, which guaranteed open housing. The vote enraged his constituents in the 7th District. Barbara Bush later wrote in her memoirs that, like so many Americans, George H.W. Bush was angered by "so many young black men . . . fighting in Vietnam for the cause of freedom [who] were denied freedom when they came home." Despite the vote, however, Bush won reelection in 1968 but found it increasingly difficult being a member of the minority party within Congress. In 1970, he decided to run for the more august U.S. Senate against another favorite Texas son, Democrat Lloyd Bentsen. Unfortunately for Bush, the conservative tide that would turn Texas into an electoral map "Red State" within a decade was still at ebb: Bush lost by a wide margin to the popular Democrat. Out of Congress, Bush returned to Texas to ponder his future. Shortly after his return home, however, Bush received a phone call from President Nixon that would give him a new lease on his political life. Nixon called the former congressional member to ask him to be the U.S. ambassador to the United Nations. Essentially, Bush was brought into the Nixon administration because of his loyalty, personality, and the ability to socialize with the right people (that is, connections)—the east coast establishment that Nixon simultaneously disdained, envied, and needed in his political camp (or, at least, needed to stop lobbing political mortars into his camp). Bush, having no other prospects, accepted the nomination. The former member of Congress, known for his party loyalty and independence, now entered the international political scene.

The experience as UN ambassador provided the future president with the opportunity to gain invaluable foreign policy experience of a kind that few modern presidents have amassed. Indeed, Bush eventually entered the Oval Office with more hands-on international experience than any modern president except for Dwight Eisenhower and, perhaps, Richard Nixon—and far more experience than Jimmy Carter, Bill Clinton, or his own son.

Bush's most important conflict during his tenure at the UN involved the People's Republic of China. In 1973, the PRC demanded a seat on the United Nations Security Council; however, the seat for China that existed on the council was already occupied by the Nationalist Chinese government in its Taiwanese exile. The U.S. faced a potential diplomatic crisis by either alienating a superpower or dismissing a cold war ally. The evolution of the U.S.-Sino détente marked by the "ping-pong diplomacy" and Nixon trip to Red China, however, made giving Beijing the seat (and the international legitimacy it implied) at the UN a necessary next step in the process of normalizing America's relationship with a quarter of humanity. The diplomatic trick was to make the move without losing face over Taiwan.

Bush, being tutored in the fine art of *realpolitik* by Nixon and his Machiavellian Secretary of State, Henry Kissinger, understood the necessity of ultimately giving in to the PRC's demand. Yet, he still chaffed at having to ultimately betray the interests of a proven and loyal American ally being sacrificed at the altar of American security. Bush played the loyal foot soldier, however, participating in the diplomatic Kabuki theater of first moving to block the PRC's security council bid and then acquiescing, following a vote by the General Assembly to oust the Taiwanese seat. Bush's loyalty to the Nixon agenda and his tenacity in the UN debates made friends within the Nixon White House. Indeed, Nixon was so impressed by Bush that, once the position had expired, the president appointed him head of the Republican National Committee— his Harris County Republican Party position writ large. Watergate was shaking the party and the nation to its foundations as Bush became involved at the top national level of the party. Bush's appointment to the RNC actually owed much to Watergate. Nixon understood that the break-in and revelations of the subsequent cover-up would be a public relations disaster (to say the least). He thus wanted someone in the RNC who could be trustworthy and loyal and not create additional trouble. Bush, a Republican stalwart and loyal follower, the good team player, played the part to perfection. As RNC chair, he traveled 97,000 miles and visited 33 states to give over 101 speeches, 78 news conferences, and appearances on 11 national news programs in defense of his president and his party (and also along the way helping to establish his own national presence and contacts that would serve him well in his later post-Nixon ambitions). However, by 1974, even his defense of Nixon had waned as the evidence of the president's guilt mounted. Nixon's resignation from the presidency marked the end of Bush's tenure as RNC chair as well. Indeed, given Bush's close connection to the Nixon White House, when he witnessed Nixon fly off into the sunset, he might well have been seeing his own political career flying off as well.

As it was, with the ascension of Gerald Ford to office, Bush was left in a kind of political purgatory. Some Republicans spoke of offering Bush the vice presidency, which had been vacated by Ford. Ford, however, now with new (if unexpected) presidential ambitions of his own, preferred a less high profile role for a man who could well be a future political rival. Instead, Ford offered Bush the post of an informal liaison to Communist China (PRC), thereby rewarding Bush for his party loyalty while moving him about as far away from the national political scene as possible while still remaining on the planet. Bush, for his own part, anxious to put the stain of his Nixon association behind him, jumped at the chance, telling the new president that he wanted to "get as far away from the stench of Watergate as possible." Accepting the post, Bush spent the next year in Beijing, but by late 1975, George and Barbara had grown weary of Beijing and its oppressive, drab, and boring Communist society. When offered the chance to return stateside as head of the Central Intelligence Agency, he jumped again (setting himself up, oddly enough, to become with former KGB head, Yuri Andropov, one of only two superpower leaders to ascend to power from the ranks of the intelligence services). Once again, Bush proved to be at the right place at the right time. The CIA was under intense scrutiny as a result of its action during the Watergate crisis, as well as a number of its activities in the third world. Congress created the Church Committee (named for its chair, Senator Frank Church) not only to investigate the illegal actions of the CIA in Vietnam and other parts of the developing world but also to demand organizational reforms for the agency. As head of the CIA, Bush supervised the reforms recommended by the Church Committee, making the agency more accountable to congressional oversight. Bush's brief tenure at the CIA (he would be out of the slot by the end of 1976 following Democrat Jimmy Carter's election) won him praise from Congress and the press and established him as one of Washington's rare breeds of "doer."

After leaving the CIA, Bush returned to Texas, becoming a truly private citizen for the first time in a decade. Back in Houston, he returned to business and numerous public activities. Among the most prominent of these were the American Heart Fund, the directorship of Baylor University and Trinity University, and fundraising for Yale. He and Barbara also traveled widely during this period, going to the Far East and the Middle East. By late 1977, Bush grew weary once again of the quiet private life. Moreover, the increasingly declining public support for Carter amidst economic woes and international setbacks made a return to public life—this time aiming at the highest possible prize—a viable option, despite the fact that by the late 1970s a new brand of conservatism—one first articulated nationally by Barry Goldwater and now taken up by former actor and California Governor Ronald Reagan (who had almost taken the party nomination away from Gerald Ford in 1976) and Congressman Jack Kemp—was rising to dominance within the rank and file, if not the institutional leadership, of the Republican Party. This new conservatism was based on a viewpoint that recast government as the enemy of the American people due to excessive taxation, economic regulation, and secular social engineering foisted upon the nation by increasingly liberal Democrats. Such conservatism directly challenged the post-Roosevelt New Deal orthodoxy of government as national advocate and steward, instead calling for government to be returned to the contained box of nineteenth century political thought through a major reduction of both taxes and spending, especially on social welfare programs. Bush's traditional conservatism cut, like Richard Nixon's wife Pat's plain cloth coat from the same material as Eisenhower's "modern Republicanism" of a generation before, seemed outdated in comparison. Ronald Reagan, who had cut taxes while governor of California (though he later was forced by fiscal realities to raise them again to a degree), was riding the wave of a new property tax revolt from the Golden State to renewed national prominence. The anti-tax revolt in California spread to Colorado and, subsequently, became a national phenomenon. By 1979, the Republican Party found itself at a crossroads between moderates such as George H. W. Bush and the conservative factions led by Reagan and Kemp. Yet, believing Reagan-style conservatism would not be able to reach out and grab the commanding heights of the moderate voters, Bush thought that the 1980 Republican nomination might be up for grabs and that he might be able to do the grabbing. On May 1, 1979, Bush announced his candidacy for president.

Across the campaign, Bush proclaimed a moderate agenda. While Bush was in concurrence with his fellow Republican candidates (in a field that initially grew to ten) on core Republican issues, such as abortion, deficit reduction, and foreign policy, Bush's traditional, pragmatic Republicanism clashed with the New Right's moral conservatism. In the candidates' debates leading up to the primaries, however, it became increasingly evident that Reagan was winning the hearts and minds of Republican voters. Indeed, after Reagan's victory in the New Hampshire primary, Reagan's nomination, though unofficial, was a foregone conclusion.

As Reagan strolled into the Republican national convention, Bush was contemplating an alternative goal. He and his closest adviser, James Baker III, figured that an offer of the vice-presidential nomination was imminent. Bush was the leader of the moderate wing of the party. He had a history of fealty to the party. He was a party activist. Reagan, however, had other alternatives. He thought Bush was a "wimp." Reagan was especially irate at Bush's criticism of his economic policies during the primary campaign. Reagan told a close friend that he had "strong reservations about George Bush." The reservations reached such a level that Reagan contemplated picking former President Gerald Ford as his vice-presidential nominee. When Ford declined the offer (after his own demand for a kind of "dual presidency" was rejected), Reagan finally bowed to electoral expediency and opted to name George Bush as his vice-presidential nominee. With Reagan's election in 1980, Bush was once again in the realm of having to show his loyalty to the party by tolerating the New Right's policies. As Bush became vice president in early 1981, the Republicans were clearly drifting to the right, and like a jellyfish afloat in the ocean, Bush was being towed helplessly by the conservative tide. During his vice-presidential term, Bush remained loyal to Reagan, as he was in his other positions. He traveled to all fifty states, four territories, and sixty-eight foreign countries. Essentially, Bush excelled in the role of vice president. He traveled extensively in support of Reagan's programs. (In the process he set a vice-presidential record for attending state funerals in lieu of the president. At one point during his tenure in office, the unofficial motto of his staff became, "You die, we fly.")

In the process Bush overcame his own initial reservations towards Reagan and became intensely fond of his boss. The intense loyalty and faith in the Republican ideology proved beneficial to Bush. During his tenure as vice president, he not only was a foot soldier in the "Reagan Revolution" but helped shape the Reagan ideology by serving on numerous committees that aimed to deregulate the economy. Following Reagan's electoral landslide in 1984, Bush again began to ponder the presidency, this time from the position of institutional—if not purely ideological—heir apparent. While many within the conservative ranks of the Republican Party were disturbed by Bush's decision to run in 1988, the vast majority of the party were pleased by his decision as the next best thing to seeing the Gipper run one more time (the presence of more than a few "repeal the Twenty-second Amendment" signs at the Republican convention that year being more a heartfelt statement by many party members as opposed to a tongue-in-cheek joke). Despite Bush's position as Reagan's assumed political heir (and in no small part because his support in the party was truly via Reagan and not because of his own personal popularity), Bush faced a strong challenge for the nomination, especially from Richard Nixon's one-time heir apparent— Senator Robert Dole. Bush ultimately returned home to the Houston Astrodome with the nomination locked up. In an attempt to reach out to the conservatives within the Republican Party, Bush offered the vice-presidential position to a young, rising (though largely unknown) conservative, Senator Dan Quayle of Indiana. Later there would be speculation that Quayle had been picked as a kind of place-holder—an innocuous vice president without any chance for presidential ambitions of his own—so that a true Bush heir (perhaps Bush's trusted aide and water-carrier Jim Baker or even one of his politically motivated sons like Jeb Bush) could safely follow him into office in 1996. As it was, the choice of Quayle became a harbinger of other fumbled political moments for the Bush presidency, as the ineptness of the young vice-presidential candidate on the campaign trail and the lack of substance to his political resume became the subject of Democratic attacks and late night television jokes.

Indeed, Bush might have had a far more difficult time winning the presidency if the Democrats, themselves bereft of strong national contenders following eight years of Reagan and four years of Carter, had not nominated an excessively liberal and almost catatonically boring candidate in the person of Michael Dukakis, the former governor of Massachusetts. The Democrats believed that Dukakis offered a strong possibility to mobilize the Democrats' voting base with his strong liberal roots. The Bush campaign ran a strongly negative campaign against Dukakis, bringing up his past record in Massachusetts of high levels of taxation and a faulty prison reform system.

(The Bush 1988 campaign marked a modern low point of sorts with its notorious running of the infamous "Willie Horton" ad. The ad, which showed the mug shot of Horton, an African American who had been released from a Massachusetts' state prison on a work furlough signed by Dukakis and had gone on to jump furlough and rape a white woman, was widely seen to be one of the most heavy-handed playing of the race card in modern presidential campaign history. While the national television ad was paid for by a political committee independent of the Bush campaign, Bush's campaign manager later took unofficial credit for the spot.)

Coupled with disastrous campaigning faux pas, such as putting on a military helmet numerous sizes too large and riding around in a tank to boost his public image as strong on defense but coming across like a geeky kid playing army, Dukakis should have lost by an even larger margin than the 53.4 percent of the popular vote and 426 electoral college votes that went to Bush. As it was, the victory proved personally monumental for Bush, as he won a larger percentage of the popular vote than Reagan in 1980 (50.9 percent). The victory was a mandate for the heir apparent to the Reagan Revolution and its continuation of the Reagan Revolution. It showed to Bush that years of loyalty had paid off in his election as president. As president-elect, the first thing that Bush did, reflecting his traditionalism, was to go to church in Houston—perhaps to pray for guidance over the next few years.

The Bush Presidency: A Positive Assessment

When Bush was elected in 1988, the two major political issues confronting the office and the nation were the American economy and the cold war. The newly inaugurated president faced a collapsing cold war paradigm, as Eastern Europe began to fall out of the Soviet orbit. On the domestic side, the federal deficit was skyrocketing to unprecedented levels after years of increasing government spending on defense and social programs amidst significant tax cuts. Federal spending had crossed the psychological barrier of a trillion dollars by 1988; the aggregate federal debt meanwhile had climbed during the Reagan years to two trillion dollars. Inflation (an expected consequence of massive deficits) was floating at 4.7 percent—sustainable, but higher than postwar averages. While the economy that Bush inherited from Reagan was much stronger than what Reagan had inherited from Carter and while most households had prospered since the 1981-82 recession, the structural weaknesses of massive federal deficits and large balance of payment deficits due to excessive imports threatened to undermine future economic growth.

Once inaugurated, it became clear that Bush's greatest area of strength would lie in his foreign policy. Indeed, like Richard Nixon before him, Bush discovered that a president often can be most successful on the international stage, where the necessity of political compromise that dilutes domestic agendas can be swept away by overriding concerns of "national security." Bush's first major move was to name longtime Republican stalwart and personal friend James Baker as Secretary of State. A no-nonsense former Treasury secretary and Reagan chief of staff, Baker had great credibility in the halls of international diplomacy. Armed with a vigorous Secretary of State and Bush's own ideas (sketchy as they might be) of a "New World Order" rising to succeed the cold war, Bush looked to deal with the impending collapse in the former Eastern bloc and the Soviet Union.

As Bush assumed office, the sclerosis of corruption and inefficiency that had been enfeebling the supposedly mighty "Evil Empire" had already passed into its terminal phase. After decades of declining economic performance, compounded by the astronomical costs of the cold war and its ill-fated Soviet sideshow in Afghanistan, the once great Soviet empire was teetering on the brink of collapse. Chairman of the Communist Party and president of the Soviet Union, Mikhail Gorbachev, who had initiated the opening of the Soviet economy and polity (*glasnost*) during the Reagan years with limited success, faced a series of major challenges. Bush, who understood what extreme disruption the events in the Soviet Union potentially foretold—the end of empires being violent, historically—paid particular attention.

As a result of Gorbachev's *glasnost*, the Soviet Union for the first time began to see the organization of groups along political and ethnic lines actively hostile to the continuation of the Soviet state. Indeed, rising challenges to Soviet hegemony both within the Soviet Union and in its satellite states held the real possibility of a complete territorial collapse of the USSR. Fearing the resulting power vacuum and instability unleashed by a wholesale Soviet collapse, Bush's initial policy was to support Gorbachev to try to work towards a peaceful renegotiation of the relationship between the Soviet state and the members of its polity. It became increasingly difficult for Bush to continue to support Gorbachev over the next two years. The reform-minded but still dedicated communist Gorbachev faced increasing pressures from Soviet bloc members for independence. Unlike Hungary in 1956 or Czechoslovakia in 1968, however, the Soviets lacked the real military ability to quell such sentiments by the traditional application of brutal force. Gorbachev, meanwhile, increasingly faced challenges to his—and Soviet—authority within the USSR proper. On March 26, 1989, under the terms of a new constitution that Gorbachev had championed in order to introduce a limited degree of electoral democracy into the Soviet system, a former politburo member turned radical democrat and Russian nationalist named Boris Yeltsin won the first free election in Soviet history, becoming essentially the "governor" of the largest Republic in the USSR, which contained the bulk of the ethnic Russian heartland by a significant majority of 60 percent. While the liberalization of the Soviet Union and the breakup of its empire boded well for America's long-term interests, Bush was concerned that the Yeltsin victory might actually destabilize an already destabilized situation even more. Thus, while supportive of Yeltsin's election, Bush continued to focus on Gorbachev as the most significant representative of the Soviet state. While Bush might be faulted for not moving more aggressively to throw his support behind the "democrat" Yeltsin, as an alternative to Gorbachev, it can fairly be argued that his policy actually provided for a more stable transition to post-communism. When Bush ultimately threw his support behind Yeltsin, following the abortive counterrevolutionary coup in 1991, his cautious approach to Russia between 1989 and 1991 aided in putting the breaks on the process of change, avoiding what could have become an uncontrolled skid and crash by helping the Russians to secure two years in which to navigate towards a peaceful demise of the Soviet state. Even then, the August 1991 coup came within a hairsbreadth (or, more literally, the fifteen or twenty minutes by which the security team that was sent to arrest—and probably kill—Yeltsin missed him when he fled his dacha outside of Moscow to return to the capitol and take refuge behind a wall of Muscovites within the confines of the Russian parliament) of a collapse into renewed dictatorship or even civil war.

Therefore, 1989 was the most crucial—and dangerous—year for Bush foreign policy. Over a period of months, the Soviet Eastern European Empire collapsed like the house of cards (or lies, if one prefers) that it was. One by one, the Soviet satellites fell out of their orbit, beginning with Poland in June and culminating with the historic collapse of the ultimate symbol of the cold war, the Berlin Wall, on November 10, 1989 (only two and one-half years after Ronald Reagan had called upon Gorbachev to tear the wall down). Within a year East and West Germany would be reunited—something unimaginable a decade or less before. The fall of the Berlin Wall and the subsequent reunification of the two Germanys in 1990 signified for Bush the victory of the United States in the cold war and the victory of the Reagan Doctrine of not just containing the Soviet Union but actively working to undermine it. Other former communist nations in the Eastern bloc followed suit. On Christmas Day 1989, the communist government of Nicolae Ceausescu ended as the communist ruler was executed in Romania. In 1989, the communist government in Czechoslovakia was ousted and later divided into two distinct nations. In Hungary and Bulgaria, the communist governments also collapsed. The final collapse with the most far-reaching implications was in Yugoslavia, which disintegrated in 1991 into seven distinct nations (Slovenia, Croatia, Bosnia-Herzegovina, Macedonia, Montenegro, Kosovo, and Serbia). The fragmentation of Eastern Europe into ethnic and political enclaves was complete by the end of Bush's presidency. To a certain degree, Bush assumed responsibility for the victory as the heir to the Reagan Doctrine. It was during his presidency that the Soviet Empire, long a mortal enemy of the United States, collapsed under its own economic and political weight. Bush led the way through the collapse but also through the more crucial period of peace and reconciliation. As with many issues concerning vice presidents who finally get to occupy the big house, since their predecessors often laid much of the groundwork for their success, much of the credit likewise escapes them. While Bush presided over the collapse of the evil empire, the public and historians alike tend to give most of the credit, where credit may be due, for this event to Reagan and not Bush. This is to at least a degree unfair, as Bush had many opportunities—through excessive rhetoric, chest-beating and flag-waving—to have turned what was ultimately a peaceful transfer of power into something far less pleasant.

Bush continued to treat Gorbachev as the legitimate head of the Soviet state right up to the 1991 coup. This was especially evident in 1991 when Bush and the politically weakened Gorbachev signed an historic nuclear arms reduction treaty, the Strategic Arms Reduction Treaty (START I). The START treaty limited delivery vehicles to 1,600 and warheads to 6,000, thus reducing both nuclear arsenals by over 50 percent. Before Bush left office, the two nations (this time with Boris Yeltsin) would sign START II, which further reduced the arsenals and eliminated altogether the multiple independently-targetable reentry vehicles (MIRV) category of weapons. Bush had an emotional connection to the signing of the arms reduction deals. He felt that they "[offered] hope to young people all around the world. Idealism is not dead and this significant reduction in these damn intercontinental ballistic missiles is a good thing." With the breakup of the Eastern bloc and the arms reduction agreements, most scholars contended that the cold war ended.

Along with leading the United States through the crucial period of Soviet fragmentation, Bush also led numerous military missions in what he believed to be an undertaking of spreading democracy and stopping the flow of drug traffic into the United States, at least in the Western Hemisphere. In this he foreshadowed the more aggressive application of American force, sans the restrictions previously imposed on unilateral action by the constraints of the cold war that would typify the administration of his son.

The most important and successful of these operations occurred in Panama. In 1983, General Manuel Antonio Noriega became the de facto leader of Panama, progressively ruling the Central American nation as his own personal fiefdom. Over the next six years, many U.S. officials, including then-Vice President Bush, urged him to step down, but Noriega refused. But the ineptitude of his rule produced its own indigenous protests, significantly diminishing his grasp on power by the fall of 1989. Noriega reacted by nullifying results of national elections and ordering his "dignity battalions" (DIGBATs—aka hired thugs) to physically beat opposition leaders. In the process, the situation in Panama had become chaotic and bordered on anarchy. Deserted by most of his allies for his ruthless behavior, Noriega began to rely increasingly on the DIGBATs to enforce his rule. By December 1989, Americans living in Panama feared for their lives. President Bush took note of the chaos, which reigned in the Central American nation, a nation of particular strategic significance given the presence of the Panama Canal. By September 1989, plans had been formulated to deal with the Panamanian crisis. While president, Reagan had signed a series of orders providing for the defense of the old Canal Zone and the neutralization of the Panamanian Defense Force (PDF) should it become a threat to U.S. interests. The operation was known as Plan Blue Spoon. In November 1989, the military had updated the plan to deal with the current Noriega situation. Tension increased greatly as Christmas inched closer. By mid-December, it was clear that Panamanian-American relations were strained to the point of damage. On December 15, with Noriega slamming a machete onto the podium, the National Assembly of Panama declared that a state of war existed between the two countries. Over the next few days, the Panamanian forces harassed Americans in Panama City and killed a Marine lieutenant. On December 17, 1989, the national command authority, with the authorization of President Bush, directed the Joint Chiefs of Staff to execute a military plan to eliminate Noriega. Bush's plan contained limited objectives, including protecting American lives, capturing Noriega, neutralizing the PDF, and supporting a U.S.-recognized government. On December 20, 1989, as Gorbachev renounced the use of military force in the Soviet Union,

Bush authorized the use of military force to "eliminate" Noriega. The 82nd Airborne Division was the first unit to jump into Panama, and they assumed control of Torrijos International Airport. After the jump, a combat air assault occurred that moved into Panama City. Operation Just Cause, as the mission was termed, eventually led to the capture of Noriega and his transportation to Florida to face criminal charges of drug trafficking. In the wake of his removal, the U.S. recognized a new government installed by American forces. Even though there were twenty-three American casualties (compared with thousands from the PDF), the operation proved successful to the Bush presidency, both in terms of outcome and public support. Bush particularly received credit from the public for his decisive actions in regards to Panama; for a short while, he manifested true leadership qualities in handling this crisis. Even though many criticized Bush for initiating an age of neo-imperialism, his actions and steadfast resolve in defending democracy in Latin America facilitated other nations on the path to democracy. The meaning of Operation Just Cause for Bush was clear: he would not tolerate the subversion of democracy—especially in light of its coming to fruition in the Soviet Union—even if that meant alienating a significant portion of the diplomatic community.

Even as Bush handled the crises in Eastern Europe, as well as Central America, a much costlier (though, compared to the collapse of the Soviet Union, ultimately less significant) situation loomed in the Middle East— a situation that allowed Bush to shine in the international spotlight as a great international leader. On the morning of August 2, 1990, the dictator of Iraq, Saddam Hussein, invaded the neighboring country of Kuwait because of the imposed 1922 boundary between the two nations. Kuwait essentially cut Iraq off from the sea and, thus, trade and military strength. Hussein also despised the Kuwaitis for flooding the global oil markets with cheap oil (sold in violation of OPEC production caps on which both Iraq and Kuwait had agreed to prop up the price of oil), thus keeping the international price of oil at a low level. This took money from Hussein that he desperately needed to pay off the huge financial costs incurred during his long, bloody, and ultimately pointless conflict with Iran in the 1980s. He also believed that, by invading Kuwait, he could become something of a populist leader of the Arab world by conquering a greedy oil nation led by a corrupt feudal elite (only in the last claim was Hussein ultimately correct). Hussein counted on the western powers staying out of the conflict, believing that, since the U.S. had given Iraq billions of dollars during the 1980s through a variety of mechanisms to help underwrite his war against Iran (at the time the number one perceived threat to American interests in the region), he was safe from reprisals. Moreover, up until the invasion, the American ambassador, April Glaspie, had advised Hussein that the U.S. would view any conflict between the two in a neutral stance—in retrospect, a tremendous diplomatic "oops." Hussein miscalculated.

Within three days of the invasion, President Bush declared publicly that the invasion "would not stand" and took the case for international intervention to repel the aggression to the international community, as Harry Truman had done in the Korean War. The United Nations gave Hussein until January 15, 1991, to withdraw his troops from Kuwait (UN Resolution 678). Meanwhile, the Bush administration launched a massive diplomatic offensive to win the approval and support from most of the Arab countries, as well as traditional American allies in Europe, Asia, and Latin America, for the use of force to expel Iraq from Kuwait.

At the same time, Bush worked diplomatic channels to try to avert actual war, hoping that the simple reality of a massive international coalition with overwhelming military capacity would be sufficient to drive the Iraqis back across their border. In a private letter to Saddam Hussein, Bush explained, "we stand at the brink of war between Iraq and the world that can be ended only by Iraq's full and unconditional compliance with UN Security Council Resolution 678." On January 5,1991, Bush sent his Secretary of State James Baker with the above letter to Geneva to work with his Iraqi counterpart, Tariq Aziz, to avert war. The two met for seven hours to no avail. Baker had asked Aziz to take the personal letter from Bush to Hussein. In an act of defiance, Aziz left the letter on the negotiating table. The moment for negotiation had withered away, along with any pretensions of rationality at the highest levels of Iraqi governance. Bush sought and received congressional approval for deploying American troops in combat in Kuwait on January 12. While the approval was a moment of triumph for Bush, with a Congress dominated by the Democrats, the vote signified a minimal level of bipartisan support for Bush's cause. Even though the vote was essentially nonbinding on Bush—he already had the men and materials necessary to wage the war in theater and had executive authority to deploy them (no one in Congress having thought to invoke the 1973 War Powers Act to demand an affirmative vote to approve the operation, reducing the act to a dead doctrine)—he was, to a certain degree, disappointed by the results. In 1999, the former president wrote, "I was disappointed that the entire Democratic leadership in both the House and the Senate opposed the resolution." In fairness to congressional Democrats, as late as January 1991 and the commencement of hostilities, a majority of Americans also favored a diplomatic solution to the crisis. Nevertheless, Bush was able to muster enough support domestically—and overwhelming support internationally, with a grand coalition of over eighty nations supporting the American effort—to send troops to Iraq after January 15.

Bush anguished over the actual deadline for war. The nervousness and tension that the commander in chief felt at the moment was clearly evident in a letter Bush wrote on the eve of hostilities: "There is no way to describe the pressure. It's 9:45 the night of the 15th. The reports from Baghdad are defiant. Their faces smile and I think, 'Oh God, save their lives.'" Bush's anguish over going to war was evidenced by his later meeting and prayer with the Reverend Billy Graham. The military tensions were coming to a head. At 2:38 a.m. on January 17, the UN war to liberate Kuwait began with air sorties over Iraq. In what would become a precedent for the later Afghani war, for the first month the war was strictly an air war with limited casualties. On the evening of Saturday February 23, the ground war commenced. Eventually, over 500,000 UN troops, most coming from the United States (74 percent), under the command of General H. Norman Schwarzkopf were committed against the vastly outnumbered Iraqi forces. The results were predictable. By February 28, with the infamous Iraqi Army on the retreat or in handcuffs, a cease-fire had taken effect between the two opposing nations. Kuwait was liberated.

More controversially, especially for a nation that appreciates the stark black and white of total victory far more than the ambiguous grays of partial triumph, Bush elected to stop military operations once the liberation of Kuwait had been accomplished rather than pushing on to Baghdad and removing Hussein from power. Bush later recalled that he made the correct decision, stating, "our mission, as mandated by the United Nations was clear: end the aggression. We did that." The conclusion of the war in favor of the United Nations saw two contradictory results. First, Hussein remained in power. Within the next few months, Hussein engaged in genocide with the ethnic minorities in the northern and southern parts of Iraq. This undermined the credibility of the military operation. Second, President Bush achieved an incredibly high level of popularity over the next few months. In January 1991 at the start of the war, Bush had a 76 percent approval rating in terms of the war, reaching a peak of 82 percent. The high approval ratings and the countless parades, at least in the short run, indicated that the American public was content with Bush's masterful handling of all of the foreign policy crises until the Persian Gulf War.

Bush clearly excelled at foreign policy, yet he also had a respectable record in his domestic agenda. Since leaving office in 1993 (and, indeed, during the election of 1992), Bush has been stigmatized as a failure on the domestic front while focusing too much attention on foreign policy. This is somewhat unfair. While Bush's domestic record of success is less flamboyant than his accomplishments in foreign affairs, they are not without note. His most immediate successes in the social arena concerned Americans with disabilities and the issue of childcare. Under pressure from a number of interest groups, President Bush sought to include disabled Americans in attaining civil rights protections against discrimination. Bush proposed and signed the *Americans with Disabilities Act of 1990*. A far-reaching piece of legislation, the law forbade discrimination by employers against disabled Americans and mandated that employers facilitate their places of employment for these Americans who had been previously excluded from any civil rights legislation. The Americans With Disabilities Act's (ADA) impact on American society fundamentally changed the way employers and educational facilities had to accommodate the disabled. The law was hailed as a great piece of legislation for Bush, as significant a social and civil rights policy as any advanced since the 1970s.

Along with the ADA, Bush took pride in his promotion of childcare. In his 1988 campaign, Bush had promised a commitment to provide childcare to the needy. Unlike the Democrats, however, who promoted a federally supervised system of governmental control and regulation, Bush promoted the idea of parental choice. Essentially, Bush believed that parents should make the decisions about their child's health care, that the federal government should support both working parents and stay-at-home parents, that the federal government should increase the range of childcare available to parents, and, finally, that new assistance should be focused on the most needy families. Armed with this philosophy, Bush proposed a series of childcare reform laws as part of the controversial *Omnibus Budget Reconciliation Act of 1990*, which Bush signed into law in November 1990. The childcare reforms included the notion that parents could choose their own childcare arrangements (not the government), the federal government would provide a large increase in the basic earned income tax credit (EITC), along with a larger tax credit for families with two or more children, and, finally, the federal government proposed the "wee tot" supplement to the EITC that aided stay-at-home mothers with children under the age of one. Essentially, the philosophy behind the legislation was choice and the utilization of the voucher and credit system over the next five years. Even though Bush was heavily criticized for his concept of parental choice, he exhibited leadership in the field of childcare reform. Extrapolating from the conservative ideology of non-government interference, Bush was able to begin the process of reform within an often-ignored area of public policy.

The Bush Presidency: A Negative Assessment

While Bush was elected five years into an eight-year economic expansion—the longest such expansion in modern American history (until the Clinton economy of the 1990s), the economic downturn of 1991-1992 ultimately defined his presidency. While no president fully (or even decisively) controls an economy as complex as the American economy, Bush's failures to deal with either the recession of 1991-1992 (or at least give the impression of competent and decisive action) or to deal with conditions in the period of 1989-1991 that directly contributed to the recession weigh heavily against any measure of the efficacy of his tenure in office.

Bush inherited federal deficits and aggregate debt that had skyrocketed to unprecedented levels during the Reagan administration. While Bush desired to deal with the problem of massive deficits head-on, he faced two obstacles at the onset. The first was largely a problem of his own political (and ideological) creation. One way to cut deficits is, of course, to raise taxes. But Bush had famously (or infamously, as things would later turn out) declared that he would never raise taxes as president, resolving in one of the most famous examples of presidential hyperbole: "Read my lips: No new taxes!" With new taxes off the table, the only alternative would be major spending cuts, but that required negotiation with a congressional Democratic Party leadership not inclined to deal in budget cuts without considering new taxes—or at least a removal of some of the more upper-income-favoring tax cuts of the Reagan years. Budget negotiations were pushed repeatedly to the political backburner by international crises such as the Panama invasion and escalating tensions in the former Soviet Union.

By the fall of 1990, the twin realities of demands for deficit reduction and a weakening economy, as well as the high cost of the savings and loan bailout (discussed below), forced Bush to tackle the problem with the opposition. Over the early months of 1990, Bush and the Democratic leadership engaged in a brutal dogfight over the budget and deficit reduction. The Democrats, led by Edward Kennedy, believed in the necessity of raising taxes to have revenue to pay for the savings and loan bailout and the military expenditures. Moreover, Democrats sensed that Bush was weak on the domestic front and, with enough intransigence on their part, might be forced into reneging on his no new tax pledge, with potentially disastrous implications for him in the 1992 election (as would be the case). Moreover, Democratic leaders who had worked well with Ronald Reagan grew to detest the arrogance they believed emanated from the Bush White House. The autocratic tendencies of Bush's first chief of staff, John Sununu (the Republican governor of New Hampshire who got the plum White House role of presidential gatekeeper at least in part because of his haloing to deliver New Hampshire to Bush in 1988), who expressed a palatable disdain for Congress only intensified this animosity. (For a while the most popular joke in the congressional cloakrooms—Democrats and Republicans alike—was alleged go as follows: Bad news: you're in a room with Saddam Hussein, Muammar Qaddafi, and John Sununu. Good news: you have a gun. More bad news: you only have two bullets. What do you do? Shoot Sununu. Twice.) After many secret meetings and demands for a solution (as the federal government was on the verge of a shutdown), Bush went on television to announce in October the passage of the *Omnibus Budget Reconciliation Act of 1990*. The budget, which had far-reaching implications, expanded Medicare coverage of poor children, gave tax credits for working class families, reformed health care for elderly Americans, reformed the childcare system, and reduced non-military expenditures. Bush, however, violated the fundamental principle of his 1988 campaign—his promise not to raise taxes! As part of the budget, in return for his plan on childcare and reducing the deficit, Bush caved in on the Democratic proposal to raise taxes. Specifically, the plan raised taxes on usage items, such as cigarettes, gasoline, and liquor. This proved, however, to be a problem for Bush, as these were taxes that disproportionately affected working class families. The public outcry against Bush's tax increase agreement reduced his popularity rating over the next year into the 30 percent range from the 50 percent plus range that he had averaged during his first year in office. More ominously, from an electoral perspective, the conservative right, which had supported Bush in 1988, viewed the tax increases as a betrayal, while moderates who had voted for him in 1988 viewed Bush as politically weak in the face of adversity. Many scholars and pundits alike have identified the signing of the tax increase as President Bush's death sentence. Many of Bush's closest advisors, however, believed that the mistake in reneging on the tax pledge was more tactical than ideological. Richard Darman, Bush's budget director, claimed, "it was a matter of timing and presentation. We never should have allowed the press release to go out when we did." Bush, however, disagreed with Darman's statement by claiming simply, "if I had to do that all over, I wouldn't do it." He understood the ramifications of his deal. It was a major cause of his loss in 1992.

Along with the politically disastrous budget deal, Bush also mishandled the increasingly volatile savings and loan crisis. The demise of hundreds of savings and loans (S & L) in the late 1980s created a massive hole in the national financial system that the federal government had to fill—before it sucked the rest of the economy down into the drain as well. As the sheer volume of S&L defaults by the late 1980s, largely driven by corporate malfeasance on a scale that still dwarfs the machinations of Enron and other energy trading companies in the late 1990s, escalated, the Federal Savings and Loan Insurance Corporation (the S&L equivalent of FDIC) was overwhelmed. The federal government ultimately had to bail out the failed savings and loans to the tune of an eventual long-term cost of over one hundred billion dollars. This bailout created a strain on the American economy, as taxpayers were forced to pay for the failures, diverting billions from deficit reduction, tax relief, or spending on necessary social and infrastructure programs. Even though Bush ordered the Justice Department to prosecute those who had committed fraud and corruption in the scandal, only a handful of corporate miscreants ever saw the interior of a courtroom, let alone a prison cell, giving new life to the old adage that the best way to rob a bank is to own one. Taxpayers, especially on the conservative right, did not necessarily blame Bush for the debacle. However, much like his predecessor in 1932, Herbert Hoover, who has been treated as a scapegoat for the 1932 Great Depression, Bush was treated as a scapegoat in his handling of the affair. Despite the fact that he introduced numerous bailout plans for the failed S&Ls, Bush was viewed as a participant in the corruption and scandal. (His son, Neil, was directly involved in the scandal.) He offered a remedy for the situation that was too late for the American electorate. For Bush, the success of his foreign policy initiatives overshadowed the corruption of the S&L bailouts. For the public, that was not entirely the case.

As Bush contended with his compromising and tardiness, it became evident that the American economy in the post-Gulf War era was headed to the dumps. Bush's popularity soared with the Persian Gulf War, reaching a 91 percent popularity rating. Yet, even this bit of good news proved ultimately disastrous for Bush's reelection efforts, vis-à-vis the economy. Bush's high Gulf War ratings led him to make a fundamental mistake: he believed he was invincible in the upcoming election. It is true that as late as the end of 1989 leading economic indicators pointed to an economy that was not weak as much as potentially weakening. By mid-1990, however, it was becoming increasingly evident that the economic boom of the 1980s was already in its terminal phase. Due to the S&L bailout, federal deficit, expanded military expenditures driven by the Gulf War, and continuing trade imbalances, the American economy went into a tailspin by the end of 1991.

The first indicator illustrating the weakened economy was the growth of the real gross national product (GNP). During the Bush presidency, especially after 1990, the GNP slowed and in 1991, retreated into the negative. In 1989, the growth of the GNP was measured at 3.4 percent, while at the end of 1990, the GNP grew by only 1.4 percent. Between 1990 and 1991, it was clear that the economy and the GNP were in trouble, as the GNP decreased by 1.1 percent. In other words, the economy was stagnant. Along with the GNP, unemployment and poverty also increased during the Bush presidency. The unemployment rate increased from 5.3 percent in 1989 to 6.7 percent in 1991. By 1992, the unemployment rate had hit an historical high of 7.4 percent. The weakened economy was also visible in the poverty rate during the Bush presidency. Between 1988 and 1992, the poverty rate increased from 12.8 percent to 14.8 percent. For the employed, the economy proved stagnant as the average hourly wage decreased between 1989 and 1993. In 1989, the average hourly wage was $7.64. By 1992, the wage had decreased by over 23 percent to $7.41. It became clear by 1991 that Bush's economic policy of deficit reduction was not functioning. By 1990, the federal budget deficit had increased to $200 billion a year (three times the 1980 levels). The total federal debt had increased to $3.2 trillion (more than three times the amount of 1980). This incredible level of debt placed entirely too much strain on the American taxpayer. The final nail in Bush's economic coffin may well have been the decision of Federal Reserve Chairman Alan Greenspan to prophylactically raise interest rates in early 1991 to offset potential inflation from increases in oil prices anticipated as a consequence of the Gulf War. When oil prices failed to seriously increase, the interest rate hikes became a further drag on the slowing economy.

As president, Bush's aloofness and perception of an economy not "that bad off" did not help. He believed that the income and standard of living of most Americans would not decrease to any significant degree. This misplaced assumption, characterized by Michael Beschloss as a "What? Me worry?" attitude, not only created a sense of alienation from the electorate, but more importantly, it alienated him from the group that brought him to power in 1988—the conservative right, chaffing under both the Bush tax increase and the busting of the Reagan-era prosperity bubble.

The result was a weakened economy, a president who offered no viable—or even unviable—solutions to a problem that he failed to fully recognize, and a public that was becoming increasingly frustrated by the lack of a coherent Bush economic program. In late 1990, his popularity ratings had slipped 20 points in one six-week period, offering an insight into what was to come once the bloom came off the Gulf War rose (and bumper stickers stating "Saddam Hussein still has a job. Do you?" became more commonplace).

As the economy floundered in the postwar period and Bush's popularity ratings quickly sank, his choice of a Supreme Court nominee further strained his credibility with the American electorate. In 1991, United States Supreme Court Justice Thurgood Marshall, the first African American appointed to the highest court in the land, symbolizing the civil rights movement and the struggle for African-American equality, decided to retire. Bush saw Marshall's retirement as an opportunity to appoint a conservative judge to the bench. After much debate, Bush decided on a forty-three-year-old conservative African American from Pinpoint, Georgia, Clarence Thomas. Bush chose Thomas primarily because of his political credentials. During the Reagan years, he served as assistant secretary for Civil Rights at the United States Department of Education (1981-1982), as well as the chairman of the United States Equal Employment Opportunity Commission (1982-1990). His appointment by the conservative Reagan and his stance on issues, such as abortion and civil rights, fit with Bush. There was intense opposition to the Thomas nomination in March 1990. The NAACP, the National Bar Association, and the Urban League, to name a few, vehemently opposed the nomination. They feared that his record in the Reagan administration might continue as a Supreme Court judge. Women's groups, such as NOW, were also concerned that an appointed Thomas would rule against legalized abortion and *Roe v. Wade*. The legal community also believed that, for the position of Supreme Court Justice, Thomas simply did not have the legal experience.

Despite opposition from these groups, the nomination proceeded to the Senate Judiciary Committee's confirmation hearings. The first few days of the hearings were uneventful, seeming as if Thomas would have a facile and supportive confirmation. After some days of outside testimony from witnesses, the nomination went to a committee vote. The committee split (7-7) the vote, reflecting the partisanship of the committee. The nomination then went to the Senate floor where the nomination almost collapsed. The vote in the Senate was stalled when a law professor at the University of Oklahoma, Anita Hill, accused Thomas of sexual harassment while working at the EEOC with his discussions of lewd sexual acts and pornographic films. The media had a field day with this accusation. The Judiciary Committee ordered a new set of hearings to investigate the matter. Thomas called the hearings "a high tech lynching for uppity blacks." The hearings became a spectacle of one person's testimony against another. Despite the accusations, the Senate voted 52-48 to confirm Thomas as an Associate Justice of the Supreme Court. The Thomas nomination despite the overall victory, was a defeat for President Bush in the long-term. At a moment of crisis for the Bush administration and with the heightened state of economic alert, the conformation proved ill-fated for an administration that needed some good publicity. The scandal heightened moral tensions in American life, as issues such as discrimination, the civil rights movement, and sexual harassment became topics on the major news networks.

At the center of those discussions was George Bush, whose popularity ratings continued to decrease. The Thomas hearings only exacerbated racial tensions that came to a boil in June 1992, only months before the presidential election. By late 1990, the Rehnquist Court had moved in numerous cases to weaken the Civil Rights Act of 1964, essentially undercutting the civil rights program of federal supervision of discrimination in the workplace. To offset this judicial incursion, the Democratic Congress brought a new Civil Rights Act to the table for negotiation with President Bush. The debate immediately became one of discrimination versus quotas. The Democrats firmly believed that the 1990 bill would strengthen the weakening civil rights programs. Bush, on the other hand, believed that the bill itself was racially discriminating as it provided quotas for African Americans. Expressing his ties to his conservativeness, he vetoed the bill despite threats of a congressional override. He justified his veto by stating that he did not "believe in quotas and [felt] that they do more harm than good." (Interestingly, as a member of Congress, Bush did *not* vote for the 1964 Civil Rights Bill on the same assumption.) Civil rights groups subjected Bush to intense criticism over the next few days. Democratic congressional member John Lewis wrote the president expressing his concerns on the consequences of the president's actions. Bush responded to Lewis that he "was moved by your [Lewis's] letter—written from the heart. I do understand how strongly you feel." He continued by noting that the new bill that Bush was sending to the Congress "does guarantee against the possibilities that quotas might be resorted to." Inevitably, a new Civil Rights Bill was signed in 1991, but like other Bush actions, the signing was considered tardy. The bill became the symbol of partisan bickering, as Bush used his veto power to debilitate an important aspect of the American political and social psyche—civil rights. It seemed that, along with the Clarence Thomas hearings, Bush was out of touch with the American electorate on the role of race and discrimination in American society. It was merely another blunder by President Bush in a series of blunders. By 1992, continued inattention to matters of race, which was exacerbated in poor communities by an economy in recession, resulted in the worst racial rioting in three decades, leaving large tracts of Los Angeles' poorest black neighborhoods smoldering in ruins and dozens dead.

Even though Bush has been heralded as a great foreign policy president, it must be noted that some of his policies at the end of his tenure proved problematic in the long term. By the end of 1991 and early 1992, Bush embarked on a new type of foreign policy—a policy based on humanitarianism and human rights. In early 1991, the political and social condition in the western African nation of Somalia collapsed. Warlords ruled the countryside. Death and destruction reigned supreme, as each warlord sought to become the ultimate leader in this African nation. The result was starvation and economic collapse. The United States and Bush in particular decided to send humanitarian aid in the form of food and medicine.

In the summer of 1992, Bush was re-nominated on the Republican ticket, having successfully fended off a challenge from the far right of his party mounted by the autarchic Pat Buchanan. By 1992, however, the tide of Bush's presidency was slipping back out to sea. The economy continued to be seriously weak, especially for average households, even though it had technically already moved out of recession by the summer of 1992. Bush now found himself pressed during the campaign by the insurgent independent candidacy of the alienated former Republican

Texan billionaire Ross Perot. Running on a populist platform lambasting a national government grown arrogant under both Democrats and Republicans, Perot would take votes from both party standardbearers come November. The consensus of pundits and pollsters alike, however, was that he took more voters from Bush by pilfering the support of many of the same conservative Republicans who had embraced Buchanan.

Two months before the election, it seemed evident to many pundits that Bush's presidency was in danger, as his popularity continued to flounder. Even Bush understood the potential for looming electoral disaster and was frustrated by it. On September 16, 1992, he wrote a personal letter in which he noted that he "[feels] much more of a frustration by the press treatment about the distortion of who I am. The record is one thing, but when they distort your character and try to make you ugly—that's a little too much." Bush's failure to distinguish himself in debates with his Democratic rival, a little-known governor from Arkansas with well-publicized woman trouble (or even against the gadfly Perot), further undercut his public support.

George H.W. Bush had been brought up during the Depression to understand that he was of a class that owed their service to the public in repayment for their good fortune, and he had spent the better part of his professional life pursuing this goal. Yet, Bush's failure to articulate a coherent message to address the rising economic anxiety of an American middle class that had been weaned on the concept of perpetual upward mobility—his weakness at "the vision thing" to which he himself confessed—left him looking the disconnected patrician—the political Nero fiddling while economic America burned—that he had spent a lifetime trying not to be.

The problem for both Bush and the American public was that the 1992 recession marked the true arrival of the "new economy" that came to define the 1990s and beyond. The accelerating rise of the globalization of production and finance in the 1980s had eroded the insular protections which the vast domestic American market had provided to generations of American middle and working class households. Outsourcing—first of low-skill industrial jobs, later of increasingly higher skill and higher paying jobs—to the increasingly technologically proficient economies of the developing world would produce a constant downward pressure on incomes of increasingly broader sectors of American workers. On paper, the 1992 recession was neither long nor particularly deep, especially compared to the 1982 Reagan recession. Economic recovery for working households from the 1992 recession, however, would take far longer than had been the case in the 1980s or, indeed, for any of the postwar recessions.

Average American households would ultimately not see a return to their 1988 buying power until 1998—well into Bill Clinton's second term, and a couple of elections too late to reinvigorate public support for Bush. Based on the aggregate economic numbers, Bush's economic team expected that by the election an economic turn around would be well established. His political team took this to mean that no significant or politically risky actions—such as increasing government spending to stimulate the economy, which would also add to the deficit—would be necessary. Thus, while Bush essentially waited for the economy to correct itself, middle-class households decided it was time to correct him. Thus, the aura of public bonhomie that had followed the Gulf War turned into a general public antipathy. A series of public gaffes during the campaign, such as the president forgetting to tip a waiter after he and his wife had dinner together in a Florida restaurant (backdrop for a classic photo-op: president as loving husband), reinforced the growing public view of the president as a rich guy from a privileged background who could not relate to the average guy. Such patrician concerns, of course, had not bothered the public during the strong economy of the 1988 campaign. Bush's failure to adequately answer a simple question addressed to him by a middle-aged African-American woman at one of the final townhall-style presidential debates—how had the current recession personally affected him—simply sealed the public perception of Bush as fundamentally out of touch with the new reality of the American middle class. Thus, Bush, the pragmatic and moderate Republican from Texas, was undone by an even more pragmatic and moderate governor with the simple mantra: "It's the economy, stupid."

Throughout his life, George Herbert Walker Bush had always been viewed as a man of conviction to principle and loyalty to party, colleague and friend, values he received from his father and grandfather and instilled in his own children. Yet, loyalty can often demand compromise to some degree of principle. Bush rose through ranks of the Republican Party where political observers noted his incredible sense of loyalty to the party.

While American politics remained awash in shades of gray between the radical extremes of ultra-autarchic Republican conservatism and neo-socialist Democratic liberalism, Bush, the political chameleon, could adjust his ideological skin colors to mesh with and fuse different factions of his own party and American society at large, therefore transcending the increasing polarization of American politics. Bush could be both a loyal Republican and a civil rights advocate during the 1960s, straddling the "in your face" conservatism of Goldwater and the "government's the answer" Great Society of Johnson divide. He could be the loyal Republican and the internationalist in the 1970s, faithfully serving both Richard Nixon and Gerald Ford. He could be the loyal vice president in the 1980s, reconciling his disdain for "voodoo economics" and commitment to traditional fiscal conservatism with his devotion to his president. But with his election in 1988, Bush was no longer in a position to be loyal to others—he was the man others were supposed to be loyal to. Historically more of a follower and supporter than a true leader, Bush failed to inspire in his party the same degree of loyalty to him that he had given to it.

Without doubt, the Republican Party that Bush led in 1992 was not the same party it had been in 1988. The Republican Party in 1988 was willing to trust Bush as the heir apparent to the legacy of Ronald Reagan. Bush's violation of his "no tax" pledge, coupled with his generally waffling on domestic issues (what was referred to by his harshest media critics as his "wimp factor") and his failure to finish off Saddam Hussein after the first Gulf War had revealed him—to conservatives at least—to be an heir unworthy of their support, a throwback to the "get along" Republicanism of the Eisenhower or Ford years, rather than the firebrand, agenda-setting Republicanism of Reagan. By 1992, the party was looking for a more worthy heir to the Reagan mantle, which it would not find at the presidential level until 2000 and the nomination of Bush's own son, George W. Bush. By 1992, the Republican Party was becoming increasingly dominated by its conservative congressional wing; House Minority Whip Newt Gingrich was soon to seize control of the Republican Party agenda, following the Bush electoral defeat and advance a far more aggressive brand of conservative activism than George H.W. Bush had ever felt comfortable with. Thus, having sipped at the nectar of power during the Reagan years, Republicans were unwilling to go back into the political wilderness because of an inept Reagan successor. In many ways, the defeat of Bush in 1992 was a necessary prerequisite for the later Gingrich revolution—the wake-up call to rally the faithful to ideological jihad (just as the 1994 Republican congressional revolution became the wake-up call to reinvigorate the Democratic administration of Bill Clinton).

By 1992, both the Republican Party and the electorate as a whole had become far more ideologically polarized. From abortion to taxes to the controversy of the Bork nomination during the Reagan years to race to feminism to gay rights to the rising debate by the emerging neo-conservative movement concerning the role American power should play in any new world order, the middle was fast falling out of American politics. American society would, for the remainder of the 1990s and into the 2000s, manifest deeper and clearer lines of political division, which for the first time since the Civil War could be said to be increasingly geographical in distinction, with an increasingly religious, traditional, and conservative suburban and rural heartland standing opposite an increasingly secular and liberal urban and coastal post-modern society. In such an environment of political black and white, George H.W. Bush, like the chameleon thrown onto a sheet of plaid, could no longer adapt and hide. Instead, he stood revealed as a moderate without a constituency—neither conservative enough to keep the loyalty of the party he had served for thirty years, nor moderate enough to attract what amounted to the disintegrating center of the American electorate.

Thus, Bush's legacy, positive or negative, is transitory in nature. Rather than serving as an extension of the Reagan Revolution or an initiator of a Bush revolution, George H.W. Bush, along with his successor, Bill Clinton, comes across to history as more of a place-holder between the first great phase of the conservative revolution consummate by Ronald Reagan in the 1980s and the second great neo-conservative phase of this political paradigm shift under his own son, George W. Bush. As Bush wrote to a friend after his loss in the 1992 election, "I think of our country and the people who are hurting and there is so much we didn't do. There are so many places we tried, and yes, we made progress. But no, the job is not finished and that kills me." Bush's ultimate failure was that he never had a clear vision of just what the job was he had to do.

(top) George H. Bush with his four sons, left to right: Neil, George H., Jeb, George W., and Marvin. 1970.
(right) President and Mrs. Bush walk with Millie at Camp David. September 19, 1992.
(bottom) President Bush signing the Americans With Disabilities Act in the Rose Garden of the White House.
July 26, 1990.
Photo credit: George Bush Presidential Library

(top) President Bush signs the Martin
Luther King, Jr. Holiday Proclamation
in the East Room of the White House.
May 17, 1989.
(right) President Bush signs the Clean
Air Act as William Reilly and Secretary
Watkins look on in the Rose Garden of
the White House. July 21, 1989.
(bottom) President Bush meets with
the Emir of Kuwait, Jabir Al-Ahmad Al
Jabir Al-Sabah in the Office of the White
House to discuss the situation in the
Gulf. September 28, 1990.
Photo credit: George Bush
Presidential Library

William Jefferson Clinton
1993-2001

In the fall of 1991, President George H.W. Bush enjoyed one of the highest approval ratings of any chief executive in the history of the Republic—91 percent. Not even FDR in the halcyon days of the New Deal even briefly approximated such a number. Bush's popularity rested largely, if not solely, on his greatest foreign policy achievement, the three-day ground war of March 1991—"Operation Desert Storm"—that liberated Kuwait from Iraqi occupation. Over the course of eight months, Bush had pieced together a multi-national coalition that initially imposed economic sanctions on Iraq and ultimately used overwhelming military force to drive Saddam Hussein's allegedly invincible army out of Kuwait and deep into Iraq. In a television war that saw CNN reporters broadcasting live from Baghdad, while the first allied bombs fell on the Iraqi capital in January 1991, from start to finish the whole nation participated in a patriotic frenzy the likes of which the country had not witnessed since World War II. For many Americans, longing for the opportunity to erase the stigma of defeat and shame of the Vietnam War, the American-led victory in the Gulf War proved the perfect catharsis. As Bush's acclaim soared through the summer months, many Democratic presidential aspirants believed there was simply no way anyone from the party could defeat such a popular incumbent in the forthcoming election—best to wait until 1996. Within months of breaking all approval records, however, George H.W. Bush's administration unraveled, and by the following summer, it appeared that he could be the victim of one of the quickest incumbent collapses in history. Although several factors contributed to Bush's rapid demise, his failure to address mounting economic problems proved to be the *coup de grâce*. From his presidency's beginning, Bush had little to no interest in domestic policy, content to mouth platitudes about things not being that bad. National unemployment was over 7 percent (much higher in many states); new jobs were concentrated in service industries; and even huge firms like IBM and Xerox were floundering. Instead of alarm, Bush responded with indifference—even complacency—certain he could stretch his Gulf War notoriety to November and use it to win reelection. Bush was mistaken. By early 1992 less than 40 percent of the American people felt comfortable with the way the country was moving.

The "malaise" about which Jimmy Carter spoke in 1979 seemed all too real—problems no one was addressing, important issues ignored for too long, such as race and civil rights, which during the Reagan-Bush years regressed significantly. Such discountenance by the Bush administration contributed to the outbreak of one of the worse race riots since the late 1960s—the explosion in April 1991 of several days of looting, burning, and violence in south-central Los Angeles. Igniting the riots was the acquittal of the LAPD officers who had been shown beating a defenseless black motorist, Rodney King, on videotape. At the same time, government officials and corporate executives were going to jail for betraying the public trust. Suddenly, an election that looked like a ritual coronation of the incumbent became a wide-open contest, with images and passions coming to the fore not seen in the political arena since the 1960s. Indeed, at its elemental level, the 1960s was what the 1992 election was all about, for the Democratic nominee who eventually emerged was a product of that era, the first postwar baby-boomer to attain such national political prominence, Bill Clinton.

Like his hero John Kennedy, with whom he was photographed shaking hands as a 16-year-old, Clinton exuded idealism and an energetic faith in the capacity of government to make things better for all Americans. For Clinton, the 1960s represented a moment of hope, a surge of moral commitment to try to make not only the United States a more equitable and just society but to bring such enlightenment to the world at large. In short, Clinton in many ways saw himself as the heir apparent of liberalism, binding him as a "child" of the 1960s, to resurrect the reform impulse and fulfill the legacy bequeathed to him by his liberal forebears—John Kennedy and Lyndon Johnson. Clinton believed, and thus his message was, that it was time for Americans to renew their faith in the efficacy of positive government and embrace once again the ideology that had in the past ameliorated so many of society's inequities. To Clinton, as it had been to Kennedy, liberalism not only improved the lives of those at the bottom but in the process instilled in all Americans a greater sense of unity and national purpose as well. It was time, Clinton believed, to get the country "moving again" after twelve years of torpid Republican rule.

Clinton was a savvy politician who knew that, although he was perceived as a liberal and did indeed embrace much of that philosophy, the majority of Americans were wary of resurrecting too much of the liberal agenda. They simply feared that once again such reform could unloosen potentially divisive and destructive forces. Clinton sensed this reservation (as did JFK in 1960) and thus modified 1960s liberalism to make it have the broadest, yet non-threatening, appeal. He claimed to be a "new Democrat," a "neo-liberal" who would reduce taxes for the middle class, cut the federal deficit, and shrink the size of government. No doubt JFK would have applauded his "heir's" strategy and image, for in reality Clinton was as much a moderate-centrist as his beloved predecessor.

By contrast, George Bush reflected the attitudes and spirit of the largely reactionary 1980s, when the conservative, self-righteous backlash of which he was part attempted to obliterate the last vestiges of the Great Society. To Bush and other conservatives, the 1960s was a time of excess, rancor, and counter-culture alienation that attacked the values and institutions that had made America great. It was also a decade of unwarranted government intervention and favoritism, especially toward the "undeserving elements" among the poor and "ungrateful" minorities, who used the government's largesse to line their own pockets and turn people against the very entity that was trying to help them. Liberalism did not unite Americans; quite the contrary in George Bush's view, it polarized them into warring factions, which came close to plunging the nation into a second civil war. Thus, the 1992 election's overarching theme wasn't the impending recession but which version of the 1960s— Bill Clinton's or George Bush's—the American people wished to honor and remember.

To the surprise of many, the electorate chose, as they did in 1960, to put their faith in the candidate who promised to get the country "moving again," who promised them strong executive leadership, and who promised them that their government would once again be an agent of social reform. The harbinger of resurrected liberalism was the forty-six-year-old, six-term governor of Arkansas who, unlike his idol, came from humble origins. Indeed, in many ways Bill Clinton was the great American success story of "rags to riches" to the White House. What was it about Clinton that catapulted him from governor of one of the nation's poorest states to the Oval Office? Like fellow Southerner Jimmy Carter, much of Clinton's appeal came from his "outsider" image, not only in the sense of "the Belt Way" but in being from the south and from a state with a strong populist tradition.

Unlike many of his presidential predecessors, Clinton was not born "with a silver spoon in his mouth." He wasn't of patrician or "blueblood stock." A nanny didn't raise him nor did he attend elite private schools as a child or adolescent. He didn't have to endure an overbearing father or a doting, controlling mother—quite the opposite on all accounts. Indeed, there was simply nothing extraordinary or romantic or "epic" about Clinton's early life other than the fact that he came from an abusive, "broken home" and did a remarkable job of overcoming such trauma, escaping relatively unscathed psychologically and emotionally to become president of the United States. Perhaps in the long run that was more noteworthy than performing momentary, heroic deeds or having a lineage that required one to enter politics and become the quintessential public servant—President of the United States. Clinton's political career should be likened to that of Harry Truman or Jimmy Carter. Like both of them, Clinton originally was of the common people, with whom he shared many sentiments and attitudes and with whom he was able to relate at varying levels. As a result of his uncanny ability to connect with plain folk, Clinton parlayed such an understanding into one of the most meteoric and impressive political ascendancies in the history of modern politics, representing as vivid and dramatic a personality as had ever run for president.

Clinton's familial roots were Southern, with forebears on both sides of his family essentially of Anglo-Scotch-Irish lineage, who followed the typical nineteenth-century pattern of moving across the region searching for better, cheaper land to improve their lot. Clinton's maternal ancestors migrated from South Carolina to Alabama, settling finally in New Hope, Arkansas, a tiny rural community about 110 miles southwest of Little Rock. Their exact arrival date in the area is unknown, although it was probably sometime before the Civil War. They were simple, poor dirt farmers, in essence part of the antebellum South's non-slaveholding rural underclass.

Bill Clinton's mother, Virginia Dell Cassidy, was born into poverty in 1923 and, over time, became one of the family's most stable and "successful" progeny, despite being considered a rebel by her parents as well as by many in the community because she had the "audacity" to wear makeup, have "relations" with boys (not sexual but lots of dates and boyfriends), drink, smoke, and play cards for money. According to Clinton, his mother relished the rebel role, purposely and often flamboyantly flaunting it just to irritate conservative town folk who considered Virginia's behavior scandalous and improper for a teenage girl. No doubt Virginia chafed at such scrutiny, and thus, no sooner did she finish high school than she left New Hope to attend nursing school in

Shreveport, Louisiana. Despite her "wild" youth, her future son admired her, for in his eyes she was the epitome of forbearance and vivacity, who refused to let the small-minded thinking of others quash her spirit.

It was while attending nursing school in Shreveport that she met her first husband, Bill Clinton's biological father, William Jefferson Blythe, a handsome, stocky, sandy brown-haired Texan from Texarkana. The twenty-year-old Blythe charmed himself into Virginia's heart, and within months of their meeting, they were married. Only twenty, Blythe already had been married three times and sired numerous children, both legitimate and illegitimate. Virginia was unaware of her husband's escapades at the time of their union (1941) and did not discover his true character until they had been married for several years. Blythe enlisted in the Army in 1943 and served in the European theater (Italy) as a member of a vehicle maintenance unit. Blythe returned home after the war and, unfortunately, resumed his drinking and philandering. Suffice it to say, Blythe's behavior caused a strain in his relationship with his wife, who became pregnant with Bill soon after her husband's return. Virginia hoped that starting a family would help settle her wayward husband, but she was deluding herself, as Blythe's wanderlust only intensified. Indeed, for no apparent reason, he would hop in his car and disappear for days on binges, leaving his pregnant wife at home worrying if she would ever see him again. In the late fall of 1945, the inevitable occurred: Blythe, inebriated and driving recklessly somewhere in Missouri, lost control of his car, flinging it into a water-filled ditch where he drowned. Blythe's death occurred three months before Bill Clinton was born. On August 19, 1946, Virginia delivered the future president of the United States, naming him after her dead husband, William Jefferson Blythe IV.

Virginia Blythe was not the "typical" post-World War II housewife/ mother, having the "luxury" of leaving the workforce and coming home to raise children while her husband supported the family. Quite the opposite: *she* would be the sole breadwinner for herself and her son. Moreover, there was a stigma attached to Virginia's current status: she was a widow with a child, which for the majority of single males at this time was simply too much "baggage" to assume. Why should they? There were plenty of "unencumbered" single women available, especially in the immediate postwar years. In short, in Virginia's reality the likelihood of her remarrying was remote. Thus, she had no choice but to continue working to support herself and her infant. For awhile Virginia worked at various odd jobs, all of them menial. She quickly concluded that she had better try to find something more meaningful and stable if she hoped to provide a better life for her son. When she married Blythe, she had quit nursing school; it was now time to return, for by becoming a nurse she would definitely have a steady income as well as a respected and "accepted" professional career, especially for a woman. Virginia took her son to her parent's house in New Hope and returned to nursing school, attending Charity Hospital in New Orleans. Before she left, she met another dissipated man, Roger Clinton of Hot Springs, Arkansas, who like Blythe was a drunk and gambler but, at least, not a womanizer. Apparently, Virginia was not a very good judge of character (or perhaps she was drawn to such individuals, believing she could "save" them from their wayward ways) and dated Clinton much to her parent's consternation. With her son being cared for by her parents, Virginia went to New Orleans to finish nursing school, which she did, graduating from Charity Hospital in 1948. She subsequently returned to New Hope to rejoin her family.

The recently arrived Virginia found Roger prospering, earning about $10,000 a year as a manager of a General Motors/Buick dealership. Roger's income was extraordinary for the time, even for a boom economy, which the United States was experiencing. Indeed, Clinton's salary was approximately $7,000 more than the national mean. He continued, however, his less than savory lifestyle, but Virginia thought Roger "good enough" to marry, which she did in 1950, eloping in order not to incur the wrath of her parents, who opposed Roger from the moment they first met him. Virginia should have listened to her parent's counsel, for no sooner did she and Roger return from their honeymoon than their marriage unraveled, largely caused by Clinton's drinking and physical abuse of both Virginia and her young son. Clinton's violent behavior caused young Bill to become his mother's protector during his stepfather's drunken rages. Bill was also a "latchkey kid"—unusual for the 1950s for in most middle-class households the mother was at home. Having to physically protect his mother while simultaneously caring for himself on a daily basis forced Bill to grow up faster than his peers. The birth of a baby brother only accelerated Bill's maturity and sense of familial responsibility, for now he not only had to defend his mother but his brother as well from his abusive stepfather. Interestingly, the theme of single-parent families and absent fathers became a leitmotif of Bill Clinton's political speeches very early in his career.

Clinton's less than idyllic home life did not affect him so adversely that he wallowed in self-pity, resigning himself to being a "victim" of an abusive family. He believed that he could rise above such travail and become more than what he saw around him. Indeed, without sounding too harsh or deprecating, Clinton in many ways grew up in a "culturally challenged" environment, which makes his rise to political preeminence all the more remarkable.

Clinton did well enough in high school to be admitted to Georgetown University in Washington, D.C. Clinton's first political foray occurred in 1966, when in the summer of his junior year he went home to work for Judge Frank Holt who was running for a local congressional seat. Although Holt lost, Clinton nonetheless gained valuable exposure to all the intricacies involved in running a campaign. However, no sooner had he returned to Georgetown for his senior year than he found himself, like many soon-to-graduate young men, confronted with the reality of the Vietnam War: the possibility, if not likelihood, of being drafted upon graduation and ultimately sent to "Nam." In 1967, Lyndon Johnson instituted the "lottery system" to try to silence those who rightly declared that the conflict was a "rich man's war but a poor man's fight." Until that year and the first lottery, the overwhelming majority of young men drafted and sent to Vietnam were from the nation's underprivileged, working classes, who could not afford to go to college. Even the majority of enlisted men or volunteers were of such background, and consequently, the stigma of "rich man's war, poor man's fight" was accurate. Pressure on Johnson to rectify the inequity led to the lottery initiative, whereby *all* eighteen-year-old males were (allegedly) now eligible for the draft based on their lottery number, which was their birth date, regardless of socioeconomic status. Thus, for example, one of the birth dates drawn in the first lottery was August 5, which happened to be number 6, and now that individual became eligible for service if troop demand required taking that many more men into active duty. In the first draft, Johnson allowed General William Westmoreland to take numbers 1-99. However, no sooner was the lottery established than white middle-class America cried out against it. Now *their sons,* not just the poor, could be shipped off to the nightmare called Vietnam. Johnson eventually cratered to middle-class insistence to establish "exemptions." Johnson thus allowed student deferments—2S's—for all males who took a minimum of 15 college credits per semester and maintained a 2.0 (a C average). If one failed to meet those requirements—i.e., flunked out of school or took less than 15 hours—they were then eligible for the draft. Also non-exempt were graduating seniors, such as Bill Clinton. Consequently, as Clinton entered his senior year, he faced the prospect of a "tour" in the jungles of Southeast Asia.

Clinton had little to worry for he had a friend on the Arkansas draft board named Cliff Jackson who made sure Bill's number was a "high one." Ironically, Jackson did not have to "pull any strings" for two reasons: first, the call up that year only took the first 99 birth dates drawn, and second, Clinton was accepted at Oxford University as a Rhodes Scholar in 1968, which allowed him to *legitimately* extend his deferment. Interestingly, when Clinton's Rhodes scholarship was finished and he was then eligible for the lottery, his number was so high—323—that the likelihood of him being drafted was remote. By 1969-70, Richard Nixon had implemented his "Vietnamization" policy, which called for turning the fighting back over to ARVN and bringing home American troops. With a high number and Nixon's new approach to the war, Clinton had little to worry about relative to Vietnam. While still at Oxford, and with such assurance that he would not be sent to Vietnam, Clinton joined other American students in an anti-war protest. At the same time, just in case the war dragged on, Clinton "hedged his bets" by joining the Army ROTC at Georgetown before leaving for Oxford. Thus, if his number came up, then at least he would be an officer and, hopefully, be assigned stateside or Europe. However, as soon as Clinton received his high lottery number, he realized there was no need for him to be in ROTC and wanted out. At first his commander refused, but after countless entreaties, Clinton was released.

Like most young white males of his generation, Clinton "dodged" Vietnam because he simply did not want to go, an understandable determination for anyone then of cannon-fodder age. (This author shared Clinton's sentiments as well as benefiting for a brief period from some of the same deferments of which Vice President Dick Cheney took advantage.) Moreover, as noted above, by the early 1970s it was becoming clear to increasing numbers of Americans (and even to Richard Nixon, who, despite his rhetoric and protestations to the contrary, was trying to extricate the United States as expediently but as politically face-saving as was possible) that "it was over"—the United States had lost the war. No doubt Clinton and thousands of other potential recruits knew this and thus rightly concluded why go and possibly die for a lost cause. At the time such a position made perfect sense to a vast majority of young American males of draft-age eligibility. However, despite such "retrospective logic," as will be seen, all of Clinton's Vietnam War era shenanigans came back to haunt him during the 1992 presidential race.

In the meantime, Clinton was admitted to Yale Law School where he received his J.D. degree in 1973. It was while attending Yale that he met Hillary Diane Rodham, a 1969 graduate of Wellesley College, who would become Hillary Rodham Clinton in 1975. Incredibly bright, multi-talented, and as ambitious as her future husband, Hillary was every bit Bill Clinton's equal. Indeed, intellectually, professionally, and politically they were a perfect match. Unfortunately, when it came to marital fidelity, Bill Clinton proved to be not nearly as "devoted" to the concept as his wife. Initially, however, in the early years of Clinton's political career they were an inseparable and formidable team, a veritable "brain trust" of political savvy and ambition.

Clinton lost his first political gambit, a seat in the national House of Representatives in 1975. While waiting for the next Arkansas election— 1976—Clinton taught law at the University of Arkansas in Fayetteville. In 1976 Clinton ran for Arkansas Attorney General and won; in 1978 he ran for the Arkansas governorship and won, becoming at thirty-two one of the youngest governors in United States history. Interestingly, he lost his reelection bid in 1980 but came back in 1982, winning that gubernatorial race as well as the next four in a row. During his tenure as Arkansas' governor, Clinton developed what essentially became his 1992 presidential platform, a neo-liberal litany of investing to create new jobs, supporting new technology, rebuilding the nation's infrastructure, and creating a new partnership between management and labor to increase American productivity and competitiveness in world markets. Young, articulate, charismatic, and an up and coming Democratic Party stalwart, Clinton was asked to give the nominating speech at the 1988 Democratic National Convention, confirming the party's choice of another governor, Michael Dukakis of Massachusetts, as the Democrats' presidential candidate. In one of the most disappointing and humbling experiences of his political career, Clinton's half-hour speech drew little positive response from the audience or from commentators. Indeed, Clinton's political career appeared over; many pundits wrote him off as simply another flash-in-the-pan wunderkind. Later than night, Clinton appeared on the *Johnny Carson Show* and "drowned his sorrows" by playing his saxophone on national television.

Although many had written Clinton off after the convention, Dukakis' route by George H.W. Bush in 1988 plunged the Democratic Party into ideological disarray, creating the perfect opportunity for a fresh face, an "outsider" to emerge (as Jimmy Carter did in 1976) to not only unite the party but breathe new philosophical life into what obviously had become in the hearts and minds of many party loyalists and voters an outdated and unappealing vision. That "messiah" emerged in the summer of 1991, and it was none other than the "come back kid," Bill Clinton, who many party power brokers believed "dead" after the 1988 convention.

Although paying respectful homage (lip-service really) to the liberal agenda of his predecessors, Clinton, along with a host of other post-Great Society Democrats, represented the "New Democracy" in ideology and vision. They were neo-liberals who believed the party had to "center" itself and cultivate a new relationship and appeal among the middle class, especially with its more upwardly mobile, affluent members who, since the 1980s, had moved to the right. In effect, to Clinton and other neo-liberals, if the Democrats hoped to win the presidency as well as maintain its status as the majority party, it had no choice but to shed its New Deal/Fair Deal heritage and shibboleths and embrace instead a "new look" that reflected the interests and concerns of the middle class. Coming of political age in the 1960s, Clinton witnessed first-hand how resentful the middle class became with Johnsonian liberalism because so much of his agenda catered to the underprivileged and disenfranchised literally at the middle-class's expense. Such "favoritism" alienated the middle class, and over the course of the next two decades increasing numbers of its members abandoned the party and voted Republican, particularly at the national level. Such occurred in 1980 and 1984 as Ronald Reagan captured many disaffected middle-class Democratic voters, henceforth referred to as "Reagan Democrats." Reagan Democrats also proved pivotal in helping George H.W. Bush win in 1988. To promote this new ethos and agenda, Clinton, along with other neo-liberals (most notably Al From) created the Democratic Leadership Council in the late 1980s. In 1990 Clinton became chairman of the DLC and from that position began putting together a new coalition of middle-class Democrats, whom he believed would be the driving force in the party's transformation. By the summer of 1991, Clinton believed the time was right for him to test whether the middle class was ready to embrace neo-liberalism and thus rejoin a redefined and refocused Democratic Party by announcing that he was running for the Democratic nomination. No sooner did he announce his candidacy than there emerged a surprising groundswell of support throughout the country for his "message." Young—in the summer of 1991 he was only 45—handsome, and articulate, Clinton was a superb politician in public with a sure grasp of issues and a winning campaign style. In private he appeared to understand well the tactics of putting together a winning coalition of supporters.

Although confident that he could bring back to the party the wayward middle-class Reagan Democrats, Clinton, more than the incumbent Bush, had to contend with the unsuspected and potentially damaging third-party candidacy of Texas billionaire Ross Perot, who many Clinton Democrats feared could hurt their candidate's presidential prospects. Perot, like Clinton, had great populist appeal with his pithy, "straight-talking," outspoken views on everything and a remarkable capacity (like Clinton) to be in the right place at the right time. Similar to Clinton, but more direct, Perot claimed to speak for "the forgotten Americans" who were sick of big government, especially the bureaucratic functionaries and self-serving party hacks who seemed to be "running the show" in Washington and who were tired of both major parties' political manipulation, falsehoods, and broken promises. He appealed to those who were ready for a take-charge kind of guy, who could look under the hood, tell them what was wrong, and proceed to fix it without fanfare, political jargon, and something in return. Perot's can-do mentality was legendary. He had sent a "rescue mission" (mercenaries) to Iran to bring back company employees who had been arrested; he initiated a movement to locate and recover U.S. POWs and MIAs thought alive but still in captivity in Vietnam and Laos. Now, he was prepared to deliver the same action to clean house at home. Perot's party (he liked the term "citizen's group" better), "United We Stand, America," called for cutting the deficit and balancing the budget. Although allegedly "a-ideological," Perot articulated a political philosophy that was essentially conservative, which his call for less government involvement in people's daily lives reflected. However, at the same time, Perot's inherent conservatism was tempered by a populist reality that many Americans still wanted a government responsive to the common people's needs and solicitous of those at the bottom. But it was Perot's "straight-talk" more than anything else that appealed to so many disaffected voters, cutting across partisan lines and causing both major parties to reevaluate their traditional third-party perceptions and calculations. Of course, Perot's immense wealth guaranteed his message would be heard. As the *New Yorker* editorialized, "to paraphrase Al Capone you can do more with an air of rough-hewn candor and a billion dollars that with an air of rough-hewn candor alone."

Helping Perot and others disseminate their respective messages to larger audiences was the emergence of talk-show journalism, hosted by such celebrities as Oprah Winfrey, Geraldo Rivera, and Phil Donohue. All provided politicians with an outlet to reach the American heartland via television. Although many Americans dismissed Geraldo and Oprah as journalistic jokes and thus their respective attempts at "serious journalism" to be a farce, they nonetheless accepted Larry King and his one-hour nightly CNN-sponsored interview program as legitimate. Indeed, King's show by the early 1990s became the prize media site for any aspiring candidate. Ross Perot used his friendship with King to persuade the *New Yorker* to let him on his program to "offer his services" to the American people as a presidential candidate—a dramatic tour de force. King allowed Perot the airtime, and in their one-hour "discussion," sans tough adversarial questions, engaged debate, or informed rebuttal, King helped catapult Perot overnight into one of the most popular third-party alternatives in several decades. (George Wallace was perhaps the last of such "threats" to Democratic-Republican hegemony in 1968.) Media control—or control of the media—suddenly took on new meaning.

Unfortunately, the power of the new journalism came to know no limits, as everything and anything about a prospective candidate became fair game to investigate and exploit, naturally, all in the name of "protecting" the people from electing a shady reprobate to lead them! Especially titillating to the new "journalists" was the relentless probing of a candidate's personal life, especially his or her sexuality. Unfortunately for the new aspirants, the revelations of previous presidents' sexual escapades had been fully exposed by the early 1990s, especially those of JFK, whose philandering while president was probably the most notorious in history. Those reporters connecting the personal to the political justified their delving by asserting there was a clear correlation between personal and public behavior. It was claimed that a candidate's questionable personal habits would adversely affect public policy decisions. Using Kennedy as the benchmark, these supposed no-nonsense, hard-nosed, objective investigative journalists contended that Kennedy's attitude toward women and sexual conquest helped explain his arrogance toward those around him and his assumption that he could always get his way. However, the majority of these pseudo-journalists were in reality nothing more than sensationalist muckrakers, out for as much publicity and "prime-time" exposure as they could possibly gain by exploiting Americans' penchant for collective voyeurism to advance their careers as rapidly as possible. In short, such journalists reduced complicated political lives to intrusive and often accusing questions about private matters. Such became the fate of the 1988 Democratic hopeful Colorado Senator Gary Hart, whose candidacy was completely destroyed by a reporter's one question: "Have you ever committed adultery?" It was now about to happen again to Bill Clinton.

Unfortunately for Clinton, long before he publicly confronted accusations of extramarital affairs, rumors abounded—though never corroborated or with devastating consequences—that he was a notorious womanizer, even while governor of Arkansas. From the moment he entered the Democratic donnybrook for president, Clinton and Hillary knew the question would arise, and his staff prepared early on to address the inevitable. Indeed, it was Clinton who first brought the issue out, telling reporters early in the campaign of the charges against him, denying their accuracy, and convincing most that it was all behind him. But then came the allegations made in a national tabloid (*The Star*) that Gennifer Flowers had engaged in a twelve-year affair with Clinton. Claiming to have taped conversations, Flowers held a live CNN press conference, announcing to all America of her relationship with Clinton. The "respectable" media picked up the story, making it front-page news, and within days of such revelations, the Clinton candidacy seemed ready to implode. At the time a front-runner in the forthcoming Democratic primary in New Hampshire, Clinton entered a "free fall" in the polls. Despite evidence that the Flowers' tapes were doctored and that the charge had already been dismissed in the Arkansas campaign, the media engaged in its own feeding frenzy about the story.

Clinton, however, was not about to bow out of the race. Instead, as one of his top advisers, James Carville, counseled and later reflected, he told Clinton, "You've got to fight back. Yes sir. And our strategy from day one was to contest at every point. And to have them [advisers] out there doing that all the time . . . the best person to give the explanation of what happened and where it was, was then-Governor Clinton and Mrs. Clinton. And that's why we did the *60 Minutes* thing, because it was the biggest deal that there was, and you had to be shown that you were out taking it on." Thus, on Super Bowl Sunday (January 1992) Clinton and Hillary chose to confront the issue directly by accepting an invitation to appear on CBS's *60 Minutes*. They did what no American political couple had ever done before—confess to having had *past* marital "problems"—Clinton's infidelity—but they had now "worked" them out. As Clinton declared, "I think the American people—at least people who have been married a long time—know what [that—marital problems] means. Listen to what I've said. . . . I have acknowledged causing pain [womanizing] in my marriage. I have said things to you tonight . . . that no American politician ever has. I think most Americans will know what we're saying; they'll get it, and they'll feel that we have been more than candid." Hillary Clinton then added: "You know, I'm not sitting here—some little woman standing by my man, like Tammy Wynette. I'm sitting here because I love him and I respect him, and I honor what he's been through and what we've been through together. And you know, if that's not enough for people, then heck, don't vote for him."

It was an amazing commentary, both on what had happened to the political media and what it now took to survive such potentially destructive onslaughts. The Clintons took one of the greatest political gambles in modern American politics by publicly "intimating" that one spouse had not been faithful and then asking for the public's "understanding" (mercy or forgiveness) for such a "momentary indiscretion." Surprisingly, the Clintons' ploy worked; the American people "understood" their problems and forgave Clinton for his "wandering." The free fall stopped. By sheer tenacity and persistence, Clinton climbed back into second place in New Hampshire, losing by 8 percentage points to Massachusetts Senator Paul Tsongas. However, after his initial defeat in New Hampshire, the Clinton campaign became a juggernaut of one primary victory after another. By the end of Super Tuesday in March 1992, Clinton had wrapped up the Democratic nomination. However, was it a nomination worth having? The attacks on his personal behavior still dogged him. He had defeated a lackluster group of Democratic challengers and now wondered if he would simply be, like Michael Dukakis four years earlier, another Democratic sacrificial lamb to a popular Republican incumbent. Indeed, Clinton was even behind in the June polls to Ross Perot. If Clinton hoped to even have a "snowball's chance in Hell" to compete, he had to find a way to define himself and his program in such a way that the American people would have a positive reason to support him.

Clinton concluded that he had to focus on the issue or issues that affected the majority of Americans. It quickly became apparent to the Arkansan what that issue was. As the sign in Clinton's Little Rock campaign headquarters blared, "IT'S THE ECONOMY, STUPID." That simple message had to be delivered, however, in such a way as to attract back to the party those Democrats who defected in the 1980s to the Republican Party but who now felt betrayed by that party's disastrous economic policies, or lack thereof. To win back the "Reagan Democrats" (mainly white middle-class America), Clinton had to articulate the neo-liberal agenda, convincing middle-class moderates that under his leadership the party would not once again become the captive of special interests. To many middle-class Democratic expatriates, it was the favoritism bestowed on such groups by 1960s liberals that had caused such widespread disaffection, leading not only to the liberal "excesses" of that decade but the party's demise as well at the national level. At the same time, Clinton had to gingerly wrap himself in the New Frontier/Great Society mantle in such a way that "old school" Democrats (traditional liberals) would not feel alienated, believing the party had forsaken its early 1960s progressive heritage. But it was to middle America who Clinton wanted to deliver his message, claiming (rightly) that it was that class (as well as the underclasses) the Reagan revolution most ignored and victimized while giving a 100 percent increase in income and wealth to the top 1 percent of the country. Although wanting to distance himself especially from Great Society liberalism, Clinton nonetheless rightly believed, like both Kennedy and Johnson, that the middle class was "the vital center" whose votes the Democratic Party had to win if it hoped to recapture the White House. It was the largest voting bloc in the country whose values and attitudes had to be embraced and reflected in party ideology and rhetoric and whose well being had to be championed above all other interest groups. Thus, in Clinton's neo-liberal litany, "fairness" meant respecting the hard work and ideals of middle-class America, getting able-bodied people off welfare, and assuring that everyone, but especially the well off, paid their fair share of taxes. In verbiage reflecting that of his idol John Kennedy, Clinton's entire economic frame of reference was premised on investment, accountability, and shared responsibility. Indeed, rarely, if ever, in speeches before middle-class audiences did Clinton call for expansion of the welfare state or greater government intervention in the private sector. To demonstrate that the Democratic Party had moved away from its dependence on special interests, Clinton went to a Jesse Jackson conference and openly criticized Sister Souljah, a black rap singer who had used lyrics that attacked white people, thereby underlining the extent to which he saw himself as a "new" Democrat.

Interestingly, although Clinton embraced and espoused the neo-liberal agenda, at the same time he was savvy enough to realize that he also had to articulate that his party was still committed to the collective hopefulness of the early 1960s. Indeed, since that decade, Republicans had run on a platform that consistently accused the Democrats of having caused the social chaos and polarization that began in the late 1960s and still haunted the nation in various manifestations. Clinton, however, reversed the tables, accusing the Republicans of having caused the latest "malaise," which he contended was the result of their discriminatory, antagonistic, and thus disastrous economic policies. Clinton presented himself as the candidate who would restore a sense of community and mutual caring to America. Like John Kennedy, he emphasized getting the country moving again economically, for if the economy expanded with jobs aplenty then everyone would be able to improve their lot. Clinton also exalted what many 1960s observers predicted at the beginning of that decade: that the United States was on its way to becoming the most diverse society in the world. By the 1990s that had become true. Clinton publicly celebrated multiculturalism, asserting it to be a positive development, one that was enriching and strengthening the American character by endowing it with a more "global" perspective and tolerance. By contrast, Clinton lambasted those Republicans who continued to see the existence of multiple cultures as negative and un-American. Interestingly, by embracing diversity, Clinton was in many ways helping to maintain the Democracy as a coalition party by welcoming into its ranks new ethnic groups and continuing to respect the membership of the old ones. Like FDR, Kennedy, and Johnson, Clinton believed he could hold all these groups together by devotion to a common set of rules and economic priorities.

Helping Clinton was the rapid unraveling of the Bush administration. By the end of 1990, all the zip had gone out of the Reagan boom. Not only was real income declining for the lower middle class and working class, but also Republicans, as well as Democrats, were expressing dissatisfaction with Bush's failure to do anything about it. Tax breaks for the wealthy, deregulation initiatives, high interest rates for investors, permissiveness toward mergers, and an enormous growth in the salaries of business executives all contributed to the disparity. So did more lenient antitrust enforcement and a general acceptance for speculative finance.

The results of the 1980s became clear by the early 1990s. According to author Tom Wolfe, the 1980s was "a decade of money fever," reflecting "the triumph of upper America." Political analyst Kevin Phillips observed, "an ostentatious celebration of wealth, the political ascendancy of the rich and the glorification of capitalism, free markets and finance." The concentration of capital increased, and the sums involved took what Phillips termed a "mega leap" forward. Now there was an extraordinary amassing of wealth at the top levels, among the dekamillionaires, centmillionaires, half-billionaires, and billionaires. "Garden-variety millionaires," Phillips noted, "had become so common that there were about 1.5 million of them by 1989. According to one study, the share of national wealth of the richest 1 percent of the nation rose from about 18 percent in 1976 to 36 percent in 1989. The net worth of the *Forbes* magazine 400 richest Americans nearly tripled between 1981-1989. Meanwhile, less fortunate Americans suffered more than they had since the Great Depression. Financial expert Felix Rohatyn decried the "huge transfer of wealth from lower-skilled, middle-class American workers to owners of capital assets and a new technological aristocracy." Millions of people, ranging from foreclosed farmers to laid-off industrial workers, were struggling to make ends meet.

Compounding Bush's economic woes was the emergence of a revitalized Republican "hard Right" led by such reactionaries as Patrick Buchanan, who waged war against the man they never believed to be a true conservative anyway. Bush tried to make peace with the conservatives, unwisely turning over the opening night of the Republican convention in Houston to Buchanan and his religiously fundamentalist colleague, Pat Robertson. The two engaged in some of the most vitriolic rhetorical overkill of the opposition ever witnessed in American political history. Both men called for a cultural and religious war to "cleanse" the nation of feminists, homosexuals, and any other alleged "deviants." It was time for 100 percent Americanism, for to Robertson and Buchanan diversity and multiculturalism were code for "mongrelization" and soon WASP America—the "true" Americans—would be no more. Buchanan also articulated a foreign policy that was both xenophobic and isolationist. There was no gentleness, no tolerance, and no humor. By contrast to the Democratic emphasis on community, inclusiveness, and warmth, the Republicans conveyed a message of prejudice, mean-spiritedness, and anger. Bush unwisely allowed the "true believers" to run roughshod over the voices of Republican reason and moderation. Even Ronald Reagan could not rescue the evening. Only an acceptance "speech of a lifetime" by Bush could have salvaged his candidacy. Instead, the president arrived at the convention with two contradictory drafts that he tried unsuccessfully to combine into one, ending with a text that offered neither vision nor hope for the party.

Bush naively believed he could win by running on his laurels, acting as though he deserved reelection simply on the basis of having been president. He believed all he had to do was invoke the pride of "Desert Storm," and he would be returned to office by acclamation. Reality, however, set in by mid-summer as Bush trailed Clinton in some polls by fifteen points. At that juncture, Bush asked long-time friend and adviser, Secretary of State James Baker, to leave his cabinet position and take over his campaign. But even an experienced operator like Baker could not do much without the president having a message he wanted to deliver, and that remained a mystery. As one highly placed staffer observed, "I still can't tell you what he stands for and I've worked for him for ten years."

As summer turned to fall and Bush still trailed Clinton by several points, the president got "nasty," resorting to some of the same tactics he had used four years earlier against Dukakis. He impugned Clinton's patriotism, even suggesting that while a student in England, Clinton made a trip to Moscow for nefarious purposes. Bush also accused Clinton of having picked up "foreign" ideas about "social engineering" while abroad, ideas that had failed "from Warsaw to Prague to Moscow." It became painfully obvious to everyone that Bush, the "old" ex-CIA director/Cold Warrior, was desperate, willing to engage in outdated red-baiting in order to find a "chink" in Clinton's armor. It was too late for such accusations or innuendo; the cold war was over; the Berlin Wall collapsed soon after Bush had become president. Consequently, few Americans cared or were concerned that over two decades earlier a young college kid might have become momentarily intrigued by Marxist-Leninist doctrine. Bush should have realized that the politics of anticommunism fortunately died soon after he became president.

Clinton was vulnerable, however, on a different character issue: his draft record during the Vietnam War. Bush had a legitimate point when he challenged Clinton to "come clean" on this matter. Clinton acknowledged that he opposed the war; however, he constantly equivocated on his draft status, saying one time he never received an induction notice while on another admitting that he had. In the end, like Bush's attempt to paint Clinton "red," the president's attempt to portray the Arkansan as a "shirker" or "draft dodger" (if not a coward) went nowhere. Polls showed that to most Americans Vietnam was a non-issue because they wanted to leave that tortured squabble behind them and not punish someone who twenty-three years earlier had opposed the war. In short, voters looked at Clinton, heard the rumors and specific allegations of his womanizing, and decided, "yeah, this is a guy who fooled around, but so what." In the same context, voters looked at Clinton's clear and even floridly literate attempts at draft avoidance, considered the circumstances already noted, and decided, "so what."

Ironically, George W. Bush hates to be compared in any way to Bill Clinton, but the president can be thankful that the Clinton "so what" effect is presently at work in his favor. Nationally, voters both in 2000 and currently, have considered Bush's sometimes dissipated youth, including his questionable military service, and decided, "so what." Like Clinton, Bush "dodged" Vietnam by "miraculously" finding (with a little help from family connections) a spot in an already-filled Texas Air National Guard. It would be interesting to know what his lottery number was, for if it was as high as Clinton's, no doubt Bush would have felt no compulsion to try to join the Guard to escape the draft and a possible tour of duty in the jungles of Southeast Asia. Indeed, as he revealed in a 1989 interview, he didn't "want to be an infantry guy as a private in Vietnam." When Bush was asked by the *Washington Post* in 1999 if he was avoiding the draft, he said, "No, I was becoming a pilot." In another interview in the same year he told the same paper that if his guard unit had been called up, "I'd have gone to Vietnam. I was prepared to go." That was an "after the fact" answer and thus does not at all count. If that seems an unfairly tough assessment, then one may not be the right age to understand it.

By contrast, for a variety of interesting reasons, some voters are not so forgiving or understanding of John Kerry's actions during the war and his protests against it. Unlike fellow Democrat Bill Clinton, Kerry appears not to have been granted his "so what" pardon. Perhaps causing such reluctance among many voters was Kerry's 1971 testimony before the Senate Foreign Relations Committee in which he appeared to defile fellow vets with his assertion that atrocities committed by American soldiers were more commonplace and legion than the public was aware at the time. Kerry compounded that indiscretion by "trashing" his military decorations in symbolic protest against the war, all such actions currently featured in disparaging ads by some of his fellow swift boat veterans, who feel betrayed by a supposed comrade-in-arms. Moreover, many veterans oppose the senator because they feel their personal honor and loyal service to the country had been sullied by Kerry's testimony. Whether Kerry's rendering of the war was accurate or not is moot; as Americans said in 1992, it's time again to say "so what." As the president self-servingly but correctly told NBC's Matt Lauer in a pre-convention interview, "I think we ought to move beyond the past," and as the nation did in 1992, focus on the more crucial domestic issues of jobs, health care, and the deficit.

To further amplify his being a new Democrat, Clinton chose as his running mate a generational peer, Tennessee Senator Al Gore, Jr. Clinton's selection of Gore surprised many primarily because he was a fellow Southerner, which many believed flew in the face of conventional wisdom, which dictated that a party's candidate never choose a running mate from his own region of the country. Clinton, however, believed that by choosing Gore he could win more Southern states, essential to a Democratic victory. Since the Nixon years, the South had been increasingly gravitating toward the Republican Party; by the end of the Reagan era, the "Solid South" now meant Republican. Thus, with a Southern running mate Clinton hoped he could at least win a few key Southern states, enough to turn the tide in his favor in the electoral college. Clinton's strategy paid off. In the election he took Arkansas, Louisiana, Georgia, Tennessee, and Kentucky, all states that four years earlier went to George H. W. Bush.

In the end Clinton won because he possessed a strategy, a vision, and a campaign apparatus prepared to implement a winning plan. By contrast, *Time* observed, Bush was "feckless, confused, whining, and rudderless." Part of Clinton's vision was to redefine the Democratic Party, making it ideologically the harbinger of neo-liberalism, and in the process, he successfully brought back to the Democrats a good number of Reagan defectors. Reflecting that philosophy, which was essentially the middle-class ethos, Clinton called his triumph, "a victory for the people who work hard and play by the rules . . . a victory for the people who are ready to compete and win in the global economy but who need a government that offers a hand, not a hand-out." Bush seemed oblivious to the average people Reagan had so skillfully cultivated. Never a "cultural Democrat" like Reagan, Bush seemed unable to shed his blue-blood persona and image and to connect with the common folk. As a result, Bush won a lower percentage of popular votes (37 percent) than Barry Goldwater, Herbert Hoover, or George McGovern—three presidential candidates "slaughtered" by their opponents. No incumbent since William Howard Taft (in 1912 against TR and Woodrow Wilson) had fared so poorly. Indeed, he won a majority only among white Protestant Southerners. In the electoral college Clinton won handily, 370 to 168, carrying 32 states and the District of Columbia. In contrast to Bush winning only a majority among white Southern Protestants, Clinton carried the Jewish, African American, and Latino vote by large margins, and he even gained a plurality among people who had served in the Vietnam War. Perot's candidacy hurt Bush more than Clinton. The Texas billionaire gained no electoral votes but did attract 19 million popular votes. Perhaps most surprising, about 55 percent of eligible voters went to the polls, a turnout that reversed 32 years of increasing voter apathy.

Perhaps such an improved turnout can be attributed to Clinton's appeal among baby boomers, for they were electing one of their own and thus took great pride in the fact that their day in the "political sun" had finally arrived. At the same time, as will be seen, such high expectations, especially among Clinton's own generation, made his job all the more difficult. In many ways Clinton was greeted with the same fanfare and hope of his idol John Kennedy, and thus the pressure was on for him to rise to such expectations and deliver the goods. Like Kennedy, Clinton projected the image of a youthful, exuberant, thoughtful, and brilliant leader with an equally accomplished wife (although one not nearly as glamorous or gracious as Jacqueline Kennedy) who promised to be a full partner in the White House, perhaps more powerful in the public arena than any First Lady since Eleanor Roosevelt. It was almost as though the best impulses of the 1960s had come together to make a reappearance—feminism, a commitment to fairness, a modern marital relationship but one framed by devotion to family, an energetic excitement about the ability to use government to make people's lives better. "What excites most people about Clinton," one magazine said, "is precisely the degree to which he speaks to their hunger for meaning and purpose, their half-conscious and often inchoate desire to transcend the selfishness and meaningless of materialistic and narcissistic society." *Time* was equally elegiac, "For years," it said in its Man of the Year issue, "Americans have been in a kind of vague mourning for something that they sensed they had lost somewhere—what was best in the country, a distinctive American endowment of youth and energy amid ideals and luck; the sacred American stuff." To the magazine, Clinton appeared to be the "messiah," providing his fellow citizens with the answer, for his victory "places him in a position to preside over one of the periodic reinventions of the country—those moments when Americans dig themselves out of their deepest problems by reimagining themselves." As one writer noted, to many baby-boomers Clinton was "our generation's second chance."

The new president himself contributed to such grandiose expectations. "Today," Bill Clinton said in his Inaugural Address, "we celebrate the mystery of American renewal. . . . In the depth of winter, we force the spring. . . .This is our time. Let us embrace it." Whether any president could live up to such high hopes represented both the challenge and the Achilles' heel of the new administration. Would it be possible for Bill Clinton to resurrect his version of the 1960s without alienating the very consensus that brought him election victory, who he assured that his brand of liberalism would keep in check the excesses of the 1960s? At the same time, if he kept his promise to the middle class that he would not allow liberalism to "run amok," then would it be possible for him to move toward fulfilling the legacy of his liberal forebears—FDR, Truman, Kennedy, and Johnson? Or would he flounder, overwhelmed by the immensity of the problems facing the Republic and victim to his own capacity for self-destructive behavior?

The William Jefferson Clinton Presidency: A Positive Assessment

Although Clinton may have fancied himself the political and ideological reincarnation of JFK, in reality his personality and temperament, and especially his "political" face, was more akin to FDR than any of his other Democratic predecessors. No doubt FDR faced problems that were far more severe than any twentieth-century president, and the American people were far more desperate during the Great Depression than their 1990s counterparts. Nonetheless, Clinton in many ways had to deal with issues far more complicated and intractable, demanding the same breadth and depth of leadership skills FDR found within himself to lead the nation through its second greatest domestic crisis. Indeed, given the array of structural dilemmas Clinton faced—the underclass, the de-skilling of industry, racial polarization, a runaway health-care system, a broken welfare state, and a widespread loss of faith in the American political process—the comparison with the Roosevelt years makes eminent sense.

Like FDR, Clinton brought to these issues a personality and set of character traits as complicated, colorful, vivid, and contradictory as his Democratic forebear. As one White House aide declared, "He is the most seductive and persuasive person I have ever met." Yet, if he was "one of the biggest, most talented, articulate, intelligent, open [and] colorful characters ever to inhabit the Oval Office," *New York Times* reporter Todd Purdum wrote, he could "also be an undisciplined, fumbling, obtuse, defensive, [and] self-justifying rogue." Purdum's colleague, Maureen Dowd, described the same paradox another way, "Clinton is naïve and sophisticated, thin-skinned and self-assured, bold and hesitant, genuine and glib." Unlike FDR and more like JFK, Clinton possessed a remarkable capacity to master the details of the most complex policy dilemma and articulate a vision of how to deal boldly with it. Yet few among his predecessors (save FDR) displayed so much "slickness," expediency, and disingenuousness. The irony, as Purdum wrote, was that "his strengths and weaknesses not only spring from the same source, but could also not exist without one another. In a real sense, his strengths are his weaknesses, his enthusiasms are his undoing, and most of the traits that make him appealing can make him appalling in the flash of an eye." Such an individual clearly had the capacity to rise to the challenges confronting him, as FDR had done. However, unlike FDR, Clinton possessed an inherent, self-destructive capacity to destroy his own best impulses and visions, giving vent to the undisciplined, careless, and self-indulgent side of his personality.

Despite an innate penchant for self-destructive behavior, which did not reach full "potential" until his second term, Clinton implemented many successful initiatives, both at home and abroad, during his tenure. For example, Clinton made embracing of diversity a reality by appointing to his cabinet three African Americans—Mike Espy as Secretary of Agriculture, Ron Brown as Secretary of Commerce, and Jesse Brown as Secretary of Veterans Affairs—and two Latinos—Henry Cisneros as Secretary of Housing and Urban Development and Federico Pena as Secretary of Transportation. Clinton's initial cabinet also included three women—Janet Reno as Attorney General, Donna Shalala as Secretary of Health, and Hazel O'Leary as Secretary of Energy. As his first nomination to the Supreme Court, Clinton chose Ruth Bader Ginsburg, only the second woman to sit on this nation's highest tribunal. And as representative to the United Nations, Clinton named Madeline Albright, who would also become the country's first female Secretary of State during his second term.

On social issues, Clinton claimed several victories during his first term. He ended the Reagan era's ban on abortion counseling in family planning clinics; pushed a family leave program for working parents through Congress; established Americorps (reminiscent of LBJ's VISTA), which allowed students to repay college loans through community service; and secured passage of the Brady Bill, which instituted a five-day waiting period for the purchase of hand-guns. In conjunction with the Brady Bill, Clinton also pushed through a crime bill that banned the manufacture, sale, or possession of nineteen different assault weapons. Limited college loan and youth training programs also received funding.

Without question, one of Clinton's most courageous accomplishments was his deficit reduction initiative, which he made a priority over the middle-class tax cut he had promised voters in the campaign. Before Clinton introduced his plan and even before his inauguration, he did his "homework" thoroughly, bringing together in Little Rock industrial leaders, financiers, and academics to educate the American people and his own team of advisors about the appropriate combination of deficit reduction and stimulus in the economic agenda he would introduce once he became president. The result was a carefully crafted package that would cut in half the annual deficit as part of total expenditures, raise taxes on the wealthy, and put in place a mechanism for sustained economic growth. To sweeten the proposal and help create new jobs, Clinton offered an economic stimulus program that would inject $30 billion into the economy through various federal programs and incentives. Despite their own avowed commitment to deficit reduction, the Republicans refused any cooperation with Clinton. Senate minority leader Robert Dole told the president that he would not get a single Republican vote. The Republicans then successfully filibustered against the stimulus package, and to secure a one-vote victory in the Senate for the overall deficit-reduction bill, Clinton sacrificed an energy tax that he had insisted House Democrats must support as proof of their loyalty to him. In the end, the legislation turned out to be a great success—even if it did pass by only one vote. Indeed, the bill proved critical to ending the seemingly interminable round of huge federal deficits, while encouraging record-setting economic growth and prosperity.

Interestingly, Clinton pushed through some of his most important initiatives during times of personal repudiation and crises. Much like FDR and LBJ, both of who responded to setbacks with even greater resolve and passion to forge ahead, Clinton did the same, never allowing the constant carping and outright personal affronts to destroy his vision and agenda for the country. Indeed, the attacks on his character and policies seemed to energize him, for Clinton possessed a confidence in his abilities—both intellectual and political—that bordered on the hubris, actuating him to persevere regardless of how crippling the issues might be at the time to his presidency. In short, Clinton simply refused to surrender to what he considered to be only momentary and thus "normal" challenges to his presidency. Perhaps at no time during his two terms did this certitude manifest itself more brilliantly than after the 1994 Republican counterrevolution, which many believed was so complete and overwhelming that even the most diehard liberals and Clinton supporters would have to believe that their man was politically dead and that the forthcoming presidential election would bring to power an even more conservative regime than that of Ronald Reagan. However, such would not be the case. In one of the quickest resurrections in American political history, Bill Clinton not only kept his job, winning by even greater numbers than he had four years earlier, but perhaps more important, progressivism (albeit a neo-liberalism) prevailed, demonstrating that when given a choice between a radical leap backward and completely dismantling the welfare state and positive government and preserving and even expanding what was good about liberalism, Americans wisely chose the latter. In many ways Clinton's reelection reflected the sufficient faith the majority of Americans still had in the ethos that had served and protected them for over sixty years from the vagaries and excesses of unbridled capitalism and reactionary Republican social policies.

Largely as a result of his failed health-care proposal, which Clinton on many levels personally mishandled from start to finish (to be discussed indepth later in this essay), the Republican opposition seized the opportunity to initiate its counterrevolution against Clintonian liberalism. Indeed, the Republican right, led by such stalwarts as Newt Gingrich in the House and Texan Phil Gramm in the Senate, had been waiting since the first day of Clinton's presidency to, as Gramm put it, "blow this train [Clinton's administration] up." After the health-care debacle, Gingrich insisted that Republicans unite in total opposition lest his plans for a Republican takeover be derailed by a Clinton foray into guaranteeing new middle-class entitlements. Finally, Senator Bob Dole, certainly no hard right ideologue, even joined with the hardliners not wanting to jeopardize his hopes for the 1996 Republican presidential nomination by holding out an olive branch to the president. In short, the Republicans were "chomping at their bits" at the prospect of bringing the Clinton administration to its knees. Clinton faced an implacable opposition that brooked no dissent and set out from day one to demonize the president. If he knew the stakes when be began his initiatives to finish the social revolution started by FDR, Newt Gingrich knew them better. The Georgia congressman was confident that Clinton's failed health-care reform initiative would be the *coup de grâce* to the last vestiges of liberalism, as well as any future attempts by Democrats to revitalize the welfare state. Gingrich (who holds, interestingly, a Ph.D. in history) believed health-care reform would be the Democrats' "Stalingrad, their Gettysburg, their Waterloo." In short, "general" Gingrich would defeat Clinton, giving no quarter, and proceed to lead a Republican counterrevolution that would attempt to destroy the liberal ramparts that the Democrats had built over the preceding six decades.

Fortunately for Bill Clinton, the United States did not have a parliamentary system of government, for if it had, Clinton's presidency would have been the shortest on record. Two years after *Time* magazine called him the "second chance" for the sixties generation, Clinton received a resounding vote of "no confidence" from the American people. Indeed, it was clearly a personal repudiation. The Republican Party gained 9 Senate seats, 52 House seats, and 11 governorships, winning control of both houses of Congress in the process. As one member of the Democratic Leadership Conference observed, "The New Deal is over. . . . The nails are in the coffin. . . . New Deal liberalism is dead and buried." All of Clinton's hopes of becoming the next FDR or LBJ were shattered; the Roosevelt coalition seemed finished, with even the Roosevelt social welfare legacy gravely imperiled. As another Democrat observed in the aftermath of the 1994 elections, "The Republicans enjoyed a double triumph, killing reform and then watching jurors—the American people—find the president guilty. It was the political equivalent of the perfect crime."

Newt Gingrich emerged as the main architect of his party's counterrevolutionary agenda, "Contract With America." The "contract" consisted of ten objectives, but the most immediate and urgent were cutting taxes, passing a balanced budget amendment, and reducing the "bloated" government bureaucracy and radical welfare reform—in short, to begin the dismantling of the New Deal state. Declaring Clinton Democrats to be "the enemy of normal Americans," Gingrich defined the election as a referendum on big government. To counter Gingrich's attacks on his presidency, as well as on his party, Clinton made himself a campaign issue by unwisely taking his health-care reform package directly to the people, passionately speaking on its behalf across the country. Unfortunately, no matter how engaging and persuasive a speaker and politician Clinton was, too many Americans had turned against him personally, as well as ideologically, and as a consequence, his presidency appeared doomed. As Democratic consultant Ted Van Dyk believed, "It's over. The president is done. He's finished. He's like the old cartoon where the guy has just had his head sliced off in a fencing match. He just hasn't noticed it yet, but as soon as he tries to turn or stand up, his head is going to topple right off his neck." Appropriately, Gingrich headquarters on election night was "filled with vengeful glee," the *New York Times* reported. The reactionaries' "glee" was a bit premature; only 38 percent of the eligible voters turned out at the polls, perhaps reflecting that the American people *did not* embrace the Gingrich revolution and the Republican "Contract With America" as enthusiastically as the party believed.

Gingrich, however, believed voters had indeed made such an ideological choice, and from his position as the newly-elected Speaker of the House, he sought to whip his minions into a phalanx of united, disciplined zealots committed to enacting their own anti-Rooseveltian "Hundred Days" of reactionary policies, certain the American people wanted such reform. One after another, bills were brought to the floor for votes. There were no hearings; legislators did not even know what they were voting on. Clinton, of course, became an object of ridicule: an emasculated, irrelevant bystander, watching an unstoppable juggernaut tear to pieces not only his agenda but the last vestiges of New Deal liberalism as well. The counterrevolution appeared triumphant. "We are finally seeing where [the Republican contract has] been carrying us," Russell Baker acidly noted in the *New York Times.*" "Dr. Kevorkian is now waiting in the parlor. He's about to be shown upstairs to finish off the government we have known for sixty years."

Although the Republicans had accused Clinton of hubris, it appeared now that Gingrich and his cohorts were exhibiting just as much arrogance as they slashed and burned their way across the liberal landscape, never stopping to think that perhaps they were pushing the people too fast and too hard to accept their counterrevolution. In short, so drunk with power they ignored the reluctance of the American people to take radical leaps, either backward or forward, without adequate discussion and negotiation. The more cautious and moderate Robert Dole-run Senate, for example, operated on a different set of assumptions and procedures than the fanatical Gingrich-led House. "There's a way to use power when you get it," Dole observed, "and my view was that maybe they've just been a little too much in a hurry [in the House]. You don't undo 40 years, 20 years or 30 years in 100 days or [even] four years." Moreover, as Russell Baker noted, what was the "end game? Do the designers of the post-government age know what they're doing? In a matter of days they have been dismantling and redesigning structures that took years to put up. . . . Who really has the vaguest idea what the results will be? Best Bet: Nobody."

Within a few months of what appeared to be the end of liberalism, the American people began to question the wisdom of what was essentially being done to them without much discussion or debate. Were there not *some* government programs worth preserving, even expanding, such as those protecting the environment? Equally alarming to many Americans was the fact that a high percentage of the new Republicans had no prior elective experience and had won simply because of their ideological connection to groups such as Ralph Reed's Christian Coalition. As a result, increasing numbers of Americans began to question whether the individuals they just elected were acting in their interests. Many concluded they were not; many Americans were dismayed to find that too many of the new Republicans were nothing more than the lackeys of extreme right special interest groups, so obsessed with vilifying Clinton and destroying the welfare state that they arrogantly disregarded their constituents' wishes. By September 1995, less than a year after their supposed mandate, the conservatives found themselves on "the run," as 58 percent of the American people disapproved of the job Congress was doing.

Although bruised and battered, Clinton, to the surprise of many (after all, he wasn't nicknamed "the comeback kid" for nothing), came out fighting, determined to triumph over the reactionaries who had tried to destroy his presidency. In the months between the Republicans' victory and his "reemergence," Clinton developed a new strategy for reclaiming and redefining the vital center of American politics. The Democrats had lost the 1994 congressional elections because Clinton's health-care proposal and other measures had alienated the middle class, who felt betrayed by the Arkansan because he had assured them in 1992 that he was a new Democrat with fresh ideas, especially about big government and a willingness to take a hard look at its excesses. In short, Clinton had promised voters that he *was not* a traditional liberal, devoted to old Democratic shibboleths. Yet, the Republicans succeeded in 1994 to paint him with that "old" Democratic brush, and he now had to escape that straightjacket and put the Republicans in one of their own. If Clinton hoped to once again "come back," he had to recast his image back into the new Democrat mold that had brought him to the Oval Office in 1992.

As early as 1993, the *New Republic* had offered Clinton a strategy for building a new "center" on the political spectrum. According to the magazine's pundits, Clinton needed to create "a liberalism that can learn from its past excesses, restore faith in the actions of a prudent, effective government, and build a constituency among the American middle class." The journal was confident that most middle-class Americans still believed in positive government as long as the reform initiatives were focused, "limited," and specific and especially if they could be enacted in conjunction with the private sector to help hold down costs and thus help reduce the deficit. Clinton heeded the magazine's suggestion, announcing to the public in an April 1995 speech, "We need a dynamic center that is not in the middle of what is left and right, but that is way beyond it." Echoing FDR's 1944 promulgation of an "economic bill of rights," Clinton declared that it was time for a "middle class bill of rights": selective tax cuts, an education credit for young people going to college, "leaner, not meaner" government, and a commitment to advance the fortunes of "hardworking Americans" who had earned their opportunities and were not asking for handouts.

Virtually all presidents have a coterie of individuals who comprise an inner circle of advisers and who are often the people most responsible for a president's image, vision, and agenda. In Clinton's quest to recast himself, one man in particular became his most important "guru," Richard Morris of New York, who had masterminded election victories for both Republicans and Democrats for several years. Morris had worked for Clinton in Arkansas, helping Clinton come back from his only electoral defeat as governor, also through recasting his image. Perhaps the most important advice Morris proffered was for Clinton not to only go on the attack but to make sure that he preempted the Republicans on the issues that could hurt the president: high taxes, crime, welfare, the federal budget, and affirmative action. In short, Morris urged Clinton to take the initiative in defining positions that would seem "reasonable" to middle-class voters. At the same time, Clinton should portray the Republicans as "radicals," seeking to destroy 60 years of progress while promoting his own agenda on issues that the center would embrace, such as education and the environment.

In Clinton's venture to resurrect his presidency, he received help from an unexpected quarter: the Republicans, who began digging their own graves by arrogantly believing they could continue to wantonly dismantle even the most sacred programs of the welfare state like Medicare. They were wrong, and Clinton shrewdly exploited their hubris to regain momentum. Although everyone agreed, including Clinton, that curbing the ever-rising cost of Medicare was essential to secure a balanced budget, the Republicans foolishly not only proposed major reductions to this program but simultaneously tried to ramrod through Congress a tax cut for the wealthy that would return to the rich almost exactly the same amount of money that was to be cut from Medicare. This was the "opening" Clinton had been waiting for to counterattack, which he promptly did by rightly accusing the reactionaries of taking money away from senior citizens, who needed it, and putting it in the pockets of the rich, who did not. Aiding Clinton were the impolitic comments of Newt Gingrich, who declared that Medicare would "wither on the vine" during his counterrevolution.

Clinton "ran" with such comments, accusing the Republicans of "killing" the entitlement program of greatest importance to middle-class citizens over 65, while at the same time making the rich richer.

By the summer of 1995, Clinton was ready to launch his counterattack. Focused and rarely, if ever, "off message," Clinton responded brilliantly. Relative to crime, a bill was passed under his leadership that put 100,000 new police on the streets; he endorsed the program of "three strikes and you're out," giving life sentences to criminals convicted three times of felonies; and he cultivated (and secured) the support of major police organizations for his anti-crime and anti-assault weapons initiatives. He addressed welfare reform by establishing a two-year limit on how long a person could remain on "the dole," while supporting as well a jobs program to help take people off the relief rolls. He proposed tax cuts that benefited the middle class, while opposing those that enhanced the rich; and he continued, with the help of a booming economy, to cut the federal deficit. Even on the controversial issues of affirmative action, he claimed the middle ground, defending the concept of correcting centuries of discrimination by seeking aid to minorities who had been victimized but agreeing that some "excesses" had to be kept in check—"mend it, don't end it."

While flooding Congress with the above initiatives, Clinton labeled the Republicans as "threats" to middle-class stability. He pilloried the Republicans for trying to destroy Medicare and other fundamental and essential social welfare programs. Under Clinton's undisputed leadership, the Democrats painted the Republicans as extremists, asking, "isn't there a better way?" By the end of 1995, Clinton's poll ratings were soaring while those of Gingrich and the Republican Congress plummeted. Less than a year earlier Republicans were certain they would obliterate Clinton in the 1996 presidential race; the opposite was about to occur, with Clinton and his fellow Democrats poised to send the Republicans reeling to one of their most embarrassing defeats in several decades. In many ways the Republicans brought such a calamity upon themselves, for they dreadfully miscalculated how long the public would tolerate their wanton arrogance and mean-spiritedness directed not only at Clinton but often at the American people as well.

For many observers, the 1996 presidential election was over the day Bill Clinton gave his January 1996 State of the Union Address, in which he declared, "The era of big government is over." With that one line, Clinton took all the wind out of the Republican sails for, in effect, Clinton was declaring to the country that "his" party had finally shed its New Deal/Great Society shibboleths and in its place had emerged a new

Democratic Party devoted to the interests and concerns of middle-class America. No longer could the Republicans criticize either Clinton or his party for being traditional liberals, advocates of big government, and still tied to the old New Deal coalitions. Indeed, no matter how hard Republicans tried to paint Clinton as a classic liberal, the president could dismiss such charges, pointing to deficit reduction, a tough crime bill, the Family Leave Act, and a commitment to welfare reform as testimony writ large that he was a new Democrat devoted to the vital center.

The Republicans chose Senator Robert Dole of Kansas as their 1996 standard-bearer. They wisely stayed away from Gingrich and other hard-right "possibilities," for Dole, despite his often vituperative attacks on Clinton, was essentially a moderate, especially in comparison to Gingrich or Jesse Helms! Moreover, people trusted Dole (he had a 62 percent approval rating in 1995, compared to 35 percent for Gingrich, and 45 percent for Clinton), and he appeared to put country over partisanship. On the downside, Dole was the oldest person ever to run for president—he was 73 at the time, a World War II "product," and despite his good health, he was of another generation and to many Americans, especially among the majority baby-boomers, he represented a step backward. Also undermining Dole's chances was the fact that extreme right groups, such as the Christian Coalition, still had overweening influence within his party. So Clinton could portray Dole and the Republicans as a candidate and party of reaction and extremism. Never a person given to soaring rhetoric, Dole's unimpassioned speeches and phlegmatic personality created the image that the senator, although an individual of unimpeachable integrity and pragmatism, lacked vision and energy. As his own chief campaign strategist observed, "Dole's strength is [that] what you see is what you get. Dole's weakness is [that] what you see is what you get."

Within weeks it became clear that the younger, more energetic, more charismatic Clinton possessed the advantage. The Clinton staff brilliantly portrayed Dole as Gingrich's clone, always picturing the two together, intimating that by association Gingrich was Dole's running mate, not New York congressman and ex-Buffalo Bills quarterback Jack Kemp, who Dole chose before the Republican convention. By Election Day it was a foregone conclusion that Clinton would triumph in one of the most amazing political comebacks in modern American history. Winning 50 percent of the popular vote and 70.4 percent of the electoral college, Clinton succeeded in his fundamental strategy of presenting himself as a dynamic centrist running against an "older generation" captive of narrow interests and extremism. In contrast to 1992, independent candidate Ross Perot's impact was minimal in 1996, and his presence hurt the Republicans more than the Democrats. Clinton without question benefited from a burgeoning economy. Typically he ran particularly well among African Americans, women, and Hispanics, winning 59 percent of female voters to Dole's 35 percent. In short, in a booming economy with a focused message dedicated to the middle class, Clinton had done what he needed to do to recapture the support he had lost in 1994.

Although soundly beating Dole, Clinton's victory was not a mandate. Despite some loss of seats in the House, the Republicans retained control of Congress, even gaining additional seats in the Senate and several new governorships. Democrats still held a majority of seats in state legislatures, a sign that many voters found ticket splitting (voting for both Democrats and Republicans at varying levels of office) to be a sensible course. Indeed, many experts concluded that voters had made a decision for "divided government," not for one party over another. To a good number of voters, such had to be the case to prevent the nation from moving too far left or right. In the minds of many Americans, a "balanced" government was what was now needed. Reforms, yes, if targeted to specific problems and limited in expense; a leaner government, yes, but not if it meant jeopardizing the environment, entitlements like Medicare, or government guarantees of fundamental rights. In essence, the American people seemed to be directing their political leaders to stay the middle course, which meant allowing the government the "flexibility" to intervene to maintain and expand, if necessary, the "fundamentals" of the welfare state but constrain as well those liberals wanting to use the government to enlarge the public sphere while curtailing or negating completely private sector participation and input. Over the course of the next four years, this new "frame of reference" that the voters had chosen would be strenuously tested, and in the end many concluded that it was not sufficient to deal with the ongoing problems challenging the nation's ability to survive and prosper.

Unfortunately, Clinton's own actions ensured that the nation would never discover whether the president's "new brand" of liberalism could have been successfully implemented. If Clinton's first term had been a roller coaster of triumph and failure, highlighted by economic recovery, failed health-care reform, and the Republican counterrevolution, his second term was even more erratic, going from great "highs" in foreign policy initiatives and domestic reforms to humiliating and debilitating "lows" that almost brought his presidency down to the same "level" as that of Richard Nixon. Indeed, not since the days of Watergate and the Nixon presidency did the American people witness such an extraordinary political spectacle. Their president, by nearly all estimates, one of the most talented and politically savvy men ever to occupy the White House, engaged in repeated acts of self-destruction and public deception that captivated Americans during two years of pre-impeachment and impeachment trauma. In the end, so consumed by the Monica Lewinsky scandal (to be discussed indepth later in this essay) did the Clinton administration become that even Clinton's positive accomplishments in domestic and foreign affairs became "tainted" and thus overlooked by his "indiscretion." Indeed, so vitiating was the transgression that Clinton forever will be remembered as only the second president in history to be impeached (Andrew Johnson was the first; Richard Nixon not only would have been impeached but removed from office as well for his improprieties) and that, even if his offenses did not rise to the level of "high crimes and misdemeanors," he had disgraced the office of the President of the United States. Nonetheless, it is the purpose of this book when discussing a president's "successes" to look beyond even his most egregious personal flaws and policy shortcomings and find those contributions and accomplishments that made them worthy of at least four years of the nation's trust and confidence. Such can be found for Bill Clinton in many areas, even during his second term, which the Lewinsky affair overwhelmed soon after it began.

No matter how embarrassing and damaging to his presidency the Lewinsky episode was, Clinton could (and can) still claim credit for a number of tangible achievements. During Clinton's tenure, the economy entered its fifth, sixth, and seventh years of unparalleled growth—an unprecedented era of prosperity for which most presidents would give anything to have on their record. At the same time, with congressional support, Clinton put into place a budget process that promised to reduce substantially the federal deficit, producing the first surpluses in post-World War II history, and offered the prospect that in a few years the entire federal debt could be retired. Continuing to target popular, previously "Republican" issues like crime and welfare, Clinton saw murder and arrest rates go down in municipalities across the country and welfare rolls decline, as his welfare reform bill sent people off to jobs rather than onto relief rolls. Even if many liberals believed Clinton's welfare reform initiatives were "callous" and "conservative," inappropriately and cruelly ending the New Deal legacy of the federal government providing for those who through no fault of their own could not provide for themselves, the statistical results of Clinton's program made this reform seem like a stunning success. And even if the rhetoric was greater than the reality, Clinton conveyed a message of caring and commitment to minorities, women, gays, and the historically disenfranchised.

Clinton also showed that he could learn politically from his blunders. He came into office envisioning and promising sweeping change, especially in the welfare state as reflected in his health-care reform proposal (to be examined shortly) that, if successful, would have been more monumental than even Social Security. However, when it failed, Clinton rebounded, lowering his expectations and pushed through an impressive list of smaller achievements ranging from adding 100,000 police officers to the police rolls to mandating 48-hour hospital stays for women giving birth, all of which conveyed a sense of doing something tangible to improve the quality of Americans' daily lives, especially for those who needed assistance. As political scientist Larry Sabato observed, "Clinton [seemed] to reach right into your heart. He pierces you with his eyes. He knows your emotions. He cares about you. Personally. It may be totally phony, or it may not, but he really seems to love you. It may be the rhetorical equivalent of cotton candy, but it works." Clinton cried easily, identified with those who were hurting, creating bonds of intimacy with those who reached out to him.

Nowhere was Sabato's assessment more accurate than in Clinton's relationship with African Americans. As *New York Times* reporter Todd Purdum noted, Clinton "used surpassing gifts of innate empathy to find a new presidential style of relating to the public, and to forge an extraordinary connection with ordinary Americans, especially minorities." Novelist Toni Morrison called Clinton "our first Black President," someone who instinctively seemed to understand the plight of black people and who identified with and championed their cause "to rise above." Political commentator Joe Klein believed Clinton's "true eloquence" was "physical, the body language he can deploy at crucial moments. The two steps he took toward a black woman questioner who was concerned about the economy during the second presidential debate in 1992 may have been the most important 'statement' he made during that campaign (especially when contrasted with the detachment of George Bush who was caught by the television cameras that same evening checking his watch)." One of Clinton's more significant moments relative to "reaching out" to the black community came at the beginning of his second term with his "national conversation on race"—a program headed by the president's good friend and renowned African-American historian John Hope Franklin, in which Clinton hoped not only to bring America face to face with its longest standing national shame but try to put the country as well on a path toward eradicating the last vestiges of the ignominy.

In foreign affairs as well, Clinton made important inroads. Like his predecessor, Clinton too faced the task of reorienting U.S. foreign policy. For nearly half a century, anticommunism and rivalry with the Soviet Union determined much of the nation policymaking agenda. However, with the breakup of the Soviet Union and the collapse of the Eastern Bloc, the United States no longer had to worry about "monolithic" communism and needed to redefine national security to fit a multipolar world. Clinton (to the surprise of many who believed his understanding of foreign policy issues and *real politique* was marginal at best) understood this and promoted an expansive, internationalist vision of improving relations with the UN, reinforcing NATO, advancing human rights and democracy abroad, reducing nuclear threats, working on global environmental concerns, and advocating free-market policies.

One of the most perplexing issues confronting Clinton involved revamping the U.S. military for the post-cold war world and under what exigencies should U.S. troops be sent abroad either as peacekeepers or to help restore order or to protect a legitimate government from revolutionary forces from either the right or the left wanting to overthrow it. Americans were torn on these issues, some believing it was time for "retrenchment" or a "new isolationism" and "America first," while others maintained that the worse thing the United States could do was to turn its back on the world, for if it did the fanatics would surely rise and threaten the world with greater violence than the cold war ever portended. Typically, Clinton sought a "middle ground" between the "isolationists" and those wanting new, more expansive international commitments.

Clinton's policies were tested early in his first administration with several trouble spots sparking debate. In the African country of Somalia, ravaged by famine and civil war, which saw powerful, brutal warlords take over the country, Clinton ordered U.S. troops to the region under the umbrella of a UN humanitarian mission to help provide food and relief support. Clinton decided that the United States should take the initiative in trying to end the bloodshed and the warlords' oppression and ordered a "raid" to capture them. Unfortunately, the mission ended up disastrous for the United States, as U.S. troops suffered well-publicized (graphically depicted) casualties. Indeed, the public, more in an "isolationist" than "humanitarian" mood, put pressure on Clinton to pull out, which he did in the spring of 1994. In Haiti, closer to home, U.S. interests seemed clearer, and Clinton vowed to help reestablish Haiti's elected president, Jean-Bertrand Aristide (who, interestingly was deposed again in 2003). In September 1994, the first 3,000 of a projected 15,000 American troops landed in Haiti, in cooperation with the UN, and last-minute negotiations by former president Jimmy Carter persuaded the Haitian military to peacefully step aside. After six months, with Aristide in power and political institutions functioning again, U.S. soldiers handed over the responsibility for peacekeeping to UN forces. In the former Yugoslavia, the United States also committed troops, under NATO auspices, to halt the massacre of Bosnian Muslims by Bosnian (Christian) Serbs and to oversee a cease-fire and peace-building process that all parties to the conflict had accepted in the 1995 U.S.-brokered Dayton (Ohio) Accords.

Beginning in 1998, the United States found itself once again in conflict with Iraqi president Saddam Hussein, who was now reneging on the agreements he had signed at the end of the Gulf War and refused to permit international inspectors to examine military sites in his country. Clinton responded by ordering a series of American bombing strikes at military targets inside Iraq. In 1999 the president faced the most serious foreign policy crisis of his presidency, once again in the Balkans. This time the conflict involved a province of Serbian-dominated Yugoslavia—Kosovo—most of whose inhabitants were Albanian Muslims. Reminiscent of the Bosnian crisis, a savage civil war erupted in the region with Serbian forces accused once again of committing unspeakable atrocities on their "enemies." Clinton and the world knew that the Yugoslav president, the Christian Serb, Slobodan Milosevic, was nothing more than a brutal dictator, pursuing another "ethnic cleansing" of his country. Clinton tried negotiating a settlement, but all such efforts failed. Thus, the president decided he had no choice but to use force to stop the genocide. Clinton unleashed a bombing campaign against the Serbians, which was successful in stopping Milosevic from engaging in further acts of genocide. Indeed, a cease-fire was established, and Serbian troops withdrew from Kosovo entirely. No doubt Clinton's resolve and his willingness to use force to stop the genocide were responsible for the Serbian withdrawal and the possibility of future peace in the Balkans.

Clinton also shaped new policies on weapons of mass destruction. He dismantled some of the U.S. nuclear arsenals and tried to curtail the potential danger from other nuclear powers. When the Soviet Union collapsed and its nuclear weapons became dispersed among several independent states, the Clinton administration feared these might be sold on the black market to terrorists. In early 1994 Clinton increased economic aid for the newly independent Ukraine, then the third largest nuclear power in the world, in return for promises to disarm its 1,600 warheads. In the same year, a highly secret "Project Sapphire" transferred enriched uranium stocks from Kazakstan, another former Soviet state, to storage facilities in the United States. Also, Jimmy Carter, responding to Clinton's request, helped negotiate a complicated agreement with North Korea over nuclear weapons, signed in 1994. North Korea agreed to begin dismantling its nuclear program and permit international inspections as soon as the United States helped it construct safer light-water nuclear reactors for its energy needs. In the Middle East, Clinton devoted endless hours and days trying to forge the foundations for lasting peace between the leaders of Israel and Palestine.

One of Clinton's principal foreign policy goals was to lower trade barriers, thus expanding U.S. global markets, which he believed essential to sustain the nation's economic boom and prosperity. (Out-sourcing of jobs, however, was not part of the Clinton initiative; American products, not American jobs, were to find greater "outlets" around the world.) Building on the Reagan-Bush legacy, Clinton argued that such policies would not only boost prosperity but help promote democracy around the world as well. Consequently, his administration consummated several historic trade agreements, one of the most important of which was in the nation's "own back yard." Despite opposition from labor unions (who feared a loss of jobs and perhaps now they were correct) and other groups that usually supported the Democratic Party, Clinton strongly backed the North American Free Trade Agreement (NAFTA), which projected cutting tariffs and eliminating other trade barriers between the United States, Canada, and Mexico over a 15-year period. After adding new provisions on labor and environmental issues, in December 1993 he muscled the bill through Congress in a close vote that depended on Republican support. NAFTA took effect on January 1, 1994. Then in early 1995, Mexico's severe debt crisis and a dramatic devaluation of its peso prompted Clinton to extend a $20 billion loan from America's Exchange Stabilization Fund, an unprecedented act that stabilized the Mexican economy, one of the United States' most important trading partners. Moreover, Clinton realized that economic chaos in Mexico could easily lead to political upheaval in that country, which in turn could impact the United States adversely, especially if violence erupted causing, as it did between 1910-1920, the massive exodus of Mexican nationals to the United States. Indeed, any United States president worth his "salt" must be cognizant at all times of the volatile nature of the Mexican economy and politics. Bill Clinton surely was.

In the same context as NAFTA, Clinton completed the so-called "Uruguay Round" of the General Agreement on Tariffs and Trade (GATT) in late 1993, and in early 1994, GATT was replaced by a new World Trade Organization (WTO), a more powerful multilateral group created to enlarge world trade by implementing new agreements and mediating disputes. Clinton also reversed his election-year position and granted China, despite its dismal record on human rights, equal trading status with other nations. To justify this about face, Clinton argued that increased trade with China would contribute to its democratization process. Similarly, in February 1994, the United States ended its 19-year-old trade embargo against Vietnam, and American businesses began establishing relations with a regime that had once been cast as a major threat to U.S. global interests. When Asian economies faltered during 1998, Clinton strongly supported acting with the International Monetary Fund to provide huge emergency credits to reform and restore financial systems from Korea to Indonesia.

Clinton rightly claimed that all of his initiatives relative to world trade not only benefited the United States by expanding and opening up new markets for American goods, but in the process they helped to stabilize the world economic order and usher in a new era of global prosperity. Moreover, as noted above, Clinton also believed that more equitable trade relations between the United States and especially developing nations went far toward helping to foster capitalism and democracy in those countries. Promoting free trade would also help to erase the long-held image among the United States' Latin American neighbors of *yanqui* economic exploitation and imperialism.

Despite the many scandals and setbacks he suffered in the White House, Clinton finished his eight years in office with his popularity higher than it had been when he had begun. Although benefiting (and thus distracting many Americans from his indiscretions and failures) from an astonishing prosperity and general world stability, Clinton's overall public approval was nonetheless consistently among the highest of any postwar president. Indeed, so skilled was Clinton in conducting the public policy part of his presidency that his opinion poll ratings went up even as his legal and moral troubles escalated into outright malfeasance. Without question, as more of his immoral behavior was revealed, compounded by his bold-faced lying, the more repulsed people became.

Yet, for almost bizarre reasons, they continued to like his ideas and thus, by extension, Clinton. Apparently, Clinton's sexual escapades no longer shocked and disgusted the American public sufficiently enough to turn them against either Clinton or his policies. No doubt the revelations of John Kennedy's notorious philandering made Clinton's womanizing seem not only "mild" by comparison but "excusable" as well. It was as if the public separated in their minds Clinton the president from Clinton the man or human being, who, like any other "normal" person, was going to make "mistakes," and as long as those personal transgressions were not un-Constitutional (which they clearly were not) and did not adversely affect the country, all was to be forgiven. In short, it was as if Americans had come to understand or expect that people in power are physically attractive and that such appeal is simply for many, such as Clinton, too overwhelming to resist.

Moreover, fresh in the memory of many Americans, particularly baby-boomers, was the horrible disgrace and embarrassment of Watergate and the resignation of a president who definitely would have been removed from office for legitimate "high crimes and misdemeanors." In 1986, during the Reagan administration, scandal again hit the Oval Office in the form of the Iran-Contra affair. Ronald Reagan, like Clinton, was personally an extremely popular president who no doubt knew enough of the "particulars" of the operation to be guilty of complicity. Yet, the American public, wanting to avoid at all costs another humiliating Watergate with the possible impeachment or resignation of yet another chief executive so soon after the first one, were willing to "look the other way," in effect exonerating Reagan of any "serious" wrongdoing. Although Clinton lied about his affair with Monica Lewinsky and did commit adultery, his actions did not violate the Constitutional provisions of his office, nor did they at any time place the nation's welfare in jeopardy. Indeed, unlike either Nixon or Reagan, Clinton's activities, while morally reprehensible, paled in comparison to the clandestine, arrogant, illegal, and nefarious doings of his predecessors and their respective henchmen. Ironically, as the more conservative Republicans vilified Clinton, with many of their attacks reflecting an obsessive personal hate, the more popular the president became with many Americans rushing to his defense. Clinton assumed an interesting celebrity or "star" status, like a box office matinee idol, especially among those Americans who responded positively to his vision and message. "Everything about such people is big," wrote one citizen who described Clinton as a classic hero, "their loves, their eagerness to do spectacular things, their deep understanding of how the world works and also their moral failings and their need to win. Clinton's enemies never grasped this; they measured him according to their own smallness."

The William Jefferson Clinton Presidency: A Negative Assessment

As noted earlier, Clinton was touted by many as being "one of the biggest, most talented, articulate, intelligent, open [and] colorful characters" to become president. Yet, he was simultaneously capable of being an "undisciplined, fumbling, obtuse, defensive [and] self-justifying rogue." Within months of his presidency, Clinton's tendency toward "political schizophrenia" became apparent. He initially created the expectation that his priority was deficit reduction and an economic stimulus package to promote job growth. Almost immediately after entering the White House, however, Clinton got "off message," declaring instead that his first major objective would be to end discrimination against homosexuals in the military rather than addressing the deficit or implementing fiscal reforms. No sooner did he announce such a policy than he was lambasted from both sides of the aisle, as well as from the military establishment. Indeed, he immediately incurred the disfavor of two of the most powerful men in the capital, General Colin Powell, Chairman of the Joint Chiefs, and fellow Democrat Senator Sam Nunn of Georgia, who was chairman of the Armed Services Committee. Both Powell and Nunn vigorously opposed the initiative. Without question Clinton believed personally in civil rights for gays, and he was right to condemn their being discriminated against in the armed services. In his mind, he was now delivering on his pledge made during the campaign to ensure gay rights. However, regardless of how courageous such an initiative might have been, it was completely the wrong timing for such a measure to be introduced. Clinton simply had not done his "political homework." He had built a consensus among middle-class Americans for his vision and agenda, and to maintain their support, he needed to give them something immediately beneficial like tax reform or some other new neo-liberal entitlement. By advocating instead something the majority of middle-class Americans believed to be not only peripheral to their lives but "deviant" as well, Clinton alienated the very class of citizens upon whom he hoped to build a new Democratic Party. For someone who was allegedly one of the most politically savvy men to inhabit the Oval Office, Clinton's proposal to end homosexual discrimination in the military quickly degenerated into his own "Bay of Pigs" fiasco, occurring, like for his hero JFK, in the first three months of his presidency. Once Clinton realized the blunder he had made, he hemmed and hawed and finally came up with a policy of "Don't ask, don't tell," which he believed would be acceptable to the gay community. For gays in the military or for those wanting to join, the words were meaningless for, in effect, those words kept them "in the closet" still. Suffice it to say, homosexuals felt betrayed by Clinton. Clinton's actions also profoundly alienated liberals, especially the "neos," who found Clinton's digression away from economic reform to be most disheartening and alarming. Clinton was now perceived by many to be a "waffler," especially when it came to sensitive social issues like homosexuality. "It was the grimmest start of any presidency in generations," the *New Republic* declared in August 1993.

From the very beginning, however, everyone knew that Clinton's presidency would rise or fall on his success in passing health-care reform, which would guarantee insurance to every American citizen. By 1992, the United States was the only developed industrial nation in the world without such a system. All the European countries had instituted national health-care programs either before the war or in its immediate aftermath. FDR had momentarily thought about making national health insurance part of Social Security but decided to hold off, largely because of right-wing opposition to such a "notion." Harry Truman tried again in 1947 to introduce such legislation, but like most of the Fair Deal's social welfare legislation, it fell victim to the politics of anticommunism, as the red-baiters and other reactionaries labeled it "communistic." Now, with the cold war over, it seemed possible for the first time in almost 50 years to resurrect the idea. Unlike gays in the military, the timing to reintroduce national health insurance was "right," for such an initiative impacted every citizen's life. Health-care costs had skyrocketed during the 1970s and 1980s, double or triple the rate of inflation, eating away any increases in real income. Moreover, nearly 40 million Americans were totally without health-care coverage. To "old time" liberals like Senator Harris Wofford of Pennsylvania, the "right" to health care was as fundamental in a democracy as the right to vote. Suffice it to say, Great Society liberals like Wofford were fully behind Clinton's initiative. For neo-liberals like Clinton, economic reform and health-care reform were symbiotic: a permanent cure for huge deficits required harnessing the explosive rate of inflation in health-care costs. Accomplishing both would put Clinton's presidency in the same league with that of FDR. Indeed, in Clinton's and other liberals' views, health-care reform represented the most massive, important social legislation in all of American history, making even Social Security pale in comparison. Moreover, Clinton was also keenly aware of the future political benefits such reform could bring both him and his party. If he could tie the middle class to the Democratic Party through providing universal national health insurance, he would solidify for at least another generation his party's dominance, much the same way FDR had used New Deal legislation to create the various coalitions that made the Democratic Party the majority party until the 1980s. The Republicans were aware of this possible reality, and from the moment Clinton introduced the measure, they were determined to defeat it.

There were a multitude of reasons why health-care reform ultimately went down to crushing defeat. One of the most important and fatal errors made by Clinton was to give responsibility for drafting his health-care reform to a task force directed by his wife, Hillary, and administered by his old friend and fellow Rhodes scholar, Ira Magaziner. By everyone's account, Hillary Rodham Clinton was brilliant, hard driving, a master of detail, and a charismatic leader. Thus, she was about to become the *first* First Lady to play a major role in determining one of the most important pieces of legislation in American history. Unfortunately, because of her marital and political partnership with the president, she became a lightning rod for hostility. A person of strong opinions (some called her dogmatic), she did not easily accept criticism or tolerate dissenting views. As one Cabinet member reported, "You make your point once to the president's wife, and if it is not accepted, you don't press it." With such a person in charge, the policy-making process might well be less sensitive than normal to political negotiation and barter. Compounding Hillary's strong presence and influence was the equally overwhelming and overbearing personality of Ira Magaziner, who, observers declared, was the quintessential "policy wonk," who believed that non-politically motivated experts could devise such legislation if left alone to do their work. Thus, all the work on the bill would take place in secret until the initiative was complete. It was policy-making by expert fiat, led by a person, who like Hillary, was often seen by others as arrogant, dismissive of views he did not share, and intent on riding roughshod over those less bright and less competent than he.

The fundamental problem with such an approach to policy was that it left out Congress, especially the wheelers and dealers who were (and are) key in getting such controversial legislation such as this passed. Not only were important legislators left out of the process but also so were equally vital members of the administration, such as Secretary of Health and Human Services, Donna Shalala, and Secretary of the Treasury, Lloyd Bentsen, who also had been the chair of the Senate Finance Committee. Both of these cabinet people had handled more health-care legislation than anyone on the task force. Suffice it to say, individuals such as Bentsen and Shalala resented being "snubbed" and so did members of Congress. The Magaziner operation seemed eerily similar to when "the best and the brightest"—the inside elite and supposed foreign policy "experts" of both the Kennedy and Johnson administrations—took over the planning of the Vietnam War. Like the Magaziner/Hillary Clinton task force, the "Wise Men" of that era often met in secret, usurping the role of Congress and other individuals in the decision-making process, ultimately leading the nation to defeat and humiliation in the catastrophe known as Vietnam. Such was about to befall the Clinton administration's health-care reform initiative.

Not surprisingly, the measure produced by this process was extraordinarily complicated, sophisticated beyond belief—with a provision for any and every eventuality—and completely incomprehensible to the average citizen. Nearly 1350 pages in length, the Clinton health-care package arrived on the Hill almost a full year after the president had taken office. It immediately incurred the venom of both Republicans and Democrats, with the former especially harsh in their criticisms. Utah Republican Senator Bob Bennett denounced it as "incredibly bloated, complex, unresponsive, and incomprehensible, . . . [symbolic of] everything people hate about government." Even supporters expressed anxiety, and the lobbyist for America's senior citizens openly worried "about the complexity of this [plan] and the ability of people to feel comfortable with something that is so complicated. If you're explaining it, people's eyes glaze over." There's little doubt Clinton could have avoided such attacks and concerns had he gone to the American people with broad outlines of a program and worked with congressional committees to draft the appropriate legislation. For a brief time, however, Clinton overcame the plan's cumbersomeness and inaccessibility. In a cogent speech before Congress and the nation in September 1993, he explained to the American people the measure's most salient points—quality care, savings, simplicity, and security. At that moment the president was clearly in his element, rising to the occasion with a memorable address that galvanized even his opponents in the audience. One Republican senator called Clinton's speech "the most comprehensive, brilliantly presented analytical dissection of everything that is wrong with the present health care system" that he had ever heard. Yet, almost immediately, Clinton allowed the momentum he had created to dissipate. Other issues distracted him—NAFTA and a military crisis in Somalia, which ended in disaster for the United States. Meanwhile, the Magaziner task force labored away trying to produce a legislative draft—a process that would take two more months. Suddenly the wind in Clinton's health-care sails disappeared, to be replaced by inaction, confusion, and demoralization, especially among reform advocates who saw passing from their control the best chance they would ever have to secure success.

Into the vacuum strode the Republican opposition, who had been waiting to savage the president's plan precisely because of its gargantuan size, its incomprehensibility, and its apparent threat to small business and individual choice. Interestingly, however, the Republicans didn't get very far in their effort to destroy the proposal for Clinton rebounded once again toward the end of his first year with some notable legislative successes such as the ratification of NAFTA, the Brady Bill, passage of his deficit reduction package, creation of Americorps, and a new, more liberal voter registration bill, all of which helped Clinton to regain momentum on his health-care initiative. Then Whitewater, sex scandals, and the suicide of White House aide Vincent Foster exploded in the national press, sending Clinton reeling for cover and crippling any chance his health-care proposal might have had. Rumors of Clinton's alleged philandering had been circulating for months, but now new "revelations" appeared about Arkansas state troopers procuring women for Clinton when he was governor, including a former state employee named Paula Jones who announced at a press conference called by a conservative Republican group that Clinton had asked her to perform oral sex. If that wasn't enough, new allegations emerged about both the president and his wife's role in the Whitewater real estate venture in Arkansas, with accusations flying that the Clintons had used improper influence with state regulatory bodies and a savings and loan association to protect and maintain their private investment. When Vincent Foster, Hillary Clinton's former law partner and counsel to the president, took his own life—declaring in a suicide note that he had become so depressed by the way "getting people" had become "a sport" in Washington's political culture—the scandal mongering and personal attacks reached new heights. Reactionary talk show host Rush Limbaugh accused the Clintons of being involved in Foster's "murder," which then sent rumors flying that the Clintons "got rid of" Foster because he had "handled" the Whitewater files. There was no truth whatsoever to Limbaugh's accusation; nonetheless, the Republicans accelerated their rantings for a full-scale Watergate-type investigation into the Whitewater matter. By March 1994, there were more Whitewater stories published in major newspapers in America than the combined total of stories on health care, welfare, and crime legislation.

All three events could not have come at a worse time for Clinton, and the damage done to his health-care proposal was enormous—both directly and indirectly. Clinton went on the defensive, struggling just to keep his own political head above water while conservatives linked the personal with the political. "I think Whitewater is about health care," Limbaugh pronounced. As the showdown over health care approached, no calumny was out of bounds. Bumper stickers proclaimed "Where is Lee Harvey Oswald now that we need him?" Hillary Clinton was accused of being a lesbian power-monger. In response, Hillary Clinton lamented, "the way a lot of unbalanced, alienated, mean-spirited people are being given license to be very disruptive. . . . There isn't any counter-balance to this incredible twenty-four-hour-a-day hate that is being spewed out." Notwithstanding a determined last-minute effort by Senate moderates to devise a compromise plan, the Clinton health-care initiative was doomed. As late as December 1993, Clinton enjoyed a 17-point margin of approval for his health-care proposal; by March 1994, all support had evaporated with a new majority now saying they opposed health-care legislation. Clinton had lost his moment to become another FDR and to redefine American politics.

To a large extent, Clinton was responsible for the defeat of health care, and he openly admitted his culpability to reporters. "We made the error of trying to do too much, took too long, and ended up achieving nothing," he declared in an interview with Haynes Johnson and David Broder. Clinton had failed to "stay on message," as he had done during the campaign. Compounding his legislative dilatoriness and digressions was the fact that Clinton went outside "the system" with his task force approach. As a result, he alienated key congressional leaders by such a slight, as well as key members within his own administration, whose knowledge and experience in health-care matters would have been most valuable to his cause. Finally, he failed on the critical terrain of timing and momentum, which any politician will admit is perhaps the most important factor in determining a bill's success or failure.

No sooner was Clinton reelected to his second term than his penchant for self-destruction began, ruining any chance of redeeming an already flawed presidency and minimizing the significance of even Clinton's positive accomplishments in domestic and foreign affairs. Clinton's "undoing" began at the height of his confrontation with Gingrich over the national budget in 1995. The government, in effect, was shut down because Congress failed to pass a year-long appropriations measure. In a crisis-style-a-la-Kennedy, the White House was operating around the clock, staffers and politicians running in and out with the latest news and strategies. One night, a 23-year-old intern named Monica Lewinsky brought dinner (pizza) to the president. Long attracted to Clinton, Lewinsky by her own admission initiated what became a torrid mutual seduction that supposedly never "escalated" to intercourse but did involve repeated rendezvous for oral sex, which on one occasion resulted in a semen stain on the blue dress Lewinsky was wearing. After about a year Clinton abruptly ended the affair. However, phone calls, notes, and presents between the two continued for several more months. Most damaging to the president was Lewinsky's "sharing" of her affair with Linda Tripp, who, unbeknownst to Lewinsky, was tape-recording their conversations. Almost a year after Clinton's second inauguration, Americans, as well as the world, began to learn, piece by piece, all the lurid details of Bill Clinton's tryst with a White House intern barely older than his own daughter.

The Lewinsky story exploded into national (as well as world) headlines. Clinton's situation worsened as Whitewater and the Paula Jones affair also hit their full impact. Compounding Clinton's problems was the appointment of arch-conservative Kenneth Starr as special prosecutor for the Whitewater gambit. In the meantime, Paula Jones had filed a federal lawsuit against Clinton, and over the president's objections, the Supreme Court unanimously ruled in May 1997 that the Jones lawsuit should not be deferred until Clinton left office, arguing that it would not sufficiently preoccupy the president to prevent him from conducting his presidential duties. On January 17, 1998, in testimony under oath in the Paula Jones case, lawyers surprised the president by asking if he ever had sex with Monica Lewinsky. Clinton declared, without hesitation, he had not. At the same time, a federal appeals court granted Kenneth Starr's request that his investigative purview in Whitewater be expanded to include the Lewinsky case. On January 21, Clinton unfortunately dug his grave deeper when he flatly denied ever having the affair with Lewinsky. "There is no sexual relationship," he said before TV cameras and later said, "I never had sex with *that* woman." Hilary Clinton, as she had in the past, "stood by her man," telling the press that the story had no validity and that it was simply another manifestation of a "right-wing conspiracy" to destroy her husband.

While Clinton swore "to the world and God Almighty" that no affair had taken place, evidence continued to mount that confirmed Clinton was lying. Clinton faithfuls wanted and needed to believe that the whole sordid business was a right-wing concoction designed to vilify the president and bring down his administration. After all, the judges who appointed Starr were conservatives who had lunch with Jesse Helms just before naming Starr. There had always been an irrational hatred for the Clintons among the far right, as if their very presence in the White House symbolized a defamation of conservative values. Moreover, the leaks from Starr's office and Linda Tripp's tawdry behavior reinforced the hope among Clinton loyalists that their man was innocent, the victim of a reactionary plot to "get" the president. Although conservatives certainly relished all that was happening to Clinton, there was no conspiracy. Clinton flat out lied to *everyone*, for the now famous (or infamous) "blue dress" stain revealed via a DNA test that the semen *did* come from Bill Clinton. Such undeniable evidence put the last nail in Clinton's coffin, making even his most ardent defenders suspicious that once again the Republican caricature of "Slick Willie" had more truth than falseness to it.

Called to testify before a grand jury Starr had convened to consider Whitewater-related allegations, Clinton finally admitted to what had now become a given, namely, "I did have a relationship with Ms. Lewinsky that was not appropriate." Even this late in the game, had Clinton gone to the American people, confessed his transgression, and asked for "forgiveness" or "understanding" or "compassion," he would have received a degree of absolution. Instead, he appeared on television and, while admitting he had dissembled, he offered a truculent and aggressive defense of himself, portraying Bill Clinton as the victim and Ken Starr and his conservative allies as the "real" perpetrators of wrongdoing. It was simply an awful, embarrassing, and unsuccessful attempt to displace the blame for his own lying and "cheating" onto someone else. By September 1998, Starr told Congress that he had "substantial and credible information" that Clinton had committed offenses that constituted grounds for impeachment. For the next three months, the nation watched as Congress heard and debated four different counts under which Starr wished Clinton indicted. On two of those four counts, most importantly that of perjury, the House of Representative voted for impeachment. In the end, the United States Senate, acting as the jury of Clinton's guilt or innocence, acquitted him of the charges, allowing him to remain in office.

In many ways, the impeachment process rendered immaterial whatever else Bill Clinton hoped to accomplish. He not only was a lame duck in the sense that he could not run again but also in his ability to push through any more meaningful legislation. Although many Americans continued to "like" Bill Clinton, more citizens were so disgusted by his questionable behavior, both sexual and financial, that they no longer had faith or confidence in his leadership. In the end, it was Clinton's "moral failings" that made tragic what might have been triumphant. "This is a tale of two presidencies," White House counselor Leon Panetta observed, "one obviously brilliant and extremely capable, with the ability to help produce the greatest economy in the history of this country and to focus on major domestic priorities, and the other. . . the darker side, the one that made a terrible human mistake that will forever shadow that other presidency." The tragedy was that the two were immutable: the "good side" reflecting the same qualities and passions that shaped the "bad side." What in the end destroyed Clinton's possibility for greatness?—hubris, an arrogance that knows no bounds and whose ambitions almost always turn into excess and wanton self-destruction. Summarizing all that had happened during the Clinton presidency, Todd Purdum wrote: "For eight years, Bill Clinton had been the bright sun and the bleak moon, embodying much of the best and the worst of times." The tragedy was that Clinton's character flaws and recklessness killed his potential for greatness. Wasted opportunities, vicious partisanship, and failure to deal with domestic challenges were the hallmarks of the last two years of his second term. To punctuate this point, Clinton, as if to spite the American people and Congress for having the "audacity" to question his integrity and leadership, spent the remaining days of his administration issuing pardons to people who had supported him throughout his political career, many of whom had engaged in dubious behavior on his behalf. Among Clinton's "friends" and associates was a fugitive multi-millionaire whose ex-wife contributed substantial sums to the Clinton Library in Little Rock. To many Americans, Clinton's eleventh-hour pardons were an appropriate end to a president who left office perhaps not in disgrace but surely not exalted—a "presidential paradox," who was the first chief executive to be impeached since 1868 while simultaneously credited with implementing fiscal policies that allowed him to preside over one of the greatest eras of sustained economic growth in the Republic's history.

Bill Clinton
shaking hands
with
John F. Kennedy.
Photo credit:
Consolidated
News, Arnie
Sachs

(Right) Bill Clinton
playing the saxophone.
(Bottom) Bill, Hillary,
and Chelsea walking
down Pennsylvania
Avenue.
January 20, 1997.
Photo credits: Clinton
Presidential Materials
Project

Bill Clinton
giving the
1999 State
of the Union
Address.
Photo
credits:
Clinton
Presidential
Materials
Project

(L. to R.) Prime
Minister of Israel,
Yitzhak Rabin, President
Clinton, and Yasser
Arafat, chairman of the
Palestine Liberation
Organization, shaking
hands in an electrifying
ceremony.
September 1993
(Bottom) President
Clinton working at his
desk in the Oval Office.
Photo credits:Clinton
Presidential Materials
Project

George Walker Bush
2001-

George Walker Bush, 43rd president of the United States of America, has been a man driven—and haunted—by extraordinary legacy. With this legacy—a legacy of birth, of generation, of political ambition—has come both great success and great controversy. It is the very complexity of these many interlocking legacies that ultimately defines both the man and his presidency.

There is the legacy of his name, that of one of America's premier business and political dynasties, the Walker-Bush clan, which has produced two oil companies, a congressman, a senator, two governors, and now two presidents. There is the legacy of a father whose name he carries and in whose footsteps he has followed from Andover and Yale to west Texas oil fields and politics to the White House itself, always a step behind his paternal namesake.

There is the legacy of his generation, the baby boomers, within whose ranks he grew up in the ease and affluence of a postwar period when success and comfort were seen as a birthright even by those not born to three generations of established money. Within that generational legacy is the narrower, more divisive legacy of the Sixties, the defining decade of the boomers, the triumphs and excesses of which still resound in our political and cultural national debate.

In this culture war, both boomer presidents, Clinton and Bush, became national screens onto which different sides of the Sixties could project their dreams and angsts. Indeed, the contrast between Bush and his predecessor is perhaps the most dramatic since Andrew Jackson replaced John Quincy Adams. The differences in popular perception between Bush and Clinton, both as men and politicians, are of different kind than those between George H.W. Bush and Bill Clinton, greater than those between Carter and Reagan, and far greater than those between Richard Nixon and Lyndon Baines Johnson.

For Bill Clinton and George H. W. Bush, the differences were perceived largely in generational terms. While the ideological divide between Carter and Reagan was vast, the general perception of their

584   George W. Bush

being men of family and faith mitigated some of the personal distinctions between them. The differences between Johnson and Nixon were more tactical than ideological. Both advanced war in Southeast Asia; both embraced anti-communism in the 1940s and 1950s and civil rights in the 1960s (albeit grudgingly on Nixon's part). Both could be easily imagined (and actually heard on various tapes) uttering gutter invectives aimed at minorities, homosexuals, and Jews. In short, both were corrupt but powerfully influential politicians that defined a postwar status quo— a status quo that the Sixties blew apart.

The political struggle between Clintonites (through the surrogate Gore—but for the Twenty-second Amendment, Democrats sighed) and Bushians by the 2000 campaign became the real life political equivalence of Oliver Stone's *Platoon*—with Bill Clinton as the slacker hippie druggie vs. Bush as the boozin', head-bashin' good ol' boy. For every action of each man, there have been equal and opposite reactions, becoming even more severe in the case of George W. Bush.

Then there is the legacy of Bush's ideological progenitors, the no-holds barred anti-liberal, red meat conservatism of Barry Goldwater, George Wallace, Ronald Reagan, and Jesse Helms, a harsher, more self-confident, more devout brand of conservatism than the moderate conservatism—"liberal on human issues, conservative on economic ones"—that Dwight Eisenhower had been content to embrace and pursue, and with which Bush's own grandfather and even father had been more comfortable.

Finally, there is the legacy of his own creation, the legacy of the Bush administration, which has already influenced the nation and world at levels deeper and more long-lasting than either Bill Clinton or Bush's own father were able to do.

The detractors and supporters of George W. Bush see him as the living symbolism of the great debate of twentieth century American politics: whither the state? From the Great Depression and the New Deal through the Civil Rights movement and the Great Society, the role of America's government dramatically expanded to encompass, support, regulate, and promote more and more of the lives of its citizens. Where some citizens of George Washington's America might never have actually even seen an agent or officer of the United States government in their entire life, all citizens of George Bush's America are in constant proximity to their federal government.

Liberals saw the expansion of government as a social good, a necessary evolution of the role of the state mirrored in all complex industrial economies to promote the general welfare and to bring fairness and justice to societies experiencing unprecedented expansions in both the scope of wealth and its concentration. Conservatives saw the rise of government as the rise of authority and control, setting the feet of a free people fully capable of seeing to their needs by their own self-determination on the fateful road to serfdom.

Detractors of George W. Bush argue that, since his election, he has systematically sought to roll back every action of the Clinton administration, turning the clock back to 1992 (or even 1982 and the heyday of the Reagan revolution). Indeed, Senator Hillary Clinton observed that George W. Bush sought not just to turn the clock back on the Clinton legacy but to turn the clock back on the New Deal itself, taking America back to the age of nineteenth century laissez faire's business unchained and, in so doing, creating a new era of post-industrial robber barons unleashed to pilfer the wealth of the middle and working classes.

Bush's supporters argue that, but for George W. Bush, the liberal vision of the super social welfare state as begun by FDR and pursued vigorously by the Clintonites with their national health-care plans and Kyoto Accords would head America down the well-trod path of twentieth century totalitarianism. And, they continue, would anyone be happier if the "draft dodger" was now our commander in chief during our new war on terror? (For the record, one cannot really fight a war against a tactic, as in "the war on high altitude strategic bombing." One can only fight wars against peoples.)

George W. Bush is a man consistently underestimated by those who oppose him and simultaneously overestimated by those who support him. He has been dismissed as a spoiled, shallow, intellectually limited, untraveled rich kid to whom the keys of the kingdom were handed without his even having to break a sweat. As Ann Richards, the Democrat whom he unseated as governor of Texas, was wont to retort, "he was born on third base and thought he hit a triple." Or as local Texas radio talk show host Mel Turner more harshly put it, "Bush never worked a day in his life. [He] was born with a silver boot up his ass."

Bush has simultaneously been praised as a man of great faith and resolute leadership, a man of focused determination who broke out of the shadow of a powerful family to establish himself as one of the pivotal political leaders of our time. To his supporters, he is simply "the right man" to lead America in a perilous time, a Texas version of Winston Churchill.

As with most things, the truth lies somewhere between the extremes. George W. Bush was born in 1946—the year that the cold war broke out and the year that Nixon launched his political career as a red-baiter—to a family well aware of its own place in society and the role that the family legacy required of them.

His great-grandfather, Samuel P. Bush, had relocated from the comfort of an upper middle-class existence in New York to Ohio, part of the western advance of later nineteenth century industry that followed the Civil War, turning farmlands from Pittsburg to Chicago into cities and cities into dynamos of industrial power. Not as flashy or wealthy as the Gettys, the Mellons, or the Rockefellers, more of a petite robber baron than the genuine article, Bush built a family fortune from steel and rail. With money comes power, and with power comes political influence. After becoming head of the National Association of Manufacturers and one of the founders of the National Chamber of Commerce, he became a director of the Cleveland Federal Reserve and confidant and advisor to 1920s Republican presidents.

Bush's grandfather, Prescott, was born into a life of privilege and was brought up with a stern sense of duty in which those of such station were to understand theirs was the responsibility of bringing order to society. From Yale and Skull and Bones membership to an officer's commission in the Great War to great success and wealth on Wall Street, the son of a titan of industry and father and grandfather of future presidents took his ordained place as part of America's early twentieth century mandarin class, which understood their role, in the finest sense of Edmund Burke, to serve as the natural aristocracy of American democracy.

Prescott's successes were in no small part bolstered by a fine marriage to another aristocratic business family, the Walker clan of Maine. Dorothy Walker, daughter of George Herbert Walker, the founder of one of Wall Street's most prominent investment banks, was a women of fierce, competitive spirit who drove her husband and children (George H.W., Prescott Jr., Jonathan, William, and Nancy) to always aspire to be better than their best, to live up to and exceed the obligation of their station. Prescott remained a creature of business through the Depression and World War II, not entering politics until his 50s, only to lose his first race for a Connecticut U.S. Senate seat in 1950. Winning the seat in a special election two years later, he went on to serve ten years in Washington, D.C. and to introduce the Bush name on a national scale.

Prescott's eldest son, George, was the only child to successfully follow his father into politics, from Congress to the vice presidency to the presidency itself (though Prescott Junior entered and dropped out of a race for his father's old Senate seat in 1982). George (or Poppy, as the family called him), like his father, excelled both in the private and public sector.

Connecticut raised, Andover and Yale educated, Skull and Bones society inducted, George H. W. Bush came out of World War II one of the Greatest Generation's legion of minor war heroes, having survived being shot down in the Pacific and a dramatic sea rescue by submarine. After the war, with several thousand dollars of family seed money, he set off for the final frontier of the west Texas oil fields to make his own fortune with his wife, Barbara (the daughter of a prominent New York family whom he married in 1941), and toddler first son George W. in tow.

The New England expatriate Bush settled in the Midland-Odessa area smack dab in the middle of some of the hardest scrabble oil lands on the planet. The local Texan social and business interests at first saw Bush as just another eastern money-kid swooping down to Texas to take advantage of the postwar oil boom that transformed the state, turning it from a rural land of ranchers and small oil men into a booming urban metropolis of steel towers built of corporate oil money. Bush spent the next decade laboring hard to complete a stunning transformation, turning himself into a successful oil man, wealthy in his own right apart from the east coast monies. By the 1950s, the oil exploration company he had founded, Zapata Oil, had become a significant player in the Texas hydrocarbon markets, expanding into offshore production by the end of the decade and absorption, at substantial profit for Bush, by Pennzoil. Along the way, George H. W. helped found a Midland bank and became a leading local civic and church leader.

Bush was less successful with his second attempted transformation, from "Connecticut Yankee in King Texas's" oil court to full-fledged son of the south. The son of the eastern senator worked the political end of things, schmoozing with local west Texas committees and civic organizations, trying to blend his good old-fashioned east coast Republican laissez faire business philosophy with the rural social conservatism that was already being prodded to reaction to the rising postwar liberalism of Democrat-controlled big cities. But the Texas of the 1950s and 1960s was still dominated by Democrats if for no other good reason than Texans were not yet ready to vote for the party of Lincoln. LBJ's Civil Rights Act, the line in the sand drawn by George Wallace, and the revolution of Ronald Reagan completed the great conservative

Republican conquest of Texas and the south that the senior Bush could
already feel rising out of the west Texas sand like gushing oil and angry
rattlers but not in time to give Bush a handy express lift towards national
prominence, as it would his son a generation later.

George H. W. Bush could not fully shake the label of "Yankee
carpetbagger," coming to Texas for a quick score. This label dogged him
in his first bid for office—a 1964 senate run—resulting in his following
his ideological mentor, Barry Goldwater, to ballot box defeat. He went
on in 1966 to win two terms in Congress, only to lose a second try for
the Senate in 1970 to the future Democratic vice-presidential candidate
and Clinton Secretary of the Treasury, Lloyd Bentsen. By then the
young Congressman with high ambitions from the prominent family
had been noticed by President Richard Nixon, who appointed Bush as
ambassador to the UN in 1970 and head of the Republican Party in
1972.

Bush survived the debacle of Watergate in part thanks to Gerald Ford,
who appointed him envoy to China in 1974 (which also conveniently got
Bush out of the country and out of any possible contention for the 1976
party nomination) and then CIA director. Bush spent the Republican
interregnum planning his own run for the highest office, only to see
himself outmaneuvered on the right—gallingly even in his own adopted
home of Texas—by the kinder, gentler voice of Wallace conservatism,
Ronald Reagan. Eight years of political house arrest as vice president
was rewarded with the ultimate prize that George H.W. Bush had been
pursuing, one way or another, since his attendance at his first Midland
Republican Club dinner forty years earlier. But the legacy would be
tainted by a weak economy and a too-smooth operator from Little Rock,
a child of the Sixties like George W. himself, only one who had strayed
far from the traditional core values of George W.'s Texan upbringing.

Through all those years of triumph and failure, George W. Bush
watched his father and learned. George W.'s early career reads in no
small part and by no small coincidence as a close copy of George Herbert
Walker Bush's life, as his father's career and achievement left a shadow-
like legacy of money, power, and success over whatever George the
younger set off to do.

While George W. Bush was the first of five children born to the Texas
branch of the Bush clan, he grew up with limited sibling companionship.
Robin, the Bush's second child, four years George W.'s junior, died from
leukemia in 1953, leaving a seven-year gap between George W. and
his closest sibling, younger brother John Ellis (the future Governor of

Florida "Jeb" Bush). Bush's formative years were spent in the company of his young Texan peers, whom he always seemed driven to be harder and wilder than. Though not born into the lap of lavish luxury, his father's early success in the oil boom coupled with deep family pockets meant the young George grew up in comparative comfort. The family's Midland home, for example, was one of the few in town with its own swimming pool.

Bush's early years carefully matched those of his father. There was prep school at Andover, where he excelled at cheerleading if not at academics, and then the inevitability that comes with being a third-generation legacy of Yale—membership in the ultimate networking secret society of Skull and Bones. Bush's Yale experience was transforming or, better put, reinforcing of the conservative values he had learned growing up in west Texas. Midland had been a place where there was no higher accolade than to be called a Veteran, one who had through service honored his family, his nation, his God: a "Good Man," a loyal man. At Yale, steeped in the anger of the anti-war movement and the rejection of all things traditional by a large segment of Bush's fellow baby-boomers run rampant, veterans were spat upon and traditional values dismissed. Bush saw the complaints of his peers—themselves overwhelmingly from the same privileged background as he—about various social, political, economic, sexual, and cultural injustices as so much whining by the privileged children of the national aristocracy wracked by their own guilt over their own good fortune.

Yale reinforced three tendencies in the young Bush: a dislike, bordering on loathing, of 1960s liberalism; a distrust, to the point of dismissal, of academic intellectualism; and a deep, unbending faith in traditional values, especially the religious values that underscored his Texas upbringing. Self-reliance, responsibility, and personal achievement were the trinity of this Texas ethos. Steeped in these ideals, the young Bush never seemed to develop a tremendous capacity for empathy with those who lacked the advantages of three generations of family privilege and power.

Coming out of Yale amidst Vietnam in 1968, Bush faced the necessity of military service or flight to Canada, an option he never explored but of which he seems to have at least been aware. Flight was truly no option. Poppy had been a pilot and a minor war hero. Not to serve was to bring disgrace on the family and dishonor the legacy. At the same time, the young Bush seems to have had no burning desire to go off and test himself in the rice paddies of Southeast Asia. Instead, he chose the option particularly appealing to families of the upper middle and upper classes during the Vietnam War, National Guard service.

There is debate about how much influence family and family friends had in securing him a coveted spot in the Texas Air National Guard. Like Bill Clinton's college deferments and Dan Quayle's own National Guard experience, supporters and detractors of the person see things with very different eyes. For his detractors, the National Guard experience would always be a point of contention, another example of how his life of privilege had allowed him to escape many of the hardships and risks to which he himself would later be willing to subject other people's sons and daughters. For his supporters, the Guard experience showed his dedication to country, honor, and duty, both familial and patriotic. Thus, when as president he landed on an aircraft carrier and emerged onto the deck in full flight suit, his detractors saw fraud; his supporters saw hero.

In any event, even with hundreds of names on a waiting list before his application, Bush soon found himself learning, like his father, to be a pilot. After quick (some have said unusually quick) promotion to second lieutenant at the end of basic training, Bush was set for six years of National Guard commitment while taking time on the side to pursue his ambitions to rival his father in the oil business and politics.

Right after basic training, Bush took a brief leave of absence from the Guard to work as an aide on the campaign of conservative Republican Edward Gurney's successful 1968 Senate race. Gurney's strategy was to focus on a handful of simple issues that resonated with southern conservatives: strong foreign policy (meaning a greater use of American military force), tougher law enforcement, and cutting federal spending. Maintaining a streamlined message to hammer on proven conservative themes later became a hallmark of Bush's own campaigns, both in Texas and nationally.

Bush spent the next year in pilot flight training at a Georgia military base. His ease of acceptance into the otherwise rigorously screened pilot program may have raised some eyebrows, as would his being flown on a presidential plane for a date with Richard Nixon's daughter during his stint. But Bush performed competently in flight training nonetheless and returned in 1970 to the Texas National Guard, where he was switched to inactive duty with only weekend warrior duties to fulfill the remainder of his four-year commitment. He worked on his father's ill-fated Texas senatorial campaign that summer and fall, crisscrossing the state and learning the fine art of working the local voters at VFW halls and coffee klatches firsthand.

With his father defeated, the National Guard a minor commitment, and no major personal attachments (an earlier marriage engagement had faded away by mutual agreement), Bush the younger floated through the next several years uncertain as to his future. A stint in law school was considered and rejected. He got a job with a family friend in the oil business in 1971 and briefly considered a run for the Texas legislature in 1972. Instead, with his father's encouragement, he spent much of that pivotal electoral year working on the campaign of another conservative Republican Senate campaign, this time in Alabama. Again he received basic training in running a Republican politician in the Democratically solid, yet increasingly and bitterly polarizing post-Civil Rights Act south.

He entered the prestigious Harvard Business School in 1973 after getting an early discharge from his National Guard commitment (the matter of his actual separation from the military itself somewhat debated) and spending several months working (at his father's urging) for an inner city charity in Houston. While his critics deride his Harvard experience as yet another example of legacy opening doors, in fairness it should be noted that Harvard Business School has always made no bones over an admission policy that stresses an applicant's ability to expand the institution's ever-growing network of alumni at least as much as the applicant's academic record. Bush received his MBA in 1975 and headed back to Texas once again to follow his father's footsteps and try to make it big in business.

By 1978, he had established himself, with help from various friends of the Bush family, as a minor figure in the Midland oil business, hustling to match venture capital, often steered his way by his uncle, Wall Street moneyman Jonathan Bush, with oil exploration projects. He also established himself as a potential political force with an unsuccessful run for Congress in which he, like his father before, was branded by his opponent as a Yankee kid from Connecticut rather than a good ol' boy from Texas. He had also met and married in 1978 a quiet librarian named Laura Welch, the daughter of a wealthy contractor, putting his bachelor days behind him. Perhaps even as significantly, from a political perspective at least, during this time he also became friends with a rising star in the world of Republican brass knuckles politics, Karl Rove. A fellow baby boomer who shared Bush's disdain for the Sixties pop culture, east coast intellectualism, and the liberal social welfare society, the two quickly bonded. Rove would go on to be Bush's most trusted strategist, advisor, and aide, becoming one of the two most influential figures in the Bush White House, perhaps even more so than Laura herself.

Much has also been made of the young George Bush's penchant for hell raising. Bush was certainly no choir boy. He could cuss with the best of the west Texas oil boys with whom he grew up. Living the life of a single man—a military pilot and a son of wealth and power at that—he had no wanting for female companionship. His predilection for raucous, alcohol-enhanced behavior in his teens and twenties has been well remarked upon. As a candidate, he dealt with the issue of youthful indiscretions head-on.

For Bush's opponents, his early personal history only underscored his image as the spoiled frat boy gone wild—the obnoxious "big man on campus" with whom everyone had gone to school who continued his boorish behaviors long after graduation while everyone else settled down to respectable adult lives. They point out that Bush's penchant for strong drink and irresponsible behavior continued into his third decade, well past the age such antics could be dismissed as just part of the usual province of boys having fun.

For his supporters, however, Bush was the embodiment of the prodigal son himself. He was a man who by his own volition and strength of personal and moral character gave up drinking cold turkey after a hellacious hangover and later quit smoking in the same way. He was a man who, with the counsel of no less than the Reverend Billy Graham himself, abandoned the follies of youth and set himself firmly on the path of faith and family. It was not that he had experienced life on the wild side that was important; it was that he abandoned the wild side for the life of propriety. Bill Clinton's biggest sin, in this viewpoint, was not that he had sinned but, as the Monica Lewinsky scandal demonstrated, that he continued to do so in the Oval Office itself.

Over the next decade and a half, George W.'s life revolved around his father's political ambitions and his own emerging business career. The younger Bush served the role as the "loyalty monitor" in George H. W.'s failed 1980 presidential primary run, being the eyes and ears of the family, protecting his father's and his family's image in the bruising blood sport of electoral campaigning. He reprised the role in 1988 and 1992. His primary focus in the 1980s was oil, however, or more aptly put, how to make his own fortune in the oil business.

Bush's oil business activities in the 1980s have engendered a substantial amount of controversy and rebuttal. He formed his own small oil exploration company, Arbusto (Spanish for "little bush"), in 1981, changing its name to Bush Oil Exploration in 1982 in the wake of all the ribbing he got over the original name. While Bush's oil concerns were never very successful in finding oil, they were more successful in finding partners. When the company was almost broke, an associate of family friend James Baker III ponied up 250 percent of the company's value to buy a 10 percent interest. Bush later merged with a slightly larger company called Spectrum 7 and profited greatly in a stock swap when that company was absorbed by an even larger company, Harken Energy. Bush would be investigated by the SEC for possible insider trading after he dumped his Harken stock just before it crashed in 1991, but no charges of wrongdoing were ever filed.

Again, Bush's supporters and detractors see his business career very differently. To his detractors, Bush's businesses were nothing more than a series of sweetheart deals arranged by friends of the Bush family for no other reason than to curry favor with a man who was vice president and then president. As the original founder of Harken Oil pointed out, in all of these dealings it did not hurt that George W.'s last name was "Bush." Thus, Bush's oil dealings are seen in this light as so much crony capitalism—a practice of inbreeding, political favoritism, and business patronage that critics would charge continued as a pattern in Bush's life right into the White House. His supporters, especially those from Texas, dismiss such criticism as so much naïveté as to the nature of real world business where who you know has always been as important—if not more important—as what you know.

Bush's big break, both financially and politically, came from his involvement with the Texas Rangers baseball franchise. When the team went on the market in 1989, a consortium of buyers invited Bush to participate in the purchase of the team in no small part to show an active local ownership in the franchise. (He ultimately bought a 2 percent share.) Even on the field of baseball, where his father had made his mark as a college star decades earlier, the younger Bush was compelled to walk as well. Bush later sold his original $500,000 dollar investment for $15 million dollars, securing his own personal fortune. As a small minority owner, his real role in the Rangers was to put a Texan public face on a partially out-of-state ownership consortium. This he did with gusto, successfully spearheading the Ranger campaign to secure a new stadium with substantial public investment by the city of Austin. Appearing at almost every team game, working the crowds and booster clubs, putting to use the skills he had acquired three decades earlier as a cheerleader at Andover, Bush became the public face of the Rangers (so much so that most people to this day think he was the solitary owner of the franchise).

Bush was such a natural in his new role as team pitchman that for awhile those around him thought he had found his final niche in life. Indeed, for a time in the early nineties, it looked as if George W. Bush had no higher aspiration than to some day perhaps be commissioner of baseball. Then came his father's unexpected and crushing defeat in the 1992 presidential election, and suddenly his family needed a new standardbearer to avenge Poppy's and the Republican Party's dishonor. Both would be found in the person of a cheerleader from Andover made good.

By 1994, George W. was no longer seen as a Yankee kid from Connecticut; he had established himself as a true Texas personality. With public appeal, party support, and the deep pockets of friends and family to back him, he was finally ready for a triumphant political run—this time for governor. Ann Richards, the self-made Democratic incumbent Texas governor, thought she would have an easy time defeating the son of an out-of-state dynasty. Like many, she underestimated the tenaciousness of her opponent. Cuing in on his lessons from past Republican campaigns, Bush hammered away on four simple themes, honed to razor-sharp political weapons by the rhetoric of Karl Rove: get tough on crime, hold education (and educators) responsible for teaching, stop lawyers and lawsuits, and get people off welfare and to work. In a state heading toward total Republican hegemony, Richards ended up being more of a holdover from the past than a real Democratic hope for the future. That November, George W. defeated Richards by the decisive margin of 56 percent to 44 percent, thus obtaining his first elected office only six years before he would ascend to the presidency.

That same year his younger brother, Jeb, continued in the family tradition by losing his first race for the Florida governorship. George W. Bush, first-born son, had always borne the mantle of following his father. During his wild wilderness years of his twenties and thirties, he seemed, at least in part, to be fighting against this legacy even as he followed his father's path almost step for step. After his father's 1992 defeat, even with his sobriety, newly found faith, and business success, it was commonly held by observers of the Bush dynasty that the mantle of succession had passed over the eldest Bush son to the more congenial and cleaner-nosed Jeb. Pundits alluded to the same notion even on the eve of the 2000 primary race, leading some to call George W.'s candidacy "accidental." Had Jeb won his 1994 race and his brother lost, things might well have turned out differently. After George W.'s 1994 victory, however, the family mantle was firmly back on the shoulders of the first son, who used the next six years to prepare himself and the nation for his run into the national spotlight.

As governor of Texas, Bush worked closely with the Democratically-controlled state legislature. From this experience he received a reputation for bi-partisanship that, while true, is a bit overstated. First, Democrats in the Texas state house took a more socially and fiscally conservative position on the whole than he would later find with the more liberal Democratic members of Congress, making outreach and compromise between the administration and the legislature much easier in Austin than it would be in Washington. Indeed, the Republican revolution in the south that ultimately would bleed many socially conservative southern Democrats out of the Congress in the 1990s would, by Bush's arrival in 2001, leave Democrats more distilled to their liberal essence than at any point in history.

Second, in Texas state politics the office of the governor is a comparatively weak position shorn of true legislative initiative. Real power is vested constitutionally in the leaders of the legislature: the speaker of the assembly and the leader of the senate, the state's lieutenant governor, which at the time was Democrat Bob Bullock. In Texas, real power historically has rested more singularly in the person of the reigning political machine master—the Lone Star State equivalency of the first man of Rome, be it a Lyndon Johnson or a Tom Delay. In the 1990s that person was Bullock. Fortunately for Bush, Bullock was a Democratic conservative far more in line with the message that Bush was advancing than he had been with the more 1990s liberal style of Ann Richards.

Thus, with a few compromises and the powerful support of Bullock, Bush was able to move the four main items of his gubernatorial campaign through the legislature. A series of welfare reforms (or drastic reductions, as his opponents would claim) were passed, as were measures to reduce frivolous lawsuits, impose tougher criminal penalties—especially on juveniles—and return more educational control to local school boards. As the keystone of the agenda, Bush achieved passage of a major tax cut, centering on a rollback in property taxes.

The upshot of this legislative record was to give Bush as governor a record as a doer and not just a campaign promiser. Bush's tenure as governor demonstrated a much greater propensity than his father for engaging in "the vision thing." "My job is to set the goal and your job is to figure out the details of how to get there," he told his staff. To that end, using the skills that he learned dealing with oilmen who made their living as a cross between con artist and entrepreneur, learning to smell the cow pies before he stepped in them, Bush established a reputation of being able to perceive an agenda and then tenaciously stick with it to completion. This view of the man coming out of Austin would be very different from the one that would emerge in the media early in his presidency as a man largely at the mercy of his staff with no real agenda of his own. The reality seems to be that the simple campaign message on which Bush ran for governor and president, with its streamlined world view of individual responsibility and limited government, was exactly the "vision thing" he held as his mandate to pursue in office.

His detractors in Texas pointed out that many of the initiatives he began in the 1990s had price tags and fallout that did not fully manifest until after he left for D.C. halfway through his second term. Indeed, they would point out subsequent to his departure from Austin, a number of his policy "victories ended up being rolled back as the combination of the legacy of his tax cuts coupled with the collapse of the 1990's economic boom left the state billions of dollars in the red."

Bush won a crushing landslide re-election against a second-tier Democratic contender, the first Texas governor to win back-to-back terms. It was an election year that underscored the consolidating polarization of the national electorate, one in which Republicans swept Texas offices statewide just as Democrats were sweeping statewide in California. Meanwhile his brother, Jeb, came back to win the governorship of Florida with all the unforeseen consequences that victory would have on the 2000 presidential race. After the 1998 election, the real focus of the Bush camp was no longer the state house in Austin but became the White House itself.

For George W. Bush and his family, 2000 was less about what was to come and more about righting what had gone wrong—that being the 1992 defeat of Poppy by Bill Clinton, the man who had come to symbolize all that conservatives felt had gone wrong with America over the preceding generation. Ultra-conservative Republicans had felt almost to an irrational degree that Clinton's election was somehow tainted and illegitimate. There was no way that a governor of a picayune southern state with no national standing—a Jimmy Carter without the morals—could beat the certified war hero and family man, conservative George H. W. Bush. The Perot run had complicated the matter to be sure (though factoring Perot out of the race would still have resulted in a narrow Clinton victory), but the real feeling was that somehow the man who had lied to his wife about his marital infidelities had also conned the nation.

George H. W. Bush was also a victim of his own conservative wing, angered beyond measure by his reversal on his (ill-conceived) campaign pledge of "read my lips, no new taxes." The elder Bush's problems with his own party's hard-core conservatives and the emerging evangelical community that was becoming a decisive voice in the party dated back to his selection as vice president by Reagan in 1980. Had Reagan listened to the Pat Robertsons or Jerry Falwells, Bush's political career would have ended that summer. Rather than holding a grudge (as he would against numerous other individuals and groups across the years) against these party factions that had almost destroyed his father's career, George W. Bush, with the guidance of Karl Rove, embraced them and sought to be their champion. Indeed, the triumvirate of hard-core fiscal conservatives, neo-conservatives, and evangelicals together with traditional big business support and disaffected white male blue-collar workers (the legacy of Reagan Democrats) would provide the key base of support for the younger Bush's campaign. Whatever tensions might exist between these groups over matters of economic justice, foreign policy, or free trade would be papered over by a constant, overriding theme: No more Clinton.

It was much easier for the younger Bush to more fully and convincingly embrace the Republican right than it had been for his father. Despite his years in Texas, the elder Bush was still affected by the east coast aristocracy's sense of noblesse oblige, which made them more open to ideas of government welfare and social programs. This Rockefeller tendency tainted the elder Bush in the eyes of the new emerging conservative southern Republicans and northern neo-cons, hence their effort to scuttle his vice-presidential nomination.

For the younger Bush, embracing the rhetoric of the right was not a transformation but, rather, an affirmation. Bush was the moral right, embodying the "3 P's" of conservative values instilled by his Texan upbringing: personal reliance, piety, and profit. More of a modern day Calvinist than the Presbyterian as he was raised, to Bush, the viewpoint that those divinely chosen through faith would manifest their faith through success in business and society that underscored evangelical political thought was as much a matter of personal faith as public policy debate.

Going into the 2000 election, there were no assurances that a popular but relatively inexperienced (having served but one and a half terms) governor of Texas would march to avenging victory in November 2000 (or December 2000, for those who prefer to be technically accurate.)

Neither could anyone foretell just how close and convoluted the election outcome would ultimately become.

The Democrats had every reason for optimism. The economy was booming, the nation was at peace, and their party's incumbent president was leaving office with one of the highest exiting approval ratings in history—this despite eight years of conservative attacks, three allegations of infidelity, and one failed impeachment attempt. The Republican's single greatest hope was that, after eight years of the soap opera that was the Clinton administration, the nation might feel enough Clinton fatigue to be willing to give the Republicans a chance.

Still, going into 1999 there was a strong sense of inevitability to the Bush 2000 Republican nomination drive. By the 1998-midterm elections, the media and national Republican leaders were already anointing the popular young governor as the coming savior of the GOP.

Bush entered the election year with over $70 million, the largest political war chest ever amassed, dwarfing the $25 million that Phil Gramm of Texas had been lauded for amassing by the start of the 1996 primary season. This largess was a testament to the fund-raising network Bush had inherited from his father's political machine, family name recognition, and the grim determination of Republican power brokers to mount a presidential campaign that would defeat the Clintonites at any cost.

Central to this goal was the perception of Republican establishment leaders that the party must quickly select a nominee in the primaries before the nominee was too bruised, bloodied, and broke from fighting off Republican rivals. Thus, long before the first caucus was held in Iowa, Bush had already secured the endorsement of the Republican governors and the majority of Republican senators, and he was the unofficial favorite of the national party leadership. In part, this locking of arms around George Bush by a party desperate for victory helps explain the almost savage assault launched on Senator John McCain by the party establishment, questioning everything from the senator's sex life to the former Viet Nam prisoner of war's commitment to national security when his unexpected good showing in the Iowa caucuses and New Hampshire primary threatened to derail the Bush juggernaut.

Core to the Bush campaign was a triumvirate of trusted political operatives: Karl Rove as his chief strategist with whom he shared a twenty-year history; Karen Hughes, his message-shaping communications director; and Joseph Allbaugh, his 1994 campaign manager and chief of staff. Of the three, Rove and Hughes would follow Bush into the Oval

Office, though Rove (sometimes referred to both cynically and admirably as "Bush's Brain") would have the longest staying power of all. Heir to the take-no-prisoner's politics of Bush's father's political svengali, Lee Atwater, Rove was renowned—and disliked by opponents—for his ability to orchestrate effective negative campaigns to discredit electoral rivals. He had not received the affectionately bestowed nickname of "Turd Blossom" from George W. Bush for nothing. Rove's detractors pointed out the constant tendency of the mud and dirt to fly in any campaign with which he was involved, with his opponents always facing unforeseen and devastating personal attacks never directly attributable to his candidate's campaign. As one participant observed, "You always see the fire and Karl Rove standing there with matches, but you can never connect the two."

The vicissitudes of the elder Bush's political fortunes—the feeling of betrayal by those who should have supported "Poppy" in his failed Senate races and failed 1980 and 1992 presidential runs—had taught the younger George that loyalty was the premier virtue in a man. To be a "good man" was to stand by those who believed in you and trusted you, and those were the people you took care of first. Thus, one of the great strengths of the Bush campaign was consistency. The Gore campaign experienced changes in both staff (including the campaign manager) and message with Gore veering from being a reformist to a populist to a centrist. The upshot was to leave a public impression of Gore as a man who put political expediency (i.e., winning) ahead of everything else. Bush's constant hammering on a cadre of core issues, even when he did not do it well, gave an image of consistency that contrasted positively with Gore's rhetorical waffling. Maintaining his inner circle for the duration of the campaign strongly reinforced this theme.

Going into the actual primary season, a field of six real Republican candidates quickly turned into a three-way contest in which favorite Bush was being attacked simultaneously from the right of his party by conservative billionaire publisher Steve "Flat Tax" Forbes with his sustained appeal to fiscal and social conservatives and on the left side by Arizona Senator John McCain's appeal to centrists and independents with his theme of political campaign finance reform and, more importantly, an image of integrity of which the outgoing administration seemed in short supply. Early on, Bush's biggest stumbling block was his own performance as a candidate, marred by massive multiple malapropisms of sufficient quantity to justify the creation of a website and the publication of a book to keep track of them. Moreover, a laid-back style on the campaign trail that seemed almost detached to the press covering him gave the impression that he was a young Ronald Reagan—"Hard work never killed anyone, but why take the chance"—in the making. This they dutifully (some would say gleefully) passed on to the public painting, as the 2000 season began in earnest, a portrait of an inexperienced, bumbling, and perhaps less than brilliant rich man's son who was running more because he felt he ought to than because he wanted or deserved to win. Bush's lackluster performance in the last of the pre-primary debates gave further fuel to Forbes and McCain.

The front-loaded 2000 primary process made the Republican race as short and rambunctious as a carnival roller coaster ride. Bush successfully dealt with the Forbes' threat by moving securely to the right, playing directly to evangelicals and social conservatives, and brandishing his Texas credentials as a fiscal conservative. McCain, unexpectedly beating Bush 49 percent to 31 percent in New Hampshire, however, (with Forbes placing a distant third) left pundits wondering if Bush was another in a long line of well-funded candidates left to crash and burn in the New England snow. McCain's victory, however, was built strongly on his appeal to independent voters allowed to vote in the Republican primary, which skewed the outcome farther to the center than would be the case in subsequent closed primaries down the line.

By the South Carolina primary two weeks later, Bush had solidified his appeal to the conservative wing of the party, while McCain was put under sustained attack by Bush boosters for being anti-evangelical (this following a tremendous backlash to McCain's own attacks on the disproportionate power of the Christian right in Republican politics) and soft on foreign policy threats (despite McCain's war record and POW status), as well as an onslaught of attacks on McCain's character. The result was a comfortable 53 percent to 42 percent Bush victory in Dixie. While McCain would limp through to win a few more primaries in the Great Lakes and the West, Bush crushed him in southern primaries, the cradle of Reagan conservatism, giving Bush the nomination before the ides of March. Bush emerged from the primaries far more the master of his party than his rival, Al Gore, would be of his own. Indeed, Bush would eventually exert greater control over the Republican Party machine than his father or any modern Republican president, rivaling that exerted by Bill Clinton and the great master of party politics, Lyndon Johnson himself.

From the primary and general campaigns, three basic emerging tendencies of what would be the Bush presidency can be discerned.

First, the campaign demonstrated Bush's ability to grow into a role. While never reaching the oratorical eloquence of a Washington, a Kennedy, or even a Clinton, by fall 2000 Bush had established his ability to give a decent speech and to handle a debate. Second, the campaign demonstrated the general tendency of Bush's opponents to underestimate his political savvy based on a false reading of his intellectual abilities. A "C" student no doubt, Bush never distinguished himself through the written or even, usually, the spoken word. His detractors took his various verbal stumbles and language mangling to be a sign of a generally weak analytical mind, which they then translated into a generally weak political mind. While Bush may have paid less than full attention to his classes at Andover and Yale, he at least remembered his Machiavelli—the good prince always surrounds himself with wise advisors whose own ambition levels are lower than his. Bush's core cadre of advisors spearheaded by the very Machiavellian Rove would follow him into the White House, providing continuity as campaign promises were translated into policy. Finally, during the campaign Bush demonstrated a focused—detractors would say narrow-minded—tenacity at staying on message and pursuing the established goals that would be the hallmark of his administration. While Al Gore had a tendency to think big and wander bigger in his campaign speeches, Bush maintained his basic trilogy of tax cuts, education reform, and social responsibility throughout the campaign and into his presidential agenda.

The famous dictum of Richard Nixon to candidate Bob Dole was "zig to the right in the primaries and zag back to the center for the general election." This is the simple strategy that successful candidates of both parties have employed since World War II to secure their party's nomination and the White House. Having secured his credentials as the champion of the social conservative wing of the party and defeated his challenger from the center, Bush went into the general election free to cast himself as a sensible centrist under the label of the "compassionate conservative." Where his father had unsuccessfully used the phrase to characterize his relatively unfocused domestic agenda, Bush the younger could point to his policy successes in Texas, paring down the welfare roles while bolstering education (at least in theory, if not in test scores and actual monies spent). He could present himself as accepting of the general ideas of the welfare state but demanding far greater accountability from both the government who provided services and the people who received them. This message would resonate strongly with both social and fiscal conservatives, as well as with the broad, tax-paying middle class. In post-Reagan America, the center of political gravity had shifted closer to the right than to the left, making it far easier for Bush to reach out to the center as a "moderate" without alienating his conservative base.

Bush's Democratic rival was not nearly as lucky. After surviving a surprisingly strong challenge from a former basketball-playing New Jersey Senator Bill Bradley, Gore's attempt to claw his way to the center was diverted by the Green Party candidacy of Ralph Nader who appealed to the most liberal Democrats. As a result, the Gore campaign struggled all through the summer and fall to develop a formula that could capture both ultra-liberals and moderates. Moreover, Gore's tendency at times to exaggerate his accomplishments became a focus of media (and his rival's) attention that developed into a public perception of untruthfulness—the precise personal failure that undermined the Clinton presidency. Ultimately, Gore was dogged by the legacy of all vice presidents with aspirations. To truly win over voters in their own right, vice presidents must walk a delicate, and often impossible, line between distancing themselves from their predecessor enough to seem new and original without repudiating the predecessor's legacy and, in so doing, alienating the key partisan base of support. In 1988, George H. W. Bush had largely run on a platform of: "Okay, you'd really rather have Reagan, but because of the Twenty-second Amendment I'm the next best thing," which worked because the economy remained strong and his opponent was fairly weak. Gore had none of these luxuries. By the summer of 2000, the economy was clearly slowing down, heading towards the following year's "Dot.com" collapse. While Clinton himself had high job approval ratings, "Clinton fatigue" and a desire for change was clearly reflected in the polls. Where Gore did attempt to distance himself from the Clinton legacy, as in his criticizing the Clinton administration's handling of the case of Ellian Gonzalez, the Cuban boy who became the subject of a legal immigration and custody battle between relatives in Florida and his father in Cuba, he appeared to be pandering for voters rather than taking principled stands.

Even despite these handicaps, Gore ran a close race through the summer and fall with polls showing him close to, and at times exceeding, Bush's popularity. Bush had his own pratfalls on the campaign stump that tended to reinforce the view that he was not necessarily the brightest bulb on the presidential marquee. The three debates between the candidates—marked more than anything, in hindsight, by their almost complete lack of discussion of foreign policy—are generally conceded to have done more for Bush than Gore. They also underlined the basic choice facing the electorate both personally and ideologically. On the personal side, the election became a choice between voting for the smart guy with the honesty problem or voting for the honest average Joe. On the ideological side, the two candidates came to personify the essential schism between the parties and the nation as a whole: the conservative view of society as a collection of individuals pursuing their own goals in which government should serve the limited role of occasional referee, and the liberal view of society as a community of individuals pursuing collective goods in which government serves the role of social advocate. This distinction in worldview, which had grown steadily since the Reagan years and the collapse of the New Deal coalition, divided the nation down the middle. Going into the November election, polls showed the race as converging towards a dead heat.

Little did anyone know.

Much has been written and, undoubtedly, much remains to be written from the standpoint of history of the electoral debacle of 2000. As with almost all aspects of the Bush presidency, it is almost impossible to separate analysis from partisanship. The failure of the electoral college to be able to decide the Bush v. Gore election due to, for all practical and statistical purposes, the dead heat in Florida produced the potential for a constitutional crisis such as the Republic had not endured since the days of Reconstruction. Indeed, the allegations on both partisan sides of duplicity, corruption, conspiracy, and illegitimacy on the part of each other are the stuff that leads to riots and even putsches in less stable political systems. As it was, the election heightened already intense partisan animosity, provoked an unprecedented political intervention by the United States Supreme Court, and produced the first minority president in modern American history. Yet, when the political dust settled and the swearing in of a new president occurred right on schedule in January 2001, a surprising degree of normalcy had returned to the American body politic.

The simple facts are these: when all the dust settled, Al Gore had won the popular vote by a plurality of less than 500,000 votes (or less than one half of 1 percent of total ballots cast). George Bush, however, won the electoral vote by 271 to 268, making him the first minority president since the nineteenth century. The election results underscored the almost perfect division of the electorate. A swing of a few thousand votes in four states (and less than three hundred in Florida and New Mexico) would have shifted the winner. Of course, barely half of the potential electorate, once again, turned out to vote, underscoring the fact that in the United States the largest electoral block is "nonvoter."

The Bush-Gore vote was particularly divided by region. The 2000 election stands out as one of the few in history that could have been discerned from outer space. Looking down on the United States from orbit at night, any part of the country that glowed in the dark voted Gore; the dark areas voted Bush. Gore commanded the coastal and interior urban centers of the country; Bush took the suburbs, countryside, and wilderness. The election underscored the growing cultural divide America had experienced since the 1960s: the urban, multi-ethnic, secular-valued "Blue States" of America that vote Democrat and the rural, white, religious "Red States" of America that vote Republican. The presidential split of the electorate carried over into the congressional and state races. The Senate was split 50-50 between the parties for the first time since the nineteenth century; moreover, Republicans enjoyed only a slim 9-vote lead in the House. State legislatures were also evenly split, with both Republicans and Democrats controlling seventeen state houses with the remaining fairly evenly divided. Republicans only maintained a clear majority in state executive mansions, which they dominated by a 3:2 margin. The sharpness of the electoral divide meant that whoever won in 2000 would face a substantial opposition not particularly disposed either political or ideologically to compromise. Of course, figuring out whom that would be took a little more time than usual.

The entire electoral brouhaha was bathed in confusion from the outset. On election night the broadcast networks first called the race in Florida for Gore based on apparently erroneous exit polls. When later actual vote tallies showed Bush ahead, the networks reversed themselves and called Bush the winner in Florida and then projected him as winner of the presidency. Gore called Bush to concede, only to have to call back shortly later to withdraw his concession when the networks again reversed themselves and called Florida too close to call, which it would remain for the next month. Gore's famous retort to Bush's less than delighted response to his retraction, "Well you don't have to get snippy about it," pretty much summarized the icy state of relations between both camps and their national supporters while the state of Florida tried to sort out the electoral confusion. The closeness of the outcome—initially Bush won the state by less than 300 votes—resulted in a legally-mandated recount that was made as muddy as Florida swamp by charges that confusion over the types of ballots used in some Florida counties resulted in a massive undercount for Gore. These claims were closely followed by allegations of intimidation of Gore voters, especially minorities, at various polling places, suppression of pro-Bush overseas absentee ballots, and general accusations of partisan and fraternal collusion in a state dominated by Republicans, including Governor Jeb Bush. In the end, the matter hinged on which ballots in which counties would be subjected to a detailed and time-consuming hand recount.

The matter also became a political battle over separation of powers between the Florida executive and judicial branches, with the state supreme court overruling the Republican Secretary of State's decision to certify Bush the winner prior to a full hand recount of ballots and a states' rights battle between the Florida supreme court and the United States Supreme Court. The United States Supreme Court intervened twice in the crisis, first warning the Florida state supreme court to reconsider its actions in ordering the recount (itself a highly unusual intervention of the high court in state legal proceedings), and then when the state supreme court reiterated its decision to uphold a recount, the nation's highest court reversed the state court, ordering effectively that the count be certified as was, with Bush the winner.

The grounds for the Supreme Court's decision in *Bush v. Gore* have been subjected to intense scrutiny and debate. While there is no real consensus between partisan sides as to the rightness of the decision, there is general consensus that the decision was, at best, unusual. Essentially, the Rehnquist Court, in a 5/4 split decision, argued that the Florida supreme court had erred in forcing the recount because, in so doing, it had usurped the constitutional role of the state legislature in managing the process by which presidential electors are selected and, more importantly, by ordering a recount in only certain counties had violated the Fourteenth Amendment provision for equal protection.

The decision was seen by detractors as a highly partisan one and, hence, an unjustified political usurpation of power by a narrow majority of five conservative Republican appointees to the bench. Critics pointed out that the Rehnquist Court consistently established itself as no friend of the Fourteenth Amendment in circumscribing state actions and, indeed, had been the most pro-Tenth Amendment Court in at least eighty years. Couple that with a web of personal connections between members of the majority to members of the Bush camp, including family members working on the Bush campaign (and later to hold positions in the Bush administration), and one has more than enough fodder for a conspiracy theorist to argue that Bush "stole" the election with the help of the Supreme Court. One should, however, never rush to assume conspiracy when simple incompetency suffices as an explanation. The extraordinary nature of the case and the extremely tight time-frame to consider the matter, with the eyes of the world riveted upon them, was never a recipe for calm judicial deliberation. In short, haste makes judicial waste. In *Bush v. Gore,* the Supreme Court became like the old *Starship Enterprise,* boldly going where no court had gone before. Unfortunately, it plowed into an asteroid, creating new precedent on far from clear legal grounds to achieve more of a political than juridical end. Be that as it may, the result was to force an ending of the Florida recount with Bush in the lead, ensuring him of the state's electoral vote and, ultimately, the presidency.

For all the drama, handwringing, and Cassandra warnings of the long-term impact the electoral impasse and its unorthodox resolution would have on American politics for years to come, the crisis seemed to fade away as unexpectedly as it began. The warnings of political scientists for decades that the electoral college was an electoral disaster waiting to happen, especially with the rise of viable third-party campaigns in the 1990s, was finally validated. Yet, especially because the sky ultimately did not fall in and the matter had been resolved within the framework of the rule of law, there has been little real constitutional fall out from the debacle. Arguments to can the electoral college that flooded the pages of the country's newspapers and echoed around Congress quickly faded away after Bush's inauguration. The rejection in 2003 by the Ninth Circuit Court of Appeals of arguments to delay voting in the California recall campaign based on the *Bush v. Gore* decision seems to have laid to rest legal speculation that the Florida decision would have long-lasting and far-reaching consequences as well.

Moreover, claims that Bush would be fatally weakened as president because of the lack of legitimacy stemming from the circumstances of his victory also faded away as Bush took the oath of office and saw his popularity experience the usual post-inaugural bounce. This occurred in part due to the graciousness of Democrats—despite early complaints of Gore's acting in a somewhat unsporting manner by continuing his challenges to the Florida count—in ultimately accepting the court-mandated outcome and moving on. The fact that, in all subsequent recounts by media organizations, George Bush consistently emerged by at least several hundred votes as the winner in Florida (though an infinitesimally small fraction of a percent of the overall ballots cast) also helped to alleviate claims of illegitimacy. To be sure, like Clinton before him, Bush would see his lack of a major electoral mandate hamper his ability to advance his legislative agenda early on. The Congress respected him but during the spring of 2001, seemed by no means in awe of him. But the often-predicted fear of a presidential meltdown due to a blurred electoral college victory did not occur—this time.

Two problems dog any contemporary assessment of George W. Bush. The first is, of course, the absence of the vantage point of time by which to assess the long-term results of a presidency, which the very immediate nature of the Bush presidency denies the observer. Given how much of the Bush presidency—from funding massive tax cuts to providing prescription drug care for seniors to fighting terrorism—have been pushed, in Washington parlance, into the out-years five or ten years down the line, the real impacts of the Bush legacy may take a decade or more to fully appreciate.

Beyond this temporal limitation is the nature of the man himself. George W. Bush, even more than his predecessor, Bill Clinton, has become a national Rorschach test not just for political policies and partisan politics but for the state of American culture and society itself. Where controversy for Clinton peaked over matters of moral character and personal action, for Bush, however, the debate, both pro and con, has been one driven by culture and ideology. He became president in a country more politically and culturally polarized than at any point since before the Great Depression, a country in which gay marriage could be tested on the nation's coasts while the existence of homosexuality itself is still scarcely mentioned in the heartland. George W. Bush has emerged as the most partisan divisive figure in modern American politics. Republicans overwhelming support their president. To them, he is a good man, a moral man, and a strong and determined leader, honest in his intentions, and righteous in his goals. Democrats overwhelmingly dislike the man, both personally and in terms of his policies. To them, he is an empty flight suit strutting on an aircraft carrier and an empty mind into which powerful people and interests pour their thoughts and self-interested aspirations. There is little middle ground. As such, any assessments of George W. Bush, positive or negative, will resound with about half the population and be condemned by the other half. Thus, we turn to an assessment of George W. Bush at the midpoint of his presidency.

The George W. Bush Presidency: A Positive Assessment

There have been to date two distinct phases of the Bush presidency or, better said, two different Bush presidencies to consider. First, there was the post-inaugural presidency lasting through the honeymoon and first hundred days into the early fall of 2001. This was a presidency at peace, though experiencing an inherited weak economy that remained sluggish, a presidency stumbling, at times flailing, but progressing towards a semblance of an agenda. Then there was the post-9/11 presidency, a presidency at war, a presidency increasingly distracted from its domestic agenda to focus instead on a new, global struggle against radical Islamic fundamentalism and to protect the homeland from further assault. An assessment of the Bush presidency must be cognitive of and distinguish between these two very different periods.

Pre-9/11

Probably the biggest single success of Bush's early months in office was the closing of the public book on Florida. Bush maintained surprisingly solid public approval ratings given the unconventional manner of his election: in the mid- to upper 50 percent level across his first months in office. While not extraordinarily high compared to twentieth century presidents in general, they were levels about which his immediate predecessor could have only dreamt during his own first six months in office. They also demonstrated that the American public was willing to put any questions as to Bush's electoral legitimacy aside and allow the new president to get on with the business of governing. From the bonhomie of the inauguration through his early policy tussles with Congress, any lingering images of an illegitimate president quickly faded from public debate. Moreover, George W. Bush inherited a presidency that had been wounded by the personal foibles of his predecessor, culminating in the ill-fated impeachment effort. Despite Clinton's high job approval ratings, his legacy of scandal and public distrust left as large a blot on the prestige and public trust of the institution of the presidency as his departing staff left on the walls and office furniture of the West Wing. Like Jimmy Carter before him, Bush's down-to-earth manner and image of trustworthiness, coupled with an image as a solid and religiously devoted family man, helped to restore a degree of public trust in his office.

Which previous presidency a new administration most seeks to emulate is often signaled by whose portrait the new president decrees be hung in the Cabinet Room. For Ronald Reagan, that figure had been (to the collective hoots and howls of media pundits) "Silent Cal" Coolidge, the man who quietly presided over much of a decade of Republican hegemony and national prosperity, which in the next Republican administration would collapse into depression, though Reagan obviously did not intend to take the simile that far. For Bill Clinton, it was fellow Southerner "Andy" Jackson, the rough and status quo shaking Westerner who rode into Washington to usher in political revolution. That the Clinton administration would resemble Jackson's more in its propensity for scandal than for radical reform was a comparison Clinton also probably did not consider at the outset.

For George W. Bush, the presidential metaphor was to be Dwight David Eisenhower, both whose portrait and bust Bush had displayed. Bush admired the fellow Texan for his calm demeanor and for presiding over an administration of peace (at least in terms of no hot shooting wars) and prosperity—the calm before the political, social, and economic storms of the next two decades, which, at least in part, Bush saw himself reversing. While Bush and Ike shared a tendency to consistently mispronounce the word "nuclear" (as in "nu-ku-lar"), their administrations would prove to actually have few things in common. Eisenhower's administration, self-described as "liberal on human issues, conservative on economic ones," would preside over a large expansion of the social security and the social welfare systems, while at the same time leaving intact an income tax system with the highest marginal rates in peacetime history. Bush would seek to whack away at the edges of social security with the long-term goal of at least partially privatizing the program and would champion substantial tax cuts for upper income households. Eisenhower, the man who made his reputation as Supreme Allied Commander during World War II by being able to deal often with recalcitrant and sometimes downright obstinate allies, would pursue a foreign policy stressing multilateralism, alliances, and international engagement. George W. Bush would pursue a foreign policy haunted more by the ghost of Robert Taft and Republican isolationism and unilateralism than Eisenhower's comparatively Wilsonian internationalism. Thus, Bush would prove to be at the other end of the continuum of postwar Republican politics from Eisenhower, far more the Goldwater and Reagan man than his father, who would have fit in quite nicely in temperament and ideology with an Eisenhower administration.

A central goal of the Bush administration was to be the "un-Clinton" White House. In this, with a staff overwhelmingly populated by straitlaced, Bible-studying (literally—while staffers were not required to attend weekly Bible study sessions, to not do so was to be in a definite minority), dark-suited, white-shirted, and solid color tie-wearing Republicans who would have looked equally at ease working at a corporate headquarters or attending Sunday services as working in the West Wing. No more hordes of Clinton's undisciplined interns and aides—both usually so young as to blur together in appearance—spreading plates of pizza over the antiques in the Roosevelt room during all-night bull sessions. No more Jerry Garcia ties, jeans, and t-shirts. The Bush White House would resemble the Bush campaign—a staid and stable nine to five operation where voices were calm and directives focused. The tradeoff would be a White House in which ideas that challenged the accepted worldview of the president would seldom be fully vetted. As former Bush speechwriter David Frum pointed out:

> If you looked around the Bush cabinet table, for example, you saw a number of very able, solid, and reliable people—but only one, Donald Rumsfeld, who could truly be said to really sparkle. And if you looked more narrowly at the White House staff, there was again a dearth of really high-powered brains. One seldom heard an unexpected thought in the Bush White House or met someone who possessed unusual knowledge.

Where the Clinton White House perpetually suffered from idea overload and second-guessed itself politically to death on numerous policy issues, from health care to North Korean nukes, the Bush's leadership style was to throw out explicit policy directives building directly on the trinity of issues he took office planning to implement: cutting taxes, reigning in the power of the federal government, and retrenching American interests abroad. The big question for the staff would not be "should we" but "how will we." Such rigid adherence to principles can be seen as a hallmark of leadership. Thus, Bush's tenacious campaign for his tax cut plan, even in the face of originally weak public and political support, can be seen as a testament to his willingness to pursue an issue even in the face of negative odds. Such tendencies can also be seen as leading towards policy myopia and tunnel vision in which policies are pursued even after objective fact begins to undermine the rationality of the position. The reported tendency of Bush to surround himself with a staff largely cut from his own stylistic mold who then work to screen the president from countervailing opinion and fact—the "group think" process that Irving Janis warned is a constant danger in presidencies—becomes particularly problematic under such circumstances. Such may be history's eventual judgment on the Bush administration's claim of Iraqi weapons of mass destruction.

Religion would also play a larger role—both subtly in the temperament of the administration and overtly in various policy initiatives—in the Bush White House than in any other of recent memory. All presidents tend to remember Machiavelli's admonition to act virtuous in public even if they were not so virtuous in private: Nixon swore like a longshoreman throughout the week but was the practicing Quaker on the Sabbath; Reagan, while never belonging to a fixed congregation nor attending services regularly, knew enough to be sure that when he did the cameras were rolling. And Bill Clinton could preach up a storm in front of a Baptist congregation even while engaging in personal behaviors that would make any good Baptist blush. George W. Bush's father, meanwhile, stuck with a quieter New Englander's genteel form of religion, sprinkling the odd religious references here and there into his speeches but never wearing them particularly on his sleeve. For George W. Bush, religion would not simply be a spice used to enhance the flavor of his message. It would be a principle ingredient in the entrée itself, providing self-evident justifications for policies ranging from education and health care to foreign policy. For Bush, educational reform, tax cuts, and the entirety of the administration's post-9/11 foreign policy would be justified not simply in utilitarian terms but in absolute imperative moral ones.

Bush went into his first year in office intent on focusing on his core three issues: tax cuts, education reform, and advancing his faith-based initiative to provide federal funding to charitable religious groups (the latter killing two birds—welfare reform and advancing a "moral" agenda—with one policy stone). He would see his goals largely derailed by summer by a host of secondary issues: flack over the energy plan advanced by his vice president, the loss of Republican control of the Senate due to an unprecedented defection and growing ideological sniping that the president's much-vaunted campaign promise to be a "uniter" was being undercut by his partisan agenda, especially in foreign policy. Along the way he would earn low marks from the press and public for environmental policy and for creating an image of government unduly controlled by business and religious interests. Yet, Bush managed to deliver on his first goal and made progress, tentative though it may have been, towards achieving the second and third, which again amounted to a more successful record than his two immediate predecessors.

Bush had a simple economic agenda made possible by the projected record budget surplus: take some of the surplus to fund campaign promises for education, some to reinvest in defense, some to repay debt and the rest (the most) for tax cuts. The centerpiece of the Bush agenda was a proposed $1.6 trillion dollar, ten-year tax reduction program. Bush had floated the tax cut idea on the 1999 campaign stump, when the federal government, flush with Dot.com capital gains revenues and benefiting from falling interest rates, projected an unprecedented sea of black ink rising into the foreseeable future. Indeed, by February 2001, the administration projected that the five trillion dollar aggregate federal debt might be paid down in full within the decade. Such projections led no less a fiscally prudent figure than Chairman of the Federal Reserve Alan Greenspan himself to warn in the spring of 2001 that too rapid a drawing down of the national debt might itself present difficulties. Once the federal debt was gone, he observed, the Federal Reserve would no longer be able to intervene in the economy through open market operations—the floating of federal securities (debt)—that would effectively deprive the government of the principle tool of monetary policy. The chairman need not have worried. Within a year of Bush's taking office, for reasons both in and out of his control, the projected surplus turned into massive deficits projected beyond the decade.

The tax-cutting agenda was in part in keeping with the general ideological goal of the administration to get government "back in the box" from whence Clinton had let it loose. Bush moved particularly quickly to set aside, within days of his inauguration, a number of new environmental rules that had been signed by Clinton in his final month in office, particularly a set of rules concerning wilderness designation to tens of thousands of acres of western lands, which would have inhibited or directly prohibited future economic development in said areas. Bush followed up on these executive actions by placing an administrative freeze, as Ronald Reagan had two decades before, on all new federal regulations pending review by his own staffers in the Office of Management and Budget. Thus, in his first months in office, Bush would successfully limit two aspects of the "big government" to which he was ideologically opposed: depriving it of revenues through his tax cut and depriving it of regulatory muscle.

His other domestic initiatives faired generally less well than his tax cut and regulatory reforms, both in terms of passage and public approval.

Three days into office Bush floated what would be known as his "No Child Left Behind Act," which sought to guarantee a national standard of education across all communities through the use of standardized testing and greater institutional accountability. The carrot in the plan was to be the possibility of increased (though unspecified) funding for improving and high-performing schools. The stick was the threat of loss of funding for under-performing schools and the possibility of introducing a voucher system to allow parents to transfer students out of those institutions. Extreme hostility by Democrats to the idea of vouchers and the general Republican dislike of anything that smacked of national interference in what they saw as matters of local control caused the Bush reforms to languish for most of the year, though just getting the matter on the table helped to address another major campaign plank.

The Bush administration proved to be surprisingly more decisive in foreign policy than in domestic policy, surprising because of the limited attention paid to foreign policy during the campaign. Nowhere can the distinction between George W. Bush and Bill Clinton be seen than in their unilateralist vs. multilateralist views and policies vis-à-vis the world at large. And nowhere was Bush more successful in transforming government policy than in the foreign arena.

The core of the Clinton-Bush difference was between a Bush conception of "American Exceptionalism," which provided the U.S. with a global manifest destiny to do what it believed right, and the Clinton view of America as a leader within a community of nations where all actions must be consensual. Bush entered office from the campaign committed to pursuing a "humble" foreign policy. Bush then, however, took the self-sufficient go-it-alone ethos of west Texas oil lands and translated it into a more unilateralist and autarchic, if not hegemonic, outlook than possibly anyone had since Alexander Hamilton dreamt of an American empire stretching the length and breadth of the hemisphere. In this outlook of America and its role in the world, Bush differed markedly with the internationalist tradition of his own party that descended from Eisenhower through Nixon and on to Nixon's protégé, George H. W. Bush. Indeed, the Bush foreign policy would eventually become even more unilateralist than that of the great postwar American Firster, Ronald Reagan.

Bush's appointments of former Chief of Staff Colin Powell, author of a doctrine bearing his name that argued for extreme caution in American foreign policy interventions, as Secretary of State was seen as a sign that the administration would be likely to continue the multilateral engagement strategy of the Bush I and Clinton administrations. The attitude of "realpolitik," fitting for an alumnus of the Nixon-Kissinger foreign policy establishment and projected by Secretary of Defense Donald Rumsfeld, gave additional credence to the administration's announced preference for a restrained foreign policy.

Early on, however, a division was apparent in the administration between the Powell "multilateralist" camp and a progressively more influential unilateralist neo-conservative cabal headed by Vice President Cheney and including, amongst others, Condoleezza Rice, Under Secretary of Defense Paul Wolfowitz (who held the same post under Dick Cheney during the Bush I administration), and Richard Perle, chairman of the Defense Policy Board. While this division predominantly manifested itself in rhetoric and debate between the two camps—some public, some private—after 9/11 the division would have profound consequences for U.S. foreign policy.

For neo-conservatives like Cheney and Wolfowitz, the collapse of the Soviet Union in the early 1990s presented the United States with a unique opportunity—and a narrow time window in which to act—to use its position as the world's sole superpower to reshape the global environment into one supportive of American security interests before rival powers or general chaos emerged to frustrate such an attempt. The broader and more enlightened long-term goals of such unprecedented application of American power would be the developing of a stable international system premised on global democracy and free markets underwritten, as necessary, by American benevolent hegemony. Accomplishing these world-shaping goals would require the U.S. to commit to maintaining absolute military supremacy and to be willing, as necessary, to engage in unilateral exercises of power unfettered by previous multilateral commitments. Such exercises of power would include pre-emptive applications of force against perceived threats before said threats could undermine America's dominant global position. The neo-conservatives argued that such applications of American power were justified by the doctrine of "American Exceptionalism" itself. The self-evident rightness of American values provided a prior legitimation of the strategies taken to defend and spread them.

This new strategy for "Pax Americana" was presented by Cheney, Wolfowitz, and other neo-cons in the early 1990s but failed to gain serious policy traction within the Bush I administration or serious academic legitimacy outside of it. For George W. Bush, however, the moral absolutism and clarity of purpose presented by the neo-con vision was far preferable and morally superior to the blurred world of multilateral engagement obfuscated by ever-grayer shades of moral pale. In contrasting the world in stark, simple terms of right and wrong—a world of good, freedom-loving peoples and freedo-hating evil-doers—Bush's foreign policy temperament would be far closer to Ronald Reagan's than that of Eisenhower. Indeed, Bush would emerge in the view of neo-cons as superior to either Reagan or his father because of his willingness not only to talk the American Exceptionalist talk but also to walk the unilateralist walk. While placing a few multilateralists in his administration, the offices closest to his own would belong to the neo-cons. While opponents of his actions tended to portray the new president as having been captured by the neo-cons, those within the administration willing to talk about such things (and the Bush administration has been much more tight-lipped about its inner workings than most previous administrations) have painted a picture of a much more engaged and decisive president than his detractors allow. Bush was willing to hear the Powell side on issues, but the decision to favor the neo-con faction within his administration came from the president himself.

Bush decisively redrew American foreign policy during his first six months in a more decisive break with the previous administration than even that between Reagan and Carter. On his first day in office, Bush reversed a Clinton policy by issuing a global gag rule that banned U.S. aid to programs that mentioned abortion or family planning. While detractors saw the decision removing millions of dollars in American support from health programs in developing nations across the globe as a clear sop to his political base on the religious right, his supporters saw it as the reassertion of a moral center to American policy.

In March, Bush stunned international opinion by pulling out of the Kyoto greenhouse gas reduction protocols that the Clinton administration had been central in creating. The accord, which would have required substantial reductions of emissions by the United States at great economic cost, had no chance of passing the U.S. Senate even before Bush took office. Clinton, however, had been willing to play the polite game of international diplomacy of continuing the convenient fiction of U.S. support for Kyoto. To the Bush administration, this was so much hypocrisy. If the U.S. would never pass the treaty, why give lip service to it? Once again, detractors of the president pointed out that in global diplomacy, appearances truly are reality. Withdrawal from a treaty process, especially when it has no current real cost to the participant, becomes a sign of international bad faith that sours negotiations and processes not even remotely connected to the original matter. Yet that, in point of fact, was precisely the reasoning behind the withdrawal. While continuation in Kyoto had no immediate cost, for the Bush administration doing so had two risks. First, it would keep the U.S. in a process that would require it to discuss making national sacrifices for a future global good, something the Bush administration ideologically felt was contrary to both American interests and its own national responsibilities. Second, it would perpetuate the post-cold war doctrine begun by George H. W. Bush and accelerated by Clinton of tying the United States' hands to act with cords of multilateral compliance. Cancellation of Kyoto amounted to a straight-out declaration of independence by the Bush administration from multilateral constraints. The United States would henceforth be Gulliver unleashed from the internationalist Lilliputians, an American Prometheus unbound.

The Bush administration resisted new multilateral commitments, continuing American refusal to join a global land mine ban (over continuing concerns regarding American security with North Korea in the demilitarized zone), halting the Clinton-initiated dialogue with North Korea, withdrawing from an active role in moderating the growing Israeli-Palestinian crisis, backing out of a new Comprehensive Test Ban Treaty, withdrawing from the Bio Weapons Convention, working to weaken a Small Arms Control Treaty (ostensibly to protect U.S. manufacturing interests of small arms, a major U.S. export, and to appease domestic Second Amendment supporters), dropping a Clinton initiative to work with the Organization for Economic Cooperation and Development (OECD) to go after international money laundering (in the face of pressure from the conservative Heritage Foundation on free market grounds and Texas border bankers on pure profit grounds), and announcing its intention to scrap the 1971 ABM Treaty that had kept the U.S. and Soviet Union from entering a new round of the arms race (this to facilitate developing the administration's proposed National Missile Defense, heir to Ronald Reagan's Star Wars initiative).   In each case, the administration's stance was derided by critics as cowboy diplomacy but applauded by supporters, including a clear majority of the American public, for reasserting the Reaganesque doctrine of American independence in pursuing its own security interests.

The administration could pursue such a radically different course in foreign policy from the previous administration because, in the spring of 2001, foreign threats to the U.S. were seen as being comparatively limited, despite several warnings from blue ribbon panels of a rising terrorist danger. The Bush administration felt emboldened to pursue a more unilateralist policy to further America's short-term economic and strategic interests and play to the interests of the administration's own domestic political base precisely because the stakes in international affairs were perceived to have declined significantly since the end of the cold war. With the stakes of going it alone diminished, the administration saw clear advantage in using America's uniquely powerful global position to pressure other nations into granting U.S. more favorable strategic and economic terms in everything from trade to military basing on a more unilateral basis. Thus, under the assumption of the moment, the administration correctly judged the advantages to America in asserting that greater global independence outweighed the costs in terms of loss of support in multilateral endeavors. While hindsight and history may show the decision to have been shortsighted, Bush did demonstrate independent leadership in pursuing a course so markedly different than that of his immediate two predecessors.

Recasting U.S. foreign policy from one based on international cooperation to one stressing international competition was clearly reflected in U.S. relations with China, which went from being designated a strategic partner under Clinton to strategic competitor under Bush. Prior to 9/11, China loomed as the single most likely long-term menace to American global hegemony (a position it still largely occupies as one must ask, "If not China, then whom?"). Bush sought to undercut China as a potential rival by taking a less conciliatory stance with this last great vestige of twentieth century totalitarianism. Bush's rhetoric was put to the test when, in March 2001, a Chinese fighter jet hot-dogging around an American reconnaissance plane off the Chinese coast collided with the plane, killing their pilot, and forcing the American plane into an emergency landing in Chinese territory. Eleven days, an official apology, and $50 million dollars paid to the Chinese later, the U.S. plane and crew were returned but not before a significant increase in hostile rhetoric between the U.S. and China. The incident, meanwhile, played to nationalist sentiment in both countries. Less than two weeks later, the Bush administration announced new arms sales to Taiwan, which domestic critics complained had been watered down to appease Beijing by not giving Taiwan cruise missiles that the island country desired. The very next day Bush startled observers by going out of his way in an interview to stress that the U.S. had an obligation to

618   *George W. Bush*

assist Taiwan if it were attacked by China, promising, "Whatever it took to help Taiwan defend herself." The declaration ended the intentional strategic ambiguity regarding Taiwan that had persisted since the Nixon years. On the whole, Bush received high marks domestically for his handling of China. Once again, his domestic supporters saw his actions as bold while his international detractors saw them as reckless.

Bush also demonstrated his willingness to break with tradition by going to Mexico rather than Canada on his first presidential foreign trip. Meeting in Mexico with fellow former border state governor and now President Vincente Fox underscored his administration's intent to shift its foreign policy focus from old alliances and regions such as Europe and NATO to the new frontier of opportunity presented in the developing world. Mexico, pundits and diplomats agreed, would be one place that Bush would be able to establish a serious and effective bilateral relationship. Both he and Fox were committed to working towards immigration reform, a topic on which both had campaigned in their respective races for office. Moreover, Bush's domestic political agenda of winning over Hispanic voters for the 2004 election clearly complimented a policy of cooperating with Mexico in working to a solution of the border problem. Fox would visit Bush at his ranch in Crawford, Texas, in May and July and return in early September for another state visit. But the Bush-Fox honeymoon would be short-lived. Bush wanted immigration reform tied to U.S. capital access to the Mexican energy industry as part of his grand strategy to replace Middle East oil with North American sources. Fox meanwhile wanted to broaden their discussion to issues of greater political cooperation and even integration, European Union (EU) style, for North America, the very kind of multilateral complications in which Bush had no real interest. The result was a tense state visit and stymied negotiations until Mexico was fully placed on the back burner by 9/11, where it would remain until the 2004 election year and the president's new election year immigration plan.

If the entirety of the Bush presidency was to be measured by its first seven and one-half months, a fair assessment of its efficacy would be mixed at best. Bush's first months in office were more productive than that of either of his two immediate predecessors, delivering on a promised tax cut and reversing whole sectors of the Clinton regulatory legacy by executive fiat. But his record of accomplishment in his first hundred days—or even two hundred—lagged far behind that of the reigning Republican titan of the twentieth century, Ronald Reagan, or the man Reagan originally idolized and whose legacy Reagan took head on, Franklin Delano Roosevelt. So too was he less successful than the second tier of presidents, such as Eisenhower, Lyndon Johnson, or Richard Nixon.

Bush went into his first summer clearly on the defensive. As one former speechwriter observed, "Green issues were killing us . . . but by the end of July, all issues were killing us." By the end of July, major questions were being asked in congressional cloakrooms and op-ed pages about Bush's ability to lead decisively. Conservatives saw too much compromise on taxes, on education, and on social security. When was the "Bush Revolution" going to begin? Meanwhile, with the Senate's rejection of the Bush plan to drill in the Arctic National Wildlife Refuge (ANWR), the stymieing of social security reform (the privatization conservatives desired and of which liberals were horrified) by the classic Beltway tactic of oblivion through special commission, and the derailing by Pentagon insiders and their congressional allies of the grand plans of Secretary of Defense Rumsfeld to radically overhaul the U.S. military, little looked promising as the Bush administration entered the dog days of its first summer.

If things had continued as they were, without the unexpected earthquake of 9/11, it is likely that Bush would have finished his first year in office with a lagging economy and a host of stalled major initiatives. This, in turn, would have left him weak for the midterm elections in which the opposition party usually does well. But for 9/11, Democrats likely would have kept control of the Senate and might have won back control of the House. For the remainder of the Bush term, the administration would have been on the defensive, which may have helped him (as it helped Bill Clinton in 1996 following the Republican 1994 revolution) but which would have left him far weaker than his current prospects would allow.

But 9/11 did happen, thrusting the nation, the world, and the Bush presidency in a few hours one beautiful September morning into a truly new world order. That September morning underscored the historical fact that more often than not the unexpected twists of fate—the Pearl Harbors, the hostage crises, the unstable dictators—define a presidency far more than the platform and agenda the president brings into office with him. The real measure of a president is his ability to adjust to the unexpected. In this capacity, George W. Bush would exceed the expectations both of those who supported him and those who did not.

9/11 and After

George W. Bush was visiting an elementary school in Florida the day his presidency changed. He was there for a photo op to push his education reform plan when he received news of the attacks on the World Trade Center and the Pentagon. Seldom, if ever, has a world leader received such black news while on camera. Bush's initial reaction, clearly captured by the cameras, was of a man both shocked and confused, as were most Americans—shocked that such an audacious act could happen on their own soil; confused as to what the attacks signaled. Were the attacks the solitary acts of a group of mad men or the first phase of a massive assault on the American homeland? Once it was ascertained by Bush's staff that the events in New York and Washington were a coordinated attack, Bush quickly exited the school, pausing before the cameras only long enough to declare, "Terrorism against our nation will not stand."

Fearing that the White House or the president's jet itself might be targets of terrorism, for the remainder of the day Bush was flown under fighter jet escort to various military bases while the threat was assessed. The absence of the president from the cameras for much of the day and, indeed, the secrecy of his whereabouts did nothing to assuage public anxiety over the attacks or to encourage confidence in their now wartime leader. Whether it is true that a frustrated Karl Rove finally forced the issue by stating that, if the president was not back at his White House desk by six o'clock that evening, he might as well resign as the public would never forgive him for the appearance of abandoning his post is unclear. By late afternoon, however, the decision was made that the commander in chief had to return to the seat of power. That evening Bush addressed America from the Oval Office. "Terrorist attacks," he told the shaken nation, "can shake the foundations of our biggest buildings, but they cannot touch the foundations of America." The speech was short, the president himself looking somewhat shaken. It would take several days for Bush to find his stride as a leader of a nation in mourning and looking for revenge. In the days following the attack, the president huddled with his national security advisors. The president characterized the deadly attacks as "acts of war." The big question was with whom was America at war?

Within days of the attack, Bush would fully assume the mantle of presidential leadership by delivering a strong address at the National Cathedral in Washington. "The conflict was begun on the timing and terms of others. It will end in a way and at an hour of our choosing." The turning point of the entire Bush presidency might well have been the moment later that day when he flew to New York to pay homage at the World Trade Center site. Slipping into an NYFD jacket, throwing his arm around a grinning, soot-streaked fire fighter, and addressing the crowd through a bullhorn, Bush was once again the Andover cheerleader, the Texas Ranger booster, a man back in his element, working the crowd. After months of seeing his political agenda bogged down in Washington compromise, the man who prized simple clarity now had a crystal clear mission to pursue: rally the home crowd and beat the other side. Forget the deep analysis and hand-wringing self-assessment that might have occurred in the Clinton White House or the realpolitik strategic assessment of Nixon and Kissinger, considering how events might now play out on the global chessboard. For Bush, September 11 transformed his duty from policymaker to crusader with a new, focused overarching goal: to transform the world into one in which an event like 9/11 could and would never occur again. The public was desperate to see a true leader, and Bush had disappointed them in his apparent confusion in the forty-eight hours following the attack. Standing on the still-smoking rubble of the former monument to American wealth and power, Bush now connected with the American people at a visceral level, erasing their previous doubt in his leadership abilities, lining the American people and the Washington political classes firmly behind him.

Approval ratings averaging in the low 50 percent levels in the days leading up to the attack shot immediately to 80 percent and above, levels at which they would stay for the next four months. For the remainder of the fall and into the winter, the United States government was George Bush's to drive. When Congress convened in emergency session, it voted 98-0 in the Senate and 420-1 in the House to authorize the president to use "all necessary and appropriate force" to retaliate against terrorists, a move that may well prove to be the granting of the biggest blank check since God told humanity, "be fruitful and multiply." The president finished his day by calling up 50,000 military reservists for "homeland defense." At that moment, it was still unclear against whom America was defending and against whom she would retaliate. Over the next month, these questions would begin to be answered.

The "War on Terrorism" would unfold along three paths: striking back militarily at perpetrators of terror, potential perpetrators of terror, and their state supporters; organization of the homeland to prevent further attacks; and finally the rallying of international support for America's global strategy. Within eight days of the 9/11 attacks, the administration had identified its two prime targets for retribution: the Al Qaeda Islamic fundamentalist terrorist movement and the Taliban regime in Afghanistan that gave shelter to the movement's leader, Osama bin Laden. Within days of the attack, a video purported to show bin Laden and supporters in Afghanistan praising the attack on the United States as acts of God reached global airwaves. Bin Laden's statements stopped short of claiming complete responsibility for the acts, but coupled with a long list of past links between Al Qaeda and previous attacks on American interests in Kenya, Tanzania, and Yemen and the earlier unsuccessful attack on the World Trade Center in 1993, the statements were more than enough to convince both the administration and the American public of bin Laden's and Al Qaeda's culpability. That bombs would fall in Afghanistan before intelligence sources had absolutely established the link between Kabul and New York would become only a minor footnote to history.

After issuing an ultimatum to the Afghani regime to turn over Osama bin Laden or else, Bush made a joint address to the Congress on September 20, announcing to the nation and the world the "Bush Doctrine." Inarguably the most important and best-delivered speech of his presidency, Bush declared a simple new axiom of international relations: "You are either with U.S. or you are with the terrorists." There were no caveats or provisos to the policy. It reflected the essence of George W. Bush. It was the stark west Texas landscape of his youth, whose razor-sharp horizon separated brown land from crystal blue sky without a sliver of equivocation, now made national policy. The world was, henceforth, black and white: the black evil of terrorist anti-Americanism and the white goodness of American ideals. While the president's sharp words raised eyebrows across the global diplomatic community, the international bonhomie felt towards the U.S. in the weeks immediately after the attacks allowed for the sentiment these words expressed—the ancient right of the aggrieved to seek justice at whatever the cost—to be accepted and even embraced. What neither America nor many of her allies comprehended at the time was how, as the war on terror unfolded into all the gray areas that wars entail, the Bush Doctrine could increasingly force countries into having to make uncomfortable choices to stay America's friend or to force America to increasingly consider former friends to be foes.

The military aspects of the Afghani campaign itself would be resolved in less than three months—eighty-six days from initial bombings to the installation of a pro-American regime in Kabul. What Alexander, the British, and the Russians had largely failed to do, the legions of America accomplished, as the French would say, *tout suite*. The Afghani victory was somewhat clouded over by the failure of American forces to capture bin Laden (though whether he was dead or alive would remain a source of great speculation for over a year) and by the fact that even Bush conceded that U.S. forces would remain in the country "for quite some time." Going into war, Americans have consistently forgotten that, like Rome, wherever the legions of the empire are sent, they seldom, if ever, come home again. The fact of American triumph on the ground served to satisfy to a degree the initial national desire to strike back, even if in doing so the entirety of the threat poised by Al Qaeda had not been eradicated. The problem that the Bush administration faced as the initial Afghani campaign wound down around Christmas 2001 was that an American public riveted before their televisions for days on end by the horror of 9/11 was already drifting back into an uneasy normalcy. While the quick success against the Taliban sent Bush's approval ratings to his personal best, pushing his father's own astounding 90 percent post-Gulf War 1 levels, once the shooting war in the Himalayas subsided, public interest in a war on terror that Secretary of Defense Donald Rumsfeld, in his trademark school principal voice, lectured would last for the better part of the century decidedly began to wain.

This might be blamed on the simple horrificness of the New York attacks, captured live and replayed to an almost pornographic extent on every television screen in America for days after the attack. Once the networks agreed to stop running the footage of jets slamming into the Twin Towers, once the normal network prime time schedules of dramas and sitcoms resumed, once football was being played again in the stadiums, the public purged itself of the horror by a massive resubmergence in the mundane. Within one month of 9/11, network news ratings that had soared to record levels had already fallen back to their usual apathetic lows. Future historians might begin to question the immediate extreme reaction of Americans to the death of 3,547 human beings even as Americans complacently lived their lives in a society in which 12 times as many of their fellow citizens died in road accidents and 4 times as many died at each others hands and guns every year—numbers that will be sadly replicated year after year while terrorist violence, to date, has fortunately not been. That the deaths were immediate, premeditated, and graphically portrayed should not rationally warrant such national fixation, they might argue.

Such future historians might wish to consider that, on September 11, America was populated by several generations of citizens for whom foreign crises and death had played out on distant battlefields that obtruded into daily life only as short news segments on the television or, at most, as a vague story of a family's loss heard from a friend of a friend of the bereaved. For those who had personally experienced human madness on a grand scale, in World War II or in Korea or in Vietnam, such memories were the faded recollections of youth long past. The greatest struggle the vast majority of Americans had personally experienced prior to September 11 was the routine daily struggle to maintain or increase their standard of living, to fight the battle of the waistline, to achieve the triumph of the wide screen TV, and live to fight the jihad of old age illness.

While 9/11 shook the notion of American stability, serenity, and insularity, it did not topple the edifice. The stock market would take a significant tumble in the weeks following the attack, but the overall behavior of the markets and the economy as a whole post-9/11 was influenced far more by global competition and the still unwinding Dot.com stock bubble. While most Americans came out of the experience with their own emotional memories of the event and, in many cases, a friend of a friend degree of separation from the tragedy itself, few were actually directly touched by it. Having chosen to defend itself as a nation with a professional army of self-selecting recruits, the resulting call to arms would likewise affect few Americans who were not already caught up in military life. Thus, life went on, but as it did, the ability of President Bush to draw on the reservoir of post-9/11 public angst to pursue his agenda likewise declined; barring a subsequent even more destructive attack, that reservoir appears to be a non-renewable resource. This trend was marked by the slow but steady decline in the president's approval rating, peaking in early December 2001 and sliding toward the 50 percent mark entering his reelection year.

Still, the administration was able to use the popular mandate for action effectively in the immediate months following 9/11. Bush's announcement of the creation of a new White House Office of Homeland Security to coordinate anti-terrorist defense efforts was in many ways a fast political ploy to give the impression of action when serious action could not yet be taken. The new office consisted primarily of its director, former Republican Governor Tom Ridge, who had no real experience in the field and a tiny staff working out of the White House itself. Ridge initially lacked any real funding or policy authority over the myriad of agencies responsible for different aspects of domestic security and anti-terrorism scattered across over a dozen cabinet departments and independent agencies. It would take a year-long battle between

Bush and his own Republican Congress to turn Homeland Security into a full-fledged cabinet department before the agency would truly gain enough real budget and enough clout to start to coordinate, however ineffectively, the disparate security fiefdoms. Bush initially opposed full cabinet status for Homeland Security because a purely executive branch office is under far less oversight by Congress than is a full-fledged cabinet department. Indeed, the Bush administration demonstrated something of an automatic reflex in its desire to maintain as much autonomy as possible in its policy-making from congressional meddling—even a Congress dominated by the president's own party. Clinton, weakened by low popularity in his first term and by scandal in his second, had been content to allow much of the policy-making initiative to slip into the hands of Republican congressional leaders and then get political mileage out of successfully blaming Congress for intransigence, as in the budget battle of 1995. Surprisingly, for a man whose only real executive experience had been as governor of a state where the legislature clearly dominated the policy-making process, as president, Bush demonstrated a strong desire to dominate policy-making, agreeing to compromise with Congress only as a last resort. Such was the case with Homeland Security. Facing a bipartisan Congress unified in its desire to one up the president on the commitment to homeland defense, Bush would embrace cabinet status as a fine idea but could not shake the impression in the media that he had somehow "lost one" on Homeland Security.

Congress would be more accommodating with the president on other domestic aspects of his war on terrorism, overwhelmingly passing on October 24 the omnibus "PATRIOT" anti-terrorism act, allowing for sweeping new governmental powers to investigate persons and groups suspected of being connected with terrorists or other enemies of the nation. While human rights activists cried foul, Congress raised scarcely an eyebrow three weeks later at the administration's historically unusual decision to detain indefinitely some of those captured in Afghanistan as "enemy combatants" (a limbo-like legal status under international law) and to use military tribunals to try foreign nationals accused of terrorism. Meanwhile, Congress approved a number of other Bush initiatives to improve security at American border crossings, airports, and commercial ports, though neither Congress nor the president would push through substantial new funding for these initiatives in subsequent budgets.

President Bush also scored a number of diplomatic victories in the aftermath of his September 20 national address announcing the new war on terror. The multilateral strategy Bush pursued appeared at first

626   *George W. Bush*

glance to greatly resemble that pursued by his father during the first Gulf War. Addressing the UN on the terrorist threat, Bush asked for and received Security Council endorsement of the Afghani operation. NATO, for the first time in its history, declared that the 9/11 attack had triggered the alliances' mutual protection clause and, henceforth, further terrorist attacks on any member would be considered an attack on all. Direct support of America's Afghani campaign would be provided by a coalition of forty-three nations, spearheaded by Great Britain, whose Prime Minister Tony Blair had provided perhaps the most eloquent oratory of any world leader after the New York attacks, calling them "an assault on civilization" itself. Like his father, George W. Bush went into the Afghani war the head of a broad, global coalition of nations who sympathized with the U.S. and accepted the 9/11 attacks as a threat to the global community at large.

In retrospect, much of the post-9/11 diplomacy seems aimed at clearing the road ahead of diplomatic hurdles to further more unilateral American goals that would follow Afghanistan. Bush secured NATO and the UN support for the Afghan war without having to cede any operational control of the war itself or political control of the postwar environment to multilateral entanglements. Moreover, having lined the nations of Europe up "with us" rather than "with the terrorists" (an absurd dichotomy, of course, for while European states might not always have agreed with U.S. policy in the past, that never meant that they "supported" regimes hostile to the U.S.—at least no more than America's own realpolitik strategies had supported regimes like Iraq when convenient), any backpedaling by European powers towards subsequent American policies could be portrayed by the administration as "bad faith," as would be the case over Iraq.

Much of the post-9/11 diplomatic maneuvering also was intent on securing the acquiescence of other non-allied major powers—most specifically the Russians and the Chinese—to allow the U.S. a free hand to pursue its aims in the war on terror in exchange for respecting those nations' strategic agendas. Meeting with President Jiang Zemin in Shanghai on October 17, Bush and the Chinese leader announced that their two nations stood "side by side" on the war on terrorism. This did not mean that China was going to commit men and material to the struggle of course. What it meant was that China would not criticize or impede military actions that the United States might take—actions China in the past might easily have categorized as those of the "running dog western imperialism." In exchange, the hard-edged rhetoric of the administration towards China on human rights, Taiwan, and trade that marked the first six months of the Bush presidency would now be softened or outright silenced.

Within days of the 9/11 attack, Russian President Vladamir Putin would declare his country's support for the U.S. in their now "mutual war" against Islamic extremism. Putin's goal was to directly link his own bloody but stalled counter-insurgency war in Chechnya with American attacks to establish a *quid pro quo*: Russian support for American actions, including even toleration of the eventual projection of American power into Russia's traditional sphere of influence in central Asia, to support the war in Afghanistan in exchange for American silence and tacit endorsement of Putin's ratcheting up the use of Russian force against Chechen insurgents and civilians. Thus, later reports from Afghanistan that Al Qaeda was being directly supported by thousands of Chechen Jihad warriors (none of which were ever subsequently identified) should be interpreted in this light. When Putin and Bush met for a November summit at the president's Texas ranch, they would reaffirm this mutual support against Islamic terrorists and continue their progress towards nuclear disarmament. Seeking to use the current crisis as leverage, Bush also pushed Putin to accept the administration's intent to withdraw from the 1972 Anti-Ballistic Missile Treaty. Though the Russian leader was hesitant to do so, when the administration did unilaterally withdraw from the accord the following month, Moscow accepted the move with little protest.

This tendency to bring all policy debate under the "War on Terror" logo was particularly applied, with mixed results, to expanding the administration's conservative agenda into areas only peripherally related to 9/11. Such would be the case with Iraq. There is considerable debate as to just when the Bush administration became committed to a war to remove Saddam Hussein from power. The administration's official stand is that the decision flowed naturally and inexorably from the 9/11 attack. Others, including Bush's first Treasury Secretary, have argued that the president was keen to remove Hussein from the moment he took office. Some attributed this to Bush's strong desire to continue the task of completing his father's unfinished legacy, be it pushing space initiatives or war. Others saw it as a desire for payback at the man who "tried to kill my dad." Whichever is true, it is undisputable that the Cheney-Wolfowitz-Rice neo-conservative faction in the administration had been disgruntled with the decision of Bush I to pull up short of Baghdad in 1991—that much they had committed to print years before

George W.'s election. To the neo-cons around the president, Iraq was like Pennsylvania: the Keystone state of the Middle East. Regime change in Iraq would serve as a warning to more radical regimes in Syria and Iran. Creation of a pro-American democracy in Iraq would serve to encourage pro-democracy movements across the region, including within authoritarian regimes like Saudi Arabia that were theoretically allies of the U.S. but were also major sources of support for radical Islamic fundamentalist movements. Turning Iraq into a U.S. "protectorate" would provide America with a stable base from which to project power into the heart of the Arab world. While the administration may have mulled over the possibility of regime change in Iraq before 9/11, afterwards such intervention became inevitable.

Bush's intent towards Iraq was made manifest at his second State of the Union address, where he warned of a new "Axis of Evil" of rogue regimes consisting of Iran, North Korea, and Iraq that threatened international stability. (According to a Bush speechwriter, Iran and Iraq were targeted as being regimes central to Islamic radicalism and Middle East instability, but an "Axis" of two seemed off, so North Korea was included at the last minute to round out the rhetorical flourish. This bit of oratorical license may well have precipitated the confrontation between North Korea and the U.S. over nuclear weapons that spring.) Two weeks later Secretary of State Colin Powell told the U.S. Senate that the president was finalizing plans for regime change in Iraq. What followed was a solid year of domestic political and international diplomatic wrangling between an administration intent on unseating Saddam Hussein and an American public and global community far from convinced of the efficacy or the legitimacy of this aim.

A power struggle developed in the Bush White House over Iraq. On one side was Colin Powell and a State Department that believed the best way to deal with Iraq was a continuation of the containment policies in place since the end of the first Gulf War. This view argued for using UN-led inspectors to identify and destroy any remaining systems that could be used for weapons of mass destruction (WMD) development or production and maintaining economic sanctions to deprive the regime of resources with which to reconstitute such programs. On the other side were the neo-cons, led by Cheney and Rice, who saw military action and regime change as the only way both to end the threat of Saddam Hussein for good and to begin a process of democratization in the region, which would over the long run eliminate the breeding grounds for Islamic radicalism itself. While this debate occurred within the White House, a storm of domestic and global opposition began to brew over what was portrayed by Bush detractors as a radical return to the unilateralism that had marked Bush's pre-9/11 foreign policy. Bush's statement on June 14, 2002, announcing that the U.S. would embrace a "new doctrine" of unilateral pre-emptive action against any real or potential foreign threat, further inflamed these concerns. Yet, Bush's bravado was also applauded by neo-conservative and mainstream Americans as a statement of strength by a nation at war.

Once Bush set himself firmly on the road to war, Powell worked as the faithful foot soldier to assuage rising global opposition to Bush's perceived unilateralism and maintain the semblance of unity and allied support the U.S. had enjoyed post-9/11. The debate would languish through the summer and fall of the year with Powell arguing the U.S. case to allies and, ultimately, to the United Nations, while NATO leaders demanded Iraq to disarm and Britain pledged support of American action. The debate on Iraq created a substantial schism between the U.S. and many of its traditional European allies. Both France and Germany refused to join the U.S. in military action or to assent to a new UN resolution explicitly authorizing American intervention, precipitating a war of rhetoric between Washington, Paris, and Berlin. A November compromise at the UN returned arms inspectors to the country, but for Bush it was now too little too late. Frustrated with the inability to organize a grand coalition of America's allies on the order of his father's in the first Gulf War, Bush now sought to organize a "coalition of the willing," consisting principally of the U.S., Britain, Australia, several of the second-tier European powers such as Italy and Spain, and a host of smaller countries, particularly eastern European, who saw support of the U.S. position on Iraq as a cheap way to ingratiate themselves with the global superpower.

In October 2002, Bush secured a second overwhelming vote from Congress to prosecute a war in Iraq (even though several of his advisors argued that such a vote was not needed, as the original terrorism vote of 2001 gave the president authority to fight a war anywhere against anyone to stop terrorism). For the next four months, the clock ticked towards war. Even as UN inspectors reported that they could find no trace of WMDs, the U.S. continued to position troops into the region in preparation for war. Finally, in March 2003, before the spring heat could fully rise off the Iraqi desert, Bush moved to resolve the issue. Warning UN inspectors to leave the country, he gave Hussein and his sons a basic "24 hours to get out of Dodge" ultimatum. When the dictator, apparently so insulated from reality by his own advisors or so egomaniacal as to have entered the realm of fantasy, refused, the cruise missiles were launched, the troops deployed. In another blitzkrieg triumph of American military superiority, Hussein's once much-vaunted forces, which the Bush administration had warned was a threat to every nation in the region with WMDs ready for release, were routed out in a matter of twenty days, with none of the much ballyhooed WMDs being deployed or found by the invading forces.

Fears that the resulting American-led coalition occupation of Iraq would degenerate into a new Vietnam were not realized after the collapse of the Hussein regime (Israeli occupation of southern Lebanon may well prove a better comparison). Post-Hussein Iraq quickly divided along ethnic and cultural lines, with majority Shi'ites in southern Iraq seeking national domination, minority Kurds in the north seeking autonomy, if not outright independence, and the former dominant minority Sunnis of the center splintered between those seeking accommodation with the rest of the country and the small minority actively resorting to insurgency to harass the American occupiers and everyone else. American policy, originally based on hope for a quick turnover of power in Iraq to a pro-American democracy, was progressively forced by the reality on the ground to morph into a long-term occupation on the German and Japanese post-World War II model likely to last several years or more. Low levels of American casualties (amidst escalating levels of Iraqi civilian casualties) allowed President Bush to avoid paying much of a political price for the prolonged deployment of U.S. troops. Moreover, as months of occupation rolled by and no hordes of WMDs or even evidence of credible development programs were uncovered, the administration's early insistence that Iraq posed an imminent threat to American interests was thrown into doubt. The absence of WMDs did not, however, undermine the credibility of the administration in the eyes of the public. Ultimately, through the summer and fall of 2003 the American people were content to have seen the U.S. military remove a particularly heinous third world dictator.

In any event, by the summer of 2003 concerns over both war in Iraq and war on terror in general that had dominated the previous eighteen months were being replaced in the public's mind by domestic concerns. In particular, an economic recovery from the mild recession of 2000-2001 was not producing as many new jobs as previous recoveries had, giving rise to public perceptions that George W. Bush might be just like his old man after all—great on winning wars, weak on winning the economy. Going into the 2004 presidential election year, anti-Bush bumper stickers might well have paraphrased those of a decade before: "Saddam Hussein doesn't have a job any more—do you?" Yet, once again, time proved to be the main ally of the Bush presidency. By the fall of 2003, the U.S. economy posted substantially higher gross domestic product (GDP) growth rates. More importantly, by the spring of 2004 even the weak job market seemed to be recovering with more new jobs being created than economists had predicted. While unemployment levels in aggregate remained higher than that to which the public had become accustomed by the late 1990s, positive job numbers (in addition to producing rounds of cheering on Air Force One when initially announced) bid well for the president's reelection hopes.

Perhaps the greatest single success of the Bush presidency has been the transformation of the public perception of the man, predominantly for the good. Bush entered office under "the shadow of a great man"—his own father—with a personal reputation of limited intellectual abilities. The high profile of so many former members of his father's administration in his own new government, especially that of Dick Cheney, once referred to as George W. Bush's "human training wheels," reinforced the election campaign's impression that he was a leadership light weight. Even before 9/11 Bush had reversed, though not completely dispensed with, these public uncertainties. His forceful handling of the spy plane and Taiwan controversies with China, his dogged and ultimately successful pursuit of his tax cut, and, more than anything else, his maintenance of an aura of personal integrity and general good humor (even if private reports revealed him to be a man of no small temper and even a tendency towards petulance) earned him high personal approval ratings and respectable job approval ones. Post-9/11, the president successfully reasserted himself as a strong wartime leader who, in a series of speeches and public appearances, showed both his human side and a hard, resolute side that few would have believed him capable of a few weeks before. Bush deserves high kudos for rallying the American public during one of the most trying moments of their history. Indeed, the fact that normalcy returned to American life so quickly is in no small part a testament to the confidence in national leadership he was able to inspire.

One of the larger ironies of the Bush presidency may turn out to be the fact that he actually emerged as a leader of stature great enough to take on a truly dangerous foreign foe—only to confront comic book character villains—men who have taken evil to the level of kitsch banality—such as Osama bin Laden and Saddam Hussein. Indeed, Bush overthrew these enemies so easily that soon the American public grew bored with the whole war matter and returned their attention extraordinarily quickly to the mundanities of comfortable American life—reality television shows and complaining about a weak economy while still enjoying one of the highest qualities of life on the planet.

Such fickleness by the American consuming classes has meant that modern presidents have enjoyed increasingly diminishing returns on foreign policy successes: witness Bush's father presiding over the collapse of the Soviet Union and Saddam Hussein's first defeat at American hands, yet enjoying no meaningful boost in public support at the ballot box. Meanwhile, even the mildest interruptions along the path towards ever increasing prosperity result in significant and immediate declines in presidential popularity. Thus, George W. Bush would go into his reelection campaign a two-time war winning president with no certainty of keeping his job.

Bush also deserves substantial credit for the success of his foreign military endeavors. While questions of their necessity, at least in the case of Iraq, and long-term strategic consequences remain open, once shooting begins, the dictum "there is no substitute for victory" is all that matters. The shockingly rapid American military triumphs in Afghanistan and Iraq, battlefields that academics and armchair generals had thought would become intractable quagmires as with the Russian Afghani nightmare or the U.S. Vietnamese experience, lay to rest doubts as to the vitality and efficacy of the U.S. war machine. Undoubtedly, the power of the U.S. military and the willingness of an American administration to deploy it—with or without global assent—has registered in the policy-making circles of the other major powers, especially China. When George Bush promised, "the people who knocked these buildings down will hear the U.S. soon," he was deadly serious. Thus, the fate of the Taliban and Saddam Hussein was noted in the palaces of other third world dictators who might now fear that they could be brought not within the crosshairs of a handful of American cruise missiles but under the heel of the entire American war machine. Such, the administration argued, was the case with the announcement by long-term Libyan strongman and international bad boy Muammar Qaddafi that, following the Iraqi defeat, his own country would abandon plans for developing WMDs. The movement by North Korea during the spring of 2003 to actually accelerate deployment of nuclear weapons can also be taken as a backhanded acknowledgement that the Bush Doctrine is being taken seriously and needs either to be accommodated or defended against.

Bush's resoluteness in pursuing his objectives, often dismissed as dogmatic or purely partisan, has resulted in more policy successes than can be attributed to his predecessor, whose leadership style was somewhat more waffling. Whether one agrees with the policies or not, one must acknowledge that Bush delivered on two of his three principle domestic policy goals—tax cuts and education reform—and accomplished two of his three principal foreign policy goals—overthrowing the Taliban and Saddam Hussein. Only his faith-based initiative and the capture of Osama bin Laden eluded him.

Meanwhile, through systematic bureaucratic and judicial appointments, executive orders, and the development of a new body of regulatory policy, Bush has engaged in a "quiet revolution" that will impact American politics for years to come. Republican control of both Congress and the presidency for the first time in a half century has allowed Bush to sow official Washington with Republican operatives and appointees at all levels of government. While much has been made of Democrats successfully blocking a handful of Bush's most conservative appellate bench appointees (one of which still got onto the bench through a recess appointment), Bush made as many appointments to the federal judiciary by the end of his first term as Bill Clinton did across his entire presidency, which will leave a conservative bias to the courts for a generation to come. While criticized for not having a substantial domestic agenda (as has been done in this essay) beyond a handful of key objectives, Bush waged a successful stealth agenda at the regulatory level, reversing years, and in some cases decades, of environmental and industrial restrictions, which conservatives have argued diminishes the efficiency and profits of the private sector. Anti-trust litigation, made an endangered species during the Reagan years, went completely extinct during Bush's first term once the administration essentially chose to take a dive on the Microsoft anti-trust case. Again, the efficacies of Bush's actions are not in debate here. It is the efficiency of the administration in accomplishing these partisan goals, largely below the public radarscope, that is most impressive.

With military victories abroad (were we truly in keeping with the Latin tradition, Bush the Younger would now be renamed Georgious Irakus or, at least, an anglicized George the Conqueror), substantial domestic victories at home, and sustained high public approval levels, George W. Bush headed into the last months of his first term as a president standing on his own record, a leader in his own right. Thus, his greatest success of all may be that, ultimately, he escaped the legacies of his past to establish a political legacy of his own. Whether that legacy will be judged well or not by future historians or the American electorate remains to be seen.

The George W. Bush Presidency: A Negative Assessment

One of the first challenges of the George W. Bush administration was to escape the legacy of the first Bush presidency. Indeed, this legacy was to loom large over the administration that George W. Bush assembled, so large, in fact, that early on the press and pundits began to conclude that, in electing the son, the public had actually only elected a shadow of the father. This legacy included most of the high profile senior White House positions: Vice President Richard Cheney (Bush 1's Secretary of Defense), Secretary of State Colin Powell (Bush 1's Chairman of the Joint Chiefs of Staff), National Security Advisor Condoleezza Rice (senior aide to Bush 1's National Security Advisor Brent Scowcroft), and Chief of Staff Andrew Card (Bush 1's deputy chief of staff). George W.'s administration was also replete with a large number of other Republican heavy-hitters from the Reagan, Ford, and even Nixon administrations, such as Secretary of Defense Donald Rumsfeld (Ford's Defense Secretary) and an economic staff heavily stocked with supply-siders from these earlier administrations.

Curiously missing from the Bush White House were the usual "friends of," the personally loyal coterie that usually constitute the behind the scenes "kitchen cabinet" that historically have great influence on a president. Bill Clinton brought his kindergarten play friend in as his first chief of staff; George H. W. Bush had old pals Brent Scowcroft and James Baker III; Reagan and Carter had their mafias of family, friends, and associates from California and Georgia, respectively. George W. Bush entered the White House with only two truly close personal loyalists—Karl Rove, who would continue as his chief political strategist, and Karen Hughes, running White House communications. First Lady, Laura Bush, meanwhile, would take a far less active role in the policy and politics of the presidency than any first lady since perhaps Pat Nixon—far less than her immediate predecessor and less even than Barbara Bush's understated and often underestimated role. The result was an unusual presidency in which those around the president were not necessarily identified as being loyal to him, first and foremost. Early in his presidency, the question arose in the minds of the press and pundits as to who would really be in charge in the Bush White House—the kid or his father's friends. The questions would continue well into his first term.

Vice President Dick Cheney emerged early in the transition as an unusually active figure in the administration. Cheney's position on the Bush ticket came as something of a surprise itself. Secretary of Defense in the Bush 1 administration (and Donald Rumsfeld's protégé during the Nixon years), Cheney had been part of the Bush convention team and was tasked originally with vetting potential vice president choices; he ultimately was chosen himself. A fellow oil man from a western state (Colorado) with strong ties to Texas through his chairmanship of Halliburton Company, his addition to the party ticket added little of the usual regional balance sought with a vice-presidential choice and, indeed, reinforced the appearance of Bush falling back under his father's shadow—a legacy administration. What with Powell, Rice, Cheney and Rumsfeld, et. al, one might not have been surprised if Bush had disinterred the bones of Harold Lassen and given him a minor cabinet posting as well. But it was precisely Cheney's similarity to Bush that made him such an attractive vice-presidential choice for the party nominee. Cheney demonstrated two key characteristics for successful service to George W. Bush: loyalty, which Cheney had demonstrated in taking hits as Secretary of Defense for Bush's father; and right thinking.

Described as a "Westerner's Westerner," this child of the postwar American West grew up with and shared Bush's core beliefs. As such, Bush would be able to use Cheney as a surrogate in the administration, standing in to make decisions and initiate policies that Bush could trust would follow his core agenda. With a bad heart and limited future political ambitions, Cheney would not be the usual vice president sitting it out for eight years before making his own run for power. Instead, he would be the right hand of power. Unfortunately for Bush, the high profile role Cheney took during the transition and first several months of the administration, chairing cabinet meetings in the president's absence, taking the lead on major policies such as energy and the budget, only reinforced the press' and public's suspicion that Bush was a disengaged leader controlled by staff. By spring 2001, a number of pundits were concluding that the U.S. now had in Dick Cheney its first prime minister, with George W. Bush acting as administration "Cheerleader in Chief," traveling the country to sell his tax cut strategy while the vice president saw to the picayune day-to-day affairs of governance. The negative reception Cheney's high profile engendered further undermined public perception of George W. Bush as his own man. Despite Bush's efforts to distance himself from his father directly—meetings between the two men, beyond purely familial, would be kept to a minimum over his first year in office—the upshot would be to give the appearance that Bush was actually less in command and more a front man for a cabal of his father's people, an appearance that would take a national crisis and two wars to begin to dissipate.

George W. Bush came out of the 2000 election with his legitimacy intact. He could not, however, make claims to possessing a major mandate from the electorate for substantial policy change. Even as Bush demonstrated that he could establish his legitimacy with the public, Congress, even one controlled by his own party, was far less impressed. That Bush did not enter his presidency as a political titan was underscored by the fact that the first major policy initiative considered by the Republican Senate was that of campaign finance reform, pushed to the front of the legislative agenda by the man Bush had defeated barely a year before in the Republican primaries, John McCain. Indeed, the very paucity of Bush's early achievements, pushing the 100-days mark with no major policy success, probably itself went a long way towards easing Democratic ire of his December victory. Bush was working the kinks out of a new administration, learning to deal with Congress and the press, and fighting the standard battles on judicial confirmations, budget, and taxes (and not being threateningly successful at them). With the transfer of power in the Senate to Democrats in May, his opposition could feel that he was not the threat to their agenda that they had once feared he might be. His public job approval figures hovered in the mid- to high 50 percent range—respectable particularly given the electoral debacle, but not overwhelming compared to more dynamic presidents like FDR or Reagan. Like both Bill Clinton and his father before him, Bush got little of a post-inaugural honeymoon with Congress.

Republican control of both houses of Congress was itself subjected to something of a controversy in the inaugural month. Senate Democrats made loud and long over the need for a bipartisan division of power given the even partisan 50/50 split in the body (and, implicitly, given the weakness of the Bush mandate). They argued this, of course, largely to seek early political advantage with the public by continuing to portray Republicans as usurpers of power, when in reality the Constitution, in giving a tie-breaking vote to Vice President Dick Cheney, assured

Republican domination of the chamber. Having quickly nailed down control of the Senate and its all-important committee chairs, the Republican leadership, however, felt it wise to initially pursue a bipartisan agenda to assuage the public. Coming on the heels of the December debacle, the idea of campaign reform enjoyed bipartisan support within the chamber and public support without. Thus, campaign finance reform consumed much of official Washington's and the press' attention for the first two months of the new administration before its passage by the Senate. The bill would go on to lag for a year in the House until passed by a coalition of Democrats and rank and file Republicans over their own leadership's objection so as to get the item off the table in advance of the midterm election season. Campaign finance reform would be one of a number of bills George Bush would eventually sign over his own misgivings but bowing to political realities.

While Bush succeeded in establishing a degree of confidence in his personal ability, his ability to follow up on his campaign promise to "change the tone in Washington" by fostering bipartisanship fell flatter. During the spring of 2001, he did not make a single major compromise with Democrats on any significant issue he advanced beyond agreeing to drop the voucher proposal from his education plan in the face of unremitting hostility to the concept by congressional Democrats and large portions of the public. Bush would argue that the appearance of partisanship on his part was simply good negotiating sense; one did not offer a compromise until one staked the position on the table. The upshot, however, was to weaken Republican claims to be pursuing the kind of bipartisanship the public seemed to desire. This was particularly evident in key appointments Bush made, especially his appointment of ultra-conservative John Ashcroft as attorney general and several controversial appointments to the federal appellate bench, which would precipitate a war of threatened filibusters by Democrats in the Senate, further poisoning the well of collegiality on which the body depends to function.

Bush initially advanced the idea of tax cuts as a way to draw down the budget surplus before Congress could appropriate it away through expansions of the government budget. The tax cut would provide both a supply-side boost to the economy, a "jobs package" by steering capital back to the investment class rather than flitting it away on less efficient (if not downright wasteful) social welfare programs, and providing a firewall against massive government expansion. But by skewing the bulk of the tax cut to the highest income brackets precisely to stimulate capital investment, Bush opened himself up to charges of being a typical Republican friend of the rich. Moreover, by April it was becoming evident that the surplus party was over before it had really started. The Clinton tax increase coupled with a booming economy (that simultaneously brought in more revenues while cushioning the outcry from those paying the taxes because of their own huge stock windfalls) had resulted in a half trillion-dollar surplus between 1998 and 2001, which was projected to exceed five trillion dollars over the next decade if nothing changed. But things did change, beginning with a precipitous drop in capital gains revenues following the collapse of the Dot.com bubble and the slide of the stock market over the winter of 2000-2001. Responding to these concerns, the Republican Senate moved to reduce the administration's proposed tax cuts by a third to half. Coupled with a tepid public response to the proposed package, Bush would be forced by June to compromise by agreeing to reduce the tax cut to $1.1 trillion dollars and add an immediate $300 rebate to average taxpayers to win the support of recalcitrant Republican legislators. Bush would be able to sign his tax cut on June 7, 2001, but it would be a smaller tax cut with a larger Keynesian-style stimulus than he originally wanted and, with the deteriorating budget situation, would still turn out to be more than he might prudently have thought to be able to afford.

Ultimately, Bush's rhetoric on the tax cut, both in working to pass it and in justifying it even as record surpluses quickly turned to record deficits, demonstrated the recurring proclivity for the administration to tailor reality to fit its ideological agenda. Initially presented as a supply-side plan to stimulate job growth, once it became clear that the surplus was gone and the economy was still lagging, Bush pushed a further round of tax cuts long after projected surpluses were disappearing. Justification for the tax cut was then recast by the administration to be a stimulus for a bad economy. Good economy or bad, the administration argued, tax cuts were the universal panacea—like blood-letting for medieval barbers—a tool to be used for whatever ails the patient, even if it means bleeding the patient to death.

During his first six months, Bush did not have a more comprehensive economic agenda beyond the tax cut plan. Reagan had quickly moved on the heels of his own massive tax cut to dismantle large portions of the business regulatory establishment and take on organized labor by busting the air traffic controller's union. Except for an early flurry of executive actions aimed at rolling back a host of Clinton environmental and ergonomic initiatives, Bush seemed content to push his tax cut and budget through Congress and to focus on selectively rolling back other elements of the Clinton social legacy through executive orders rather than advancing substantial new legislative initiatives of his own.

Bush's Faith-Based Initiative, known officially as the Community Solutions Act, a centerpiece of his campaign's "compassionate conservatism," was aimed both at reforming welfare by bringing in more private participation and at partisan political engineering. The reformist goal was to allow religious groups providing community services to be eligible for federal funds, thereby bringing the vast private religious charitable infrastructure into the federal social welfare umbrella. The political goal of the initiative was to allow the administration to move beyond its core base of support with white suburban evangelicals and to reach out to urban blacks, Hispanics, and Catholics—core Democratic constituencies—through federal financial largess. The initiative stalled out amidst infighting between evangelical interest groups, each wanting a bigger piece of pie and jealousy over losing any to urban ministries. This was followed up by the resignation of the director of the White House Office of Faith-Based and Community Initiatives, John Dilulio, seen as an ally of inner city ministries, which left the very communities that Bush had sought feeling sold out to the white suburbs. The matter was further complicated by an apparent deal reached by Karl Rove with the Salvation Army to leverage federal support against cities and states that pressured religious groups not to discriminate in hiring gays. What started out as an effort by the administration to show that it was independent of the evangelical right ended with the administration under assault from minorities and gays for caving into pressure from the evangelical right.

Meanwhile, Republican business lobbyists and corporate interest group leaders long excluded from the executive mansion seemed over-eager to translate their new-found partisan advantage into access and influence in a pell-mell race to slash environmental regulation and reshape tax law. As had been the case when Republicans took over the Congress in 1994, a public perception—fanned by the media—developed of an administration increasingly rift with corporate influence beyond public scrutiny and without reference to the broader public good. A case in point was the energy task force that Vice President Dick Cheney organized in the spring. Cheney had been tasked with developing a comprehensive energy policy dealing with supply, in particular looking at ways that deregulation and tax incentives could lead domestic producers to expand exploration production. Cheney viewed the energy "problem" from an industrial perspective—one of lack of expansion of domestic supply versus overuse. Conservation, while a "personal virtue," according to the vice president, was not "a sufficient basis for a sound, comprehensive energy policy." To make America more "energy independent," the Cheney task force ultimately concluded that a variety of environmental laws such as those applying to the refitting of coal-fired power plants would need be reconsidered and access to more public lands such as the Arctic National Wildlife Refuge (ANWR) opened to exploitation.

All this occurred against the backdrop of the California energy crisis, the product of the kind of energy free-marketing that the Cheney task force seemed bent on fostering as national policy. By spring 2001, the state's utilities verged on bankruptcy as wholesale prices under deregulation skyrocketed from less than $20 megawatt-hour to over $1000. Meanwhile, gasoline prices were skyrocketing, going on to spike at almost $2 a gallon in spring and early summer of 2001 (which, while adjusted for inflation, was far lower than the prices resulting from either the 1973 or 1979 oil shocks but had still crossed the psychological barrier of $2 which consumers were just not ready to face). As Bush's communication director Karen Hughes had warned, the public perceived the task force as pro-energy industry (an industry which the public generally distrusted) at the expense of the environment. When the press reported that the vice president had created the draft plan after extensive meetings with energy industry executives and lobbyists, including the disgraced head of ENRON, the Texas energy giant that had come to symbolize what all detractors felt was wrong with American corporations run amuck, the issue became a public relations nightmare for the administration. Given the president's and vice president's history with the energy industry, the resulting image was one of an administration that had sold out the national environment to its business buddies—crony capitalism, Texas style. The consequences were a substantial public relations failure for the administration and on-going legal battles over the vice president's right to keep attendance at the task force meetings secret.

Bush's environmental and energy policy initiatives only served to reinforce an early portrait of the administration as being in the pockets of business interests at the public expense—a portrait Democrats and the press were set to frame and hang on the political wall. Bush's appointment of former Republican Governor Christine Todd Whitman, billed as an eco-moderate, as head of the EPA was quickly undercut by a slew of executive orders setting aside Clinton administration environmental initiatives, including the reopening of tens of thousands of acres of western lands to economic exploitation. In many cases, business-restrictive EPA and Department of Interior rules that had been the better part of a decade in formulation were swept away with one stroke of the Bush presidential pen, leaving Whitman to try and reconcile the rhetoric of environmental concern with actions clearly positioning short-term economic benefits ahead of long-term ecological effects. The final nail in the administration's environmental integrity coffin was the ill-fated decision to reverse the Clinton administration on arsenic levels in water supplies. President Clinton had reduced allowable levels for arsenic by 80 percent, despite arguments that the change would have questionable health benefits and came with high compliance costs. Bush moved to rescind the reductions in part for economic reasons of cost but also in part because much of the extra cost in removing arsenic would be borne by New Mexico water users. (Bush had lost New Mexico in 2000 by a few hundred votes.) The result was a public backlash to the obvious impression that Bush was willing to trade public health and environmental safety for heavy-handed political advantage.

Bush's campaign promises of bipartisanship were also quickly undercut by his extremely partisan and ideologically conservative appointments. It is hard to see what positive gain Bush derived from the appointment of John Ashcroft (a man so religiously conservative as to put drapes over the classical nude statues that have graced the Justice Department since the 1940s and request that cats be kept from his sight as they are associated with the devil) as attorney general beyond serving up a big sop to the religious right. Ashcroft proved to be one of the most divisive figures in the Bush cabinet, from his contentious Senate confirmation to his zealous pursuit of ever more governmental investigative powers, which produced an odd alliance of conservative libertarians and civil liberties advocates such as the ACLU. Ashcroft's appointment, as well as several high-profile appointments of ultra-conservative jurists hostile to abortion, affirmative action, and large portions of modern civil rights orthodoxy to the federal appellate bench, might simply be dismissed as Bush's pandering to the political and religious right. Well that may be, but Bush's dogged defense of these appointees underscored his own strong commitment—detractors might cite zeal—to advance a very partisan social agenda under the mask of bipartisan compassionate conservatism. The Bush administration's tendency towards pushing its ideological agenda even at the expense of objective fact has been alleged in decision-making on everything from Iraqi weapons of mass destruction to freezing stem cell research to global warming. Evidence of the reality of this tendency could be found in an accusation in early 2004 by a coalition of concerned scientists, including twenty Nobel prize winners, that took the unprecedented step of accusing the Bush White House of a pattern of deliberately suppressing scientific studies that disagreed with the administration's policy objectives. While many administrations have been accused of playing fast and loose from time to time with the facts, such strategies appeared to be the standard method of operation of the Bush White House. Such heavy-handed tactics backfired initially, contributing to the defection of one irritated Republican senator, tipping the evenly split body to the Democrats and thereby hamstringing the president's legislative agenda for eighteen months.

Ultimately, even return of the Senate to Republican control by 2003 did little to embolden the Bush domestic agenda, giving rise to the criticism that the administration suffered from the policy equivalence of not being able to chew gum and walk. Going into the fourth year of the administration, the once-lauded Bush discipline of staying focused on a handful of core issues had come to look like liability governing a multifaceted society that demands simultaneous attention to a host of macro social and economic issues. Waging war was an excuse the public credited from 9/11 to the fall of Baghdad, but as the months since Saddam's fall rolled by with no major domestic initiatives appearing, public patience, reflected in declining approval ratings, wore thin. It would appear that "vision thing" phenomenon might well be genetic, running from father to son. In the vacuum of no significant initiatives, Bush's domestic policy appeared captive to the same core business special interests—energy, finance, health care, and manufacturing—that always rise to prominence during Republican administrations. Bush's 2003 move towards protectionism on steel imports and increases in agricultural subsidies flew in the face of the administration's goal of pursuing greater levels of global free trade, alienating major trading partners and developing nations seeking greater access to U.S. markets and undercutting U.S. efforts to expand global and hemispheric trade talks, all to appease domestic economic interests with an eye towards buying political support for the 2004 election. Meanwhile, his heavy-handling of environmental policy opened his administration up to even more charges of collusion with industry. An administration with so many deep ties to resource extracting companies would have had to bend over backwards to be inclusive of environmentalists from the outset if it really wanted to establish pro-environmental bona fides. The almost cavalier attitude of Dick Cheney in forming his energy task force and the exclusion of environmentalists from any real policy-making roles could only look like the callous collusion between Bush and industry that became the public perception, if not the complete reality.

Bush went into the 2004 election year with a surprisingly light record of a domestic policy achiever. Admittedly, domestic policy was overshadowed by the rumor and reality of war through most of 2002 and 2003. And after Congress reconvened in January 2004, Republican leaders basically adopted a policy of riding things out until the November election. As a result, Bush had a very narrow window of opportunity to initiate and push through major domestic policy initiatives. Still, the paucity of Bush's domestic agenda leads one to conclude that, like Bill Clinton before him, his is best categorized as a "Bart Simpson" presidency: "underachiever and proud of it"—this despite the historically unusually strong showing of the president's party in the 2002 mid-term elections. Democrats went into the mid-terms with every possible disadvantage—a popular opposition president with a strong war record on which to run, Democratic waffling on the vote to authorize war with Iraq just weeks before the election and an economy that, while not sterling, also was not weak enough to trigger middle-class anxiety. The result was that the Republicans took back control of the Senate and added to the House majority, which should have given Bush ample political support to begin a "Bush Revolution," whatever that might have been. Instead, the president tepidly continued to advance his core agenda, signing in January 2002, a compromise education reform bill and pushed for an expansion of his tax cut, now touting it as necessary to stimulate a still lackadaisical economy. He continued his pro-business environmental agenda, signing legislation easing clean air regulations on utilities and industry in November 2002. Much of Bush's legislative record was defensive. He signed over his own misgivings the McCain-Feingold campaign finance reform legislation in March 2002, which House Republicans had rebelled against their own leaders to pass. He also signed with limited enthusiasm a July law increasing penalties for corporate malfeasance that came out of Congress as a reaction to Enron and other corporate scandals. The only major domestic accomplishment of Bush's third year in office was to finally deliver, in part, on a campaign promise to provide a Medicare prescription drug benefit. Even here,

Bush was criticized for supporting a plan that provided too small a benefit at too great a cost. Moreover, like much of Bush's initiatives, the plan would not take effect for several years, and its costs later turned out to be far higher than originally stated with large portions of the costs going to increased health-care company profits.

Meanwhile, the president presented budgets to Congress in 2003 and 2004 that substantially increased defense spending but also drastically expanded federal budget deficits ($300 million for federal year 2003 and a projected $500 million for federal year 2004—a record in size though not in percentage of GDP). Rapidly rising federal deficits reignited the domestic deficit debate that had dominated the Washington fiscal debate in the 1980s and 1990s. This time, though, it was Democrats arguing about the harm of deficits and Republicans defending them. Vice President Dick Cheney dismissed arguments that huge federal deficits hurt the economy because federal borrowing "crowded out" private borrowers and sent interest rates up as "Rubinomics" (after Clinton Treasury Secretary Robert Rubin), ignoring that Republicans had made precisely the same claim since the 1970s (and across the nineteenth century as well). Rising federal deficits did not adversely affect the economy, however, which posted substantial gains towards the end of 2003. But even administration booster Alan Greenspan, who had reversed his initial opposition to Bush's 2001 tax cut plan after Bush had made noises about dumping him as Federal Reserve chief, began to express his concerns over the sustainability of deficits of the Bush magnitude. Going into the 2004 election year, George W. Bush showed signs of mimicking another Texan president of yore—Lyndon Baines Johnson. Like Johnson, he chose to finance a major war abroad without raising taxes so as to avoid diminishing public support for the war at home. Whether this policy will contribute to economic stagflation in years to come, as Johnson's policy did, remains to be seen.

The large budget deficits also provided Democrats ammunition to attack the Bush tax cuts and argue for their repeal on the grounds that, during times of war, all must share the national burden. Worse for Bush, in the face of rising deficits and an economic recovery that still had not been realized in most households in terms of lost jobs replaced or incomes expanded, by 2004 his public approval ratings began to slide below the 60 percent level, returning to what they had been before 9/11. Even the capture of Saddam Hussein in October 2003 seemed something of an anticlimax. Hussein's capture did not end the insurgency, which continued to inflict pinpricks of pain on the

U.S. occupation forces. Thus, after three years in office, one horrific terrorist attack, two successful military campaigns, and a tepid economy, George W. Bush went into his re-election year far more vulnerable to Democratic challenge than might have been imaged the previous year.

Ultimately, while George W. Bush entered office promising a new, non-partisan tone and a conservative agenda tempered by compassion, his actual legislative and executive record has been strongly partisan and only partially compassionate. His tax cut, while billed as giving money back to all Americans, continued the supply-side dogma of flooding capital to the investment class—whether done in the belief that this would some day help average people on the street or simply help rich political supporters notwithstanding—in the same mode as the Reagan tax cuts two decades before. Like Reagan and his father, he continued to expand federal spending, arguably for the same irresistible reason of fighting a war of national defense, which, coupled with the tax cuts and declining revenues from a weak economy (the lowest rate of revenue as a percentage of GDP since 1950), produced the massive deficits that will dog the domestic policy debate for years to come. This will inevitably produce a crowding out effect on any attempts to expand social spending programs over the next decade, which will be made all the worse by the coming tidal wave of social security and Medicare red ink produced by baby boomers jumping en masse into the entitlement pool. While failure to address the looming social security crisis has been a failure of all recent presidencies, the temporal proximity of Bush's to the coming disaster underscores his failure to act. Meanwhile, the true insidious problem of massive deficits on the heels of tax cuts that has been compounding for two decades continues to grow. Deficits produced by tax cuts now require the government to borrow back at interest the money it had previously taken by law. Repayment by the government of the interest on this accumulated debt effectively transfers tens of billions of dollars in revenues collected from mid- and lower income tier households to those in the upper tier, the wealthiest 5-10 percent of the population. Thus, Bush's policies have directly increased the propensity towards income inequality in a society that already has the most extreme levels of such inequality in the industrial world. At current rates, within a few short decades the gap between the richest and poorest 20 percent of American society will reach that of third world countries like Guatemala. The long-term legacy of Bush fiscal policy may well be a country eventually as torn by divisive class and social schisms as such societies as well.

There has also been a marked tendency of the administration to give lip service to ideas of expanding free trade while subverting trade initiatives to satisfy domestic political concerns. While lambasting China and other exporters for protectionist policies, the administration did not hesitate to slap high tariffs on steel imports. Bush's justification of these tariffs as a response to unfair "dumping" practices by European and Asian producers was later rejected by the World Trade Organization, precipitating a dropping of the sanctions before countersanctions against the United States could be authorized. Most observers saw the tariffs as a direct political sop to the American steel industry and its employees in key electoral states such as Michigan, Ohio, and Pennsylvania, which Bush needed to secure for the 2004 campaign. While all administrations manipulate global trade agreements to appease domestic producers (such as the high U.S. subsidies to protect American sugar producers), the Bush steel tariffs were particularly transparent and heavy-handed, undermining the administration's position in other ongoing trade discussions.

The administration's "weak dollar" policy adopted in 2003 has even more potentially harmful long-term consequences. The American dollar was exceedingly strong in comparison to other currencies by the late 1990s, fueled in part by a tremendous influx of foreign capital looking for riches in the booming American economy. Thus, the Euro, introduced to trade at parity with the dollar, quickly declined to 85 percent of the dollar's value by 2000. The strong dollar helped to exacerbate America's traditional balance of trade deficit, as it made American exports less competitive against foreign goods and made imports cheaper for Americans to buy. The move to allow the dollar to decline in value was seen by many economists as a natural, desirable, and necessary policy for Bush to pursue. A cheaper dollar would make imports more expensive, stimulate U.S. exports, and add jobs to the American economy.

Unremarked by most experts was the impact of foreign exchange markets and, particularly, actions by Asian central banks in light of the U.S. move to weaken the dollar. Fearing a declining dollar would make their own exports to the U.S. less profitable (as economic theory would indicate), Asian banks have dumped tens of billions of dollars back into the U.S. Treasury by loaning dollars to the U.S. government to finance the massive Bush deficits. These actions kept the dollar from sliding enough to have a major impact on U.S./Asia trade (though its impact on European exporters had a more immediate impact leading to accusations from the other side of the Atlantic that the Bush policy was in part punishment for the failure of Germany and France to support its war over Iraq). While any job growth generated by the weak dollar would not have an impact on the overall economy until 2005 at the earliest, the massive infusion of Asian capital to underwrite the U.S. deficit meant that the U.S. did not have to otherwise raise interest rates to attract lending, which would have dampened the U.S. recovery heading into the fall 2004 election. The Bush weak dollar policy smacked, as did its steel tariff plan, of more than a little election year manipulation. The downside of this policy was a huge increase in American national indebtedness to foreign lenders and the real possibility that sometime after the 2004 election foreign lenders might decide, either because of continuing huge deficits, an economic downturn, some foreign policy setback, or all of the above, to ease out of American markets, resulting in a sudden and dramatic decline in the value of the dollar and a major upturn in interest rates. As a result, Bush economic policies that worked well during an election year—massive federal spending and tax cuts to woo the public funded by foreign borrowing—could become a major dampening factor on the economy after the 2004 election, triggering a slide back into an even deeper recession than that of 2000-2001. Given the fragile nature of the global economy, such a renewed American recession could have significant global impact.

The tendency of the administration's international policy to score political points with domestic interest groups would be replicated in the areas of health and social policy as well. When the administration replaced the usual AMA medical delegation sent to July's UN's World Health Organization conference with a specifically selected pro-life delegation, lacking in scientific expertise but solid in conservative credentials, the delegation would go on to vote with the most conservative Islamic nations on a host of resolutions dealing with women's and reproductive health. Growing international wariness—and indeed anger—with the Bush administration was reflected in a May 2001 vote by the UN Commission on Human Rights to boot the U.S. for obstruction. The administration, joined by conservative supporters, denounced the action (which left such notorious human rights abusers as Syria and China on the commission) as further evidence of how irrelevant international organizations had become. But for being forced to seek international support post 9/11, the administration would have been more than content to have pursued an international policy stressing unilateral American prerogatives at a cost to global support unprecedented since the Vietnam war days.

Like his father, the defining foreign policy event of the George W. Bush administration was not initiated by the president. While Bush's initial response in the hours after 9/11 unfolded on the television screens of America was shaky, he achieved his finest hours in the days and weeks thereafter. Yet, with the passage of time historians may be inclined to suggest that the Bush administration overstated the threat that Al Qaeda and terrorism poised to overall American security and overreacted at least to some degree. Whether this harking on the terrorist threat was purely legitimate or contained at least some elements of opportunistic fear mongering for political advantage has and will be the subject of intense partisan and academic debate.

For example, shortly after 9/11 the administration announced the creation of a new "Shadow Government" (an ill-considered phrase that gave conspiracy theorists everywhere grist for their internet websites and chatrooms), which was to be relocated from Washington, D.C. to a secure bunker location outside of Greenbriar, West Virginia, to guarantee that, in the event of a devastating terrorist attack on Washington, the central government would continue to function. The Greenbriar complex had been developed during the 1950s to provide long-term shelter to high-ranking government officials from nuclear attack. Eisenhower, however, had scoffingly refused to even consider retreating to such a hole in the ground, even in the face of Soviet atomic might. The Bush administration, however, apparently felt the threat level poised by terrorism to be sufficient to institute policies that Eisenhower, facing nuclear Armageddon, did not. Dick Cheney seems to have spent a fair amount of the months immediately after 9/11 buried in West Virginia.

Indeed, the Bush administration responded to Al Qaeda with policies that in many cases exceeded those kept in place during the cold war years. Bush used the terrorist threat to justify the adoption of a new doctrine of military and a strategic force plan that called for the possibility of first use of nuclear weapons—something the U.S. studiously rejected for fifty years following World War II. While the administration would claim that its tough stance on Iraq was instrumental in bringing rogue power Libya back into the international fold, it could easily be argued that the doctrine of preemption has served to drive at least North Korea and possibly Iran to accelerate their WMD programs so as to provide a deterrent against precisely such American preemption. After 9/11, the president and his supporters also made constant reference to America being "at war" and "on a war footing," comparable to the cold war; yet the administration took few of the domestic steps usually associated with being at war. That Bush chose to fund the war with deficit spending is not unusual. Debt and war historically go hand in hand. That he chose to fund the war with deficit spending while pushing significant tax cuts is somewhat unusual, though one need look no farther back than Ronald Reagan to find another president who did precisely the same thing. But Bush never backed up his rhetoric of a nation sacrificing at war with any meaningful domestic policies—not even a call for greater fuel conservation to cut dependence on Middle Eastern oil and certainly not a tax on new energy inefficient SUVs. While the president eventually acquiesced on the creation of a new department of Homeland Security, little real money and presidential initiative was put into the new department beyond federalizing airport screeners (while depriving them of rights of collective bargaining in the name of national security) and adopting a color code threat alert system that quickly became the butt of late night television comedians—the post-9/11 equivalent of a Gerald Ford's "WIN" button.

Herein lay another characteristic of the Bush administration, post-9/11: the strategy of bringing every aspect of its foreign and domestic policies under the "brand name" of the "War on Terror" to advance a broad domestic conservative and global neo-conservative agenda. Once the initial shock of 9/11 subsided in Washington, D. C., the very real, raw, and deep partisan divisions within the Congress naturally returned. At every turn, where Democrats sought to question, modify, or block administration policy, both the White House and congressional Republicans played the war card, calling for "bipartisanship" (bipartisanship [n]: to call upon others to shut up and do what you say) in times of war. Forgetting a long history of loyal opposition in times of war (including contested wartime presidential elections in 1864, 1916, 1944, 1952, 1964, 1968, and 1972, as well as the famous instance of war leader Winston Churchill's parliamentary defeat in 1945), Republican politicians and conservative media accused disagreeing Democrats of undermining the war effort (if not giving outright aide and comfort to the other side or even committing treason). Thus, drilling in ANWR was reintroduced (though no more successfully) as now necessary to make America energy-independent in times of war. Congress passed a law federalizing airport security workers and then pushed through the administration's request that these workers and a host of others now working under the Homeland Security umbrella be denied rights of collective bargaining on national security grounds (thereby also dispensing as irrelevant a long history of the government employing union workers in security-related jobs even during times of war). The president's call for a second round of tax cuts in 2002 would be justified on the national security grounds of keeping the wartime economy strong; his reaffirmed call for the confirmation of conservative nominees to the federal appellate bench was now justified for the need to keep the judiciary strong to handle the challenges of terrorism; and even the "No Child Left Behind" initiative was pursued with renewed vigor as a patriotic duty in times of struggle.

George W. Bush was one of the least cosmopolitan figures to achieve the presidency in modern times, a man who had seldom traveled abroad, not out of lack of opportunity or means but out of simple lack of interest and a professed disdain for things "un-American." What some would call a "focused" approach to other nations, dealing with them from an exclusive prism of American strategic and domestic political interests others would call narrow-minded. Be that as it may, one can only help but feel that a president who would get visibly irritated with an American reporter for asking questions of the president of France in French at a joint press conference between the American and French presidents in Paris might be at least somewhat ineffective at maintaining the *entente cordiale* with traditional European allies. Indeed, the only foreign leaders with whom Bush established a sustained rapport were British Prime Minister Tony Blair (the erudite prime minister and the malaproping president becoming something of a verbal odd couple who seemed to personally get along surprisingly well) and Russian President Vladamir Putin. Bush was raked in the press for seeming to fawn over Putin at their first meeting in June 2001, remarking afterwards that he had been "able to get a sense of the ex-KGB officer's soul." Bush saw in Putin a potential ally in an area of mutual concern: Islamic radical fundamentalism of the sort that had led to the abortive attack on the World Trade Center in 1993 and fueled the flames of separatism in the break-away Russian province of Chechnya. Bush would also require Putin's acquiescence in dismantling the 1972 IBM treaty, which Bush received, allowing the administration to formally terminate the agreement in December 1972 amidst European Union and Chinese ire but only minor Russian grumbling. The only price tag on Russian support would be American silence on an increasingly violent war of suppression by the Russians against the Chechens, with its resulting rise in human rights abuses (something with which the administration would become painfully familiar firsthand with the Iraqi prison abuse scandals in the spring of 2004). Thus, prior to 9/11, Bush's foreign policy progressively isolated the U.S. in the global community, which his supporters gave nary a worry about given their "go it alone" preference. While the world community rallied to the U.S. immediately following the terrorist attacks, the continued preference of the administration for an "America first," "with us or against us" foreign policy worked to undermine U.S. support, sending it again to levels not seen since the early Reagan years or the Vietnam era. This global division would be intensified by the decision to go to war with Iraq in 2003.

No aspect of the George W. Bush presidency has proven to be as controversial and open to future historical judgment than the decision to go to war with Iraq. Bush's justification for war with Iraq boiled down to three claims: Saddam Hussein was endeavoring to develop weapons of mass destruction, including chemical, biological, and nuclear, which he might use against the United States or its allies; he supported terrorists even to the point of potentially arming them with these devastating weapons; and he was a heinous dictator who brutalized his people. Of the last claim there is no doubt. Over his twenty-five years in power, Hussein wracked up a horrifyingly impressive record of human rights abuses and mass murder. Even though his last major round of mass murder had arguably subsided in 1991, following his brutal crushing of an insurrection by Iraqi Shi'ite Muslims in southern Iraq following the first Gulf War, human rights abuses continued right up to the American invasion. President Bush presented evidence establishing a peripheral link between the Hussein regime and Al Qaeda—several Al Qaeda operatives had transited through Iraq in the past, and Iraqi facilities created to train anti-Iranian insurgents may have also trained mujeheen associated with the terrorist network. At no time did the administration present anything amounting to a smoking-gun directly connecting Hussein to the 9/11 attack, this despite substantial public belief, fed by both administration innuendo and media rhetoric, to the contrary.

The administration based its most critical claim that Hussein was pursuing WMDs on his previous history of using chemical weapons in the past (against separatist Kurds in the 1970s and Iranians during the 1980s Iran-Iraqi war), on UN weapon inspectors' reports from the 1990s that could not account for all materials Hussein possessed that could be used to develop WMDs, and Clinton-era intelligence, reaffirmed by the current CIA director held over from the Clinton years, that Hussein still actively desired to produce such weapons. Over the next year the administration would make numerous clear statements and present evidence both to the American public and the global community proving "beyond doubt" that Saddam Hussein not only desired such weapons but also had already developed, operationalized, and deployed them, making him a clear and present danger to American interests. As of this writing, in the more than eighteen months following the successful American invasion of Iraq, no significant evidence of such weapons or even of operational development programs has as yet been discovered, which casts doubt on either the administration's veracity or the quality of the intelligence upon which the war was based. Final verdict on this matter awaits the passage of time. The net effect of the controversy over WMDs would be to rob the administration of at least some of the luster of victory after the main shooting war stopped, as critics would raise the cry of "where are the weapons?" thereby diminishing the legitimacy of the war itself.

George W. Bush entered office with a nation at peace and a federal budget in surplus. How to spend the surplus would be the defining feature of his first six months in office. That these wholesale reversals of budget and peace occurred on George W. Bush's watch is not in and of itself a condemnation. Inheriting an economy already in recession and a foreign environment already populated with known enemies of the United States—Osama bin Laden and Al Qaeda had made the American hit parade of terrorist threats a decade before—Bush was only in part reaping what had been sown before him. His own policies, however, intensified the deficit problem and, to date, have less than decisively dealt with the terrorist threat.

The Bush legacy, however, will be judged ultimately on the success of his foreign policy, the boldest assertion of American power since Reagan certainly and perhaps even Teddy Roosevelt a century before. Americans judge the success or failure of a military intervention by three simple criteria: how much did it cost in money and, more importantly, blood; why did we do it; and, most critically, did we win or lose? World War II is the archetype successful war. While its costs were high, the costs of defeat would have been infinitely higher because we were fighting for the survival of our civilization, and it ended in the unconditional vanquishing of our foes. By the reverse token, Vietnam is the archetype failure: high costs, confused reasoning, and clear defeat. How George W. Bush's wars will be measured over their entirety remains to be seen, as neither the struggle in Afghanistan nor Iraq are concluded as of this writing, and the war on terror is projected to last for a generation or more.

Though public support for the war in Iraq remained high a full year after the initial invasion, a slew of negative news coming out of the country in the spring of 2004 began to seriously erode public support for, and confidence in, the Iraqi operation. The capture of Saddam Hussein in the fall of 2003 gave heart to an American public looking for a sign of a neat ending to the war, à la the death of Hitler and the capitulation of the Japanese at the end of World War II. Continued low-scale harassment of American forces by a hodgepodge of displaced remnants of the *ancien regime*, foreign agitators, and domestic political factions looking to establish their own claims to a share of the postwar political and economic pie gave lie to hopes for any such easy conclusion of the American-led "liberation" of Iraq. Claims by 2004 that Iraq was turning into a Vietnam-style quagmire were most certainly overstated. American forces endured casualties averaging over a hundred killed per week in the Vietnam war; American weekly losses in Iraq over the period amounted to less than ten per week—a tenfold difference. Yet, the continued reports of steady, if light, casualties coming from a country in which the commander in chief had announced the successful end to military operations a full year before led the public to conclude that the mission to Iraq was far from a successful and final solution. While the administration pointed out that it required years of occupation to restore order and democracy to Germany and Japan, critics pointed out that only a handful of American troops were killed by hostile action across the entirety of that occupation. Nor did any organized, militant anti-American opposition ever develop in either defeated nation to undermine the process of democratization. Thus, while critics of the occupation in Iraq erred in comparing it to Vietnam, supporters likewise erred in comparing it to Germany or Japan. Time may well prove better comparisons to be the British occupation of Northern Ireland (a long but, ultimately, politically successful instance) or the Israeli occupation of southern Lebanon (long, ugly, and unsuccessful).

Public support for the Iraq conflict was further and significantly undermined by numerous confirmed reports of brutality by American military police and intelligence operatives at the Abu Ghraib prison complex used to house suspected terrorists and other agitators, plus a number of others apparently apprehended in round-ups following the collapse of the Hussein regime. The actual actions at Abu Ghraib may arguably be attributable to misconduct of a relatively few members of the American occupation force. Yet, the failure of the Bush administration to swiftly deal with the crisis in a public way, establishing a clear chain of accountability up the line of command to higher ranking military officers or civilian administrators (who, if not guilty of actually authorizing the misconduct, might at least be considered guilty of sins of omission in failing to properly oversee operations at the prison) even as lower ranking service personnel were indicted for their actions gave the public and critics an impression of either a cover-up in the making or massive incompetence.

Moreover, the global circulation of graphic photographic evidence of American abuse of Iraqi prisoners undercut the Bush administration's claim to the moral high ground in its dealings with Iraq and other authoritarian regimes. Abu Ghraib had been used by Saddam Hussein to torture his people; to see the "liberators" using the facility for the same purpose gave massive quantities of grist to every anti-American propaganda machine from Pyongyang to Tehran (despite the obvious differences in moral magnitude of the actions involved, with torture and mass executions being a standard policy of the Hussein regime, while prisoner abuse is an aberration to the norms espoused and embraced by any American administration). The administration added an almost Orwellian twist to the scandal when President Bush announced that the U.S. would deal with the problems at the prison by bulldozing it and building a new one.

The most surprising aspect of the Iraqi prisoner-abuse atrocity may well be that the administration—having in its ranks numerous members who served in uniform or in government during the Vietnam war with its own record of occasional atrocities committed by U.S. troops—was not better prepared to deal with the crisis when it erupted. That such veterans of the Vietnam experience (such as Donald Rumsfeld and Colin Powell) were not prepared to swiftly and effectively deal with the inevitable atrocious acts that a few soldiers in any conflict will always engage in underscored two disturbing tendencies of the Bush administration: a failure to learn from past American mistakes and over-optimism in estimating the costs and outcomes in formulating foreign policy. Going into the spring of 2004, the turnaround in public opinion was unanticipated by politicians and pundits alike, helping to make the fall election in 2004 far closer than anyone might have imagined in the months following 9/11 and Bush's overwhelming popularity.

However the Iraqi campaign plays out in the public mind, the fact of the matter is that, by embracing the neo-conservative world view as American policy, George W. Bush took a tremendous national gamble that neo-con voices within the White House are correct in their fundamental assumption that the United States is now confronted with a narrow window of opportunity in which it can unilaterally reshape the world in its own image. In 1950, America strode the world like a colossus; the dollar was undisputed global king, America controlled half the planet's industrial capacity and was the world's clear dominant nuclear power. By 2000, even as the gap between the U.S. and its nearest national competitor swelled to unprecedented proportion, the gap in power between the U.S. and the world at large had narrowed dramatically. The dollar now accounts for less than 70 percent of global trade—a significant decline, as has been the rapid decline of the dollar versus other currencies in 2003-2004. Whatever the short-term value, national greatness has seldom been predicated upon a weak currency. The U.S. now accounts for less than 20 percent of the world's industry, and now even small, impoverished nations, or even smaller fanatical groups, can aspire to belong to the WMD club. The real and most destabilizing lesson of Iraq was not that a ruthless, bloodthirsty Hollywood caricature of a third world tin-plated dictator might *seek* to acquire weapons of mass destruction. Destruction, mass or otherwise, was what Saddam Hussein specialized in. The real issue of Iraq was that, by the beginning of the twenty-first century, a ruthless, bloodthirsty Hollywood caricature of a third world tin-plated dictator could indeed actually *acquire* weapons of mass destruction. Thus, like Rome before her, the United States faces the real possibility that the very technological superiority that has protected her from her enemies, civilized and barbarian alike, is now eroding. Rome ultimately fell 1,500 years ago because of its inability to integrate the "barbarian" peoples—barbarians whose technologies of war and destruction had caught up with "civilization's"—of northern and eastern Europe into the Roman economic, cultural, and political sphere. Denied access to the rewards of the Roman regional game, with no vested interest in its continuation, these peoples simply kicked the game board over, sending the Roman world into a thousand-year political and economic depression. So too are the stakes of the current global game. Unless the United States and the developed world can find a way—soon, within a handful of generations at most—to integrate the five billion people on the planet who do not currently have a stake in the modern global game, they too may well kick the global board over sending humanity into a millennium—or longer—dark age.

The neo-con argument is that the best way for the U.S. to maintain its security amidst such rising global instability is the creation of a "New World Order" based on pure American military hegemony. When the administration published "The National Security Strategy of the United States" in September 2002, it basically laid out the policy foundation for such Pax Americana by asserting that the U.S. would maintain military superiority over any other nation or group of nations and would consider the employment of any weapon in its arsenal in pursuit of national security, even the preemptive use of such weapons, thereby setting aside fifty years of American no-first-use doctrine. America has faced the prospects of proclaiming its own Imperium three times in its history. At the conclusions of each of the major wars of the twentieth century, the U.S. was revealed as the single strongest military and economic power. For a brief time after World War II the U.S. alone had the "bomb," and quite a few voices urged its use, or the threat of its use, to create an American-dominated order before the window of opportunity closed and rival powers arose to hold America back. After the collapse of the Soviet Union, America was the last standing superpower. Yet, each time the nation chose not to seek empire, turning instead to the creation of multinational institutions constituted on liberal values of national self-determination and multilateral consensus building. Wilson gave the world the League of Nations, and FDR and Truman the United Nations. Following the U.S.S.R.'s demise, George H.W. Bush turned to the UN and to a global grand coalition to deal with the Iraqi menace. George W. Bush alone stands out as a president who turned from the multilateral path to pursue a unique American course. The payoff of Bush's gamble would be a world made safe by American resolve to use power effectively and crushingly against all "evil doers" who seek to destabilize the international system. Achieving this goal, however, will take more than the conquests of two Islamic countries. Indeed, leading up to Iraq, neo-con thinkers both in and outside of the administration were asking the question—who next? Tehran? Damascus? Riyadh? The "joke" going around Washington in the heady post-Afghanistan days was, "Everyone wants to go to Baghdad. Real men want to go to Tehran." In this view, until the whole of the world, Islamic and otherwise, is brought within the American sphere of democracy and free markets, America will remain at risk from those on the outside.

The alternative to the Bush Doctrine would be a return to the multilateral processes of global conflict resolution that dominated much of postwar history. One of the price tags of Bush's foreign policy to date, however, has been a reversal of the general global support of the United States generated by 9/11—squandered, critics of the president would say; necessarily sacrificed for U.S. freedom of action, neo-con supporters argue—and an unprecedented rift between the U.S. and several of its principle postwar allies. Given the American strategy of deliberately snubbing multilateral institutions and processes over the first Bush term, it is questionable if and how well relationships might be repaired with such institutions and nations should the U.S. discover that the cost of going it alone exceeds either its resources or resolve. Ultimately, this could leave the United States in the worst of all foreign policy environments: bogged down in failed nation-building exercises in Afghanistan and Iraq, isolated from its allies and multinational institutions, and facing rising challenges from regimes accelerating their efforts to acquire WMDs as an insurance policy against a future application of the Bush Doctrine. Such has arguably been the case with North Korea. The fact that the Bush administration withheld the use of force against a hostile country claiming to already possess nuclear weapons after going to war against another country only alleged to have such weapons has also undoubtedly been noticed in capitols around the world. In the wake of Iraq, possession of WMDs may now be seen by numerous regimes hostile to American interests as a necessity for survival. The ultimate pay-off of the Bush gamble may be a world less, not more, stable than it was in the days following 9/11.

George W. Bush is the ultimate president of the twentieth century, not the first president of the twenty-first. On his watch, the social cleavages exposed and deepened by the cultural revolution of the 1960s and the conservative counter revolution of the 1980s and 1990s, as well as the international political uncertainties produced by the ending of the cold war, have all come to a head. Until these uncertainties are resolved, we continue to live haunted by the legacy of the last century, unable to clearly perceive what twenty-first century life will be about. George Bush himself entered office in the shadow of the legacy of his father, his generation, and his century. He headed into his re-election campaign certain of only one thing—the legacy he has already amassed as president—that of a veritable revolution in American foreign policy thinking that will affect the international order for decades to come—far outstrips the legacies left by either of his two immediate predecessors. As president, George W. Bush has become the master, and captive, of his own legacy.

George W. Bush at Yale University,
1964-1968.
Photo credit:
George
Bush Presidential Library

George W. Bush in
the Texas Air National
Guard,
1968-1973.
Photo credit:
George Bush Presidential
Library

George W. Bush
holds his twin
daughters,
Barbara and
Jenna, born in
Dallas, Texas, on
November 25,
1981.
Photo credit:
George Bush
Presidential
Library

George W. Bush congressional campaign poster, circa 1978. Photo credit: George Bush Presidential Library

George W. Bush talks with workers in the Midland, Texas, oil fields while campaigning for Congress, 1978. Photo credit: George Bush Presidential Library

President Bush with son, George W. Bush, and baseball broadcaster, Joe Morgan, in the locker room in Dallas, Texas, April 8, 1991. Photo credit: George Bush Presidential Library

THE 2004 PRESIDENTIAL ELECTION

In retrospect, one should not have expected any other outcome. A presidency as dramatic and controversial as that of George W. Bush simply could not be contained within only one term of office. For Bush to have lost his bid for reelection would not have been unusual by any means—of his five immediate predecessors, three had failed in winning reelection to office (though, to be accurate, Gerald Ford had never been elected in the first place). Despite having achieved public approval ratings in the aftermath of September 11, 2001, rivaling that of his father in 1991, having a recovering economy, having won two wars, and having no high profile popular Democratic opponent at the threshold of the 2004 campaign, Bush's election was not a given. Indeed, across the tumultuous battleground of 2004, there would be no moment at which politicians and pundits could agree that Bush had nailed down his reelection, right up until the moment ballots were cast. Yet, for Bush to have followed in his father's footsteps—footsteps he had chosen to follow for most of his life—would have been a rejection of the sense of inevitability that had been the hallmark of his political life since his first run for the governorship of Texas barely a decade before. Such was not to be the final legacy of George W. Bush.

The 2004 election was a testament to the polarization of the Bush years, which had further divided an America divided since the 1960s into two ideological colors, Red and Blue, with little unifying purple in between. The 2004 election pitted fear versus loathing in America. The loathing was the intense dislike that a substantial portion of Americans (overwhelmingly Democrats) had for George W. Bush personally and for most of Bush's policies, from the environment to the economy to foreign affairs. For this bluest of "Blue America," Bush had come to represent the most reactionary aspects of the conservative revolution that had been unfurling its battle flag since Barry Goldwater in 1964. The fear was two-fold. On the one hand, it was the fear of terrorism shared across America and fed by the shock of an actual attack on the homeland and the promise that future such attacks were inevitably in the wings. On the other hand, it was the fear felt particularly by "Red America," and most particular amongst the reddest of the Red, that since the 1960s America had progressively lost its moral center, sinking into a secular sump of moral ambiguity or outright moral corruption.

In 1980, Red America had voted for Reagan, expecting a real conservative revolution that would reverse the social and moral excesses of the Democrat-dominated 1960s. Instead, they got a partial revolution: strong on tax cuts, strong on foreign policy, but weak on engineering real social reversion. In 2000, Red America voted for George W. Bush as a candidate superior to the "son" of Clinton, Al Gore, who, like any good son, had rebelled against his father in his own campaign, but with little hope that Bush would be the one to lead them to the Promised Land. So disheartened were the reddest of Red America after eight years of a popular immoralist like Bill Clinton that millions of their numbers stayed home, almost denying Bush victory. Expecting moderate change, they got in Bush's first term the foundation for a true conservative shift in American politics and society and, possibly, the final coming of the revolution foretold and promised by the Reagan years.

Indeed, the 2004 presidential election will go down in history alongside other elections that served to solidify the revolution set into play by the previous election. Such watershed reelections included that of U.S. Grant's 1876 reelection, cementing Republican hegemony (but for two disconnected terms by Grover Cleveland) for the balance of the century, FDR's reelection in 1936 that set the New Deal revolution firmly on track for the next 40 years, and Reagan's own 1984 reelection that promised a conservative tinge to American politics through the end of the twentieth century. Then, it would turn even more conservative under the consecutive victories of George W. Bush, victories that firmly entrenched Republican hegemony with the first back-to-back Republican presidential victory in twenty years (coupled with the Republicans maintaining control of both the House and the Senate, giving them a solid decade of congressional dominance—something they had not achieved in over a century).

Despite all the 2004 election might have delivered for Republicans, it delivered far less than it should have for the Republic. For the American political system, what was needed from the 2004 election was a clean, decisive election victory for one side or the other to dispel from the winner any lingering vestiges of political illegitimacy such as had dogged both Bill Clinton across two terms and George W. Bush during his first term. What Americans could have used was a crushing victory by a candidate and a party to demonstrate a newfound unity and center to

American politics and establish an environment in which brutal partisan divisions emerging in the 1990s and the early 2000s could be narrowed. Alas, it wasn't to be.

PRIMARIES

Both the voters and the public at large (the two groups need be distinguished between, as fewer than half of eligible adult voters have bothered both to register and to vote in recent elections) for the most part had accepted the outcome of the 2000 election, legally disputed though it might have been. The Democrat outrages in December were largely forgotten by the inauguration of George W. Bush the following January. That is not to say that all the "Bush is illegitimate" protesters went quietly into the night. A large number of protesters showed up in Washington, D.C. on Bush's big day, sufficient in numbers and loudness as to precipitate a change in the new president's inaugural route. The protesters, however, got scant coverage from a media generally together in presenting a story line "package" of America together once more. The media perception quickly became the public reality, and the wounds of division from the 2000 election seemed to have scabbed over nicely during Bush's first term. Even if polls continued to show that substantial numbers of Americans felt in their hearts that the Bushes slept in the White House under false pretenses, for the most part such talk did not breach polite discussion, especially after 9/11. By the 2004 election, however, memories of the alleged injustices of 2000 for Democrats and Republican fears of a reprise of Clinton's reversing victory in 1992 had resurfaced—lock, stock, and two-party smoking electoral barrels.

The events of September 11, 2001, and the subsequent war in Afghanistan served to have a similar quelling effect on the emergence of Democratic candidates for president as the Gulf War had had in 1991. With the nation coming together in the wake of the terrorist attack and George W. Bush experiencing public approval ratings of 80 percent, potential Democratic candidates, such as Al Gore or House minority leader Dick Gephardt, avoided the unnecessary partisan antagonism of actually organizing to run against a popular war president. By the end of 2002, however, Bush's popularity was sagging. Controversy was rising over the looming war with Iraq. International opposition to the Bush policy agenda was becoming louder and more universally felt, and with the midterm elections out of the way, Democratic minds could turn to unseating an opposition president who might prove vulnerable after all.

The Democratic battle to pick a standard bearer to revenge 2000 started less than halfway into George W. Bush's first term. On May 31, 2002, Vermont Governor Howard B. Dean III formed a presidential exploratory committee. Dean had limited national name recognition except amongst a strata of liberal Democratic Party activists. A medical doctor, he did have a reputation within political circles as a competent administrator and an intelligent centrist-liberal, but he lacked any real record of significant policy achievement. Democrats had shown a penchant for throwing their nomination over the past three decades to little-known governors of smaller states, as with Jimmy Carter and Bill Clinton. The last Democratic candidate to win election who was not a Southern governor was Southerner Senator Lyndon Baines Johnson in 1964. The last Democratic New Englander or Midwesterner to win both the party nomination and the general election was Senator John F. Kennedy in 1960. Thus, Dean was seen early on as both a long shot and lightweight candidate.

The field for Democrats opened up on December 16, 2002, when former vice president and 2000 presidential candidate Al Gore announced that he would not seek his party's nomination for a second time. Gore (having recently wrapped up a nationwide book tour) had been widely expected to run again, reclaiming the party standard for a campaign of revenge. But the last defeated standard bearer to reclaim his party's nomination (in consecutive elections) was Democratic Governor Adlai Stevenson, who went down to defeat at the hands of Republican Dwight Eisenhower both in 1952 and 1956. Nixon had won the Republican nomination and lost in 1960, only reclaiming the party crown after an eight-year interregnum (following Goldwater's fabulous failure in 1964). Since the 1960s, the label of "loser" has apparently become harder to shake. Defeated party nominees have faded away into the quieter (and often more lucrative) world of the private sector (as Gerald Ford, George H.W. Bush, and Bob Dole did after their defeats), into the world of public and humanitarian service (as Jimmy Carter and Walter Mondale did), into the high profile world of publishing, or into the role as senior statesman of the party, as Ronald Reagan (who would have continued as a force to be reckoned with for years had Alzheimer's not intervened) or Bill Clinton. As no defeated party nominee had reclaimed his party leadership in thirty-six years, Gore's decision not to run was not seen as too great a surprise.

The prospect of Gore reclaiming as rightfully his the party mantle and nomination had caused a number of potential serious contenders to hold off entering the fray. Taking Gore out of the equation released the floodgates of Democratic presidential contenders. Connecticut Senator Joseph Lieberman, Gore's 2000 vice presidential running mate and a widely considered Democratic centrist, had previously promised not to run should Gore seek their party's nomination. With Gore's decision, Lieberman now joined the fray.

John F. Kerry, U.S. senator from Massachusetts, announced his plans to form an exploratory committee for a possible 2004 presidential run that December. Kerry wisely, however, did not build on many of the similarities to JFK, "initial"-wise or otherwise, even though both were war veteran Massachusetts' senators. Kerry would, however, be the third Massachusetts' Democrat to make a run for the presidency in two decades, joining Governor Michael Dukakis, who won the nomination in 1988 but lost the presidency, and former Senator Paul Tsongas, who failed to win the nomination in 1992.

By the end of January 2003, first term U.S. Senator John R. Edwards of North Carolina, veteran congressional leader Dick Gephardt of Missouri, and the activist Reverend Al Sharpton of New York had all thrown their hats into the nomination ring. Meanwhile, Tom Daschle, the United States Senate Minority Leader, also widely expected to run, announced that he would not. (Daschle ultimately ended up defeated in a surprisingly close race just to hold onto his seat in South Dakota, following former Democratic Speaker of the House Tom Foley onto the recent list of Democratic congressional leaders who were turned out of office.) By the end of February, three more contenders jumped into the arena: Carol Moseley Braun, former senator from Illinois; Dennis Kucinich, Representative from Ohio; and outgoing Senator Bob Graham of Florida.

In addition to Daschle, Senators Christopher Dodd and Joseph Biden, both considered potential candidates, chose not to run. Yet, there really were strong first-tier Democrats who could have had a shot at winning but who sat the 2004 race out—no Ted Kennedys of 1976 or Mario Cuomos of 1992 waiting in the wings for next time round—with the possible exception of the freshman junior senator from New York, Hillary Clinton. Despite much speculation in the media (with conservative AM radio talk show hosts vacillating between terror and glee at the prospect) the former First Lady apparently came to the realization that she cast a polarizing shadow over the 2004 race, potentially resurrecting all the damage Clinton-fatigue had caused her party in 2000. Plus, there was the simple fact that she was a first-term senator, barely two years in elected public office with a scant record of senatorial accomplishment leaving her only credentials as First Lady with all the accompanying controversy on which to run. Beyond Clinton, just about any and every Democrat with a real national reputation and a shot at winning in 2004 joined the fracas.

The Democrats "Fellowship of the Nine" dwarfed even the large Republican 1996 field (a group referred to at the time as "The Seven Dwarfs," which Bob Dole would finally come to dominate after a bruising primary season). A huge field forming against an incumbent works to the incumbent's advantage, as his eventual opponent from the other party will have to have waged bloody infighting, as Dole did against Pat Buchanan and Steven Forbes. Weakened by a hotly contested primary fight, already having tested epithets of derision pinned to him by his own party member primary opponents and having spent a hunk of cash just winning the nomination, Dole entered the general election campaign at a huge (and ultimately insurmountable) disadvantage with incumbent Bill Clinton, who had won his own renomination without having to fire a shot. Republican strategists could only hope that Democrats would experience the same thing in 2004 as their divided party waged cruel war upon itself to produce a nominee.

In the collective minds of the media, at least, Gephardt, Graham, and Dean emerged the closest thing to front-runners early on. Gephardt benefited from his senior party position as minority leader in the House, making him one of the top ranked Democrats in the country. Graham, meanwhile, benefited from his gravitas as a moderate senator from a critical electoral state. Dean, however, was emerging as a new kind of post-modern "E-candidate." Having used the year and a half of relative quiet between his own joining the race in 2001 and the flood of candidates in 2003 to organize a powerful system of grassroots activists through unprecedented use of the Internet, he had created a new funding stream of electronically-solicited small donations that was both cost effective and removed from control by established party interests. By 2003, Dean sat at the center of a web of liberal activist websites that provided a powerful tool to steer millions of dollars in small donations and hours of effort by tens of thousands of activists—"Deaniacs" as they were called—to create a "virtual" party within the Democratic Party—a party that bypassed much of the entrenched power structure that flowed through the fingers of party leaders like Gephardt or Graham.

While Republican spokesmen, such as House Majority Leader Tom Delay, publicly salivated at the chance to run against another liberal

Democrat from New England like Dean and repeatedly tried to paint him as a wild-eyed populist left-wing ideologue (indeed, the story line of Dean as "Wildman of the Left" would become a central feature of media coverage, setting up his eventual demise from the "Dean Scream" in early 2004), the sheer amount of Republican attacks on Dean leading up to the primary season gives pause for analysis. Did Republicans protesteth too much? It may well be that Dean's ability to organize a massive movement outside of traditional channels of political control posed exactly the kind of grassroots threat Republican strategists felt could challenge Bush's own grassroots support built through the more traditional media of evangelical churches.

Dean was the only governor running for the Democratic nomination in 2004. The remainder of the "Fellowship" consisted of four senators, a former senator, two congressmen, and an activist. The presidential bug has bitten many members of Congress across history. The perception (if not always the reality) of the power of members of Congress and senators helps at least to persuade many of them that Congress makes a perfect platform from which to reach for the top political prize. Overwhelmingly, however, this has not proven to be the case, especially since the 1970s. No man has been elected president since Lincoln (1860) after only having served in the House of Representatives. Senators have been more successful in achieving the presidency, especially between World War II and Watergate. But, while 4 of 5 American presidents elected between 1948 and 1968 had served in the U.S. Senate (Truman, Kennedy, Johnson, and Nixon), only Kennedy had been elected directly from the Senate, the other three doing stints as vice president before their eventual elevation.

The collapse of the New Deal coalition in the 1960s and 1970s and the parallel rise of the "Washington is the problem" rhetoric from George Wallace to George W. Bush has served to turn the power senators' derive from their "insider" political status into a significant liability when running outside of their home states and outside of the Washington Beltway. Indeed, since World War II, and even before, the more secure route to the presidency was either through the vice presidency (Truman, Johnson, Nixon, and George H.W. Bush reaching the highest office by that route) or through state executive office (as with Governors Carter, Reagan, Clinton, and George W. Bush). While literally dozens of senators have run for their party nominations since John Kennedy's election, only Barry Goldwater, George McGovern, and Bob Dole actually received it, with disastrous results in the first two instances and just disappointing results in the third.

In 2004, the Democrats' only viable vice president had bowed out of the race, and only one governor had bowed in. The eventual emergence of Senator John Kerry as head of the ticket and Senator John Edwards in the number two spot would seek to turn history and conventional wisdom on its head by postulating that a dual-senatorial ticket could repeat what no one had since the Kennedy-Johnson ticket in 1960: emerge triumphant. In retrospect, history appears to have been a more difficult trend to buck than Democrats assumed. As every presidential election since 1976 has shown, running as an outsider against a Washington insider (even if the outsider is the incumbent president who at least originally won as an outsider) is the surest ticket to victory. The election of 2004 reaffirmed that the best route to the presidency does not lie through the U.S. Senate.

Democrats, therefore, entered the dawn of the real election campaign in the spring of 2003 having fielded a true "Odd Fellowship of the Nine," weak on governors and top heavy on senators. Yet, the senators emerged with an early advantage, at least in the money wars of campaign fund-raising. By the end of the first quarter of 2003, John Edwards and John Kerry led the pack, having raised $7.4 million and $7.0 million, respectively. Congressman Dick Gephardt and Senator Joe Lieberman had each raised about $3.0 million, while Howard Dean, relying on his grassroots Internet campaign, had raised only $2.6 million. (Graham, Kucinich, and Braun had each raised $1 million or less, an early indication of their lack of traction as candidates.)

The first formal debate of the Democratic primary campaign was held on May 3, a full nine months before the casting of the first primary ballots. The campaign kicked off, however, under the shadow of the war in Iraq. Only two days earlier, on May 1, George W. Bush landed on the aircraft carrier *USS Abraham Lincoln*, in a Lockheed S-3 Viking, and gave a speech announcing the end of major combat in the Iraq war. Clearly (and strategically) visible in the background was a banner stating "Mission Accomplished." While Bush's landing was criticized by opponents as overly theatrical and expensive, Bush's approval ratings, which had sagged after the initial burst of war-driven patriotism when the shooting started in March, rose back to a comfortable 66 percent, according to a CNN-USA Today-Gallup poll. As the Democrats gathered at the University of South Carolina for their first debate, national attention was far more fixated upon the president and the war. The candidates disagreed on their support for the war against Iraq, with Howard Dean leading the anti-war charge. All four Democratic senators had voted for the resolution authorizing the war, which put them in a weak position to suddenly develop a significant criticism of it. The candidates also disagreed on core domestic policy concerns, such as health insurance and even President Bush's tax cuts, but were united in criticizing Bush's handling of the economy in general. The first debate helped illustrate the difficulties Democrats would have in framing a national campaign the following year. Neither the candidates nor the public at large had reached a consensus on the Bush war-policy. Moreover, with the economy recovering but not roaring, with unemployment falling but not plummeting, and with the stock market rising but not booming, the public had also not reached a consensus on the efficacy of Bush's economic policies. As long as public opinion on foreign and domestic issues remained a muddle, the Democratic primary debate would remain a muddle, too.

Of course, to call public opinion of the George W. Bush presidency a "muddle" by the spring of 2003 is to overly simplify things. Substantial percentages of the population had a very clear view of the Bush presidency, with Democrats overwhelming rejecting it and Republicans overwhelmingly embracing it. That was precisely the problem for the Democratic candidates. Neither of the two parties has been able to win the presidency since the 1940s by simply mobilizing their own party loyalists. Political players as diverse as Nixon and Clinton realized that in the postwar period a party could only win nationally by reaching out to the mushy moderate middle. For Democrats, that has meant convincing moderates that they could be stronger on defense and less the social liberal activist. For Republicans, that has meant showing they could be peaceniks as well as war hawks and could embrace a "compassionate conservatism"—as both Bush presidents would frame it—and accept the continuation of popular social welfare programs. By the 2004 election, however, much of this mushy middle had disappeared with polls showing an electorate increasingly polarized in its worldview between laissez-faire social conservative Republicans and socially liberal and economic statist Democrats. Meanwhile, the so-called independent voters had been revealed as something of a political myth in the 2000 and 2002 elections. Such voters, independent in name, were increasingly and consistently being found actually to vote with either the left or the right. True independents who might swing their vote from party to party within and between elections have been becoming a progressively smaller share of the electorate.

The increasing polarization of the electorate through the 1990s into the 2000s presented a challenge to political strategists of both parties but proved in the 2004 election cycle to be a bigger problem for Democrats. The increasing social conservatism of the electorate and the loss in faith in Washington since the 1960s as a force for economic growth and egalitarianism had shifted the median of American politics more to the right, making it easier for Republicans to reach out to the "middle" without risking alienating the GOP right wing too greatly. This was a more difficult task for both George H.W. Bush to accomplish in 1988 and 1992 and Bob Dole in 1996 than it proved to be for George W. Bush in 2004, post-9/11. The specter of terrorism and war had helped to whip up public feelings of patriotism, which tend to become linked to ideas of traditional values—social conservatism—when translated into policy debates. Thus, Bush moved into 2003 in control of the commanding heights of patriotic fervor with which to dominate both the right and center of American politics. But for the divisiveness of his decision to wage war in Iraq amidst less than overwhelming public support, this advantage alone probably would have been sufficient to guarantee retention of office.

The polarization of the 2004 electorate created a greater dilemma for Democrats. In a population apparently politically divided down the partisan middle, as the 2000 election results and polls in 2003 indicated, reaching out to an increasingly less significant center becomes less important than mobilizing the entirety of the party base. Developing strategies that would get the party faithful to register and to vote in droves, therefore, becomes a larger concern than reaching out to the center. Thus, Democratic presidential candidates for 2004 faced two very different strategic options. They could go the route of Bill Clinton and reach out not only to independent moderates but even go the extra electoral mile and reach out to moderate Republicans as well, stressing such moderate conservative values as governmental fiscal and personal responsibility. Under this strategy, it was assumed that liberal Democrats would have no choice but to buck up and vote for the Democratic candidate as the lesser of evils (provided, of course, there was no repeat of the left-wing insurgency campaign of a Ralph Nader to offer liberals a faux choice). Or they could abandon the Clinton consensus and shift left, adopting a more "in-their-face" opposition to Bush and the Republicans to motivate and mobilize Democratic activists and rank-and-file party members, as well as to recruit more Democrat-in-all-but-name independents to the party rolls. (Al Gore had tried to do both in 2000, vacillating between

Clinton centrist and Liberal populist, which worked well enough to actually garner him a plurality of the popular vote.)

The Democratic contenders ended up splitting down the middle on the question of tactics. Howard Dean, David Kucinich, Carol Moseley Braun, and the irascible Al Sharpton played to the party's left wing, with an anti-war, anti-Bush pro-Great Society style economic agenda and an anti-Republican social-conservatism message. The four senators, however, played more of a Clinton game in varying degrees, ranging from Lieberman's neo-Bob Dole-esque agenda to John Edwards' economic populist/social moderate platform. In general, though, the four senators embraced the concept of the Bush war on terror and even the Iraqi war (with gradations of qualifications) and further embraced the hitherto quaint Republican ideal of balanced federal budgets, which Reagan had run on and which Clinton by his second term had co-opted but that Bush and the Republican Congress had apparently forgotten. The big issue for Democrats on the eve of the 2004 primary season would be which strategy would produce a viable nominee.

Through the summer and into the fall of 2003, that candidate increasingly seemed to be the run-for-the-heart-of-the-party candidate, Howard Dean. By the summer of 2003, Dean had already surprised political observers (that is, the less than 1 percent of the population who actually pay attention to such things—mostly because they are paid to do so—more than a year before the general election) by now out-fund-raising the more established senatorial candidates by several million dollars on average. Dean's appeal in part came from his effective Internet campaign that helped to bring loose organization to a wide-ranging group of liberal activist groups united mostly by their dislike (read "extreme dislike") of George W. Bush. Chief amongst these was an umbrella organization that had arisen from the small but vocal anti-Iraqi war movement, MoveOn.Org. MoveOn and similar groups, both on the left and the right, marked a new innovation in American interest group politics: the web-based virtual interest group that, in addition to using the Internet to link up and more effectively coordinate the activities of many smaller groups, could function as an effective virtual-grassroots fund-raising mechanism.

Across the dog days of summer 2003, as reports of insurgency in Iraq increased and the rising rate of American casualties began to register on the American public, opposition to the "new Vietnam" was fast becoming a cohesive issue for the Dean candidacy. The Democrats' bread-and-butter issue of the economy failed to really mobilize public opposition to the president's economic numbers because jobs and the stock market continued to improve, at least anemically. But the increasing perception transmitted by the media that things in Iraq simply were not progressing as shiningly as prewar rhetoric said they would be (where Iraqis were first supposed to greet liberating GI's with flower garlands and not with car bombs) and postwar claims said they would be quickly and efficiently with Iraqis creating the regions first Islamic democracy made the war an issue, which gave Dean increasing traction. The entry of retired General Wesley Clark into the race in September on a platform based largely on criticism of the president's war record added legitimacy to Democratic claims that Bush was a war botch. (While Clark's entry into the race pushed the number of Democrats running to a massive ten, Bob Graham's dropping out of the race in October, citing his inability to inspire either money donations or public support, would bring the number back down to the slightly more manageable nine.) That same month, amidst the growing Iraqi snafu, Bush's public approval rating sank to a record low of 50 percent. For the first time, Democrats could truly smell blood in the water from a wounded, vulnerable incumbent.

The big issue dividing Democrats over the war was whether their opposition was based on rejecting the concept of the war itself or rejecting the manner in which Bush had prosecuted the war. Pundits, politicians, and historians will no doubt argue over precisely that same point for decades to come (precisely because it may well take decades to fully assess the ramifications of the Bush Iraqi War Doctrine). For Democrats, the political stake was how opposition to a war still largely popular with Americans would be perceived. While Dean's anti-war rhetoric might touch a strong nerve with liberal Democrats, his views on the war could be used by Republicans to reaffirm the cliché of Democrats as foreign policy wimps, running from a fight. By fall 2003, as animosity towards the war rose and Dean began to look increasingly like the party front runner, many Democratic strategists (and more than a few gleeful Republicans) began to see Dean as the second coming of George McGovern—a candidate who would lead his party out of the political mainstream and into electoral Armageddon.

Even as more moderate Democrats began to worry about Dean's anti-war bluster, going into the final months leading into the 2004 caucus and primary season, the Dean candidacy began to self-destruct. In a November 1 interview with the *Des Moines Register* (in the first pivotal Democratic battleground of Iowa), Howard Dean was quoted as saying, "I still want to be the candidate for guys with Confederate flags in their pickup trucks. We can't beat George Bush unless we appeal to a broad cross-section of Democrats." While the off-the-cuff remark aimed at illustrating a legitimate strategy for Democrats—reclaiming the allegiance of southern "Reagan" Democrats—the comment immediately produced a small firestorm of criticism both within and without the Democratic Party. Liberals, especially civil rights activists, reacted with horror to Dean's idea that they would ever be in the same party again with Southern reactionaries. Republicans, meanwhile, derided Dean for essentially calling Southern voters redneck racists with his Rebel flag imagery (not withstanding the fact that a fair number of southern Republican voters do seem to have a particular affection for the old battle flag—as well as do several southern states). That Democratic hopes of recapturing a South that not only voted for Reagan's party but also had now largely joined the party were only pipe dreams, receiving scant analysis.

Still, by December 2003, little more than a month before the first ballots were to be cast, polls showed Dean receiving a plurality of party support (23 percent) more than double that of his nearest rivals, newbie candidate Wesley Clark and the establishment Senator Joe Lieberman (10 percent each). The remainder of the field sagged in the single digits (Richard Gephardt at 6 percent, Al Sharpton at 5 percent, John Kerry at 4 percent, John Edwards at 2 percent, Carol Moseley Braun at 1 percent, and Dennis Kucinich at 1 percent). The big question for Dean and the Democrats would be how the remaining 28 percent of undecided Democratic voters would break once they held a ballot or caucus slip in their hand and, as importantly, how voters would shift once the field inevitably slimmed down following the first primary season events.

Democrats would not have to wait long for the whittling away to begin. Following the mid-January non-binding Washington, D.C. Democratic primary, Carol Moseley Braun, who placed third with 12 percent, dropped out of the race and endorsed Howard Dean, the winner with 43 percent of the vote. While such an early victory in a minor venue was in no way determinant, the D.C. vote did help to make Dean stand out from the crowded pack, giving him momentum going into the Iowa caucuses a few days later similar to the way Pat Buchanan had in 1996 following his unexpected win over Phil Gramm of Texas at the Louisiana Republican delegate convention. Fresh from his first "win," Dean visited Plains, Georgia, to meet with former President Jimmy Carter. While Carter reiterated in a press conference following a church service the two men attended, "I have made an announcement in advance that I'm not going to endorse any particular candidate," he went on to add, "But I have been particularly grateful at the courageous and outspoken posture and position that Governor Dean has taken from the very beginning." Armed with the almost-endorsement of a senior party statesman to bookend the outright endorsement that he had received the month before from Al Gore, Dean set out for the snows of Iowa. That his endorsements came from two Democratic losers might have given him pause.

In recent elections, the Iowa caucuses have done a much better job of ruining candidates rather than anointing nominees. In 1996, Phil Gramm's third-place finish largely ended his candidacy, while Bob Dole's first-place win merely reaffirmed what he was expected to do in a neighboring state. Pat Buchanan's second-place victory, however, suddenly took the largely fringe candidate from the party's right wing and made him a possible serious contender—something his follow-up win in New Hampshire almost turned into a reality—and what would have been a McGovernesque tragedy for Republicans. Iowa was not kind to Howard Dean. For a variety of factors ranging from the increasingly harsh press that Dean was receiving subsequent to his Confederate remark, to the negative impression that the invasion of liberal "Deaniacs" from east and west coast political activist groups and college campuses had on Iowa locals (grassroots are all well and good, but the emphasis must be on the "roots" aspect, e.g., the local connection), to the failure of his antiwar rhetoric to really engage the voters of a largely socially conservative, flag-waving state, Dean fumbled in Iowa, coming in third with only 18 percent of the caucus vote. While that might not have been a fatal blow to the Dean candidacy, two other factors emerged that would prove his ultimate undoing.

The first was the victory of John Kerry, largely discounted to this point by pundits and the press, who pointed out precisely how unlikely the Democrats would be to go with a liberal senator from Massachusetts for precisely the same reasons discussed above. Kerry's winning of 38 percent of the state's delegates and Senator John Edwards' taking of 32 percent was a testament to both Dean's own weakness in the state and the power U.S. senators can bring to mobilizing the establishment side of a political party to their support. With the Iowa results, Dean now faced a clearly defined and potent threat from the Democratic Party establishment in the form of two senators who, while liberal, operated within channels that the party elite more comfortably dominated: the world of mainstream interest group endorsements and established contributor lists, as opposed to Dean's less predictable—and controllable—cyber-base.

The second factor in Dean's Iowa demise proved to be his infamous "Howard scream," a late night exhortation of the faithful to keep fighting to the other primary states despite his weak showing that degenerated into a loud, if inarticulate and incoherent, "Heeyah!" Played relentlessly in the following days not just by conservative AM radio talk shows but mainstream drive-time radio stations, TV news broadcasts, and on every late night television show from coast to coast, Dean immediately went from looking presidential to looking ridiculous—if not actually mentally unbalanced and dangerous. Dean attempted to mend the damage with a series of television interviews (most of which would not air for several days while the "I have a scream" tape played relentlessly to a national chorus of hoots and howls). While many in the national broadcast news media later expressed some regret about overplaying the story, especially after it became clear that audio engineering (in which the speech was deliberately electronically manipulated for maximum comic—and maniacal—effect) played a significant role in his speech sounding so bad. But like Edmund Muskie's infamous 1972 tear while defending his wife from slander in the snows of New Hampshire (which a number of witnesses later attributed to a melting snowflake on the candidate's cheek and not a sign of emotional weakness), Dean never recovered from the flap. How much of the Dean destruction was truly self-inflicted and how much was inflicted upon him remains for history to judge. The fact was, though, that Dean faced a Democratic establishment unwilling to risk a second McGovern and a mass media more than willing to run with a story line of Dean and his "Deaniacs" as maniacs rather than a substantial grassroots movement with truly strong roots.

Iowa was no kinder to the rest of the Democratic field either. Following his disappointing showing in his neighboring state of Iowa, Dick Gephardt dropped out of the presidential race to return to private life, following the expiration of his congressional term in 2005. The remaining four members of the pack had not chosen to actively participate in Iowa, but none would be able to mobilize serious support after the caucus in the face of Kerry's and Edwards' surprisingly good showings, with the limited exception of General Wesley Clark. Clark himself would benefit, albeit briefly, by the Clinton factor. A fellow Arkansan, Clark had been actively encouraged by the former president and titular senior statesman of the Democratic Party to jump into the race in the face of the early popularity of Howard Dean. Dean had attacked the Clinton legacy of moving the party to the middle by sacrificing the core New Deal values, derisively referring to Democrats who favored continuing such policies as "the Republican wing of the Democratic Party." Clinton saw Clark, with his military bona fides, as the ideal candidate to blunt the Dean leftward-insurgency. It would all prove for naught. Clinton's standing with the Democratic establishment had suffered along with his national reputation over the doings of his second term, and his public approval in general had fallen with revelations of what he did not do to stem the Al Qaeda threat. Having been kept at arm's distance and thus out of the 2000 Democratic campaign, the former president lacked the political muscle to be a party kingmaker in 2004. Given Clark's own limitations as a candidate—weak on the stump, mixed record as a military man, and no real political record to speak of—it would have been unlikely that even a fiendishly popular Clinton could have tipped things to Clark.

John Kerry's follow-up win a few days later in the New Hampshire primary with 38.4 percent of the vote solidified his position as the nomination front-runner—a position almost no professional observer thought likely just a month before. Howard Dean's 26 percent of the vote, while putting him in second place with more than double the vote of either third place Wesley Clark (12.4 percent) or fourth place John Edwards (12.0 percent), only served to reinforce a media-fed public perception that he could not win after the "scream heard around the world." The fickle gods of momentum had quickly and decisively shifted the mantle of "winner" to Kerry, leaving Dean labeled "loser." The fifth place finish of Joe Lieberman, the most conservative of the Democratic contenders, finished the former vice-presidential nominee's chances. He would withdraw from the race within weeks.

The New Hampshire primary had achieved an iconic stature from the 1960s (when primaries first really emerged as a decisive factor in determining party nominees) through the 1980s. During that period, no candidate would win both their party's nomination and the presidency without first emerging triumphant in the snows of the Granite State. This conventional wisdom was set on its head by the 1992 Democratic New Hampshire primary, which Bill Clinton lost to Paul Tsongas before going on to crush the former Massachusetts senator in the southern primaries, thereby going on to win the nomination and, eventually, the presidency. In 1996, Bob Dole lost in New Hampshire to Pat Buchanan and seriously considered dropping out of the race. Dole continued on to the southern primaries where he, too, emerged triumphant with the party nomination—though the presidency eluded him. And in

2000, George W. Bush was famously upset by John McCain in New Hampshire, only to go on and sew up the party nomination in the south. Both Dole's and Bush's victories in the cradle of the Civil War provided the critical firebreaks they needed to stop the insurgencies of Buchanan and McCain, respectively.

Since 1988, the primaries in southern states, particularly South Carolina, had displaced New Hampshire as the critical test for party candidates. With the Reagan southern realignment in the 1980s, southern states shifted hue in mass in presidential elections (and, increasingly, in congressional, state, and local elections) from Democratic Blue (never a particularly comfortable color for the states of Dixie) to the more natural Republican Red. With this realignment, the center of American politics moved both right and south, turning the South increasingly into the king-maker of both parties and the presidency-maker for Republicans. The new rule of political thumb that emerged in the 1990s, therefore, was no party candidate could secure the party nomination without winning most of the southern primaries, and no nominee could become president without winning at least some southern states (for Republicans, that would be "all" southern states).

John Kerry's campaign flew in the face of this new, conventional wisdom by winning in New Hampshire and then going on to win his party nomination—the first to do so since 1988. Securing the nomination would only take a matter of weeks, as things turned out. In the follow-up to New Hampshire, the February 3rd "mini-Tuesday," Kerry won primaries in the border state of Missouri, the western states of Arizona and New Mexico, the plains state of North Dakota, and the mid-Atlantic state of Delaware. John Edwards of North Carolina won in his state of birth, South Carolina, and scored a string of second-place finishes. Wesley Clark, meanwhile, emerged a whisker ahead of Edwards to win in Oklahoma. For the media, the Democratic nomination had now become a contest between liberal New Englander Kerry and populist Southerner Edwards, with General Clark being consigned the role of possible vice-presidential nominee. Howard Dean ceased to exist as a candidate after mini-Tuesday, having failed to achieve any first place wins. Within a matter of three weeks, a contest of nine candidates, none of whom had been perceived to have a truly insurmountable advantage over their rivals four weeks before, had been reduced to a contest between two senators from the more liberal wing of their party.

Yet, John Edwards never really had a shot for the party nomination. Edwards was a single-term senator with a scant record of senatorial achievement from a southern state from which he likely could not win reelection to the Senate. Benefiting from his deceivingly youthful good looks (appearing to be in his early forties, he was actually a decade older than that), which made him a natural favorite of the television cameras, he based his campaign on arguing that the average man was not getting his fair share of the American pie. Blasting Bush's tax cuts as a giveaway to the rich at the expense of the middle class and attacking the 1990s free trade regime as having gutted middle-class jobs to line the pockets of big business interests, Edwards came across as much more the neo-late nineteenth century-style Great Plains populist than the southern Clintonite "New Democrat." Edwards' problem was that his rhetoric rang truer in states outside of his perceived zone of advantage, which conventional wisdom took to be in the south. The states of the "Rust Sea"—the Great Lakes region's equivalence of the Eastern "Rust Belt," including Michigan, Wisconsin, Illinois, Pennsylvania, and Ohio—which had lost tens of thousands of manufacturing jobs in the steel, automotive, and consumer products industries would prove more fertile ground for Edwards' anti-tax cut, anti-free trade message than would the land of his birth and political power base.

But these Great Lakes "rust states" were also the states in which Northerner John Kerry was presupposed to have a significant advantage in. Thus, John Edwards paradoxically ran a campaign that would play strongest in states where he was weakest. At the same time, though, Edwards was weak in the states he was supposed to be strong in, namely, the south. A number of pundits and Democratic strategists argued that Edwards' southern roots might help tilt the south back towards its party of tradition. Yet, as his Republican detractors observed, Edwards would probably not have won reelection had he run for his Senate seat again in North Carolina, a seat that he owed in no small part to the 1998 Clinton-inspired Democratic upset in the congressional midterm elections. That he could deliver an increasingly conservatively hegemonic South—or even a piece of it—to the Democrats was a flight of fancy, at best, as the Republican sweep of southern states in November 2004 ultimately demonstrated.

What Edwards did offer to the Democrats in 2004 was a photogenic populist candidate who could reach out to Democratic and independent moderates on the Democrats' core issue of economic inequality—and the related issues of inequality in health care and education. Meanwhile, Edwards could take a pass on the more divisive issues of social morality thanks to the assumed social-moderate credentials his status as a

Southerner gave him. What Edwards offered the Democrats was not a truly viable party but, rather, a candidate with the right credentials to back a potentially winning nominee. While Edwards consistently insisted during the primaries that he was in the race to win the party nomination, his run had all the earmarks of a man who would be vice president, as history would shortly validate.

Having emerged from Iowa, New Hampshire, and mini-Tuesday the first-place winner, the momentum of victory would now carry John Kerry to the party nomination in a matter of weeks. Just as with the nominating processes of 1992, 1996, and 2000, the front-loaded primary schedule that each party had created to avoid the horror of a protracted nomination fight—especially against an opposition incumbent who would face no real primary challenge and thus be able to raise and save every contributory dime for the fall campaign—quickly produced a party winner. Whether that candidate was the best the party had to offer, however, remained to be seen. As the old adage wagged, political haste often makes electoral waste.

Between February 7 and March 2, 2004, Kerry won by large margins primaries and caucuses in ten states (Michigan, Washington, Maine, Tennessee, Virginia, Nevada, Wisconsin, Utah, Hawaii, and Idaho) and Washington, D.C. Along the way, Wesley Clark, who had little to offer as a candidate beyond his credentials as a military man, his opposition to Bush's foreign policy, and his vague similarity to Dwight Eisenhower, withdrew from the race and endorsed the front runner. And Howard Dean, failing to achieve one significant primary victory (though consistently out-polling John Edwards), finally bowed to what had become inevitable since the media's relentless barrage of the "scream," dropping out of the race within days of his failure to even come in second in Wisconsin, a state assumed to be one of his surer bets. Kerry's decisive victories on March 2 in California, Connecticut, Georgia, Maryland, Massachusetts, New York, Ohio, Rhode Island, and Minnesota cinched the nomination (though formally securing the necessary majority of delegates to win would still take a little over of week) with John Edwards withdrawing from the contest the following day. Securing the nomination had required a scant forty-six days. The general election campaign, which can fairly be said to have begun within hours of President Bush's calling Senator Kerry on March 2 to congratulate him on his victory (the Republican's first pro-Bush and anti-Kerry ads would air within days of that telephone call), would last more than five times as long.

The GOP race for the nomination held none of the horse-race drama of the Democrats, with George Bush joining the ranks of Ronald Reagan and Bill Clinton as an incumbent who could claim his party's nomination by right with no opposition. Jimmy Carter had faced a damaging insurgency from Ted Kennedy and the liberal wing of his party in 1980, and George H.W. Bush had similarly suffered the attack of Pat Buchanan from the right wing of his party in 1992. Both incumbents subsequently lost. Bush, however, facing no opposition, would be able to act and look presidential during his own primary season while the wheels of the nominating process ground relentlessly towards awarding him all Republican delegates in primary after primary—looking presidential while quietly raising vast amounts of campaign cash, that is. Republicans had decried the fund-raising mania of the Clinton administration as being unseemly, if not outright corrupt (though one often detected at least a smidge of fund-raising envy in the Republican griping). George W. Bush, however, proved even more adept at getting interest groups and the public at large to cough up massive amounts of cash to fill the Republican electoral coffers. By the beginning of the Republican primary season in January 2004, Bush's campaign manager, Ken Mehlman, announced that the president's reelection campaign had already raised a record $130.8 million from almost a half million individual donors. The campaign, meanwhile, targeted raising almost $200 million by the convention, a goal it would actually exceed. (The Bush campaign would ultimately raise more than $360 million, more than half again as much as the $194 million raised in 2000. Kerry proved no slacker either, raising just over $300 million, better than double the $133 million raised by Al Gore. All totaled, the 2004 election marked the nation's first billion dollar presidential campaign. For whatever problems the two campaigns had in getting their messages out, neither could complain about being cash-starved.)

The record-setting fund-raising occurred despite the efforts of Congress to inhibit the flow of influence money, particularly the influence of "soft money"—the unlimited amounts of campaign cash that could be contributed to political parties and candidates for "party-building" activity. The McCain-Feingold campaign finance reform had sought to end the influence of soft money on American political campaigns, effectively abolishing it by legislative statute. But money in campaigns is like air in a balloon—squeezing it in one place only causes it to flow into another, as the groups with money to give will remain intent on giving it. The result in 2004 was a shift of money into so-called 527 groups, e.g., tax-exempt independent political groups seeking to advocate an issue rather than a candidate *per se*. In 2000, $500 million in soft contributions flowed into the political campaign. In 2004, that money seems to have shifted into the 527s, which collectively spent over $500 million. Independent groups spending their own money on campaigns have always been a feature of modern politics. (Indeed, in 1988 such a group funded the infamous Willie Horton ad, as discussed below.) But with the rise of soft money in the 1980s and 1990s, interest groups had little reason to pour lots of cash into the independents—better to simply write big checks to the parties and let them have the headache of figuring out how to spend the money. Just like with political action committees (PACs), which had been legal prior to the campaign finance reforms of the 1970s but only took off once the reforms made them a more rational vehicle for funneling campaign donations, after McCain-Feingold, 527s became a more effective legal way to influence campaigns, and their numbers (and share of the campaign cash) skyrocketed.

Intuition might indicate this loophole would have benefited Democrats more than Republicans, as they had become hooked on big soft money donations during the Clinton years and desperately needed a funding alternative. Because the moderate and lower income households that formed the core of Democrats' constituency had less disposable income available to them to spend on something as arcane as politics, the party of the little man found itself ironically (and, some would say, embarrassingly) dependent on the largess of the big man—well-healed individual and corporate interests who could be counted on in the past for the big soft money check. Republicans, the party of wealth, could count on both large chunk contributions from individuals and corporations but also could tap a large pool of upper middle-class contributors. But Republican strategists also learned in 2004 to play the 527 game as well as the Democrats, raising tens of millions of dollars and reaffirming that whatever a Democrat could do with a buck, a Republican could do one better. Whether the will and strength will be shown by 2008 to close the 527 loophole remains to be seen. What history shows, however, is that whatever reforms may come down the pike, the highwaymen of political influence will be laying in wait to waylay them.

Bush's having no opposition, meanwhile, did not entirely empty all drama from the story of Republican ticket-making in 2004. Through the summer and fall of 2003, there was increasing speculation that Bush might move to replace controversial Vice President Dick Cheney with someone younger and less divisive. Such talk proved to be simply that: talk. At no time during his first term had Bush given the slightest indication to anyone that he held anything other than the highest trust and confidence in his vice president. Indeed, it well might have been said of Bush and Cheney in their first term that, when they walked in the sun together, they cast but one shadow. That this would be any different for a second administration was pure fantasy.

The real sense of drama brought to the Bush renominating process was the palatable sense of destiny that seemed to surround it. For both Bush's campaign operatives and the Republican Party's rank and file in general, the Republican primary season and subsequent nominating convention would be more a matter of coronation of the good king, a reaffirmation of the party's commitment to its leader (and its increasingly operational master). For Republicans, Bush had delivered that which even the icon of later twentieth century presidential conservatism, Ronald Reagan, had not: namely, a secure Republican national hegemony. Under President Bush, Republicans had not only maintained their dominance in the Congress but, after the 2002 midterms, had expanded and solidified it (the short Democratic resurgence in the Senate being a temporary deviancy). As the party's congressional leaders were the first to point out, the credit for their incumbent party's unusual midterm gains lay with one man and one man alone: George W. Bush. By 2004, the image of Ronald Reagan for Republicans—including both their high priests of policy and politics and their laity—had begun to morph from that of the messiah himself into that of a modern John the Baptist, foretelling the coming of the true messiah to lead the GOP forever out of the political wilderness. (Reagan's own passing in June 2004 would further help weld the mantle of true conservative mastery unto Bush's shoulders.) By the summer convention, all that was missing to complete the metaphor would be the laying of palm fronds at the nominee's feet as he trod into the hall to give his acceptance speech.

SPRING/SUMMER

Once the Democrats had succeeded in selecting their champion to challenge the Republican incumbent, the political question now shifted to what the nature of that challenge would be. What would be the issues that would emerge to dominate the summer and fall campaign? Would it be the economy, recovering nicely in terms of the raw numbers but still leaving many households with fiscal anxiety, if not in outright distress? Would it be security and war, with fear of terrorism competing for dominance in the minds of the American public with growing discontent over the progress—or lack thereof—in postwar Iraq? Would it be the traditional grab bag of social concerns—rising health-care costs, declining schools, increasingly insolvent social security, inefficient welfare programs, and skyrocketing budget deficits, which had grown to dominate much of the political debate right up to 9/11? Would it be the special interest wedge issues like the environment and gun control? Or would it be the smoldering embers of the moral culture war with all its hot button issues—gay rights (including marriage), civil rights (and affirmative action), women's rights, and abortion and its clone issues, such as stem cell research or the separation of church and state—which always lay just below the surface of political debate until the winds of some new event *du jour* blow them back into a political blaze?

Both the Bush and Kerry organizations would struggle to define the campaign on terms favorable to themselves. The advantage in this struggle lay with Bush, as with every incumbent who can use the formidable powers of the office of the presidency to set the national political agenda. One of the hallmarks of Bush's first term in office, particularly after 9/11, had been precisely its well-ordered ability to make its agenda the national agenda. What the Bush White House wanted to discuss the Congress, the news media, and the national "punditocracy" ended up discussing. The Bush organization would continue to flex its conscious-shaping muscles across the campaign, working fairly effectively to keep the national focus on issues that accorded with its own strengths.

Even as the Democratic field was forming in the spring of 2003, Bush was shaping one of the defining issues of the 2004 campaign on the battlefield of Iraq. The United States' "shock and awe" campaign of the war would translate into a Republican shock and awe campaign by the spring of 2004, with the Bush campaign relentlessly (and effectively, as events would play out) hammering Democrats as "soft" on the war on terror and unpatriotic in their opposition—no matter how muted—to the war in Iraq. In this, the Bush campaign pursued a familiar wedge issue, painting Democrats in general and John Kerry in particular as cliché un-American peaceniks, something Republicans had done as consistently as election year fall leaves turned brown ever since the anti-war movement engulfed the Democratic left in the 1960s. That the Democratic nominee, John Kerry, had established himself on the public scene in the early 1970s as a Vietnam veteran vocally against the war made the attack appear all the more credible. The beauty of playing the war hawk-equals-patriot card for Republicans was that it consistently helped split Democratic candidates from a significant portion of their traditional New Deal base: blue collar workers to whom the Democrats' economic populist agenda appealed but who were social conservatives, especially when it came to issues of patriotism and support of country in times of war. Given that the United States had been in some form of war for almost all of the post-World War II period, this argument could be trotted out at just about any opportunity by Republicans to their advantage. The one time that advantage was denied them, during the false peace of the 1990s (in retrospect, the dawning age of terror), Democrats succeeded in electing their first two-term president since FDR.

Tied seamlessly by Republicans to the war theme was the issue of presidential character—or the Democratic nominee's alleged lack thereof. Within days of both parties having wrapped up their nominations, Republicans began to air TV spots branding Democratic nominee John Kerry as weak presidential material. The case in point, to be harpooned again and again by Republican advertisements, spokesmen, candidates, and the mass of the conservative media from March to November, was that John Kerry had voted in the Senate to authorize the president's use of force in Afghanistan and Iraq but had later voted against an $87 billion appropriation bill to support Afghani and Iraqi occupations. The reality of the matter was that Kerry had been presented with two versions of an appropriation bill, the first of which contained language inserted by Democrats as an amendment, stating that the $87 billion appropriation should be offset by rescinding some of the Bush tax cut to pay for it, and the second version with the defeated Democrats' amendment stripped out. Kerry had voted for the Democrats' version but voted against the Republicans' version as a protest against running up the deficit in times of war while not asking all households, especially affluent ones, to share in the war's fiscal burden.

In the arcane world of senatorial procedure and partisan politics, such votes are both routine and mundane. But in presidential politics, where any and every action and word by a candidate, past and present, will be dissected, parsed, and reframed for optimum political advantage, such actions are the stuff of effective attack ads. When questioned about his apparent inconsistency in these votes, Kerry compounded the problem by explaining before a group of veterans the day after the ads first aired, "I actually did vote for his $87 billion, before I voted against it!" True enough, but hardly the sort of straightforward admission that the 99.5 percent of Americans who were not experts in senatorial procedure

2004 Presidential Election 685

would actually understand. Indeed, Kerry's very words were to be used against him repeatedly for the rest of the campaign, with Republican ads and President Bush himself relentlessly hammering away at the senator's inconsistency with the chant: "Voted for it before he voted against it." With one single stroke, the Bush campaign had framed public perception of John Kerry, reducing that perception to the simple label of "flip-flopper."

Bush, by contrast, could then claim the label of the solid, consistent, dependable candidate, the true leader who will always "say what I mean," as he would repeat over and over again in his stump speeches. Whether the media and the public simply chose to ignore Bush's own many "flip-flops" as president—first opposing, then supporting the McCain-Feingold campaign finance reform package once its passage was inevitable; first opposing, then supporting the congressional proposal to create a cabinet-level Department of Homeland Security once its passage was inevitable; first opposing, then supporting the creation of an independent commission to investigate the catastrophic failure in intelligence leading up to 9/11 once its creation became inevitable; first refusing to allow himself or key staffers to testify before the commission then allowing it when public pressure became irresistible—or whether Democrats were simply incompetent in making the case coherently that the president also suffered from "flip-flopperitis" is a matter of debate.

To at least some degree, however, it is unquestionable that the Republican success in framing Kerry as a flip-flopper so early and so enduringly in the campaign was a function of the increasing predilection of both the media and the public for comprehending complex political campaigns through the creation of a simple (or, better said, simplistic) story line. Over the last thirty years, the media has shifted from trying to portray news events as a reconstruction of a historical record to portraying them as part of a running story line with a clearly identifiable plot and clearly identifiable characters. Attribute it to the serialization of the American culture through the omni-present conditioning agent of mass entertainment with standardized plot lines and stock characters presented over and over to the public in motion pictures and serialized television shows that want audiences to be able to identify and feel comfortable with characters and plots within the first few minutes of the presentation. (It is not an accident that almost all successful Hollywood pitches try to link any new ideas to proven old ideas—"it's Star Wars meets Gone With The Wind," as the pitching screenwriter might observe.) Attribute it to the incursion of the profit-motive into previously insulated television news operations that, in the face of corporate parent company demands to increase profits and ratings, have cut back on staff and focused increasingly on trying to hook viewers with emotional versus rational content. Attribute it to a society so overwhelmed in its modern complexity (previous generations did not have to try to comprehend the myriad of complex political concepts that have inevitably emerged in a multicultural, post-industrial nation of over three hundred million people while simultaneously trying to comprehend how to program their VCRs, computers, and cell phones) that it simply cannot focus as intently on the mundane and removed world of government.

For whatever reason, simple labels in political campaigns work because the media is overjoyed to use them, and the public is overjoyed to embrace them. In recent campaigns the media has sought early on to identify candidates with a particular label: Clinton as the great seducer, or Reagan as the Teflon great communicator. In 2000, Al Gore was tagged as the exaggerator (who claimed he had "invented the Internet") and flip-flopper. Bush, meanwhile, was labeled the friendly country-western bumpkin—a kind of Andy Griffith with a speaking problem. The problem is that there is only room in any campaign, as far as the media is concerned, for one archetype, for one candidate bearing a particular label. Once Kerry was branded the "flip-flopper," there was simply no room for another flip-flopper in the story line, no matter how hard Democrats tried to stick the same label on Bush. To give two candidates the same label would be to invite confusion for both the media covering the story and the public following it, requiring both to have to dig deeper and think harder about the real underlying issues than either would be comfortable with.

Given the news coming out of Iraq in the spring of 2004, using the war as a wedge issue might not, at first glance, have appeared to be the soundest strategy for the incumbent president. Indeed, the Bush campaign's first foray into campaigning focused on the more visceral subject of 9/11 and terrorism. It was too visceral a subject, as things turned out. On March 5, just three days after Kerry scored his victory-clincher, Republicans aired an ad that transposed a pro-Bush message across footage of the aftermath of the 9/11 terrorist attacks. Unfortunately for Bush, public reaction was swift and negative. The fallen Twin Towers have iconic stature in post-9/11 America, which denies its heart-wrenching imagery for any partisan political advantage, at least directly, that is. During the campaign, Bush would advance the thesis that Democratic softness on terror during the Clinton years was in no small part responsible for the 9/11 attacks. Dick Cheney would also famously (or infamously, for Democrats) chime in that a Democratic victory in November would almost certainly result in another terrorist attack on the order of 9/11. But to actually use footage of the attack crossed a clear, public-drawn line.

The efficacy of using the war on terror as a bully-club with which to bash the Democrats also had some of its impact diminished with the March 22 release by President Bush's former chief counter-terrorism aide, Richard Clarke, of a book harshly critical of the Bush administration's handling of Al Qaeda before the 9/11 attacks. Clarke also challenged most of the administration's principle assertions used to justify the 2003 invasion of Iraq. Testifying before the 9/11 Commission that week, the former Clinton and Bush aide reiterated claims that the Bush team had been far more focused on regime change in Iraq prior to 9/11 than on Al Qaeda and, in the days immediately after the attack, had determinedly sought to connect Iraq to the strikes on New York and Washington. The Bush administration and pro-Republican news and pundit media immediately launched a counteroffensive to discredit Clarke, arguing that the book contained many factual errors and amounted to sour grapes from a man pushed out of government for having a less than stellar record of service. The Clarke book, as well as the public focus on the proceedings of the 9/11 Commission, however, served for the first time to drive the Bush administration into a serious defensive mode, justifying a record on fighting terror that the public had previously simply accepted at face value.

Yet, while the news out of Iraq of rising violence and instability did the administration little good, Democrats would find the war's problems hard to capitalize on. When John Kerry observed on April 2, "We need a regime change not just in Iraq. We need a regime change here in the United States," the Republican establishment from Congress to the outraged punditocracy unleashed a firestorm of criticism on him for speaking out against a wartime president. Indeed, for the balance of the campaign, the gold standard Republican response to any Democratic challenge to the Bush foreign policy was to ignore the substance of the challenge and simply blast the concept of any challenge to a wartime president as being unpatriotic—if not outright treasonous. Of course, such assertions fly in the face of historical precedent. Eisenhower blasted Truman's record in Korea when running against Democrat Adlai Stevenson in 1952. Goldwater and Nixon blasted Johnson over Vietnam. Reagan blasted Carter over the Iranian hostage crisis, and congressional

Republicans blasted Clinton for firing cruise missiles at Sudan and Afghanistan and for bombing Iraq in the lead up to the impeachment. The list is endless. But the party in power has always reserved the right to blast the party out of power as unpatriotic for its foreign policy criticisms, just as every party out of power has always reserved the right to blast the party in power for incompetence in foreign policy. Partisan politics has never ended at the water's edge, except in times of abject national danger, such as during the Cuban missile crisis or in the months after Pearl Harbor. What most Americans forget, however, is that Kennedy faced increasing political pressure on his cold war policies by 1963, and even FDR faced mounting public discontent as the war dragged on into the winter of 1944. (Indeed, Hitler's gamble on the Battle of the Bulge was not aimed at winning the war—just prolonging it long enough for the public of the Allies to become discontented enough to pressure their governments to seek a negotiated end to the struggle.) The problem for Democrats would be that news from Iraq, while grim, would not become bad enough to cause significant portions of the Bush supporters to desert him at the polls the way voters defected from the Democrats amidst the drag of Vietnam in 1968 and from the humiliation of the Iranian crisis in 1980.

The shocking revelations of photographs showing Iraqi prisoners in the Abu Ghraib prison outside Baghdad being abused and humiliated by U.S. soldiers and their sparking of global outrage came closest to decisively tipping public opinion away from the administration in the run up to the election. Calls for the resignation of Secretary of Defense Donald Rumsfeld over Abu Ghraib prisoner abuse were rebuffed by the president. Instead, Bush issued a strong statement of support for Rumsfeld, saying the Secretary of State was "doing a superb job" in the war on terrorism and attributed the problems at the prison to a few bad apples who would be dealt with. Democrats seized on the prison scandal as indicative of both the administration's failures in Iraq in general and Bush's consistent inability to ever admit any mistakes in the handling of any issue. That no senior administration official—or even a senior military office—would be held accountable for the Abu Ghraib human rights abuses (to date, only low-ranking soldiers on duty at the prison have been charged or convicted of misconduct) would further tarnish the Bush reputation. In the wake of the scandal, Bush's overall job approval plummeted to 42 percent (from highs more than double that in the wake of 9/11), and his approval for handling Iraq dropped to 35 percent, compared with 44 percent prior to the scandal, which itself had been a significant drop from the previous year. More ominously for Republicans, polls also showed Kerry besting Bush 46 percent to 45 percent for the first time. For a brief time in the spring of 2004, George W. Bush began to show signs that he was inheriting his father's legacy: winner of war but loser of reelection.

But whatever excesses in which coalition forces may have engaged during the Iraqi occupation were overshadowed in the American public's mind by the rash of hostage-takings and horrific videotaped beheadings of Westerners, particularly Americans, that became an increasing modus operandi of particularly radical insurgents across 2004. Between the primaries and the November general election, dozens of such groups would seize foreign nationals in Iraq, and more than thirty would be executed. The immediate impact of these barbaric acts was to offset public disgust with America's own moral failings in the occupation and bolster the administration's justification of the war on humanitarian grounds: liberating Iraq from dictatorship and radicalism. Indeed, the more horrific the hostage-takers acted, the easier it became for the administration to sell its argument that Iraq was a struggle between good and evil. While it is common to demonize the enemy in times of war, it is especially easy to do so when the enemy behaves like demons. And if the insurgents were evil, questioning the war against them made one, by default, soft on evil.

As a result, while the increasing level of violence in Iraq eroded the president's public approval ratings, allowing John Kerry to post far better poll numbers than had been expected in a contest with a war-time president, the deteriorating situation did not produce a coherent and broad-based anti-war movement that might have decisively turned the electorate to Kerry either. Thus, the Iraqi war simply did not offer Kerry a significant strategic political advantage. Kerry had repudiated the anti-war wing of the Democratic Party with his attacks on Howard Dean during the primaries. Despite his own antiwar history after Vietnam— or, indeed, because of that very history—Kerry went into the general campaign on the record as having voted for the war and being supportive of its basic ends. What that left for Kerry was to run on two issues: Bush had failed in his conduct of the war in Iraq and in the broader war on terror, and therefore, that Kerry would be the better man to lead the country out of the mess Bush supposedly had created.

To prove that he had what it took to be commander in chief, Kerry offered up as evidence his own record as a warrior in Vietnam, despite the fact that Kerry had later repudiated the war and despite the fact that thirty years later Vietnam continues to be the third rail of American foreign policy: seizing it with both hands has never done any politician much good. Conservatives would spend the campaign attacking Kerry's Vietnam record on two fronts. First, they would condemn his anti-war rhetoric (with pundits and bloggers trying to link him up to the antiwar movements most radical—and even violent—fringes) and offer it up as evidence that he was unworthy of the title "Commander in Chief." Second, they would pick away at his actual war record, trying to reveal him as yet another Democratic fraud. They would be successful to various degrees on both fronts.

Meanwhile, the trio of perennial domestic issues—jobs, health care, and social security—that were at the core of the Democratic agenda and on which George W. Bush had focused effectively in 2000 were reduced to a secondary concern in the 2004 campaign. This was despite no end of polling that showed domestic concerns ranked ahead of either the war in Iraq or the broader war on terror. Yet, while would-be voters told pollsters what they, the voters, were worried about, they did not apparently tell pollsters exactly what they were actually listening to. In 2004, the public protested too much that it was more concerned about domestic problems than international problems. Poll data showed that Bush and Kerry rose and sank in the polls against each other concurrent with events in Iraq and in the war on terror. The famous injunction of the 1992 Clinton campaign, "It's the economy, stupid," simply did not apply in the war terror year of 2004. Rather, it was foreign policy and, most importantly, perceptions of credible leadership, all filtered through a screen of heightened patriotism, that mattered. Patriotism and another related issue were largely missed by pollsters as well: the "Moral Question."

The moral question in 2004 was the question of which party—Republican or Democrat—would best be able to lead an America increasingly divided on fundamental issues of morality, such as abortion (and related themes like stem-cell research), public prayer, and gay marriage. The situation in Iraq was not bad enough to drive large numbers of moderate independents and moderate Republicans from the president's banner. While the situation in Iraq continued to deteriorate through the summer of 2004, the relatively low level of American casualties defied comparison to Vietnam or Korea (though, of course, if those same casualty rates continue for four more years, they will become an issue in the 2008 campaign, just as will the liberty of Osama bin Laden should he not be apprehended by then). And the economy was not good enough to drive large numbers of moderate Democrats and independents to Bush's standard either. The moral question, therefore, turned out to be the issue upon which the campaign hinged, something about which the pollsters and Democrats—though not Republicans—remained largely ignorant. And of the various moral issues, gay marriage would prove to have the greatest practical and tactical influence on the outcome of the 2004 vote.

The sleeper issue of the campaign fell into Republican hands in February when the Massachusetts Supreme Court ruled that marriage between people of the same gender had to be recognized under the state's constitution. The court's decision unleashed a firestorm of public criticism (and a sigh of relief from the U.S. Ninth Circuit Court of Appeals for no longer being pilloried as the most liberal court in America!) from conservative politicians and pundits and howls of protests from religious conservatives. But the protests did not only come from the right wing of American politics. While majorities of Americans favored some form of legalized union short of marriage for gay couples (an odd condition of being "a little" married), even larger majorities clearly rejected the legalization of full-blown gay marriage.

For Democrats the issue of gay marriage had been the sleeping dog of social policy that they would just as soon have let lay. Ever since Congress overwhelmingly passed and Bill Clinton signed the Defense of Marriage Act (DOMA) in 1996, thereby giving states a free pass on the "full faith and credit" clause of the Constitution, the nation could comfortably live the lie that the institution of marriage had been legislatively "saved." The only problem, of course, was that acts of Congress could not contravene the Constitution, so it was likely that the Defense of Marriage Act would not pass judicial review. However, since no state allowed gays to marry, the issue was mute—no one had standing to challenge the law. Meanwhile, states could play with and Democrats could endorse the idea of civil unions as a half-way measure to appease gays while "protecting" marriage. Not so after the Massachusetts ruling.

It was one thing for liberal Democrats to support gay marriage when it was a hypothetical "some day when we cross that bridge" kind of issue. The February court ruling ordered the state of Massachusetts, however, to begin allowing and recognizing such marriages within a matter of months. By May 2004, therefore, that bridge was crossed, and the stakes in this game went from theoretical to real. Once the first "I do, I do's" were exchanged amidst the azalea blossoms, the gay community—at least in Massachusetts—was inevitably forced on the road towards having to

692   2004 Presidential Election

eventually fight tooth and claw to protect what some of its members
had so long sought to achieve. Those who opposed gay marriage faced
the danger of it spreading from Massachusetts like a contagion, either
through similar judicial action in other states or through a court case
that might rule against DOMA. The decision of a California superior
court judge that spring to order the issuance of marriage licenses in that
state, followed by the decision of the mayor of San Francisco to issue and
honor gay marriage licenses as well, only underscored the fact that the
old status quo prohibiting gay marriage had been shattered. (That higher
courts in California would quickly shut down the gay marriage license
tap and the fact that, up through the election, no lawsuits were filed
challenging DOMA could be taken only as the calm before the eventual
renewed political firestorm.)

For Republicans, the big question presented by the gay marriage flap
was how to use it to inflict the greatest possible damage on Democrats.
The answer, of course, was twofold. First, Republicans would use the
issue to try and to force every Democratic candidate from president
down to local dogcatcher to either come out firmly against gay marriage
(appealing to the majority of the population but alienating a key activist
constituency) or come out for it and thereby lose the political middle.
Making matters worse for Democrats was that the issue of gay marriage
polled badly even in solidly Blue states and with core constituencies like
African Americans and Latinos (who would end up voting in record
numbers in November for Bush). To get Democrats on the record,
Republican Senate and House leaders played tag team with the issue, first
offering a constitutional amendment (which President Bush had called
for after the Massachusetts ruling) in the Senate in July and reintroducing
it in the House in September.

The Senate version of the amendment, introduced in July, was timed
to remind Americans of the Democrats' opposition to it (opposition
which Democrats shared with a majority of the public) just as Democrats
were gearing up for the national nominating convention later that month.
The matter never even technically came up for a full vote, as Republicans
could only muster 48 votes of 60 needed to end debate, but the record
was established. Democrats opposed the amendment, which could be
easily tweaked to mean they supported gay marriage, even if most did
not. The October vote in the House was closer (227 to 186, 49 votes
shy of the necessary two-thirds) and served to refocus attention on the
gay marriage issue just weeks before the election. (The House leaders
were busily getting other issues on the record, voting 250 to 171 to

overturn a 28-year municipal ban on handgun ownership in the District of Columbia and voting 247 to 173 to protect the words "under God" in the Pledge of Allegiance from court challenge.)

Democrats dismissed these legislative hijinks as so much typical political grandstanding and "raw political cynicism" on behalf of GOP leaders looking to "create the fodder for a demagogic political ad." Kerry himself weighed in after the July Senate vote saying the vote had been "designed to divide us for political purposes," adding, "Even Republicans concede that this amendment is being offered only for political gains." Democrats in general downplayed the damage the issue might do them, with some Democratic strategists even arguing that Republicans were taking a risk of inciting a backlash from moderates across the country by pushing the anti-gay marriage constitutional amendment. The problem was that Democrats apparently could not read an electoral map, confusing the fact that polls showed the majority of Americans agreed with the position John Kerry and John Edwards had both embraced opposing both same-sex marriage and a constitutional amendment to bar it with the damage that the issue would do them amongst concentrated groups of voters in key swing states such as Pennsylvania and Ohio. Democrats simply failed to grasp the critical role this issue would play in mobilizing the Republican's ultimate November surprise and the secondary role for which the issue would be used—part of a good one-two combination punch.

The second fist of that punch was the rallying call the issue of gay marriage sounded to Christian Evangelicals across the country. This played directly into Karl Rove's Evangelical strategy: the Republican goal to get the four million Evangelicals who Rove said stayed home in 2000 out to the polls for Bush in 2004. Prior to the Massachusetts decision, Rove had to be content with attacking John Kerry for being 1 of only 14 votes in 1996 against DOMA, portraying the Democratic front-runner as another loony marriage-wrecking liberal. After Massachusetts, Rove could use the image of Democrats destroying marriage (forgetting for a moment that none of the millions of heterosexuals were showing any signs of suddenly chucking their sexual preference of choice to marry someone of their own gender) to ignite the critical Evangelical base. From spring 2004 to the election, from the pulpits of thousands of Evangelical congregations and in tens of thousands of Evangelical Bible groups, the issue of gay marriage—and the perception that a Kerry victory would lead inevitably to its legalization, just as Bush's reelection would lead to the passage of a prohibiting constitutional amendment (basic principles of our constitution regarding the role of the president versus that of Congress and the states in passing constitutional amendments not receiving equal perusal apparently)—would be harped and reharped upon. Ultimately, the gay marriage flap seemed to have the single biggest impact on mobilizing this community to show up in massive numbers and vote Republican. While the Rove strategy may have brought more liberal protest voters to the polls in states like California and New York (where they would do no additional good for Kerry), it also unquestionably brought more conservative voters to the polls in states like Iowa, New Mexico, Florida, and Ohio, which may well have been the decisive factor in the Bush victory.

Republicans followed up with an additional strategy to take advantage of the marriage issue: getting propositions onto the ballots of eleven states that would declare marriage to be only between heterosexual couples. While the Bush campaign played some role in helping to organize such movements, given the intensity of the backlash of many people to the Massachusetts court decision, it seems likely that the initiatives were heading to the ballot one way or the other. What the Bush campaign succeeded in doing was to integrate these movements into the extended Bush campaign—voters showing up to vote against gay marriage would more than likely vote for George W. Bush. The gay marriage issue also played into Republican hands in congressional and state legislative races. The issue received a heavy focus in South Dakota, where former Republican representative John Thune played the gay card in his successful race upsetting Senate Minority Leader Thomas A. Daschle (D-S.D.), who opposed the marriage amendment. Of all the issues Democrats would just as soon not had to fight in 2004, gay marriage topped the list. Indeed, political historians may come to decide that, in ruling in favor of gay marriage in February 2004, the Massachusetts' Supreme Court had inadvertently handed George W. Bush his reelection on a silver wedding tray.

While the seeds of the Democrats' ultimate defeat were being sown with the gay marriage issue, the presidential campaign proceeded through the summer months at the same lackadaisical pace that summer presidential campaigns typically do. On July 6 John Kerry ended what had been only middling speculation in selecting John Edwards as his running mate. Edwards' only real rivals were General Wesley Clark, who had proven himself an inept campaigner during the primaries, and perhaps Bill Richardson of New Mexico, a Latino governor of a small state who had some national following but no real national base. As remarked above, the Kerry-Edwards ticket would fly in the face of recent history that said that since 1960 such a combination was a loser (as the 1996 Republican senatorial duo of Bob Dole and Jack Kemp could affirm). The subsequent Democratic convention at the end of July on Kerry's home field of Boston became a harbinger of sorts of the difficulty that the Democrats would have capturing the public's attention and affection that fall. But for a stirring speech by a new rising star (conventions have a habit of producing "rising stars" who subsequently seem to sink back into obscurity), Illinois senatorial candidate Barak Obama, the convention itself seemed to get lost amidst the public run up to the Olympics and the miasma of the summer doldrums.

More ominously for the Democrats, Kerry failed to receive the usual post-convention bump in the polls (typically in the 5 percent or greater range) that serves to jumpstart most nominees' fall campaigns. By early August, Kerry had either stayed even with the president in the polls or had dropped by a point or so. While this was not devastating, it marked the first time since 1972 (and the disastrous Democratic convention of that year) that a party standard bearer had not gained an advantage from his nominating convention. Within days, things would get much worse for Kerry.

What little afterglow the nomination ceremony provided Kerry was swiftly sunk by an advocacy group called Swift Boat Veterans For Truth. The group was one of the "527" independent groups allowed unlimited campaign spending up to sixty days prior to an election under a loophole in the McCain-Feingold reform. On August 5, the Swift Boat Veterans debuted a television ad calling into question John Kerry's account of how he earned his Purple Heart medals in Vietnam. Kerry had continued since the primaries to make his service in Vietnam a centerpiece of the character component of his campaign since the primaries—having served in war, he now presented himself to be best able to lead in war. (The juxtaposition with George W. Bush's own more controversial record of service—or lack thereof, according to critics—was left on the table for all to see though Kerry himself made no real reference to it.) Indeed, Kerry had accepted his nomination with the words, "John Kerry, reporting for duty." The Swift Boat group (bankrolled in part by Texas Republicans with more than a passing interest in the reelection of George Bush) directly sought to undermine this issue, essentially alleging that Kerry had actually acted with cowardice under fire and had earned his military commendations through politics, not deed. While the ad was only aired in a limited number of markets, the ad and the issue were immediately pounced on by the broadcast and cable networks, which gave the ads repeated national airings. While the accusations were the subject of tremendous debate and debunking with numerous other Swift Boat veterans and comrades in arms of the senator rallying to his defense, the effect of the Swift Boat Veterans' ad was to neutralize Kerry's record as a combat veteran as a campaign advantage. Across the month of August, Kerry slowly sank in the polls, setting up George W. Bush to deliver a killing blow with his own convention in early September (a blow that never really fell however).

The Swift Boat Veterans' ad became the Willy Horton ad of the 2004 campaign. In the fall of 1988, having seen his lead over rival Michael Dukakis decline significantly after Dukakis' post-convention boost, an increasingly desperate George H.W. Bush was left scrambling to blunt the Democratic drive. Bush's problem was that his campaign lacked the money to wage an effective, massive media attack on Dukakis. Then, out of the blue, an independent advocacy group aired a devastating national ad that painted Dukakis as soft on crime (and criminals, especially violent African-American felons whom he allowed out of jail to rape white women, as the ad deliberately underscored, playing the race card). The Swift Boat Veterans' campaign appears to have been planned for similar effect and execution, well before the Democratic convention, with its release timed precisely to blunt any bump Kerry might have gotten in the polls. With the new prohibition of 527-ad spending within sixty days of the election, early August (ninety days out) marked the absolute ideal time for the ad's release, allowing thirty days for it to percolate into the public consciousness and allowing no real time for a significant counter-ad campaign to be produced and aired. The marketing of the Swift Boat message was extraordinarily sophisticated, with Swift Boat spokesmen popping up on all the news and talk shows, particularly on cable and AM radio, and with a best-selling book released within days of the original ad. All that was missing was Swift Boat Veterans lunchboxes, coloring books, and baseball caps to turn it into the political marketing equivalent of "Shrek." The "independent" group responsible for the Willy Horton ad was later directly connected to George H.W. Bush's political strategist Lee Atwater. Whether political historians will ever connect the Swift Boat group directly to George W. Bush's political Svengali, Karl Rove (a disciple of Atwater), remains to be seen (though several members of the Bush campaign would resign for having had association with the group). Suffice it to say, the ad played a critical role in undercutting Kerry's claims to leadership based on his war experience—a matter on which Kerry would dwell less and less as the fall unfolded—at a convenient time for the Bush campaign, thereby blunting Kerry's ability to gain ground on Bush across the dog days of summer. Kerry's own extraordinarily ineffective response to the Swift Boat challenge (actually ignoring it for several days while the firestorm grew) only went to underscore the old adage of cowboy comedian Will Rogers: "I don't belong to an organized political party—I'm a Democrat."

What Kerry discovered in the Swift Boat incident was what Bob Dole, John McCain, and Al Gore had previously discovered. Simply being the candidate with the stronger record of military service does not necessarily translate into public respect or political success. Dole's record as a World War II veteran, who had been critically wounded (and permanently disabled) in combat, bought him little advantage in his campaign against non-warrior Bill Clinton, who had sat out Vietnam in Oxford, England. John McCain's record in Vietnam with the personal courage and character that he displayed as a POW did not save him from a savaging at the hands of the Bush campaign in 2000 in South Carolina. And Al Gore's record of serving in uniform and in combat in Vietnam did not help him against National Guardsman Bush in the fall campaign of that year. While Americans honor their veterans, they honor their own commitment to issues and self-interest more.

Bush held his own coronation ceremony from August 30 to September 2, in New York City. While some pundits had questioned the wisdom of holding the convention so late and so long after the Democrats' convention (which could have given Kerry a full month to bask in its afterglow), holding the convention when and where it did proved to be a masterstroke for the Bush campaign. Kerry conveniently did not get an August boost, in thanks to the Swift Boat attack. And coming right after the Olympics (and, hence, after any real distractions to the public's attention) and in the run up to the third anniversary of 9/11, the Bush campaign was able to build on the president's image as a war leader, delivering his acceptance address blocks from ground zero without having to be gauche about using 9/11 overt imagery. While the convention offered table scraps to GOP moderates in the personages of new California Governor Arnold Schwarzenegger and Rudy Giuliani, the gathering's main themes were red-meat conservatism, as underscored by the unusual appearance of an apostate Democrat—Senator Zell Miller—hammering the leftward drift of his own party and driven home with the patriotic image of George W. Bush as war leader and moral leader of a nation endangered by gay marriage, abortion, and other righteous failures. These themes were distilled at the convention into a simple message for the remainder of the fall campaign: Bush was a strong, moral leader. John Kerry was not. Of the economy or the war in Iraq, little was said in New York. These issues would prove to have only a marginal impact on the outcome of the fall race, in any event.

While Democrats and Republicans completed the political kabuki theater of anointing their party standard bearers, another significant issue that would impact the fall election was revealing itself to be a dog that did not bark. The dog in this case was Ralph Nader. The Nader insurgency in 2000 had damaged Al Gore (some argued, decisively, given the 90,000 votes that the consumer activist had received in Florida). This time around, the Democratic establishment was united in its determination not to allow Nader to do similar damage. As early as February, a chorus of Democratic voices, including John Kerry, DNC chairman Terry McAuliffe, Democratic Party strategist Dane Strother, and the liberal magazine *The Nation*, sought to drown out a Nader run. Within days, however, the man in the wrinkled old suit announced his intention to do precisely that on NBC's *Meet the Press*, saying, "There's too much power and wealth in too few hands." In 2000, Nader had qualified for the ballot in twelve states as the Green Party candidate. In 2004, however, the Green Party refused him their nomination, in part seeking to avoid the backlash the party had suffered in public opinion over the 2000 election results. Lacking an established party's endorsement, Nader would have to run as an independent, making it far harder to qualify for ballot access. Lacking a broad grassroots movement to gather petition signatures to qualify for state ballots such as Ross Perot had in 1992 further undercut the Nader bid. Despite fighting in court for ballot access (successfully) in states like Oregon, New Mexico, and Florida, Nader would end up on the ballots of only thirty-five states and the District of Columbia (versus forty-three in 2000), and ultimately received only .35 percent of the vote (versus 2.75 percent in 2000). In this, Nader repeated electoral history, which has shown that repeat third-party candidates achieve half or less (substantially less in this case) of their original vote the second time out.

Within days of accepting his party's nomination, Bush's own post-convention bliss would be blunted by an attack on his own military record of service. On September 8, the CBS news program *60 Minutes II* announced the alleged discovery of newly uncovered records of President George W. Bush's service in the Air National Guard that purported to show that then Lieutenant Bush disobeyed orders and that the Bush campaign had lied about having made all such records public. Within days of its release, the story took a wild twist after a number of pro-Bush bloggers took the CBS report to task, attacking the newly found memos as forgeries based on inconsistencies in type fonts and style. Within a week CBS would be forced into the humiliating (and credibility-shattering) admission that the news organization could not verify the memos authenticity. Unlike the Swift Boat attacks, which served to undercut Kerry support, the public backlash against the bogus National Guard memos actually served to bolster support for Bush. A fall-out of the affair was the diminishing of the credibility of the mainstream media in the eyes of the public (or, rather, a reinforcement of the belief held by a goodly portion of the public that the mainstream media was biased against conservatives in general and George W. Bush in particular). Any subsequent media reports questioning Bush would thereafter be seen through a jaded lens. So punch drunk had Democrats become seeing themselves apparently outfoxed at every turn by Republicans that some desperate Democrats tried to blame the whole memo-mishmash as a trap deliberately set by Karl Rove precisely to discredit them and the mainstream media.

What the memo incident did underscore was the huge power the new media of the Internet was now wielding over the political process, muscling in on the traditional print, broadcast, and cable media. "Blogging" (from "weblogs") is a more stream-of-consciousness, real-time form of commentary and reporting (more dynamic than traditional print commentary, though unbound from that medium's prerequisites of reflection and attempts at accuracy). While the bloggers' messages reach only a tiny fraction of the public who pay attention to the chatting of what is referred to as the "blogosphere," it reaches the hyper-attentive portion (fellow bloggers, pundits, politicians, activists, and members of the traditional media) that will then amplify and distribute the blogger message to the broader public. Indeed, by 2004 the medium of blogging, practically nonexistent four years before, had integrated itself into the food chain of modern media as a kind of information plankton that bigger, established media would then feed upon. Successful cable media such as Fox, in fact, had learned how to distribute its content across such news media, integrating their traditional television operations with radio broadcasts and their own websites and bloggers. The power of this new media nexus to create and amplify any message with electron speed into an omnipresent media event was demonstrated continually in 2004.

FALL CAMPAIGN

For all the strengths that George W. Bush brought into the fall campaign (the power of incumbency, war leader and winner, a reasonably robust economy, a public perception of trustworthiness, and generally positive approval ratings) and all of Kerry's weaknesses (a liberal senatorial insider with a limited record of accomplishment in the age of dominance by conservative outsiders, a former anti-war activist in an age of hyper-patriotism) the race remained surprisingly close. Indeed, the final two months of 2004 were even tighter than those of 2000. During September and October of 2004, Bush and Kerry averaged within 1 to 3 percentage points of each other in polls (with Bush usually narrowly in the lead though with Kerry pulling even or surpassing the president on several occasions). In 2000, Bush and Gore had been separated by margins as wide as 5 to 10 percent (waffling the lead back and forth between them) until the race ended in its gnat's eyelash finish. Unlike fellow successful incumbents, Reagan in 1984 or Clinton in 1996, both of whom opened up and maintained large leads over their rivals months before the election, George W. Bush would prove himself unable to decisively capture the middle ground and thereby open up a decisive lead over Kerry. Of course, by 2004 there was far less middle to capture.

Typically, a winning presidential candidate first solidifies his own base during the spring and summer and then moves to capture the undecided middle ground from the convention onwards. What made the 2004 election stand out was how small that middle ground turned out to be and how consistent early poll results between Bush and Kerry remained across the entirety of the campaign. From March onwards, Bush and Kerry typically remained within 5 percentage points of each other. Moreover, by summer an amazing 90 percent of voters had identified themselves as basically committed to one of the two candidates. As the summer wore on, the number of undecided voters continued to shrink, such that by fall, only 5 percent of likely voters might realistically be said to possibly swing either way, the smallest pool of undecided voters in years. The three October presidential debates proved the last opportunity to tip the few remaining undecideds or to shake the other side's base.

While modern American presidential debates may never have risen to the oratorical level of Lincoln-Douglass, they have often had significant impacts on the outcome of campaigns. Indeed, the importance of the first televised debate to challenger John Kennedy's victory over the party in power's candidate, Richard Nixon, was the reason why it was the last televised debate until 1976 (in which incumbent Gerald Ford was made to look less than competent by challenger Jimmy Carter). Reagan was helped in both 1980 and 1984 by his overall debate performances, as was Clinton in 1992 and 1996. The 2000 debates, while more of a draw, tended to make George W. Bush look more potentially presidential than much of the public and media had credited him to be. The 2004 debates would have a similar positive effect for Kerry. Though the debates did not ultimately tip the balance to him on Election Day, they contributed significantly towards narrowing the margin of his defeat.

The first presidential debate, held at the University of Miami, focused on foreign policy, particularly the war on terror, and the war in Iraq. While foreign policy was supposed to be the president's strong suit (polls consistently gave him a substantial lead with voters on foreign policy matters), the post-debate consensus among mainstream pollsters and pundits gave Kerry a decisive debate victory. (And in debate politics, winning the post debate buzz, which almost all conscious Americans will hear, outweighs winning the debate itself, which perhaps 20 percent of the population will watch.) Kerry had appeared in command of both the facts and his emotions during the debate, while the president was perceived as being weak on the facts—often reduced to repeating portions of his campaign stump speech—and combative. The Kerry campaign, which had drifted through September carrying the wounds inflicted by the Swift Boat Veterans while flailing about unsuccessfully for a wedge issue to use against Bush, came out of the debate reinvigorated. Indeed, John Kerry left Miami looking for the first time in the campaign, both in the eyes of the public and perhaps in his own, like a man who could be president. The president's supporters, meanwhile, were reduced to claiming that image did not matter (which is post-debatese for "my candidate choked"). The vice presidential debate held between Dick Cheney and John Edwards a few days later helped to restore confidence in the Republican ticket. Billed by pundits as "Darth Vader versus Robin" and again focusing on Iraq and the war on terror, the often combative vice president came across in a kinder, gentler mode (though not hesitating to take the gloves off to box Edwards' and Kerry's ears at several points), while Edwards came across as somewhat lighter weight material than many had presupposed.

Bush performed better during the two subsequent debates (which anti-Bush bloggers attributed to his using a radio receiver and being fed answers—speculation that pictures of an apparent hump under the back of Bush's jacket helped to fuel). Indeed, most observers credited him with his strongest performance in the final debate, even though the focus of that contest was on domestic policy, Kerry's supposed long suit. While both candidates showed an ability to grapple with particulars of policy (including diving into the minutiae of dual-party versus multiparty American/North Korean negotiations, a subject that no doubt drove millions of viewers to the restroom for a timely break), Kerry was generally credited with having a better command of facts and issues and a better oratorical style. For all the issues debated (including spirited exchanges on gay marriage and rights, during one of which Kerry raised eyebrows and Republican ire by going out of his way to point out the homosexuality of Dick Cheney's daughter), the real essence of the debate boiled down to the issue of presidential character. The big issue coming out of Arizona was which candidate had ultimately convinced the public that he was the best to lead America abroad and at home with integrity and courage. The goal of presidential debaters is to perform competently enough not to give their own supporters reason to reconsider their commitment while giving undecided voters reason to now commit. Both candidates succeeded in the first goal. Unfortunately for Kerry, there simply were not enough truly swing-voters remaining by mid-October to influence the race decisively in his favor.

No issue crystallized to produce a last-minute defection to one candidate or the other in the final weeks of the campaign. Bush was helped by the October release of a report by the Iraq Survey Group, headed by the U.S.'s top former arms inspector Charles Dueffer, which claimed that Saddam Hussein was able to mitigate many of the effects of the sanctions through corruption of the Oil for Food Program, adding credibility to the administration's claims that sanctions alone would not have contained the dictator. That the report also implicated France, Russia, and China in helping Hussein thwart the sanctions was also helpful to Bush, as it eroded the credibility of Kerry's promise that the U.S., under his administration could work effectively with such countries to combat terror. But the Iraq Survey Group's conclusions that Iraq had produced no weapons of mass destruction after 1991 undercut the administration's claim as to the necessity of war in 2003, giving support to Kerry's claim that the war was unnecessary and unjustified.

Ultimately, the debate over Iraq was something of a push. Kerry argued that Bush had isolated the U. S. from its traditional allies and that Iraq distracted American attention away from the true threat of Al Qaeda and global terror. Bush offset this by arguing that Kerry was going to hamstring the U.S. by submitting American foreign policy to a "global test," leaving the U.S. dependent on the kindness of strangers, such as France and Russia, which the Dueffer report had revealed to be less than trustworthy. That Kerry repeatedly rejected the claim that he would only act with a global permission slip could not repair the perception that the repetition of the phrase "global test" created. Moreover, Bush would use Kerry's too clever by half alliteration of "wrong war, wrong time, wrong place," in damning the Iraqi venture during the debates to question his ability to now effectively lead in that "wrong war" should he be elected. In essence, what was really under debate in relationship to foreign policy for the U.S. in the 2004 election was not the particulars of a war in Iraq or on terror. What was in play was a debate between two fundamentally opposed worldviews of America's relationship with the world. Would the United States pursue its security by being a partner in the community of nations, working through multilateral processes to do so, as had been the dominant approach under both George H.W. Bush and Bill Clinton? Or would the U.S. seek to dominate the community of nations, relying first and foremost on its own strength and alliances based on "coalitions of the willing," meaning those states willing to recognize U.S. leadership in initiating global strategies, e.g., a continuation of the Bush doctrine. Thus, the isolationist/internationalist debate that had separated Republicans and Democrats in the 1940s and 1950s was resurrected as an American exceptionalist versus internationalist debate in the 2000s. That Kerry's message of multilateral engagement and internationalist worldview resounded strongest (electorally) on the coasts, closer both physically and psychologically to the broader world, while Bush's America-first message resonated strongest in the interior of the country was more than just a coincidence of geography.

Both campaigns went into the final stretch deprived of last-minute events that might tip things in their direction. Even the surfacing of a last hour video tape by Osama bin Laden condemning America and promising the usual litany of divine vengeance being unleashed on the great Satan did not really benefit either candidate. Instead, each campaign focused in the last weeks on using the other side's words against them. Thus, Bush seized on an out-of-context quote of Kerry in *The New York Times Magazine* saying the U.S. needed to get to the point where terrorism could again be considered more of a nuisance than a civilization-threatening danger as evidence that Kerry just "didn't get it" and would be weak on terrorism. Meanwhile, in a speech at Newton, Ohio, vice-presidential candidate John Edwards blasted Bush for abandoning federal support of embryonic stem cell research arguing that it could mean "people like Christopher Reeve are going to get up out of that wheelchair and walk again." The recently deceased Reeve had supported embryonic stem cell research and the Kerry-Edwards campaign. Senate Majority Leader Bill Frist, a medical doctor himself, blasted back, saying that John Edwards' claims raised false hope and were "shameful" and "crass." Thus, the 2004 campaign went to the ballot not on notes of ringing rhetoric and high ideals, but on the same tin notes of "gotcha" politics that had been its hallmark since the spring.

A simmering issue for many Americans going into actual balloting was how fair and honest the balloting process would be. Given the large number of allegations of electioneering improprieties leveled by both parties and their partisans at each other across the campaign season, such concerns were not without merit. No elections anywhere are without their allegations (and, indeed, real acts) of corruption. In an electoral system as large and complex (or, better said, ridiculously arcane and inefficient) as that used by the oldest Republic on the planet, such machinations by party machines or other groups and individuals are to be expected from time to time. The public perception, however, since the 1960s and the dawn of the era of open government is that such behaviors are the serious exception to the clean election rule. Gone in theory are the days when ballots for Landslide Lyndon Johnson would be recounted until enough were found for victory, or when the motto for Cook County, Illinois, was, "Vote early and vote often" and one's political obligation to vote for one's party did not end at the grave. The closeness of the 2000 election, however, particularly in infamous Florida, had caused the light of public scrutiny to be shone in higher intensity on American electoral practices. It is one thing to tolerate electoral fraud when it was perceived to account for a fraction of a percentage point of the vote when elections are won by large margins. It is quite another to do so in an era of tight political races. What close scrutiny of electoral practices in Florida revealed was not pretty, with tales (some substantiated, others not) of voter intimidation, registration and ballot fraud, outright destruction of ballots, wholesale purging of voters by state officials from voter rolls without due process, and a whole litany of other election-rigging endeavors from the spreading of walking around money to get out a targeted group of voters to the creation of sophisticated but untraceable call centers spreading deliberate misinformation on elections to suppress those voters. Congress, responding to public discontent over such threats to the sanctity of the ballot, passed the "Help America Vote

Act" in 2002, which, amongst other things, mandated that each state provide provisional ballots for voters with registration problems and provide states fiscal help in upgrading their voting machines to move America away from the now infamous punch-card ballot. Despite such congressional action, concerns of electoral manipulation resurfaced and, with these concerns, so too would a slew of allegations such as electoral manipulation. Whether this was the result of heightened awareness of, anxiety over, and sensitivity to such potential campaign shenanigans in the wake of Florida in 2000 or whether this represented a real trend towards increasing dirty campaigning remains to be determined. But from a simply anecdotal perspective, 2004 may have been the most divisive and hard—if not dirtily—fought campaign since perhaps 1972 and the bitter Nixon/McGovern race. Indeed, both parties accused the other of engaging in patterns of dirty tricks reminiscent of those played by "Tricky Dick and company."

Democratic Party offices in Toledo, Ohio, and Scottsdale, Arizona, and Republican offices in the state of Washington were reportedly broken into and computers containing campaign information stolen (which means that either violence against campaigns were on the rise or campaign offices have become a favorite target of quick thieves). Reports of harassment of and violence towards political partisans also poured in from around the country. A Bush-Cheney headquarters in Knoxville, Tennessee, was hit by two gunshots, apparently from a passing vehicle, and a West Virginia Republican Party headquarters was shot at during Bush's acceptance speech. Vandals burned an 8-by-8-foot swastika into the lawn of a Madison, Wisconsin, Bush supporter. In September, a Republican campaigner, Phil Parlock, claimed John Edwards assaulted him and his daughter at a public appearance. (It was later revealed that he had made similar claims during previous presidential elections.) In early October, union members took part in AFL-CIO-coordinated protests of new federal restrictions on overtime pay at local Bush-Cheney headquarters across the nation. In Orlando, union protesters injured two Bush supporters and defaced Bush posters, with similar acts reported in twenty cities. The Bush campaign blasted the AFL-CIO for tolerating, if not outright organizing, union activities, while less restrained Republicans compared the actions to those of Hitler's "Brown Shirts." The conservative-leaning Drudge Report, meanwhile, cited a Democratic field manual to accuse Democrats of being ready to unleash "pre-emptive strikes" against Republicans to stop voter intimidation—essentially using intimidation to stop intimidation. The Democratic Party web site responded by stating that Drudge had "unfairly characterized" the manual, but Republicans seized on the matter to paint the Democrats as being the real party of intimidation.

Allegations also surfaced in October that a for-profit voter registration outfit—Voters Outreach of America—operating in the state of Nevada collected and submitted Republican voter registrations while collecting and shredding Democratic registrations. Similar charges against the group also arose in Oregon. Meanwhile, Republicans alleged that Democrats had systematically sought to illegally register pro-Democratic voters, charges backed up by anecdotal reports from states like Ohio and Colorado of people registering Democrats thirty-five times or under names like Mary Poppins. Such allegations unleashed a tirade on talk radio stations against Democrats trying to stuff the ballot boxes with phony votes. (Perhaps nothing so well defines the differences between the two parties as how each is alleged to commit electoral fraud, with Democrats trying to illegally maximize the vote and Republicans seeking to illegally minimize it.) Other voter registration drives came under fire as well. When stars supporting MTV's "Rock the Vote" campaign urged students to register and vote against Bush to avoid his implementing a draft, RNC Chairman Ed Gillespie threatened with legal action, challenging the group's tax-exempt status.

Dirty politics of false accusations have been a part of the American tradition since the mudslinging days of Adams and Jefferson, and playing on the ignorance and gullibility of voters has an equally long lineage (such as in the delightfully apocraphyl tale of Democrat Claude Pepper winning his first race for Congress by telling rural Florida voters that his opponent was a notorious "heterosexual"). Such political mudslinging, however, has become electron-fast and world-wide-web omnipresent thanks to the rise of the alternative media universe of the blogosphere, where any rumor or innuendo can circle the world a dozen times before the mainstream media can identify and debunk it. Such was the case in July after the Department of Homeland Security asked the Justice Department's office of legal counsel to research on the legal requirements for postponing the November elections as a contingency plan should terrorist attacks or their threat disrupt the elections. Internet rumor mills went into overdrive following the first posting of the report. (While overplayed by some bloggers as a sinister plot of some kind, the decision of Homeland Security to even look into such a contingency was more borderline bonehead than seriously disturbing. Yet, such suggestions to tamper with the legal rhythm of elections out of security concerns, like the foolishness of suggesting Rudy Giuliani should not have to step down at the end of his term in 2001 because of the 9/11 attack, represent either a profound misunderstanding of the sanctity of the electoral process or a diminishment of it verging on contempt. While it may be far from the intent of those who make such suggestions, it would be well for them to realize that of such ideas, in truly perilous times, is the stuff of dictatorship borne.)

Moreover, the art of bare knuckles politics resurrected and refined by the first wave of bloodsport political consultants like Lee Atwater in the 1970s and polished to a Madison Avenue perfection by the second generation Karl Roves and Dick Morrises has become progressively more effective and efficient. (For example, the notorious though hard to nail down process of pushing polling where voters are systematically called under the pretense of a poll but actually to impart a negative imagine of a candidate, as in, "Do you think it is right for candidate X to advocate the execution of all people over the age of 65 to save money?") Such techniques have raised the fine art of character assassination to new heights, with the lifeless campaign bodies of smeared candidates often hitting the ground, victim of an Internet assault before the candidate even knows he or she was attacked. What was shocking in 2004 was not that outrageous claims were made about the candidates but that outrageous claims were made in such huge numbers in so many venues by seemingly legitimate political groups and players.

Such was the case with Michael Moore's film *Fahrenheit 9/11*, awarded the Palme d'Or at the Cannes Film Festival. While the film was billed as offering a critical look at the administration of George W. Bush and the war on terror, it was truly a polemical work aimed at destroying the Bush image more than establishing a true historical record. A pay-TV distributor backed away from a deal to air the film in the fall out of "legitimate business and legal concerns" (a decision driven at least in part by a massive protest from the right. Conservative media had its day as well. In October the Sinclair Broadcasting Group (whose owner had strong Republican ties) ordered its sixty-two television stations—many of them in battleground states—to air *Stolen Honor: Wounds that Never Heal*, a purported documentary that attacked Kerry's anti-Vietnam war record as unpatriotic. The Sinclair group had refused to broadcast an episode of *Nightline* in April that reported on American military casualties in Iraq, based on the premise that it would undermine the war effort and hence risk harm to American troops, although critics argued it was for fear that a review of casualties would hurt the Republican campaign.

Meanwhile, a veritable avalanche of anti-Kerry books (culminating in the Swift Boat book) hawked daily on AM talk radio stations and anti-Bush books filled the sales tables of club-stores across America. So poisoned had the political atmosphere become with vitriol and distrust that, when ultra-conservative groups circulated a petition asking Attorney General John Ashcroft to disqualify John Kerry from running for office and to prosecute him for treason over his anti-war activities in the 1970s, more than 170,000 signed it.

Both Republicans and Democrats, distrustful of each other and fearful that somehow the election might be stolen from them, went into Election Day mobilized for full-scale legal war. Both national parties were reported to have teams of lawyers standing by on runways like legal commandos, waiting to be dropped within hours into any disputed ballot-counting firefight—conjuring up images of a post-election "Apocalypse Now," with the parties reduced to partisan guerilla warfare, trying to win the election literally ballot by ballot in key states. Both parties fielded record numbers of poll observers—Republicans largely to challenge the legitimacy of voters' registration status to avoid voter fraud, and Democrats to challenge the challenges and protect voter ballot access. And both parties announced that they would not be giving in without a fight—there would be no early concession while ballots were still being counted, as had been the case with Al Gore after the networks called Florida for Bush. It was widely accepted that Gore's retracting of his concession had undercut his standing with the public at large during the subsequent protracted election dispute. Neither Bush nor Kerry, therefore, were going to make a concession call until all significant ballot disputes were resolved, which in an election expected to come down to the balloting in a handful of swing states might take days, if not weeks, once the dogs of law were unleashed.

It was against such a backdrop of uncertainty and mistrust that voters finally went to the polls on November 2. Early exit poll reports (which television networks faithfully did not report so as to avoid a repeat of 2000 and Florida but which webbloggers felt no compunction about sharing near and far) showed Kerry leading, particularly in key swing states like Ohio, by 2 to 5 percentage points. But as polls closed and state winners were projected, a Red tide rose across the heartland reversing Kerry's early exit poll lead. One by one, most swing states swung Republican with some, like Florida, swinging by reasonably large margins (5 percent). By midnight on the East Coast, the only big apple that had not fallen from the electoral tree was Ohio, which was hanging by a stem over the

Bush basket. But given Bush's popular vote majority, most people went to bed fairly certain that, barring some incredible Florida-style repetition, George W. Bush had won reelection (and by doing so, as a little footnote to history, turned the 2004 election into the first back-to-back successful reelection since the founding of the Republic when Thomas Jefferson, James Madison, and James Monroe followed each other in successive 8-year stints).

The 2004 morning after the night before was, therefore, anticlimactic. While Bush's lead in Ohio was statistically razor-thin at little over 100,000, compared to a Florida of 500 votes it looked like a landslide in the public eye. Moreover, Bush emerged as the clear national winner with 51 percent of the popular vote—the first presidential victor to be able to claim an outright majority of the vote since his own father in 1988. Given the clear popular vote majority with 58.9 million votes to Kerry's 55.4 million (a 3.5 million vote advantage compared to Gore's 500,000 votes in 2000) and a 34-vote electoral victory (286 to 252 compared to a 4-electoral-vote margin of victory in 2000), there simply seemed to be no clear reason for either party to challenge the election outcome. By midday, Kerry made his concession call and speech, acknowledging what the networks and cable channels had indicated was the outcome since around sunrise. The legions of lawyers mobilized for a war that never came faded silently into the dawn. (However, accusations would start to percolate on liberal websites and talk radio stations within days of the election, with questions being raised over the discrepancy between the exit polls and the final tallies. While these accusations remained out of the mainstream in the weeks after the election, they served as an early warning that the taint of illegitimacy would continue to follow Bush into his second term.)

When the electoral dust of 2004 had settled, little had changed on the national political landscape in comparison to 2000. The 3 percent swing from Democrats to Republicans was the smallest for a presidential election in modern history. Bush won in only two states that he had not won in 2000—New Mexico and Iowa—while losing New Hampshire to the forces of Blue. The 2004 electoral map neatened up the geographical divisions in the country that had been clearly delineated in 2000, with Democrats dominating the west coast, Great Lakes and New England and Republicans everything else. Indeed, as county-by-county results showed, Republican hegemony was even more pronounced, with Democrats winning in those counties upon which an ocean or a lake lapped and Republicans dominating where the sea gulls stopped flying.

Of course, the distorting effect of the geographic electoral map made the Republican margin of victory seem huge, with all the Red states of the interior rich in land but poor in population. It is worth remembering that, while Democrats won fewer states (20, including the District of Columbia, versus 31 for Republicans), those states tended to be the more populous ones.

Yet, the basic geographically observable political division in the country manifested in 2000 seems to have intensified, if anything, in 2004. In most states, the election was nowhere near as close as it was at the national level: Kerry tended to win states by 5 to 10 percent margins; Bush tended to win by 10 to 20 percent. There were only nine states where the margin of victory for Bush or Kerry was 3 percent or less. Ominously for Democrats, six of these states (Oregon, Michigan, Minnesota, Wisconsin, Pennsylvania, and New Hampshire) voted for Kerry. These will, no doubt, be the battleground states for Republicans in 2008. What the increasingly wide margins of victory for candidates (i.e., Kerry by 22 percent in Massachusetts, Bush by 45 percent in Utah) seem to indicate is that in, turn of the century America, Nixon's sage twentieth century advice to Bob Dole—zig to the right in the primaries and zag to the center in the general election—no longer applies. Indeed, over the last ten years, it would seem that American politics has begun its own slouch towards a Bethlehem where the political center no longer holds. Ultimately, Bush's victory in swing states such as Ohio, Iowa, and New Mexico came not from appealing to moderates but from rallying the battle-Red conservative faithful. Similarly, Kerry did best where his liberal bona fides were considered a badge of honor rather than a scarlet letter. One would anticipate that this will be observed by strategists of both parties who in 2006 and 2008 can be expected to chuck their mushy-middle defensive playbooks in favor of a more aggressive rally of the base offense—which should make upcoming elections even more partisan and divisive.

Foreshadowing such an intensification of the partisan wars, despite the relative closeness of the vote, Republicans immediately seized on the opportunity of Bush's victory with an outright majority of the vote to proclaim a clear "mandate" from the voters. This despite the fact that Bush's 3 percent margin of victory would be the smallest for any incumbent since Woodrow Wilson in 1916 and significantly smaller than the margin of victory for the two recent successful incumbents. Bill Clinton had won reelection in 1996 by a 9 percent margin, and Reagan had won reelection against Walter Mondale by a crushing 18 points. Indeed, while Bill Clinton won election with only a plurality of the vote in both 1992 and 1996, his minimum margin of victory was 5 percent against George H.W. Bush in 1996. Bush senior had dispatched Massachusetts liberal Democrat Michael Dukakis with an 8-point margin in 1988 and Ronald Reagan had defeated incumbent Carter by 9 points in 1980. Bush's 34-vote electoral majority was also small in comparison to recent elections. (Reagan's margins: 440 in 1980; and 512 in 1986; Bush's margin: 315 in 1988; Clinton's margins: 202 in 1992 and 220 in 1996) Thus, compared to recent electoral history, Bush's 3 percent margin might, at first blush, not be seen as anything to crow about. But crow Bush could and would, stating at his first post-victory press conference that he had "earned [political] capital" and intended to spend it.

What separated Bush's reelection victory from that of recent predecessors, however, was the fact that he did, indeed, have a legislative "bank" in which to invest his electoral capital. Both Ronald Reagan and Bill Clinton faced opposition-dominated Congresses in their second term that had no incentive to help a soon-to-be lame duck continue a record of accomplishment that might keep his party in the presidency. While Democrats were content to blunt any further rightward drift in Reagan's second term (including the famous rejection of Supreme Court nominee Robert Bork), Republicans were even more in-your-face with Clinton, emasculating his second term through impeachment. George W. Bush, however, emerged from his reelection with a Congress even more solidly in the hands of his party, with House Republicans extending their majority by four seats (to 231) and Republican senators seeing their number swell to a century-mark high of 55—only five short seats away from the holy grail of political hegemony, a filibuster proof 60 (making achieving that margin the undoubted sacred political quest of the GOP in the coming 2006 midterm elections).

Conventional wisdom holds that presidents are always less effective in their second lame-duck term than in their first term. Conventional wisdom also holds that second term presidents will become increasingly concerned about their historical legacy and to ensure a final record of accomplishment worthy of a presidential library (if not a monument on a mall or a carved visage on a mountain side), will be increasingly willing to compromise with the opposition. Conventional wisdom, however, has increasingly been turned on its political ear as the nation adjusts to a twenty-first century world progressively deviating from its twentieth century roots, driven by the realities of the replacement of the cold war with the war on terror and domestic economies by global economies. Thus, the prospects of a Bush second term that conforms to past wisdom—less aggressive, more willing to compromise, less focused on big ideals, and more focused on achieving a moderate, respectable agenda—should be discounted.

George W. Bush began his first term with the weakest mandate of any president since perhaps Rutherford Hayes. A minority president ultimately confirmed by Supreme Court intervention with slim majorities in Congress that would actually be reversed in one chamber within a matter of months, expectations at the beginning of Bush's term were for a humble and limited presidency. Yet, from that slender thread of legitimacy, Bush wove an aggressive agenda in domestic policy and a radical agenda on the global stage. Armed now with an outright majority mandate and unassailable (but for the prospect of endless Democratic filibustering in the Senate) majorities in the Congress, Bush is better positioned than any second-term president since FDR to aggressively tackle his agenda. That he would then go quietly into the second term night seems like hopeless optimism on the part of a party now more fully out of power than it has been since the late nineteenth century.

Shortly after reelection, Bush laid out precisely how aggressive his second term would be. His near term domestic agenda targeted extension of his already substantial tax cut regime, further simplification of the tax code, and privatization of at least part of Social Security. Should he be successful in the last instance, he will have significantly rolled back one of the last remaining pillars of the New Deal (with the pillars of progressive taxation, overtime pay, the minimum wage, and the goal of full employment having been weakened or toppled by successive conservative administrations from Reagan to Bush's own first term). Having admitted no foreign policy mistakes in his campaign, it must be assumed at least that lip service will continue to be paid to the Bush Doctrine of defensive preemption, if not its outright extension to new targets. Given the dynamic nature of the unsettled post-cold war world, opportunities for new applications of the Bush Doctrine may indeed be forced on the administration.

Bush's first new cabinet appointment after his reelection underscored his intent to give no ground to the center or left in his second term. When Bush's controversial Attorney General John Ashcroft (blasted as reactionary and dangerous by his most vocal liberal critics, acknowledged as clearly socially conservative by everyone else) tendered his resignation for reasons of health, pundits immediately began to debate which more centrist figure Bush might appoint to show his willingness to reach out to the middle. Moderate Republican Rudy Giuliani became the center of short-lived speculation along those lines. Instead, Bush reverted to form, appointing a member of his inner circle, White House counsel Alberto Gonzales, to take Ashcroft's place. The media tended to see Gonzales, the first Latino to be nominated to so high a cabinet post, as a sign of Bush taking a more conciliatory line in replacing the divisive arch-conservative Ashcroft. (If the person is an ethnic minority like Gonzales, the reasoning seemed to be that he must be at least a political moderate, if not a liberal). More cautious voices observed that appointing a man who helped author the administration's controversial enemy-combatant detainee policy and liberalization of the rules relating to torture of suspects and who referred to the Geneva Convention as dated and quaint hardly created a sea change in the attorney general's office.

Meanwhile, when moderate Senator Arlen Specter, in line to become chairman of the Republican-dominated Judiciary Committee, suggested that Bush would have to be circumspect in his second term judicial selections—particularly on the divisive issue of abortion, making appointments more from the moderate middle than had been done in the first term—he was vehemently attacked by conservative politicians and pundits. Indeed, heading into the 109th Congress, Specter's possible tenure as chairman of the Judiciary Committee appeared to be called into doubt. Given the illness of Supreme Court Chief Justice William Rehnquist and the high average age of members of the highest Court, the possibility of Bush having a chance to defy Specter's injunction seems high. Indeed, if Bush would make trusted loyalist Alberto Gonzales (who Bush had appointed while governor to the Texas Supreme Court) his first cabinet appointment, it would be logical to assume that, after a year or two in the attorney general's seat, Bush might well appoint him as the first Latino to a vacancy on the Court.

After the election, many voices in Washington and around the country repeated the politically correct mantra that it was now time to "heal the country's wounds," wounds both parties had willfully spent months rubbing partisan salt into for political advantage. In an America in which liberals think conservatives are stupid and conservatives think liberals are evil, bipartisanship becomes difficult, if not outright impossible. The reality of the intensely partisan voting patterns in 2004 would seem to argue against such moderation by the two parties, at least from a rational political perspective. The 2004 election showed that mobilizing the base now outweighs reaching out to the center in national politics. For Democrats who, according to House Minority Leader (in apparent perpetuity) Nancy Pelosi, "lost just about everything that we can lose," the big question after the election became "where next?" Had Democrats truly hit bottom with nowhere to go but up, or were they still in free fall to political oblivion? Democrats had dumped their candidate of partisanship, Howard Dean, fearing he would set them up for a replay of 1972, and gone more to the center with Kerry. While such Clintonian moderation had won Democrats two elections, by the end of 2004 it had also lost them two, though by close margins. Yet, the margin of loss was greater the second time around, which presented Democrats with a less than rosy future trend line. For the nation's oldest party, the popular primary season bumper sticker, "Dated Dean, Married Kerry," took on true irony after the election. Marrying safe, the Democrats had remained losers. Whether the party will mimic Republicans and begin moving more to solidify their own base in elections remains to be seen. And whether that base is any longer stable and large enough to produce national victory also remains to be seen. One of the most disturbing outcomes of the election for Democrats for the long term was the record-setting share of the Latino vote (42 percent—a 7-point increase over 2000) captured by Bush. The fastest growing minority group in the country and hitherto largely Democratic stalwarts, socially conservative Latinos seem increasingly drawn to the Red banner. If such trends continue and Democrats see their base further erode, they may be left an increasing minority party.

For Republicans, the clear message of 2004 was carpe diem. The initial partisan rumblings from Republican opinion shapers and policy makers in the weeks after the election, stressing their party's mandate to reshape the American political landscape, seemed to reinforce the notion that, for the near term at least, politics in the world's oldest Republic will stay partisan. Bush's foreign policy during his first term in office became dominated by a neo-conservative view that argued that the U.S. was presented in the post-cold war world with a narrow window of opportunity to reshape the global order through American power to America's benefit. The retirement of Secretary of State Colin Powell, seen as a lone significant counter-voice to the administration's neo-cons and Bush's rapid appointment of National Security Advisor Condoleezza Rice (part of the dominant neo-con troika with Vice President Cheney and Secretary of Defense Donald Rumsfeld in Bush's first term) would seem to reaffirm the critical role this view will have in the second Bush term. Rice's appointment reaffirmed two additional aspects of the Bush presidential style: the president's commitment to a leadership style based on the advice of a small, inner coterie of trusted, loyal aides and his commitment to "staying the course" in all policy matters, large and small, foreign and domestic.

It may well prove that in his second term Bush will apply a neo-conservative view towards his domestic agenda, recognizing that his electoral victory provides himself and Republicans a narrow window of opportunity to reshape the domestic landscape by reversing fifty years of liberal orthodoxy and replacing it with Republican conservative ideals, thereby solidify a GOP political hegemony that could then last another quarter century—or more. Whether Bush will succeed in implementing such a "Domestic Bush Doctrine," abandoning the pretense of bipartisan moderation in favor of aggressively solidifying the policy dominance of the conservative worldview will be the political story of the next decade. That he will try to implement such a doctrine will be the political story of his second term. Whether successful or not, the attempt to reverse the liberal legacy of the twentieth century will be the lasting legacy of George W. Bush, arguably the most significant Republican politician since Abraham Lincoln.

BIBLIOGRAPHY

Franklin Delano Roosevelt

Other than Abraham Lincoln, no president has been written about more than Franklin Roosevelt. Indeed, FDR biographies are legion. However, for this particular essay, the following were found to be the most useful: James MacGregor Burns's two volumes, *Roosevelt: The Lion and the Fox* (1956), and *Roosevelt: The Soldier of Freedom* (1970); Frank Freidel's one volume, *Franklin D. Roosevelt: A Rendezvous with Destiny* (1990); Patrick Maney, *The Roosevelt Presence* (1992); and Conrad Black, *Franklin Delano Roosevelt: Champion of Freedom* (2003). The *Public Papers and Addresses of Franklin Roosevelt* (13 volumes, 1938-1950), edited by Samuel I. Rosenman, is an indispensable source on FDR's presidency as is *The Complete Presidential Press Conferences of Franklin Delano Roosevelt* (1972); and Russell D. Buhite and David W. Levy, eds., *FDR's Fireside Chats* (1992). Also useful is Elliot Roosevelt, ed., *FDR: His Personal Correspondence, 1928-1945* (2 vols., 1950).

In addition to the above, also found helpful and insightful were Geoffrey C. Ward, *A First Class Temperament: The Emergence of Franklin Roosevelt* (1989), and *Before the Trumpet: Young Franklin Roosevelt* (1985); Robert E. Sherwood, *Roosevelt and Hopkins* (1948); Frances Perkins, *The Roosevelt I Knew* (1946); John Morton Blum, *Roosevelt and Morgenthau* (1970); William E. Leuchtenburg, *The FDR Years: On Roosevelt and His Legacy* (1995). On Eleanor Roosevelt and her relationship with Franklin, as well as her invaluable contributions to the New Deal and liberalism, see Blanche Wiesen Cook, *Eleanor Roosevelt: A Life* (1992); Lois Scharf, *Eleanor Roosevelt: First Lady of American Liberalism* (1987); Joseph T. Lash, *Eleanor and Franklin* (1973).

The general histories of the New Deal central to this essay were David M. Kennedy, *Freedom From Fear: The American People in Depression and War, 1929-1945* (1999); Robert S. McElvaine, *The Great Depression, 1929-1941* (1984); William E. Leuchtenburg, *Franklin D. Roosevelt and the New Deal, 1932-1940* (1963); Arthur M. Schlesinger, Jr., *The Age of Roosevelt* (3 vols., 1956-1960); Anthony J. Badger, *The New Deal* (1989); Paul Conkin, *The New Deal* (third edition, 1992); Harvard Sitkoff, ed.,

Fifty Years Later: The New Deal Evaluated (1985), a summary of several generations of New Deal scholarship. Also informative are Michael Parrish, *Anxious Decades: America in Prosperity and Depression* (1992); James T. Patterson, *America's Struggle Against Poverty, 1900-1994* (1994); Richard Polenberg, *Reorganizing Roosevelt's Government: The Controversy over Executive Reorganization, 1936-1939* (1966), and "The Decline of the New Deal State," in *The New Deal: The National Level,* ed. John Braeman, et. al. (1975); Page Smith, *Redeeming the Time: A People's History of the 1920s and the New Deal* (1987); Alan Brinkley, *The End of Reform: New Deal Liberalism in Recession and War* (1995).

The best general works on FDR during the war years are John Morton Blum, *V Was for Victory: Politics and American Culture During World War II* (1976); Richard Polenberg, *War and Society: The United States, 1941-1945* (1972); David M. Kennedy, *Freedom From Fear* (1999); Doris Kearns Goodwin, *No Ordinary Time: Franklin and Eleanor Roosevelt and the Home Front in World War II* (1994); William O'Neill, *A Democracy at War: America's Fight at Home and Abroad in World War II* (1993); George H. Roeder, *The Censored War: American Visual Experience During World War II* (1993), and Patrick S. Washburn, *A Question of Sedition* (1986). Allan Winkler's *The Politics of Propaganda* (1978) examines the Office of War Information through which FDR censored the war and used as his "propaganda machine." John Dower's *War Without Mercy: Race and Power in the Pacific War* (1986) explores American and Japanese racial propaganda in the Pacific theater and its impact on their respective homefronts. On Roosevelt and the internment of Japanese-Americans, see Roger Daniels, *Prisoners Without Trial: Japanese Americans in World War II* (1993), and *Concentration Camp, U.S.A.: Japanese Americans in World War II* (1971); and Peter Irons, *Justice at War: The Story of the Japanese American Internment Cases* (1983). The best treatments of FDR's response to the Holocaust are David Wyman, *The Abandonment of the Jews: America and the Holocaust, 1941-1945* (1984), and *Paper Walls: America and the Refugee Crisis, 1938-1941* (1968); P. Leonard Dinnerstein, *America and the Survivors of the Holocaust* (1982); Henry Feingold, *Politics of Rescue: The Roosevelt Administration and the Holocaust, 1938-1945* (1970); and Saul Friedman, *No Haven for the Oppressed* (1973); and Deborah E. Lipstadt, *Beyond Belief: The American Press and the Coming of the Holocaust, 1933-1945* (1986).

The black experience in World War II America and during FDR's presidency has received significant attention in recent years. However, Gunnar Myrdal's *An American Dilemma: The Negro Problem and Modern*

Democracy (1944) remains the standard, especially for African Americans and the war years. Also see Richard Polenberg, *One Nation Divisible: Class, Race, and Ethnicity in the United States Since 1938* (1980). The condition of Southern blacks during the 1930s is the focus of John Dollard's *Caste and Class in a Southern Town* (1937); and Hortense Powdermaker's *After Freedom* (1939). A good, general survey of African Americans during the New Deal years can be found in Raymond Wolters' *Negroes and the Great Depression* (1970); and Harvard Sitkoff's *A New Deal for Blacks* (1979). Nancy Weiss, in *Farewell to the Party of Lincoln: Black Politics in the Age of FDR* (1983), argues that blacks voted for FDR because many of his work programs and other policies benefited African Americans economically, which at the time was more important to the majority of blacks than equality, which (as noted in the essay) FDR was reluctant to push. Also see Neil Wynn, *The Afro American and the Second World War* (1976); Lee Finkle, *Forum for Protest: The Black Press During World War II* (1975); and Louis Ruchames, *Race, Jobs, and Politics: The Story of the FEPC* (1948). Racial violence during the war is discussed in Robert Shogan and Tom Craig's *Detroit's Race Riot* (1964); and Dominic J. Capeci Jr.'s *The Harlem Riot of 1943* (1977). Jervis Anderson's *A. Philip Randolph: A Biographical Portrait (1973)* offers a detailed account of one of the primary leaders of black civil rights during the war years.

The foreign policies of the four Roosevelt administrations are ably presented in Robert Dallek's encyclopedic *Franklin Roosevelt and American Foreign Policy, 1932-1945* (1979); Robert Divine, *The Reluctant Belligerent* (1965), and *The Illusion of Neutrality* (1962); Waldo Heinrichs Jr., *Threshold of War* (1988); Lloyd Gardner, *Economic Aspects of New Deal Diplomacy* (1964); Warren F. Kimball, *The Juggler* (1991); and Frederick W. Marks, *Wind Over Sand: The Diplomacy of Franklin Roosevelt* (1988). On FDR's struggle with the isolationists, see Wayne S. Cole, *Roosevelt and the Isolationists* (1983). On FDR and the Spanish Civil War, see Allen Guttman, *The Wound in the Heart: America and the Spanish Civil War* (1962); and Douglas Little, *Malevolent Neutrality: The United States, Great Britain, and the Origins of the Spanish Civil War* (1985). On the formulation of the Good Neighbor Policy, see Irwin F. Gellman, *Good Neighbor Diplomacy* (1979). On FDR and Pearl Harbor, see Herbert Feis, *The Road to Pearl Harbor* (1950); Paul Schroeder, *The Axis Alliance and Japanese-American Relations, 1941* (1958); John Toland, *Infamy: Pearl Harbor and Its Aftermath* (1982); and Roberta Wholsetter, *Pearl Harbor: Warning and Decision* (1962). The best coverage of FDR's relationship with Stalin and the origins of the cold war can be found in

Walter LaFeber, *America, Russia, and the Cold War, 1945-1996,* 9th ed. (2002); John L. Gaddis, *The United States and the Origins of the Cold War, 1941-1947* (1972); William Hardy McNeil, *America, Britain, and Russia: Their Cooperation and Conflict, 1941-1946* (1953); Herbert Feis, *Churchill, Roosevelt, and Stalin: The War They Waged and the Peace They Sought* (1957); *Between War and Peace: The Potsdam Conference* (1960); and *The Atomic Bomb and the End of World War II* (1961). For a revisionist view of FDR's wartime conduct, strategy, and relationship with the other Allies, most notably the Soviet Union, see Gabriel Kolko, *The Politics of the War: The World and United States Foreign Policy, 1943-1945* (1968).

Harry S Truman

The best single volume biographies of Harry Truman are David McCullough, *Truman,* (1992), and Alonzo Hamby, *Man of the People: Harry S. Truman* (1995). The most comprehensive political overview of the postwar years can be found in Alonzo Hamby, *Beyond the New Deal: Harry S. Truman and American Liberalism* (1973). Also see Cabell Phillips, *The Truman Presidency* (1956); Bert Cochran, *Harry Truman and the Crisis Presidency* (1973); Robert Donovan, *Conflict and Crisis* (1977); and Robert Ferrell, *Harry Truman and the Modern American Presidency* (1982). In *Future of American Politics* (1952), Samuel Lubell presents a provocative interpretation of the postwar years' hostile and rather mercurial political climate, and Barton Bernstein, ed., *Politics and Policies of the Truman Administration* (1970), assesses the goals, accomplishments, and failures of the Truman presidency. Two of the more scathing indictments of the Truman presidency can be found in I.F. Stone's *The Truman Era* (1953); and Paul G. Pierpaoli, *Truman and Korea: The Political Culture of the Early Cold War* (1999). Two of the best general histories of the postwar years that assess the Truman presidency evenhandedly are William H. Chafe, *Unfinished Journey: America Since World War II,* fifth edition, (2003); and James T. Patterson, *Grand Expectations: The United States, 1945-1974* (1996).

There are numerous books that focus on specific issues that Truman had to contend with during his presidency. Some of the most informative are R. Alton Lee, *Truman and Taft-Hartley* (1966); Allen J. Matusow, *Farm Policies and Politics in the Truman Administration* (1967); Steven Bailey, *Congress Makes a Law* (1950), which is a study of the full employment act; Richard O. Davies, *Housing Reform During the*

Truman Administration (1966); and Susan M. Hartman, who examines congressional-executive relations in *Truman and the 80ᵗʰ Congress* (1971). Truman's civil rights policies are the subject of several good books, most notably Steven Lawson's *Black Ballots* (1977); William Berman, *The Politics of Civil Rights in the Truman Administration* (1970); and Donald R. McCoy and Richard Ruetten, *Quest and Response: Minority Rights in the Truman Administration* (1973).

Since Truman was "present at the creation" of the cold war, his role and responsibility for creating America's cold war policy is the central topic of the best general surveys, which include John L. Gaddis, *The United States and the Origins of the Cold War, 1941-1947* (1972); Walter LaFeber, *America, Russia, and the Cold War, 1945-1996,* 9ᵗʰ edition (2002); Daniel Yergin, *A Shattered Peace: The Origins of the Cold War and the National Security State* (1977); Stephen Ambrose and Douglas Brinkley, *Rise to Globalism: American Foreign Policy Since 1938,* 8ᵗʰ rev. ed. (1997); and Thomas Patterson, *On Every Front: The Making and Unmaking of the Cold War* (1992); Melvyn Leffler, *A Preponderance of Power: National Security, the Truman Administration, and the Cold War* (1992). All of these works are generally "traditionalist" in their interpretation; that is, they are supportive of Truman's cold war initiatives although they do let the reader know when they believe Truman "overreacted" or simply blundered. Such is not the case in the revisionist assessments, which contend that the United States aggressively and needlessly initiated the cold war and that Truman led the charge. That is the opinion found in Joyce and Gabriel Kolko, *The Limits of Power: The World and U.S. Foreign Policy, 1945-1954* (1972); D.F. Fleming, *The Cold War and Its Origins* (two volumes, 1961); Richard Barnett, *Intervention and Revolution* (1969); and David Horowitz, ed., *Containment and Revolution* (1967). Relative to cold war specifics and the Truman presidency, see Gar Alperowitz's *Atomic Diplomacy: Hiroshima, Potsdam* (1965, rev. ed. 1986). On the hydrogen bomb, see Richard Rhodes, *Dark Sun: The Making of the Hydrogen Bomb* (1995). John Gaddis discusses the formation of the Truman Doctrine and containment in *Strategies in Containment: A Critical Appraisal of Post-War American National Security Policy* (1982); Michael Hogan, *The Marshall Plan: America, Britain, and the Reconstruction of Western Europe, 1947-1952* (1987).

The symbiotic relationship between the cold war and the emergence of the politics of anticommunism at home during the Truman years is assessed in David Caute's *The Great Fear: The Anti-Communist Purge Under Truman and Eisenhower* (1978); Allen D. Harper, *The Politics* of Loyalty: *The White House and the Communist Issue, 1946-1952* (1959); and Michael Belknap, *Cold War Political Justice: The Smith Act, the Communist Party, and American Civil Liberties* (1977). The most thorough and critical rendering of Truman's responsibility for the politics of anticommunism is Athan Theoharis' *Seeds of Repression: Harry Truman and the Origins of McCarthyism* (1972).

Among the many books on the Korean War, some of the more informative are Dorothy Foot, *The Wrong War: American Policy and the Dimensions of the Korean Conflict, 1950-1953* (1985); Burton Kaufman, *The Korean War: Challenges in Crisis, Credibility, and Command* (1986); William Stueck, *The Road to Confrontation: American Policy Toward China and Korea, 1947-1950* (1981); Callum MacDonald, *Korea: The War Before Vietnam* (1986). Bruce Cumings, *The Origins of the Korean War* (two volumes, 1981, 1990), is very critical of American policies, thus of Truman's handling of the conflict from start to finish.

Dwight D. Eisenhower

Historian Stephen Ambrose provides a comprehensive biography of Dwight David Eisenhower in his two-volume set: *Eisenhower: A Soldier and President* and *Eisenhower: The President* (1984 and 1990). Rich in detail and balanced in analysis, the book explores all facets of the man and his presidency. Fred Greenstein's *The Hidden-Hand Presidency: Eisenhower As Leader* (2000), providing an early edition (1982 with an update for the newer addition), is characteristic of the more positive assessment of Eisenhower's effectiveness as a leader that has evolved over the past several decades. In a similar vein, Chester J. Pach's update of Elmo Richardson's *The Presidency of Dwight David Eisenhower* (revised edition 1991) systematically builds on the revisionist literature to paint a much more successful assessment of both Eisenhower as leader and the efficacy of his policies. The view of Eisenhower as engaged leader gives validity to the portrait painted by his aide and confident, Sherman Adams, in the 1961 insider's account, *First Hand Report: The Story of the Eisenhower Administration*. Somewhat dismissed at the time as faithful loyalists, the book looms more authoritatively in the light of subsequent academic investigations. Eisenhower's policy of peaceful engagement with the Soviet Union is carefully and favorably assessed in Robert Bowie's and Richard Immerman's analysis, *Waging Peace: How Eisenhower Shaped an Enduring Cold War Strategy* (2000), in light of the recent resurgence of more aggressive neo-conservative orthodoxy. Eisenhower's own take on his presidency, *Mandate for Change* (1963), and *Waging Peace* (1965), both republished by Doubleday in 2000), are well worth reading but tend to be more politically sensitive than his early classic history, *Crusade in Europe*.

John Fitzgerald Kennedy

The most comprehensive works dealing with John Fitzgerald Kennedy are Thomas Reeves, *A Question of Character: A Life of John Fitzgerald Kennedy* (1991); and Herbert S. Parmet, *Jack: The Struggles of John F. Kennedy* (1980), and *JFK: The Presidency of John F. Kennedy* (1991). The most systematic portrayals of JFK within the context of the Kennedy family is Doris Kearns Goodwin, *The Fitzgeralds and the Kennedys* (1986). See also Judie Mills, *John F. Kennedy* (1988), as well as Ted Schwarz, *Joseph P. Kennedy: the mogul, the mob, the statesman and the making of an American Myth* (2003), and Michael Beschloss, *Kennedy and Roosevelt: The Uneasy Alliance* (1984).

The most compelling account of cold war liberalism in the 1950s, which places the Kennedy liberalism in a cold war context, is David Burner and Thomas R. West, *The Torch is Passed: The Kennedy Brothers and American Liberalism* (1984).

JFK's presidency has undergone a significant historiographical shift in recent years. The traditional and authoritative work by a contemporary on the Kennedy presidency is Arthur Meier, Jr. Schlesinger's *A Thousand Days: John F. Kennedy in the White House* (1996). See also David Halberstam's *The Best and the Brightest* (1972) for an accurate assessment by a valuable contemporary. A more balanced assessment of the JFK presidency is James Giglio's *The Presidency of John F. Kennedy* (1991). Giglio's work may in turn be supplemented by Herbert S. Parmet's authoritative *JFK: The Presidency of John F. Kennedy* (1983). On the other hand, Bruce Miroff's *Pragmatic Illusions: The Presidential Politics of John F. Kennedy* (1976) offers a critical (yet balanced) assessment of the Kennedy presidency.

The most significant issue in the Kennedy presidency was foreign policy, specifically the cold war, Europe, Cuba, and the Far East. The best general survey of Kennedy's cold war foreign ideology is Walter LaFeber, *America and the Cold War* (1993). Other works that analyze Kennedy's cold war initiatives include Richard Walton, *Cold War and Counterrevolution: The Foreign Policy of John F. Kennedy* (1973); and Louise Fitzsimmons, *The Kennedy Doctrine* (1972). Within the context of the cold war, Kennedy had to contend with Nikita Khrushchev and the Berlin Wall Crisis. The best works dealing with these issues are Michael R. Beschloss, *The Crisis Years: Kennedy and Khrushchev, 1960-1963* (1991); and Burner and West, *The Torch is Passed* (1984). Other works include Honore Catadal, *Kennedy and the Berlin Wall Crisis* (1980); Robert A. Slusser, *The Berlin Crisis of 1961* (1971); Eleanor Dulles, *The Wall: A Tragedy in Three Acts* (1972) and Curtis Cate, *The Ides of August: The Berlin Wall Crisis, 1961* (1978). While the aforementioned works offer a neutral or positive interpretation of Kennedy's policies in Berlin, Thomas G. Paterson offers a critical appraisal of JFK's policy in "Bearing the Burden: A Critical Look at JFK's Foreign Policy," *Virginia Quarterly Review* 54 (Spring 1978), pp. 193-212.

The literature on Kennedy's handling of Cuba is divisive and contentious. Kennedy's decisions in regard to the Bay of Pigs provide fuel for historiographical debates. An authoritative work is Trumbull Higgins, *The Perfect Failure: Kennedy, Eisenhower and the CIA at the Bay of Pigs* (1988). Among other important sources dealing with the Cuban incident include Irving Janis, *Victims of Groupthink* (1972); Peter Wyden, *Bay of Pigs* (1979); and Haynes Johnson, *The Bay of Pigs* (1964). Another crisis dealing with Cuba involves the Cuban Missile Crisis. The best work dealing with this crisis and offering a balanced perspective is David Detzer, *The Brink* (1979). Other works, which generally offer a balanced account, are Ernest May, *The Kennedy Tapes: Inside the White House During the Cuban Missile Crisis* (1997); Thomas G. Paterson, *Contesting Castro: The United States and the Triumph of the Cuban Revolution* (1994); and Robert Kennedy's classic, *Thirteen Days* (1969) (along with Kevin Costner's film by the same name).

Kennedy's role in the Vietnam conflict in expertly analyzed in George Herring, *America's Longest War: The United States and Vietnam, 1950-1975* (1986). Other scholars have analyzed Kennedy's Vietnam policy such as Stanley Karnow, *Vietnam: A History* (1983). Scholars dispute the role that Kennedy played in the escalation of American intervention in this civil war.

Kennedy's domestic policy has received less attention than his foreign policy initiatives. JFK's economic agenda is adroitly analyzed by a number of economists and scholars. Contemporaries like Schlesinger and Halberstam agree that JFK's economics were considered moderate. Other contemporaries argue for his economic liberalism and activism. Herbert Rowen, *The Free Enterprisers: Kennedy, Johnson and the Business Community* (1969), argues the former, while Theodore Sorenson, *The*

Kennedy Legacy (1979), supports the contrary position. Kennedy's patchy civil rights records has received ample analysis from scholars and academicians. A viable general survey is Robert Weisbrot, *Freedom Bound: A History of America's Civil Rights Movement* (1990). A critical analysis of JFK's civil rights views is Victor Navasky's *Kennedy Justice* (1971), while Carl M. Brauer, *John F. Kennedy and the Second American Revolution* (1977), offers a more favorable interpretation of his civil rights policies. Scholars have also explored JFK's relations with prominent civil right leaders. The most authoritative works on this complex relationship continues to be Stephen B. Oates, *The Life of Martin Luther King, Jr.*, (1986); and David J. Garrow, *Bearing the Cross: Martin Luther King, Jr. and the Southern Christian Leadership Conference* (1986).

The literature on Kennedy's assassination is truly vast. A good starting point would be the Warren Commission Report.

Lyndon Baines Johnson

Four biographies of Lyndon Johnson were especially insightful in helping to evaluate his presidency: Doris Kearns's sympathetic and overall favorable evaluation, *Lyndon Johnson and the American Dream* (1977); Paul Conkin's "balanced" but more critical, *Big Daddy From the Pedernales* (1986); Robert Caro, *The Years of Lyndon Johnson: The Path to Power* (1982), and *The Years of Lyndon Johnson: Means of Ascent* (1990); and Harry McPherson, *A Political Education* (1975). Also consulted were Eric Goldman's *The Tragedy of Lyndon Johnson* (1969); Ronnie Dugger's *The Politician* (1982); George Reedy's *The Twilight of the Presidency* (1971); and Tom Wicker's *JFK and LBJ* (1968).

General works particularly helpful in assessing the Johnson presidency relative to the Great Society, 1960s liberalism, and the history of the era were William H. Chafe, *The Unfinished Journey: America Since World War II* (fifth edition, 2003); James T. Patterson, *Grand Expectations: The United States, 1945-1974* (1996); Jim F. Heath, *Decade of Disillusionment* (1976); Allen J. Matusow, *The Unraveling of America: A History of Liberalism in the 1960s* (1984); Irwin Unger, *The Best of Intentions: The Triumph and Failure of the Great Society Under Kennedy, Johnson, and Nixon* (1996); and Irwin and Debi Unger, *America in the 1960s* (1988). Also of great value are William Leuchtenburg's *In the Shadow of FDR: From Harry Truman to Ronald Reagan* (1983); Todd Gitlin's *The Sixties: Years of Hope, Days of Rage* (1987); and Terry Anderson's *The Movement and the Sixties: Protest in America From Greensboro to Wounded Knee* (1995). One of the best studies of politics and public policy during the 1960s is James Sundquist, *Politics and Policy: The Eisenhower, Kennedy, and Johnson Years* (1968). Books focusing on other Great Society legislation are Sar Levitan and Robert Taggert, *The Promise of Greatness* (1976); Theodore Marmer, *The Politics of Medicare* (1973); Daniel P. Moynihan, *Maximum Feasible Misunderstanding* (1970); and Stephen M. Rose, *The Betrayal of the Poor: Transformation of Community Action* (1972). For critical overviews of the Great Society, see Marvin E. Gittleman and David Mermelstein, eds., *The Great Society Reader: The Failure of Liberalism* (1975); and Charles Murray, *Losing Ground* (1984). Jonathan Schwarz offers a more positive assessment of the Great Society and its legacy in *America's Hidden Success* (1983).

Relative to civil rights and the Johnson presidency, the works found most beneficial were Harvard Sitkoff, *The Struggle for Black Equality* (rev. ed., 1993); Taylor Branch, *Pillar of Fire: America in the King Years, 1963-1965* (1968); Steven Lawson, *In Pursuit of Power: Southern Blacks and Electoral Politics, 1965-1982* (1985); and Robert Weisbrot, *Freedom Bound: A History of America's Civil Rights Movement* (1990). On the emergence of Black Power and its impact on the "rights revolution" of the 1960s, see William L. Van Deburg, *New Day in Babylon: The Black Power Movement and American Culture, 1965-1975* (1992). The urban revolts of the decade spawned largely by LBJ's failure to "deliver the goods" that his Great Society promised are chronicled in numerous books, including Joe F. Feagin and Harlan Hahn, *Ghetto Revolts: The Politics of Violence in American Cities* (1973); Robert M. Fogleson, *Violence as Protest: A Study of Riots in Ghettoes* (1969); Paul Jacobs, *Prelude to Riot* (1969); and Robert Conot, *Rivers of Blood, Years of Darkness* (1968).

It was Vietnam, of course, that constituted the major foreign policy crisis of the Johnson presidency, ultimately destroying LBJ personally and his cherished Great Society. The best single book on Vietnam is George Herring, *America's Longest War: The U.S. and Vietnam, 1950-1975* (1981, 2002), a survey of U.S. involvement beginning with the Truman administration and ending with the April 1975 fall of Saigon. Also see Herring's *LBJ and Vietnam: A Different Kind of War* (1994). A good complement to Herring are Larry Berman's *Lyndon Johnson's War* (1989), and *Planning a Tragedy* (1982). Both works chronicle the debates within the Johnson administration relative to Vietnam, with the first work emphasizing that in many ways it was not Johnson but rather his "Wise Men" who were most responsible for the debacle, for it was based on their advice that LBJ escalated the war, often contrary to his own best judgment not to do so. Invaluable in any study of the war is Neil Sheehan's *The Pentagon Papers* (1975), for they reveal the perceptions that shaped LBJ's decisions on the war throughout his presidency. Also of importance are the early works of Bernard Fall, *The Two Vietnams* (1967), and *Street Without Joy* (1964). See also David Halberstam, *The Making of a Quagmire* (1965), and *The Best and the Brightest*, (1972); Gunter Lewy, *America in Vietnam* (1978); and Stanley Karnouw, *Vietnam: A History* (1984). Also see David Kaiser, *American Tragedy: Kennedy, Johnson, and the Origins of the Vietnam War* (2000). On the Tet offensives, see Don Oberdoffer's *Tet* (1971); and Peter Breestrup's *Big Story* (1978). For two contrasting approaches to the war, see Frederick Levegall, *Choosing War: The Lost Chance for Peace and the Escalation of War in Vietnam* (1999); and Rhodri Jeffreys-Jones, *Peace Now! American Society and the Ending of the Vietnam War* (1999). Lovegall asserts that other countries, America's allies, provided Johnson with ways of "getting out" without the disgrace he so feared. However, he was so obsessed with not being the first American president to lose a war that he ignored their ideas and entreaties and "stayed the course," which only led to disaster. Jeffreys-Jones argues that powerful citizens groups had a greater impact on the war than many believe. Indeed, according to Jeffreys-Jones, key groups such as students, African Americans, and labor initially supported the war as a means of obtaining Great Society entitlements. However, once satisfied and "inside" the Great Society's circle of benefits, they turned against Johnson and the war. In short, they "used" LBJ and liberalism to gain access to power and largesse, believing that the only way they could have gotten such status and rewards was to "pretend" to support Johnson and his war.

Richard M. Nixon

Because of the notoriety of Watergate, several people associated with the Nixon administration found markets for their autobiographies, examples of which include Charles Coleson's *Born Again* (1993); John Dean's *Blind Ambition* (1976); and Nixon himself in a work entitled *The Memoirs of Richard Nixon* (1978). Though the scope of all three men is on their life stories, the events of the Nixon White House garner a great deal of attention. Because of the widespread vilification of Nixon, it is interesting to read the accounts of insiders like Coleson and Dean who respect the man's talents, even as they expose some of his shortcomings. (Dean is especially interesting, since he helped authorities close in on

Nixon.) Nixon does a better job of glossing over and explaining away his shortcomings than his subordinates do for him, almost making it seem believable that the man was not guilty of much (if the reader lived in a vacuum).

Nixon's Chief of Staff, H.R. Haldeman, provides another insider's account of the Nixon administration with *The Haldeman Diaries* (1995). Because of its format, this work is not as riveting as some pertaining to Nixon, but it is a valuable resource for learning about what went on in the Nixon White House. However, given Haldeman's role in various alleged improprieties, it would be a mistake to accept everything in his diaries as the unvarnished truth.

Many outsiders have tried to understand who Nixon was, including Kenneth Franklin Kurz in *Nixon's Enemies* (1998), and Anthony Summers with his book *Arrogance of Power* (2000). Kurz focuses on how Nixon interacted with his political enemies and comes to the conclusion that, while Nixon could be surprisingly gracious in defeat, he was an extremely poor winner. Though not as harsh towards Nixon as many writers, Kurz nevertheless did not shy away from writing about the more unpleasant characteristics of the former president. On the other hand, Summer's personal dislike of Richard Nixon is obvious, and this impacts some of his assessments. At times, events are interpreted in such a way as to cast Nixon in the worst possible light (besides the times when Nixon deserves to be seen in such a light). But the book is very thorough in its use of the sources and more objective than Nixon himself. Summers provides an interesting and useful counterbalance to Nixon's autobiography and the writings of conservatives like Ann Coulter.

Another category of works on Nixon includes those books that do not focus on Nixon primarily, yet still have informative things to say about him. Relevant books include Kati Marton's *Hidden Power* (2002); Peter Schwiezer's *Reagan's War* (2002); and David C. Whitney's *The American Presidents* (1985). Marton looks at the marital relationships of twelve of the more recent presidents and analyzes how these relationships impacted the presidential administrations—a unique and interesting angle. According to Marton, one of Nixon's shortcomings was his terrible treatment of his wife, Pat. Though Nixon was not a serial adulterer like John Kennedy or Lyndon Johnson, in every other respect Richard Nixon was a much worse man with whom to live. It might also be worth noting that Pat Nixon had less influence and input on the running of the White House and/or political affairs than all subsequent first ladies with the possible exception of Laura Bush. Schwiezer provides a conservative's look at Ronald Reagan's battle against communism from Reagan's Hollywood days through his presidency. Among other things, the book is a useful tool for understanding Reagan's conservative views on Nixon's foreign policy. Though Nixon is generally perceived as a war hawk, Reagan's relatively unique perspective was that Nixon's problem (or at least one of Nixon's problems) was that Nixon was not strong enough when it came to communism. Whitney wrote brief backgrounds of the presidents through Reagan. It briefly covers the major events of Nixon's time in office, thus providing a historical context for more detailed treatments of his administration.

Gerald R. Ford

With a presidency that only lasted about one-third the time of Nixon's, and a level of controversy that was a much smaller fraction of Nixon's own, Gerald Ford has had much less written about his time in office than his immediate predecessor. One insider account was written by Ford himself in *A Time to Heal: The Autobiography of Gerald Ford* (1979), while another perspective came from long-time Ford aide Robert Hartmann, *Palace Politics: An Inside Account of the Ford Years* (1980). Ford's autobiography was not as compelling as Nixon's, but then Nixon's administration had a lot more intrigue. Ford's book is an honest reflection of the man himself: moderate in its positions and temper. While this makes the work useful for understanding Ford, it is sometimes frustrating when the author shies away from certain events when it would be beneficial for the reader to know what the president thought on the matter. Hartmann, a senior aide and speech writer for Ford, displays a genuine admiration for his boss, but Hartmann is also candid with his opinions on Ford's shortcomings and mistakes. One of the more interesting aspects of this book is Hartmann's blame of the Nixon holdovers for many of the internal and external problems in the Ford White House. In Ford's autobiography, however, the president blames Hartmann for some of the internal problems. Ford thought Hartmann could be difficult to work with, but Hartmann glosses over his personality issues when he writes about himself.

Many other books help round out the picture on Ford, like Kati Marton's *Hidden Power* (2002); Peter Schwiezer's *Reagan's War* (2002); Bob Woodward's *Shadow: Five Presidents and the Legacy of Watergate* (2000); and David C. Whitney's *The American Presidents* (1985). Marton's look at the marital relationships of twelve of the more recent presidents sheds light on Betty Ford's mental breakdown early in her marriage and how the future first lady ultimately emerges stronger, more outspoken, and closer to being an equal partner with her husband. Marton speaks glowingly of Betty Ford's confident expression of her liberal views as first lady, but Marton fails to mention how Betty Ford's views hurt her husband's standing with conservative voters whose support was essential for a Republican presidential candidate. Schwiezer's book on Ronald Reagan's lifelong battle against communism is a useful tool for understanding Reagan's views on the foreign policy of Ford. Schwiezer helps the reader to understand the difficulties that Ford had in keeping the support of his party as he ran for election in 1976. The staunchly conservative Reagan finds Ford's foreign policy more distasteful than Nixon's had been. Of course, Reagan and Schwiezer do not seem to appreciate the legal limits on Ford's power. Woodward's book gives a very balanced account of how the first five presidents after Watergate managed scandals (real and alleged) under an increasingly skeptical media scrutiny. Ford comes across as a decent fellow who was not completely prepared to be president. This lack of preparation is cited as a leading culprit behind Ford's lapses in judgment. Ford's lack of ambition for the presidency, more so than the unusual circumstances of his ascendancy, is Woodward's explanation for why this president was so ill-prepared for his office. Whitney's brief backgrounds of the presidents contain an overview of the major events of Ford's time in office, thus providing a historical context for more detailed treatments of his administration.

James Earl "Jimmy" Carter

Two useful books for understanding Carter's rise to the White House are Carter's own *Why not the Best?* (1976); and Gregory Paul Domin's *Jimmy Carter: Public Opinion, and the Search for Values* (2003). Carter's early autobiography shows what Carter stood for and what his background was leading up to the 1976 election. Carter's talent, intellect, work ethic, and decency all come through clearly. Carter's commitment to civil rights also manifests itself. Conversely, it is evident that Carter did not have much political experience, and one gets the sense that Carter never developed an ability for compromising on political issues, which was one of the reasons for his difficulties as president. Domin's work is very brief (104 pages) and poorly edited, thus making it tempting to dismiss the book altogether. But Domin sheds an interesting light on Jimmy Carter's candidacy and his presidency. Though he ran on his character, Carter's policies were often driven by opinion polls, says Domin. While this would not be surprising for a candidate/president in the twenty-first century, it does stand out in the 1970s, especially because of Carter's reputation for staking out principled positions and clinging to them even when they were unpopular.

Jody Powell's *The Other Side of the Story* (1984) is an insider's account of a presidency, and Powell has some insightful things to say about how the media sometimes overbuilds stories in an effort to secure market share. On occasion, however, Powell's sense of humor makes it hard to distinguish what was real from his hyperbole, which makes this book a frustrating source for understanding Carter and his times. Perhaps because he served as Carter's press secretary, Powell regards many of the problems Carter experienced as simply examples of poor communications when the real sources of the trouble were more substantive.

Foreign policy critiques were offered by Peter Schwiezer's *Reagan's War* (2002), and Frederick Kempe's *Divorcing the Dictator* (1990). Schwiezer's conservative book is not that unique in what it says about Carter, though it does trumpet Reagan's virtues more than some other books. Of course, the more credit Reagan is given, the more respectable Carter's loss to him in 1980 becomes. Kempe examines the relationship between the United States and Panama's Manuel Noriega. Kempe is critical of Carter, which is not that extraordinary in light of the fact that the author is also critical of the other presidents about which he writes, Reagan and Bush I. But given that Carter is usually praised for his Latin America policy, this is an interesting perspective.

Among other books that are not solely devoted to Jimmy Carter, Kati Marton's *Hidden Power* (2002), David C. Whitney's *The American Presidents* (1985), and Bob Woodward's *Shadow: Five Presidents and the Legacy of Watergate* (2000), are relevant. Marton's book on twelve presidential marriages shows that Rosalynn Carter was an active and vocal first lady when the country was not quite ready for one. While Rosalynn may have hurt her husband politically, she was his most trusted advisor, and like the Fords, at least the Carters had a good marriage. Whitney covers the backgrounds of the presidents and the major events of their terms in office, thus providing a historical context for other, more detailed treatments of Carter's administration. Woodward portrays Carter as a president who suffers from some major problems (besides the economy and the hostage crisis). In the seamy world of Washington D.C., the principled, uncompromising Carter does not know how to fit himself into the political process, and he is not able to completely live up to his honesty pledge. Also, Carter was not good at setting politics aside and just forming relationships with the people of Washington, including (surprisingly) many Democrats in Congress and members of his own White House staff. Through it all, Carter's morality still manages to shine through to the reader.

Ronald Reagan

Journalist (and Reagan confident) Lou Cannon's three-volume set *Ronald Reagan, Governor Reagan: His Rise to Power*, and *President Reagan: The Role of a Lifetime* (2000), provides Reagan readers with a comprehensive, and fairly balanced in-depth review of the life and times of the 40th president. Insider accounts of the Reagan presidency are more generally positive than with those by Reagan's successors. Such is the case with Michael Deaver's *A Different Drummer: My Thirty Years with Ronald Reagan* (2001); Peggy Noonan's *When Character Was King: A Story of Ronald Reagan* (2001); and Dinesh D'Souza's *Ronald Reagan: How an Ordinary Man Became an Extraordinary Leader* (1997).

Least one think all was rosy in the Reagan years, look no farther than *Washington Post* columnist Haynes Johnson's indictment of the corruption and policy failures that tarnish the Reagan legacy in *Sleepwalking Through History: America in the Reagan Years* (1991). Sitting somewhere in the middle between hero worship and abject condemnation is Michael Shaller's *Reckoning With Reagan: America and Its President in the 1980s* (1994), which attempts to look beyond the image and illusion generated by the ultimate showman of American political history.

Finally, Reagan's autobiography *An American Life* (1990) provides a uncomplicated narrative that captures the optimistic nature that propelled Reagan from his simple beginnings to the ultimate seat of power.

George Herbert Walker Bush

The literature on President George Herbert Walker Bush, though not as divisive as the literature on Clinton and George W. Bush, can be placed into three distinct categories. By far, the most relevant of the literature deals with the personal upbringing of the president. Stressing the elitist upbringing, most of the authors argue that the president's sense of political loyalty was directly attributable to the morals and ethics that his father imbued his son within the young years. The earliest account of the link between Bush's loyalty and ethics is Nicholas King's compelling *George*

Bush: A Biography (1980). King stresses Bush's sense of loyalty during the turbulent years of the Nixon and Ford terms. Building on King's work, Herbert Parmet, in *George Bush: The Life of a Lone Star* (1997), provides an insightful narrative of the life of George H.W. Bush. Gaining unprecedented access to many personal documents and interviews, Parmet offers insights into Bush's political evolution especially from within the Rockefeller wing of the Republican Party. Most significant, the author provides insight into the dubious relationship between Bush and the Panamanian dictator, Manuel Noriega. Supplementing the historical biographies of President George H.W. Bush, many authors have debated the more interesting issues involving Bush's role in the cold war. With the demise of the Soviet Union, some scholars argue that Bush's tough stance towards the Soviet Union essentially acted as a catalyst in destroying the evil empire. Others argue that Bush was the final phase in the Reagan era of an aggressive foreign policy. For examples of the former argument, see Walter LaFeber, *The United States and the Cold War: Twenty Years of Revolutions and Response, 1947-1967* (1967), while the proponents of the latter ideas have their spokesman in Sidney Blumenthal's *Pledging Allegiance: The Last Campaign of the Cold War* (1991). Another major point of analysis is Bush's policies towards the Middle East, specifically the Persian Gulf War. The most comprehensive work is Lawrence Freedman and Ephraim Kirsch's *The Gulf Conflict, 1990-1991, Diplomacy and War in the New World Order* (1994), which analyzes in detail the diplomatic maneuvers of the United States in the years prior to the outbreak of the conflict. It offers an in-depth analysis of the daily meetings of the top diplomats. In addition to Freedman's work, Bob Woodward's *The Commanders* (1991) details the meetings between Colin Powell and other cabinet members in the Bush presidency in the preceding years. It essentially offers an "insider" approach to Bush's foreign policy. Bush's diplomatic failures and successes are analyzed in David Mervin's *George Bush and the Guardianship Presidency* (1996), as well as Martin Mayer's skewed, yet insightful *The Greatest Ever Bank Robbery: The Collapse of the Savings and Loan Industry* (1990). The analyses of Bush's domestic policy tends to be hypercritical, without considering the long-term decline in the American economy prior to Bush's election. In conclusion, the former president has contributed his interpretation of his life and political philosophy in the compelling *All the Best: My Life in Letters and Other Writings* (1999). *All the Best* is a collection of letters from his World War II stories through his presidency. The letters offer a personal glimpse into the mindset of Bush at critical points in his life.

While Bush's letters are by far the most important primary manuscript, a collection of essays entitled, *The Bush Presidency: Ten Intimate Perspectives of George Bush* (1998), offers glimpses of the Bush presidency from the perspective of ten of the presidents' advisers. Coupled with the Bush letters, this work offers an entirely different perspective on the key events in the Bush term.

William Jefferson Clinton

The best single source of William Jefferson Clinton is his autobiography, *My Life* (2004). Offering a detailed narrative of his life and times, the youngest ever elected president argues that much of his political and personal philosophy was shaped by his early years, specifically the manner in which his domineering mother and grandmother guided his upbringing. At times, the argument loses its cohesiveness as a result of the minutiae, but in general, the work offers an excellent and detailed account of the presidency from Clinton's perspective. In addition to Clinton's autobiography, other first-hand accounts provide a differing glimpse into the presidency and Clinton's life. Virginia Kelley, Clinton's mother, in *Leading with My Heart* (1994) related the manner in which her son dealt with four marriages, a drug addiction, and a broken home. It is evident that Clinton's difficult boyhood contributed to his political and personal difficulties later in life. In addition, Hillary Clinton, in *Living History* (2003), provides her insights into the travails and tribulations of her husband's eight years in office.

Along with the autobiographies, numerous works have focused on Clinton's early years. In a surprisingly sympathetic work, Nigel Hamilton's *Bill Clinton: An American Journey* (2003), details the early life and maturation of the 42nd president. Approaching Clinton from a psychological methodology, Hamilton contends that Clinton's behavior and politics in life were a direct result of his upbringing in a broken home. He convincingly argues that Clinton's domineering mother was a crucial factor in Clinton's development as a person and politician. David Marannis' *First in His Class: The Biography of Bill Clinton* (1996), takes the reader on a long and at times chaotic look into Bill's and Hillary's relationship within a psychological context of Virginia Kelley and Clinton's womanizing in his younger years in Arkansas, Washington D.C., and London. In an interesting conclusion, Marannis offers an interesting comparison of Clinton's impeachment with Watergate and the Iran Contra scandal.

The works dealing with Clinton's presidency devolve into two distinct camps. There are scholars who criticize Clinton for his haphazard foreign policy initiatives, while others argue that Clinton's balance of promoting a domestic agenda with a vigorous foreign policy contributed to a successful first term. An engaging analysis of Clinton's domestic agenda is Bob Woodward's *The Agenda: Inside the Clinton White House* (1994). Obtaining access to many Clinton "cabinet makers," Woodward offers a compelling narrative of Clinton's brainstorming on his domestic agenda. Other works that examine Clinton's domestic agenda include Stanley A. Renshon's *The Clinton Presidency* (1993), and William Berman's *From the Center to the Edge: the Politics and Policies of the Clinton Presidency* (2001).

The literature on Clinton's foreign policy focuses on two themes. For a general view of Clinton's foreign policy, President Clinton's *The Clinton Foreign Policy Reader* (2000), offers a first-hand synopsis of his foreign policy views. In addition, for the first theme of Clinton's role in obtaining peace in the Middle East, see Rich Lowry's *Legacy: Paying the Price for the Clinton Years* (2003). Along with a discussion of Clinton's Middle East policies are works that deal with Clinton's role with Iraq and his attempts to curtail terrorism. The most consistent work is Yosseff Bodansky's *The High Cost of Peace* (2002), which traces Clinton's historical legacy in the Middle East.

The most controversial issue that plagued Clinton's second term was his impending impeachment. The best work dealing with the impeachment and the issues involved in the process is Richard A. Posner's *An Affair of State: The Investigation, Impeachment and Trial of President Clinton* (1999). For a partisan interpretation, see Ann Coulter's *High Crimes and Misdemeanors* (1998), and Nathan Aaseng's *The Impeachment of Bill Clinton* (2000).

George W. Bush

The literature on George W. Bush, while still evolving, can be divided into three camps. First there are those assessments that have emerged from the seemingly growth industry field of Bush-bashing books. Then there is the smaller but growing body of texts by Bush-defenders, seeking to refute the allegations and innuendo that imbue books in the first category. Finally, there are the texts attempting to take an objective look (the thinnest body of the three genres) at Bush's still evolving presidency.

Bush's predecessor, Bill Clinton, was no stranger to hostile texts attacking every aspect of his presidency from the personal to the public. What differentiates George W. Bush is the number of such hostile titles that have emerged in the first years and, indeed, with no small number emerging even before his inauguration in January 2001. Books of note challenging the entire matter of George W. Bush's selection (as these texts would categorize it, as opposed to "election") include David Kaplan's *The Accidental President: How 413 Lawyers, 9 Supreme Court Justices, and 5,963,110 Floridians (Give or Take a Few) Landed George W. Bush in the White House* (2001); and Alan Dershowitz, *Supreme Injustice: How the High Court Hijacked Election* (2001). Kaplan's book approaches the 2000 election from the perspective of a dramatic narrative, focusing on the personality and the foibles of fortune that helped elevate Bush to the highest office. Dershowitz, the noted Harvard law professor, meanwhile, performs a vivid vivisection of the Rehnquist Court decision to overturn the Florida supreme court, effectively certifying the election for Bush.

There are a slough of books evaluating the Bush family tree and its current reigning bough with Bill Minutaglio's *First Son: George W. Bush and the Bush Family Dynasty* (1999), and Elizabeth Mitchell's *W: Revenge of the Bush Dynasty* (2000), a more balanced treatment than most. Bush's public policies, both before and after occupancy of the White House, have also been subjected to great and unflattering scrutiny as in *Shrub: The Short but Happy Political Life of George W. Bush* and *Bushwhacked: Life in George W. Bush's America* (2000 & 2003, respectively), both by the journalistic duo of Molly Ivins and Lou Dubose.

Meanwhile, former Bush Treasury Secretary Paul O'Neill provided one of the first insiders account (negative though it is) in *The Price of Loyalty: George W. Bush, the White House, and the Education of Paul O'Neill* (written by journalist Ron Suskind, 2004). Mismanagement of the war on terror is the theme of another former administration terrorism advisor, William Clarke, in *Against All Enemies: Inside America's War on Terror.* (2004). One should anticipate a further avalanche of such titles as more Bush insiders become outsiders in the months and years to come.

A more positive assessment of George W. Bush, man and president, can be found in the work of another insider, former Bush speechwriter David Frum, *The Right Man: The Surprise Presidency of George W. Bush* (2003), which examines the foibles of the 43rd president while underscoring Bush's substantial record of achievement on both the domestic and international fronts. Likewise, veteran journalist Bob Woodward paints a largely positive portrait of the Bush's response to the horrors of 9/11 and his ultimate ability to abruptly adjust to the position of wartime president in *Bush At War* (2002), though Woodward seems to have bitten the administration hand that fed him through more access than that granted to any other journalist with his follow up tone, *Plan of Attack* (2004), which paints a less flattering portrait of Bush's Iraqi venture.

A more academically-oriented assessment can be found in *The George W. Bush Presidency: An Early Assessment* (2003). Edited by Fred I. Greenstein, the volume provides commentary, both pro and con, by a group of academic experts contrasting the Bush presidency, its policies, and its politics with previous administrations.

And, finally, while George W. Bush has not reached the stage of serious autobiographical writing, his obligatory 2000 election work, *A Charge To Keep* (1999), provides some insight into what the man deems important, both by what is included in the discourse and what is not.

Index